THE ULTIMATE
BIRTHDAY BOOK

TALISMANS FOR EVERY DAY ✳ ENIGMAS OF TIMELESS FAITHS AND DIVINATION SYSTEMS WITH PREDICTIONS, INFLUENCES AND TALISMANS INFLUENCES

THE ULTIMATE
BIRTHDAY BOOK

REVEALING THE SECRETS OF EACH DAY OF THE YEAR

CLARE GIBSON

CHANCELLOR PRESS

This edition published in 1998 by Chancellor Press, Michelin House, 81 Fulham Road, London SW3 6RB.

Design © Ziga Design

ISBN: 0-7537-0048-4

Printed in China

10 9 8 7 6 5 4 3 2 1

PROJECT EDITOR: Nicola J. Gillies

ASSOCIATE EDITORS: Jennifer Ditsler, Peter C. Gillies, Sara Hunt, Robin Langley Sommer, Barbara Paulding Thrasher

CONSULTANT: Robert Currey

ART DIRECTOR: Charles J. Ziga

GRAPHIC DESIGNER: Wendy Ciaccia Eurell

SUPPLEMENTARY RESEARCH: Veronica Langley

To order your personal horoscope, interpreted by leading astrologer Robert Currey of Equinox™, please complete the information below and send to: Equinox, The Astrology Shop, 78 Neal Street, Covent Garden, London WC2H 9PA. Tel: 0171 497 1001. Fax: 0171 497 0344.
e-mail: eqxbb@eqx.net
website: http://www.equinox.uk.com
A cheque or credit card details should be enclosed for £18.00 per chart requested. Postage within the UK is included; for air mail outside the UK, add £1.50 per chart.

Full name
Address
Sex: M/F
Date of birth (day/month/year)
Time of birth (hour/minute)
Place of birth (if small, include nearest town).

Note: The time of birth should be recorded as the local time on the clock. If not known within the nearest hour, specify a "flat chart," which will be more accurate than one cast for an inaccurately guessed time.

Robert Currey, who holds a degree in psychology and a diploma from the Faculty of Astrological Studies, is the founder and director of Equinox™ and The Astrology Shop in London's Covent Garden. He has been an astrological consultant since 1981 and is recognised around the world as a leading practitioner of his craft. While the publisher gratefully acknowledges his invaluable contribution as a special consultant to this book, it should be noted that the astrological profiles herein reflect the expertise and methods of the author.

For Mike Haworth-Maden

CONTENTS

FOREWORD

It is not widely known that Western astrology is split into two mutually exclusive camps: one claims the professional high ground and the other claims the hearts of the public at large. The "quality" camp is led by academic astrologers who see astrology as a discipline that can be attempted only after years of study. They contend that a chart can be read only by taking into account all the planets, aspects and houses—otherwise, interpretive or predictive statements are meaningless. The "quantity" camp, celebrated through newspaper and magazine columns, known as the Sun Sign astrologers, argue that astrology should be accessible to all and that it should be both informative and entertaining.

The beauty of *The Ultimate Birthday Book* is that it bridges these schools of thought. Information is targeted specifically at you on a most personal level. This is because it homes in like a laser on your birthday rather than generalizing across the much wider target of your Sun sign, like the scattershot of a "blunderbuss." Yet the information presented in this volume remains highly accessible despite its detail and focus. Everyone knows his or her date of birth. The interpretation for each day of the year encompasses the academic, the technical and the mystical by providing additional information about well-known people who share your birthday and key events that occurred on that day.

I was fascinated to learn that the novelist F. Scott Fitzgerald was born on my birthday (September 24). Before I was interested in astrology, one of the main contributions to my degree was a thesis about one of Fitzgerald's autobiographical short stories. At the time, the parallels with my life struck me. Somehow his life story resonated deeply within me and only now begins to make sense. I am sure that by reading about the events that occurred on your birthday, a similar inner chord will strike.

Glancing through this book, one has to marvel at how world events so often reflect the powerful emphasis of the Sun sign (whichever sign the Sun was in at the time). It is true that the build-up of planets in different years make the pattern highly complex. But still a trend shines through. For example, why have stock markets changed direction sharply or crashed when the Sun went into Scorpio—the one sign connected with other people's money? Why have so many of the major developments and disasters connected with flight and aviation occurred when the Sun passes through the signs of travel: Gemini and Sagittarius?

In earlier times, we understood the rhythms of nature, but now this attunement is perceived as less relevant to our urban lifestyle and less apparent due to the effects of scientific control of our environment. As we enter the third millennium, we should become aware once again of the natural rhythms of human experience and endeavour.

Robert Currey
London, 1998

DIALOGVS
DE SYSTEMATE MVNDI,
Autore
GALILÆO GALILÆI LYNCEO,
SERENISSIMO
FERDINANDO II. HETRVR. MAGNO-DVCI
dicatus.

CL. PTOLEM.

N. COPERNICVS

INTRODUCTION

It is the stars,
The stars above us, govern our conditions.

William Shakespeare, *King Lear* (1605–06), Act 4, Scene 3.1

Since time immemorial the heavenly bodies—luminaries, planets and stars—have exerted a mysterious fascination upon their Earth-bound observers. Even today, when the scientific precepts of astronomy have come to marginalize (some even say, discredit) the astrological beliefs that prevailed for millennia, we remain captivated by their ethereal beauty and elusive promise of worlds as yet undiscovered.

Ancient stargazers, who lacked instruments like the telescope with which to study the heavens in accurate detail, still discerned that certain astral bodies comprised fixed formations that moved in predictable fashion through the night sky, their appearance and disappearance heralding the changes of season. They believed that the universe was geocentric, and that the positions and majestic progressions of the Sun, Moon, planets and stars influenced the lives of human beings and all of the events that occurred on Earth. This concept is encapsulated in the word "astrology," a composite of the Greek words *astron* ("star") and *legetin* ("speak"). It was only through the groundbreaking work of such later astronomers as Nicolaus Copernicus (1473–1543), who first postulated that the Earth did not, in fact, occupy the center of the universe, but rotated on its axis while revolving around the Sun; and Galileo Galilei (1564–1642), who described it as part of a solar system, that the geocentric view began to change, if slowly. (The Vatican, for example, did not formally accept Galileo's findings until 1979). Their successors built upon the work of these pioneering astronomers to provide us with knowledge undreamed of by the ancients. In learning more about our universe and the celestial bodies that it contains, we have learned that many aspects of the astrological beliefs professed by our ancestors were correct. We also know that numerous cosmic truths have yet to be discovered.

Today astronomy is regarded as a scientific discipline distinct from astrology, which most scientists dismiss as simply a naive divinatory system. Yet our affinity with astrology endures: Why is it that even astrological nonbelievers cannot resist sneaking a glance at their "stars" for the day? The human psyche, through the collective unconscious that we all share, clearly has a profound and complex connection to the stars. In order to understand the reasons underlying this attraction, we need to trace the history of astrology through time to its ancient origins.

Page 8: Born Nikolaj Kopernik in Poland, the astronomer Nicolaus Copernicus began to observe the Sun, Moon and planets in 1497. As a result, he abandoned the Ptolemaic theory and introduced his revolutionary heliocentric system, whereby the Earth rotates on its axis daily and, with other planets, revolves around the Sun.

The Origins of Western Astrology

Blessed as we are with our inherited legacy of millennia of human thought, experience and discovery, our current level of intellectual sophistication and knowledge—though still increasing—is unprecedented in human history. Scientific advances have enriched our lives and understanding immeasurably, but have also in some respects detracted from the awe with which our forebears regarded the natural world. Especially mysterious to them were the celestial bodies: the life-giving, yet also destructive, powers of the brightly burning Sun; the apparently magical ability of its nocturnal counterpart, the Moon, to regulate the ebb and flow of the oceanic tides; and the regular cycles of these two luminaries (as well as those of the constellations), which helped humans to determine the measurement of time—night and day, months and years. In fact, the regular movements of the heavenly bodies, and their corresponding influence over the passage of the seasons, have long been understood as related to one another.

In trying to comprehend the role of the luminaries in governing natural life on Earth, many ancient cultures ascribed supernatural properties to the Sun and Moon, and later also to the planets and stars: the subsequent personification of the solar, lunar, planetary and stellar bodies as deities was an entirely logical progression. Star-worship (also termed astrolatry or Sabaism) was practiced in differing degrees by most of the world's early civilizations, especially those that depended upon agriculture for subsistence. Thus, for example, the ancient Egyptians venerated their supreme deity, the Sun god Re, who was believed to traverse the sky in his solar boat. Such megalithic structures as the standing stones of northern Europe (many aligned with the position at which the Sun rises on the summer and winter solstices), the Native American medicine wheels of North America, the pyramids of ancient Egypt and the ziggurats of Mesoamerica and Mesopotamia also attest to a widespread veneration of the celestial bodies.

Historians believe that the roots of Western astrology are embedded in Mesopotamia—the Near Eastern region comprising the land between the rivers Tigris and Euphrates, which was ruled successively by the Sumerians, Babylonians and Assyrians. Elements of the preceding culture's beliefs were adopted by each subsequent civilization, and yet although the Babylonians absorbed many Sumerian sacred concepts, it is they who are generally believed to have formalized the first astrological precepts. (It should be noted that there is some confusion as to whether the credit for the evolution of this astrological expertise should be given to the Babylonians or the Chaldeans. Chaldea was a region of Babylonia, and the two terms have become interchangeable, although there is reason to believe that the Chaldean astrologers, as priests of Baal, were especially renowned astrologers. Even the Bible refers to the astrological prowess of the Chaldeans, and during the classical period all astrologers were generically known as Chaldeans.)

It is estimated that by 3000 BC the Babylonians believed that their Sun god, Shamash; their lunar deity, Sin; and the goddess of the Morning Star (Ishtar) had special power to regulate Earthly life. To keep track of their movements, the Babylonians built stepped pyramids, or ziggurats, which served as both observatories and temples (as they had in Sumeria). By about 500 BC, the Babylonians had extended their concept of stellar influence to the individual: they introduced the idea that the position of the luminaries, planets and stars at the time of a person's birth had a direct bearing on the course of his or her life. One of the world's oldest horoscopes was cast in Mesopotamia for a baby born on April 29, 410 BC. It would be some time, however, before astrology's primary purpose would shift from its role as a leading form of state divination—used to ascertain, for example, the most auspicious time to undertake military campaigns—to that of predicting an individual's destiny.

Mesopotamia was the cradle that nurtured nascent astrology. From there it spread eastward, to India and beyond, evolving into different astrological traditions. In terms of Western astrology, it was the assimilation of the Babylonian tradition by the ancient Greeks that proved the most significant, both in clarifying astrological precepts and extending them to Greece's Mediterranean neighbors, and thence to other parts of the European continent. It is estimated that the ancient Greeks—enthusiastic diviners and readers of many different oracles—embraced Babylonian astrological beliefs between 600 and 500 BC. The first written Greek allusion to astrology was made during the following century by the philosopher Plato. Through Hellenistic influence, it reached into Macedonia and, after Alexander the Great's conquest, to Egypt and the Roman Empire, where it was probably introduced around 250 BC by Greek slaves.

The Greco-Roman formalization of astrological concepts shaped the system into one that is recognizable today. The Romans adopted the Greek pantheon of Olympic gods virtually wholesale, although they endowed them with Latin names. Thus the leading Greek deities who were associated with the planets were renamed as follows: Zeus became Jupiter; Ares, Mars; Aphrodite, Venus; Hermes, Mercury; and Kronos, Saturn. The luminaries did not enjoy such a simple translation, however. The Moon and its several phases was variously associated with Diana, Selen and Luna, among other goddesses, while the all-powerful Sun was the shared province of Apollo, Sol Invictus ("the unconquered Sun") and Mithras. The cult of the latter deity was particularly associated with astrological tenets, for it had seven grades of initiation, each of which corresponded to a planet.

Below: Monumental Stonehenge, near Salisbury, England, the mysterious Druidic circle of standing stones believed to have been built in alignment with the stars, the solstices and the paths of the Moon.

Above: *The zodiacal system of twelve celestial symbols used in Western astrology has been known since the second century AD, as seen in this Arabic zodiac.*

Just as astrology thrived in imperial Rome, so it spread to the outposts of its empire—a vast entity that dominated much of Europe, the Near East and northern Africa. It was the advent of Christianity that heralded astrology's decline, for the emphasis that the former placed on individual free will and potential redemption contradicted the principles inherent in the latter, especially the belief that an individual's destiny is pre-ordained, or "written in the stars." The first Christian emperor, Constantine (AD 274–337), pronounced astrology "demonic" in 333: from then on, Christianity's ascent in Europe was inversely paralleled by astrology's decline. However, not all parts of Europe became Christianized. Some regions were subject to the influence of Islamic culture—specifically Spain, which was conquered by the Arab-Berber Moors in 711 and reconquered by Christian forces by 1250 (apart from Granada, which remained Islamic until 1492).

There are many reasons why, during Europe's astrological dark age, the tradition continued to be the subject of serious and concerted study in Islamic lands, initially according to the translation of the *Almagest* along Ptolemaic lines. Between the eighth and tenth centuries, astrological treatises from India, Persia and Syria, as well as Greece, were also transcribed into Arabic. For the ritual observance of the Islamic believer, it was important that both the correct times for prayer and the direction of Mecca be identified accurately, and they could be determined only by charting the movements of the various celestial bodies. Scientific knowledge was encouraged as a means of attaining

tawhid, or "the oneness of Allah." The simultaneous flowering of such mathematical disciplines as trigonometry advanced the Arab astrologers' understanding of the "science of the decrees of the stars," and dedicated observatories were established at Maragha in Azerbaijan in 1259 and at Samarquand during the fifteenth century. There astronomers worked meticulously with such instruments as the astrolabe and quadrant.

Following the fall of Arab Granada to the Spanish monarchs Ferdinand and Isabella, Christians were reintroduced to astrology at the city's celebrated Moorish universities, partly as a result of the influence of Judeo-Spanish scholars, who reconciled many astrological principles with those governing their own mystical system of belief, the Kabbalah. From the fifteenth century, astrology enjoyed an unprecedented renaissance in Europe. Taught as a science at universities, it was regarded as a vital source of medical knowledge and treatment, for according to the macrocosmic-microcosmic principles of melothesia, the human body was a microcosm of the celestial macrocosm, or *imago mundi* ("image of the world [or universe]"). Hence each of its component parts was subject to the influence of the planet that rules it. It was also considered a prophetic system, and as a result, such astrological practitioners to royalty as John Dee (1527–1608) and Michel de Nostredame (1503–66)—Nostradamus—enjoyed the respective patronage of the English monarch Elizabeth I and the French queen Catherine de' Medici and her son Charles IX. Ordinary citizens, too, consulted popular astrologers like the

Englishman William Lilly (who is said to have predicted London's plague year of 1665 and the city's great fire in 1666), and printers could barely satisfy the demand for astrological almanacs.

Even the previously hostile Roman Catholic Church now accepted the system that it had so vehemently condemned. The dates of papal coronations were set according to the auspices indicated by the stars, while zodiacal symbols decorated churches, their presence subtly justified by their reinterpretation as Christian symbols (Virgo, for example, representing the Virgin Mary, and Pisces referring to Christ's role as the fisher of men). Yet although Roman Catholic authorities now acknowledged the influence of the constellations as indicators of fate, they never regarded them as agents of destiny. Furthermore, the roles of the planets, with their dangerously pagan names, were minimized in relation to those of the zodiacal signs.

It is interesting to note that some commentators have suggested fascinating parallels between many events described in the Bible and possible astrological occurrences. For example, the star that Matthew mentions hovering over Bethlehem, guiding the Magi from the east to the birthplace of Jesus Christ (2:1–12), has been variously interpreted as: a supernova; Halley's Comet (thought to have been visible in the skies around 11 BC); the conjunction of Jupiter and Saturn in the constellation of Pisces (believed to have occurred around 7 BC); or the "dog star." A related theory is that the three wise men were astrologers from Persia, who followed the star in the belief that it indicated the imminent fulfillment of a prophecy made by Zoroaster (c.628–551 BC).

Another school of astrological beliefs reconciles the characteristics of the zodiacal signs said to govern two-thousand-year eras with human, and specifically Judeo-Christian, behavior. Thus the astrological age of Taurus, the bull (from about 4000 to 2000 BC), was indicated by the idolatrous worship of the golden calf; that of Aries, the ram (lasting for 2000 years from c.2000 BC), by the near-sacrifice of Isaac by Abraham and the substitution of a ram in his place. These episodes occurred in the Old Testament, while the birth of Christ heralded the age of Pisces, the fish, predicted to end about AD 2000. Because the vernal equinox has slipped over the millennia, the age of Aquarius has been calculated as starting at any time between 1904 and 2160).

Inevitably, the cumulative result of the discoveries made by such notable astronomers as Copernicus, Tycho Brahe (1546–1601), Galileo, Johann Kepler (1571–1630) and Isaac Newton (1642–1727), was a diversion of the study of the celestial bodies into two discrete spheres. Astronomy was considered "scientific," while astrology was a dubious kind of divinatory art. The discovery of three planets unknown to the ancient stargazers— Uranus (in 1781), Neptune (1846) and Pluto (1930)—seemed to cast new doubt on astrological principles. However, modern astrologers have reconciled such findings with traditional principles (which provide the answers to previously puzzling anomalies), and astrology remains as significant and enlightening a subject today as it was four thousand years ago.

Above: The French astrologist Michel de Nostredame, better known as Nostradamus, advised sixteenth-century monarchs and published his famous book of rhymed prophecies under the title Centuries *in 1555.*

Astrology Re-evaluated

During the twentieth century, in conjunction with the emergence of the discipline of psychology, the role of astrology has undergone a change of emphasis. The work of American astrologer Marc Jones (1888–1980) popularized the Sabian symbols (channeled by a clairvoyant in 1925), which impart an evocative image to each degree of the zodiac to enable psychological inspiration and illumination through free association and meditation. In this respect, "the battles of life actually are fought, and won or lost, in the purely psychological and intangible areas of being.... Here, in the individual's ability to create at will, is the dynamic of his being and the essence of his functional or actual identity. It is with this that any effective astrology must have its primary concern," wrote Jones in his seminal work *The Sabian Symbols in Astrology* (1953).

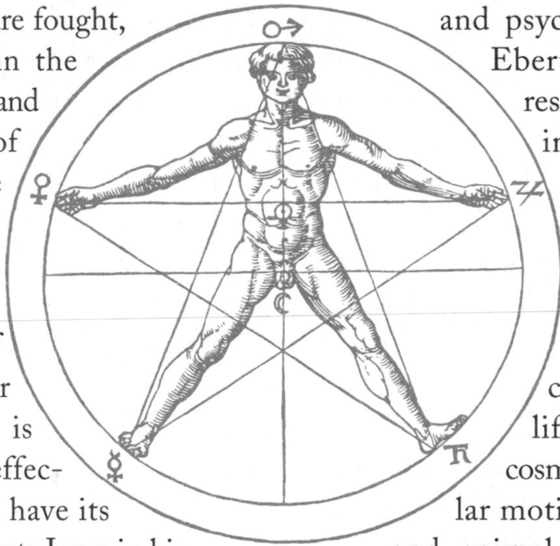

The pioneering psychologist Carl Gustav Jung (1875–1961), who also made a serious study of alchemy and mythology, thought that astrology and its symbols were an integral part of humanity's collective unconscious—that part of the human psyche that contains the archetypes, the universal blueprints of human experience. Through studying the horoscopes of certain clients, he also came to believe in synchronicity ("the 'acausal' correspondences between mutually independent psychic and physical events"). After evaluating a study of nearly five hundred married couples' horoscopes to ascertain whether mutual compatibility was determined by astrological influences, he stated: "The statistical material shows that a practical as well as a theoretically improbable chance combination star occurred which coincides in the most remarkable way with traditional astrological expectations."

Some scientists are still unwilling to deny the possible truth of astrological tenets. The noted German astrologer and psychologist Reinhold Ebertin (b. 1901) was responsible for initiating a new realm of study: cosmobiology, "a scientific discipline concerned with the possible correlations between cosmos and organic life and the effect of cosmic rhythms and stellar motions on man...plant and animal life as a whole." Undeniably, the gravitational pull of the Moon affects the tides. The decreasing Apogean tide, for example, occurs when the Moon is farthest from the Earth, while the increasing Perigean tide flows when the Earth is nearest to the Moon. Since ancient times, it has been observed that the Moon (Latin, *luna*) directly affects some people's behavior—hence the words "lunacy" and "lunatic" (the latter derived from *lunaticus*, meaning

Right: The diagram of Cosmic Man seen here reflects the Pythagorean theory that five is the perfect number of the human being as a microcosm of the universe. The wheel that encircles the figure bears the signs of the five planets (besides Earth) known to ancient astronomers.

"moonstruck"). Statistical evidence indicates that violent crime tends to increase when the Moon is full. Why, then, should the other "planets" be disbarred from exerting a similar influence?

Many scientific studies have, in fact, attested to the macrocosmic influence of other planets over the microcosmic Earth. Noted German seismologist Rudolf Tomascheck, for instance, discovered that when Uranus is positioned within 15° of the meridian, violent earthquakes sometimes occur, a phenomenon that could be explained by the gravitational influence exerted by Uranus over the Earth's molten core. And although the French psychologist and statistician Michel Gauquelin, in a series of tests begun in 1949, concluded that he had disproved many astrological precepts, he did identify a curiously frequent series of "coincidences" in examining the birthdates of selected physicians, athletes and high achievers in other professional spheres, which he termed the "Mars effect." In noting the common occurrence of a shared Sun, Moon or rising sign between parents and their offspring, he also suggested that humans may somehow be biologically attuned to celestial forces, and that the fetus may unconsciously "choose" the moment of its birth.

The South African-born astronomer Dr. Percy Seymour, in his compelling study *Astrology: the Evidence of Science* (1988), concurs: "According to my theory, [in the womb] we are all genetically 'tuned' to receiving a different set of 'melodies' from the magnetic 'symphony' of the Solar System." He goes on to state that: "the cosmos cannot alter our inherited characteristics but, by causing the actual moment of birth,... [our connection with the cosmos] is determined by our genes." Many scientists are becoming increasingly willing to explore, rather than reject outright, the ancient theory that human characteristics and behavioral patterns, along with those of other Earthly components, may be conditioned by the planets.

The Principles of Western Astrology

There are four leading systems of Western astrology: horary astrology, which is used to answer questions; electional astrology, employed to determine the optimum time when an intended course of action should be undertaken in order to ensure its success; mundane (or judicial) astrology, which is concerned with the forecasting of global, national or communal events; and natal astrology, whereby a person's characteristics and prospects are interpreted through the birth chart, or horoscope (a word derived from the Greek for "I look the hour," or "hourwatch"). Another type, natural astrology, has since been eclipsed by astronomy. It was used for practical purposes, for example, to set calendrical dates (such as Easter). Astrology is still sometimes used for predictive purposes, by calculating the planets' progressions or transits, their future positions or aspects, and then relating them to a specific birth chart.

Below: The Swiss psychologist and psychiatrist Carl Jung, who developed the theory of the collective unconscious, searched mythology and astrology for the meaning of the universal symbols that recur through the ages in diverse cultures.

Above: *Jung was fascinated by the symbolism of the mandala, a timeless image of the universe and being. He equated it with the quest for personal individuation, and, indeed, the horoscope itself may be regarded as both mandala and representation of the Self.*

THE ZODIAC

The zodiac may be defined as a circular belt extending for 8° on each side of the ecliptic, the path followed each solar year by the Sun, through which the twelve constellations pass cyclically. It is represented symbolically as a circle with the Sun at its center, with the zodiacal constellation arranged in a band around the perimeter, each occupying 30° of the 360° circle.

In the interests of scientific precision, it should be noted that because of the precession (simply described as a sort of wobble caused by the Earth's revolution on its axis) of the equinoxes—the vernal, around March 21, and the fall, around September 23—when the Sun crosses the celestial equator, the zodiacal constellations no longer occupy the same areas and dates traditionally assigned to them. For example, the Sun now traverses Leo between August 16 and September 15, whereas Leo's traditional dates ranged from July 23 to August 22. Therefore, effectively there are two zodiacs: the astrological zodiac, which is discussed here, and the movable.

Ancient star-gazers from many cultures observed that the constellations and planets seemed to follow the same cycle every year, each constellation reappearing at the same point in the night sky annually. Thus it was that the zodiacal cycle came to be used as a method of measuring time. The concept of the zodiac—derived from the Greek words *zodiakos kuklos*, "circus/circle of animated creatures," or *zoe* ("life") and *diakos* ("wheel")—is now believed to have originated in Mesopotamia around 3000 BC. During the earliest periods of astronomical observation, the Moon was considered more significant than the Sun, for not only were the constellations visible at night, but many ancient cultures venerated a lunar (often feminine) over a solar (usually masculine) deity. In contrast to today's convention, it was the Moon's, rather than the Sun's, progress through the zodiac that was charted. It is believed that the ancient Egyptians assimilated the Mesopotamian zodiac, incorporating a new refinement: the decans (the three periods of approximately ten days into which the zodiacal "month" is divided). Each of the thirty-six divisions that resulted was equated with an astral deity.

Many of these deities were allotted patronage of a specific constellation, according to the image that the starry pattern appeared to paint in the sky: Isis, for example, was associated with the creature whose shape was seen in Virgo. Indeed, it is probably this pairing of astral spirit and zodiacal constellation that resulted in some members of the original "circus" (comprised solely of animals) assuming human or demihuman form. By extension, the influence of the macrocosm (the zodiacal constellation) on the microcosm (a person born under that sign) was seen as imparting the characteristics inherent in, for instance, Aries, to the natal Arian: like the heavenly ram, people born under this sign were said to be headstrong and energetic. This astrological belief has endured over the millennia, although modern astrologers recognize that many other natal influences must also be taken into account.

The zodiacal signs were also thought

to affect human health. In microcosmic-macrocosmic thought ("as above, so below"), the macrocosm comprised the celestial components of the universe, which were mirrored exactly in the microcosm (the human body), over which they exerted a corresponding influence. This belief is graphically demonstrated in the medieval melothesic figure of "zodiacal man," in which each sign of the zodiac is strategically placed over the part of the body that it is said to govern. The theory underlying such representations profoundly influenced both medical diagnosis and treatment.

The symbolism associated with the twelve zodiacal signs is reflected in both the Jewish as well as the Christian religions. Eusebius (c.260–c.340), bishop of Caesarea (the modern city of Qisarya in Israel), chronicled the Jewish belief that Abraham was the father of the zodiac, and that each of the twelve tribes of Israel (named for the twelve patriarchs, the sons of Jacob) was associated symbolically with

a sign of the zodiac. Within Christianity, not only are there twelve apostles, but St. John's Book of Revelation in the New Testament describes the post-Apocalyptic holy city of Jerusalem as resting on twelve cornerstones inscribed with the apostles' names, and as having twelve pearly gates. Medieval Church authorities Christianized the name of the zodiac itself to the Latin *corona seu circulus sanctorium apostolorum,* "the crown of the circle of the Holy Apostles." They also tried to reinterpret the pagan signs into Christian symbols (Aries, for example, becoming the lamb of God), but this attempt never captured the popular imagination. The zodiac also assumed a symbolic role in Christian legends, as when King Arthur's knights took their places at the table equated with its circular form.

By astrological convention, the zodiacal signs have various groupings, all of which add symbolic meaning to their interpretations. Aries, Taurus, Gemini, Cancer, Virgo and Leo—called the septentironal signs from the Latin *septem* ("seven") and *triones* ("oxen") for the seven stars in the constellation of the Great Bear or Plow—are found in the northern hemisphere; Libra, Scorpio, Sagittarius, Capricorn, Aquarius and Pisces are southern-hemisphere constellations. Each sign is also accorded either feminine or masculine characteristics, which Ptolemy mentioned: "as the day is followed by the night, and as the male is coupled with the female." Each may also be balanced against its opposite, or polar, counterpart in a conflicting-complementing relationship similar to that of *yin* and *yang*. Thus Aries is paired with

Far left: The full Moon, associated with unity and completeness, is the final phase of a cycle identified by astrology with life, death and rebirth.

Below: In ancient Egypt, the key-shaped ankh, held here by the goddess Isis, signified the union of heaven and Earth.

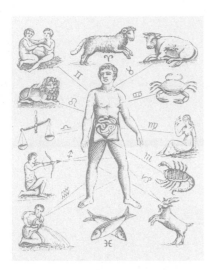

Above: *A medieval image of "Zodiacal Man," diagramming the relationship of the celestial signs to various parts of the human body.*

Far right: *Christianity "baptized" the traditional signs of the zodiac by equating them with the twelve apostles and the twelve gates of Jerusalem, as described by St. John the Evangelist in the New Testament Book of Revelation.*

Libra; Taurus with Scorpio; Gemini with Sagittarius; Cancer with Capricorn; Leo with Aquarius; and Virgo with Pisces.

Also important to defining the type of character imparted by each zodiacal sign is its mode (or "quadruplicity," denoting the four signs allocated to it, each of which represents a different element), which is said to reflect a quality of life. These can be one of three: cardinal (representing creativity and activity—Aries, Cancer, Libra and Capricorn); fixed (signifying preservation and passivity—Taurus, Leo, Scorpio and Aquarius); and mutable (denoting destruction and changeability—Gemini, Virgo, Sagittarius and Pisces).

THE PLANETS

"Observe how system into system runs/What other planets circle other suns," wrote Alexander Pope in his work *An Essay on Man*, Epistle I, li.25 (1733). And, indeed, the extent to which the astrological, calendrical and esoteric systems of world cultures and beliefs interact is astonishing, even in the light of syncretization and cross-fertilization of ideas. Nowhere is this more evident than in the influences associated with the planets, elements and seasons.

Perhaps the most significant figure in the history of astrology is Ptolemy (AD c.100–c.170), the Greco-Egyptian astronomer who grouped more than a thousand stars into forty-eight constellations. His key astrological treatise *Tetrabiblios*, written around AD 140, and specifically his *Almagest*, postulated that the Earth stood at the center of the universe, while the celestial bodies revolved around it. The Ptolemaic system prevailed until Copernicus disproved it in his posthumous opus *De Revolutionibus Orbium Coelestium* (1544), but by then the belief that the planets and constellations orbited the Earth, rather than the Sun, had become deeply entrenched in astrological theory and symbolism. In examining the role of the planets, it must also be remembered that early astrologers not only regarded the Sun and Moon—the luminaries—as planets, but that the existence of the three planets mentioned earlier was unknown. For millennia the "planets' were defined as seven bodies: the Sun, Moon, Mercury, Venus, Mars, Jupiter and Saturn.

Modern astrologers follow Copernican rather than Ptolemaic principles, but many of the concepts popularized by Ptolemy endure, especially in terms of symbolic associations. The original seven "planets,"

for instance, were equated with the seven heavens, directions, days of the week, metals, and also—with the ascendance of Christianity—the cardinal virtues and sins, and gifts of the Holy Spirit. Yet Ptolemy did not originate, but rather perpetuated, the symbolic significance of the seven planets. The seven stepped levels that make up the Mesopotamian ziggurat, for example, were believed to represent the hierarchy of the seven "wandering stars" within the structure (the word "planet" is derived from the Greek *planetes*, "wanderer," because they appeared to move erratically in comparison to the fixed stars). They also signified the ascending stages leading from Earth to the heavens (representing increasing spiritual enlightenment). Called *etemenanki*, the "temple of the seven spheres of the world," or "house of the seven directions of heaven and Earth," the ziggurat's seven levels were painted to accord with the colors associated with the deities (whose Romanized names are given here): black (Saturn), orange (Jupiter), red (Mars), gold (the Sun), yellow (Venus), blue (Mercury) and silver (the Moon). The Mesopotamians regarded the Moon, rather than the Sun, as being most important, both in astronomical and sacred belief, and placed it at the ziggurat's zenith.

In microcosmic-macrocosmic thought, astrologers credit the planets with a more important role than the zodiacal constellations, for it is their position in the sky that is said to exert the greatest influence over everything that occurs on Earth, as well as over personalities. While the sign of the zodiac under which a person is born may be said to impart potential, the planets are the energizing factors that activate and direct these innate possibilities. For example, while each zodiacal sign was believed to hold sway over a specific part of the human body—the Sun was said to be the spirit and the Moon, the soul—the remaining planets were assigned one of the five senses. According to a related theory from antiquity—that of the Greek philosopher Pythagoras (570–496 BC)—the seven planetary spheres were arranged hemispherically above the Earth: their independent turning created the "music of the spheres" (as our musical scale consists of seven principal notes). When a human soul descended to Earth from the eighth sphere (the Empyrean), traveling down through each level, it received the attributes of the individual ruling planet, so that when it was manifested on Earth as a new-born baby it possessed the corresponding virtues—and vices. Given the awesome power supposedly invested in them, it is hardly surprising that the planets were believed to be gods, and under Greco-Roman influence, the older Mesopotamian deities were transformed first into the Olympians and then into Roman gods.

The geocentric Ptolemaic system ordered the cosmos as follows: the Earth at the center, surrounded by the circular spheres of the Moon, Mercury, Venus, the Sun, Mars, Jupiter and Saturn. In a further refinement, Plato (427–347 BC) regarded the universe as a "cosmic soul" rotating on its own axis, while Tycho Brahe believed that while

Above: *The seven circles of the heavens identified by early astronomers were reflected in the stepped temples of the Babylonians and the monuments built by the Aztec and Mayan civilizations of the Western hemisphere.*

Above: The pyramid has profound implications as the "cosmic mountain" or world axis linking Earth and heaven. Correspondingly, it is an ancient symbol of the arduous path to enlightenment.

the Sun and Moon revolved around the Earth, the planets rotated round the Sun. Today the order of precedence used by astrologers accords with the updated heliocentric Copernican system, in which the Sun—the center of the solar system—is followed by the Moon (actually the Earth's satellite), then the nearest planet, Mercury, and subsequently by Venus, (Earth), Mars, Jupiter, Saturn, Uranus, Neptune and Pluto. In astrological interpretation the planets are categorized into three groups, indicating the level of influence that each exerts over people and the Earth: the fast-moving, "personal" planets, the Sun, Moon, Mercury, Venus, and Mars; the middle, or "transpersonal," planets, Jupiter and Saturn, which revolve at a more stately and sedate pace; and the "impersonal" planets: Uranus, Neptune and Pluto, which move so slowly that they are thus described as having a generational, rather than a personal, effect.

The Sun ☉

Sigil: a dot within a circle
Zodiacal rulership: Leo
Associated deity: Apollo, the Roman god of the Sun, music, poetry and prophecy (also the Roman *Sol Invictus*, the Persian Mithras, the Greek Helios, the Egyptian Ra, the Babylonian Shamash, and the Hindu Surya)
Day: Sunday
Zodiacal cycle: 1 year
Characteristics bestowed: vitality and individual consciousness

The Moon ☾

Sigil: a crescent
Zodiacal rulership: Cancer
Associated deity: Diana, the Roman goddess of the Moon and of the hunt (also the Roman Selene and Luna, the Greek Artemis, the Egyptian Isis, the Babylonian Sin, as well as the Hindu Chandra)
Day: Monday
Zodiacal cycle: approximately 28 days
Characteristics bestowed: profound emotions and intuition

Mercury ☿

Sigil: the caduceus
Zodiacal rulership: Gemini and Virgo
Associated deity: Mercury, the Roman messenger of the gods (also the Greek Hermes, the Egyptian Thoth, and the Hindu Hanuman)
Color: dark blue
Metal: mercury/quicksilver
Day: Wednesday
Zodiacal cycle: 88 days
Characteristics bestowed: intellectual ability and communication skills

Venus ♀

Sigil: a mirror or necklace
Zodiacal rulership: Taurus and Libra
Associated deity: Venus, the Roman goddess of love and beauty (also the Greek Aphrodite, the Egyptian Hathor, the Babylonian Ishtar, and the Hindu Lalita or Shukra)
Day: Friday
Zodiacal cycle: 225 days
Characteristics bestowed: the quest for beauty and harmony; benevolence

Mars ♂

Sigil: a shield and spear
Zodiacal rulership: Aries (traditionally, also Scorpio)
Associated deity: Mars, the Roman god of warfare and bloodshed (also the Greek Ares, the Egyptian Horus, the Babylonian plague god Nergal, and the Hindu Mangal)
Day: Tuesday
Zodiacal cycle: 687 days
Characteristics bestowed: energy, leadership and aggression

Jupiter ♃

Sigil: the Greek letter *zeta* (Z)
Zodiacal rulership: Sagittarius (traditionally, also Pisces)
Associated deity: Jupiter, the chief Roman god and deity of the sky (also the Greek Zeus, the Egyptian Amun-Re, the supreme Babylonian god Marduk, and the Hindu god Indra, Guru or Vrihaspatri)
Day: Thursday
Zodiacal cycle: 11 years, 315 days
Characteristics bestowed: expansive energy and optimism

Saturn ♄

Sigil: a sickle
Zodiacal rulership: Capricorn (traditionally, also Aquarius)
Associated deity: Saturn, the Roman god of agriculture and time (also the Greek Kronos, the Egyptian Sebek, the Babylonain Ninib or Ninutra, and the Hindu Brahma or Shani)
Day: Saturday
Zodiacal cycle: 29 years, 167 days
Characteristics bestowed: growing wisdom and maturity

Uranus ♅

Sigil: the letter "H" bisected by an orb
Zodiacal rulership: Aquarius
Associated deity: Uranus, the primeval Roman sky god (also the Greek Ouranos)
Zodiacal cycle: 84 years
Characteristics bestowed: transcendental energy, unpredictability and inventiveness

Neptune ♆

Sigil: a trident
Zodiacal rulership: Pisces
Associated deity: Neptune, the Roman god of the sea (also the Greek Poseidon)
Zodiacal cycle: 168 years, 292 days
Characteristics bestowed: psychic powers, idealism, escapism and confusion

Pluto ♇

Sigil: an orb enclosed by a crescent; the initials "P" and "L"
Zodiacal rulership: Scorpio
Associated deity: the Roman god of the underworld (also the Greek Hades)
Zodiacal cycle: 248 years, 183 days
Characteristics bestowed: the power to effect transformation

THE ELEMENTS

Just as the numbers twelve (the total zodiacal signs) and seven (the sum of the traditional planets) are symbolically important within astrology, so the number four assumes additional significance, for each of the four elements (fire, air, water and earth) is associated with three signs of the zodiac.

From classical through medieval times, and even for some centuries later, it was believed that everything in the universe was made up of the four elements, differences in form and character arising from the attractive and repulsive properties and relationships of elements, as well as the varying proportions of the four vital ingredients. Solid matter (represented by the element of earth), liquid (water) and vapor (air) were each believed to be inherent in any object or living being, while fire provided animating energy. The basest or heaviest element was earth, followed by water, the lightest or most elevated elements being air and fire. (In esoteric thought, originated by the ancient Greeks, there is also a rarefied fifth element, ether, the perfect element which contains and generates the other four, from which the ethereal stellar and planetary bodies are made, and which exists only in the heavenly sphere.)

Although it was the ancient Greeks, and specifically Empedocles (c.490–30 BC), who formalized the elemental theory, they had inherited a concept so ancient that scholars believe it stretches back to Neolithic times, and perhaps even beyond. Some speculate that it was derived from the early human realization that corpses can only be disposed of satisfactorily by four means: burying them in the earth; throwing them into a body of water, there to sink to the bottom of a river, sea or lake bed; allowing carrion birds, such as vultures, to swoop from the air and feast on the remains; or cremating them on a pyre. Thus the human body was perceived to be reclaimed by the elements after death, to dissolve into its elemental component parts, and then to be ecologically reconstituted. And just as the planets were personified as gods, so most sacred beliefs elevated the elements to deified status, venerating an Earth Mother, such as the Greco-Roman Demeter (Ceres) or a divine ruler of the Underworld like Hades (Pluto); a god of water, such as Poseidon (Neptune); a deity whose realm was the air, most notably Zeus (Jupiter); and a fire god like Hephaestos (Vulcan).

In medieval times, and also in alchemical thought, each element was associated with an appropriate spirit: gnomes represented the earth; undines, water; sylphs, air; and salamanders, fire. In this respect, too, astrological and Christian symbolism are linked, for the form of the "astrologer's cross" was traditionally used to represent the Evangelists: St. John's eagle (equated with Scorpio and the element of air) standing on the northerly point; St. Luke's ox (related to Taurus and the element of earth) in the south; St. Matthew's angel (Aquarius and water) in the west; and St. Mark's lion (Leo and fire) in the east.

In a further refinement of the macrocosmic-microcosmic elemental concept in relation to the human body, medieval physicians not only believed that each zodiacal sign governed a particular limb or organ, but also that four elemental "humors" flowed through the body, and that certain ailments were caused by an imbalance of these. The element of earth was equated with black bile, and the melancholic humor; water with phlegm, and thus the phlegmatic humor; air was associated with the blood, and hence with the sanguine humor; and fire with choler (yellow bile), and the choleric humor.

The twelve zodiacal signs are divided into four trigons, or triplicities, each of which corresponds to an element: the fiery (masculine) trigon, comprising Aries, Leo and Sagittarius; the airy (masculine) trigon, containing Gemini, Libra and Aquarius; the watery (feminine) trigon, consisting of Cancer, Scorpio and Pisces; and the earthy (feminine) trigon of Taurus, Virgo and Capricorn. Each element is believed to influence the personality: fire bestows vitality and aggression; air, intellectual aspiration and volatility; water, gentleness and changeability; and earth, patience and solidity. People born under the first zodiacal sign within each trigon (e.g., Aries within the fiery trigon) are said to manifest these characteristics in their purest form, while those whose natal signs are second and third in a trigon will possess these traits in gradually decreasing degrees.

THE ASTROLOGICAL GOVERNANCE OF TIME

Astrological precepts are inextricably linked with the measurement of time—cosmic and Earthly. Thus the symbolism of the number four is harnessed to the planets, which are associated with the idea

Left: Agricultural societies looked to the skies for portents not only of the best times to sow, reap and celebrate the deities of fertility, but to placate forces inimical to an abundant harvest.

of dividing time into "world periods," a concept that exists within most sacred traditions, from the Mesoamerican to the Zoroastrian, to the Hindu, Greco-Roman and Christian, among others. Ovid (43 BC–AD 18), in his work *Metamorphoses I*, specifies four such ages, of decreasing levels of perfection: the Golden Age, under the rulership of Saturn; the Silver Age, dominated by Jupiter; the Bronze/Brazen Age, and the Iron Age (the governing deities of the latter are not specified). St. Augustine of Hippo (354–430) specified seven ages in *De Civitate Dei* (*The City of God*), connected to the number of days listed in the Old Testament book of creation, Genesis (but also, in esoteric thought, with the planets).

The four elements are said to correspond to the cardinal directions and seasons: earth representing the south and fall; water, the west and winter; air, the north and spring; and fire, the east and summer (although these designations can vary). The Mesopotamian civilizations distinguished three seasons: spring, summer and winter; while the inhabitants of more northerly, harsher, climes recognized only

Below: The evergreen tree is an enduring symbol of eternal life, especially in northern climates, where its layered branches offer shelter from winter's cold and the promise of seasonal renewal.

two: summer and winter. As with so many conventions, it was the ancient Greeks who introduced the additional season of fall, thus harmonizing the seasons both numerically and symbolically with the elements and directions. In fact, the Greek word *horae* ("hours"), signifying the four goddesses who represented the seasons, was also used to describe the four quadrants of the cosmos.

Spring denotes the time when nature awakens after its long sleep. The vernal equinox, which falls around March 21, was especially significant in sacred pagan rites: for example, it marked the beginning of the ancient Roman *hieros gamos* (held between March 22 and 24). By April 30, May Eve, the burgeoning of nature was evident, and the Romans dedicated their licentious festivities of May 1 to the fertility goddesses Floralia or Maia, while the Celts honored their Sun god Beli at the feast of Beltane. In the medieval Christian books of hours, the spring zodiacal constellations were equated with agricultural "labors of the months," Aries being associated with the pruning of vines, for instance; Taurus with the planting of flowers and training of vines; and Gemini with the scything of grass.

The arrival of summer is heralded by the summer solstice, which usually falls around June 21, a time when the prospect of the Sun's descent and the coming winter caused pagan peoples to burn fires to the Sun to encourage its eventual return. Important summer festivals included the Celtic Lughnasha on August 1—a sociable occasion when the grain god Lug was celebrated with games and feasting. Traditional summer activities include the

reaping of harvests sown in spring, and the summer zodiacal signs reflected this emphasis—Cancer, haymaking; Leo, the scything and threshing of corn; and Virgo, the gathering of fruits.

Fall is a somewhat melancholy period, a transitional season when winter's chill begins to manifest itself even while the Sun still warm the Earth. The labors over which the zodiacal signs held sway reflect this duality, for Libra presided over the trading of grapes; Scorpio over the distillation of wine into casks; and Sagittarius over the harvesting of olives and the collection of kindling. Pagan tribes held ceremonial rites to mark the fall equinox around September 21, but perhaps the most important Celtic festival was that of Samhain, on November 1, when, according to the lunar calendar, it was believed that the old year ended and the new one began. The fact that it was regarded as a dangerous night, when a cosmic crack in time allowed the ghostly inhabitants of the "other world" to roam abroad, is still reflected in today's Hallowe'en celebrations.

Winter is a barren, cheerless season, but also promises the coming of spring, and at the winter solstice (around December 21), which ancient civilizations equated with the rebirth of the solar god, this promise of regeneration was celebrated in such festivities as the Roman Saturnalia, those in honor of Sol Invictus, and the Teutonic Yule. (Thus the Christian commemoration of the birth of Christ on December 25, and the riotous behavior associated with New Year's Eve in modern times, both recall ancient pagan festivals). Other fertility rites, including the

Celtic Imbolc (February 1), also looked forward to the spring with activities traditionally associated with the zodiacal signs of winter: Capricorn governing the slaughter of pigs and baking; Aquarius, the felling of trees; and Pisces the grafting of fruit-bearing trees.

Lunar Calendars

Today the Western world measures time in accordance with the solar calendar, and dates its years from the birth of Christ. (Since 1582, when the Gregorian calendar of Pope Gregory XIII replaced the Julian calendar devised by Julius Caesar in 46 BC, inaccuracies have been prevented by restricting century leap years to those divisible by four hundred.) Yet many of the world's major religions order their sacred calendars by lunar months according to ancient custom. Archaeological and historical evidence indicates that the Mesopotamian astronomers disregarded the position of the Sun in their observations, concentrating on that of the Moon for the purposes of lunar worship. Indeed, most ancient religions venerated the Moon, both because of its constantly changing shape which associated it with the cycle of life: birth (the new Moon); growth (the waxing, crescent Moon); maturity (the full Moon); decline (the waning, crescent Moon); death (the "black" Moon, comprising the three or four days when the Moon appears to be invisible); and rebirth (the new Moon again.) Another factor in its worship was the mysterious lunar effect on the ebb and flow of tides and its apparent effect upon menstrual cycles. It is said that the Roman emperor Numa Pomphilius (8th century BC) increased the number of months comprising a year from ten to twelve in order to regulate the lunar and solar cycles, thus instigating a conscious shift in importance from the Moon to the Sun in Western thought.

The Jewish calendar (*huach ha-shanah*) is primarily lunar, although it includes adjustments (the addition of an extra month between February and March seven times within every nineteen years) related to the solar cycle. Thus ritual celebrations of agricultural origin, such as the *sukkoth* harvest festival, do not fall out of synchronicity with the seasons (the lunar year is some eleven days shorter than the solar). Such is the ancient importance of the Moon in Judaism that it is symbolically equated with the children of Israel, while the Sun represents Gentiles (all other peoples). At the start of each month, the birth of the new Moon (*molad*) may be greeted with ritual rejoicing called *rosh chodesh*. Since medieval times, years have been counted from the date when God is believed to have created the world, that is, 3760 BC.

Like the Jewish calendar, that of Hinduism is lunar-based, although it is modified by the addition of a month every two-and-a-half years to bring it into line with the solar cycle. Each lunar month is thought of as consisting of two light (*shukra*), positive weeks, indicated by the waxing of the Moon, and two dark (*krishna*), negative weeks, heralded by the Moon's waning. The Islamic religious calendar is also lunar-based, from the date of

Mohammed's migration (*hejira*) from Mecca to Medina (September 622 AD). This is the starting point not only for the calculation of years, but also for the month (in this case *muharram*) that opens the new year. Even Christianity, most of whose feasts and saints' days are celebrated on fixed annual dates, retains the influence of the lunar calendar in the moveable date of Easter Sunday (commemorating Christ's resurrection), which may fall on any Sunday between March 21 and April 25, according to when the Moon first becomes full after the vernal equinox. (Christianity and Judaism's shared sacred history closely links this date with that of the Jewish Passover, when Christ suffered).

Although astrology is heliocentric rather than lunacentric today, the Moon remains an extremely significant force: as it progresses through the zodiacal signs, it exerts a strong influence over the Earth and its inhabitants. During those periods when it is between the signs, it is said to be "void in course," its absence threatening dangerous instability.

Of further significance in astrological calculations are the Moon's two nodes, or "dragon points" (so called because a dragon was envisaged as swallowing and then regurgitating the celestial bodies). The Dragon's Head (*Caput Draconis*), the ascending, northern node, denotes where the Moon's orbit crosses that of the Earth's ecliptic as the latter rotates around the Sun; and the Dragon's tail (*Carda Draconis*), or southern node, which lies directly opposite. The Dragon's Head and Tail are respectively termed Lo-hou and Chi-tu by Chinese astrologers, and Ratu and Ketu by Indian astrological practi-

tioners. In ancient times the lunar nodes were important to the calculation of solar and lunar eclipses, but today Chinese and Indian astrologers consider them especially important for the interpretation of horoscopes. They are beleived to represent the subject's karma—the northern node showing areas in which improvements should be made in life; and the southern, the subject's genetic inheritance (or the characteristics that stem from a former existence).

The Americas

Remarkably sophisticated calendrical and astrological calculations were made by the early inhabitants of present-day Central and South America. Archaeological evidence from Mexico and Guatemala, including the ancient Zapotec culture, can be traced to the sixth century BC. After the invasion of the Spanish *conquistadores* in the sixteenth century, the Mesoamerican astrological tradition perished with its practitioners. However, enough of its legacy endures in cultural artefacts and folk practices among highland Mayans and Oaxacan peoples to show its overriding importance, especially in the Mayan and Aztec societies.

Extant records bear witness to the detailed solar and lunar observations made by the Mesoamerican astrologers to set the dates of their most important festivals, or otherwise determine the best times for placating their ferocious gods or undertaking civil action. The link between the Mesoamerican deities and the measurement of time, as dictated by solar and lunar cycles, is inseparable, and the position and movement of the celestial bodies represent cosmic mythological beings and events. Many kinds of calendars were used in Mesoamerica, but perhaps the most important was that which operated according to a 260-day cycle (the Aztec *tonalpohualli*), in which individual gods were associated with twenty "day names," as well as the twenty groupings of thirteen-day "weeks" into which the cycle was divided. Each of the thirteen days had dual patron deities—a "lord" of the day and night—and a specific color, direction and bird.

A less clear-cut, approximately 365-day, solar cycle (called *xihuitl* by the Aztecs) was used by the postclassic Mayans in conjunction with the 260-day calendar. The solar calendar omitted leap-year days, and was divided into eighteen groups of twenty days (the Aztec *veintena*), each category falling under the patronage of a named deity. The annual balance of days was made up by five inauspicious days (*nemontemi*, or "nameless days") falling at the end of the aforementioned period, which were considered unlucky as birthdates.

The Aztecs also charted a "calendar round" of fifty-two solar years (the end of which "century," or *ziumolpilli*, was celebrated with the New Fire ceremony to appease the gods). A new cycle was initiated when the new year's day of each of the two primary calendars coincided. Nor was this cyclical system limited in scope. The classic Mayans' conception of time encompassed a truly heroic scale, the long-count *baktun* cycle beginning on August 2, 3114 BC, and forecast to end on December 23, AD 2010. The periods of time used to compute this cycle were divided into days (*kin*), 20-day periods (*uinal*), 360-day years (*tun*), 20 years (*katun*), 400 years (*baktun*), and so on, up to a staggering 160,000 *tuns* (*calabtun*).

The completion of any calendrical cycle assumed apocalyptic significance, for it was regarded as a dangerous time that could potentially herald the cataclysmic ending of the current world age and the dawning of a new one. Solar eclipses (when the Sun was said to be under attack), lunar eclipses (less dangerous than the solar, but still threatening) and the first manifestation—the heliacal rising—of the planet Venus (regarded as a malevolent, masculine deity) as the Morning Star all engendered anxiety. Thus the movements of the Sun, Moon and Venus were studied with special care.

Mesoamerican birthdates were believed to preordain one's future, and Aztec diviners consulted the *tonalamatl* almanac on behalf of those who wished to know their destinies. An astrologer, *adivino*, was invariably asked to divine a baby's future shortly after its birth.

Despite lacking a homogenous astrological system comparable to that of the Western tradition, North American native peoples give important roles to the celestial bodies within their mythologies and folk tales. The Pawnee tribe of the Plains, for example, celebrate the Morning Star ceremony in remembrance of the masculine Morning Star's part in creating humanity with the feminine Evening Star. Pawnee "star charts," as well as those of other tribes, feature intricate representations of the night sky, but are regarded

Above: The stars and four cardinal directions are a frequent motif in the artwork of tribal societies like those of Native America. Note the resemblance to the yin/yang *symbolism of the Far East.*

more as articles imbued with magical power than as accurate recordings of astrological knowledge.

There are many Native American tribes, each cherishing its own cultural, sacred and astrological lore—too many to do justice to here. Suffice it to say that celestial observation related to mythology and the celebration of seasonal festivals are of vital significance within the various traditions, and that ancient beliefs still have relevance today. The exact principles underlying the ancient medicine wheels of the Plains, for example, are unknown. These impressive structures may have played a symbolic role in ritual, besides aiding calendrical calculation, for—like the ancient northern European megaliths—they were probably constructed in alignment with the summer solstice. Most have twenty-eight spokes radiating from the center, associating them with the lunar cycle.

Chinese Astrology

The Chinese calendar is among the most ancient of the world's surviving cultures. Based primarily on the lunar cycle, along with numerical and other astronomical observations, it is not only extremely complex, but is inseparable from the indigenous system of astrology—one that now rivals that of the West in terms of popularity. In a modified form, Chinese astrology also forms the basis of the Japanese tradition, as well as that practiced by Lamaist priests in Tibet. Chinese astrology, *ming shu* ("the reckoning of fate"), is said to have been instituted by the "Yellow Emperor," Huang Ti, in 2637 BC. He and his successors were divinely generated—"sons of heaven," who were considered directly responsible for ensuring celestial harmony in the realm. Chinese astrologers regard their craft as more predictive than that of their Western counterparts (who prefer to regard their conclusions as indicative), and in order to ascertain a person's destiny, knowledge of the precise time and place of birth is crucial.

Since the fifth or sixth centuries AD, the Chinese have divided the week into ten, rather than seven, days, the names of the days being termed collectively the "ten heavenly stems" ("stem" is equivalent to the Chinese word for "Sun"). The number of hours comprising a day are twelve (consisting of two-hour groupings), known as the "twelve terrestrial branches." The same branch names are applied to the twelve lunar months (of twenty-nine or thirty days) that make up a year. (Through the influence of Buddhism, which was imported from India, the names of the twelve branches were eventually replaced by those of the twelve animals comprising the Chinese zodiac.) The stem-and-branch cycles, within which the elemental and polarity cycles are also intercalated, combine to make an additional cycle of sixty years (*chia-tzu*); the present cycle began in 1984 and will end in 2044. In order to regulate the lunar calendar, an additional month is intercalated every two-and-a-half years. There is another calendrical system based on the solar cycle, which is used as an aid to agriculture: the "farmer's calendar" is divided into twenty-four periods, each lasting approximately fifteen days.

Given such an intricate system of measuring time, it is small wonder that expert astrologers are consulted regularly, and that most Chinese households need the help of an annual almanac to keep track of the days on which important festivals fall each year. The most important of these is the new-year festival, celebrated on the occasion of the second full Moon occuring after the winter solstice, and considered as representing every person's birthday. (In fact, in the Chinese way of reckoning, people regard the new year of the year in which they were born, and not their actual birthdays, as the starting point at which to determine their age.) According to ancient belief, the course of an imaginary planet, *t'i sui* ("the great year," personified as the "minister of time," rotating in a reverse direction to Jupiter) determines the start of the year, and hence the subsequent dates that are ritually significant. Other important festivals with strong astrological associations include the lantern festival, which anticipates the coming of spring and is celebrated on the full Moon of the first lunar month; and the midfall festival, held on the occasion of the fall equinox, when offerings are made to the Moon by its Earthly *yin* representatives—women.

THE CHINESE ZODIAC

Although they are said to date back to 3000 BC, it is speculated that the creatures now associated with the zodiac entered Chinese astrology around the first century AD, and that they were derived from a Western exemplar brought to China by Turkish traders. The more con-

Left: In Chinese astrology, the year of the horse denotes both optimism and inconstancy. It is linked with the element of fire.

ventional view is that they were introduced during the T'ang dynasty, around 600 AD, and indicated the animals that should be sacrificed on the opening of each month or year, for unlike the Western signs, these creatures do not represent the names of the zodiacal constellations. The identities of the twelve signs are explained by the Buddhist legend that before his death Buddha summoned all the animals on Earth to him: only twelve responded (the rat narrowly beating the ox to arrive first), and he rewarded them by naming a year after each. The twelve are neatly divided into two additional categories: wild creatures (the rat, tiger, rabbit, dragon, snake and monkey) and domesticated ones (the ox, horse, goat, cock, dog and pig); and those that are respectively *yin* and *yang*. Such signs alternate throughout the cycle of the zodiac, with each *yang* creature paired with a *yin* animal (the *yang* rat and *yin* ox, for example) in a conflicting-complementing partnership.

Although the animals are now said to govern each month, as well as two hours of every day, their real importance lies in each creature's rulership of a year, resulting in a zodiacal cycle of twelve lunar years. The zodiac itself is represented as a "year tree," consisting of twelve branches under which the creatures graze. People's personalities are said to be influenced by the nature of the creature in whose year they were born. Just as Western astrology acknowledges the importance of the ascendant sign at time of birth, so in the Chinese system the influence of the creature that prevailed at the hour of birth is said to affect the way in which people present themselves to others, according to the "personality" of the animal that governs the double-hour concerned.

The Rat (*da shu*)

Polarity: yang
Element: water
Direction: north
Western equivalent: Sagittarius
Hours of ascendance: 11 p.m. to 1 p.m. (*tzu*)
Characteristics bestowed: positive action, fortune, wealth and expansion

The Ox (buffalo or cow, *nion*)

Polarity: yin
Element: water
Direction: north-northeast
Western equivalent: Capricorn
Hours of ascendance: 1 a.m. to 3 a.m. (*ch'ou*)
Characteristics bestowed: patience, industriousness and responsibility

The Tiger (*po hon*)

Polarity: yang
Element: wood
Direction: east-northeast
Western equivalent: Aquarius
Hours of ascendance: 3 a.m. to 5 a.m. (*yin*)
Characteristics bestowed: power, aggression and impulsiveness

The Rabbit (or hare, *tu ze*)

Polarity: yin
Element: wood
Direction: east
Western equivalent: Pisces
Hours of ascendance: 5 a.m. to 7 a.m. (*mao*)
Characteristics bestowed: good fortune, harmony and sensitivity

The Dragon (*long*)

Polarity: yang
Element: wood
Direction: east-southeast
Western equivalent: Aries
Hours of ascendance: 7 a.m. to 9 a.m. (*ch'en*)
Characteristics bestowed: energy, egotism and enthusiasm

The Snake (or serpent, *sue*)

Polarity: yin
Element: fire
Direction: south-southeast
Western equivalent: Taurus
Hours of ascendance: 9 a.m. to 11 a.m. (*zu*)
Characteristics bestowed: shrewdness, stealth and mystery

The Horse (*ma*)

Polarity: yang
Element: fire
Direction: south
Western equivalent: Gemini
Hours of ascendance: 11 a.m. to 1 p.m. (*wu*)
Characteristics bestowed: determination, optimism and fickleness

The Goat (ram or sheep, *yang*)

Polarity: yin
Element: fire
Direction: south-southwest
Western equivalent: Cancer

Hours of ascendance: 1 p.m. to 3 p.m. (*wei*)
Characteristics bestowed: sensitivity, compassion and gentleness

The Monkey (*hou*)

Polarity: yang
Element: metal
Direction: west-southwest
Western equivalent: Leo
Hours of ascendance: 3 p.m. to 5 p.m. (*shen*)
Characteristics bestowed: intelligence, versatility and humor

The Rooster (cock, *ji*)

Polarity: yin
Element: metal
Direction: west
Western equivalent: Virgo
Hours of ascendance: 5 p.m. to 7 p.m. (*yu*)
Characteristics bestowed: critical faculties, pride and independence

The Dog (*gou*)

Polarity: yang
Element: metal
Direction: west-northwest
Western equivalent: Libra
Hours of ascendance: 7 p.m. to 9 p.m. (*hsu*)
Characteristics bestowed: loyalty, fairness and straightforwardness

The Pig (or boar, *zhu*)

Polarity: yin
Element: water
Direction: north-northwest
Western equivalent: Scorpio
Hours of ascendance: 9 p.m. to 11 p.m. (*hai*)
Characteristics bestowed: good humor, sensuality and honesty

THE LUNAR MANSIONS

Another significant convention to be considered is the Chinese custom of dividing the year into twenty-eight lunar *hsiu*, "mansions" (the palaces in which the Moon goddess resides every night in rotation during her passage across the sky). Each is equated with a ruling spirit and animal, as well as a Taoist disciple of the immortal T'ung-t'ien Chiao-chu (the first, for example, is the dragon's horn, whose animal is the scaly dragon; whose spirit is Teng Yo, and whose disciple is named as Po-lin Tao-jen), and whose name also corresponds to a day. In many respects, a greater parallel can be drawn between these lunar mansions and the Western zodiacal constellations than between the latter and the twelve Chinese beasts of the constellations, for the *hsiu* are said to exist within the constellations that lie along the celestial equator, through which the Moon passes.

THE CHINESE ELEMENTS

A vital component of Chinese astrology, as of Western astrology, is the modifying influence of the elements (*wu hsing*). However, in Chinese astrological thought—also said to have been originated by Huang Ti, but formalized by Tsou Yen (305–240 BC)—these number five, rather than four: water, fire, earth, metal and wood (the latter two replacing and supplementing the fourth Western element of air, which the Chinese regard as *ch'i*, the breath of life). The Chinese elemental theory is bound up with the Taoist belief in the cosmic polarities of *yin* and *yang*, which exist in opposition yet possess the potential to produce

Above: *Those born in the Chinese year of the rooster are said to be proud and independent, with acute powers of discernment.*

perfection when in harmony, each element possessing both *yang* (the masculine, solar, active principle), and *yin* (the female, lunar, passive force) aspects. The twelve zodiacal creatures and the years over which they preside are, however, one or the other—each positive year (perhaps that of the rat), being followed by a negative one (the year of the ox).

The theory underlying the five elements is similar to the Western view: all manifestations of cosmic energy (also called *ch'i*) are contained within them. The elements exist in a constant, cyclical state of engagement and battle for supremacy, explained by the fact that metal implements can be used to fell trees (wood); wood takes essential nourishment from the earth; earth hinders the flow of water; water extinguishes fire; and fire can melt metal. In the reverse aspect, metal can be used to contain water; water gives life to trees, and thus wood; wood gives energy to fire; the ashes produced by fire nurture the earth; and metal ore comes from the earth.

As in Western thought, the five Chinese elements are also associated with the seasons (the fifth season briefly separating summer and fall). The twenty-eight constellations are traditionally divided among the four quarters of the universe, each quadrant being allocated a season and guardian creature. East is the season of spring, protected by the green dragon; south, summer, and the scarlet phoenix (*feng huang*); west, fall and the white tiger or unicorn (*kylin*); and north, winter, with a black tortoise encircled by a snake. The center of this quadrant represents China. Just as much

Western symbolism is largely informed by the number four—the number of the Western elements—so the elemental number of five is used to represent such sacred concepts as the number of virtues, blessings and books of ritual, as well as the five emperors of heaven (*wu ti*). The elements also play a vital part in the practice of *feng shui*, which seeks to identify and rectify any kind of elemental imbalance in the landscape.

In order to determine your own personal element, it is necessary to consult tables to discover, in order of their significance: the element of your year of birth (perhaps positive fire); the element associated with the animal sign that governs your natal year (perhaps the rooster, which is negative); the element that governs your hour of birth; the element that presides over the month of your birth; and the element that is linked with your country of birth. The element that occurs most frequently is regarded as your dominant sign, and thus the strongest personality indicator, although ideally each element should be represented within this grouping of five in order to produce a well-balanced personality.

Metal
Direction: west
Season: fall
Color: white
Characteristics bestowed: fairness, determination, inflexibility and melancholy

Water
Direction: north
Season: winter
Color: blue

Characteristics bestowed: compassion, flexibility, nervousness and hypersensitivity

Wood
Direction: east
Season: spring
Color: green
Characteristics bestowed: creativity, cooperation, impatience and lack of focus

Fire
Direction: south
Season: summer
Color: red
Characteristics bestowed: dynamism, passion, egotism, pride, frustration and recklessness

Earth
Direction: the center
Color: yellow
Characteristics bestowed: patience, practical skills, caution and stubbornness

Other Traditions

It is generally (though not universally) accepted that the form of astrology practiced in India today originated in Mesopotamia, the "cradle of civilization." Indian astrology is closely interlinked with other forms of Hindu mystical tradition, such as *kundalini* yoga, and shares the microcosmic-macrocosmic theories that assumed such vital importance in traditional Western astrology. Thus, for example, it is said that while a fetus is growing in the womb two *chakras* ("wheels") are simultaneously being formed within the unborn child. One,

the twelve-segmented *pingala*, corresponds to the signs of the solar zodiac, and the other, the *ina*, comprises twenty-eight components, each of which is equated with a house of the lunar zodiac. This theory implies that people harbor these dual forms of physical horoscope within their bodies.

Based primarily on the Chinese system of astrology, the Tibetan tradition differs subtly from its parent. The Chinese rat, for instance, is replaced by a mouse, the rabbit by a hare, and the rooster by an unspecified bird. The influence of Indian astrological beliefs is also evident in those of its geographical neighbor, and the Lamaist astrologers (*tsi-pa*) practice any of three types of interpretation and prediction: the Chinese-influenced system of *jung-tsi*, in which *yin* and *yang*, the five elements, and twelve animals all play a crucial part; *kar-tsi*, whose origins are believed to lie in Hindu *kalachakra* tantric principles, and which employs nine planets, twelve houses (i.e., zodiacal signs), and twenty-seven constellations; and *wang-char*, a numerological and talismanic system that its adherents believe was taught to human beings by the Hindu god Shiva himself.

Constructing a Horoscope

Astrologers believe that by charting the positions of the luminaries, planets and zodiacal constellations at the exact time of a person's birth (or, indeed, a nation's inception), valuable conclusions as to that person's personality and potential, as well as possible future challenges, can be drawn by interpreting the influences that prevailed when they came into the world.

The charting of a horoscope is a highly skilled art, which requires a profound knowledge and understanding of the complex principles and interrelationships that govern astrology. Consulting an experienced astrologer, or perhaps taking advantage of the detailed, but now readily accessible, information stored in dedicated computer-software packages, is recommended. In order to compile as accurate a picture as possible, it is vital to know the subject's exact time of birth, and also his or her birthplace: any variation in these two crucial factors can lead to a distorted or false reading.

Once armed with the date and place of the subject's birth, the astrologer will consult a tabular daily listing (ephemeris) to ascertain the positions of the Sun, Moon and planets within the zodiac at that particular moment in "sidereal" time (astronomical, rather than artificially regulated time, such as Greenwich Mean Time). An atlas is also needed to calculate the latitude and longitude of the place of birth, which will then be added or subtracted from the sidereal time to calculate the astronomically correct time of birth. This information, in turn, will enable the astrologer to draw up a horoscope according to a prescribed circular format, in which the zodiacal signs occupy the outer band at 30° intervals, with the sigils of the luminaries and planets placed at the appropriate points. The tenth and twentieth degree of the circle are often differentiated by long lines, while the fifth, fifteenth and twenty-fifth are identified by dotted, or shorter, lines. Within the elliptic of each sign are further subdivisions: the thirty degrees themselves, and the three groups consisting of ten degrees (the decans).

THE HEMISPHERES

The circle is further divided into four quarters, or hemispheres, signifying the four cardinal points: the ascendant (ASC) in the east; the descendent (DSC) in the west; midheaven, or *mediumcoeli* (MC) in the north; and the *immum coeli* (IC) in the south. Thus the horoscope may be regarded as a sort of cosmic map of the heavens at the time of the subject's birth. The Sun sign, that is, the zodiacal constellation occupied by the Sun at the time of birth, is the most important component in the horoscope, for this indicates the subject's dominant personal characteristics. The second most significant indicator is the ascendant, or rising sign (for which knowledge of the subject's time and date of birth is especially vital). Situated on the cusp of the first house, it reveals further information about the subject's personality, especially his or her means of expression. The planet that rules the zodiacal sign situated on the ascendant is the subject's ruling planet. The descendant sign, on the cusp of the seventh house, imparts information about the subject's unconscious mind, while the midheaven sign, on the cusp of the fourth house, represents the zenith, or highest point in terms of potential success, and the *imum coeli*, on the cusp of the tenth house, indicates a person's lowest point, or nadir.

THE HOUSES

Next the astrologer will consider the implications of the planets' position within the twelve houses (represented as twelve segments) that hold sway over various aspects of daily life, and through which the zodiacal bodies pass every twenty-four hours. According to the mundane-house system, which equates the houses with the zodiacal signs, each house has a specific area of influence traditionally dictated by its zodiacal sign and its ruling planet:

I: personality, appearance and beginnings (Aries/Mars)

II: financial concerns, possessions and growth (Taurus/Venus)

III: communication skills, siblings and mundane matters (Gemini/Mercury)

IV: the childhood environment, parents and background (Cancer/The Moon)

V: creativity and children (Leo/The Sun)

VI: health and work (Virgo/Mercury)

VII: relationships (Libra/Venus)

VIII: spirituality, inner motivations and change (Scorpio/Pluto)

IX: philosophical considerations and learning (Sagittarius/Jupiter)

X: professional concerns and ambition (Capricorn/Saturn)

XI: friendship and group activities (Aquarius/Uranus)

XII: uncertainty, privacy and karma (Pisces/Neptune)

If planets fall within their "own" houses, they are said to exert a harmonious influence. Yet just as the location of planets within zodiacal signs can cause subtle changes in personality, their placement within the houses also indicates a distinctive synergy between house and planet (the Moon in the first house, for example, indicates a self-absorbed character, while Jupiter suggests an expansive, optimistic personality). The houses are numbered counterclockwise from the eastern horizon, running full circle through the zenith. Those houses that fall within the eastern half of the circle are in the ascendant (as indicated by the first), and those on the western are descendant (marked by the seventh). The houses are further categorized as angular (comprising I, IV, VII, and X); succeedent (II, V, VIII, and XI); and cadent (III, VI, IX, and XII), in which the angularly placed planets initiate particular circumstances, to be modified by the succeedent and finally the cadent houses.

THE ASPECTS

An additional consideration to be evaluated is the planetary aspects, or the angular relation of the planets to each other according to the number or degrees between them. Because each planet travels through the zodiac at a different speed, their position varies, and may be determined either by mathematical calculation or by means of a useful device termed an aspect finder. The aspects may exert either a positive or negative influence. The conjunction (and also the self-explanatory parallel), in which planets occupy the same point, within 8° of each other, can be either beneficial or difficult, depending on the characteristics of the specific planets. The quincunx or inconjunct, in which planets are placed 150° apart, can indicate complications, while the quintile (72°) and biquintile (144°) exert a mildly positive influence.

The positive, or "benefic" aspects are: The semisextile, 30° = an easy relationship; the sextile, 60° = communication ability; the trine, 120° = great creativity. The negative, or "malefic" aspects are: the semisquare, 45° = difficulties; the square, 90° = a tense relationship; the sesquiquadrate, 135° = stressful interaction; and the opposition, 180° = conflict and frustration.

Note that conflicting aspects may cancel each other out. The aspects of the planets should be recorded in the following order: the Moon in relation to Mercury, Venus, the Sun, Mars, Jupiter, Saturn, Uranus, Neptune and Pluto; then Mercury in relation to the subsequent planets, followed by a similar process for Venus, the Sun, Mars, Jupiter, Saturn, Uranus, Neptune and Pluto.

THE CUSPS

Some individuals are born on the "cusp" of two zodiacal signs, that is, "on the line" between the ending of one zodiacal sign and the beginning of another, may be said to have a combination of the characteristics inherent in each. Because the exact date of the Sun's entry into each zodiacal sign varies from year to year, a natal chart specific to the individual is necessary, in order to determine exactly where the subject's birthday lies in relation to the two, and therefore whether the influence of the departing sign is greater, or (more usually), if it is that of the incoming sign. In determining potential compatibility with others born under different signs, those born on the cusp should be especially aware of their decanates, which must be determined accurately to serve as reliable clues to harmonious relationships.

Advice to Readers

The personality profiles and listings of significant events for each day of the year that follow have been constructed broadly on the principles of the Western astrological tradition. In discussing the evolution and tenets of the various forms of astrology and calendrical traditions that were—and still are—practiced throughout the world, it is clear that no system stands alone: each is predicated upon similar, and sometimes identical, beliefs—especially with regard to macrocosmic-microcosmic theory—even if specific names and refinements of practice vary to some degree. Thus astrology is both global and holistic in its nature and resonance, and no variant should be regarded as separate from, or contradictory to, another. Indeed, each could be regarded as a vital strand in a richly variegated fabric.

There are a number of points that the reader should bear in mind when consulting this book. The day on which the Sun enters each sign of the zodiac is not a fixed date, but varies from year to year. Therefore, while the dates marking the beginning and end of each zodiacal period (sign and decan) as given here are traditional, they were originally instigated for reasons of convenience rather than accuracy. This means, for example, that a person born on July 21, 1929—on the cusp of Cancer and Leo—should be aware that the degree of the zodiacal sign—the correct indicator—may not accord with the day of the month on which he or she was born, and that the nearest personality profiles on either side of this birth date may, in fact, be more pertinent to the individual than that given for July 21.

Each degree (or day) is part of a larger grouping of ten—a decan, or decanate—a system devised by the ancient Egyptians to help them locate fixed stars. Each sign is subdivided into three decans (the first decanate covering 0° to 10° of the segment of the zodiacal circle occupied by the sign; the second, 11° to 20°; and the third 21° to 30°). In this book, the decans have their traditional positions, but remember that just as the correspondence of degrees to dates varies by specific years, so do the starting and ending dates of each decan's period of influence (because there are 360 degrees in the zodiacal circle, but 365 days in the year—except for leap years).

To gain more than a general understanding of, and guide to, the astrological influences that govern an individual's personality, it is vital to consult a reputable astrologer, who will draw up a detailed horoscope showing the exact position of the planets and zodiacal constellations that prevailed at the time of birth, and will help interpret and draw lessons from the complex information revealed. Astrology does not promise concrete answers to specific questions: like life itself, it operates in subtle and infinitely variable ways. The information that it yields should be regarded as an enlightening guide to one's potential rather than as tablets set in stone.

The noted British astrologer Robert Currey offers the following observation, which he urges his clients to remember while they are digesting the "cosmic inheritance" detailed in the horoscopes that he prepares for them: "Your genes and environmental conditions, such as your upbringing, are also key influences...astrology can reveal the impact of these conditions and your perception of them in surprising ways." Every person is an individual—no one else shares the genetic inheritance, the experiences that have shaped him or her since birth, his or her knowledge, perceptions and desires. So in reading the natal observations and advice contained here, the birthday person should remember that they represent a framework within which individual characteristics and predilections may vary greatly. Currey also points out that we are all constantly evolving, so that while one may not immediately recognize or concur with the personality summary presented, the passage of time and intervening events may make the words ring truer when consulted later. To order a personal horoscope interpreted by Robert Currey, refer to the details on page 4 of this book.

Finally, the question of free will must be taken into account. Throughout their lives people are presented with choices, faced with paths whose direction, if followed, may change them irrevocably. Astrology guides, but does not dictate, and while it offers sound advice, it is up to individuals to take responsibility for themselves and determine their own destiny—for better or for worse. For, as Paracelsus commented astutely in *Astronomia Magna* (1537): "The stars must obey man and be subject to him, and not he to the stars. Even if he is a child of Saturn and if Saturn has overshadowed his birth, he can master Saturn and become a child of the Sun."

THE DAYS OF THE YEAR

INFLUENCES AND TALISMANS FOR EVERY DAY • ENIGMAS OF TIMELESS FAITHS AND DIVINATION SYSTEMS WITH PREDICTIONS, INFLUENCES AND TALISMANS FOR EVERY DAY

ARIES

March 21 to April 20

Ruling planet: Mars   **Element:** Cardinal fire

Symbol: The ram   **Polarity:** Positive (masculine)

Physical correspondence: The head and brain

Stones: Amethyst, ruby, diamond

Flowers: Hollyhock, carnation, poppy, thistle, geranium

Colors: White, red

Aries is traditionally regarded as the initial sign of the zodiac, for its ascendancy during the first month of the Northern Hemisphere's spring associates it with the burgeoning of life and the renewal of solar energy following the fallow winter months, and thus with new beginnings of all kinds. The ancient Egyptians identified the ram that represents this sign with their creator deity, the Sun-god Amon-Ra, who was usually portrayed crowned with rams' horns. According to the Arab astronomer Abumasar, the cosmos itself was created when the major planets were conjoined within the sign of Aries. While the Hindu zodiac equates Aries, as Mesha or Aja, with a ram or goat respectively, and the Persians termed it "the lamb," Varak, the Babylonian astronomers regarded the sign as either Zappu, "the hair," or Hunga, "the worker." The ancient Greeks called the ram of their zodiac Krios, and linked it with the fabled golden-fleeced ram—the offspring of the sea-god Poseidon and the Thracian princess Theophane—who carried Phrixus and the doomed Helle, the children of the Boeotian King Athamas, to Colchis before being sacrificed to Ares, the Greek god of war. Its golden fleece subsequently adorned Ares' temple at Colchis, guarded by a fire-breathing serpent, until it was later claimed by Jason and his Argonauts. The association of this mythical ram with the zodiacal sign is apparently confirmed by the proposition that the Latin name Aries (which means "ram") is etymologically derived from Ares, the Greek name for Mars, the Roman god of war whose name is used for the red planet that rules this constellation.

It is Aries's association with the qualities traditionally attributed to the planet Mars—leadership, courage, aggression and egotism—that in part defines the personal characteristics of those born under this sign, complemented by those that are suggested by the element of fire: heated emotions, vitality and enthusiasm, but also the potential for impatience, impulsiveness and destruction. And, of course, the headstrong and active nature of the ram itself further reinforces these dual associations.

Planetary Influences
Ruling planets: Mars and Neptune.
First decan: Personal planet is Mars.
First cusp: Aries with Piscean qualities.

Sacred and Cultural Significance
Saints' day: Benedict (c.480–c.550), patron saint of monks and speleologists; Enda (d. c.530); Nicholas of Flue (1417–87).

MARCH 21

Others respect March 21 people for their forthright directness and the practical way in which they approach life. Although they are intuitive people, they prefer to express themselves through activity rather than remaining passive in the face of a stimulating challenge. This is not to say that those born on this day do not possess great powers of perception and reflection—on the contrary—just that they have a deep-rooted urge to act upon their convictions, and to see progress being made. These individuals are often attracted to extremes, espousing the highest ideals and the most radical solutions, and displaying a remarkable level of tenacity in promoting them. As a result of their considerable energy and vision, combined with their practical gifts of logic and organization, little withstands these people's drive and determination to succeed. Furthermore, they have real leadership potential, which they will put to especially good use in business or military careers, or as educators, where they can blaze an inspirational trail.

These people have a tendency, however, to isolate themselves inadvertently from others, for not only can they intimidate weaker characters with the intensity and strength of their opinions, but they are also prone to spectacular bouts of temper when frustrated or opposed. Particularly in regard to their personal lives, it is vital that these people relax their standards and expectations and demonstrate the pragmatism of which they are unquestionably capable. By slowing down and opening themselves up to others, they will find that they will receive greater understanding and affection.

VIRTUES: The individuals born on this day are forceful, vigorous and clear-sighted in the pursuit of their aims. Quick-thinking and yet also practical, they have the dedication and capability to realize their ambitions.
VICES: Because they are self-confident and decisive, as well as being independent agents, these people are not afraid of incurring the opposition of others to their goals. In the process, however, they may alienate those whom they would do better to placate.
VERDICT: March 21 people should try to moderate their impatience—both with those people who do not agree with them and with the more impersonal impediments to their progress. By cultivating a judicious use of tact when necessary, and accepting that success does not always result from following a direct path, they will find greater self-fulfillment.

On this day of courageous action and determination in pursuit of goals, Dr. Martin Luther King, Jr., led a mass of civil-rights demonstrators in a march from Selma to Montgomery, Alabama, in 1965.

On This Day
Famous Births: Johann Sebastian Bach (1685); Benito Pablo Juàrez (1801); Modest Petrovich Mussorgsky (1839); Albert Chevalier (1861); Florenz Ziegfeld (1869); Raoul Lufbery (1885); Geoffrey Dearmer (1893); Paul Tortelier (1914); Antony Hopkins (1921); Peter Brook (1925); Brian Clough (1935); Roger Whittaker (1936); Timothy Dalton (1944); Matthew Broderick and Rosie O'Donnell (1962).

Significant Events and Anniversaries: On a day that is governed by the element of fire, the first Protestant archbishop of Canterbury, Thomas Cranmer, ultimately refused to recant his religious convictions and was burned at the stake for heresy in England (1556). March 21 is a day that indicates self-belief and courage, and marks the anniversary of the fighting of a bloodless duel over Catholic emancipation between the Duke of Wellington and the Earl of Winchelsea (1829); two political demonstrations unfortunately had more violent results, however: when fifty-six people were killed by South African security forces in what became known as the "Sharpeville Massacre" (1960); and when many protesters against the newly instituted "poll tax" were injured by police in London (1990). In an altogether more harmonious statement of political opinion, this was the day on which John Lennon and Yoko Ono enacted their "Beds in Peace" demonstration in a hotel room in Amsterdam (1969).

MARCH 22

The sort of people who bluntly speak their minds, those individuals born on March 22 are uncompromisingly honest, valuing truth over anything else. Since they are brave and persistent types, they furthermore have no fear of the consequences of either discovering or expressing the actual facts of a situation. It is just as well that these rabble-rousing independent agents are generally impervious to opposition because few people relish hearing an unvarnished critique of their faults, while those who harbor ulterior agendas will resent having their real motives exposed to the world. It is not that these people are insensitive—on the contrary, they are extremely intuitive, and use this skill to bolster their position—it is merely that they are willing to jeopardize their popularity by refusing to pander to flattery or to submit to subterfuge.

Such uncompromising qualities suit them especially well to such technical areas as scientific or medical research, in which concepts can indeed be seen in black-and-white terms, but they will be less successful in those professions in which interpersonal and diplomatic skills are an important component. In their personal liaisons, the onus is on these people to temper their natural predilection for criticism—particularly if they were also born in the Chinese year of the dragon—and to realize that not only are they not always right, but that they will run the risk of driving away those who care for them.

VIRTUES: These energetic and honorable people are unswervingly direct in their quest to uncover the real nature of a situation, employing their prodigious powers of astuteness and perception in their mission. Their refusal to be diverted from their chosen course of action augurs well for their success.

VICES: Those born on this day are prone to dismiss the feelings of others as a result of their inherent need to be frank and cut to the bones of an issue. They furthermore typically refuse to compromise over what they perceive to be clear truths and thereby run the risk of alienating other people and possibly condemning themselves to a solitary existence.

VERDICT: March 22 people must recognize that it is not always expedient or judicious to express their convictions so outspokenly, and must learn to appreciate the value of the occasional use of tact when possible. They should, moreover, try to be less strident, and could benefit by listening to the viewpoints of others.

On This Day

Famous Births: Holy Roman Emperor Maximilian I (1459); Anthony van Dyke (1599); Carl August Rosa (1842); Hamish MacCunn and Robert Andrews Millikan (1868); Nicholas John Turney Monsarrat (1910); Karl Malden (1914); Marcel Marceau (1923); Gerard Hoffnung (1925); Lynden Oscar Pindling and Stephen Joshua Sondheim (1930); William Shatner and Leslie Thomas (1931); J.P. McCarthy (1933); George Benson (1943); Andrew Lloyd Webber (1948); Bob Costas (1952).

Significant Events and Anniversaries: That this day features the confident promotion of perceived truths was reflected in the national and political realm by the formation of the Arab League in Cairo, Egypt (1945), and Jordan's proclamation of independence from Britain (1946). In Melbourne, Australia, the first official "mercy killing" was carried out (1988); difficult ethical issues such as this illustrate the challenge of this day—that not all things can be seen in black-and-white terms, and that one person's truth is anathema to another. It is newspapers' proud claim that they are reporting events objectively to their readership, and on this day the first color image to be published in a newspaper appeared in the U.S. *Daily Illustrated Mirror* (1904), while Britain's broadcasting service, the B.B.C., started to transmit reports to the French Resistance in Morse code during World War II, to avoid accurate information falling into the hands of Nazi Germany (1942). This day is ruled by the parching element of fire and marks the day on which the Niagara Falls cascaded less spectacularly than usual on its U.S. side, due to drought (1903).

Planetary Influences
Ruling planets: Mars and Neptune.
First decan: Personal planet is Mars.
First cusp: Aries with Piscean qualities.

Sacred and Cultural Significance
In ancient Rome, the Procession of the Tree-Bearers.
Saints' day: Deogratias, bishop of Carthage (5th century AD).

The most visited waterfall in the world, Niagara Falls was at its lowest level on this day in 1903, as a result of an unseasonal, severe drought.

Planetary Influences
Ruling planets: Mars and Neptune.
First decan: Personal planet is Mars.
First cusp: Aries with Piscean qualities.

Sacred and Cultural Significance
The National Day of Pakistan; Dance of the Sali in ancient Rome; Marzenna celebrated in Poland.
Saints' day: Gwinear (dates unknown); Turibius of Mogroveio (1538–1606), patron saint of missionary bishops.

Islam, the official religion of Pakistan, is professed by 93 percent of its population: illustrated below is the Great Mosque of Vazir Khan in Lahore. March 23 is the national day of Pakistan.

MARCH 23

March 23 individuals are fascinated by the workings of the world—with what makes things tick—and this propensity is especially pronounced in their dealings with other people. Although they will use their intuition and keen powers of observation to gather information, these people are generally too objective and emotionally detached to be truly fired by compassionate sentiments and, if asked for advice, will give a detailed summary of the situation as they perceive it, unclouded by emotion. Yet although they may be somewhat lacking in empathy, human behavior as a whole intrigues those born on this day, and they are therefore clearly well equipped for careers in teaching, psychotherapy or, indeed, for any type of medical specialty. They also have the potential to be gifted actors, for they possess the ability to model their fictitious characters on the traits of individuals whom they have closely observed in life.

Yet this highly developed capacity to keep their intellects and emotions separate does not mean that these people are cold fish—far from it. They enjoy the company of others, are blessed with an infectious sense of fun—particularly if they were also born in the Chinese year of the goat—and approach most ventures in an enthusiastic and positive manner. In their personal relationships they should, however, try to moderate their critical tendencies, and offer those closest to them a greater level of unquestioning support.

VIRTUES: These extraordinarily perceptive people are always inquisitive and eager to learn, and never stop observing and analyzing all that occurs around them. Their astuteness and enthusiasm to act upon their findings can have startling consequences.
VICES: These people must beware of imposing their predilection for impartial analysis—which, in extreme cases, can resemble the painstaking dissection that a forensic scientist would make—upon their more intimate relationships, within which such tendencies are often negative and destructive.
VERDICT: It is vital that March 23 people recognize the importance of other people's—as well as their own—emotional needs. They must strive to achieve a healthy balance between their intellects and instincts in order to gain all-round fulfillment.

On This Day
Famous Births: William Smith (1769); Horatio William Bottomley (1860); Muirhead Bone (1876); Juan Gris (1887); Joan Crawford (1908); Akira Kurosawa (1910); Wernher von Braun (1912); Jimmy Edwards (1920); Donald Campbell (1921); Doc Watson (1923); Roger Bannister (1929); Chaka Khan (1953); Amanda Plummer (1957).

Significant Events and Anniversaries: This day highlights logical action, regardless of the human or emotional consequences, and marks the anniversary of the passing of the Stamp Act by the British government, a measure of indirect taxation that so upset the colonists in America that it can be regarded as a major cause of the subsequent American Revolution (1765), as well as the devastating barrage unleashed by the notorious German gun "Big Bertha" on the citizens of Paris during World War I (1918). On a day of objective analysis, the first issue of the first Canadian newspaper, the *Halifax Gazette*, was published (1752). Fascist propaganda can be regarded as the calculated manipulation of the masses, which may be a danger of the emotional detachment inherent in this day on which Benito Mussolini formed the Italian Fascist Party (1919) and Adolf Hitler became the Nazi *de facto* dictator of Germany (1933); yet impartiality can also result in a willingness to move forward by means of compromise, as is reflected in this day being the anniversary of the first meeting in four hundred years between the the primary representatives of the Roman Catholic and Anglican churches, Pope Paul VI and Michael Ramsey, the archbishop of Canterbury (1966).

MARCH 24

These charismatic individuals prefer simple solutions and a direct approach in favor of more complicated and difficult alternatives, a result of their incisive intellectual powers and their predilection to take action rather than prevaricate. These are the sort of people who make snap decisions—often influenced by their intuitive perceptions—and then stick to their initial resolutions through thick and thin, regardless of any obstacles that may be put in their paths. While this typically straightforward method frequently results in success, it does, however, mean that these individuals may either blindly follow an unfortunate course, or that they may ignore small, but important, details. Since they are multitalented people, they will find fulfillment in any professional field in which they can act independently and imaginatively to achieve tangible results, but will be miserable if relegated to a passive role or required to deal with excessive bureaucracy.

Others are attracted to the optimistic, invigorating qualities that March 24 people radiate, and hence they may find themselves in popular demand, a position which they rather enjoy. Indeed, they are quick to reciprocate displays of affection and, as in all other things, are open and honest in their dealings with other people. Although they generally make excellent partners, parents and friends, they should ensure—especially if they are men—that they take care to moderate their natural propensity to speak their minds bluntly on all occasions, and that they do not ignore other people's emotional needs when fired by an all-consuming interest in a project.

VIRTUES: Vigorous, enthusiastic and action-oriented, these people are stimulated by challenge, to which they respond in a typically forthright fashion. In addition, their ability to tenaciously pursue a cherished vision promises great success.

VICES: March 24 people have a tendency to behave impulsively, without having carefully thought through the implications of their actions, a propensity that may have unexpected and unwelcome results. Because they are eager to pursue their own interests and typically throw all their energies into pet projects, they may unwittingly neglect their family and friends.

VERDICT: In all areas of their lives, those born on this day must ensure that they do not get carried away with the excitement generated by envisaging the big picture. They should take time to reflect on the perhaps less interesting details of an issue, and should remember to also devote more attention to those closest to them.

On This Day

Famous Births: Fanny Crosby (1820); William Morris (1834); Harry Houdini (1874); Roscoe "Fatty" Arbuckle (1887); Ub Iwerks (1901); Malcolm Muggeridge (1903); Tommy Trinder (1909); Lawrence Ferlinghetti (1919); Steve McQueen (1930); Benjamin Luxon (1937); Bob Mackie (1940); Archie Gemmill (1947); Nick Lowe (1949); Robert Carradine and Vince Jones (1954).

Significant Events and Anniversaries: March 24 is a day that heralds directness, and marks the anniversary of Denmark's decisive action in abolishing capital punishment (1911), as well as the uncompromising action of a military junta in Argentina in deposing President Isabel Perón (1976). In a genealogical illustration of this characteristic, this was the day on which Queen Elizabeth I of England died, and her direct heir (although not her son), James VI of Scotland, acceded to the throne as James I of Britain, thereby uniting England and Scotland (1603). As an example of the dangers that can result from paying insufficient attention to the risks inherent in a major undertaking, the *Exxon Valdez* oil spill that occurred on this day off the coast of Alaska caused one of the worst environmental disasters of the twentieth century (1989).

Planetary Influences
Ruling planets: Mars and Neptune.
First decan: Personal planet is Mars.
First cusp: Aries with Piscean qualities.

Sacred and Cultural Significance
In ancient Rome, the Day of Blood was commemorated.
Saints' day: Macartan (d. c.505); Hildelith (d. c.712); Dunchad (d. 716); Catherine of Sweden (1331–81).

The aftermath of the disastrous Exxon Valdez *oil spill, an event that brought home the terrible risks of routing oil tankers too close to a coastline. March 24 is a day of action, but is sometimes characterized by insufficient attention to details.*

Planetary Influences
Ruling planet: Mars.
First decan: Personal planet is Mars.

Sacred and Cultural Significance
The vernal equinox and traditionally the first day of spring; National Day of Greece; Festival of Joy in ancient Rome.
Saints' day: The Annunciation of the Blessed Virgin Mary (d. 1st century AD), patron saint of mothers, nuns and virgins; Dismas the Good Thief (d. c.30), patron saint of prisoners and thieves; Alfwold (d. 1058).

March 25 is believed to be the day of the Annunciation of the Virgin Mary, illustrated here in Fra Angelico's painting of 1441.

MARCH 25

M arch 25 people are regarded as rocks of support by those who depend on them for advice, practical help and empathetic commiseration. And indeed, these compassionate individuals have a highly developed sense of natural justice, while their strong protective instincts arouse in them a fierce desire to champion the underdog and reverse any perceived social abuses. It helps that they are also emotionally robust, self-confident and vigorous individuals, who, when certain of their motives and mission, will not allow their sense of purpose to be swayed by the censure of those who hold conflicting convictions. Neither are they afraid of taking an independent—even isolated—stance when convinced of the need to do so. All these qualities equip these people extremely well for such public-service-oriented careers as the military, medicine, law enforcement or social work, and this is especially true if they were also born in the Chinese year of the tiger.

Despite their externally directed energies, March 25 people also have a profound requirement for periods of solitude and reflection. It is essential that they make time in which to relax and be themselves, away from the demands of those who seek their assistance. Since they are loving and generous in their personal liaisons, they will find great comfort in the simple joys of friendship and domesticity, but will understandably be deeply wounded if the loyalty that they proffer to others is unreciprocated or—far worse—betrayed. Their nearest and dearest should therefore remember that, despite their apparent strength and invincibility, these people are also vulnerable.

VIRTUES: March 25 people are self-reliant, independent types, who are fueled by a desire to act on behalf of the vulnerable or oppressed, and to set wrongs right. Fair-minded, perceptive and energetic, they typically direct their considerable gifts of generosity and compassion toward the world's improvement.
VICES: When determinedly engaged in their personal struggles, there is a danger these people may forget that they too have personal needs and, if their inner equilibrium is disrupted, have a tendency to lash out at others in their frustration.
VERDICT: These people generally maintain an even balance between their introverted and extroverted sides, but must nevertheless ensure that they do not neglect themselves in their ardent desire to serve others. If driven to exhaustion, they will often become prone to feelings of depression, from which they will have difficulty extricating themselves.

On This Day
Famous Births: King Henry II of England (1133); Joachim Murat, King of Naples (1767); Arturo Toscanini (1867); Béla Bartók (1881); A.J.P. Taylor (1906); David Lean (1908); Howard Cosell (1920); Simone Signoret (1921); Gloria Steinem (1934); Anita Bryant (1940); Aretha Franklin (1942); Paul Michael Glaser (1943); Elton John (1947); Bonnie Bedelia (1948); Mary Gross (1953); Sarah Jessica Parker (1965).

Significant Events and Anniversaries: In many ways, the qualities of this day indicate leadership, and on March 25 Robert the Bruce was proclaimed king of the Scots (1306). A feature of this day is fearless independence, as was illustrated by the departure of the English explorer and navigator Henry Hudson on his last journey of exploration, which would result in his discovery of Hudson Bay, subsequently named in his honor (1609). Committed humanitarianism is a characteristic of March 25, on which the British House of Commons abolished the slave trade (1807); while a desire to effect economic greater good influenced six European nations to sign the Treaty of Rome, which would inaugurate the European Economic Community (E.E.C.) (1957).

MARCH 26

To many who do not know them well, it appears that those born on March 26 are easy-going people who wish for nothing more than a simple life, and this is, to some extent, the case. This does not mean that they are intellectually or physically lazy—quite the reverse—just that they do not believe in making things unnecessarily difficult or complicated for themselves. Because they are inherently perceptive and quick-thinking people, they are blessed with the enviable gifts of clarity of vision and purpose, having the capacity both to cut straight to the heart of a problem and to fix their sights firmly on a long-term target. This mental directness is furthermore complemented by their vigor, tenacity and preference for taking positive action rather than endlessly prevaricating. Along with these personal qualities, those born on this day have an intuitive sense of right and wrong, and both their human empathy and high ethical standards suit them especially for public-service careers.

Hand in hand with their intellectual abilities also go marked qualities of sensuality and sensitivity, and hence these people often make talented artists, writers, musicians or actors. When "off duty," they will pursue their relationships, interests and hobbies with the energy and enthusiasm that characterizes their approach to their work, and thus they make popular friends and much-loved family members. These people will often find themselves in great demand, but it is vital for their emotional equilibrium that they periodically withdraw from the company of others and find time to be themselves.

VIRTUES: These people adopt a straightforward approach to everything that they undertake, a characteristic that is informed by their compulsion to effect progress as quickly as possible. Because they are moreover exceptionally clear-sighted and practical, they make their achievements appear deceptively easy.

VICES: March 26 people have a propensity to form firm judgements that are shaped by their innate sense of morality, and then stick by them. They must beware of a tendency to close their minds to the validity of conflicting viewpoints.

VERDICT: Those born on this day must remember not to overextend themselves, thereby giving themselves the space within which to indulge in quiet reflection.

On This Day

Famous Births: George Smith (1840); A.E. Housman (1859); Robert Frost (1874); Chico Marx (1891); Tennessee Williams (1911); Elizabeth Jane Howard (1923); Pierre Boulez (1925); Sandra Day O'Connor (1930); Leonard Nimoy (1931); Alan Arkin (1934); James Caan (1939); Erica Jong (1942); Bob Woodward (1943); Diana Ross (1944); Kyung-Wha Chung (1948); Jon English and Vicki Lawrence (1949); Teddy Pendergrass and Martin Short (1950); Curtis Sliva (1954); Marcus Allen (1960); Princess Eugenie of York (1990).

Significant Events and Anniversaries: Artistic potential is a feature of this day, on which George Bernard Shaw's play *St. Joan* was first performed (1924), as was the film *Funny Girl*, starring Barbra Streisand (1964). This day is furthermore one that augurs well for the overcoming of any obstacles blocking the path of tenaciously pursued ambitions, as is reflected in the achievement of the first woman stockbroker to break into the previously all-male bastion of the London Stock Exchange (1973), and the unprecedented signing of a peace treaty between Israel and Egypt by Prime Minister Begin and President Sadat (1979). It is appropriate, on a day governed by the element of fire, that the first funerary cremation in Britain should have taken place on this day (1885).

Planetary Influences
Ruling planet: Mars.
First decan: Personal planet is Mars.

Sacred and Cultural Significance
Saints' day: Liudger (d. 809); William of Norwich (d. 1144).

A scene from the London Stock Exchange of old, before a woman stockbroker first entered this all-male environment on this day in 1973. March 26 is characterized by the achievement of goals in spite of obstacles.

Planetary Influences
Ruling planet: Mars.
First decan: Personal planet is Mars.

Sacred and Cultural Significance
Liber Pater honored in ancient Rome;
in India, the goddess Gauri celebrated.
Saint's day: Rupert (d. c.710).

MARCH 27

Appearances can be deceptive, and especially so in the case of March 27 people, who frequently hide their steely determination and capacity for incisive thought beneath a delightfully laid-back manner. Although they are blessed with considerable social skills—in part a result of their recognition that more can be achieved by charming rather than alienating people—they are generally concerned less with gaining the approval of others than with following their own original path through life. Indeed, those born on this day are independent thinkers who set themselves high targets and then work single-mindedly to achieve them. While they may be fired by social ideals, they are usually far more interested in getting to the heart of a more abstract or technical issue and then reinterpreting it in their characteristically logical manner—but also with some flair. These people typically make gifted and dedicated academics, scientists or lawyers, particularly if they were also born in the Chinese year of the rooster.

Because March 27 people are intellectually curious, they are interested in soliciting other people's opinions, but sometimes more because they want to know what makes them tick than out of a sense of empathy or a need to be advised. As well as being sociable, they are extremely self-reliant people, and cope equally well alone or within group situations. Usually supportive and nonjudgemental with regard to their friends and family, they should try to ensure, however, that they do not ignore the basic emotional needs of those closest to them when carried along by a cause or an enthusiasm.

VIRTUES: Perceptive, logical, fascinated by theoretical concepts and technical problems and possessed of great powers of concentration, these people have the potential to blaze a trail in their chosen professions. They are additionally blessed with enormous personal charm, which draws others to them.
VICES: Those born on this day have a tendency to become completely consumed by their intellectual interests, to the extent that they can neglect their own physical and emotional needs and isolate themselves from others.
VERDICT: Although March 27 people usually strike the correct balance between inner and outer needs, they must guard against their propensity to sacrifice their personal lives on the altar of work, and remember the value of paying attention to things that may appear less urgent, particularly within their domestic environments.

On This Day
Famous Births: King Louis XVII of France (1785); Georges Eugène Haussmann (1809); Wilhelm Konrad von Röntgen (1845); Henry Royce (1863); Heinrich Mann (1871); Ferde Grofé (1892); Gloria Swanson (1899); James Callaghan (1912); Sarah Vaughan (1924); Mstislav Rostropovich (1927); David Janssen (1931); Michael York (1942); Tom Sullivan (1947); Duncan Goodhew (1957); Quentin Tarantino (1963); Mariah Carey (1970).

The Salvation Army, a highly organized international institution dedicated to alleviating suffering, adopted its familiar uniform on this day of focused action in 1880.

Significant Events and Anniversaries: Technical advances are indicated by this day, on which Guglielmo Marconi made the first international radio transmission, between England and France (1899), and the first successful blood transfusion took place, in Brussels, Belgium (1914). Unfortunately the capacity for error exists, and this day marks the anniversary of the death of the Soviet cosmonaut Yuri Gagarin, whose plane crashed above Moscow (1968); the collision of two jumbo jets at Tenerife airport in the Canary Islands, with the loss of 574 lives (1977); and the malfunctioning of an elevator at the Vaal Reef mine in South Africa, resulting in the death of twenty-three people when it plummeted for over a mile (1980). Organized action is a further feature of March 27, on which the U.S. Navy was officially created (1794), the Nazi U-boat base at St. Nazaire in France was destroyed by a British commando raid (1942) and the first women traffic wardens began ticketing in Leicester, England (1961).

MARCH 28

Paradoxically, although March 28 people are naturally somewhat solitary and reflective individuals, they frequently find themselves at the center of attention and beset with others' demands—requests either for the pleasure of their company or for their services. Other people admire them for their optimistic and practical approach to life, as well as for their personal charm and perceived empathy, and therefore turn to them for advice and support. And, indeed, these individuals respond magnificently to a crisis, mustering their great qualities of originality and steadfastness in the face of a challenge and thereby often achieving the desired outcome. Rather than being motivated by feelings of profound compassion, however, it is the testing of their intellectual powers and stamina to which these people respond. This quality of emotional detachment when occupied with the details of an issue will benefit them in such professions as the police or military, as well as in business and the building trades.

Although they are blessed with the ability to be objective and realistic in their dealings with the outside world, those born on this day need to feel cocooned by the loving devotion of those closest to them at home. It would surprise those who do not know them well to discover that these apparently confident and capable individuals are often subject to nagging feelings of self-doubt—which is perhaps the reason why they feel compelled to prove their worth. A stable domestic framework within which they can retreat from outer demands and be themselves is therefore crucial to these people's emotional well-being.

VIRTUES: March 28 people present an engagingly positive and helpful face to the world, marshaling their qualities of clear-sightedness, energy and determination and placing them at the disposal of any who request it. Underneath their public personae, however, lie sensitive and rather reclusive souls.

VICES: These people can be prone to feelings of insecurity, which they try to overcome by seeking the affirmation of others, and also by being high achievers. This tendency can cause them to perform in overdrive, sometimes to the point of exhaustion and to the exclusion of their true needs.

VERDICT: It is vital that these people listen more to their inner voices and remain true to their intuitive convictions. Although they make loyal and generous partners and parents—and attach enormous importance to family life—they should ensure that their need for privacy and autonomy is not compromised by domestic demands.

On This Day

Famous Births: Fra Bartolommeo di Paghola (1472); St. Teresa of Avila (1515); King George I of England (1660); Maxim Gorky (1849); Aristide Briand (1862); Paul Whiteman (1891); Flora Robson (1902); Rudolf Serkin (1903); Dirk Bogarde (1921); Leonard Stern (1938); Neil Kinnock (1942); Richard Eyre (1943); Ken Howard (1944); Dianne Wiest (1948); Reba McEntire (1955); Vince Vaughn (1970).

Significant Events and Anniversaries: Indicated by this day is potential conflict between national duty and personal emotion—a friction that is inherent in martial situations—and this day marks the anniversary of the founding of Britain's Women's Army Auxiliary Corps (W.A.A.C.) (1917); the conclusion of the Spanish Civil War, when Franco's Nationalist forces captured Madrid (1939); the victory of the British over the Italian Navy at the Battle of Cape Matapan, off Crete (1941); and the last V2 rocket to be launched by the Germans on Britain (1945). Indeed, the somewhat schizophrenic nature of this day can result in crises of identity, as was illustrated by the renaming of Constantinople to Istanbul and Angora to Ankara by the Turkish leader, Kemal Atatürk (1930). Determined action is a feature of this day, on which the first seaplane took off near Marseille, France (1910). March 28 is ruled by the element of fire: flames threatened disaster when the nuclear power station at Three Mile Island, Pennsylvania, suffered a meltdown (1979).

Planetary Influences
Ruling planet: Mars.
First decan: Personal planet is Mars.

Sacred and Cultural Significance
Saint's day: Alkeda of Middleham (d. c.800).

Neil Kinnock, the British Labour Party leader from 1983 to 1992, was born on March 28, 1942. Throughout his political career he displayed the abundant energy and optimism that characterize this day. His personality is more forceful, confident and ambitious than many March 28 people because of the presence of the Moon in Leo at the time of his birth; with Jupiter in Taurus, he is also a versatile, quick thinker and naturally skilled in debating.

Planetary Influences
Ruling planet: Mars.
First decan: Personal planet is Mars.

Sacred and Cultural Significance
Pagan Festival of Ishtar; masquerade ritual of Bobo people of Africa.
Saints' day: Gwynllyw and Gwladys (6th century AD).

Elle MacPherson, who was born on this day in 1963, achieved fame and success at a young age. Her ruling planet, Pluto, was in Leo on the day of her birth, reinforcing her enthusiasm and capacity for hard work. As a Chinese water rabbit, she is sensitive, sociable and appreciates comfort and elegance.

MARCH 29

Although not driven by burning ambitions for personal success, those individuals born on this day may—somewhat to their surprise—find themselves in positions of authority, for while self-glorification is not one of their qualities, tenacity, perceptiveness and reliability are. March 29 people typically approach life in a calm and steady manner, their laid-back style and tendency toward self-effacement often masking the critical and astute way in which they observe everything that is going on around them. Undoubtedly sensitive, they will nevertheless use their intuitive powers like tools, taking time to consider every aspect of a situation, carefully working out their chosen strategy, and then implementing it with unwavering determination—a method that will rarely prove unsuccessful. So positive and varied are their many talents, that they will thrive in almost any career, especially one in which their observational and organizational skills can be best employed.

These self-disciplined individuals generally keep their emotions to themselves in professional scenarios, but are, in fact, highly opinionated, having arrived at their ideological convictions by means of the same considered route that characterizes their response to any intellectual challenge. However, because they are extremely confident of their ground, they will stubbornly assert the validity of their convictions, even while remaining emotionally detached. March 29 individuals are deeply affectionate and supportive in their personal liaisons—perhaps instinctively recognizing that family ties and friendship offer a vital emotional release from work constraints—and are valued by their nearest and dearest for their loyal and steadfast qualities.

VIRTUES: March 29 people are coolly intelligent, employing their powers of perception, analysis and logic in meeting a challenge. They display consistency and reliability in their professional and personal lives, and therefore have the potential to achieve all-round fulfillment in both these areas.
VICES: Once they have arrived at an opinion, these people are so certain of its veracity that they have a tendency to obstinately refuse to open their ears to alternative arguments—a policy that may sometimes be inadvisedly inflexible.
VERDICT: Those born on this day are usually extremely well balanced, paying equal attention to work and play. Because they are not natural limelight-seekers, however, they should try to ensure that their qualities do not go unrecognized, that their loyalty is not abused, or that others do not take the credit for their achievements.

On This Day
Famous Births: John Tyler (1790); Elihu Thomson (1853); Cy Young (1867); Edwin Landseer Lutyens (1869); William Turner Walton (1902); Ed Burra (1905); Frederick Mackenzie (1912); Chapman Pincher (1914); George Chisholm (1915); Eugene McCarthy (1916); Pearl Bailey (1918); Ruby Murray (1935); Richard Rodney Bennett (1936); John Major (1943); Eric Idle and Julie Goodyear (1945); Billy Thorpe (1946); Elle MacPherson (1963); Lucy Lawless (1968); Jennifer Capriati (1976).

Significant Events and Anniversaries: March 29 is a day that indicates quiet determination, a characteristic that can result in outstanding success, as was reflected in the launching of one the world's most popular beverages, Coca-Cola, after years of research on the part of Dr. John Pemberton of Atlanta, Georgia (1886), and the setting of a land speed record of 203.841 mph. by Henry Segrave, on Daytona Beach, in his vehicle *Mystery* (1927). The organizational powers that are inherent in this day can be described as military in character, and on this day Edward VI became king of England by defeating Henry VI's Lancastrians at the Battle of Towton (1461), while the French Marshal Foch was appointed commander-in-chief of the Allied forces during World War I (1918). Although neither gave any ideological ground—a stubborn tendency of this day—British premier Margaret Thatcher nevertheless had an amicable meeting with Mikhail Gorbachev in Moscow (1987).

MARCH 30

* *

March 30 people cannot help but arouse strong emotions in others—and not always positive ones—for not only are they larger-than-life characters who dominate their immediate surroundings but, like their Arian attribute, the ram, will typically put their heads down and charge at a challenge, regardless of the consequences. Inevitably, their stubbornness and drive will lead them to make mistakes, but these people have the intelligence to learn from past experiences. Such is their relish for experiencing everything that the world has to offer, that they will discover far more from life than from books. They approach everything with passionate enthusiasm in their quest for stimulation, knowledge and success, and are the types to make things happen rather than standing passively on the sidelines. In doing so, they will either elicit feelings of intense admiration or, conversely, of profound irritation in others, but will never be ignored.

Because of their great sensuality and creative abilities, these people will often achieve outstanding success in the arts, although their talents will usually only be recognized later in life, when their youthful rebelliousness has been tempered by maturity. Because they react negatively to external constraints, they are unsuited to being small cogs in large organizations, and will only flourish when they can act independently. If their personal relationships are to succeed, their friends and partners will have to match their strength of character, but will also have to provide the emotional stability necessary to ground March 30 individuals.

VIRTUES: Headstrong, driven, vigorous and imaginative, those born on this day may be compared to forces of nature, approaching all aspects of life with fearless energy and passion. They have the potential to be extraordinarily successful, but will inevitably encounter many difficulties in the process.

VICES: March 30 people have a propensity to rush headfirst at everything that they encounter, an instinctive approach that can have disastrous consequences. Their irresistible compulsion to express themselves forcefully and honesty can alienate more sensitive types.

VERDICT: These people must recognize that the very impulsiveness that fuels them can also sabotage their best efforts. They must strive to develop greater patience in everything that they do, and take time to consider the effects of their actions and words before it is too late.

On This Day

Famous Births: Maimonides (1135); Francisco José de Goya y Lucientes (1746); Anna Sewell (1820); Paul Verlaine (1844); Vincent van Gogh (1853); Melanie Klein (1882); Sean O'Casey (1884); Frankie Laine (1913); Tom Sharpe (1928); John Astin and Rolf Harris (1930); Warren Beatty (1937); Astrud Gilberto (1940); Eric Clapton (1945); Paul Reiser (1957); M.C. Hammer (1962); Tracey Chapman (1963); Celine Dion (1968).

Significant Events and Anniversaries: March 30 promises ardent—and sometimes ill-advised—confrontational action, and on this day the South African government declared a state of emergency in response to the A.N.C.'s campaign against apartheid (1960); I.R.A. terrorists, passionately devoted to their cause, used a car bomb to kill the British member of parliament Airey Neave at the House of Commons in London, causing public outrage in Britain (1979); while in Washington, John Hinkley III shot and wounded U.S. President Ronald Reagan in a misguided demonstration of his obsession with actress Jodie Foster (1981). Reflecting the opportunism inherent in this day, U.S. Senator William H. Seward purchased Alaska from the Russian Empire for $7.2 million (1867).

Planetary Influences

Ruling planet: Mars.
First decan: Personal planet is Mars.

Sacred and Cultural Significance

In Iran, New Year's celebration begins.
Saints' day: John Climacus (d. 649); Zosimus of Syracuse (d. c.660); Osburga (d. c.1018); Leonard Murialdo (1828–1900).

On this day of adventurous action in 1842, ether was used as an anesthetic for the first time.

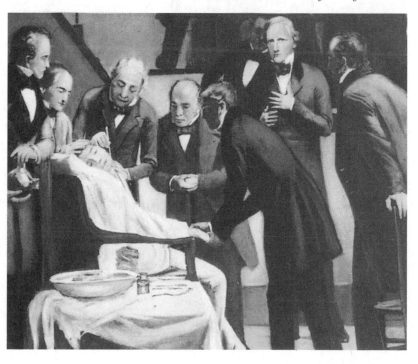

Planetary Influences
Ruling planet: Mars.
First decan: Personal planet is Mars.

Sacred and Cultural Significance
Feast of Luna in ancient Rome.
Saints' day: Benjamin, deacon of the church of Persia (5th century AD).

René Descartes, born on this day in 1596, is best known for his philosophical phrase "cogito ergo sum" *("I think, therefore I am"), but his contribution to mathematics and science in the field of geometry cannot be overstated. His logical, rational approach was typical of March 31 people, but he neglected his personal life and was never fully settled.*

MARCH 31

Individuals born on this day are valued by their coworkers and family alike for their calm and steady qualities. They typically keep firm control, imposing their logical methods on everything and everyone that they encounter, thereby ensuring that their professional and personal environments remain organized to their liking. Although they work determinedly toward their ideals and ambitions, these are never unrealistic or unachievable, and, indeed, their world view is conditioned by the pragmatism that allows them to readjust their approach—and compromise if necessary—if this will give them a better chance of success. Such willingness to be flexible if the circumstances require it is an undoubted asset in the business world, to which these people's qualities suit them extremely well, especially if they were also born in the Chinese year of the monkey.

Inherent in these individuals' desire to effect progress in an orderly and direct manner is their impatience with what they regard as unnecessary complications—be they impersonal obstacles impeding their path, or the objections of others. And while they will eventually accommodate most differences of opinion in the interests of pushing ahead, the sources of their irritation will first have been subject to their wrath. In their personal liaisons, March 31 people—particularly if they are men—display magnanimity, affection and loyalty, and expect those closest to them to reciprocate in kind. If, however, they perceive signs of insubordination, they have a tendency to lose their tempers spectacularly.

VIRTUES: March 31 people are resourceful, realistic and steadfast, qualities which, when combined with their energy and ambition, augur well for success in every aspect of their lives. Of further benefit to these individuals is their tendency to recognize that compromise is an unavoidable and necessary fact of life.
VICES: Those born on this day are prone to suppressing their emotions, believing that mental control and rational methods are preferable to imprecise, sentimental responses. When frustrated, however, their emotions can gain the upper hand, and may be released in a startlingly forceful—if short-lived—explosion of temper.
VERDICT: These individuals should recognize that few people—including themselves—can maintain the rigorously disciplined standards that they promote. They should therefore relax their expectations of constant control and learn to respect the importance of emotional expression.

On This Day
Famous Births: René Descartes (1596); John Harrison (1693); Joseph Haydn (1732); Edward Fitzgerald and Nikolai Vasilievich Gogol (1809); Robert Wilhelm Bunsen (1811); Arthur Griffith (1872); Jack Johnson (1878); Henry Morgan (1915); Richard Kiley (1922); Gordie Howe (1928); Shirley Jones (1934); Herb Alpert and Richard Chamberlain (1935); Christopher Walken (1943); Gabe Kaplan (1945); Rhea Perlman (1946); Al Gore (1948).

Significant Events and Anniversaries: This day promises success achieved by disciplined organizational methods, a characteristic that is reflected in the business and manufacturing realm, and on this day: Germany's Daimler plant produced its first automobile, a 53-mph, four-cylinder car that he named after his daughter Mercedes (1901); Whitcomb L. Judson patented the first zipper (1896); the Eiffel Tower, designed by Gustave Eiffel, was officially opened in Paris (1889); while in Argentina, the Buenos Aires police force imposed a singularly bureaucratic approach to crime-fighting by inaugurating the world's first fingerprinting establishment (1892). Achieving recognition and success after imposing self-discipline in developing her literary talent, Toni Morrison became a Pulitzer Prize winning author for her 1987 novel *Beloved* (1988). An inherent feature of March 31 is pragmatism, a quality illustrated by Japan's action in abandoning its policy of isolation and sanctioning trade with the United States (1854). The element of fire rules this day, on which the south wing of England's Hampton Court Palace was destroyed in a blaze (1986).

APRIL 1

Those born on April 1 exude an aura of quiet confidence that instantly inspires the trust of others. Nor is this faith in their abilities misplaced, for they are consistently competent and reliable in all their undertakings. Indeed, in many respects they represent the complete antithesis of the fool with which their birthday is popularly associated: dignified rather than madcap personalities; focused and tenacious instead of flighty; and prudently cautious rather than impulsively daring. Probably the only similarity that can be identified between the archetypal jester and those born on this day is the affection that they arouse in other people. They are admired for their typically perceptive, methodical and determined approach to life, an approach, moreover, that is always positive. And, although their main motivation is to achieve success in everything that they do, their ideals are usually realistic and rarely prompted by a desire for self-aggrandizement.

Because they are primarily task-oriented, they work equally well as independent agents or as team members, and in the latter situation will often find themselves elected to leadership positions—a tribute to their great professionalism, thoughtfulness and personal magnetism. So varied are their talents that they will usually excel in any career they choose, but they are probably best suited to those fields in which practical action is required. They generally make concerned and caring partners, parents and friends, whose loved ones rely on their unfailing support. An inherent disadvantage of being regarded as a pillar of strength, however, is that their own emotional needs may not be perceived or nurtured by others.

VIRTUES: These people are characterized by their calm and considered outlook. They respond positively to life's challenges by making pragmatic assessments of situations, structuring intelligent and organized plans of action, and promoting these with unflagging energy.
VICES: Those born on this day find it impossible to turn their backs on other people's requests for assistance, prompted more by their urge to find practical solutions to problems than by feelings of empathy. This propensity may result in their becoming overburdened and hence emotionally fraught and less effective.
VERDICT: April 1 people must try to moderate their inherent predilections to throw themselves single-mindedly into their work, and to take the load off others' shoulders. Unless they learn to relax their expectations of themselves and to delegate responsibility they may grind themselves into a state of exhaustion and depression.

On This Day

Famous Births: William Harvey (1578); Abbé Prévost (1697); Otto von Bismarck (1815); Edmond Rostand (1868); Sergei Rachmaninov (1873); Edgar Wallace (1875); Lon Chaney (1883); Wallace Beery (1885); Cecily Courtneidge (1893); Toshiro Mifune (1920); Anne McCaffrey (1926); Jane Powell (1929); Gordon Jump and Debbie Reynolds (1932); Ali MacGraw (1938); J.J. Williams (1948); David Gower (1957); Jennifer Runyon (1961).

Significant Events and Anniversaries: April 1 is a day of martial organizational powers which promise practical and pragmatic advances, as was illustrated by: the formation of Britain's volunteer, part-time Territorial Army (1908); the merging of Britain's Royal Naval Air Service and Royal Flying Corps into a new entity, the Royal Air Force (1918); the ending of the Spanish Civil War (1939); and the invasion of Okinawa by U.S. forces during World War II (1945). In a more negative manifestation of these qualities, the Berlin blockade was instituted by the city's Soviet occupying powers, with the intention of forcing their erstwhile U.S., British and French allies to cede the city to East Germany (1948). The determined idealism and focus indicated by this day is evident in the first woman being signed by a minor league baseball team (1931), and—in the political realm—in the Ayatollah Khomeini declaring Iran an Islamic republic (1979). These same qualities naturally culminate in scientific and technological achievements, illustrated by the completion of the first telephone link between London and Paris (1899) and by the launching of the first U.S. weather satellite (1960).

Planetary Influences
Ruling planet: Mars.
Second decan: Personal planet is the Sun.

Sacred and Cultural Significance
April Fool's Day (All Fools' Day).
Saints' day: Tewdric (5th to 6th century AD); Walaric (d. 620); Agilbert (7th century AD); Hugh of Grenoble (1052–1132); Gilbert of Caithness (d. 1245).

The singular trait April 1 people share with the clown or fool typically associated with this day is their appealing warm nature. Otherwise they tend toward pragmatism and thoughtfulness.

APRIL 2

✳✳✳

Planetary Influences
Ruling planet: Mars.
Second decan: Personal planet is the Sun.

Sacred and Cultural Significance
Saints' day: Mary of Egypt (5th century AD), patron saint of repentant prostitutes; Francis of Paola, patron saint of sailors (1416–1507).

Demonstrating the humanitarianism that is common to those born on April 2, Hans Christian Andersen wrote a play deploring the evils of slavery. Born in the Chinese year of the ox, which can impart a need for stability, Andersen worked relentlessly to overcome his personal insecurity.

Inherent in the characters of those born on April 2 is a curious mixture of prodigious organizational skills and extreme idealism that almost tends toward the otherworldly. Hence although they exhibit a propensity for taking direct and practical action—a gift of their ruling planet, Mars—the causes that fire them may seem to others to be inadvisable at best, and ludicrously fanciful at worst. Because those born on this day possess an intuitive sense of social justice and therefore feel compelled to channel their energies toward protecting the vulnerable, weak or abused, their ambitions are typically of the humanitarian variety. The problem, however, is that while their motivations are eminently laudable, they have difficulty in inspiring others with a similar sense of zeal in the pursuit of their mission. It may be that they express their convictions too forcibly and hence frighten more cautious types, or when in the thrall of all-encompassing visions appear to lose their sense of realism and thus fail to convince others of the veracity of their beliefs.

Professionally, they find greatest satisfaction in those situations in which they can promote their progressive visions, but not necessarily within conventional structures—they are too intellectually libertarian to submit to someone else's party line or organizational method. When they can express themselves as independent agents—especially as writers or artists—however, they have the potential to achieve great success and be acclaimed for their visionary powers, although the recognition of others will probably not come immediately. During all of life's trials, they find enormous solace in the close emotional bonds that they typically form, and they are valued by their nearest and dearest for the loving concern that they display.

VIRTUES: April 2 people tend to passionately espouse a cherished humanitarian ambition and pursue it with outstanding enthusiasm, vigor and tenacity, thereby simultaneously impressing and alarming others with their intensity.
VICES: Because those born on this day are so convinced as to the correctness of their opinions, they find it almost impossible to believe that others might not agree with them. This gives rise to a dual danger: that they may refuse to consider other viewpoints, and that they may alienate themselves from others by their inability to compromise.
VERDICT: These people must try to develop a more accurate view of the impact that their sometimes radical opinions has on other people, and should try to find more pragmatic ways in which to enlist their support. Recognizing that not everything can be seen in black-and-white terms, accepting differences of opinion and tempering their intensity with realism, will augur better for success and protect them from otherwise inevitable disappointment.

On This Day
Famous Births: Charlemagne (742); Giovanni Jacapo Casanova (1725); August Heinrich Hoffmann von Fallersleben (1798); Hans Christian Andersen and Léon Gambetta (1805); William Holman Hunt (1827); Emile Zola (1840); Max Ernst (1891); Alec Guinness (1914); George Macdonald Fraser (1925); Jack Brabham (1926); Marvin Gaye (1939); Emmy Lou Harris (1947); Dana Carvey (1955); Linford Christie (1960).

Significant Events and Anniversaries: This day highlights the desire to effect humanitarian progress, and marks the anniversary of: the first meeting of Italy's national parliament in Turin (1860); the closing of Britain's notoriously inhumane debtors' prison, the Fleet, in London (1884); and the visit of Israeli Prime Minister Begin to Egypt for peace talks with President Sadat (1979). Another, different type of advance was also made on this day, when the sub-Alpine Simplon Tunnel between Switzerland and Italy was opened (1905). A potential danger inherent in this day is the conflict that can result from the single-minded pursuance of a strong belief, as was illustrated when Argentina invaded the British Falkland Islands, claiming that the "Malvinas" were rightfully theirs, and thereby provoking the Falklands War (1982).

APRIL 3

Those born on April 3 are highly sociable individuals, who enjoy surrounding themselves with other people and directing their activities. They do not necessarily crave leadership positions out of a desire to dominate, merely that their energy, natural charisma and strong views tend to attract less vibrant people. It is, however, indubitably the case that these strong-minded people believe that their convictions and organizational methods are unquestionably correct and therefore seek to promote them by enlisting the support of those around them. Their considerable powers of persuasion are aided by intuitive gifts that also play a large part in informing their opinions: others' moods are assessed and then their own words and actions are adjusted appropriately to achieve optimum results. Such interpersonal skills equip them well for positions in which they can take charge of teams, and their capabilities are such that they may achieve success in any profession they choose, although they have the potential to star especially well as politicians, movie directors or actors.

There are certain dangers inherent in their characteristic self-certainty and predilection to guide others. Although they usually display a sunny, magnanimous and outgoing face to the world when things are going their way, in difficult situations their introverted and some-what insecure side comes to the fore. When they are crossed or let down by others, they have a tendency to react badly, typically either exploding with anger, or retreating into their shell and brooding introspectively over the cause of their annoyance. It is therefore important that they become more realistic in their personal relationships, and do not punish others who fail to meet their own sometimes unreasonably high expectations.

VIRTUES: April 3 people are intuitive and perceptive thinkers, instinctively attuned to others' moods, and geared toward achieving progress. Their clarity of vision, vigor and enthusiasm endow them with great personal magnetism, which they exploit in winning over others to their cause and orchestrating individuals toward a common goal.
VICES: Although generally good-humored, those born on this day have a tendency to be oversensitive when they encounter opposition, or when people do not comply with their demands, taking any manifestations of dissension personally. As such, they may be prone to sulking or temperamental outbursts.
VERDICT: These people usually keep their introverted and extroverted sides in harmony, but should not allow their more negative emotions to intrude on their dealings with others. They must accept that others expressing different views are not necessarily launching personal attacks on them, and should temper their propensity to react with hostility.

On This Day

Famous Births: King Henry IV of England (1367); Washington Irving (1783); Reginald De Koven (1859); J.B. Hertzog (1866); Daisy Ashford (1881); Leslie Howard (1893); Henry Luce (1898); Marlon Brando and Doris Day (1924); Helmut Kohl (1930); Marsha Mason and Wayne Newton (1942); Alec Baldwin (1958); Eddie Murphy (1961).

Significant Events and Anniversaries: This is a day that indicates that dissension may be perceived as betrayal, and indeed, on April 3 Robert Ford abandoned his loyalty to fellow outlaw Jesse James and shot him in the back in St. Joseph, Missouri, a treacherous action motivated by his desire to receive a $5000 reward (1882). Leadership potential is bestowed by this day, on which, in England, Emmeline Pankhurst was found guilty of encouraging her fellow suffragettes to bomb the home of the chancellor of the exchequer, David Lloyd George (1913); and Joseph Stalin became general secretary of the Soviet Communist Party (1922). A predilection for action in the cause of progress is highlighted by this day, on which the Pony Express began carrying mail between St. Joseph, Missouri, and San Francisco (1860), and socially disadvantaged British youths dramatically displayed their disaffection by initiating a series of violent riots in the Brixton area of London (1981).

Planetary Influences
Ruling planet: Mars.
Second decan: Personal planet is the Sun.

Sacred and Cultural Significance
Persephone's annual return from the Underworld, in classical mythology.
Saints' day: Pancras of Taormina (1st century AD); Agape, Irene and Chione (d. 304); Richard of Chichester (1197–1253), patron saint of coachmen.

In 1913 Emmeline Pankhurst was found guilty of conspiring, with fellow suffragettes, to bomb the home of political opponent David Lloyd George on this day when astrological forces favor the convergence of leadership, idealism and direct action.

Planetary Influences
Ruling planet: Mars.
Second decan: Personal planet is the Sun.

Sacred and Cultural Significance
Saints' day: Ambrose (339–97), patron saint of beekeepers; Isidore of Seville (c.560–636).

America's eminent author Maya Angelou was born on April 4 in the Chinese year of the dragon, reinforcing the lively and forthright aspects of her personality. Her writings strike a chord—connected with the day's tendency—of tremendous determination in the pursuit of a vision.

APRIL 4

Underlying all of the actions of those born on April 4 is a compulsion to effect their visions, and to do so on their own terms. Their ambitions may well be humanitarian ones, for these protective people typically exhibit great compassion and kindness to the vulnerable as a collective entity, and may therefore become fired with enthusiasm to implement social progress. Surprisingly, however, they are less empathetic toward individuals. This apparent paradox may have various explanations: they may feel that the concerns of those closest to them are less urgent or serious than those of the world's downtrodden as a whole; they may have a misplaced suspicion of others' motives as a result of disappointments experienced in the past; or they may simply be uninterested in the problems of those for whom they do not feel personal sympathy. When they are inspired, however, they will typically throw their considerable energies, tenacity and organizational talents into a project, giving them immense potential for success, especially in the business and financial spheres, but also in the literary and performing arts.

Those born on this day possess a great sense of self-certainty; so convinced are they of the veracity of their convictions and approach to life that they expect others to conform to their views unquestioningly. Although they are typically affectionate and involved parents, partners and friends, they tend to demand that their personal liaisons operate on the terms that they have set. Just as they impatiently dismiss the validity of alternative opinions in the workplace, so do they regard any incidences of nonconformity by their nearest and dearest as tantamount to betrayal—an emotional reaction that they must strive to temper.

VIRTUES: These strong-willed individuals are stimulated by challenge and, when their interest is fired, typically marshal their formidable talents of determination, drive, tenacity and organization in developing and promoting effective strategies.
VICES: Underpinning the actions of April 4 people is an overwhelming belief in themselves and their motives, resulting in a level of self-confidence that may refuse to countenance the possibility that other approaches may be not only justified but also better. They may also lack forbearance and empathy.
VERDICT: It is vital that these people keep their ears and minds open to different viewpoints, and that they do not stubbornly persist in promoting their own convictions at the expense of others. They will find great emotional—and material—rewards by cultivating an increased sense of empathy and tolerance.

On This Day
Famous Births: Grinling Gibbons (1648); Pierre Paul Prud'hon (1758); Linus Yale (1821); William Siemens (1823); Hans Richter (1843); Pierre Monteux (1875); Maurice de Vlaminck (1876); William Russell Flint (1880); Isoroku Yamamoto (1884); Arthur Murray (1895); Robert Emmet Sherwood (1896); John Cameron Swayze (1906); Frances Langford (1914); Muddy Waters (1915); Maya Angelou (1928); Anthony Perkins (1932); Craig T. Nelson (1946); Marilu Henner (1952); David Garvin (1963); Robert Downey, Jr. (1965).

Significant Events and Anniversaries: The success that can result from tremendous determination in the pursuit of a vision is highlighted by this day, on which: the English mariner Francis Drake was knighted on board *The Golden Hind* by Queen Elizabeth I in recognition of his achievement in having circumnavigated the world (1581); gold was finally discovered in the Yukon area of North America after many previously unsuccessful attempts (1896); and the British jockey Bob Champion, in remission from cancer, rode to victory on his horse Aldaniti, winning the Grand National (1981). April 4 indicates intolerance toward conflicting beliefs, and in two extreme illustrations of this tendency this day marks the anniversary of the murder of U.S. civil-rights leader Dr. Martin Luther King, Jr., in Memphis, Tennessee, by James Earl Ray (1968), and the execution of Zulfikar Ali Bhutto, the former president of Pakistan, in Rawalpindi (1979).

APRIL 5

T hose born on this day are admired for their strength of purpose and the forceful, determined way in which they work toward achieving their ambitions. Indeed, once enthralled by the light emanating from a star of inspiration, they will firmly set their eyes on their vision and refuse to allow themselves to be deflected from making steady progress toward its attainment. The motivations that inspire such tenacity may be varied: some April 5 people are fired by a social or humanitarian mission, others by their desire to achieve perfect artistry, while all yearn to be the best. This propensity is even more pronounced in those also born in the Chinese year of the dragon. The urge to climb to the top of their professions is not fueled by personal vanity or a craving to be showered with acclaim: rather it arises because they are perfectionists and feel compelled to conquer any challenge that presents itself. Their prodigious organizational powers, as well as their steadfast and logical approach, bestow on them enormous potential to realize their lofty aims.

Despite the seriousness that they accord to their intellectual pursuits, they are not wholly absorbed by their work and, when "off duty," play hard and enjoy themselves. They are caring friends and family members, who enjoy bringing pleasure to others and are typically extremely indulgent with their children. Particularly for the men, however, their attention may frequently be distracted by the irresistible lure of their impersonal ambitions, and insufficient attention may be paid to meeting the emotional needs of their intimate associates.

VIRTUES: April 5 people possess outstandingly well-developed personal qualities, including clarity of vision and a logical intellectual focus. This gives them the ability to form highly methodical strategies, the will-power and energy to introduce them and the tenacity to continue until success has been achieved.

VICES: Despite their recognition that, when away from work, it is important to relax and recharge their mental batteries in order to make them more effective, their overriding priority is their intellectual pursuits, and they may therefore neglect the more mundane—though equally important—requirements of their family and friends.

VERDICT: Although they usually manage to separate and compartmentalize their professional and personal lives, their commitment to the visions that inspire them may sometimes cause them to take a physical or emotional leave of absence from their family and friends. They must therefore guard against their intellectual preoccupations causing hurt to others.

Planetary Influences
Ruling planet: Mars.
Second decan: Personal planet is the Sun.

Sacred and Cultural Significance
Festival of Kuan Yin in China.
Saints' day: Derfel (d. c.250); Vincent Ferrer (1350–1419), patron saint of builders.

The Festival of Kuan Yin—the Chinese goddess of healing, mercy, compassion and forgiveness—takes place on April 5.

On This Day
Famous Births: Thomas Hobbes (1588); Elihu Yale (1649); Jean Honoré Fragonard (1732); Joseph Lister (1827); Algernon Charles Swinburne (1837); Booker T. Washington (1856); Chesney Allen (1894); Spencer Tracy (1900); Bette Davis and Herbert von Karajan (1908); Gregory Peck (1916); Arthur Hailey (1920); Gale Storm (1921); Roger Corman (1926); Nigel Hawthorne (1929); Frank Gorshin (1934); Colin Powell (1937); Michael Moriarty (1941); Agnetha "Anna" Faltskög (1950).

Significant Events and Anniversaries: One of the multitude of talents indicated by this day is artistic prowess, and in a musical manifestation of this talent, April 5 marks the anniversary of the first performance of the younger Johann Stauss's operetta *Die Fledermaus* (1874), while in the realm of film, the movie *Ben Hur* received outstanding acclaim, winning ten Oscars (1960). This day is governed by the element of fire, as was sadly reflected in Ireland when numerous tax offices and police stations were set ablaze to mark the anniversary of the Easter Rising in Dublin in 1916 (1920). Not only is April presided over by the Roman god of war, Mars, but it highlights martial characteristics of organization, and on this day a British task force set sail for the Falkland Islands to eject the Argentinian invaders (1982).

Planetary Influences
Ruling planet: Mars.
Second decan: Personal planet is the Sun.

♂ ☉

Sacred and Cultural Significance
Saints' day: Irenaeus of Sirmium (d. 304); Elstan (d. 981).

A drawing of St. Paul's Cathedral in London depicts its impressive architecture. In 1580 on April 6—a day notable for restlessness and instability—the cathedral was devastated by an earthquake.

APRIL 6

The driving force behind those born on April 6 is their restless quest for knowledge, their urge to uncover the true nature of a person or situation. And, because they learn from experience, the discoveries that they make upon their voyages of learning not only inform their future actions, but also bestow upon them the ability to be open-minded, and to accept the possibility of sometimes otherworldly concepts. Yet despite their intellectual restlessness, they are by no means deficient in staying power, and when they meet a subject that truly absorbs their interest, will employ their considerable powers of logic, mental organization and tenacity in analyzing and subsequently building upon their findings. Such talents give them the potential to be real innovators, especially in the scientific field, although since they are typically all-rounders, they may also make gifted musicians, writers or even philosophers.

Indeed, such is the variety of talents and interests with which they are blessed that those born on April 6 may initially have difficulty in either settling on their life's vocation or committing to a life partner. Once they are finally established in a stable domestic situation they generally make loyal and supportive family members, and are particularly cherished as generous and indulgent parents. The irresistible siren call of a fascinating idea, however, may cause them to drop everything in its hot pursuit.

VIRTUES: These multitalented and original individuals are motivated by a burning compulsion to discover as yet unknown truths, a need which can lead them into previously uncharted areas of knowledge. Once set upon a particularly exciting trail, they marshal their prodigious methodological talents and energy into its proper investigation.
VICES: There is a danger that April 6 people may become so enthralled by pet projects that they will single-mindedly promote them to the exclusion of everything else. This propensity may cause them to neglect their own need for relaxation, as well as the emotional requirements of those closest to them.
VERDICT: While never abandoning the direction into which their intellectual curiosity leads them, those born on this day must try to maintain a sense of perspective in life and not push themselves so hard toward the realization of their visions that they become both physically and mentally exhausted and isolated from others by their obsession.

On This Day
Famous Births: Raphael (1483); Maximilien Robespierre (1758); Harry Houdini (1874); Walter Huston (1884); Leo Robin (1900); John Betjeman (1906); Richard Murdoch (1907); David Moore (1927); James Dewey Watson (1928); André Previn (1929); Merle Haggard and Billy Dee Williams (1937); Michelle Philips (1944); Bob Marley and Peter Tosh (1945); Ari Meyers (1969).

Significant Events and Anniversaries: April 6 highlights a range of talents, as is reflected in the individual achievements that were attained on this day, including George Washington's appointment as the first president of the United States (1789); Joseph Smith's establishment of the Church of Jesus Christ of the Latter Day Saints in New York (1830); William Wordsworth's naming as the British poet laureate (1843); Baron de Courbertin's realization of his Olympic vision with the opening of the first modern Olympic Games in Athens (1896); the successful culmination of U.S. explorers Robert Peary and Matthew Henson's quest to be the first to reach the North Pole (1909); and Pierre Trudeau's election as the prime minister of Canada (1968). The inherent restlessness indicated by this day is paralleled in seismic action, when an earthquake in Britain devastated many buildings in London, including such notable ecclesiastic structures as St. Paul's Cathedral (1580).

APRIL 7

✶ ✶

There are two distinct sides to the characters of those born on April 7: a positive and idealistic side, which inspires them to work unstintingly toward progress; and a more negative, impatient side, which has a tendency to manifest itself when these individuals are frustrated. Although it may seem that these characteristics are in direct opposition to each other, they are, in fact, interlinked by cause and effect. When April 7 people are seized by the desire to bring about improvement—be it in the humanitarian sphere or, more specifically, with regard to a work-related task—they will enthusiastically and whole-heartedly invest their considerable gifts of imagination, logic and tenacity into the project. When, however, they encounter obstacles in their paths, they are prone to rush headlong at them, and then, like the Arian goat that is their astrological attribute, explode with anger when their repeated butts fail to clear the way. This temperamental reaction is even more pronounced if they were also born in the Chinese year of the dragon.

The talents of those born on April 7 are versatile: their idealism and sensitivity indicates potential success in literary, musical and dramatic pursuits, while their inquiring minds and methodical approach suits them for scientific research. In whatever field they make their profession, they need to be given as much autonomy as possible; they make good leaders, but usually only on their own terms. Similarly, although generally sunny and relaxed in their personal relationships, they will chafe if restricted by others' ground rules—especially in adolescence—and here again, if things are not going their way, they are prone to temperamental outbursts.

VIRTUES: Those born on this day are blessed with unlimited zeal, determination and optimism when inspired by an intellectual or social vision. They are motivated by a fervent wish to make their dreams become reality and, indeed, have the ability and drive to succeed in this.
VICES: April 7 people have a propensity to react aggressively if others disagree with them, or if they are prevented from acting as they wish. Such negative responses may take the form of eruptions of temper, hurtful, sarcastic comments or the nurturing of grudges.
VERDICT: It is vital that these people do not sabotage their efforts to effect good by alienating others in the above ways when they feel disgruntled. Adopting a calmer and more considered approach, of which they are undoubtedly capable, and listening coolly and objectively to the views of others will benefit them in every area of their lives.

On This Day

Famous Births: St. Francis Xavier (1506); William Wordsworth (1770); Charles Fourier (1772); Ole Kirk Christiansen and David Low (1891); Irene Castle (1893); Billie Holiday (1915); Ravi Shankar (1920); James Garner and Alan J. Pakula (1928); Andrew Sachs (1930); Wayne Rogers (1933); Jerry Brown (1938); Francis Ford Coppola and David Frost (1939); Jackie Chan (1954).

Significant Events and Anniversaries: This day indicates a fiery temper (and is, indeed, ruled by the element of fire), and on April 7 the first safety matches, the brainchild of John Walker of Stockton-on-Tees in England, were sold commercially (1827), while over a hundred people lost their lives when Mount Vesuvius erupted in Sicily (1906). Further violent manifestations of this day's confrontational tendencies include the hanging of the highwayman Dick Turpin in York, England (1739); the victory of General Ulysses Grant's Union forces at the Battle of Shiloh when they forced the Confederate Army to retreat (1862); and the sinking of the world's largest battleship at that time, the Japanese vessel *Yamamoto,* by U.S. aircraft during World War II (1945). This day highlights both scientific and artistic talents, as is reflected in the achievement of Swiss scientist Albert Hoffman in synthesizing L.S.D. (1943), and the first performance of Rodgers and Hammerstein's musical *South Pacific* (1949). Humanitarian concern is another characteristic inherent in this day, on which the World Health Organization (W.H.O.) was established in Geneva (1948); the Swede Dag Hammarskjöld became head of the United Nations (1953); and an estimated 15,000 people protested at the Atomic Weapons Research Establishment at Aldermaston in England (1958).

Planetary Influences
Ruling planet: Mars.
Second decan: Personal planet is the Sun.

Sacred and Cultural Significance
Blajini celebrated in Romania.
Saints' day: Finan Cam (d. c.600); Goran (dates unknown); Celsus (12th century AD); Jean-Baptist de la Salle (1651–1719), patron saint of teachers.

Born on April 7 in 1915, Billie Holiday mirrored characteristics common to this day, especially for those born—as she was—in the Chinese year of the rabbit: creativity combined with a sensitive and mercurial nature.

Planetary Influences
Ruling planet: Mars.
Second decan: Personal planet is the Sun.

Sacred and Cultural Significance
Saints' day: Walter, abbot of Pontoise (c. 1030–99).

Former first lady Betty Ford was born on April 8, a day favoring humanitarian concerns. Her achievements in overcoming her own addiction and working tirelessly to help others with similar issues were aided by her pragmatism, confidence and attraction to challenges—traits reinforced by her being born in the Chinese year of the horse.

The ambitions that fuel the actions of those born on April 8 are rather noble ones, for they yearn to bring about global improvement, especially in social issues. Their humanitarian concerns and consequent ideals are motivated in part by feelings of compassion for unfortunate individuals suffering abuse, and in part by their inherent recognition of what is correct and morally just behavior. Such characteristics and ideals equip them especially well for careers in the judiciary, military or other law-enforcement agencies, but the attainment of sporting goals is also starred by this day and, whether or not they pursue athletics professionally, most will derive great enjoyment from energetic physical pursuits. In the great race of life, these strong-willed individuals typically map out well-considered and direct courses of action, which they then follow single-mindedly, a strategy that augurs well for success.

Despite their great empathy, the incisive and logical intellects of those born on April 8, as well as their desire to effect justice, give them a propensity to see the world in black-and-white terms, impatiently dismissing the myriad shades of gray opinion as being manifestations of mental and emotional confusion, or even unequivocally wrong. Since they furthermore keep their emotions on a tight leash, they may appear to others to be somewhat remote, lofty beings who find it hard to form truly intimate relationships. When among trusted friends and family members they are, however, generally deeply loyal and affectionate, and may develop a specially close rapport with their children.

VIRTUES: April 8 people are blessed with prodigiously incisive and methodical minds, as well as with enormous vigor and determination, qualities which they have a propensity to employ in the service of others, especially the more vulnerable members of society.
VICES: Those born on this day are prone to suppress their own emotional requirements in their quest to bring about improvement in the lives of others, a tendency which may ultimately be unhealthy. They may additionally be extremely rigid in their convictions, refusing to admit the veracity of views that conflict with their own.
VERDICT: Although the altruism and concern that these people feel for humanity as a global entity is admirable, it is vital that they address their own needs in order to avoid sacrificing their personal lives and losing their mental equilibrium. They should try to develop a more tolerant attitude to those who hold different opinions and should also relax and demand less of themselves.

On This Day
Famous Births: Giuseppe Tartini (1692); August Wilhelm Hofmann (1818); King Albert I of the Belgians (1875); Adrian Boult (1889); Mary Pickford (1893); E.Y. "Yip" Harburg (1898); Josef Krips (1902); Sonja Henie (1912); Betty Ford (1918); Ian Smith (1919); Sheckey Greene (1926); Eric Porter (1928); Dorothy Tutin (1930); John Gavin (1932); Hywel Bennett (1944); John Schneider (1954); Julian Lennon (1963).

Significant Events and Anniversaries: A predilection toward taking active measures in the cause of perceived justice is indicated by this day, on which the Roman emperor Caracalla was assassinated, thus putting an end to his cruel and tyrannous rule (217); the British General Horatio Kitchener captured the Mahdi, the leader of a revolt against Egypt, at Atbara River in the Sudan (1898); Jomo Kenyatta was imprisoned by the Kenyan authorities for his alleged leadership of the Mau Mau guerrilla movement (1953); and actor Clint Eastwood was elected mayor of the town of Carmel in California (1986). The vision and tenacity inherent in this day can result in technical advances, as was illustrated when the *Great Western*, the steamship built by British engineer Isambard Kingdom Brunel, inaugurated the first such transatlantic passenger service when she set off on her maiden voyage from Bristol to New York (1838); in landmark achievements, as when baseball legend Hank Aaron hit his 715th career home run, shattering Babe Ruth's record (1974); and in the attainment of artistic goals, as when Nicholas Maw's symphony "Odyssey" was first performed (1989).

APRIL 9

Those born on April 9 are resolutely practical, preferring action to reflection, and displaying great vigor and competence in the process. They are not given to abstract ideological visions, instead concentrating upon the immediate aims of their professional and domestic lives. In doing so, their drive, tenacity and strength of purpose come to the fore, and their capacity for organizing both their own ideas and other people's resources is put to good use. Such methodical and determined qualities, as well as a remarkable clarity of focus, augur well for their success. However, their tendency to see things in black-and-white terms, and their impatience with those who do not concur with their approach may ultimately hinder their progress. Because they manifest both artistic and scientific talents, they are suited to careers in either field, but will probably find greatest satisfaction in those areas where tangible results can be achieved, such as in business, the military or as mechanics.

Many of those born on this day regard their home environment as being of greater importance than their careers, and they will typically run it—and their immediate family—with enormous efficiency. Indeed, such is their energy and compulsion to be active, that they frequently devote their leisure hours to home improvements and other domestic activities. While offering considerable practical support and stability to those nearest to them, they do have a propensity to dominate their loved ones, and should try to develop a more relaxed and accepting view of any differences of opinion.

VIRTUES: Being blessed with prodigious energy, organizational skills, resourcefulness and single-mindedness, April 9 people have a great capacity to achieve their ambitions.
VICES: Reflecting their strongly held views and urge to effect progress, they are prone to give insufficient consideration to those who hold alternative convictions, or who advocate less clear-cut methods than their own.
VERDICT: It is vital that, in all areas of their lives, April 9 people should strive to develop the more intuitive and sensitive qualities that they undoubtedly possess, giving genuine attention to the needs of others, and moderating their propensity for taking control. Such equality and reciprocal communication within their professional and personal relationships, will ultimately provide profound emotional fulfillment.

On This Day

Famous Births: James Scott, Duke of Monmouth (1649); Isambard Kingdom Brunel (1806); Charles Pierre Baudelaire (1821); King Leopold II of the Belgians (1835); Erich von Ludendorff (1865); Léon Blum (1872); Paul Bustill Robeson (1898); Anatole Dorati and Hugh Todd Naylor Gaitskell (1906); Robert Murray Helpmann (1909); Hugh Marston Hefner (1926); Tom Lehrer (1928); Jean-Paul Belmondo (1933); Dennis Quaid (1954); Sevériano Ballesteros and Paulina Porizkova (1957).

Significant Events and Anniversaries: April 9 is a day which indicates unwavering commitment to passionately held convictions—a tendency which may lead inevitably to violent confrontation—and marks the anniversary of the execution of Lord Lovat for high treason in England for his espousal of the Jacobite cause (1747); the triumph of the Unionist General Ulysses S. Grant in receiving the Confederate General Robert E. Lee's surrender at Appomattox during the American Civil War (1865); the launching of the Canadian assault on German positions at Vimy Ridge during World War I (1917); the German Army's invasion of Norway and Denmark during World War II (1940); and the physical attack on South African Prime Minister Hendrik Verwoerd by David Pratt (1960). On a more positive note, the determination inherent in April 9 promises potential success, as was reflected in the first flight made by the supersonic aircraft Concorde 002 from Filton in England (1969). Practical concerns are also a factor of this day, on which Paul McCartney took the first step toward the legal dissolution of the Beatles (1970).

Planetary Influences
Ruling planet: Mars.
Second decan: Personal planet is the Sun.

Sacred and Cultural Significance
Portuguese Feast of A-Ma; in England, Hocktide Festival.
Saints' day: Madrun (5th century AD).

On April 9—a day that highlights enacting passionately held convictions and abhors compromise—General Ulysses S. Grant accepted the surrender of General Robert E. Lee at Appomattox (1865), marking the end of the American Civil War.

Planetary Influences
Ruling planet: Mars.
Second decan: Personal planet is the Sun.

Sacred and Cultural Significance
In Celtic folklore, the day the Sun dances; the Day of Bau in Babylonia.
Saints' day: Beocca and Hethor (d. 870); Hedda of Peterborough (d. 870).

Whatever it is that especially motivates those born on April 10—be it a humanitarian, spiritual, scientific or artistic vision—they will typically devote their single-minded attention and enormous energy to its exploration, shrewdly examining its inherent aspects in minute detail and then evolving a soundly considered plan of action with which to take it farther. Although they are geared toward achieving results, these pragmatic people are rarely impulsive, and will first employ their incisive intellects and practical skills in researching and formulating the most feasible strategy with which to realize their ambitions. So while those who do not know them well are sometimes taken aback by what they perceive to be their radical approach, April 10 people are, in fact, confident of success, secure in the knowledge that they have carefully evaluated any potential risks. This conjunction of methodical and adventurous characteristics equips them for a variety of careers, but professions such as stockbroking, surveying, advertising or marketing are likely to be especially fertile fields.

Although those born on this day place great value on the bonds of family and friendship, and genuinely desire the happiness of those closest to them, their propensity to become overly involved in work-related projects may result in an unequal division of their interests. This tendency is particularly pronounced in men born on this day, as well as in those individuals who were also born in the Chinese year of the tiger, who are similarly often distracted by more pressing—but no less important—interests outside the home.

VIRTUES: Inherent in those born on this day is a variety of talents, including intellectual perspicacity, technical expertise, steadfastness of purpose and a willingness to take carefully calculated risks. This combination is auspicious for potential success.
VICES: Because they are so intent on confronting challenges head on, on proving their mastery of difficult circumstances and achieving tangible results, there is a danger that they may either become addicted to, or obsessed by, situations in which they can test themselves, to the ultimate detriment of their well-being.
VERDICT: April 10 people are unequivocally dynamic and positive individuals, who are geared toward overcoming obstacles and making progress. In all areas of their lives, however, it is crucial that they learn to relax, occasionally to switch off the questing sector of their minds, so that they may receive the emotional fulfillment inherent in personal relationships.

Triumph over challenge and a drive to enact humanitarian visions are characteristics of April 10, a day on which the U.S. Senate passed the Civil Rights Bill, in 1960. This landmark achievement was made possible by groundwork laid by such civil rights activists as (left to right) John Lewis, Whitney Young, Jr., A. Philip Randolph, Dr. Martin Luther King, Jr., James Farmer and Roy Wilkins.

On This Day
Famous Births: King James V of Scotland (1512); Christian Hahnemann (1755); William Hazlitt (1778); Lew Wallace (1827); William Booth (1829); Joseph Pulitzer (1847); Ben Nicholson (1894); Clare Boothe Luce (1903); Chuck Connors (1921); Max von Sydow (1929); Omar Sharif (1932); Stan Mellor (1937); Don Meredith (1938); Paul Theroux (1941); Steven Segal (1951).

Significant Events and Anniversaries: This day highlights a relish for confronting and triumphing over challenging situations, and marks the anniversary of various manifestations of this tendency, including the victory of the Duke of Wellington's forces over Marshal Soult's French Army (1814); the landing of the first British settlers at Algoa Bay in South Africa, after an arduous journey at sea (1820); and golfer Nick Faldo's achievement in becoming the first Briton to win the Masters tournament in the U.S.A. (1989). Inherent in April 10 is a burning desire to effect practical progress, and, indeed, many innovations and ground-breaking achievements occurred on this day: the passing of the Copyright Act by the British Parliament (1710); the publication of the first issue of the *New York Tribune* (subsequently renamed the *Herald Tribune*) (1841); the patenting of the safety pin by New Yorker Walter Hunt (1849); the publication of the world's first crossword-puzzle compendium in New York (1924); and the enacting of the Civil Rights Bill by the U.S. Senate (1960). Personal success is indicated by this day, on which George Eliot published *The Mill on the Floss* (1860); Sun Yat-sen became president of China (1921); and Paul von Hindenburg was voted president of Germany (1932).

APRIL 11

Grand ideas fascinate those born on April 11, especially those that promise progress for humanity—either in terms of global social advancement or by means of scientific and technical advances. Blessed by an inherent sense of natural justice and a desire to champion the causes of those who are disadvantaged, they have both a strong sense of empathy with those who experience suffering and the determination to improve their lot. Eternally optimistic when it comes to the development of a strategy with which to realize their ambitions, these people will typically invest their prodigious energy, clarity of vision and considerable interpersonal skills in the formulation of a plan of action, and then promote it with single-minded tenacity. Not only are they intellectually incisive, but they are realistic and practical enough to know that they will need to enlist the support of others if they are to succeed. As a result, they will often consciously set out to charm potential opponents and convert them to their cause by means of skilled diplomacy.

Such skills and concerns suit them especially well for public-service careers, including the spheres of politics, the diplomatic service, social work or scientific research. They perform particularly well when given charge of a team, and have the capability to encourage and inspire their coworkers. For many of them, however, their personal environments may be less than harmonious, and within which their drive and tenacity may be struggling to find a satisfying outlet. They may, moreover, be bored by mundane domestic chores and may therefore gain a reputation for shirking their responsibilities in the home because of their preference for more stimulating pursuits.

VIRTUES: Fueled by their progressive ideals, April 11 people will work tirelessly toward their objective, mustering their enormous powers of persuasion, tenacity and clear-sightedness into a dynamic package that gives them great potential for success.
VICES: Because they are so actively oriented towards achievement, they will react badly if—despite their considerable efforts—they find themselves in an impasse, taking out their annoyance on the nearest available target, or becoming deeply depressed. They are furthermore prone to impatience when unstimulated.
VERDICT: It is vital that those born on this day adapt the same realistic outlook to their personal liaisons that they do to their professional work, accepting people as they are and recognizing that domestic life is important precisely for the relaxation and quiet emotional fulfillment that it offers as a counterbalance to work demands.

On This Day
Famous Births: George Canning (1770); James Parkinson (1775); Charles Hallé (1819); Nick La Rocca (1889); Dean Acheson and John Nash (1893); Percy Lavon Julian (1899); Oleg Cassini (1913); Cameron Mitchell (1918); Ethel Kennedy (1928); Ronald Fraser (1930); Joel Grey (1932); Jill Gascoine (1937); Louise Lasser (1939).

Significant Events and Anniversaries: This day of progress promises diplomatic solutions to conflicts of interest, as was reflected in the coronation of William III and Mary II of Britain, thus resolving the crisis engendered by James II's pro-Catholic policies (1689); the ending of the War of the Spanish Succession, by which Britain gained Newfoundland and Gibraltar by the Treaty of Utrecht (1713); and Britain's granting of self-government to Singapore (1957). April 11's high humanitarian ideals were mirrored by the founding of the International Labor Organization (1919), while the horrors that can result from inhumanity and abuse of power were exposed by Allied forces when they liberated Buchenwald, the first Nazi concentration camp to be freed (1945). The justice inherent in this day was reflected in the opening of the trial of former Nazi Adolf Eichmann for crimes against humanity (1961).

Planetary Influences
Ruling planet: Mars.
Third decan: Personal planet is Jupiter.

Sacred and Cultural Significance
Anahit honored in Armenia.
Saints' day: Guthlac (c.673–714); Stanislaus of Cracow (1010–79).

The Nazi concentration camp Buchenwald was liberated on April 11—a day reinforcing humanitarian concerns in the crusade to relieve suffering and champion justice.

Planetary Influences
Ruling planet: Mars.
Third decan: Personal planet is Jupiter.

Sacred and Cultural Significance
Chu-Si-Niu honored in Taiwan; ancient Roman festival Cerealia celebrated.
Saint's day: Zeno of Verona (d. 371).

The first shot of the American Civil War—signaling the Confederate attack on Fort Sumter—occurred on April 12, a day when idealism and zeal can converge to bring about confrontation.

APRIL 12

Those born on April 12 are generally externally oriented, typically projecting their strongly held ideals and humanitarian visions outward in their desire to create a more perfect, just and effective society. They are impatient with those who espouse personal interests, believing that achieving the greater good is of far more importance than, for example, making money or drifting idly through life. Indeed, although their commitment and strength of purpose may intimidate less driven people, they generally manage to mitigate their almost magisterial, aloof image by means of both their often self-deprecating wit and their concern not to alienate others. They are prone to employing their considerable verbally persuasive talents in enlisting and encouraging support for their mission, but are prepared to strike out courageously on a solitary—but morally justified—path if diplomatic methods fail. They have the potential to achieve success in whatever profession excites their interest, but are especially well equipped for military and political careers, as well as for those artistic styles—such as satire—in which they can make a moral statement.

It is ironic, given that these people are motivated by the desire to further human progress, that away from work they may be somewhat lonely individuals. Because they set others—as well as themselves—such high standards, they may not only find it difficult to find a partner who lives up to them, but also experience profound disappointment when the behavior of friends and family members incurs their disapproval. Yet once they moderate their propensity for criticism and become more indulgent of the failings of others, they can be extremely supportive of, and generous toward, their nearest and dearest.

VIRTUES: April 12 people are defined by their ideals, which are usually humanitarian and always progressive. In working toward the achievement of their ambitions, they will display outstanding tenacity, great practical capabilities and unwavering focus.
VICES: There is a danger that they may become obsessed with realizing a vision, which they may regard as their life's work, to the extent that they cut themselves off from other people, either because they have no energy to spare, or because they may feel that if people are not with them, they must be against them.
VERDICT: It is of crucial importance that in every aspect of their lives these individuals moderate their predilection to devoting all of their time and energy to crusading missions. They must strive to recognize the emotional and physical benefits that come from relaxation and the quiet enjoyment of the simpler things in life, and they should especially strive to make time to indulge in family pursuits.

On This Day
Famous Births: Henry Clay (1777); Imogen Holst (1907); Lionel Hampton (1913); Maria Callas and Ann Miller (1923); Tiny Tim (1925); Montserrat Caballe (1933); Alan Ayckbourn (1939); Herbie Hancock and Jack Herbert (1940); Bobby Moore (1941); David Letterman (1947); David Cassidy (1950); Andy Garcia (1956); Shannen Doherty (1971); Claire Danes (1979).

Significant Events and Anniversaries: The idealistic zeal inherent in this day has the potential to result in head-on confrontation, as was mirrored in the capture and pillage of the Islamic city of Constantinople (Istanbul) by Christian members of the Fourth Crusade (1204); the defeat inflicted on the American rebels by the British Navy at the Battle of the Saints off Dominica during the American War of Independence (1782); the victory of English settlers over the Zulus in the Battle of Tugela in southern Africa (1838); and the outbreak of the American Civil War, when Confederate forces laid siege to Fort Sumter in Charleston Harbor (1861). Determination in the pursuit of a cherished ambition can result in individual triumphs, as is reflected on this day when the French pilot Pierre Prier became the first person to fly from London to Paris nonstop (1911), and when *Volstok 1*, the spacecraft of Soviet cosmonaut Yuri Gagarin, blasted off, and he become the first man to orbit the earth (1961).

APRIL 13

✱✱✱✱✱✱✱✱✱✱✱✱✱✱✱✱✱✱✱✱✱✱✱✱✱✱✱✱✱✱✱✱✱✱✱

It may seem paradoxical, in the opinion of those who do not know April 13 people well, that these solitary, strong-willed and silent types are totally geared toward moving humankind forward. And, indeed, it is through their work that these essentially private and rather introverted individuals connect with the world, sometimes even making their indelible mark on history. Yet their external orientation is not as contradictory as it might appear at first sight, for when one considers their intellectual curiosity, their power of penetrating thought, their methodical approach, as well as their predilection toward progressive ideals, it is logical that they should employ their prodigious talents in projects for the benefit of humanity. Professionally, success beckons from a diversity of areas—politics, the judiciary and military, scientific research, and also such artistic spheres as music, literature and drama, in which they can translate their frequently radical visions into reality.

They are skeptical of conventional truths, and therefore feel compelled to seek out their own interpretations and solutions to social issues. Their quest may inevitably, however, either baffle or alienate less intellectually adventurous souls, who may respond to their ideas with incomprehension or derision. And, since they are deeply sensitive to the opinions of others, they will thus experience personal hurt, while nevertheless refusing to be deflected from the pursuance of their chosen course of action—particularly if they were also born in the Chinese year of the ox. Should they be fortunate enough to enjoy the understanding of friends and family, they will derive great comfort and encouragement from the support of those who know them best, and will reciprocate many times over.

VIRTUES: April 13 people are profound—almost philosophical—and incisive thinkers, who are not afraid to act independently when convinced of the veracity of their beliefs. Since they also possess great qualities of realism, practicality and tenacity to back up their visions, they are blessed with enormous potential for success.
VICES: When others react negatively to their revolutionary, albeit meticulously researched, proposals, they tend to regard this as personal slight, and may isolate themselves from their detractors or become embittered.
VERDICT: While rarely doubting their own abilities, they may have difficulty in persuading others to take a similar viewpoint. It is therefore crucial to their emotional well-being that they learn to cope positively with discouragement and to draw on the strength and love of those dearest to them, who will also help them to maintain a healthy sense of perspective.

On This Day

Famous Births: Catherine de Medici (1519); Lord Frederick North (1732); Thomas Jefferson (1743); Richard Trevithick (1771); Frank Winfield Woolworth (1852); Arthur "Bomber" Harris and Robert Watson-Watt (1892); Philippe de Rothschild (1902); Samuel Barclay Beckett (1906); Eudora Welty (1909); Howard Keel (1919); John Gerard Braine (1922); Stanley Donen (1924); Don Adams (1926); Lyle Waggoner (1935); Edward Fox (1937); Jack Casady (1944); Tony Dow (1945); Al Green (1946); Ron Perlman (1950); Gary Kasparov (1963); Ricky Schroder (1970); Jonathon Brandis (1976).

Significant Events and Anniversaries: This day highlights artistic and creative achievements, often attained against great odds, and marks the anniversary of the appointment of John Dryden, the satirical dramatist and poet, as the first English poet laureate (1668); the premiere of Georg Friedrich Handel's oratorio the *Messiah*, nine years before he became totally blind (1742); and the bestowing of an Oscar on Sidney Poitier—the first African-American actor to receive one—for his performance in *Lilies of the Field* (1964). The strength of conviction inherent in this day may ultimately lead to conflict, and on this day the German Anti-Semitic League was formed, tragically prefiguring the racial views promoted by the Nazis (1882), and British troops fired on Sikhs demonstrating at their holy shrine of Amritsar in the Punjab region of India, killing 379 people and injuring over 1,200 (1919).

Planetary Influences
Ruling planet: Mars.
Third decan: Personal planet is Jupiter.

Sacred and Cultural Significance
Buddhist festival of water.
Saints' day: Carpus, Papylus and Agathonice (d. c.170); Martin I (d. 655); Guinoch (d. 838).

One of the greatest statesmen in American history, Thomas Jefferson was born on April 13, 1743. Qualities reinforced by astrological attributes of the day include intellectual acuity, progressive vision and a humanitarian orientation.

Planetary Influences
Ruling planet: Mars.
Third decan: Personal planet is Jupiter.

Sacred and Cultural Significance
Maryamma honored in Hinduism.
Saints' day: Tiburtius, Valerian and Maximus
(dates unknown); Caradoc (d. 1124); Benezet
of Avignon (c.1163–84), patron saint of
bridge-builders.

*On April 14, a day that highlights strong—
even extreme—political convictions, President
Abraham Lincoln was assassinated by John
Wilkes Booth in 1865.*

APRIL 14

Their surroundings are of supreme importance to the well-being of those born on April 14, be it their professional or domestic environment or, indeed, the country in which they live. They possess a curious conjunction of apparently conflicting qualities: intellectual and physical restlessness and yet a strong emotional need to feel grounded within a societal group— usually the family. When each characteristic is taken to its extreme, they may be intrepid travelers, who delight in exploring foreign lands and cultures, or committed home-bodies, who direct their considerable energy and enthusiasm into beautifying their home and taking charge of the activities of their families and friends. And there is no doubt that they like to be in control, a predilection that may be manifested in their urge to act as independent agents, or in their tendency to impose their own regulations and methods on others.

Because they are capable organizers, with a practical turn of mind, they thrive in professions in which they can combine their love of creating order with their enjoyment of personal contact. Therefore tourism augurs well as a career choice, as does the retail trade, a variety of business pursuits and also the performing arts. Despite the autocratic conduct to which they are prone, they are extremely intuitive; since they are blessed with the ability to tune into others' moods, and because they wish to receive approval, they will generally quickly realize when their behavior is annoying others and adjust it accordingly. They should remember, however, to adopt a similarly flexible approach toward their nearest and dearest—who, moreover, provide them with the security that they crave—whom they would otherwise expect to conform unquestioningly to their views.

VIRTUES: April 14 people are ceaseless seekers of intellectual stimulation, who typically channel their optimism and energy into the projects that interest them. Possessed of a strong sense of self-belief which derives from their considerable organizational abilities, and geared toward directing others, they enjoy taking leadership roles.
VICES: Intent as they are on implementing their preferred *modi operandi*, they are prone to dominating others, riding roughshod over objections in their quest to run things on their own terms. Although they may recognize the need to compromise in work situations, this tendency is strongest with regard to those of whose support they are most certain, including, especially, their families.
VERDICT: In their personal lives in particular, April 14 individuals must remember not take other people for granted. It is crucial that they recognize the value of a stable domestic environment, and thus treat any expressions of dissent as healthy manifestations of individuality which can be amply accommodated within the family unit.

On This Day
Famous Births: Ortelius and King Philip II of Spain (1527); Christiaan Huygens (1629); Arnold Toynbee (1889); Barbara Wootton (1897); John Gielgud (1904); François "Papa Doc" Duvalier (1907); Valerie Hobson (1917); Bishop Abel Muzorewa and Rod Steiger (1925); Loretta Lynn (1935); Julie Christie (1940); Pete Rose (1941); Julian Lloyd Webber (1951).

Significant Events and Anniversaries: The intellectual curiosity of this day may lead to scientific breakthroughs, as was illustrated by the discovery of the typhus vaccine by Dr. Harry Plotz of New York (1903), and the unveiling by the telecommunications companies British Telecom and Fidelity of the first cordless telephone able to operate up to 600 feet (183 meters) away from its base (1983). Strong—almost autocratic—political and national convictions are highlighted, which can sometimes lead to violent conflict, and April 14 marks the anniversary of the defeat of the Lancastrians by the Yorkists at the Battle of Barnet during the English Wars of the Roses, resulting in King Edward IV's restoration to the throne (1471); the fatal shooting of U.S. President Abraham Lincoln by John Wilkes Booth at Ford's Theater in Washington, D.C. (1865); the enforced abdication of King Alfonso, resulting in Spain becoming a republic (1931); and the rioting of civil servants, provoked by pay cuts, in New Zealand (1932).

APRIL 15

those born on April 15 possess a remarkable grasp of practicalities, and are methodical and organized in the extreme. Their intellectual incisiveness enables them to formulate a well-structured strategy in response to a stimulating challenge, and they are extraordinarily tenacious when it comes to implementation, capably overseeing the contributions of others and refusing to be deflected from their objective. Although the methodology underlying their actions is sound, the visions that inspire them may be regarded by others as being uncharacteristically unrealistic and fanciful, if not downright bizarre. And, indeed, it may be that the world is not yet ready for such imaginative ideas: yet no matter how strange they may seem to others, their feasibility will generally have been researched in depth by their originators. Many areas may inspire them, including commerce and business issues, but they have a gift for working with their hands, especially when they can also be creative, as chefs, caterers, beauticians, interior designers or decorators, for example, where their talents can be accepted and admired by more conventional types.

Because these dynamic people are convinced of the validity of their ideals, they will not only be infuriated when others do not take them seriously, but will also suffer great personal hurt, so bound up are their identities with their idealistic ambitions. And this inherent inability to accept dissent also applies to their personal liaisons, within which (particularly if they are men) they typically expect the unwavering loyalty and support of their partners, friends and family members. Consequently, they may inadvertently suppress in others the individuality and freedom of thought which they themselves hold so dear.

VIRTUES: The combination of great imagination, faultless organization and single-mindedness inherent in April 15 people is a rare one, and, when channeled in a direction that is palatable to others, may not only elicit their applause, but also be truly inspirational.
VICES: They have a propensity to react badly if others do not fall into line with their views, usually robustly dismissing their objections as being uninformed. Ironically, when they find themselves in positions of influence, they too may resist accepting new approaches.
VERDICT: It is vital that those born on this day accept that they will never be able to win everyone over to their cherished causes, and therefore evolve a means of protecting themselves from the wounds inflicted by the skepticism of others. They will find humor a valuable release for pressure, as well as the simple, uninhibited joys of family life.

On This Day

Famous Births: Leonardo da Vinci (1452); Guru Nanak (1469); Etienne Geoffrey Saint-Hilaire (1772); Friedrich Georg Wilhelm Struve (1793); James Clark Ross (1800); Théodore Rousseau (1812); Wilhelm Busch (1832); Henry James (1843); Bessie Smith (1894); Joe Davis (1901); Hans Conried (1917); Roy Clark and Elizabeth Montgomery (1933); Claudia Cardinale and Marty Wilde (1939); Jeffrey Archer (1940); Emma Thompson (1959).

Significant Events and Anniversaries: April 15 is a day that promises innovations so unusual that while they may initially be mocked by contemporaries, history often confirms their importance. In illustration, on this day the English author Dr. Samuel Johnson published his *Dictionary*, the world's first lexicon (1755); François Joseph Belzung patented the first screw-top bottle in Paris, France (1852); and the Japanese company Canon unveiled the first electronic pocket calculator (1970). The humanitarian concerns of this day are reflected by the action of Scottish playwright James Barrie in donating the copyright proceeds of his play *Peter Pan* to London's Great Ormond Street Hospital for Sick Children (1925), and the awarding of the George Cross, Britain's highest award for civilian gallantry, to the people of Malta in the face of German attacks during World War II (1942). The immovability of this day had its tragic reflection when, after hitting an iceberg, the *Titanic* liner sank, with the loss of over 1,500 lives (1912), and when an excessive number of spectators caused ninety-four soccer fans to be crushed to death at the Hillsborough ground in Sheffield, England (1989).

Planetary Influences
Ruling planet: Mars.
Third decan: Personal planet is Jupiter.

Sacred and Cultural Significance
Tellus honored in ancient Rome.
Saints' day: Paternus of Wales (5th to 6th century AD); Ruadhan (d. c.584).

The combination of tenacity, single mindedness and immovability indicated by April 15 can have disastrous results. It was on this day in 1912 that the "unsinkable" Titanic went down.

APRIL 16

Planetary Influences
Ruling planet: Mars.
Third decan: Personal planet is Jupiter.

Sacred and Cultural Significance
In ancient Greece, Hiketeria was celebrated.
Saints' day: Paternus of Avranches (d. 564); Magnus (c.1075–1116), patron saint of fishermen; Benedict Joseph Labre (1748–83), patron saint of beggars, homeless people and tramps; Bernadette (1844–79).

On April 16—a day indicating fiercely idealistic determination—conflict came to a head in the Battle of Culloden (1746), when the Duke of Cumberland's army defeated Jacobite rebels fighting in support of Bonnie Prince Charlie's accession to the throne.

Those born on this day are very aware of their roots, of their place within their family and community, perhaps instinctively recognizing that they need to feel grounded within their home environment before taking flight from this solidly stable base. For while they cherish the familial bonds that surround them with the supportive and affectionate framework that is so important to their emotional well-being, April 16 individuals are adventurous thinkers, who feel compelled to seek out knowledge and truths and then, having assimilated as much information as they can, build upon their interests and move forward. There are thus two sides to their natures: the side that desires a quietly happy domestic life, causing them generously to nurture the needs of their friends and family members, and the side that adopts a determinedly individualistic approach to the wider world and fiercely fights for those issues that motivate them. They are usually cheerful, balanced and popular.

Many subject matters interest those born on April 16, but underlying all is a concern with humanitarian issues and making progress. Because they are blessed with great powers of logic, organizational skills and unwavering steadfastness, whatever profession they choose to follow—be it within the scientific or technical fields, jurisprudence or academia, or the various pursuits that the artistic sphere encompasses—they will bring a solid backing to their imaginative visions. They also have great leadership potential, for not only do others admire them for their inspirational strength of purpose, but their fine sense of humor and gentle demeanor attract others to them.

VIRTUES: Caring and committed in their relationships with other people, yet firmly unbending when it comes to espousing those causes that fuel their ambition, those born on this day manage to remain true to their beliefs without simultaneously alienating others.
VICES: Because others regard them as pillars of strength and sources of wisdom, there is a danger that they will assume too many burdens, for they find it difficult to turn away those in need, and equally hard to resist the lure of a particularly exciting impersonal concept.
VERDICT: April 16 people generally strike a healthy balance between their introverted and extroverted selves, exploring and championing those intellectual concepts that fascinate them, while at the same time recognizing the importance of remaining rooted in reality. In order to avoid becoming overstressed, it is crucial that they accept that they are not superbeings and cannot accomplish everything that they demand of themselves.

On This Day
Famous Births: Jules Hardouin-Mansart (1646); Hans Sloane (1660); John Franklin (1786); Ford Madox Brown (1821); Anatole France (1844); Wilbur Wright (1867); John Millington Synge (1871); Charlie Chaplin (1889); Ove Arup (1895); Spike Milligan (1918); Peter Ustinov (1921); Kingsley Amis (1922); Henry Mancini (1924); Queen Margrethe II of Denmark (1940); Ellen Barkin (1955); Martin Lawrence (1965); Selena Quintanilla (1971).

Significant Events and Anniversaries: Imagination and tenacity in pursuit of a goal or ambition are dual features of this day, on which two women achieved remarkable milestones: when Harriet Quimby became the first woman to fly across the English Channel (1912); and when Geraldine Monk of West Germany became the first female solo pilot to fly around the world (1964). The determined championing of a strongly held conviction is a characteristic of this day, which may often, in certain circumstances, result in head-on confrontation, as was illustrated when the Duke of Cumberland's army, in the last such conflict on British soil, defeated the Jacobite rebels fighting for the accession to the throne of Bonnie Prince Charlie, James II's Stuart heir, at the Battle of Culloden near Inverness, Scotland (1746); when Paul Kruger, whose pro-Boer policies would subsequently provoke the Second South African War with the British, became president of the Transvaal (1883); and when communist Khmer Rouge troops forced the surrender of Cambodia's capital, Phnom Penh (1975).

APRIL 17

The impression that those born on this day make on others is undoubtedly a strong one, for they vigorously promote their lofty ambitions with unrelenting certainty and expect others to fall in line with their wishes and convictions. Because they have a highly developed sense of natural justice and possess a burning, protective desire to champion the cause of the downtrodden, April 17 people will often make their careers in such humanitarian-related fields as politics, jurisprudence or the military, although their predilection for paying attention to detail and their prodigious organizational skills will also equip them superbly as accountants or businessmen. And, because they typically translate their profound thoughts into energetic action, they may frequently find themselves leading the less imaginative or dynamic, or—especially if they are women—working as self-employed people on their own account.

Yet despite the laudable nature of their ideological concerns and their considerable practical talents, April 17 people may find enlisting the support of others an arduous task. One inherent problem with their direct, often forceful, approach—which is particularly pronounced if they were also born in the Chinese year of the dragon—is that they may appear somewhat unyielding individuals, who are furthermore not afraid to voice their criticism if they feel it is justified. Others may be intimidated by the austere, judgemental image that they project, and hasten to remove themselves from the line of fire. Those nearest to them may similarly believe themselves unable to live up to their high ideals and expectations, and thus these people may become emotionally isolated and prone to feelings of disillusionment and depression.

VIRTUES: Blessed with incisive intellectual qualities, including penetrative vision and the ability to focus on a distant aim, as well as considerable methodological and practical skills, those born on April 17 possess the talents and convictions to achieve their ambitions.
VICES: These people have a tendency to see the world in black-and-white, dividing its components into positive and negative categories rather than appreciating its many complexities. In terms of their personal relationships, there is an ever-present danger that this condemnatory propensity will not only drive away potential friends and partners, but that they will become solitary and morose figures.
VERDICT: It is vital that these individuals try to develop a more relaxed and tolerant approach within every area of their lives. By accepting their own and others' shortcomings and working round them rather than rejecting them out of hand, and by furthermore remembering the importance of making time for the simple pleasures of life, they will become more well-rounded beings and gain enormous emotional benefits.

On This Day

Famous Births: Henry Vaughan (1622); J.P. Morgan (1837); Constantine P. Kavatis (1863); Robert Tressell (1870); Leonard Woolley (1880); Artur Schnabel (1882); Nikita Sergeyevich Khrushchev (1894); Thornton Wilder (1897); Mikhail Moiseyevich Botvinnik (1911); Sirimavo Bandaranaike (1916); William Holden (1918); Lindsay Anderson and Harry Reasoner (1923); James Last (1929); Clare Francis (1946); Olivia Hussey (1951).

Significant Events and Anniversaries: April 17 highlights judgemental beliefs which can result in uncompromising action, and on this day Martin Luther, the German Protestant reformer, appeared before the imperial Diet (assembly) of Worms, where his refusal to recant his criticism of the Roman Catholic Church resulted in his excommunication (1521); and, during a protest in London against the policies of the Libyan ruler, Colonel Gaddafi, British policewoman Yvonne Fletcher was shot dead by a gunman firing from within the Libyan People's Bureau (1984). This is also a day which indicates progressive vision, reflected in Queen Elizabeth II's signing of the Canada Act, which gave Canada itself, rather than Britain's parliament, the right to amend its constitution (1982). The bottling-up of emotions that is a danger inherent in April 18 may find destructive outlets, tragically illustrated when the sea burst through dikes at Dort in Holland, causing the deaths of around 100,000 people (1421).

Planetary Influences
Ruling planets: Mars and Venus.
Third decan: Personal planet is Jupiter.
Second cusp: Aries with Taurean tendencies.

Sacred and Cultural Significance
Chariot Festival of the Rain God in Nepal.
Saints' day: Donan and Companions (d. 618).

Forceful, ambitious and decisive, Nikita Khruschev was a typical April 17 personality who employed his formidable energies and intellect to the full in succeeding Stalin as Soviet premier (1953). Khruschev espoused the Bolshevik cause relentlessly: he fought in the Russian civil war as a young man and, when in power, introduced "de-Stalinization" to reverse much of the former leader's egotistical agenda.

Planetary Influences
Ruling planets: Mars and Venus.
Third decan: Personal planet is Jupiter.
Second cusp: Aries with Taurean tendencies.

Sacred and Cultural Significance
In India, Festival of Rama-Navami.
Saints' day: Apollonius (d. 183); Laserian (d. 639).

On a day on which overcontrol can sometimes result in the loss of equilibrium, April 18 saw the devastation of San Francisco in the disastrous earthquake and subsequent fires, which left 503 people dead and caused $350 million in damages (1906). The ruins of City Hall stand as stark testimony to the destruction.

APRIL 18

★★★

April 18 individuals may secretly regard themselves variously as the upholders of tradition, the torch-bearers of justice or the champions of the vulnerable and abused. Possessed as they are of clear-cut views regarding the governance of human society and the importance of implementing justice, the driving forces behind their actions are often the maintenance of social order and the promotion of human equality. They will therefore often find a fulfilling outlet for their concerns and ambitions in those professions in which they can effect tangible improvements—national or civic politics, for example, the military, judiciary or other public-service bodies, as well as the caring professions. When engaged in their battles for the furtherance of human civilization, April 18 people will typical marshal their prodigious talents of energy, zeal and intellectual focus and employ them with determination and tenacity.

Despite their seriousness of intent, however, most people born on this day are redeemed from becoming overly obsessive in their single-mindedness by their intuitive recognition of the need to recharge their batteries by means of relaxation and fun. Indeed, some April 18 people have a markedly mischievous streak, and relish playing devil's advocate for the sheer enjoyment of provoking a stimulating argument. Concerned and magnanimous friends, partners and parents, they will stick loyally to those closest to them, but will inevitably suffer deep disappointment if they feel personally let down in any way, either through perceived abuses of their kindness, or by others failing to live up to their exceptionally high standards.

VIRTUES: Those individuals born on this day are typically oriented toward maintaining the smooth and equitable regulation of human society, and will act determinedly to rectify any perceived wrongs. Blessed with great compassion, perspicuity and high ideals, they are nevertheless also practical and organized in developing effective strategies with which to achieve their humanitarian and personal ambitions.
VICES: Although they will generally keep tight control of their emotions, the disadvantage that can result from having such lofty standards is their negative response to either their own failures or the shortcomings of others. When they are thus disappointed, they may become disillusioned, unmotivated and withdrawn, or even furious, when they may take out their frustrations on the nearest available target.
VERDICT: April 18 people generally balance their professional and private interests extremely well, but should nevertheless beware of a tendency to project their sometimes unrealistic or unattainable ideals onto other people. They should therefore strive to adopt a more pragmatic approach toward their interpersonal relationships, and accept that no one is perfect.

On This Day
Famous Births: Lucrezia Borgia (1480); Louis Adolphe Thiers (1797); George Henry Lewes (1817); Franz von Suppé (1819); Clarence Darrow (1857); Humphrey Verdon Roe (1878); Leopold Stokowski (1882); Hayley Mills (1946); Cindy Pickett and James Wood (1947); John James and Eric Roberts (1956); Malcolm Marshall (1958); Nick Farr-Jones (1962); Conan O'Brien (1963).

Significant Events and Anniversaries: Action on behalf of the wider community is a characteristic highlighted by April 18, on which: the day before the outbreak of the American War of Independence, Paul Revere rode from Charlestown to Lexington to alert the minutemen to the impending arrival of hostile British troops (1775); the Natural History Museum was opened in London, with the intention of educating the British populace (1881); and, on a more mundane note, the first "washeteria" opened for business in Fort Worth, Texas (1934). Acting in the collective interest is an inherent feature of nationalism, and on this day the nation of Eire was established when the Republic of Ireland left the British Commonwealth (1949); Colonel Gamal Nasser became prime minister of the new republic of Egypt (1954); Robert Mugabe became the prime minister of the recently independent Zimbabwe, formerly the British-ruled Rhodesia (1980). Reflecting the mischievous tendency that is inherent in April 18, British playwright Joe Orton's black comedy *Entertaining Mr Sloane* had its premiere (1964).

APRIL 19

Those born on this day cannot bear disorder, indecisiveness or stagnation, and therefore seek to introduce efficient, smoothly running and progressive systems into both their work and domestic environments. Nothing gives them more satisfaction than setting a drifting individual firmly upon a focused course of action, or turning an unprofitable operation into a success. Attaining tangible results is important to April 19 people, who regard the fruits of their labors as the validation of their efforts. Whatever career they choose to pursue, they will therefore experience the greatest fulfillment when their input is counterbalanced—if not outweighed—by the output, the physical proof of their success, that they generate. Such professions as teaching, manufacturing, project management, construction, design and the creative arts are especially well starred, as well as business pursuits, although it should be stressed that they rarely hunger for materialistic rewards.

Their highly achievement-driven determination can, however, lead them to become overly controlling. Because they possess great confidence in their intellectual capability, as well as in their practical and organizational talents, they are often reluctant to relinquish the reins of control to others that are, as yet, unproven. When they do delegate, they will sometimes succumb to the urge to point out how they think things could be better done, this tendency being particularly pronounced in women born on this day. Despite this regulatory predilection, they generally make generous and affectionate partners, parents and friends, who unselfishly wish for the greatest happiness and success of those closest to them.

VIRTUES: Those born on April 19 are oriented toward bringing order and efficiency to everything that they do, and derive considerable satisfaction from achieving perceptible results. They are not usually motivated by personal or financial ambitions, but rather by a somewhat perfectionist desire to see tasks done as well and effectively as possible.
VICES: When rewarded by the attainments for which they have striven, they tend to take such successes as evidence and confirmation of the veracity of their approach. They may, therefore, find it hard to indulge those who favor different methods, and as a consequence become inflexible and dominating.
VERDICT: These hard-working and kind people typically maintain the correct equilibrium between their intellects and their emotions, as well as between their professional and their domestic lives. They should, however, recognize that, in the interests of gaining experience and thus furthering personal development, it is sometimes necessary to adopt new and untested approaches, and especially to allow others to do so.

On This Day

Famous Births: Herbert Wilcox and Germaine Tailleferre (1892); Richard Hughes (1900); Eliot Ness (1903); Jim Mollison (1905); Don Adams (1926); Alexis Korner (1928); Dickie Bird and Jayne Mansfield (1933); Dudley Moore (1935); Elinor Donahue (1937); Alan Price (1942); Tim Curry (1946); Paloma Picasso (1949); Trevor Francis (1954); Al Unser, Jr. (1962).

Significant Events and Anniversaries: Self-belief is a strong characteristic of this day, which, in the global arena, may result in martial action in the defense or promotion of nationalistic ideals, as was illustrated by: the outbreak of the American War of Independence, provoked when British troops under General Thomas Gage fired at a hostile crowd in Lexington, Massachusetts (1775); the U.S. *Mongolia*'s destruction of a German submarine, signaling the United States' entry into World War I (1917); the abortive invasion of Cuba at the Bay of Pigs by U.S.-sponsored Cuban exiles (1961); and the embarkation of Australian troops to participate in the Vietnam War (1966). April 19 highlights great practical and methodical talents, and marks the first occasion on which a war correspondent—the representative of the British newspaper *The Times* during the Second Afghan War—telephoned a report from a battlefield, that of Ahmed Khel (1880); and also commemorates the launching of the Soviet *Salyut* space station following years of detailed research (1971).

Planetary Influences
Ruling planets: Mars and Venus.
Third decan: Personal planet is Jupiter.
Second cusp: Aries with Taurean tendencies.

♂ ♀ ♃

Sacred and Cultural Significance
Saints' day: Alphege (c.953–1012); Leo IX (1002–54).

Tibet's Dalai Lama was forced into exile by Chinese troops in 1959 on April 19—a day on which strong self-belief can tend, in the global arena, toward domination and nationalism.

ARIES

Planetary Influences
Ruling planets: Mars and Venus.
Third decan: Personal planet is Jupiter.
Second cusp: Aries with Taurean tendencies.

Sacred and Cultural Significance
Saints' day: Caedwalla (d. 689); Agnes of Montepulciano (1268–1317).

The Hotel Aubecq in Brussels, designed by architect Victor Horta, illustrates the Art Nouveau style first introduced to the world at a Paris exhibition in 1902, on April 20—a day which augurs well for artistic success.

APRIL 20

✳✳

Those born on April 20 hunger for success, partly as a result of their burning desire to see their idealistic ambitions realized, and—since they may often be somewhat insecure individuals—partly to feel validated by the admiration and approval of their peers. It is this quest for perfection that fuels their great zeal, and these perceptive people typically observe their surroundings critically, noting any inherent shortcomings and then formulating complex strategies for bringing about improvement. When in the thrall of a fascinating vision, they will devote their considerable energy, tenacity and organizational skills toward its achievement, allowing nothing or no one to stand in their way. And although they are intuitive types, this quality is not usually manifested in empathetic action, but rather in the conscious manipulation of others in order to enlist their support—or at least to quell their objections—for the mission which they regard as being of paramount importance. Such enormous focus, ambition and pragmatism augurs well for April 20 people, especially if they work as freelancers, where any success achieved will not usually be at the expense of others.

Their extreme clarity of vision and strength of purpose will inevitably incur extreme reactions, and these people will inspire either ardent support or strident opposition. Since they are convinced of the veracity of their ideas and methods and, moreover, crave the recognition of others, those born on this day will feel profoundly hurt when their opinions are subjected to criticism or derision, and have a tendency to close their ears to negative comments in order to protect their sensibilities. It is important that they recognize this propensity, as well as the inherent dangers of such an inflexible approach. By grounding themselves in the love and support of their families and diversifying their interests and priorities, they will gain a greater level of emotional equilibrium.

VIRTUES: Blessed with qualities of intellectual incisiveness and vision, as well as prodigious energy and organizational skills, those born on this day utilize their various talents to great effect in their enormous drive to achieve the ambitions that inspire them.
VICES: Not only does their strong self-belief lead them to dominate other people, but their aversion to criticism furthermore instills in them an intolerance of alternative viewpoints. Both propensities are potentially destructive and may cause them to live in a fantasy world, isolated from both reality and the affection that they desire.
VERDICT: It is vital for their emotional well-being that they do not take constructive criticism as a personal affront, but instead recognize the importance of maintaining an objective and open mind, accepting that they are not always right. Learning to relax their drive for perfection and high expectations, and becoming more tolerant in all things, will ultimately bring those born on April 20 great fulfillment.

On This Day
Famous Births: Napoleon III of France (1808); Nikolay Myaskovsky (1881); Adolf Hitler (1889); Joán Miró (1893); Harold Lloyd (1894); Donald Wolfit (1902); Tim Burstall (1929); Debbie Flintoff-King (1930); Betty Cuthbert (1958); Ryan O'Neal (1941); Jessica Lange (1949); Luther Vandross (1951); Nicholas Lyndhurst and Don Mattingly (1961).

Significant Events and Anniversaries: Potential success in the artistic world is promised by this day, on which Edgar Allen Poe's gripping short story "The Murders in the Rue Morgue" was first published in the U.S. magazine *Graham's* (1841), and the Art Nouveau style was introduced to the world at a Paris exhibition (1902). Near-autocratic tendencies are characteristic of April 20, on which Oliver Cromwell dissolved the "Rump" of the English Long Parliament (1653) and—appropriately, on the birthday of the world's most notorious Fascist dictator, Adolf Hitler—on which King Victor Emmanuel III inaugurated the first Italian parliament to consist solely of Fascist representatives (1929). The determination in pursuit of a cherished ideal that is a highlight of this day was reflected in Captain James Cook's discovery of the Australian region now known as New South Wales (1770).

TAURUS

☉

April 21 to May 20

Ruling planet: Venus   **Element:** Fixed earth

Symbol: The bull   **Polarity:** Negative (feminine)

Physical correspondence: The neck, ears and throat

Stones: Alabaster, topaz, rose quartz, emerald

Flowers: Lily, lilac, daisy, mallow, poppy, violet

Colors: Pale blue, lilac, pink

Virtually every astrological tradition has equated the constellation of Taurus with a bull: the ancient Greeks, for example, called it Tauros; the Persians, Tora; the Hindus, Vrisha; and the Mesopotamians Gudanna, the heavenly bull that the goddess Inanna/Ishtar prevailed upon her father, An/Anu, to create in order to avenge her rejection by the hero Gilgamesh. A sign that is governed by the planet Venus, this astral grouping includes the seven stars known as the Pleiades, or "Seven Sisters," who, in Greco-Roman mythology, were said to be the daughters of the Titan Atlas and the sea-nymph Pleione, and who guarded Aphrodite/Venus' "pearly gates." The bull's association with the goddess of sexual love is clear, for this creature not only embodies fecundity and procreative powers, but its horns may be said to represent the crescent Moon, and its head the full Moon (both of which are reflected, some scholars believe, in Taurus's sigil), and the Moon is the preserve and symbol of the Goddess, as is the element of earth that governs this sign. Indeed, the tauroctony rites devoted to the Persian deity Mithra and the Roman Sol Invictus, among others, were propagated in the belief that the body and blood of the sacrificed bull gave birth to, and nurtured, all forms of vegetal and animal life. Many other ancient peoples, including the Babylonians, also sacrificed white bulls at the time of the Taurean new Moon. It is therefore appropriate that Taurus presides over the seasonal period in which spring life burgeons and thrives.

Those born under this sign are said to be influenced by the earthy element that rules their birth sign in that they are regarded as practical and materialistic types who have the capacity to initiate and steadily cultivate plans of action, while Venus is said to bestow her sensuality, love of pleasure and artistic affinity upon Taureans. Less positively, however, the Taurean personality may sometimes be obstinately resistant to change, fiercely possessive of loved ones, and roused to spectacular displays of anger when its plans are thwarted—all forms of behavior that may be said to be demonstrated by the bull.

✦✦

Planetary Influences

Ruling planets: Venus and Mars.
First decan: Personal planet is Venus.
First cusp: Taurus with Arian qualities.

♀ ♂

Sacred and Cultural Significance

In ancient Rome, the Palilia festival held to commemorate the birthday of Rome.
Saints' day: Beuno (6th century AD), patron saint of sick animals; Ethilwald of Farne (d. 699); Maelrubba (c.642–c.722); Anselm (1033–1109).

English novelist Charlotte Brontë was born in 1816 on April 21, a day on which qualities of perfectionism, self-discipline, aesthetic sensibilities and intellectual clarity converge to favor artistic achievement.

Those born on April 21 are proud individuals who set themselves high standards and are mortified if circumstances prevent their being achieved. Such is their capability, efficiency and self-discipline—as well as their strong self-knowledge which allows them realistically to assess their abilities and limits—that when faced with a task, its completion will usually be hindered only by unforeseeable obstacles beyond their control. These are dignified and self-possessed people, who typically harness their prodigious powers of perspicacity and reflection (qualities born of their sensitivity), and their organizational skills and single-minded tenacity, in their drive to succeed—a package that endows them with great potential to achieve their aims. Because they are both reliable and unafraid of voicing their deeply held opinions, they will often find themselves assuming leadership roles, and will be accorded respect for both their ability and their talent for motivating others by means of positive encouragement. These qualities bode well for success in such interpersonal careers as teaching, although their inherent distaste of being dictated to means that they will generally be unhappy in large, rigidly structured organizations.

April 21 people are bent on achieving perfection—or as close a state possible to this ideal—rather than receiving financial rewards, but they appreciate money for the good things that it can buy, for these are somewhat sybaritic types who relish sensual stimulation of all kinds and therefore have a profound affinity with all things artistic. People are drawn to them for their infectious, pleasure-seeking propensity, as well as their endearing desire to bring happiness to others. They typically make indulgent, yet responsible, friends, parents and partners, but may occasionally annoy others by their often unconscious tendency to control them or, for those who are closest, by attempting to impose their personal outlook on them.

VIRTUES: Those born on this day are blessed with qualities of self-reliance, objectivity, intellectual clarity, strength of purpose and enormous tenacity when faced with a challenge. Yet they are also sympathetic, positive and energetic types, who recognize the importance of relaxation and will use it to counterbalance their own intensity.
VICES: The main danger that arises from the inherent characteristics of those born on this day is that they may gravitate toward extremes, becoming either overly controlling of those around them, or uncontrollably hedonistic and sensation-seeking.
VERDICT: April 21 people intuitively recognize the importance of striking a healthy balance between their professional and personal lives, and thus generally devote equal time and attention to work and play. They should, however, beware of allowing those characteristics that are of great value in one sphere to cross over to another, neither dominating their friends and family, nor adopting a frivolous approach to their careers.

On This Day

Famous Births: Jan van Riebeck (1634); Friedrich Froebel (1782); Charlotte Brontë (1816); Norman Parkinson (1913); Anthony Quinn (1915); John Mortimer (1923); Queen Elizabeth II of Britain (1926); Angela Mortimer (1932); Charles Grodin (1935); Iggy Pop (1947); Patti Lupone (1949); Tony Danza (1951); Jesse Orosco (1957); Andie Macdowell (1958).

Significant Events and Anniversaries: The organizational qualities and drive to dominate that are indicated by April 21 have their parallel in warfare, as was reflected in three martial triumphs that occurred on this day: when Texan forces defeated their Mexican opponents at the Battle of San Jacinto (1836); when an R.A.F. fighter shot down the near-legendary German pilot, Baron Manfred von Richthofen (the "Red Baron") (1916); and when Canadian troops wrested Vimy Ridge from the German Army during World War I (1917). The artistic promise inherent in this day was illustrated by the first performance of Irish dramatist George Bernard Shaw's play *Arms and the Man* (1894), the unveiling of French sculptor Rodin's sensational seminude portrait of Victor Hugo (1901), and the premiere of Welsh composer Ivor Novello's musical *Perchance to Dream* (1945).

APRIL 22

Others admire those born on April 22 for their instant grasp of potential problems inherent in a situation and their apparently effortless ability to counter and overcome them. Indeed, the efficiency, energy and positive outlook—as well as the empathy—manifested by these capable people means that not only are they often consulted for objective and realistic advice, but they are also frequently entrusted with projects that less reliable people wish to offload. In such circumstances, they will accept total responsibility for the tasks and will typically work tirelessly, and with deceptive ease, to achieve beneficial outcomes, motivated by both their personal desire to test their abilities and their sneaking wish to elicit the approval and gratitude of others. There is a risk, however, that the cooperation and goodwill that they offer may be abused by others, and that they may end up overburdened and exhausted, while less scrupulous characters claim the glory for their achievements.

In their personal lives, they display a similar level of magnaminity and dependability, also bringing an element of fun to their interpersonal relationships since they are themselves deeply receptive to sensual stimuli and enjoy bringing pleasure to their nearest and dearest. In their professional lives, they supplement their organizational talents with a combination of clear-sighted vision, a pragmatic outlook and a tendency to take risks, thus endowing them with great entrepreneurial potential. Such a conjunction of meticulous and far-sighted qualities augurs well for careers in business, as well as in the realm of scientific research, depending on the personal predilection of the individual. They do, however, crave material rewards, both as recognition of their efforts and as a means of enabling them to indulge themselves— and deservedly so—when work is over.

VIRTUES: April 22 people typically combine their inherent qualities of steadfastness, empathy and determination with their methodical organizational talents, orderliness and intellectual objectivity, and generously direct their energies toward helping others in their quest to attain tangible progress.
VICES: Such is their self-confidence, pride and determination not to be beaten by a demanding challenge, that they may not only become obsessive in the pursuit of their ultimate aims, but may also become overworked and stressed, a state which is clearly detrimental to their physical and emotional well-being.
VERDICT: In every area of their lives, it is crucial that April 22 people retain a sense of perspective regarding life's priorities. They should therefore beware of overcommitting themselves to the service of others and guard against their propensity to measure their success—and flaunt it—by overspending monetary gains.

On This Day

Famous Births: Henry Fielding (1707); Immanuel Kant (1724); Madame de Staël (1766); Käthe Kollwitz (1867); Nikolai Lenin (1870); Alexander Feodorovich Kerensky (1881); Robert Oppenheimer (1904); Eric Fenby (1906); Eddie Albert (1908); Kathleen Ferrier (1912); Yehudi Menuhin (1916); Sidney Nolan (1917); Aaron Spelling (1928); Glen Campbell (1936); Jack Nicholson (1937); Peter Frampton (1950); Lloyd Honeyghan (1960).

Significant Events and Anniversaries: This day combines individual adventurousness with an awareness of collective responsibility, as was reflected in: Pedro Alvarez Cabral's "discovery" of Brazil, which he claimed for his nation, Portugal (1500); the first crossing of the Atlantic, by the British packet steamer *Sirius* (1838); and British yachtsman Robin Knox-Johnston's achievement in circumnavigating the world single-handedly (1969). The conjunction of organizational skills and national loyalty inherent in April 22 is reflected in the martial arena, as obsessive extremism in the German Army's unprecedented use of poison gas during the second battle of Ypres (1915), and the British Admiral Keye's action in attempting to block German U-boat stations at the Battle of Zeebrugge (1918) during World War I.

Planetary Influences
Ruling planets: Venus and Mars.
First decan: Personal planet is Venus.
First cusp: Taurus with Arian qualities.

Sacred and Cultural Significance
Earth Day celebrated.
Saint's day: Theodore of Sykeon (d. 613).

German artist Käthe Kollwitz was born on April 22, 1867. Her opposition to social injustice, powerfully depicted in her art, was reinforced by her birthday's characteristics of empathy, overcoming and social responsibility.

APRIL 23

✴ ✴

Planetary Influences
Ruling planets: Venus and Mars.
First decan: Personal planet is Venus.
First cusp: Taurus with Arian qualities.

Sacred and Cultural Significance
St. George's Day, the national day of
England; in ancient Rome, the Vinalia
was celebrated.
Saints' day: George (d. c.303), patron saint
of archers, England, husbandmen, knights,
soldiers and syphilis sufferers; Adalbert
of Prague (956–97).

*A frieze depicts St. George's fabled slaying of the
dragon. April 23—a day that indicates a natural sense of social justice and thirst for knowledge—is St. George's Day in England.*

Those born on April 23 possess a rare combination of introverted and extroverted qualities—namely, intellectual individuality and, conversely, a marked social orientation. These perceptive and curious individuals need to be able to explore the abstract concepts that hold their interest yet, at the same time, seek to ground themselves in a stable base from which to launch themselves on their quest for knowledge, perhaps intuitively recognizing that without such an anchor of security their darting imagination may lead them into fantasy worlds, causing them to lose touch with life's realities. Despite their independent leanings, however, they are gregarious types blessed with a sense of natural justice, born of their keen empathy with others. Such a well-balanced combination of characteristics enables them to find success in any professional situation in which they can exercise their talents for innovation and interpersonal contact; the various possibilities offered by artistic pursuits would therefore appear ideal career options for those born on April 23.

In their personal lives, April 23 people display a similar interest and concern for the well-being of those closest to them. They aim to create a happy and relaxed domestic environment, within which, while emotional bonds are paramount, the capacity for having fun is also encouraged. Others are drawn to them both for the steady aura of reliability that they exude (especially if they are women) and the infectious *joie de vivre* that they generate: the disadvantage of such popularity is that they may become overburdened with the expectations of less dynamic individuals.

VIRTUES: On the one hand kind, compassionate and sociable beings, and on the other blessed with acute intellectual powers of perspicacity, inquisitiveness and tenacity, they have the potential to make a real mark on the world without incurring the enmity of less talented or imaginative individuals.
VICES: April 23 people have a profound—often unconscious—desire both to receive the acceptance and approval of their peers and to direct their attention toward fulfilling the needs of others, laudable qualities which may nevertheless result in an ultimately damaging neglect of their own desire for independent action and thought.
VERDICT: Although typically blessed with great emotional equilibrium and a sensible recognition of the importance of balancing their private and professional lives, they must ensure that their capacity for intellectual concentration and their predilection for a certain level of hedonism do not become out of synch, thus resulting in extremes of behavior.

On This Day
Famous Births: William Shakespeare (1564); Joseph Mallard William Turner (1775); James Buchanan (1791); Max Planck and Ethel Smythe (1858); Henry, Viscount Allenby (1861); Lester Pearson (1897); Ngaio Marsh and Vladimir Nabokov (1899); Ronald Neame (1911); J.P. Donleavy (1926); Shirley Temple (1928); Roy Orbison (1936); Lee Majors (1942); Judy Davis (1956); Jan Hooks (1957); Valerie Bertinelli (1960); Jean Kinloch Read (1974).

Significant Events and Anniversaries: This is a day that promises personal popularity, and marks the anniversary of the coronation of King Charles II of England and Scotland—one of history's best-loved monarchs (1661). On the day that is believed to be the birthday of the world's most famous playwright, the first Shakespeare Memorial Theatre was opened in the bard's birthplace, Stratford-upon-Avon, in England (1879). The potential for beneficial innovation that is highlighted by this day was reflected in the opening of the Moscow underground railway by Josef Stalin (1935), and the announcement that U.S. scientists had identified the AIDS virus—this being the first step on the path to finding a possible cure (1984). The natural sense of fairness that is a characteristic of this day was illustrated in the U.S.A., where Sirhan Bishara Sirhan was found guilty of murdering Robert F. Kennedy (1969), and in Spain, where the notorious British Great Train Robber, Charlie Wilson, was shot dead after having eluded capture for many years (1990).

APRIL 24

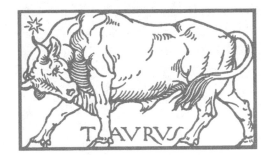

****

Those born on April 24 often feel torn between their careers and their families, for the urge to devote their whole-hearted attention to both is strong, and they do nothing by half measures. At work, they are driven by the desire to perform tasks as perfectly as humanly possible. Their searching intellects are supported by their methodical approach and organizational talents, as well as their sometimes obstinate refusal to quit until they have accomplished their aims. A further facet of their natures is manifested by their great humanitarianism and concern with the feelings of others which, in professional scenarios, makes them cooperative and approachable colleagues. They have the potential to succeed in any field that they chose, provided that they have interpersonal contact, as well as the scope to act relatively independently. That they can be relied upon to deliver whatever is required of them is rarely in doubt, particularly if they were also born in the Chinese year of the ox.

Away from the workplace, April 24 people typically make loving and protective friends, partners and parents, whose somewhat controlling behavior is motivated by the desire to set their loved ones on stable and productive paths. Although undoubtedly sensible and steady types, they have a prodigious sense of fun, which bestows upon them an endearing ability to enjoy life and thereby also bring pleasure to others, qualities for which they are valued and which inspire genuine affection in others.

VIRTUES: Those born on this day are kind and empathetic, blessed with enormous organizational capabilities and single-mindedness when addressing projects entrusted to them, and are furthermore imaginative and intellectually perceptive individuals.

VICES: Unless they feel especially strongly about an issue, they find it difficult to refuse the demands of others, whose problems they typically address with great seriousness. This propensity may, however, result in them becoming both emotionally and physically overburdened and unable to concentrate on their own affairs.

VERDICT: Although April 24 people instinctively recognize the need to draw a clear dividing line between their personal and professional spheres, they must not allow their tendency to respond to every request made of them to encroach on areas to which they do not properly belong. Learning confidence in the judicious use of the word "no" will help them to control this predilection.

On This Day
Famous Births: William I, Prince of Orange (1533); Edmund Cartwright (1743); Anthony Trollope (1815); Marcus Clarke (1846); Henri Philippe Pétain (1856); Hugh Dowding (1882); Stafford Cripps (1889); Robert Penn Warren (1905); William Joyce, "Lord Haw-Haw" (1906); Bridget Riley (1931); Shirley MacLaine (1934); Jill Ireland (1936); John Williams (1941); Barbra Streisand (1942); Chipper Jones (1972).

Significant Events and Anniversaries: This day highlights the dual qualities of humanitarian concern and collective responsibility which have obvious nationalist and political parallels, and on April 24: the soldier Claude Rouget de Lisle composed the rousing "*La Marseillaise,*" which would subsequently become the French national anthem (1792); Sinn Fein sympathizers began their nationalist rebellion against the British on Easter Monday in Dublin, Ireland (1916); and Robert Menzies was elected prime minister of Australia (1939). The adventurousness and tenacity that are features of this day were reflected in the daring feats of two individuals: solo seafarer Joshua Slocum, when he left Boston, Massachusetts, in his ship *Spray*, beginning his successful circumnavigation of the world (1895); and pilot Amy Johnson, who landed in Darwin to become the first woman to fly single-handedly from England to Australia (1930). This day is governed by the element of earth, and marks the tragic death of Soviet cosmonaut Vladimir Komarov, when his spacecraft *Soyuz I* plummeted back to earth (1967).

On April 24—a day favoring national achievement as a culmination of humanitarian concern and collective responsibility—the Library of Congress was dedicated in Washington, D.C., in 1800.

Planetary Influences
Ruling planet: Venus.
First decan: Personal planet is Venus.

Sacred and Cultural Significance
Anzac Day; Arbor Day.
Saints' day: Mark the Evangelist, patron saint of secretaries (d. c.74).

Legendary vocalist Ella Fitzgerald was born on April 25, 1918. The combination of vigor, intuition and steadfast striving indicated by this day augured well for her artistic success.

Those born on April 25 typically favor action over reflection, possessed as they are of a burning need to actually make progress rather than just musing on the possibility of achieving it. These are strong-minded types, whose enormous vigor and desire to effect tangible manifestations of their drive to succeed often inspires the somewhat intimidated awe of those who are less self-assured. Very little can resist the combined will and energy of April 25 people, despite their unwitting tendency to sabotage their own efforts by considering neither their personal motivations nor the implications of their actions sufficiently carefully. Indeed, such is their aversion to both mental and physical inactivity that they are prone to make snap decisions and then tenaciously stick to them, steadfastly ignoring the objections of others. Such unwavering sense of purpose and single-minded commitment equips them for a variety of business, scientific or artistic careers, but the fields of law enforcement and politics are especially well starred.

Although they are natural leaders and seem to effortlessly command respect, April 25 people have a tendency to be overly blunt in their dealings with others, a propensity that applies equally to their colleagues and their family and friends, and one that can be deeply wounding. Although they play every bit as hard as they work, and moreover have a deep-rooted urge to protect and promote the well-being of their nearest and dearest, they tend to run their interpersonal relationships on their own terms and may thereby engender—and merit—resentment and rebellion.

VIRTUES: These dynamic individuals are geared toward attaining success, and employ their prodigious qualities of energy, intellectual focus and determination in working toward the achievement of their aims, thereby bestowing them with enormous potential.
VICES: Inflexibility is their greatest enemy, and their typically straightforward outlook can lead them to disregard the validity of alternative convictions or methods. They may also be impatient with less direct people, and have a tendency to express their irritation in unambiguous and less than tactful terms.
VERDICT: It is crucial that April 25 people make time for periods of reflection and introspection to ensure that they have fully evaluated any inherent risks arising from their actions and the reasons underlying them. They should also devote greater attention to the opinions and feelings of other people, an approach which will gain them allies rather than opponents.

On This Day

Famous Births: Louis IX, King of France (1214); King Edward II of England (1284); Oliver Cromwell (1559); C.B. Fry (1872); Walter de la Mare (1873); Guglielmo Marconi (1874); Wolfgang Pauli (1900); Edward Murrow (1906); Marcus Morris (1915); Ella Fitzgerald (1918); Paul Mazursky (1930); David Shepherd (1931); Patrick Lichfield (1939); Al Pacino (1940); Bjorn Ulvaeus (1945); Talia Shire (1946); Johann Cruyff (1947).

Significant Events and Anniversaries: April 25 highlights the active pursuit of visions, and on this day work started on the construction of the Suez Canal, the brainchild of French engineer Ferdinand de Lesseps (1859), while the Hubble Space Telescope, which would send unprecedented images back to earth, was released into space by the U.S. shuttle *Discovery* (1990). A pronounced danger inherent in this day is the enthusiastic promotion of ideas that may not have been properly thought through, as was reflected in: the landing of Anzac (Australian and New Zealand) forces in Gallipoli during World War I, a campaign that would end disastrously (1915); the U.S.A.'s ill-fated rescue mission of hostages held at the U.S. Embassy in Tehran, Iran (1980); and the German magazine *Stern*'s confidence in publishing what it believed to be Hitler's diaries, which were later proved to be fakes (1983). The energetic manifestation of intellectual focus inherent in this day favors success in the arts, as was illustrated by the publication of Daniel Defoe's novel *Robinson Crusoe* (1719) and by it being the day Toscannini conducted the first performance of Puccini's *Turandot* (1926).

APRIL 26

It may seem contradictory to those who do not know them well that although those born on April 26 are proponents of bold and visionary ideas, they also manifest a meticulous attention to detail. Yet these propensities are not so paradoxical when one understands that these realistic people recognize that a project's success cannot generally be achieved without careful forethought and planning involving the minute examination of all inherent issues and the subsequent setting in place of sound systems of organization, with contingency plans. Having considered and catered for all eventualities, those born on this day thereby bestow themselves with the potential to preside over smooth-running and effective projects which they control with great capability while rarely relinquishing their focus on their ultimate objective. They are admired for their efficiency and reliability, and will therefore flourish in any profession they chose as long as they are able to retain their autonomy of thought and action.

It is perhaps inevitable, given their efficacy and practical talents, that April 26 people are extremely self-confident as regards to the veracity of their outlook and methods. There is a risk, however, that they will become too rigid in their beliefs, and will seek to mold others—or else dismiss them—into their preferred form. This controlling predilection will not generally result in harmonious personal relationships—particularly with their children—and it is therefore important that they should learn to relax their expectations of others, respect indivuality and embrace diversity of conviction.

VIRTUES: April 26 people combine qualities of great intellectual independence and penetratingly clear-cut vision with prodigiously effective managerial skills, resulting in inspired and productive strategies which they carry forward with considerable energy and single-mindedness in successfuly achieving their goals.
VICES: However, prompted by the success they achieve by tried and tested methods, they are often lulled into a potentially dangerous sense of security and become set in their ways and opinions, rejecting those approaches that do not accord with their own.
VERDICT: In all areas of their lives, those born on this day should remember to apply their unquestionable capacity for objective thought to themselves and should periodically honestly examine their own motives to ensure that they do not become inflexible, narrow-minded and closed to alternative *modi operandi*.

On This Day
Famous Births: Marcus Aurelius (AD 121); David Hume (1711); John James Audubon (1785); Ferdinand Delacroix (1798); Alfred Krupp (1812); Syngman Rhee (1875); Michel Fokine (1880); Anita Loos (1893); Rudolf Hess (1894); John Grierson (1898); Charles Francis Richter (1900); Charlie Chester (1914); Carol Burnett (1933); Duane Eddy (1938); Bobby Rydell (1942); Prue Acton (1943); Peter Shaufuss (1949); Roger Taylor (1960).

Significant Events and Anniversaries: The certainty of conviction that is indicated by this day can have both positive and negative consequences; positive manifestations can be seen in the first performance of Frederick Ashton and William Walton's collaborative, groundbreaking ballet *Façade* (1931), and the holding of the first democratic elections in Portugal for half a century (1975), while negative examples include: the pre-emptive death, by either shooting himself or being shot, of Lincoln's assassin John Wilkes Booth (1865); the opening in London of the trial of Irish playwright Oscar Wilde for homosexual offenses (1895); and the bombing of the city of Guernica by German bombers in demonstration of their solidarity with the Fascist General Franco during the Spanish Civil War (1937). Highlighting April 26's organizational skills, this was the day on which the layout of the town of Deadwood, Arizona, was officially planned (1876), and the day on which the first motorcycle police patrols began operating in London (1921). On this day which features a tendency toward careful forethought and meticulous attention to detail, the largest U.S. bank robbery of all time—$3.3 million—was committed (1981).

Planetary Influences
Ruling planet: Venus.
First decan: Personal planet is Venus.

Sacred and Cultural Significance
New Year's Day in Sierra Leone.
Saints' day: Cletus (1st century AD); Riquier (d. c.645).

The Basque city of Guernica y Luno, near Bilbao, northern Spain, was immortalized as a symbol of Fascist destruction by Picasso's famous painting, which depicts women and children in the aftermath of its devastating bombing on April 26, 1937. This day is characterized by strong convictions and their consequences, as seen in the 1937 photograph of the city, below.

TAVRVS

APRIL 27

Planetary Influences
Ruling planet: Venus.
First decan: Personal planet is Venus.

Sacred and Cultural Significance
Tyi Wara honored in African republic of Mali.
Saints' day: Machalus (d. 498); Zita (1218–72), patron saint of bakers and servants.

Mary Wollstonecraft, English writer and champion of women's rights, was born in 1759 on April 27, a day that favors compassion and conviction. Her Vindication of the Rights of Women *(1792) made an early and eloquent case for equality of the sexes.*

Those born on April 27 have a tendency to direct their attention and energies inward, preferring the exploration of their rich inner world of ideas and visions over the distraction of more trivial or unproductive pursuits. These are self reliant and somewhat solitary types, who are rarely lonely in their own company and do not need to feel validated by the affirmation of others, especially if they are also women. More extroverted people may regard them as diffident or even antisocial, but this perception is far from the case; indeed, not only are these people comfortable with themselves, but they are furthermore blessed with qualities of profound intuition and compassion and will rarely withhold their help when it is truly required. Those born on this day will typically be happiest when working on their own account, or within small organizations where their individuality and imagination can be given full rein, and will often find great fulfillment in the humanitarian, artistic or scientific realms.

Despite their natural reserve and need for periods when they can be alone, April 27 individuals do not confine themselves exclusively to their self-imposed ivory towers and can often amaze those who do not know them well with their marked sensuality, appreciation of beauty and highly developed sense of humor. While rarely gregarious, they display great affection and loyalty to their friends, partners and family, who in turn cherish them for the emotional support and stability that they offer.

VIRTUES: Remarkably perceptive, discerning and reflective individuals, those born on this day are fueled by their fascination with the realm of concepts and knowledge, a propensity which, when coupled with their strong sense of realism and intellectual focus, as well as their sensitivity, bestows on them great potential.
VICES: There is a risk that April 27 people may take their predilection for self-sufficiency to extremes, and may thus cut themselves off from the stimulating benefits that can result from social and intellectual interaction.
VERDICT: Although they are typically emotionally and intellectually well-balanced, and do not seek the approval of others, they should recognize that their introverted characteristics may be misinterpreted as aloofness or even arrogance. It may therefore be necessary at times to demonstrate greater emotional openness, especially in their private lives.

On This Day
Famous Births: Edward Gibbon (1737); Mary Wollstonecraft Godwin (1759); Samuel Morse (1791); Friedrich Flotow (1812); Herbert Spencer (1820); Ulysses S. Grant (1822); Edward Whymper (1840); Wallace Corothers (1896); C. Day-Lewis (1904); Jack Klugman (1922); Sheila Scott (1927); Anouk Aimée, Pik Botha and Casey Casem (1932); Sandy Dennis (1937); Judy Carne (1939); Sheena Easton (1959).

Significant Events and Anniversaries: April 27 is a day that promises considerable artistic talent, and marks the anniversary of the premiere of German composer Georg Friedrich Handel's *Royal Fireworks Music*, a performance which was, perhaps not unsurprisingly, abruptly ended by the outbreak of a fire (1749). The concern with furthering human knowledge that is highlighted by this day was reflected in the opening of London's Zoological Gardens (1828) and in the opening in Montreal of the international fair Expo '67 (1967). Self-belief is a strong characteristic of April 27, on which John Watson became Australia's youngest prime minister (1904), and on which Judy Johnson, riding Lone Gallant in a Baltimore steeplechase, became the first female professional jockey (1943). Illustrating the day's characteristic of self-sufficiency gone to extremes and introversion to the point of no return, Watergate FBI director Patrick E. Gray resigned after admitting he destroyed evidence (1973). On April 27—a day on which perceptive introspection can lead to bold and independent-minded results—the British government recognized the state of Israel (1950) and abortion was legalized in Britain (1968).

APRIL 28

Those born on April 28 are geared toward achievement, be it the attainment of personal goals or the realization of more abstract visions—either way, their drive for success compels them constantly to push forward until they finally reach their objectives. They are aided in their quest by their acute perspicacity, their great physical and mental vigor, their formidable organizational talents and their stubborn refusal to be deflected from their course. And because they are sensitive and intuitive individuals, they may not only direct their energies toward bringing about humanitarian progress, but also in so doing manifest a remarkable facility for tuning in to the emotions of others; they are not above using this ability to manipulate other people in order to enlist their support. Their independence of thought and action, as well as their interpersonal skills, mark them out as potentially inspirational leaders in whatever field they choose to make their careers, especially if they were also born in the Chinese year of the dragon.

April 28 people typically project a similar intensity of focus onto their private lives. Since they are averse to inactivity, they fill their private time with physical and sensual pursuits, a tendency which, when taken to its extreme, may result in uninhibited hedonism. Although they feel deep affection for those closest to them, they generally seek to direct the lives of their children in particular, without perceiving that they may be thereby suppressing the individual expression that they themselves hold so dear.

VIRTUES: April 28 people are driven by an overriding desire to achieve tangible and impressive results, and display their considerable intellectual powers of pragmatism and resourcefulness when single-mindedly working toward the fulfillment of their objectives.

VICES: There is a danger that the self-certainty that plays such a large part in motivating those born on this day may have two negative consequences: that they may dismiss out of hand those who hold conflicting opinions, and they may furthermore become vain, open to flattery and intellectually arrogant.

VERDICT: If April 28 people are not to become emotionally isolated, it is vital that they moderate their predilection for taking exclusive control of both people and situations. Their inherent desire to get their own way may have destructive implications, not least on their own holistic equilibrium.

On This Day

Famous Births: Edward IV of England (1442); James Monroe (1758); Charles Sturt (1795); Anthony, Lord Shaftesbury (1801); Lionel Barrymore (1878); António de Oliviera Salazar (1889); Odette Hallowes (1912); Reg Butler (1913); Kenneth Kaunda (1924); James Baker (1930); Saddam Hussein (1937); Ann-Margret (1941); Mike Brearly (1942); Jay Leno (1950).

Significant Events and Anniversaries: This day highlights an unwavering determination to realize personal visions, and the potential for success was reflected in explorer Captain James Cook's achievement in landing in what later became known as Botany Bay, Australia, in his vessel *Endeavour* (1770), and in anthropologist Thor Heyerdahl's launching of his balsa-wood raft *Kon-Tiki* on his voyage proving that ancient native Peruvians could have colonized Polynesia (1947). April 28 indicates leadership talents, and on this day Fletcher Christian led the crew of the *Bounty* in their mutinous uprising against Captain William Bligh (1789). Leadership, however, often carries the implicit dangers of arrogance and consequent retribution, and on this day the Italian dictator Benito Mussolini, along with his mistress Clara Petucci, was executed by Italian partisans (1945), and President Charles de Gaulle resigned when his proposed reforms were rejected by a French referendum (1969). Indicating the global humanitarian concern featured by this day, the League of Nations was established in the aftermath of World War I (1919). On a day favoring the energetic drive toward the realization of goals, Broadway's *A Chorus Line* closed after fifteen years as one of the Great White Way's most successful shows ever (1990).

Planetary Influences
Ruling planet: Venus.
First decan: Personal planet is Venus.

Sacred and Cultural Significance
Floralia celebrated in ancient Rome.
Saints' day: Vitalis (3rd century AD);
Louis Grignion de Montfort (1673–1716);
Peter Chanel (1803(41).

Born on April 28, 1758, James Monroe became the fifth president of the United States (1817–25). Highlighting the day's tendency toward the stubborn pursuit of ideals, and further aided by a forceful character reinforced by being born in the Chinese year of the tiger, Monroe promulgated the Monroe Doctrine, an important foreign policy statement tolerating no European interference in America.

Planetary Influences
Ruling planet: Venus.
First decan: Personal planet is Venus.

Sacred and Cultural Significance
National day of Japan; Pagan Tree Day.
Saints' day: Endellion (6th century AD);
Wilfred II (d. 744); Hugh of Cluny
(1024–1109); Robert of Molesme (1027–1110);
Peter the Martyr (1205–52); Joseph
Cottolengo (1786–1842).

*The national day of Japan is also the birthday
of the potent, self-confident emperor who led
his nation aggressively through World War II:
Showa Tenno Hirohito. His April 29 capacity
for organization and strategy and his Chinese
ox stubbornness were evident in his
military leadership.*

The conjunction of their meticulous and determined approach to work with the often flamboyant personal image that April 29 people present to the world is a rare combination, and one that has a potent, although sometimes confusing, effect on others. These people are incisive and independent thinkers, who may be inspired by bold concepts but would rarely start to implement them without careful prior consideration. Recognizing the value of organization, when planning a project they will typically examine every inherent aspect, anticipating potential pitfalls and then working out an appropriate course of action, with the result that although they may champion daring strategies, these will be soundly researched. And, because they understand the importance of image, they will "sell" their conceptual package to the skeptical with their enthusiasm and persuasive skills. Such talents are clearly suited to the world of business—and especially marketing, advertising and public relations—but they will also be effective in any professional area in which interpersonal relationships are important components.

Physically as well as intellectually dynamic, those born on this day are admired for their vigor, strength of will and infectious zest for life. In their personal lives, they are bent on having a good time, on enjoying to the full all that the world has to offer, and thereby they effortlessly attract friends and followers. Yet even when caught up in the excitement of a giddy social life, they never abandon their more sober and realistic characteristics, perhaps instinctively realizing the importance of grounding themselves in emotionally stable and supportive domestic relationships.

VIRTUES: April 29 individuals generally reconcile their introverted and extroverted tendencies extremely well, manifesting the best features of each: on the one hand attention to detail, intellectual focus and steady dependability, and on the other prodigious interpersonal skills, optimism and great self-confidence.
VICES: These people have a tendency to believe their own powerful propaganda, a propensity that means that they run the risk of becoming obdurate and resistant to accepting the (sometimes justified) counterarguments of those who espouse opposing viewpoints.
VERDICT: Despite their intuitive respect for the need to maintain an even intellectual and emotional equilibrium, they may on occasion become overly committed to alluring concepts, causing them to lose their typically balanced sense of perspective.

On This Day
Famous Births: Arthur Wellesley, Duke of Wellington (1769); Czar Alexander II of Russia (1818); William Randolph Hearst (1863); Thomas Beecham (1879); Harold Urey (1893); Malcolm Sargent (1895); Duke Ellington (1899); Emperor Hirohito of Japan (1901); Rudolf Schwarz (1905); Fred Zinnemann (1907); Jeremy Thorpe (1929); Lonnie Donegan (1931); Zubin Mehta (1936); Jerry Seinfeld (1955); Daniel Day-Lewis and Michelle Pfeiffer (1957); Andre Agassi and Uma Thurman (1970).

Significant Events and Anniversaries: The propensities for independent thought and committed pursuit of inspirational aims inherent in this day highlight innovation, as was reflected in the patenting of the zipper in Sweden by Gideon Sundback (1913), and the appearance of "cats' eyes" on British roads—these aids to motorists at night were invented by Percy Shaw (1935). April 29 is a day of irresistible dynamism, and marks the anniversary of the collapse of the Axis powers during World War II in the face of Allied advances, when the German forces in Italy surrendered unconditionally, and when inmates of the Nazi concentration camp of Dachau, in Germany, were liberated by U.S. troops (1945). This day's unwavering support of cherished ideals was reflected by U.S. boxer Muhammad Ali's refusal to be inducted into the U.S. Army during the Vietnam War; he was relieved of his world heavyweight title in punishment for his uncompromising stance (1967).

APRIL 30

Those born on April 30 are deceptively calm individuals, their pronounced sense of humor, appreciation of the good things in life and relaxed and affectionate approach to other people often masking their highly perceptive and tenacious professionalism. Indeed, contrary to initial appearances, such is their intellectual drive that they will feel unfulfilled unless they can immerse themselves in their work, and this will often be directed toward achieving progress of a humanitarian nature—a result both of their empathy and of their ability incisively to identify faults in existing systems and then formulate strategies for improvement. And because they wish to attain their aims as quickly and effectively as possible, and realistically recognize that they will be much more successful by winning others over to their cause rather than alienating them, they employ their considerable charm in the cultivation of open and friendly interpersonal relationships.

These multitalented individuals have the potential to make their mark on whichever area of professional expertise interests them. They are valued by their coworkers for their optimistic and encouraging outlook, as well as their great reliability. Within their personal liaisons, too, they are generally at the center of their social and domestic circles, for their ability to combine the provision of solid emotional support with a light-hearted, fun-loving approach is a rare and invigorating one and furthermore makes them especially gifted parents.

VIRTUES: Although these independent, strong-willed, determined and practical individuals are primarily motivated by the urge to bring about progress, they instinctively appreciate the importance of counterbalancing their serious intellectual quest with the enjoyment of the simpler things in life.

VICES: These responsible individuals find it hard to refuse requests for practical or emotional help, and may therefore find themselves overburdened—a potentially physically and emotionally damaging propensity.

VERDICT: It is vital that these people occasionally make time for periods of quiet reflection and remove themselves temporarily from the demands imposed by others, thereby allowing themselves not only to recharge their batteries, but also to concentrate upon their own needs and ambitions.

On This Day

Famous Births: Jean Baptiste, Abbé de la Salle (1651); Queen Mary II of England (1662); David Thompson (1770); Karl Friedrich Gauss (1777); Franz Lehar (1870); Jaroslav Hasek (1883); Joachim von Ribbentrop (1893); Juliana, Queen of The Netherlands (1909); Eve Arden (1912); Cloris Leachman (1926); Willie Nelson (1933); Gary Collins (1939); Burt Young (1940); Bobby Vee (1943); Jill Clayburgh (1944); King Carl XVI Gustaf of Sweden (1946); Jane Campion (1954).

Significant Events and Anniversaries: April 30 is a day that indicates collective humanitarian visions, a characteristic that is paralleled in national concerns, and this day marks the anniversary of three defining events in U.S. history: the inauguration of George Washington as the nation's first president (1789); the acquisition by the U.S. of the French territories of Louisiana and New Orleans (1803); and Hawaii's gaining territorial standing in the U.S. (1900). Realism is a further feature of this day, on which the Roman emperor Galerius Valerius Maximianus, recognizing that Christianity could not be eliminated by persecution, issued the Edict of Nicodemia which acknowledged the religion (311), and on which the German dictator Adolf Hitler, along with his new wife Eva Braun, committed suicide in Berlin, thereby conceding the total defeat of the Nazis (1945).

Planetary Influences
Ruling planet: Venus.
First decan: Personal planet is Venus.

Sacred and Cultural Significance
National day of the Netherlands; Walpurgisnacht in Germany.
Saints' day: Erkenwald (d. 693); Catherine of Siena (1333–80); Pius V (1504–72).

A depiction of Walpurgisnacht in Germany, which begins at sunrise on April 30. To protect the home from evil spirits, birch boughs are placed on all doors and windows, and traditional bonfires and torches of herbs are lit. According to legend, witches can be seen riding across the sky on broomsticks.

Planetary Influences
Ruling planet: Venus.
Second decan: Personal planet is Mercury.

Sacred and Cultural Significance
May Day; in ancient Rome, the Spring goddess Maia honored; international day of labor and unions.
Saints' day: Joseph (d. 1st century AD), patron saint of bursars, carpenters, the dying, fathers, holy death and workers; Philip (1st century AD) and James the Less (1st century AD); Corentin (dates unknown); Marcoul (d. c.558); Brioc (6th century AD); Asaph (d. 7th century AD).

The Pagan May Day fertility festival, associated with the Celtic Beltane, is still widely celebrated in northern Europe. It is marked with the gathering of flowers in the early morning to decorate a maypole. In Rackham's illustration, Queen Guinevere goes "a-maying."

MAY 1

✳✳✳✳✳✳✳✳✳✳✳✳✳✳✳✳✳✳✳✳✳✳✳✳✳✳✳✳✳✳✳✳✳✳✳✳✳✳

Perspicacity is the greatest strength of those born on May 1. There is very little that escapes these observant individuals—neither the occurrences of the physical world, nor actions reflecting the more nebulous range of human emotions. For, blessed as they are with acute powers of intellectual perception, these are also highly intuitive types, who often rely upon their instincts in forming their initial opinions of people, situations and predicaments. Then, once they have gleaned sufficient information, they will typically apply their talent for sound, logical and realistic thought to building an effective strategy for action. Their great sensitivity toward the feelings of others makes them kind and empathetic people, who will generally do their utmost to help when approached—as they frequently are—with a problem. This propensity, coupled with their other natural abilities, equips those born on this day especially well for the caring professions in general and for psychiatry or counseling in particular, although less altruistic types also have the potential to make gifted salespeople.

Within their personal relationships, also, May 1 individuals usually find themselves playing an actively supportive role, bolstering the confidence of those closest to them while at the same time encouraging them to enjoy life, for they love company, as well as such sensual domestic pleasures as cooking for others. But in assuming somewhat static positions as linchpins, around whom others revolve, they will need to guard against the risk of being taken for granted and, furthermore, of neglecting their own personal development.

VIRTUES: These people-oriented individuals are compassionate, concerned with the welfare of others, and desirous of creating harmonious situations. Blessed with profound intuitive qualities, as well as impressive skills of mental organization and tenacity, they are adapt in combining their various gifts to form a particularly effective whole.
VICES: There are two risks inherent in these individuals' nurturing approach toward others: that they may ignore their own emotional needs in favor of assisting other people, and that they may be deeply disappointed when their carefully considered advice is disregarded, becoming cold and withdrawn, or even furious and accusatory.
VERDICT: While those born on this day are generally successful in striking the right balance between their professional and personal concerns, they will need to take extra care to maintain a similar equilibrium between fulfilling others' requirements and their own. It is vital that they should develop a more relaxed and pragmatic view of human nature and others in following their own paths through life, even if this involves their making mistakes.

On This Day
Famous Births: Rudolf I of Habsburg, King of Germany (1218); Joseph Addison (1672); Mary Jones (1830); Hilaire, Comte de Chardonnet (1839); Mark Wayne Clark (1896); Kate Smith (1909); Glenn Ford (1916); Jack Paar (1918); Joseph Heller (1923); Terry Southern (1924); Judy Collins (1939); Rita Coolidge (1944); Joanna Lumley (1946); Steve Cauthen (1960).

Significant Events and Anniversaries: The enormous sensitivity indicated by this day was reflected in the artistic realm when the ballet *L'Après midi d'un faune*, composed by Claude Debussy and with Nijinsky in the lead, had its premiere (1912); while on this day artist Pablo Picasso began work on his masterpiece *Guernica* (1937). May 1 highlights the desire to act in the best interest of others, a propensity that can take many progressive forms, as was illustrated when, on this day, the pain-killing compound aspirin was first marketed in powder form by the German pharmaceutical company Bayer (1889); the fictional hero Batman was introduced to the world by *Detective Comics* (1939); tourist-class flights were introduced by the U.S. airline T.W.A. (1952); and when the doors of the Legoland theme park were opened to enthralled children in Billund, Denmark (1968). The element of earth governs May 1, and on this day New York's Empire State Building—then the world's tallest skyscraper—was opened by U.S. President Hoover, its unprecedented height made possible by the great stability of its solid constructional methods (1931).

MAY 2

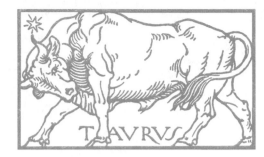

To those who at heart desire nothing more than to enjoy stable and harmonious interpersonal relationships, it might seem strange that those born on this day often upset others with their propensity to express themselves bluntly. Yet these honest individuals do not consciously set out to wound others with the unvarnished accuracy of their observations, it is just that, as acutely perceptive people possessed of an almost clinical fascination with what makes others tick, they tend to reach logical conclusions unclouded by emotional complications and then to voice their findings with undiplomatic objectivity. Such people-oriented qualities of curiosity and interest, as well as their tenacious determination to effect improvement, bestow upon May 2 individuals a marked potential for success not only in the more technical of the caring professions, such as medicine and scientific research, but also in social campaigning: these talents and inclinations are even more pronounced if they were also born in the Chinese year of the pig.

In the domestic sphere, these people long to create steady and enduring ties of affection and greatly value the bonds that they form with their family members and friends. They are often extremely gregarious types, who are stimulated by social gatherings and relish seeing others enjoying themselves, yet they will also derive profound pleasure from being alone with nature—a predilection that often makes them inspired gardeners. They have a dangerous tendency, however, to apply their own standards to their nearest and dearest, expecting them unquestioningly to conform to their mores: thus they may themselves generate the sort of confrontational situations that they abhor by engendering a clash of wills—especially with their parents or children. It is vital, therefore, that they should learn to relax their high, albeit well-meaning, expectations of others.

VIRTUES: Those born on this day are blessed with outstanding intellectual skills, perspicacity and inquisitiveness, as well as with the ability to marshal their thoughts with logical coherence. Their concern for bringing about human progress, coupled with their talents, gives them a great capacity to work for the common good.
VICES: These people's typical directness of approach extends to their liaisons with others, and they may therefore become not only overbearing in their attempts to set others on what they perceive to be the right track, but also impatient and tactless in comments regarding their behavior: although both tendencies are well-meaning, they will ultimately be destructive.
VERDICT: It is important that, in all their endeavors, these people maintain a balanced sense of perspective, lest they end up sabotaging their own efforts through either a misplaced sense of urgency or a less-than-diplomatic approach. They should cultivate a greater awareness of the sometimes devastating effect that their words and deeds can have upon others.

On This Day

Famous Births: Alessandro Scarlatti (1660); Empress Catherine II (the Great) of Russia (1729); Ebenezer Cobham Brewer (1810); Elijah McCoy (1843); Jerome K. Jerome (1859); Theodor Herzl (1860); Vernon Castle (1887); Baron Manfred von Richthofen (1892); Benjamin Spock (1903); Satyajit Ray (1921); Theodore Bikel (1924); Roscoe Lee Browne (1925); King Faisal II of Iraq (1935); Bianca Jagger (1945); Lesley Gore (1946); Brian Lara (1969).

Significant Events and Anniversaries: The day's certainty of conviction may result in confrontation, which, in the martial sphere, is reflected in three events that occurred on this day: the approaching Italian Army forced the Abyssinian Emperor Haile Selassie to flee his capital, Addis Ababa (1936); the Lebanese Army reacted violently to the provocation of Palestinian refugees, thus initiating the outbreak of the Lebanese Civil War (1973); and the British submarine *Conqueror* controversially torpedoed the Argentinian battleship *General Belgrano* during the Falklands War, with the loss of 362 lives (1982). The quality of determined tenacity that is inherent in this day was mirrored by the achievement of Lieutenants Kelly and Macready, when they became the first aviators to cross the U.S.A. nonstop, flying from Long Island to San Diego (1923).

Planetary Influences
Ruling planet: Venus.
Second decan: Personal planet is Mercury.

Sacred and Cultural Significance
Ysahodhara, the consort of Buddha, honored in India.
Saints' day: Athanasius (c.296–373); Gennys (dates unknown), patron saint of St. Gennys, Cornwall, England; Mafalda of Portugal (1184–1257).

Empress Catherine the Great of Russia, born on this day in 1729, is remembered as an ambitious, strong and successful ruler, but she also embodied the negative characteristics of May 2 people: she was overbearing and ruthless in both the personal and political realms.

Planetary Influences
Ruling planet: Venus.
Second decan: Personal planet is Mercury.

Sacred and Cultural Significance
In Christianity, the feast of the finding of the Holy Cross.
Saints' day: Glywys (dates unknown); Philip (1st century AD) and James the Less (1st century AD); Theodosius of Kiev (c.1002–74); Pellegrino Laziosi (1265–1345).

Israeli stateswoman Golda Meir, born on this day in 1898, was a successful and influential prime minister who demonstrated the insight and concern for others that characterize May 3 people. Although her personal life was marked with some sadness, she was greatly admired throughout her life.

MAY 3

✦ ★

Those born on May 3 are astute judges of character, utilizing their highly developed skills of intuition, perception and intellectual objectivity to make often extremely realistic assessments of others. They can also apply these interpersonal talents to collective human situations, thus giving them a profound understanding of the reasons underlying both individual behavior and group dynamics. In observing others and trying to determine why people act as they do, they are driven by an almost scientific curiosity, and the nature of this inquisitiveness, together with the information they glean in the process, endows them with genuine concern for their fellow beings. Linked with the necessary emotional detachment, this equips them admirably to become psychologists, psychiatrists or counselors: careers as market researchers or advertising executives are also favored. Combined with their human awareness, their ability to think pragmatically additionally promises success in the political sphere. These are furthermore energetic types, who will not rest until they have implemented their chosen solutions to their satisfaction.

Although those born on this day manifest a healthy hedonistic streak, which enables them to discard their professional personae and enjoy life to the full when appropriate, they may have difficulty in committing themselves to a single partner, a problem that derives from their inherent propensity to judge people with their head rather than their heart. While others are attracted to May 3 people for the fun that they generate, as well as the sound advice that they proffer, those seeking more enduring relationships may be disappointed. Once strong emotional bonds are formed, however, these people remain steadfastly affectionate and caring toward those closest to them.

VIRTUES: Those born on this day manifest a profound interest in their fellows, marshaling their considerable powers of conscious and unconscious perspicacity in studying others, and generally arriving at sound conclusions. Not only are they valued by others for this rare gift of insight, but they are also appreciated for their optimistic and enthusiastic approach.
VICES: Because they are so adept at impartially analyzing the behavior and motivations of others, their own personal relationships may be unintentionally restricted by their failure to accept others as they are and, in the worst-case scenario, reject some relationships that have the potential to bring them great happiness.
VERDICT: Despite the usual ability of May 3 people to separate their professional and domestic lives, it is important that they do not allow the analytical qualities that make them so successful at work to impinge upon their personal relationships. They should overcome their tendency to reject those who wish to strengthen emotional ties with them and should try harder to reciprocate expressions of affection.

On This Day
Famous Births: Niccolo Machiavelli (1469); Richard D'Oyly Carte (1844); John Scott Haldane (1860); François Coty (1874); Marcel Dupré (1886); Gabriel Chevallier (1895); Dodie Smith (1896); Golda Meir (1898); Bing Crosby (1904); Mary Astor (1906); William Inge (1913); Pete Seeger (1919); Sugar Ray Robinson (1920); James Brown (1928); Henry Cooper (1934); Engelbert Humperdinck (1936); Frankie Valli (1937); Doug Henning (1947); Christopher Cross (1951).

Significant Events and Anniversaries: May 3 falls under the sign of Taurus, indicating dogged determination in the pursuit of visionary ambitions, as was illustrated by the rewarding of explorer Christopher Columbus's tenacity when he "discovered" Jamaica (1494). This day indicates great physical and intellectual energy, qualities that were highlighted when the British poet Lord Byron swam across the Hellespont (the Dardanelles), a feat that his legendary inspiration, Leander, had failed to achieve (1810); and when the first world badminton tournament was held in Malmö, Sweden (1977). The humanitarian concern that is a feature of this day is reflected in the medical realm, when a pioneering team at London's National Heart Hospital in Britain carried out the world's first heart-transplant operation (1968).

MAY 4

****

One of the strongest—and most endearing—qualities manifested by those born on May 4 is their concern with the well-being of others and their commensurate desire to place their considerable talents and energy at the disposal of those who require their help. Their enlightened powers of perspicacity and realism, in conjunction with their genuine empathy, steadiness and optimistic outlook, not only give them the potential to help solve others' problems effectively, but also win for them esteem and gratitude. Their ability to combine their great intellectual and practical skills with their typically emotion-driven gifts of compassion and kindness is an unusually potent talent, and whether they make a career of counseling or not, they will generally find that their sound advice is much sought after by others. Indeed, whatever profession they choose, they will generally flourish best in those work-based situations which offer a significant degree of personal interaction.

Within their personal relationships too, May 4 individuals make heartening friends, partners and parents, who typically tend to place the needs and desires of those closest to them above their own. Because they are so used to being consulted for their advice, there is a danger that, if their carefully considered words of wisdom are ignored, they will feel deeply disappointed and express their annoyance forcefully. They should guard against subsuming their own—equally important—ambitions to those of others.

VIRTUES: May 4 people are unusually concerned with resolving the problems of other people and furthering their potential: they draw upon their prodigiously rational, sensible and yet imaginative intellectual talents in offering remedial counseling to others.
VICES: Because they inevitably neglect their own desires in making the lives of others their main priority, they may either succumb to feelings of resentment, typically masked with an unappealing aura of martyrdom, or ultimately explode with frustration when they fail to gain fulfillment from their selfless work.
VERDICT: It is vital that those born on this day take care not to sacrifice their own emotional and physical requirements upon the altar of altruism. Their selfless motives may be commendable, but they must also consider and nurture themselves if they are not to become worn down in the service of others.

On This Day
Famous Births: Bartolommeo Cristofori (1655); Thomas Lawrence (1769); Thomas Henry Huxley (1825); John Hanning Speke (1827); Emil Nikolaus Reznicek (1860); Sylvia Pankhurst (1882); Archibald McIndoe (1900); Heloise (1919); Eric Sykes (1923); Muhammed Hosni Mubarak (1928); Audrey Hepburn (1929); Roberta Peters (1930); Gennady Rozhdestvensky (1931); Manuel Benitez Pérez, "El Cordobes" (1936); George F. Wil (1941); Pia Zadora (1956); Keith Haring (1958); Randy Travis (1959).

Significant Events and Anniversaries: May 4's inherent tendency to bring about improvement in humanity's collective life can take various forms, and on this day: the Cunard Shipping Line was founded (1839); Charles Rolls and Henry Royce agreed to manufacture cars together (1904); and the Trades Union Congress (T.U.C.) called for the first general strike in Britain, in an attempt to improve working conditions (1926). The strong convictions felt on behalf of the general good can sadly result in confrontation, as was reflected in the events that occurred on this day at Kent State University, Ohio, when members of the U.S. National Guard fatally shot four students who were protesting against President Nixon's decision to send troops to Cambodia (1970); in the Falklands Islands War, when the British ship H.M.S. *Sheffield* was sunk by an Argentinian Exocet missile, with the loss of twenty-one lives (1982); and in the U.S.A., when Colonel Oliver North, a key figure in the Irangate scandal, was convicted of supplying arms to the Contra rebels in Nicaragua (1989). Highlighting the Taurean determination of this day, Margaret Thatcher made history when she became Britain's first woman prime minister (1979).

Planetary Influences
Ruling planet: Venus.
Second decan: Personal planet is Mercury.

Sacred and Cultural Significance
In Irish folklore, Fairy Day.
Saint's day: Florian (d. 304).

Perhaps the most sought-after luxury car, the Rolls Royce was born from the partnership of Charles Rolls and Henry Royce that was made on this day in 1904. The relationship-oriented May 4 augurs well for new partnerships.

MAY 5

* *

Planetary Influences
Ruling planet: Venus.
Second decan: Personal planet is Mercury.

Sacred and Cultural Significance
Saint's day: Hydroc (dates unknown).

Born on this day in 1818, Karl Marx embodied the passionate convictions and humanitarian vision of May 5 people. His works in economics and political philosophy gave rise to a coherent framework of historical and political beliefs that was named for him.

Those born on May 5 are convinced of the veracity of their remarkably strong opinions, which they feel compelled to transmit to others in order to convert them to their viewpoints. Since they are extremely concerned with the welfare of people as a collective entity, and furthermore blessed with a highly developed sense of fairness and justice, their convictions are more than likely to be inspired by a radical humanitarian vision—a desire to bring the greatest happiness to the greatest number of people. When working toward the implementation of their aims, they typically manifest great pragmatism, using every weapon in their armory of skills to effect their ambitions: talents that include objective perspicacity, meticulous attention to detail, profoundly methodical organizational abilities, and enormous energy and tenacity. It is also pertinent that those born on this day are natural salespeople, who instinctively understand how to motivate and inspire others—and thereby, sometimes, to manipulate them toward their own ends, too.

Careers in the retail trade, as well as in politics, therefore augur especially well for May 5 individuals, but they also have the potential to find fulfillment in such academic areas as philosophy or medical studies, as well as in the arts, with which they have a remarkable affinity. For, however serious the purpose that drives their intellects, these are sensual people who relish such pleasurable experiences as fine food, haunting music and aesthetic beauty, this being especially true if they were also born in the Chinese year of the goat.

VIRTUES: The combination of their prodigious imaginative powers with their truly compassionate feelings orients these inspirational people toward helping others. Once set upon the course of effecting progress, they typically utilize their fiercely down-to-earth talents of organization and tenacity in seeking to attain their ideals.
VICES: A somewhat ambivalent result of their joint fixity of conviction and drive to help others is the tendency of May 5 people to become overly authoritarian in their personal liaisons, particularly in their relationship with younger or less mature people, including their children.
VERDICT: Although those born on this day are motivated by laudable intentions, it is vital that they resist their desire to dominate others' lives, a controlling propensity that may anger and ultimately cause the objects of their concern to rebel against them. They must recognize that it is important for others to learn life's lessons for themselves and, even if they regard this to be injudicious, sanction independent behavior, in the interest of their gaining experience.

On This Day
Famous Births: Louis Hachette (1800); Søren Aabye Kierkegaard (1813); Eugène Martin Labiche (1815); Karl Marx (1818); John Batterson Stetson (1830); Henryk Sienkiewicz (1846); Nellie Bly (1867); Gordon Richards (1904); Tyrone Power (1914); Alice Faye (1915); Pat Carroll (1927); Michael Murphy (1938); Tammy Wynette (1942); Michael Palin (1943); Roger Rees (1944); Tina Yothers (1973); Danielle Fishel (1981).

Significant Events and Anniversaries: An inherent danger of this day's intellectual certainty is that it may engender dissent and thereby cause alienation, and on May 5 Napoleon Bonaparte, who was regarded by his enemies as a powerful adversary and inspirational leader, died in exile on the island of St. Helena in the Atlantic (1821); while during a period of political dissent French students clashed with police in a serious riot in Paris (1968). The desire to bring about human progress is highlighted by events that occurred in space on this day, such as when astronaut Alan B. Shepherd became the first American to complete a suborbital flight in his spacecraft *Mercury-Redstone III* (1961), and when Britain launched its first satellite, *Ariel III* (1963). A lesson that this day imparts is the value of autonomy, a message that is mirrored in the national sphere when West Germany became a sovereign federal state (1955). A further feature of this day is action motivated by feelings of justice, as is reflected when members of the British elite fighting force, the S.A.S., successfully stormed the Iranian Embassy in London, freeing nineteen persons who were being held hostage by terrorists (1980).

MAY 6

In common with many of their Taurean fellows, those intuitive people born on May 6 are acutely attuned to the emotions of others, and moreover often feel profound empathy with less fortunate individuals, who arouse a fiercely protective instinct in them. Whether or not their interest in humanity takes an active compassionate form, these people cannot help but be fascinated by the mechanics of the human psyche, seeking to understand what exactly it is that motivates others. And, because these are perceptive, articulate and logically thinking individuals, who feel compelled to pass on their wisdom to others, they typically make gifted and insightful problem-solvers, whose advice is frequently sought. Given such inherently people-oriented talents and inclinations, they will usually find career fulfillment in the medical, psychiatric or caring professions, but they are also suited to politics and the arts, both areas in which they can utilize their sensitivity and urge to help humanity progress.

Despite the seriousness with which they apply themselves to their work, however, May 6 individuals retain the capacity to enjoy the simpler things in life, perhaps instinctively appreciating that relaxation is a vital release from intellectual pressure. They typically make deeply supportive and affectionate friends, partners and parents, whose marked sense of humor, infectious optimism and generosity draw others to them, particularly if they were also born in the Chinese year of the horse.

VIRTUES: Extremely sensitive and intuitive, yet also blessed with highly developed powers of organization and determination, those born on this day have the capacity to form deep relationships with other people and to direct their prodigious energy toward being of service. **VICES:** The inherent desire of May 6 people to ensure the happiness of others may cause them to be overly tolerant in their dealings with others, particularly their nearest and dearest, when a firmer stance might be more appropriate.
VERDICT: Despite their instinctive appreciation of the importance of having fun out of working hours as a means of recharging their mental batteries, May 6 people may sometimes lose sight of the value of self-indulgence when another's cause appears more pressing, a propensity that may ultimately lead to physical and emotional burnout, and one that they should consciously try to control.

On This Day

Famous Births: Maximilien Robespierre (1758); Sigmund Freud and Robert Edwin Peary (1856); Rabindranath Tagore (1861); Willem de Sitter (1872); Alan Cobham (1894); Rudolph Valentino (1895); Max Ophuls (1902); Stewart Granger (1913); Orson Welles (1915); Willie Mays (1931); Bob Seger (1945); Tony Blair (1953); George Clooney (1961); Janet Jackson (1966).

Significant Events and Anniversaries: May 6 indicates great concern with implementing progress, a tendency that may take many forms, and on this day the city of Ville Marie (later renamed Montreal) was founded in Canada (1642); the pioneering "Penny Black" postage stamps went on sale in England (1840); the U.S. inventor Linus Yale patented his revolutionary lock (1851); the British runner Roger Bannister broke the four-minute mile, achieving a then record time of 3 minutes, 59.4 seconds (1954); and the Channel Tunnel was opened, linking England to France (1994). Human innovations are not necessarily infallible, however, as was manifested on this day by the explosion at Lakehurst, New Jersey, of the German airship *Hindenburg*, tragically claiming the lives of thirty-six individuals (1937). This day highlights an enjoyment of such relaxing pastimes as sporting activities, and also marks the anniversary of the staging of the first international boxing match, between a British and an Italian pugilist, in London (1733), as well as of the inaugural Kentucky Derby in Louisville, Kentucky (1874). The collective determination associated with nationalist sentiments that is a feature of this day was reflected when of Irish Fenian assassins murdered the British politicians Lord Cavendish and Thomas Henry Burke in Phoenix Park in Dublin (1882), and Icelandic gunboats fired over the bows of British fishing trawlers during the "Cod War" (1959).

Planetary Influences
Ruling planet: Venus.
Second decan: Personal planet is Mercury.

Sacred and Cultural Significance
Saints' day: Marian and James (d. 259); Edbert (7th century AD).

The explosion of the Hindenburg *airship on May 6, 1937, illustrates the "burnout" that can characterize this day, when the compelling desire to achieve a goal can cause inadequate attention to the potential risks and dangers.*

Planetary Influences
Ruling planet: Venus.
Second decan: Personal planet is Mercury.

Sacred and Cultural Significance
Thargelia celebrated in ancient Greece to honor Apollo.
Saints' day: Liudhard (d. c.603); John of Beverley (d. 721).

Pontiac's Rebellion began in 1763 with a dramatic siege on the British garrison at Detroit on this day of taking action to effect change. A powerful orator, the Ottawa tribe's chief inspired this attack on a day when communication is also favored.

MAY 7

Inherent in those born on this day is a profound mixture of inward-looking spirituality and externally-oriented concern with personal image. Thus while the former characteristic leads these people to recognize that life's most important truths and values are of the nonmaterialistic, intellectual and emotionally elevated variety, the latter endows them with an altogether more superficial desire to make the best possible impression on others. Yet this image-consciousness is not necessarily a negative quality, for once May 7 people have become aware of it, they may consciously influence others to achieve their ends. Indeed, as well as being deeply sensitive and often compassionate, these individuals are gifted communicators, with an outstanding ability to convey their strongly held convictions to others and thereby inspire them with their visions. Reflecting their skills and leanings, these people have the potential to excel in the artistic sphere, not only as writers, poets and composers, but also as spiritual or even political evangelists.

Despite their best intentions, however, those born on May 7 may have less-than-idyllic personal lives, for their interest in idealistic concepts and their desire to influence the wider world may leave them with little energy or attention to devote to those closest to them, a tendency that is particularly pronounced in the men born on this day. Indeed, it is ironic that, while they may devote enormous effort to winning allies when at work, they may unintentionally neglect the feelings of their partners, children and friends, despite the genuine affection that they feel for those closest to them.

VIRTUES: Those born on this day possess both introverted and extroverted characteristics, in that they are fueled by the desire to uncover profound abstract truths and at the same time are aware of the importance of making a personal impact, dual qualities which, when used astutely, endow them with enormous potential for success.
VICES: May 7 people have an unwitting tendency to take the emotional support of friends and family members for granted when trying to enlist the support of others for whatever specific missions drive them. They should recognize that such professional success may ultimately result in emotional isolation.
VERDICT: In all areas of their lives, it is vital that these people examine the motives that underlie their urges and actions. They should consider, for example, whether their concern as to how others perceive them, and their quest to find fulfillment in spirituality, result from unresolved feelings of insecurity? When they are able to truly understand themselves, May 7 people will be better placed to satisfy their innermost yearnings.

On This Day
Famous Births: David Hume (1711); Robert Browning (1812); Johannes Brahms (1833); Peter Ilich Tchaikovsky (1840); Lord Rosebury (1847); A.E.W. Mason (1865); Gabby Hayes (1885); Archibald MacLeish and Josip Broz Tito (1892); Gary Cooper (1901); Edwin Land (1909); Maria Eva Perón, "Evita" (1919); Darren McGavin (1922); Ruth Prawer Jhabvala (1927); Teresa Brewer (1931); Johnny Unitas (1933); Peter Carey (1943); Robin Strasser (1945).

Significant Events and Anniversaries: Outstanding artistic potential is promised by this day, on which the German composer Ludwig van Beethoven conducted the premiere performance of his *Ninth Symphony* (1823). The desire to inspire direct action in the cause of a collective ideal is a further tendency inherent in May 7, on which Pontiac, the chief of the Native American Ottawa tribe, rebelled against the English forces garrisoned at Detroit (1763); the Cunard liner *Lusitania* was sunk off Ireland by a German submarine during World War I, with the loss of some 2000 lives (1915); Allied forces received the final unconditional surrender of their German adversaries at Rheims in France (1945); and the ideologically committed communist Leonid Brezhnev assumed the leadership of the Soviet Union (1960). Reflecting this day's determination to make progress, U.S. photographer George Eastman patented the Kodak box camera (1888).

MAY 8

Those born on this day harbor extremely strong convictions, which they will typically maintain with stubborn determination and strive to propagate as widely as possible. Although they are possessed of a highly developed sense of fair play, which may compel them to direct their efforts toward improving the lot of less fortunate individuals by serving, for example, as politicians, May 8 people generally feel a greater connection with the environment—be it with the natural world, or their immediate, perhaps man-made surroundings—a sympathy that is heightened by their profound innate appreciation of beauty. Hence they will often be found playing a leading role in preserving or improving landscapes, historically important buildings or—in the more personal realm—their own homes. When in the grip of crusading zeal, they may occasionally put their ideas across forcefully, sometimes overly so when they are particularly impassioned: but, since they instinctively understand the value of converting rather than alienating others, and are gifted and effective communicators with the persuasive talents of a salesperson, they usually prefer to be persuaded.

Despite the unwavering loyalty and affection that they manifest toward their friends, partners and families, those born on this day may be difficult to live with because of their high standards and ideals. Their aesthetic concern with their personal environment, for example, may result in simmering resentment when those with whom they share their homes fail to fall in with their exacting requirements, particularly untidy teenage children, and this tendency is unusually pronounced in May 8 men. Their energy and self-certainty may furthermore instill in them a propensity to control the actions of their nearest and dearest rather than let them explore their own avenues independently.

VIRTUES: May 8 individuals are motivated by global, nonmaterialistic ideals, ambitions that are aroused by their intellectual and intuitive perspicacity, their sure sense of the morally correct course, and their burning desire to bring about improvement. Their success seems assured, when they supplement these visions with their systematic approach and tenacity.
VICES: Those born on this day are fired by what they perceive to be the unquestionable veracity of their beliefs, a predilection that may lead them not only to seek to impose their convictions on others in a domineering fashion, but also to close their minds to the possible validity of alternate approaches.
VERDICT: In order to find fulfillment, it is important that these people learn to relax the expectations that they have for both themselves and others, although never at the expense of compromising their most cherished opinions. Learning to embrace diversity of all kinds, and to adopt a more light-hearted attitude to life, will benefit them immeasurably.

Planetary Influences
Ruling planet: Venus.
Second decan: Personal planet is Mercury.

Sacred and Cultural Significance
In Cornwall, England, the annual Furry Dance celebrates Springtime.
Saints' day: Victor (d. 303); Indract (d. c.700); Wiro (d. c.753); Odger (8th century AD); Peter of Tarentaise (c.1102–74).

On This Day
Famous Births: Francis Quarles (1592); Jean Henri Dunant (1828); Harry S. Truman (1884); Bishop Fulton Sheen (1895); Fernand Constantin (1903); John Snagge (1904); David Attenborough and Don Rickles (1926); Sonny Liston (1932); Jack Charlton (1936); Peter Benchley and Rick Nelson (1940); Toni Tennille (1943); Gary Glitter (1944); David Keith (1954); Melissa Gilbert (1964).

Significant Events and Anniversaries: The firm convictions highlighted by this day may be displayed in national, political or ethical arenas, as was reflected when: Sweden abolished capital punishment (1921); South Africa adopted Afrikaans as its official language (1924); the British spy George Blake was jailed for his ideological commitment to the Soviet Union (1961); and the alleged Nazi collaborator Pieter Menten was brought to trial in The Netherlands (1977). This day indicates a close affinity with the natural world, a propensity that is underlined by two respectively negative and positive events: when a volcano erupted on the outskirts of St. Pierre in Martinique, causing the deaths of around 30,000 people (1902); and when the Thames Barrier, constructed to prevent the flooding of the English tidal river, was opened (1984).

Hernando de Soto, a ruthless Spanish conquistador, found his boundless ambition furthered on this crusading day in 1541, when he "discovered" the Mississippi River.

TAVRVS

Planetary Influences
Ruling planet: Venus.
Second decan: Personal planet is Mercury.

Sacred and Cultural Significance
National day of the Czech Republic.
Saints' day: Gregory Nazianzen,
Cappadocian father (329–89).

On a day characterized by both social concern and aesthetic sensitivity, Australia's landmark Parliament House (pictured below) was opened in Canberra in 1927.

MAY 9

Those born on this day can astonish those who do not know them well with their awesome flashes of temper, colorful pyrotechnical displays that are at variance with their generally steady and calm approach to life. Such tantrums are rarely gratuitous, however, instead being provoked by what May 9 people believe to be manifestations of perversity that hinder implemention of their progressive visions. For these are judgemental—almost magisterial—people, who feel compelled to adopt the champion's mantle when moved by examples of injustice or abuse, desiring to protect the downtrodden and reverse their misfortunes. And, in such instances, when faced with a humanitarian challenge, May 9 people typically draw deep on their prodigious resources of energy, determination and courage, thus making inspiring leaders. While such qualities suit them extremely well for careers in politics, the caring professions or the judiciary, their enormous sensitivity also endows them with outstanding artistic potential.

Because these people are overridingly possessed by highly developed instincts of moral rectitude, they generally find it hard to forgive the all-too-human failings of their nearest and dearest, expecting them to live up to the lofty ethical standards on which they themselves place such great value. When they experience inevitable disappointment within both their professional and personal relationships, their temperamental tendencies surge to the fore, a propensity that is especially marked if they were also born in the Chinese year of the dragon.

VIRTUES: When responding to a humanitarian cause that deeply moves them, May 9 people draw upon their considerable powers of compassion, vigor, tenacity and bravery, ultimately displaying leadership qualities and a level of passionate commitment that is both unrivaled and potentially irresistible.
VICES: Their tendency to succumb to irascibility makes these people, in many respects, their own worst enemies, for by directing their feelings of frustration toward others they may wreak devastating—and sometimes irreparable—damage to relationships that they strived so hard to establish.
VERDICT: In order to achieve the success toward which they are directly oriented, it is crucial that those born on this day apply their considerable capacity for self-control toward containing their emotions. Developing a more pragmatic outlook on life, as well as accepting the more harmless vagaries of human behavior without complaint, will help them in this.

On This Day
Famous Births: John Brown (1800); J.M. Barrie (1860); Harry Vardon (1870); Lilian Baylis and Howard Carter (1874); Mike Wallace (1918); Richard Adams (1920); Pancho Gonzáles (1928); Alan Bennett (1934); Terry Downes, Albert Finney and Glenda Jackson (1936); James L. Brooks (1940); Candice Bergen (1946); Billy Joel (1949); Jane Wendt and Gough Whitlam (1956); Tony Gwynn (1960).

Significant Events and Anniversaries: May 9 indicates a desire to effect real progress, an urge that may manifest itself in a diversity of actions and spheres, and on this day Australia's first federal parliament met in Melbourne (1901); U.S. aviators Richard Evelyn Bird and Floyd Bennet made their pioneering flight over the North Pole (1926); the world's first eye "bank" was inaugurated at the Ear, Nose and Throat Hospital in New York (1944); and, in the aftermath of its inglorious Fascist past, Italy became a republic upon the abdication of King Victor Emmanuel III (1946). Serious intent underlies even the artistic pursuits and attainments of this day, on which Australia's Parliament House was opened in Canberra (1927), and insightful British playwright John Osborne's acerbic, socially critical play *Look Back in Anger* was premiered (1956).

MAY 10

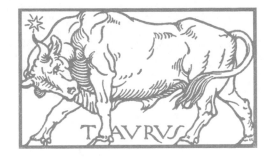

****

Many of those born on May 10 tend to be obsessive in exploring and promoting those concepts that fuel their imaginations and passions. Indeed, their capacity to become totally absorbed in pet projects can leave them with little time, energy or even interest to devote to unrelated people or projects. Without the unconditional tolerance and understanding of friends and family members, they are unlikely to experience any of the joys of personal interaction and close emotional support; this is especially the case for men born on this day, who often turn a blind eye to what they regard as the trivial, relatively unimportant chores and obligations of normal family relationships. While there is no single captivating ideal or topic of interest that can impel these individuals to sacrifice their personal lives in this manner, these sensitive people generally feel a strong affinity with the arts, and also with politics, both areas which allow scope for their great imaginative powers and ambitious urge to attain success.

Such qualities endow these people with the potential to make their mark on the world as far-seeing innovators, and when they are working toward fulfilling their innate promise, they are aided enormously by their vigor, their willingness to take a lone stand when necessary, their ability as gifted communicators to enlist the support of others, their capacity for logical thought and their outstanding tenacity.

VIRTUES: These people possess the prodigious ability to focus single-mindedly on achieving their ambitions, devoting their great powers of intellectual and physical energy, determination, and frequently also pragmatism, to their chosen mission. Dynamic and driven, their progress can be irresistible.

VICES: Although they can often make affectionate and enlivening partners, friends and parents, those born on this day have a pronounced tendency to take the support of their nearest and dearest for granted. When held in the grip of an alluring passion they may neglect their emotional requirements.

VERDICT: In order to inject a greater sense of equilibrium into their lives, it is vital that May 10 people should develop the empathetic feelings of which they are undoubtedly capable. Moreover, they should also recognize that their almost compulsive propensity to pursue their intellectual interests can engender great hurt in others.

On This Day

Famous Births: Claude de Lisle (1760); Augustin Jean Fresnel (1788); John Wilkes Booth (1838); Thomas Lipton (1850); Léon Gaumont (1864); Karl Barth (1886); Dimitri Tiomkin (1894); Fred Astaire (1899); David O. Selznick (1902); Arthur Marshall (1910); Dennis Thatcher (1915); Nancy Walker (1922); Gary Owens (1936); Taurean Blacque, Donovan and Maureen Lipman (1946); Sid Vicious (1957); Paul Hewson, "Bono" (1960).

Significant Events and Anniversaries: This day indicates dynamic action in the propagation of strongly held convictions, a tendency that is particularly manifested in the realm of warfare, and on this day English forces wrested Jamaica from Spain (1655); Sepoy troops in Meerat, India, mutinied against their British masters (1857); German Zeppelin airships bombed London for the first time during World War I (1915) and Luftwaffe bombers unleashed a devastating attack on the same city during World War II (1941). In a dramatic demonstration of their determination to eliminate "un-German" art forms, Nazi stormtroopers began burning "degenerate" literature in Germany (1933). May 10 furthermore highlights leadership potential, and on this day martial events diversely affected the lives of four noted individuals: the Confederate general "Stonewall" Jackson, who was killed by inadvertent "friendly fire" (1863) and the president of the Confederacy, Jefferson Davis, who was captured by Union troops at Irvinsville (1865), both during the American Civil War; Winston Churchill, who became the British prime minister in response to the demands imposed by World War II (1940); and Nazi politician Rudolf Hess, who parachuted into Scotland independently to negotiate a cessation of hostilities, and was subsequently incarcerated (1941).

Planetary Influences
Ruling planet: Venus.
Second decan: Personal planet is Mercury.

Sacred and Cultural Significance
In Madurai, India, the sacred marriage of Shiva to the goddess Meenakshi is celebrated; Tin Hau, Chinese goddess of the North Star, honored in Hong Kong.
Saints' day: Gordian and Epimachus (d. c.250); Conleth (d. c.520); Catald (7th to 8th century AD); Antoninus of Florence (1389–1459); John of Avila (1500–69).

The powerful Hindu god Shiva, known as the Lord of the Dance, is often depicted within a circle of flames. His marriage to Meenakshi is celebrated on May 10.

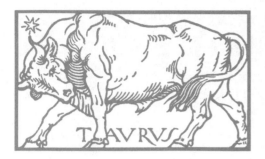

MAY 11

Planetary Influences
Ruling planet: Venus.
Third decan: Personal planet is Saturn.

Sacred and Cultural Significance
Saints' day: Credan (dates unknown);
Tudy (6th century AD); Comgall (d. c.601);
Fremund (d. 866); Maieul (906–94); Ignatius
of Laconi (1701–81).

*Perhaps the most prominent member of the
Surrealist movement, Salvador Dalí was an
outstandingly original thinker who possessed
a generous degree of May 11's energy and
independence. As a wood dragon, he was also
creative, volatile and attention-seeking.*

Although they may be exceptionally self-disciplined when they choose, those born on May 11 refuse to be constrained by others' narrow rules and regulations or ideas and ideals. Fiercely independent in both thought and deed, they are perhaps best characterized by their burning desire to discover the world's truths for themselves, an inherent compulsion that inevitably causes them to reject the mores of conventional beliefs and behavior patterns. Their questing and imaginative intellectual qualities are typically supplemented by outstanding powers of perception, methodical attention to detail, true originality and stubborn tenacity when investigating or defining concepts that especially fascinate them. And, although they are naturally attracted to abstract ideas and are therefore suited to academic or technical research, these are sensitive individuals, whose interest in every aspect of the human condition endows them with feelings of considerable empathy, which may impel them to pursue careers in the judiciary or politics.

In their interpersonal relationships, their humanitarian concern and appreciation of individuality makes them remarkably tolerant of behavior that others may regard as being extreme or eccentric. When also coupled with their inherent gifts of intuition, protectiveness and loyalty, they make gifted parents, who encourage the natural enthusiasm and inquisitiveness of their children are rarely authoritarian or judgemental. In addition, they appreciate that a stable domestic life provides the best background for their more radical propensities. Their professional relationships, however, may be less harmonious, since they have a tendency to alienate more conventional souls, who may feel threatened by their tendency to subvert or debunk society's norms.

VIRTUES: Imaginative, vigorous and possessed of great determination to seek out knowledge and new ideas for themselves, May 11 people are committed individualists who are blessed with the potential to blaze an innovatory trail through life, inspiring and informing others in the process.

VICES: Their pronounced independence of mind and profound dislike of following the herd may serve to isolate these people from others, thereby removing them from potentially diverse and beneficial societal influences and friendships.

VERDICT: In order to guard against the negative responses of others engendering feelings of profound disappointment, these people should develop a more realistic awareness of the effect that their sometimes radical ideas may have on those who are less enlightened, or simply more conservative.

On This Day
Famous Births: Baron Karl Friedrich von Münchhausen (1720); Ottmar Mergenthaler (1854); Joe "King" Oliver (1885); Irving Berlin (1888); Paul Nash (1889); Margaret Rutherford (1892); Martha Graham (1893); Salvador Dalí (1904); Phil Silvers (1912); Richard Feynman (1918); Denver Pyle (1920); Jackie Milburn (1924); Mort Sahl (1927); Louis Farrakhan (1933); Eric Burdon (1941); Ian Dury (1942); Gary Foley and Randy Quaid (1950).

Significant Events and Anniversaries: The propensity for independent action highlighted by May 11 promises great innovatory potential, and on this day there appeared in China what is believed to be the world's first printed book, the *Diamond Sutra* (868); the French liner S.S. *France*—then the world's longest—was officially launched (1960); and the groundbreaking, perennially popular musical *Cats*, by British composer Andrew Lloyd Webber, had its premiere (1981). Demonstrating a more destructive manifestation of this independent tendency, John Bellingham, a disgruntled bankrupt, shot dead the British prime minister, Spencer Perceval (1812). Appropriately, it was on this day that Siam changed its name to Muang Thai ("Land of the Free"), or Thailand (1939).

MAY 12

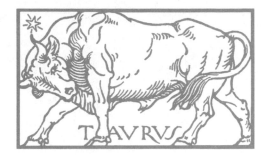

Those born on May 12 are valued by coworkers and family members alike for their dependability, for they have both a highly developed sense of responsibility and a somewhat protective desire to help those for whom they care by assuming their burdens. These are immensely capable individuals, who typically combine their urge to actively make progress with impressive intellectual gifts, including remarkable perspicacity, an unremitting ability for logical thought and unwavering tenacity. Because they are direct and guileless, they tend to speak their minds bluntly, a characteristic that is not always advisable, however. Their steadfastness of purpose and independent outlook often propels those born on this day into leadership positions, roles that, although they do not crave, they will rarely reject or fail to execute well, such is their determination to fulfill the trust that has been placed in them. With their wide range of interests, these individuals are well equipped to succeed in virtually any career that they choose, but their marked orientation toward others may encourage them to work in the caring professions, while their overall sensitivity may furthermore bestow upon them great artistic talent.

Those who do not know May 12 people well may be surprised to find that lurking behind the somewhat serious face that they present to the world is an apparently uncharacteristically adventurous and hedonistic streak, especially if they were also born in the Chinese year of the goat. For these are intellectually curious types, who are stimulated by contact with the different or unusual and enjoy new experiences and situations. They instinctively understand the importance of relaxation and, since they are gregarious individuals, like nothing better than to be hospitable to others and entertain them lavishly.

VIRTUES: Although they manifest somewhat introverted qualities, being methodical, quietly determined and deep-thinking individuals, those born on this day are also externally oriented, for they are largely geared toward supporting and assisting other people—a rare and potentially extremely effective conjunction.
VICES: Despite their wish to create a positive impression on others and to make friends rather than enemies, May 12 people may unwittingly sabotage their best efforts by failing to use diplomacy and tact when expressing their viewpoints, thereby unintentionally wounding others with the unvarnished—albeit usually justified—nature of their comments.
VERDICT: These people generally balance their personal and professional lives with extraordinary facility but, since they tend to invest as much energy and attention as possible in each activity they undertake, they should recognize that they may spread themselves too thinly and thereby risk suffering mental or physical exhaustion. They should learn to assess and sometimes refuse the demands made upon them by others.

On This Day

Famous Births: Lady Emma Hamilton (1765); Baron Justus von Liebig (1803); Edward Lear (1812); Florence Nightingale (1820); Dante Gabriel Rossetti (1828); Jules Massenet (1842); Gabriel Fauré (1845); Lincoln Ellsworth (1880); Wilfred Hyde-White (1903); Leslie Charteris and Katharine Hepburn (1907); Tony Hancock (1924); Yogi Berra (1925); Burt Bacharach (1929); Tom Snyder (1936); George Carlin (1937); Susan Hampshire (1942); Alan Ball (1945); Steve Winwood (1948); Emilio Estevez (1962).

Significant Events and Anniversaries: This day highlights a desire to provide practical assistance, as was reflected by the founding of the Alcoholics Anonymous (A.A.) organization in Akron, Ohio, by William Wilson (1935). Further manifestations of the urge to act as an instrument of guidance indicated by May 12 can be seen in the journalistic sphere by the publication of the first editions of two influential journals: the British *John Bull* (1906) and the Soviet *Pravda* (1912). Potential for success is promised by this day's tenacity in the cause of humanitarian aims, as was demonstrated when the Allied airlift to supply Berlin with provisions caused the Soviet Union to lift its blockade of the West German city (1949).

Planetary Influences
Ruling planet: Venus.
Third decan: Personal planet is Saturn.

Sacred and Cultural Significance
In Belgium, the annual Cat Parade is celebrated; Aranya Sashti, god of the woodlands, honored in India.
Saints' day: Nereus and Achilleus (2nd century AD); Pancras of Rome (d. 4th century AD); Ethelhard (d. 805).

On this day of practical and responsible progress in 1926, Britain's General Strike was resolved, an agreement that was widely celebrated, as seen in this view of the Guardsmen returning to their London base.

TAVRVS

Planetary Influences

Ruling planet: Venus.
Third decan: Personal planet is Saturn.

Sacred and Cultural Significance

Saint's day: Robert Bellarmine (1542–1621).

On May 13, 1933, Diego Rivera's recently completed mural in New York City's lavish Rockefeller Center was scraped off because the building's owner found another of Rivera's paintings, Man at Crossroads *(below), politically offensive. Rockefeller's impulsive, spontaneous decision was characteristic of this day.*

MAY 13

In comparison to those who find it something of a struggle to attain their ideals, those born on May 13 appear to breeze through life, effortlessly notching up success after success, charming others in the process. And indeed, these are undeniably gifted people who are able to harmonize their often contradictory personal qualities to produce a remarkably effective holistic package. Thus while their great intellectual curiosity stimulates them to think and act independently, their enormous sensitivity and intuitive perspicacity makes them extremely receptive to the people and circumstances that surround them. Similarly, while many May 13 people manifest a profoundly serious sense of purpose when engaged in tasks that truly absorb them, their inherent earnestness is balanced by their infectious and enthusiastic enjoyment of life. Although their multitude of interests may lead them to consider a variety of careers in the professional spheres, their artistic aptitude marks them out for particular success in this realm.

Their skills and people-oriented approach generally make these people valued team members—both at work and within the family—and they typically display a remarkable level of affection and loyalty to their nearest and dearest, whose lives they seek to enrich while simultaneously assuming a supportive and protective role. Yet because May 13 individuals, and especially the men born on this day, respond so immediately to the stimulus of an exciting challenge, they may occasionally appear to be somewhat flighty, preferring to investigate an alluring new passion rather than sticking doggedly to a less attractive, but perhaps more critical, option.

VIRTUES: Those people born on May 13 are both interested and interesting, their desire to thoroughly explore uncharted territory often leading them into new and important fields of interest. Their huge sensitivity is usually manifested within their interpersonal relationships, not only making them attractive to other people but also endowing them with concern for the welfare of others.

VICES: In some instances, these people allow their attention to be diverted from their routine day-to-day activities by what may appear to be a more enlivening alternative, a tendency that may ultimately lead to restless dissatisfaction rather than serene fulfillment.

VERDICT: In order to achieve more fulfillment in life and also gain more happiness, these people should moderate their predilection for pursuing what in retrospect will often turn out to be temporary fascinations. Before responding to such impulsive urges, they should stop to consider their motives carefully; grounding themselves within the stability of strong bonds of friendship and kinship will give them a greater sense of perspective.

On This Day

Famous Births: Maria Theresa, queen of Hungary and Bohemia (1717); Josephine Elizabeth Butler (1828); Alphonse Marie Léon Daudet (1840); Arthur Sullivan (1842); Ronald Ross (1857); Georges Braque (1882); Daphne du Maurier (1907); Joe Louis (1914); Bea Arthur (1926); Clive Barnes (1927); Harvey Keitel (1939); Bruce Chatwin (1940); Joe Brown and Richie Valens (1941); Tim Pigott-Smith (1946); Peter Gabriel and Stevie Wonder (1950); Dennis Rodman (1961).

Significant Events and Anniversaries: May 13 highlights a relish for adventure and experiencing new situations, as was reflected when English soldiers founded the first permanent English settlement in North America, at Jamestown, on the Virginian coast (1607), as well as when the first Australian team arrived in England for a cricket match with the host nation (1868). Impulsive behavior is indicated on this day, as when a lone Islamic gunman, Mehmet Ali Agca, shot and wounded Pope John Paul II in St. Peter's Square, Rome (1981).

MAY 14

✳ ✳

A lthough their enormous sensitivity bestows upon them the capacity to have deep feelings and compassion for those who are less fortunate, it is the realm of abstract ideas rather than of interpersonal relationships that really excites May 14 individuals. Thus while they may indeed be found devising strategies for alleviating global human suffering, it is the excitement engendered by the challenge that stimulates them, rather than the end result of their labors. Their marked—often extreme—powers of imagination instill in them an enthusiasm for exploring new concepts and techniques, a trait which is backed up extremely effectively by their great intellectual and intuitive perceptiveness, their steadfast commitment to the mastery of detail, and their obstinate refusal to concede defeat. Such qualities indicate particular success in the realm of science, for example in information technology, or in the social sciences, although they also have an innate talent for such artistic pursuits as music, drama, literature and painting.

Such an overriding commitment to the world of ideas is usually the mark of the introvert and, while those born on May 14 may indeed sometimes appear to be solitary and obsessive types, their interest and concern for their coworkers, friends, partners and relations, combined with their sense of humor and healthy appreciation of pleasure and beauty—especially if they were also born in the Chinese year of the rabbit—typically give them strong interpersonal roots that ground them in the real world. Their knack for problem-solving, dependability and kindly attitude frequently encourage others to seek their advice.

VIRTUES: Those born on May 14 are "nuts and bolts" individuals, whose passion for identifying the components of a situation or idea, and then patiently sifting through the whole gamut of possibilities in their quest to find the best method of proceeding, endows them with outstanding technical or academic expertise as well as the potential to attain outstanding success.
VICES: Their capacity to lose themselves entirely within their work carries the risk that those born on this day may inadvertently isolate themselves from people or circumstances that are not directly involved in their topic of interest. Their huge drive and capacity for overwhelming commitment furthermore make them prone to mental stress or physical exhaustion.
VERDICT: Despite an instinctive recognition of the importance of maintaining balance in all things, their intellectual curiosity and stubborn determination can lead them to forsake all else in the pursuit of a particularly irresistible and absorbing concept. This tendency heralds clear dangers in terms of their emotional and physical health, and is one that they should learn to temper by maintaining a better sense of perspective.

On This Day
Famous Births: Gabriel Daniel Fahrenheit (1686); Thomas Gainsborough (1727); Robert Owen and Thomas Wedgwood (1771); Claude Dornier (1884); Otto Klemperer (1885); Sidney Bechet (1897); Hastings Banda (1905); Eric Morecambe (1926); Lazlo Kovacs (1933); Sian Phillips (1934); Bobby Darin (1936); Chay Blyth (1940); George Lucas (1944); Season Hubley and Robert Zemeckis (1951); David Byrne (1952).

Significant Events and Anniversaries: This day indicates the potential obsessiveness that is inherent in the determined promotion of a belief, as was confirmed by the murder of the religiously tolerant King Henri IV of France by the Catholic fanatic François Ravaillac (1610), and the anti-government coup attempted by Sitivina Rambuka in Fiji (1987). The stubborn and active commitment that is a feature of this day augurs well for success, as is reflected by the many advances that occurred on May 14, including administering the first successful vaccination against smallpox by English physician Edward Jenner (1796); the establishment of the British "Home Guard," the Local Defence Volunteers, to protect against a possible German invasion during World War II (1940); the founding of the independent state of Israel, with Chaim Weizman as president and David Ben-Gurion as prime minister (1948); and the launching of the first U.S. space station, *Skylab I* (1973).

Planetary Influences
Ruling planet: Venus.
Third decan: Personal planet is Saturn.

Sacred and Cultural Significance
National day of Paraguay; in Norway, the Pagan Festival of the Midnight Sun is celebrated.
Saints' day: Matthias (1st century AD); Maria-Domenica Mazzarello (1837–81); Gemma Galgani (1878–1903).

On a day noted for strong commitment, the independent state of Israel was founded in the Jewish peoples' ancient spiritual homeland on May 14, 1948. Pictured below is Damascus Gate in Old Jerusalem.

Planetary Influences
Ruling planet: Venus.
Third decan: Personal planet is Saturn.

Sacred and Cultural Significance
Annual purification rite performed in ancient Rome.
Saints' day: Pachomius (d. 346); Dympna (7h century AD), patron saint of epileptics and the mentally ill; Bercthun (d. 733); Hallvard (d. 1043); Isidore the Farmer (c.1080–1130), patron saint of agricultural workers and Madrid, Spain.

Innovations in communication are starred by this day, which saw the first permanent airmail delivery service instituted in the eastern United States in 1918.

AIR MAIL
is Socially Correct

MAY 15

Those born on this day are often perceived by others as being rather dreamy individuals, who live in worlds of their own devising and therefore possess a somewhat otherworldly quality. And in many respects this somewhat superficial judgement is correct, for these are profoundly introspective beings, who not only have a near-irresistible urge to attain knowledge but, once they have accumulated sufficient information on subjects that excite their interest, to expand and develop it with unusual imagination and creativity. Thus while their mental agility and independence, their open mindedness toward mystical concepts and their tenacity of purpose endow them with innovative potential, their steady and methodical approach provides them with the concrete means with which to support and validate their visions. Underlying all their actions is their enormous sensitivity, a defining characteristic which, in their professional lives, may manifest itself in areas where it can be employed to effect humanitarian progress, or in the artistic sphere, where their work can be shared with, and inspire, others.

Despite their often solitary interests and *modi vivendi*, the sensitivity of May 15 people is so all-encompassing that it propels them toward interpersonal contact, and is often manifested in unusual levels of empathy and compassion toward others, especially those closest to them. Perhaps because they recognize that, in turn, their nearest and dearest understand them, respect their interests, and accept them as they are, they are typically fiercely devoted to long-standing friends and families and, if they are parents, particularly to their children. They are encouraged by the emotional support that they receive to share their talents with the wider world.

VIRTUES: These people are blessed with strong visionary powers, the intellectual ability to actively develop the abstract concepts that fuel their interest and the capacity to ultimately present the inspirational fruits of their mental endeavors to the less enlightened world. As well as being inward-looking, these sensitive individuals long to bring happiness and illumination to their fellow beings.
VICES: Such is the level of their self-reliance, of their tendency to immerse themselves within their own worlds of ideas and ideals, that those born on May 15 have an inevitable and marked propensity to cut themselves off from the distractions of day-to-day mundanities, even including communal and social responsibilities.
VERDICT: It is vital for reasons of emotional health that, while never suppressing their soaring and unique powers of thought, May 15 people venture farther into the real world, toughening up their sensibilities in the process. Participating more in group activities will give them a new and ultimately fulfilling dimension to their lives.

On This Day
Famous Births: Prince Clemens Metternich (1773); Frank Baum (1856); Pierre Curie (1859); Katherine Anne Porter (1890); Jimmy Wilde (1892); Joseph Cotten (1905); James Mason (1909); Eddy Arnold (1918); Anthony and Peter Shaffer (1926); Ted Dexter (1935); Anna Maria Alberghetti (1936); Trini Lopez (1937); Brian Eno (1948); George Brett and Mike Oldfield (1953); Lee Horsley (1955); Emmit Smith (1969).

Significant Events and Anniversaries: May 15 has the potential to transform dreams into reality, a conjunction which is reflected in a number of innovations whose anniversaries are marked by this day including: the patenting of the first machine gun, by Londoner James Puckle (1718); the opening of the first U.S. baseball stadium at Union Grounds, Brooklyn (1862); the instigation of the first enduring airmail delivery service, between New York and Washington, D.C. (1918); the introduction of the "flying-doctor" service by Dr. Vincent Welsh at Cloncurry, Queensland, Australia (1928); Spain hosting England for the first international soccer match, in Madrid (1929); the deployment of the first commercial air hostess, Ellen Church, for United Airlines (1930); the first recorded sale of nylon stockings in the U.S.A. (1940); and the detonation of Britain's first hydrogen bomb, on Christmas Island in the Indian Ocean (1957).

MAY 16

If only one word were to be used to sum up their personalities, the most apt would probably be "flamboyant," for although they themselves might not regard themselves as individualists and especially not in terms of their attitude toward the predilections and foibles of others, those born on May 16 typically blaze a highly idiosyncratic and dynamic trail through life. Indeed, in many respects those born on this day are larger-than-life characters, determined to impose their forceful wills upon people and circumstances and receive maximum possible attention and acclaim for their actions in the process. Despite these controlling and attention-seeking qualities that are such a vital part of their personal make-up, others thoroughly enjoy their company. Indeed, life is rarely dull when around them, for not only do they present awesome spectacles when in full flight, but their indomitable vigor and infectious *joie de vivre* draws others to them for the sense of fun—and sometimes danger—that they generate. Professionally, they will fare best when they can assume leadership or performing roles, and they are therefore especially well equipped for careers in such artistic fields as acting or music-making, in which their talents will be appreciated by their audiences.

The direct approach favored by these people is fueled by their strength of purpose and orientation toward success, which usually takes the form of personal ambition. While they are generally loyal and affectionate to those who unquestioningly support them, family members in particular, they may brush aside, or even trample over, those who appear to stand in their way. When impeded, they may express their frustration by means of spectacular outbursts of temper, a tendency which may, unless controlled, ultimately sabotage their success.

VIRTUES: May 16 people are fundamentally classic extroverts, who profess passionately held convictions and are driven by an irresistible urge to effect their cherished aims. Dynamic, tenacious and self-confident, they impress others with their courageous resolution.
VICES: Despite their often unconscious desire to receive the applause and adulation of others, those born on this day are prone to intimidate or even alienate those around them, not only because of their aggressive impatience with conflicting viewpoints, but also their propensity to fly into uninhibited furies when thwarted. Unless stemmed, this trait can lead them to become overwhelmingly egotistical and uncompromisingly intolerant.
VERDICT: In all areas of their lives, it is crucial that these people adopt a more considered and disciplined approach, both to themselves and others. Periods of honest introspection will help them to understand their inner selves better and give them greater insight into the best ways of achieving their ambitions. Cultivating self-discipline will additionally save them from misdirecting their energy and efforts.

On This Day

Famous Births: Louis Vauquelin (1763); William Seward (1801); David Hughes (1831); Richard Tauber (1891); H. E. Bates and Henry Fonda (1905); Studs Terkel (1912); Woody Herman (1913); Liberace (1919); Billy Martin (1928); Roy Hudd (1936); Pierce Brosnan (1953); Olga Korbut, Hazel O'Connor and Debra Winger (1955); Janet Jackson (1966); Tracey Gold (1969); Tori Spelling (1973).

Significant Events and Anniversaries: The compulsion to actively promote deeply held beliefs that is indicated by this day has a clear parallel in warfare, and on May 16, during the Napoleonic Wars, General Beresford's British forces inflicted a decisive defeat on Marshal Soult's French Army at the Battle of Albuera in Spain (1811). The courage and determination that are twin features of this day augur well for innovation, as was reflected in the achievement of Japan's mountaineer Junko Takei, on becoming the first woman to climb Mount Everest (1975), and in the attainment of the medical team at Britain's Brook Hospital, who carried out the first successful hole-in-the-heart operation (1989) on this day. The potential acclaim for artistic pursuits that is highlighted by this day was mirrored in the movie world by the holding of the first Academy Award ceremony in the U.S.A. (1929).

Planetary Influences
Ruling planet: Venus.
Third decan: Personal planet is Saturn.

Sacred and Cultural Significance
Saints' day: Peregrine of Auxerre (d. c.261); Brendan the Navigator (c.486–c.575); Carantoc (6th/7th century AD), patron of Crantock, Cornwall, Llangranog and Carhampton, Somerset, England; Simon Stock (d. 1265); John of Nepomuk (c.1345–93), patron saint of bridgebuilders.

On this day in 1990, a Japanese businessman paid a record-setting price at auction for Vincent van Gogh's Portrait of Dr. Gachet *(1890). This ostentatious action reflects the flamboyant qualities of May 16, as well as the artistic appreciation bestowed by the ruling planet, Venus.*

TAVRVS

Planetary Influences
Ruling planet: Venus.
Third decan: Personal planet is Saturn.

Sacred and Cultural Significance
National Day of Norway; in the Philippines, a three-day Neo-Pagan fertility ritual honoring Santa Clara begins.
Saints' day: Madron (6th century AD); Paschal Baylon (1540–92).

Born on May 17, 1900, Ayatollah Khomeini, the architect of Iran's "Islamic Revolution," possessed in generous measure the defining characteristics predicted by his birthdate: driving ambition, zeal and a sense of certainty in the rightness of his convictions. As a metal rat, his style was ruthless and intolerant, but his achievement in reforming his nation and instilling in its citizens strict religious observance marked him as an extraordinary spiritual and political leader.

MAY 17

✳✳✳✳✳✳✳✳✳✳✳✳✳✳✳✳✳✳✳✳✳✳✳✳✳✳✳✳✳✳✳✳✳✳✳✳✳

Those born on May 17 are fueled by their fierce wish to see their ambitions realized: although these may involve personal betterment, they are above all concerned with the improvement of the lot of humanity as a whole. For these are not only perceptive people whose clear-sightedness helps them to readily identify faults and failings, but they are also individuals whose deep, people-oriented sensitivity bestows upon them the urge to work toward improving the lives of those who are less fortunate than themselves. Yet despite their prodigious energy (which they typically devote with single-minded zeal toward the achievement of their ideals), their capacity for original and logical thought, and their obstinate refusal to be diverted from their missions, many May 17 people seem doomed to failure. It may be that they have a tendency to set their sights too high, possibly recognizing that their aims are inherently unfeasible but nevertheless assuming that they can overcome any obstacles in their path through sheer determination and force of will.

Once they have developed a greater sense of realism, these people will thrive in those professions where their great practical skills and intellectual idealism can find best expression. The artistic sphere promises special potential for success, for those born on this day have a highly developed sense of the aesthetic, as well as enormous creativity, talents that are even more pronounced if they were also born in the Chinese year of the goat. They may also find satisfaction in the world of finance or in tourism, where they can cater for the enjoyment of others. Within their personal relationships, these people typically show great commitment to those closest to them, perhaps in inherent recognition of the emotional rewards that result from a stable and supportive domestic life.

VIRTUES: Caring and sensitive toward others, ambitious and desirous of achieving progress, the motivations of those born on this day are often geared toward improving human welfare, a positive predilection that is supported by their organizational and practical talents.
VICES: Their natural sense of justice can lead these people to condemn behavior that does not accord with their ideals and to pronounce their displeasure in unambiguous terms; this is an overly judgemental tendency that frequently augurs badly for the attainment of their goals.
VERDICT: Developing a more pragmatic—and in certain instances more tolerant—approach will be of considerable assistance to May 17 people both in pursuing their aims and realizing a greater sense of equilibrium: this strategy will lessen the possibility of emotional disappointment and open up for them new areas of potential that might otherwise remain closed.

On This Day
Famous Births: Edward Jenner (1749); Joseph Norman Lockyer (1836); Timothy Michael Healy (1855); Erik Alfred Lesley Satie (1866); Ayatollah Ruhollah Khomeini (1900); Jean Gabin (1906); Maureen O'Sullivan (1911); Robert Maugham (1916); Märta Birgit Nilsson (1918); Dennis Brain (1921); Dennis Christopher George Potter (1935); Dennis Hopper (1936); "Sugar" Ray Leonard and Bob Saget (1956); Jordan Knight (1970).

Significant Events and Anniversaries: This day highlights an active desire to bring enlightenment that is supported by strong organizational skills, qualities that are mirrored in the tourism industry; it is therefore appropriate that May 17 marks the anniversary of the start of the first vacation package run by Thomas Cook, from London to Paris (1861). The determination of this day to realize a cherished aim is reflected in the achievement of Irishman Tom McClean, who became the first person to row across the Atlantic single-handedly when he arrived in Blacksod Bay, Ireland, from Newfoundland (1969). The committed promotion of a collective ideal indicated by this day is mirrored in martial undertakings, as was illustrated when General Baden-Powell's British forces relieved their besieged compatriots at Mafeking, in southern Africa, during the Boer War (1900), and when the British R.A.F. 617 Squadron, led by Wing Commander Guy Gibson, undertook its daring "Dam Busters" raid on German dams at Mohne, Eder and Sorpe during World War II (1943).

MAY 18

Those born on May 18 favor a straightforward approach in everything that they do, possessed as they are by a driving urge to push onward, ever onward, rather than prevaricating or even stagnating. Their strong compulsion for direct action does not, however, mean that these individuals are not profound thinkers: to the contrary, they are blessed with an outstanding intellectual ability to cut incisively to the heart of an issue and then, employing their remarkable analytical powers, to build up their own, often extremely effective, strategy with which to achieve their aims. And, because these are sensitive types who cannot bear to see injustice being done, and who are furthermore endowed with a keen sense of natural justice, their energies will often be directed toward the alleviation of suffering or the improvement of social systems. Indeed, when convinced of their moral veracity in the face of a perceived abuse of power, those born on May 18 will not flinch from taking a brave stance and tenaciously persevering with their mission until the challenge has been overcome. Others admire their strength of intent and ability to inspire, and will thus frequently elevate them to positions of responsibility, roles which they will discharge with dedication.

Individuals born on this day will flourish in any career in which they can attain tangible progress, but, given their latent humanitarian and often philosophical leanings, they will find special satisfaction when they can provide guidance to others. Despite their predilection for independence of thought and action, these are empathetic people who would rather not have to act in isolation, preferring instead to work as part of a harmonious and committed team, this being especially true in the case of women born on this day. Indeed, in both their professional and personal liaisons they typically exhibit great charm, consideration and loyalty, qualities that make them valued coworkers, friends and family members.

VIRTUES: The dynamic force that results from their vigor and steadfastness, their methodical organizational talents and their considerable perspicacity and compassion combine to make May 18 people committed humanitarians and energetic campaigners for progress.
VICES: These people tend to form unshakable convictions, which they will defend and seek to advance at all costs. One of the negative consequences of such intellectual obstinacy is that they may fail to recognize the respective merit of conflicting viewpoints.
VERDICT: Those born on this day have two innate characteristics that they would be well advised to recognize and address: their paradoxical propensity to become intolerant of those who express different opinions, despite their otherwise fierce defense of victims of intolerance; and their predilection to wholeheartedly devote their energies to others. The latter is a laudable tendency but one which may ultimately have a detrimental effect on their own emotional and physical well-being.

On This Day

Famous Births: Lionel Lukin (1742); William Steinitz (1836); Czar Nicholas II of Russia (1868); Bertrand Russell (1872); Walter Gropius (1883); Frank Capra (1897); Fred Perry (1909); Richard Brooks and Perry Como (1912); Charles Trenet (1913); Boris Christoff and Margot Fonteyn (1919); Pope John Paul II (1920); Pernell Roberts (1930); Robert Morse (1931); Dwayne Hickman (1934); Nobby Stiles (1942); Reggie Jackson (1946).

Significant Events and Anniversaries: The combined qualities of this day promise outstanding leadership potential, as was evidenced when Napoleon Bonaparte was declared Emperor of France (1804). May 18's determination to achieve progress has been manifested in a variety of ways, for example in the technical field, when the Vickers Valiant, the British four-engined jet bomber, made its first flight (1951), as well as in the sporting realm, when the British motor-racing driver Graham Hill won his fifth Monaco Grand Prix (1969). The justice that is indicated by this day was mirrored in the award of $10.5 million to Karen Silkwood by the U.S. government in compensation for the contamination that she suffered while working in a nuclear plant (1979).

Planetary Influences
Ruling planets: Venus and Mercury.
Third decan: Personal planet is Saturn.
Second cusp: Taurus with Gemini tendencies.

Sacred and Cultural Significance
The Feast of Twins is held in Nigeria.
Saints' day: John I (d. 526); Elgiva (10th century AD).

On this dynamic, forward-focused day in 1642, the French-Canadian city of Montreal was founded. Pictured below is a nineteenth-century view of the city's Windsor Street.

TAVRVS

Planetary Influences
Ruling planets: Venus and Mercury.
Third decan: Personal planet is Saturn.
Second cusp: Taurus with Gemini tendencies.

Sacred and Cultural Significance
Saints' day: Pudentiana (1st/2nd century AD); Dunstan (909–88), patron saint of blacksmiths, the blind and goldsmiths; Peter Celestine (1215–96); Ivo of Brittany (c.1235–1303), patron saint of judges and lawyers.

The dynamic, uncompromising activist and leader Malcolm X possessed the strong convictions and profound sense of natural justice that characterize May 19 people. As a fire tiger, his passion, eloquence and magnetism were reinforced—and sometimes outweighed the tact that can be notable in May 19 people.

MAY 19

★★★★★★★★★★★★★★★★★★★★★★★★★★★★★★★★★★★★★★★

The steadfast kindness and dependability of those born on this day, as well as their aura of capability and efficiency, marks them out as people to whom others turn for support and encouragement in times of difficulty. When asked to advise upon problems, they typically muster their prodigiously practical talents to devise realistic and yet positive solutions and then devote their energies wholeheartedly toward implementation. And, although they harbor extremely strong convictions, which are generally informed by their sense of natural justice, they pass on their opinions to others with a judicious use of tact, tailoring the manner in which they impart their ideas without ever compromising the essence of their beliefs. Such pragmatic characteristics, when combined with their humanitarian concern and idealism, suits those born on May 19 to a number of people-oriented careers, including politics, teaching and the caring professions, and, indeed, they will usually only find true satisfaction in work involving interpersonal contact.

These individuals will similarly assume a central role in their private lives, acting as rocks of stability and reliability, especially if they are also women, around which their more flighty friends and relations flit back and forth, always returning for support, however, to their grounding May 19 linchpin. Two dangers are thus presented: that these people's sense of responsibility, protective urge and commitment to those nearest to them may sometimes cause them to suppress their own needs and desires in the interests of others; and that unless they are also able to pursue their personal interests their frustrated desire for independence may find a somewhat destructive outlet in the control of those around them.

VIRTUES: May 19 individuals manifest great concern for the well-being of others, a propensity which may be expressed either within the limited circle of the family, or toward humanity as a whole. The conjunction of their sensitivity and empathy, combined with their calm and sensible approach to life's challenges, is particularly efficacious.
VICES: If taken to its extreme, their otherwise laudable orientation toward serving the needs of others can have potentially negative consequences, such as physical and mental exhaustion. More dangerously, a simmering—if unconscious—resentment may arise when others, confident of their support, sometimes unthinkingly place burdens upon them.
VERDICT: It is vital that those born on this day do not sacrifice their personal ambitions on the altar of altruism, a propensity that is conditioned by their reluctance to turn away those in need, and one which may ultimately prove pernicious. Ensuring that they always make time for their own interests will give them a healthier emotional equilibrium and help to make their efforts more effective.

On This Day
Famous Births: Johann Gottlieb Fichte (1762); Nellie Melba (1861); Nancy Astor and William Waldorf Astor (1879); Albert Richardson (1880); Ho Chi Minh (1890); Michael Balcon (1896); Sandy Wilson (1924); Malcolm X (1925); Edward de Bono (1933); David Hartman (1935); Nora Ephron (1941); Pete Townshend (1945); Grace Jones (1952); Victoria Wood (1953).

Significant Events and Anniversaries: A marked feature of May 19 is the determined propagation of deeply held beliefs, a quality that can be manifested in war, and on this day French forces under the Duc d'Enghien won a notable victory in the Ardennes against allegedly "invincible" Spanish forces at the Battle of Rocroi (1643). The natural justice that is heralded by this day can be positively expressed by the rewarding of noble actions, as when Napoleon announced the institution of the *Légion d'honneur,* with which to honor outstanding instances of civil and military deeds (1802), or by penitential punishment, as when the Italian actress Sophia Loren began her month-long sentence in prison in Naples for tax evasion (1982). The emotional repression that is inherent in this day was dramatically paralleled in a natural disaster that occurred in the U.S.A., when after being quiescent since 1857, Mount St. Helens volcano, Washington, erupted, resulting in the deaths of eight people (1980).

MAY 20

The apparently limitless energy of those born on May 20, and their appetite for savoring new intellectual or sensory experiences, arouses both awe and exhaustion in others. The awe is inspired by the variety of interests that fascinate them, and the exhaustion by the relentless pace with which they seek out and explore novel ideas and situations. Yet despite the speed with which they move from subject to subject, from place to place, or from person to person, the knowledge that they gain is rarely superficial, for their quick wits and intuitive capability to absorb the essential elements of a concept enable them to process the information thus garnered into a coherent and remarkably accurate précis of the prevailing state of affairs. Moreover, when they encounter an area that truly absorbs them, and the humanitarian, philosophical or artistic spheres are especially propitious for those born on this day, they manifest a remarkably highly developed capacity for detailed investigation and a single-minded tenacity for its development and implementation.

Despite their apparently ceaseless quest for stimulation, these people are typically steadfast, supportive and loyal in their personal relationships, although they may initially find it hard to commit themselves to a life partner. Not only is the welfare and happiness of their nearest and dearest—particularly their children, if they are parents—of paramount importance to these caring individuals, but they are furthermore blessed with an endearing *joie de vivre*, which has an enlivening effect on those around them. In return, the ties that they form with their long-standing friends and family members provide a grounding and supportive framework from which to launch themselves on their voyages of discovery.

VIRTUES: Their intellectual curiosity makes these individuals both interested and interesting. They combine their somewhat mercurial tendencies with a solidly logical and practical approach, as well as a profound appreciation of the importance of forming and nurturing strong emotional bonds.
VICES: There is a risk that unless they are able to cultivate a rigorous awareness both of those priorities that are truly important and their own needs for self-discipline and restraint, their predilection for seeking out new and exciting experiences will lead them into random and inconstant behavior patterns, ultimately causing them to feel dissatisfied.
VERDICT: Although these people generally understand the importance of maintaining balance in every area of their lives, they should be aware of, and moderate, their propensity to pursue too many fascinating ideas simultaneously, otherwise they may spread themselves too thinly.

On This Day
Famous Births: Henry Percy (Harry Hotspur) (1364); Hieronymous Fabricius (1537); William Thornton (1759); Honoré de Balzac (1799); John Stuart Mill (1806); William George Fargo (1818); Emile Berliner (1851); Wladyslaw Sikorski (1881); Reginald Mitchell (1895); Margery Allingham (1904); James Stewart (1908); Moshe Dayan (1915); Stan Mikita (1940); Joe Cocker (1944); Cher (1946); Bronson Pinchot (1959).

Significant Events and Anniversaries: Inherent in this day is a predilection for adventure and a determined desire to experience new situations, characteristics that were exemplified on this day by the Portuguese navigator Vasco da Gama, who achieved his ambition of discovering a sea route from Portugal to India when he landed at Calicut (1498), and by U.S. aviator Charles Lindbergh, who set off from New York in his monoplane *Spirit of St. Louis* to fly solo across the Atlantic (1927). Intellectual innovation, especially in the artistic realm, is also indicated, and on this day, Norwegian playwright Henrik Ibsen's seminal play *Ghosts* had its premier (1895). The daring willingness to innovate that is highlighted by this day was mirrored in the realm of warfare, when Crete was invaded by German paratroopers during World War II (1941) and when the first hydrogen bomb was tested over Bikini Atoll by U.S. researchers (1956).

Planetary Influences
Ruling planets: Venus and Mercury.
Third decan: Personal planet is Saturn.
Second cusp: Taurus with Gemini tendencies.

Sacred and Cultural Significance
Plynteria celebrated in ancient Greece in honor of Athena.
Saints' day: Ethelbert of East Anglia (d. 794); Bernardino of Siena (1380–1444), patron saint of advertisers, preachers and weavers.

Amelia Earhart arrived in Londonderry, Ireland, on May 20, 1932, to become the first woman to have completed a solo transatlantic flight. Her remarkable 2,206-mile journey, which originated in Newfoundland and lasted for 13 hours, 30 minutes, marked the fifth anniversary of the departure of Charles Lindbergh's famous solo transatlantic flight—a fact that underlines the pioneering, adventurous nature of this day.

GEMINI

May 21 to June 21

Ruling planet: Mercury   **Element**: Mutable air
Symbol: Twins   **Polarity**: Positive (masculine)
Physical correspondence: The lungs, shoulders, arms and hands
Stones: Beryl, garnet, citrine, amber, agate
Flowers: Verbena, balm, tansy, yarrow, orchid, myrtle
Colors: Red, yellow, orange

The constellation of Gemini comprises the stars Castor and Pollux, and these brothers have popularly become associated with the zodiacal sign. The twin analogy is common to most traditions, though not all the characters are male, or even siblings. The ancient Egyptians, for example, envisaged the Gemini couple as a man and woman, while in Hindu belief the pair are lovers known as Maithuna. It was probably the Babylonian astrologers (who named Gemini Mastabagalgal or "the great twins") who first regarded the stellar duo as androgynous beings, a concept adopted by the Persians and Greeks, who named the sign Dopatkar and Didumoi ("twins") respectively. The ancient Greeks told of the seduction of Leda by Zeus, who transformed himself into a swan for the purpose; Leda laid two eggs, one containing her children by her mortal husband Tyndareos, Kastor (Castor) and Clytemnestra, and the other her immortal offspring, Polydeuces (Pollux) and Helen. Castor was killed, and Pollux mourned his brother's death so deeply that Zeus raised his dead twin to immortality. While the myth of Castor and Pollux has come to prevail, it was also believed that the Gemini twins represented Romulus and Remus, who were nursed by the Sabine wolf and who later founded Rome.

The primary characteristic associated with Gemini is duality, symbolically represented by the opposition of masculinity and femininity, or mortality and divinity. This ambivalence, as well as its potential reconciliation and synthesis, is compounded by Gemini's planetary ruler, Mercury (the Roman name for the Greek messenger god, Hermes), who, in various traditions was a hermaphroditic deity. As well as being blessed with mercurial minds and outstanding powers of communication, those born under this sign are intellectually diverse but occasionally indecisive and impulsive, torn as they sometimes are between conflicting viewpoints. The element of air confers the qualities of versatility and idealism, but also a potential lack of direction and restlessness.

MAY 21

In many respects, those born on this day can be characterized by their total commitment to whatever it is that excites their devotion and inspiration, be it their families, their hobbies, or their work. Blessed with tremendous physical and intellectual energy and never known to do things by halves, these dynamic individuals typically throw themselves into the pursuit of their interests and ideological aims with boundless enthusiasm and optimism, tenaciously investigating, developing and implementing until they have achieved their purpose. Since they have the potential to be stubborn in the extreme, they may sometimes be regarded by others as obsessive and obstinate, yet because they are deeply practical and furthermore possess an ingenious turn of mind, their eventual success will often prove their doubters wrong. Their visionary and pragmatic tendencies augur particularly well for finance-related professions—as well as the more unusual realm of technical invention—but their great sensitivity also bestows upon May 21 people enormous aptitude for humanitarian work and a wide range of artistic endeavors.

Although they may cut themselves off from society when engaging in what they may perceive to be their vocational labors, these people by no means prefer solitary lifestyles. Not only are they interested in other individuals, and experience great concern for their welfare, but they are gregarious and sensual types, who enjoy relaxing with friends and family members and ensuring that everyone has a good time. One disadvantage of their generally guileless and affectionate approach toward others, however, is that they run the risk that are more manipulative people may take advantage of them.

VIRTUES: These vigorous individuals have a strong propensity to immerse themselves single-mindedly in their chosen area of interest, concentrating their entire attention on making progress and, in so doing, displaying their pronounced talents of intellectual clarity and determination. Although they are geared toward achievement, they still manage to remain caring within their personal relationships.

VICES: Those born on this day possess strongly held convictions and ideals, as well as the courage to profess them, undaunted by any criticism that they might thereby incur. They therefore run the risk of not only imposing a state of voluntary isolation upon themselves, but also becoming overly rigid in their beliefs and behavior.

VERDICT: The considerable drive and dedication of May 21 people, which may be manifested in many ways, may leave them with little opportunity to indulge in quiet periods of introspection. It is important that they should periodically take time not only to recharge their mental and physical batteries, but also to take stock of themselves as regards their motivations, opinions and actions, as well as their interpersonal relationships.

On This Day

Famous Births: Albrecht Dürer (1471); King Philip II of Spain (1527); Alexander Pope (1688); Joseph Fouché, duc d'Otranto (1759); Elizabeth Fry (1780); Henri Rousseau, "Le Douanier" (1844); Willem Einthoven (1860); Claude Auchinleck (1884); "Fats" Waller (1904); Peter Hurkos (1911); Harold Robbins (1916); Raymond Burr and Dennis Day (1917); Andrei Sakharov (1921); Peggy Cass (1924); Malcolm Fraser (1930); Mary Robinson (1944); Gwydion Pendderwen (1946); Mr. T (Lawrence Tero) (1952).

Significant Events and Anniversaries: May 21 highlights a conjunction of curiosity and tenacity, qualities that are reflected in the realm of adventure and can be seen in the achievements on this day of two pioneering individuals: the navigator Joao de Nova, who discovered the Atlantic island of St. Helena (1502); and U.S. aviator Charles Lindbergh, who became the first person to complete a nonstop flight across the Atlantic single-handedly when he landed the *Spirit of St. Louis* in France (1927). The firmly held convictions inherent in this day can result in violent confrontation, as was illustrated when the Indian premier Rajiv Gandhi was assassinated by a Tamil separatist adherent (1991).

Planetary Influences
Ruling planets: Mercury and Venus.
First decan: Personal planet is Mercury.
First cusp: Gemini with Taurean tendencies.

Sacred and Cultural Significance
Saints' day: Collen (dates unknown); Godric (c.1069–1170); Andrew Bobola (1591–1657).

On this day of sheer determination, details and ordinary caution are sometimes overlooked. Below, the Art Nouveau landmark L'Innovation, *a Brussels department store designed by Victor Horta, was destroyed on May 21, 1967, in a disastrous fire that claimed 322 lives.*

Planetary Influences
Ruling planets: Mercury and Venus.
First decan: Personal planet is Mercury.
First cusp: Gemini with Taurean tendencies.

Sacred and Cultural Significance
Saints' day: Helen of Carnarvon (4th century AD); Rita of Cascia (1377–1447), patron saint of desperate causes and unhappily married women.

MAY 22

Inherent in the behavior of those born on May 22 is an apparently paradoxical tendency to concentrate on one specific area of interest in meticulous detail, while flitting from fascination to fascination in an apparently superficial manner. Yet this dual propensity is not really so contradictory when one considers that these individuals have a profound urge to search for knowledge and thereby gain greater understanding. This compulsion encompasses their tendency to gather a minutiae of information on subjects that truly arrest their attention and, when these are exhausted, to renew their quest for new areas of enlightenment. Indeed, their twin capacity to devote their energies single-mindedly to the thorough exploration of a concept, as well as their abhorrence of intellectual stagnation, is an unusual and potentially extremely fulfilling combination. In addition to the artistic and scientific spheres, these people will find satisfaction in working in such arts-related business activities as journalism and advertising, as well as politics.

Perhaps the key to what exactly it is that motivates those born on May 22 is their desire to work for the improvement of humanity, be it by acting as inspirational innovators or—more pertinently—by imparting the truths that they have learned in their own quests for illumination to guide the beliefs and actions of others. Whether within their professional or domestic relationships, these individuals effortlessly assume a leadership and mentoring role. Although this tendency makes them wise and effective parents and friends, it may also cause them to become overly controlling. In either event, their care and concern for their loved ones is never in doubt.

VIRTUES: Those born on May 22 combine within their personalities outstanding capacities for intellectual inquisitiveness and profound analytical thought, characteristics which give them the potential to pioneer new, but soundly researched, ideas. Their deeply empathetic feelings toward others endow them with a strong protective urge, manifested in the desire to set friends and family members on the correct path through life.
VICES: The combination of their polymathic tendencies, the firm convictions that result from their studies and observations, and their desire to use their talents and knowledge in helping others can lead these people to seek to control—even manipulate or dominate—the lives of those around them.
VERDICT: Although they recognize intuitively the importance of balance within their lives, May 22 people may inadvertently upset their emotional equilibrium if they become either obsessive or intellectually restless. They should therefore acknowledge and seek to control their potential for extreme behavior, as well as allowing others to learn their own lessons.

The Wright brothers' innovative airplane, developed over many years of dedicated work and commitment to a seemingly impossible dream, was finally patented on this day in 1908. May 22 is a day on which long-cherished ideals have often come to fruition.

On This Day
Famous Births: William Sturgeon (1783); Richard Wagner (1813); Arthur Conan Doyle (1859); Daniel Malan (1874); Ernest Oppenheimer (1880); Laurence Olivier and Georges Remi (Hergé) (1907); Charles Aznavour (1924); Kenny Ball (1931); Peter Nero (1934); Richard Benjamin and Susan Strasberg (1938); Michael Sarrazin (1940); Paul Winfield (1941); Betty Williams (1943); George Best (1946).

Significant Events and Anniversaries: This day indicates the twin tendencies of adventurousness and careful research, both of which are manifested by various events that occurred on this day, including: the embarkation of the Scottish navigator Mungo Park on his first voyage of discovery to Africa (1795); the patenting of the Wright brothers' airplane (1908); and the first official visit of a U.S. president, Richard Nixon, to the Soviet Union (1972). Twelve months later, to the day, Nixon admitted his role in the Watergate scandal (1973). The urge to implement ideals that is a feature of this day can ultimately result in conflict, as was reflected when Lancastrian forces defeated the Yorkists at St. Albans during the English War of the Roses (1455), and when French and Austrian armies clashed at the Battle of Aspern-Essling (1809).

MAY 23

The vibrancy, enthusiastic outlook and great personal charm exuded by those born on May 23 make them popular and magnetic characters who seem to effortlessly draw others to them, inspiring affection and admiration in equal measure. A further potent ingredient that adds to their overall appeal is their orientation toward other people, a leaning inspired by their empathy, their genuine concern for the well-being of others, their natural gregariousness and, to some extent, their desire for approval. Yet it is not only other individuals that excite the interest of these intellectually inquisitive people, for their insatiable curiosity instills in them the urge to discover as much as they can of life's mysteries, and furthermore to pit their skills against any challenges that they encounter. They typically combine their sharp wits with highly imaginative minds, as well as a redoubtable talent for practical action, a hands-on approach that is particularly marked if they were also born in the Chinese year of the goat.

Their humanitarian bias, artistic sensibilities, acute intellectual powers, and urge to effect progress, equip them for a variety of careers, including those within the caring professions, the performing arts and also diplomacy, for May 23 people are gifted communicators. Whatever career they choose to pursue, however, they will usually only flourish if their work involves significant interpersonal contact. Similarly, they will usually wish to be actively involved in the lives of those closest to them—a predilection that is very pronounced in the women born on this day—and will have the outstanding ability both to enliven and provide close support to their personal relationships. They should, however, temper a certain compulsion to behave impulsively without having fully thought through the implications of their actions.

VIRTUES: Those born on this day are blessed with a rare combination of intellectual incisiveness and solidly practical capabilities, a conjunction that is auspicious in terms of achieving their aims. They furthermore augment these talents with a genuine concern for others, and a deeply felt urge to place their prodigious energy at the service of other people.
VICES: There are two main characteristics that these individuals must regulate if they are not to become extreme: the first is their tendency to flit impulsively from subject to subject without exploring any in sufficient depth; the second is their propensity to involve themselves in the affairs of others, which may be perceived as being overly controlling.
VERDICT: In order to gain maximum self-fulfillment in all areas of their lives, these people should occasionally take time out from their activities to indulge in brief periods of introspection. In so doing so, they should not only honestly examine the motivations that underlie their behavior toward others, but they should also strive to identify and focus on what it is that they truly desire in life.

On This Day

Famous Births: Carolus Linnaeus (1707); Franz Mesmer (1734); Thomas Hood (1799); Otto Lilienthal (1848); Douglas Fairbanks, Sr. (1883); Libby Holman (1906); Scatman Crothers and Artie Shaw (1910); Denis Compton (1918); Helen O'Connell (1920); Humphrey Lyttleton (1921); Rosemary Clooney and Nigel Davenport (1928); Joan Collins (1933); Richard Moog (1934); John Newcombe (1944); Anatoli Karpov (1951); Marvin Hagler (1952).

Significant Events and Anniversaries: Implicit in this day is a tendency to act independently without considering any inherent risks or, if these have been recognized, dismissing them, a propensity that may demand the ultimate price, and on this day the Dominican monk and prime mover of Florence's Democratic Party, Girolamo Savonarola, was executed for heresy (1498); the Scottish pirate William Kidd was hanged (1701); Gaetano Brecci, the anarchist who murdered of King Umberto I of Italy, took his own life (1901); the notorious U.S. bank robbers Bonnie Parker and Clyde Barrow were ambushed and killed by police in Louisiana (1934); Gestapo boss Heinrich Himmler committed suicide when in British military custody (1945); and Nazi fugitive Adolf Eichmann was flown from Argentina to Israel to stand trial for war crimes (1960).

Planetary Influences
Ruling planets: Mercury and Venus.
First decan: Personal planet is Mercury.
First cusp: Gemini with Taurean tendencies.

Sacred and Cultural Significance
In ancient Rome, the sacred rose festival Rosalia, which honors Flora and Venus.
Saints' day: Montanus and Lucius (d. 259); William of Rochester (d. 1201); translation of Alexander Nevski (1220–63).

The Roman goddess of Spring, Flora (pictured below holding a bouquet of roses), was honored on May 23 in the ancient Roman festival of roses, Rosalia. The rose was an attribute of Venus, the goddess of love and beauty, who was also honored in the festival.

GEMINI

Planetary Influences
Ruling planet: Mercury.
First decan: Personal planet is Mercury.

Sacred and Cultural Significance
Sacred Furrow Day, an annual harvest ritual in Cambodia; in ancient Greece, the birthday of Artemis.
Saints' day: David of Scotland (c.1085–1153).

A New York City landmark, the Brooklyn Bridge was opened on this day in 1833, linking the increasingly popular residential neighborhood of Brooklyn, Long Island, with Manhattan Island. May 24 is a day when communications are favored.

MAY 24

✦✦✦✦✦✦✦✦✦✦✦✦✦✦✦✦✦✦✦✦✦✦✦✦✦✦✦✦✦✦✦✦✦✦✦✦✦✦✦

In many ways, the people born on May 24 can be compared to catalysts, for they have a gift for making things happen to others without being in any way affected themselves, whether this be done by changing the opinions of those around them or by spurring them into action. Because they are blessed with incisive powers of thought and analysis, those born on this day typically approach a problem by first examining the diversity of issues associated with it, and then honing in on one specific area in which real improvements can be made. Indeed, little stimulates these individuals more than an intellectual challenge to which they can apply their considerable energy and talents; once their roving minds have settled on a subject that excites their interest, they will commit themselves to its development with great resourcefulness. These people furthermore possess the facility to communicate their ideas, apparently effortlessly, both verbally and in writing, giving them the ability to persuade and inspire others. Such loquacious and people-oriented qualities mark them out for careers as salespeople, politicians, teachers, or artists and performers.

Although it is the realm of abstract concepts that truly fascinates them, May 24 individuals are not content to lead solitary, contemplative lives, preferring instead to share their ideas with other people. But, even so, they tend to seek an acquiescent audience rather than a open forum for debate, and may become impatient and frustrated if, despite their efforts, they fail to win converts to their cause. This somewhat controlling propensity also applies to their closest personal relationships—and particularly to their children if they are parents—for their strong sense of self-belief can lead them to expect—and often demand—unquestioning submission from their nearest and dearest.

VIRTUES: Their great imagination and insatiable intellectual curiosity generate wide-ranging interests in those born on May 24, and their articulacy gives them an enormous advantage over less decisive types. Because of their strong communication skills, they have great potential to influence and direct others.

VICES: Although they may act with the best of motives in mind, these people are often prone to imposing their opinions on others, whether or not their advice is sought. When they are unable to get their viewpoint across, they may express their annoyance in devastatingly acerbic fashion.

VERDICT: To improve their sense of self-fulfillment, May 24 people should learn to accept others as they are, and become more relaxed and tolerant of differences of opinion. Grounding themselves in the supporting bonds of strong relationships should help lessen their judgemental tendencies.

On This Day
Famous Births: William Schwenck Gilbert (1540); Jean Paul Marat (1743); Queen Victoria of Britain (1819); Arthur Wing Pinero (1855); Jan Christiaan Smuts (1870); Mick Mannock (1887); Suzanne Lenglen (1899); Mikhail Sholokhov (1905); Joan Hood Hammond (1912); William Trevor (1928); Arnold Wesker (1932); Tommy Chong (1938); Bob Dylan (1941); Gary Burdhoff (1943); Patti LaBelle (1944); Priscilla Presley (1945); Roseanne Cash (1955); Joe Dumars (1963); Liz McColgan (1964).

Significant Events and Anniversaries: This day indicates great strength of belief, and marks the anniversary of the conversion of John Wesley, the founder of Methodism, to evangelism (1738); the John Brown-led anti-slavery "massacre" of five pro-slavery farmers at Pottawatomie Creek in the U.S.A. (1856); and the sinking of the British vessel H.M.S. *Hood* off Greenland by the German battleship *Bismarck* during World War II, resulting in the loss of 400 lives (1941). The communicative talent that is highlighted by this day found expression when Samuel Morse transmitted the U.S. Telegraph's first coded message, from Washington, D.C., to Baltimore (1844); while in the realm of entertainment, the first Eurovision Song Contest was staged in Switzerland (1956).

MAY 25

At the core of the personalities of May 25 individuals lies an intractable sense of honor, natural justice and decency, a deeply held moral code that underlies the majority of their personal convictions and actions. This is not to say that these people are intellectually rigid: to the contrary, they possess a mercurial turn of mind that leads them to embrace new ideas or innovations easily, albeit with the proviso that these do not conflict with their ethical or ideological beliefs. Their sensitivity toward the suffering or misfortunes of others endows them not only with a great sense of compassion for the downtrodden, but also the desire to actively work toward the improvement of their lot: in the course of their struggle they typically draw upon their enormous energy and powerful communication skills. And, although they possess the courage to stand alone if necessary, their favored option is to inspire an equally determined and enthusiastic band of like-minded individuals. Such characteristics endow May 25 people with pronounced leadership potential, and they gain greatest satisfaction when blazing an artistic, political or humanitarian trail.

Within their personal lives, too, these people are oriented toward protecting and ensuring the happiness of their loved ones, a propensity that is further emphasized for those also born in the Chinese year of the pig. Yet despite the indulgence and generosity that they typically display within their domestic relationships, their ethical convictions remain paramount. Should these be transgressed, they will experience deep hurt and disillusionment even to the point of abruptly withdrawing their affection and support from the offender, no matter how close the relationship.

VIRTUES: Their empathetic tendencies, combined with their innate recognition of right and wrong, endow these people with strong ideological convictions that are usually directed toward the improvement of human life—be it in the global or personal sense. Charismatic and dynamic figures, they typically work toward the implementation of their aims with prodigious vigor and determination.
VICES: Those born on this day have a propensity to be overly judgemental of other people and expect them to adhere to the same lofty moral standards as themselves.
VERDICT: Developing a greater sense of realism as to what can or cannot be achieved, as well as a more pragmatic view of life, will assist May 25 people to achieve their goals without alienating others and thereby rendering themselves isolated, ineffectual and frustrated.

On This Day
Famous Births: Ralph Waldo Emerson (1803); Tom Sayers (1826); Pieter Zeeman (1865); Luther Bill "Bojangles" Robinson (1878); William Aiken, Baron Beaverbrook (1879); Igor Ivanovich Sikorsky (1889); Gene Tunney (1898); Richard Dimbleby (1913); Claude Akins (1918); Jeanne Crain (1925); Miles Davis (1926); Robert Ludlum (1927); Beverly Sills (1929); Tom T. Hall (1936); Dixie Carter and Ian McKellan (1939); Leslie Uggams (1943); Connie Sellecca (1955); Paul Weller (1958).

Significant Events and Anniversaries: The ideological conviction that is such a strong feature of this day is typically manifested in the realms of politics, religion and humanitarian activities, and it is therefore appropriate that May 25 marks the anniversary of the meeting of the Philadelphia Convention which formulated the U.S. constitution (1787); the opening of the "Monkey Trial" of teacher John Scopes in Tennessee, which showcased the conflict between Darwinist and Christian principles (1925); the defection of the British spies Guy Burgess and Don Maclean to the Soviet Union (1951); and the "Race Against Time," organized by Bob Geldof, in which 30 million people all over the world took part in a fun run to raise money to alleviate starvation in Ethiopia (1986). Active determination in the pursuit of an ideal is further highlighted by this day, on which Captain Cook, in the *Endeavour*, launched his first voyage of discovery (1768), and the U.S. athlete Jesse Owens smashed six world records in under an hour at Ann Arbor, Michigan (1935).

Planetary Influences
Ruling planet: Mercury.
First decan: Personal planet is Mercury.

Sacred and Cultural Significance
Saint Sarah of the Gypsies honored in Europe; the birthday of Apollo celebrated in ancient Greece.
Saints' day: Urban (d. 230); Zenobius of Florence (d. c.390); Gregory VII (c.1021–85); Madeleine Sophie Barat (1779–1865).

The handsome Apollo, twin brother of Artemis, was the Greek god of healing, light and oracles. His birthday was celebrated on May 25. He is often portrayed with a lyre, as in the sculpture below, or with his other main attribute, a bow.

Planetary Influences
Ruling planet: Mercury.
First decan: Personal planet is Mercury.

Sacred and Cultural Significance
In ancient Rome, the Fortinalia festival;
Sacred Well Day, a Pagan celebration.
Saints' day: Priscus (d. c.272); Augustine
of Canterbury (d. c.604); Philip Neri
(1515–95).

*Like many fellow May 26 people, John Wayne
was naturally drawn to the performing arts;
as an actor, he was able to pursue a dynamic
and varied career, exploring new roles and
avoiding the constraints of a more conventional
life in which he might have felt restless. Rising
to fame as the Ringo Kid in* Stagecoach *(1939),
Wayne made over eighty films and became an
icon as an all-American hero. His on-screen
personality often reflected aspects of his Chinese
birth influences: as a fire goat, he exuded
charisma and persistence, and had an
easy-going manner.*

MAY 26

✳✳✳

Many of those born on May 26 may regard life as something of a struggle, particularly in their quest to find both intellectual and emotional fulfillment. Indeed, it may seem somewhat paradoxical that it is their own talents, which they employ so effectively on others' behalf, that impede their own search for happiness. For inherent in these individuals are both firmly held ideological convictions and a restless urge to gain new knowledge and experience. While having the potential to embrace new ideas and thus be startlingly innovative, these people may also strive to impose or maintain their strong social ideals. These two characteristics can be remarkably efficacious when in harmony, but if imbalanced they may result in double standards and alternately impulsive and intolerant behavior. Nevertheless, the dynamism of those born on this day frequently inspires the admiration of others, and they may therefore assume leading roles in those professions that naturally attract them, such as the performing arts, with which they have a special affinity and where they may enjoy autonomy of action and influence over others.

Because intellectual and physical independence is of such fundamental importance to them, May 26 people—and especially the men born on this day—will inherently resist submitting to another authority. Their innate dislike of being constrained within rigid organizational or personal structures means that not only do they find it difficult to conform to corporate life, but they may also be reluctant to commit themselves to a single life partner. Within established personal relationships, however, they tend to reserve the freedom that they cherish for themselves exclusively, while at the same time expecting their nearest and dearest to conform to their expectations.

VIRTUES: Introverted in that they have the power of concentrated and incisive thought, and extroverted by virtue of their insatiable curiosity and social orientation, these people are blessed with the capacity to impart their strong views to others in inspirational fashion.
VICES: Despite requiring others to conform to their high standards and expectations, they may have some difficulty in so conforming themselves because of their strong need for freedom of thought and action. If these propensities are not reconciled, May 26 people may find themselves accused of hypocrisy.
VERDICT: Those born on this day should strive to cultivate their undoubted capacity for candid introspection in order to gain a more profound level of self-knowledge. Directing their talents more positively and moderating any potentially destructive tendencies will bring them greater personal happiness and professional success.

On This Day
Famous Births: John Churchill, Duke of Marlborough (1650); Edmond de Goncourt (1822); Henri Farman (1874); Al Jolson (1886); Aaron Douglas (1899); George Formby (1904); John Wayne (1907); Robert Morley (1908); Matt Busby (1909); Janos Kadar (1912); Peter Cushing (1913); Peggy Lee (1920); Jay Silverheels (1922); James Arness (1923); Alec McCowen (1925); Brent Musburger (1939); Stevie Nicks (1948); Philip Michael Thomas and Hank Williams, Jr. (1949); Sally Ride (1951); Genie Francis (1962).

Significant Events and Anniversaries: Indicated by this day is a talent for implementing innovation and thereby effecting progress, as is reflected in the patenting of Englishman John Kay's "flying shuttle," used in conjunction with Richard Arkwright's "spinning frame" to speed up the cotton-spinning process (1773); and in the first significant oil strike in Persia (1908). A propensity for taking daring action is also highlighted, and on this day the first 24-hour car race was held at Le Mans, France (1923); the evacuation began of British forces stranded at Dunkirk in France, during World War II (1940); and U.S. stuntman Evel Knievel was gravely injured when his car failed to clear thirteen buses over which he was attempting to leap (1975). Confirming the charismatic leadership powers bestowed by this day, Napoleon Bonaparte was crowned king of Italy (1805).

MAY 27

Although they are incisive and imaginative thinkers who possess the enviable capacity to easily absorb the intricacies of complex abstract theories, those born on this day are not really interested in pondering undisturbed in isolated ivory towers; instead they feel compelled to share the fruits of their knowledge with the wider world. Indeed, these people are fueled by the desire to be of benefit to humanity as a whole, and their favored approach is to take practical action to implement their progressive ideals. Their interest in the human condition is but one manifestation of their general intellectual inquisitiveness, and, although they are sympathetic to human suffering, they manage to remain somewhat emotionally detached, perhaps instinctively recognizing that too deep a level of emotional involvement would limit their ability to be of effective help. Such characteristics equip May 27 people particularly well for the medical, teaching or diplomatic professions, as well as for those artistic realms where they can express themselves freely; the only vital requirement being that there should be an opportunity to guide or care for other people.

Their confidence, as well as the infectious optimism generated by their strength of purpose, endow these individuals with great magnetism, and they are generally well respected and greatly liked by those with whom their work brings them into contact. Yet their personal relationships may be less harmonious for a number of reasons, including the amount of time and attention that they devote to their work, their tendency to control the lives of those closest to them, and their strong self-belief, which makes it difficult for them to accept criticism.

VIRTUES: As well as possessing keenly analytical intellectual qualities, those born on this day are innovative, practical and dynamic. They are typically geared toward assisting other people and achieving tangible progress, in the process utilizing their considerable talents and energies in a remarkably clear-sighted and committed fashion.
VICES: Since they have a natural inclination for mentoring or leading others, there is a danger that in extreme cases these people may become overly dominating. This tendency is in part a result of their inherent self-belief which admits few, if any, personal failings, and in part a consequence of their urge to actively involve themselves in others' affairs.
VERDICT: Although these people's desire to place themselves at the service of humanity is commendable, in the interests of gaining greater self-awareness, and to ensure that they do not become victims of their own propaganda, they should periodically re-examine their motivations and strategies—especially with regard to their personal liaisons.

On This Day
Famous Births: Henry Parkes (1815); Amelia Jenks Bloomer (1818); Julia Ward Howe (1819); "Wild Bill" Hickok (1837); Arnold Bennett (1867); Georges Rouault (1871); Isadora Duncan (1878); Louis Durey (1888); Dashiell Hammett (1894); Hubert H. Humphrey and Vincent Price (1911); Herman Wouk (1915); Christopher Lee (1922); Henry Kissinger (1923); Louis Gossett, Jr. (1936); Allan Carr (1941); Morning Glory Zell (1948); Todd Bridges (1965).

Significant Events and Anniversaries: Inherent in this day is a pronounced talent to think tactically and act strategically, qualities that are reflected by a variety of events that occurred on May 27, including: the staging of the first International Masters chess tournament in London (1851); the victory of the Japanese Navy under Admiral Togo over its Russian adversary at Tsushima Straits (1905); and the sinking of the German battleship *Bismarck* by British forces during World War II (1941). This day endows leadership potential, as is confirmed by the election of Jomo Kenyatta to be the first prime minister of Kenya (1963), and Jacques Chirac to be premier of France (1974). The practical implementation of innovative visions that is a feature of this day is implicitly mirrored in a number of pioneering achievements, for example: when Belgium, the first country to do so, elected its government according to proportional representation (1900); when the liner *Queen Mary* set sail on her maiden voyage from England to New York (1936); and when San Francisco's Golden Gate Bridge was opened (1937).

Planetary Influences
Ruling planet: Mercury.
First decan: Personal planet is Mercury.

Sacred and Cultural Significance
Secular Centennial Games observed in ancient Rome.
Saints' day: Julius the Veteran (d. 304); the Venerable Bede (673–735), patron saint of scholars.

The confluence of pragmatic, dynamic and pioneering forces that often occurs on May 27 was demonstrated in 1937 by the opening of San Francisco's most famous structure, the Golden Gate Bridge.

Planetary Influences
Ruling planet: Mercury.
First decan: Personal planet is Mercury.

Sacred and Cultural Significance
Plythian Games enacted every four years
in ancient Greece.
Saint's day: Bernard of Aosta (d. 1081),
patron saint of mountaineers.

*Born on this day in 1968, Australian television
and pop star Kylie Minogue became a teen
idol at a young age, capitalizing on the
communication skills that are strong in May 28
people. Her personal horoscope has five planets
in Gemini, including her ruling planet,
Mercury, giving her an even stronger
communicative bent and a thirst for stimulation
and variety. As an earth monkey, her Chinese
astrological influences bestow a craving for
attention and a perfectionist streak, as well
as an ultra-feminine personal style.*

MAY 28

✱✱

Those born on May 28 are stimulated by the grand picture, by visions that are so progressive
that others may find them radical and unrealistic. Yet because they are blessed with
soaring imaginative powers, the ability to accept and investigate innovative ideas rather than
reject them out of hand, and sound intellectual investigative talents, the proposals that they
advance rarely seem to be fantastic and unfeasible. Indeed, in many ways those born on this
day are ahead of their times, and, in retrospect, it will probably be their detractors who are
proved wrong. The problem is that, although they are able to communicate their ideals
effectively to those who are sympathetic and like-minded, and provide them with inspiration
and leadership, their words will fall on deaf ears when they preach to those who are less
enlightened and adventurous. Given the generally unenthusiastic reception to be expected
for their enterprising proposals, they are likely to achieve greatest success when able to work
apart from mainstream bodies in those areas where their personal flair and originality can
be showcased. Thus, they can make very successful artists, writers or stage performers for
example, or business entrepreneurs.

Because these people yearn to influence others and institute progress in their own, inimitable
way, they have to learn to deal with the inevitable disappointment of having their most deeply
cherished ideals disparaged by others. Some of those born on this day are able to cope with
this by putting on a brave and defiant face, others by withdrawing into their own worlds.
All, however, value the unquestioning respect, support and affection of their friends, partners
and families, and usually reciprocate such loyalty in kind, especially if they were also born in
the Chinese year of the rat.

VIRTUES: Their creative imagination and practical inventiveness invests those born on this
day with a rare originality that gives them the potential to be remarkably innovative. Their
great sensitivity and willingness to embrace the new and the different furthermore bless them
with the gift of intellectual tolerance, as well as of far-sightedness.
VICES: These people have a tendency to respond to skepticism or criticism by resorting to
two behavioral extremes: by becoming aggressively defensive, or by abandoning their dreams.
The former propensity may lead to their isolation; the latter may engender destructive feelings
of lack of fulfillment.
VERDICT: It is vital that May 28 individuals should not compromise their beliefs and visions
by conforming to the more conventional norms of their critics: when seeking to impart and
implement their ideas, they should develop a more pragmatic approach by adapting their
inherent gift for communication to suit those who are less intellectually advanced.

On This Day
Famous Births: Joseph Ignace Guillotin (1738); William Pitt the Younger (1759); Thomas
Moore (1779); Warwick Deeping (1877); Eduard Benes (1884); Jim Thorpe (1888); Ian Fleming
(1908); Rachel Kempson and Patrick White (1912); Dietrich Fischer-Dieskau (1925); Edward
Seaga (1930); Caroll Baker (1931); the Dionne Quintuplets: Emilie, Yvonne, Cecile, Marie
and Annette (1934); Gladys Knight (1944); Sondra Locke (1947); Kylie Minogue (1968).

Significant Events and Anniversaries: May 28 features innovation and progress, qualities that
may be mirrored in a variety of fields, and on this day the first indoor swimming pool was
opened in England (1742); Londoner Erasmus Bond patented tonic water, a palatable form of
the quinine used to combat malaria that was then rife in British-ruled India (1858); and the
world's largest sea dam was completed across the Zuider Zee in The Netherlands, by which
the Ijsselmeer was also created (1932). The success that is promised when the visions of this
day are adhered to was confirmed when British yachtsman Francis Chichester completed his
single-handed navigation of the world in *Gypsy Moth IV* (1967); Amy Johnson made the first
solo flight from England to Australia (1930); and the yacht *Maiden* finished the Whitbread
Round-the-World Race, the first to do so with an all-woman crew (1990).

MAY 29

Others are drawn to May 29 people, attracted by their kindness, endearing charm and infectious *joie de vivre*, and in turn these gregarious individuals ensure that a good time is had by all. Not only are they fundamentally concerned with trying to bring happiness to others, but they believe in sharing their talents and, when they are blessed with it, good fortune. They therefore exhibit both hedonistic and altruistic tendencies, characteristics that are often incompatible in others, but which those born on this day manage to reconcile extremely effectively. So determined are they to experience all that life has to offer—a compulsion that results from their inquiring minds and need for stimulation—that it may take them some time to alight on and settle into a fulfilling career, but once they have found their professional niche they will commit their prodigious energy and incisive analytical skills to the realization of their imaginative ideals. Because these are strongly people-oriented types, who wish to act as the instrument that improves the lot of humanity as a whole, they will thrive in such diverse fields as politics, business and the arts.

In all their ventures, those born on May 29 typically seek to enlist approval and support from as many people as possible, and they are not above exploiting the power of their natural charisma if this will aid the common cause. In both their professional and domestic lives they will therefore generally be surrounded by enthusiastic admirers, whom they will treat with generous affection and gentle humor. Exemplary friends and parents, these people may be less successful as partners, however, on account of their tendency to keep an open house, as well as to respond to new challenges: it is therefore of paramount importance that their partners should have a high tolerance level.

VIRTUES: The extraordinary appeal that these magnetic characters exert over those around them results from their good-natured charm and their genuine interest in the well-being of others. Their apparently languid approach masks their fierce determination, and their potential is enhanced by their relish for testing themselves in demanding situations.
VICES: Those born on this day may find it difficult to find their true vocation in life, for their wide-ranging interests may inhibit their ability to focus on a single field, a tendency that also applies to their intellectual activities and their personal relationships.
VERDICT: In order to maximize their potential and gain emotional satisfaction, May 29 people should strive to develop the ability to define priorities, for unless they control their predilection to address every challenge, they may spread their energies too thinly.

On This Day
Famous Births: King Charles II of England (1630); Patrick Henry (1736); Philippe Lebon (1767); John Walker (1781); Isaac Albéniz (1860); G.K. Chesterton (1874); Oswald Spengler (1880); Joseph von Sternberg (1894); Erich Korngold (1897); Leonard Huxley (1902); Bob Hope (1903); T.H. White (1906); John F. Kennedy (1917); Paul Elrich (1932); Alvin Schockemohle (1935); Al Unser (1939); LaToya Jackson (1956); Annette Bening (1958); Melissa Etheridge (1961); Melanie Janine Brown (1975).

Significant Events and Anniversaries: The progressive urge that is inherent in May 29 may result in confrontation, and this day marks the anniversary of the fall of Constantinople to Turkish forces, thereby ending the Byzantine Empire (1453); as well as of the challenge mounted by Patrick Henry in the Virginia Assembly against the British-imposed Stamp Act (1795). Illustrating the less aggressive, but equally visionary, tendencies of this day, Charles Stuart entered London to be restored as king of England and Scotland (1660); Wisconsin joined the union of the United States (1848); Edmund Hillary and Sherpa Tenzing Norgay became the first to conquer Mount Everest (1953); Rhodesia gained its first African prime minister, Abel Muzorewa, one year before becoming the independent state of Zimbabwe (1979); and Pope John Paul II began his tour of Britain, the first pontiff to visit the nation for over four-and-a-half centuries following its split from Rome (1982).

Planetary Influences
Ruling planet: Mercury.
First decan: Personal planet is Mercury.

Sacred and Cultural Significance
In England, Oak Apple, or Royal Oak Day; Mars honored by farmers in ancient Rome.
Saints' day: Alexander (d. 397); Mary Magdelene de' Pazzi (1566–1606).

Gregarious, charming, people-oriented and socially concerned, John F. Kennedy, thirty-fifth president of the United States, was the definitive May 29 personality. In his public life he brought his persuasive leadership style and passionate humanitarian convictions to the world stage, focusing on the Cold War and, at home, desegregation. In the personal arena, few could resist his magnetic appeal, and he was known to reciprocate the attentions of a number of female admirers throughout his married life. A fire snake, his qualities of lively sociability, ambition and concern with his public image typify people with his Chinese birth influences.

Planetary Influences
Ruling planet: Mercury.
First decan: Personal planet is Mercury.

Sacred and Cultural Significance
Saints' day: Hubert (d. 727), patron saint of healthy dogs and hunters; Ferdinand III (1199–1252), patron saint of engineers; Joan of Arc (1412–31), patron saint of France.

Queen Victoria was definitely not amused when an attempt was made on her life on May 30, 1842, by Jon Francis. Sudden, impulsive and dramatic actions have been a feature of this day, on which almost anything could happen.

Perhaps the defining personal characteristic inherent in those born on this day, and the one that informs and influences the majority of their actions, is their irresistible fascination with imaginative and innovatory concepts. Indeed, the adjective "mercurial" perfectly encapsulates the restless inquisitiveness of their intellectual approach, which leads them to search ceaselessly for knowledge and truth and makes them remarkably receptive and sympathetic to new ideas and proposals. Although their curiosity and need for stimulation endow those born on this day with the potential to become gifted polymaths, it also carries the inherent risk that they may fail to settle on any interest long enough to develop it fully. Well able to inspire and direct the thoughts and actions of others by means of their enthusiasm, optimism and communication skills, they have a propensity to leave others to finalize the less intriguing aspects of their projects while they themselves move on to more alluring pastures.

Professionally, May 30 people are suited to those areas in which they have the best chance of utilizing their talents and the least chance of becoming bored with the minutiae of working life. Finance-related careers, such as in stockbroking, are especially indicated, as are artistic and sporting pursuits. In their personal relationships, too, these people tend to shy away from sustained commitment and the constraints imposed by familial obligations; nevertheless they typically care deeply for their nearest and dearest.

VIRTUES: Their quick-wittedness, enthusiasm for the novel and wide-ranging interests, combined with their limitless imaginative powers and refusal to be bound by convention, bless these people with great innovatory potential, as well as with the capacity to motivate others with their visions.

VICES: Ironically, their tendency to sabotage their own aims and efforts reflects one of their greatest strengths: their intellectual restiveness. For, unfortunately, their innate skittishness may cause them not only to lack staying power, but also to develop a reputation for unreliability.

VERDICT: It is vital that these people do not waste their considerable talents. Developing their powers of concentration, and resisting the urge to respond impulsively to the lure of a new fascination before the possibilities of an existing venture have been exhausted, will help them gain greater personal satisfaction and optimize their potential to achieve success.

On This Day
Famous Births: Mikhail Alexandrovich Bakunin (1814); Alfred Austin (1835); Peter Carl Fabergé (1846); Pierre Janet (1859); Leslie Dawson (1906); Mel Blanc (1908); Benny Goodman (1909); Ray Cooney (1932); Keir Dullea (1936); Michael J. Pollard (1939); Meredith MacRae (1944); Bob Willis (1949); Wynona Judd (1964).

Significant Events and Anniversaries: The adventurousness that is a strong feature of May 30 is mirrored by three events that occurred on this day: Christopher Columbus embarked on his third voyage of discovery, to the Caribbean (1498); the Indianapolis 500 automobile race was inaugurated (1911); and the first hovercraft was launched, the brainchild of British scientist Christopher Cockerell (1959). A propensity for behaving impulsively is highlighted by this day, on which the English playwright Christopher Marlowe lost his life when involved in a violent tavern altercation (1593), and Jon Francis attempted to assassinate Queen Victoria (1842). Grand visions, which may take a variety of forms, are indicated by this day, and this predilection was expressed when the British R.A.F. launched its first "thousand-bomber" raid, on the German city of Cologne during World War II (1942), and when the Auckland Harbour Bridge—a triumph of engineering—was opened on North Island in New Zealand (1959). And on this day Joan of Arc, whose patriotic words and actions provided enormous inspiration to the French people, was burned at the stake in Rouen by English forces (1431).

MAY 31

Many of those who do not know them well can be bewildered by the apparent inconsistency of those born on this day: they can be enthusiastic about a new venture at one moment, and almost doctrinaire in their upholding of traditional values at the next. Similarly, their tendency to alternate between exuberant optimism and dark pessimism can make these people difficult to know and understand. Such seemingly conflicting patterns of behavior reflect their prodigious imaginative power, a gift that can have both positive and negative influences. While this endows them with enormous innovatory potential, it also bestows on them the ability to see all sides of an issue, thereby sometimes making them indecisive or reluctant to take potentially disastrous risks, instead opting for the safer, albeit more static, option. Yet once convinced of the veracity of a particular course of action, May 31 people will typically pursue it with directness and great capability, devising ingenuous means of overcoming obstacles, and gearing themselves toward influencing others by their work and vision.

Because they are independent in both thought and action, those born on this day fare best when unconstrained by the rules and regulations of thers. They are especially attracted to artistic pursuits, but may also find fulfillment when engaged in humanitarian work. They are generous of their time and attention in both their professional and personal relationships, provided, that is, that they do not feel trapped or stifled by the demands of others, a propensity that is particularly pronounced in the men born on this day.

VIRTUES: Individualistic, imaginative and innovative, these people are furthermore blessed with considerable practical talents, as well as a straightforward and determined approach when working toward the attainment of their aims. Although they may hold profound convictions, they understand the importance of pragmatism in achieving success.
VICES: These people have a tendency to profess jealously their intellectual and physical freedom and to react negatively to what they perceive to be any attempt to exercise control over them. Conversely, they may be authoritarian toward others when expressing a viewpoint in which they firmly believe.
VERDICT: The key to the happiness of those born on May 31 lies in forming and maintaining strong emotional bonds. By grounding themselves within stable relationships they will gain greater equilibrium and thus be better placed to direct their intellectual energies effectively.

On This Day
Famous Births: Alexander Cruden (1701); Walt Whitman (1819); Walter Sickert (1860); William Heath Robinson (1872); Fred Allen (1894); Norman Vincent Peale (1898); Don Ameche (1908); Denholm Elliott (1922); Prince Rainier III of Monaco (1923); Clint Eastwood (1930); Peter Yarrow (1938); Terry Waite (1939); Johnny Paycheck (1941); Sharon Gless and Joe Namath (1943); Tom Berenger and Gregory Harrison (1950); Lea Thompson (1961); Brooke Shields (1965).

Significant Events and Anniversaries: May 31 highlights a quest for freedom, a quality that may be manifested in nationalistic actions, and on this day the Union of South Africa was established, to be self-governing (1910); its full independence from Britain was similarly proclaimed on this day (1961). Further expressions of this desire for autonomy are illustrated by the actions of Czech resistance fighters during World War II, when Reinhard Heydrich, the Nazi "protector of Bohemia and Moravia" was assassinated (1942); and by the refusal of U.S. playwright Arthur Miller in refusing to divulge the identities of communist sympathizers to Congress, resulting in his conviction for contempt (1957). Inherent in this day is also an innovative urge, reflected in the technical sphere when London's famous clock, Big Ben, was set in motion on this day (1859), and when construction work started on the Trans-Siberian Railway in Russia (1891).

Planetary Influences
Ruling planet: Mercury.
First decan: Personal planet is Mercury.

Sacred and Cultural Significance
The national day of South Africa; Theravada Buddhists honor and observe the Triple Blessing of the birth, enlightenment and passage of Buddha into nirvana.
Saints' day: the Visitation of the Blessed Virgin Mary (d. 1st century AD), patron saint of mothers, nuns and virgins; Petronilla (dates unknown).

May 31, a day on which practical and technical achievements are favored, marks the anniversary of the first day the hands swept around the world's most famous clock, London's Big Ben.

Planetary Influences
Ruling planet: Mercury.
Second decan: Personal planet is Venus.

Sacred and Cultural Significance
Pagan festival of the Oak Nymph.
Saints' day: Nicomedes (dates unknown);
Justin (c.100–65), patron saint of
philosophers and travelers; Gwen Teirbron
of Brittany (dates unknown); Ronan of
Brittany (dates unknown); Whyte (dates
unknown); Wistan (d. 850).

*With the considerable energy and adroitness
with the media common to those born on June 1,
Marilyn Monroe realized much of her enormous
potential in her meteoric film career. Being
born in the Chinese year of the tiger (1926)
enhanced her natural magnetism but also
perhaps contributed to the impulsiveness and
melancholy that brought about her premature
and tragic end.*

JUNE 1

✱✱

Like most people born under the sign of Gemini, June 1 individuals possess the pronounced characteristic of mercurial inquisitiveness, which is manifested by their almost insatiable desire for intellectual stimulation and manifold interests. While their inherent curiosity endows them with a natural predilection for exploring abstract concepts and—if their attention is captured by a subject that really fascinates them—for delving deeper in truly innovative fashion, it may, however, equally prohibit those born on this day from concentrating on one topic alone. Indeed, they have a remarkably low boredom threshold, as well as a horror of being stifled and stultified by petty details. But there is one subject that rarely fails to intrigue these individuals, and that is human behavior, for observing other people and speculating about their characters and motivations provides them with an endless challenge. This orientation, when combined with an openness to change and progress, gives them the aptitude for, and potential to achieve success within, such fields as marketing, advertising, the media and politics, or perhaps psychology or detective work.

Despite their almost compulsive interest in other people, however, those born on June 1 are often extremely private individuals, who guard their own personal lives jealously. It may be that they recognize the value (in terms of protecting their emotional equilibrium) of keeping the professional and domestic spheres in which they operate separate, or that—for a multitude of reasons—they do not wish the personae that they have adopted with colleagues to be unmasked to reveal their "real" selves. Whether plagued by insecurity or not, they tend to resist committing themselves to a life partner, but once they are firmly enmeshed within bonds of family and friendship, these people typically enliven their personal liaisons, and make particularly affectionate and effective parents.

VIRTUES: These vigorous individuals are driven by their quest for knowledge, a propensity that may find its expression in a range of interests, but usually includes a marked proclivity toward human personality and conduct—whether of the individual or a wider social grouping. Because they direct their considerable energy and quick-wittedness toward achieving progress, they are blessed with enormous potential to attain tangible results.
VICES: There is one significant propensity inherent in their personalities that June 1 people would do well to recognize and address: their tendency to move restlessly from one passing enthusiasm to another without gaining more than a superficial understanding of any area that attracts their interest.
VERDICT: June 1 people appreciate the importance of privacy as a healthy means of providing a refuge from professional demands, but they must ensure that they do not take this predilection to its extreme, and thereby cut themselves off from potentially rewarding friendships. They should also resist the tendency to dilettantism.

On This Day
Famous Births: Henry Francis Lyte (1793); Nicolas Carnot (1796); Brigham Young (1801); Mikhail Ivanovich Glinka (1804); John Masefield (1878); John Drinkwater (1882); Frank Whittle (1907); Andy Griffith and Marilyn Monroe (1926); Edward Woodward (1930); Pat Boone (1934); Gerald Scarfe (1936); Morgan Freeman (1937); Cleavon Little (1939); Robert Powell (1944); Jonathan Pryce and Ron Wood (1947); Alanis Morissette (1974).

Significant Events and Anniversaries: The adventurous nature that is bestowed by this day may result in pioneering discoveries or actions, as when James Clark Ross located the site of the magnetic North Pole (1831), and when Captain Robert Falcon Scott set sail from Britain in the *Terra Nova* on his ultimately tragic quest to reach the South Pole (1910). In the artistic sphere, this innovative tendency was reflected when the Beatles released their seminal and highly acclaimed album, *Sergeant Pepper's Lonely Hearts Club Band* (1967); while in the realm of nationalism it was expressed when Greece proclaimed itself a republic (1973), and when Napoleon Bonaparte swore fidelity to the French constitution (1815).

JUNE 2

The lives of those born on June 2 rarely seem to run smoothly: no sooner has one hurdle been cleared, than another appears to impede the path of progress. Such is the frequency of these crises in their lives, that others often secretly wonder whether they have been manufactured—consciously or unconsciously—by the individuals themselves as a means of spicing up their daily routine. It is indeed true that June 2 people thrive on challenge, relishing the opportunity to pit their skills against the difficult or unexpected, particularly if they were also born in the Chinese year of the monkey. These are quick-witted individuals, who can readily analyze the many facets inherent in a situation, more often than not devising an ingenious and effective course of action. And, because they enjoy sharing their considerable talents with others, they will frequently flourish in the artistic sphere—especially as performers—but also sometimes as scientific researchers or as corporate trouble-shooters; in any career, in fact, in which they are allowed autonomy of thought and action.

Their predilection for exposing themselves to new stimuli may, however, complicate their personal lives. Not only do they typically find it hard to take the plunge in committing themselves to a life partner, but they may also lack the capacity to stick with a relationship once it has lost its initial bloom of excitement. This is not to say that they do not possess profound feelings for their nearest and dearest, but rather that they may helplessly succumb to the irresistible lure of the unknown—or even the unattainable.

VIRTUES: The defining characteristic of those born on June 2 is their urge to test their impressive intelligence and moral fortitude against demanding situations. The combination of their mercurial, flexible minds, their determination to succeed, and their courage (especially when taking risks) endows them with enormous potential.
VICES: These people tend to disrupt their emotional and professional lives by seeking change for its own sake. Their natural enjoyment of challenge and finding imaginative solutions may even become an extreme compulsion, causing them to become permanently restless and dissatisfied and to perceive their everyday lives to be boring and unfulfilling.
VERDICT: Although they demonstrate great determination when it comes to achieving the aims that truly inspire them, June 2 individuals should develop greater staying power when they find themselves in situations or relationships that do not provide them with the short-term stimulation to which they respond so positively.

On This Day

Famous Births: Comte Donatien de Sade (the Marquis de Sade) (1740); Thomas Hardy (1840); Edward Elgar (1857); Felix Weingartner (1863); Hedda Hopper (1890); Lotte Reiniger (1899); Johnny Weissmuller (1904); King Constantine II of the Hellenes (1940); Stacy Keach and Charlie Watts (1941); Marvin Hamlisch (1944); Michael Leunig (1945); Jerry Mathers (1948).

Significant Events and Anniversaries: Innovative artistic pursuits are starred by this day, on which the celebrated dancers Nijinsky and Pavlova took part in the premier of the ballet *Les Sylphides*, choreographed by Fokine (1909); and on which *Lulu*, the opera by Alban Berg, had its first performance (1937). Pioneering achievements of all kinds are also highlighted, as is variously illustrated by the patenting of Guglielmo Marconi's electromagnetic-wave wireless (1896); the opening of the world's first children's zoo at Regent's Park in London by the U.S. ambassador's young sons, Robert and Edward Kennedy (1937); the televising of Queen Elizabeth II's coronation, the first such ceremony to be beamed to the public (1953); and the start of Polish-born Pope John Paul II's tour of his homeland, the first papal visit to a communist state (1979). June 2 indicates potential confrontation, and marks the anniversary of the Gordon Riots in Britain against the abolition of the penalties imposed on Roman Catholics by the Catholic Relief Act (1778); the formation of the anti-Israeli Palestine Liberation Organization (PLO) (1964); and the death of over one hundred prodemocracy protesters at the hands of the Chinese Army in Tiananmen Square, Beijing (1989).

Planetary Influences
Ruling planet: Mercury.
Second decan: Personal planet is Venus.

Sacred and Cultural Significance
In Christianity, St. Elmo's Day; in classical mythology, the birthday of Apollo; Shapatu of Ishtar, a Pagan festival.
Saints' day: Erasmus (d. c.300), patron saint of intestinal-disease sufferers; Marcellinus and Peter (d. 304); Oda (d. 958).

Depicted on a lion, Ishtar is the ancient Assyrian and Babylonian deity of love, fertility and war. Her festival, Shapatu of Ishtar, is celebrated on June 2.

GEMINI

Planetary Influences
Ruling planet: Mercury.
Second decan: Personal planet is Venus.

Sacred and Cultural Significance
Festival of Cataclysmos in Cyprus.
Saints' day: Kevin (d. c.618); Genesius of Clermont (d. c.660), patron saint of actors; Charles Lwanga and Companions (d. 1885–87).

Born on June 3, 1808, Jefferson Davis utilized the charm, sharp-witted intelligence and dedication favored by his birthday to construct a remarkable military and political career. A veteran of the Mexican War and secretary of war from 1853 to 1857, Davis became president of the Confederacy during the Civil War, highlighting domineering and confrontational traits common to the influences of this day.

JUNE 3

Despite the marked independence of thought that June 3 people not only manifest but cherish zealously, they are not the types to distance themselves from the company of others in order to explore concepts that interest them. To the contrary, whether or not they make a career choice based on their relish for personal interaction and their desire to advance humanitarian goals, they feel a need to share their ideas with others, indeed, often to impose them on those around them. In common with many of their Gemini fellows, June 3 people are somewhat intellectually restless, yet their strong urge to achieve tangible results by implementing the visions that inspire them gives them the ability to concentrate upon their chosen aims with single-minded dedication, thus giving their mercurial tendencies an outlet for resolving new problems. Such qualities, when supplemented by their impressive communicative talents, give these people the potential to succeed especially in such spheres as teaching, research and the performing arts.

Coupled with their predilection for putting across their occasionally idiosyncratic opinions—even in the face of a hostile audience—is these people's (often unconscious) desire to bask in the acclaim of others, a combination that is not easily reconciled. For June 3 people sometimes alienate others and forfeit the goodwill and admiration that they seek to elicit. This reaction is usually due to the forceful and impatient manner in which they present their beliefs. While charming and benevolent when things are going their way, they may become negative and domineering when their path is blocked. This propensity is especially pronounced in confrontations with recalcitrant family members and friends, particularly in men born on this day.

VIRTUES: Blessed with sharp-witted intelligence as well as with great personal charm and a gift for communication, those born on June 3 have the capacity both to initiate pioneering work and to inspire others to take part in it.
VICES: These individuals are governed by the urge to move forward—usually on their own terms—and react extremely badly if their progress is impeded. They are particularly demanding of people who are in a position to lend their assistance to a pet project, and are prone to losing their tempers, or veering off on extreme tangents when "let down."
VERDICT: Despite their innate understanding of the power of words and personal image in enlisting support, June 3 people easily become frustrated when others fail to fall in with their schemes. They should therefore strive to cultivate a more genuine respect for the equal right of others to the same freedom of thought and deed that they claim for themselves.

On This Day
Famous Births: James Hutton (1726); Frantisek Jan Skroup (1801); Richard Cobden (1804); Jefferson Davis (1808); Charles Lecocq (1832); William Flinders Petrie (1853); King George V of Britain (1865); Raoul Dufy (1877); Josephine Baker (1906); Paulette Goddard (1911); Leo Gorcey (1915); Tony Curtis (1925); Colleen Dewhurst and Alan Ginsberg (1926); Curtis Mayfield (1942); Suzi Quatro (1950).

Significant Events and Anniversaries: June 3 highlights a strong determination to proceed on a chosen course, regardless of the consequences, as is illustrated when the Duke of Windsor married the U.S. divorcée Wallis Simpson (after abdicating from his position as King Edward VIII of Britain) (1937). Determination joined with force on this day when the Duke of York led the English Navy to victory over the Dutch of Lowestoft (1665); and the World War II Battle of Midway began between the Japanese and U.S. Navies (1942). A day that indicates progress of all kinds, June 3 marks the anniversary of the introduction to the astonished world of the first bikini swimsuit (a name inspired by the testing of atomic bombs by U.S. researchers at Bikini Atoll) by Louis Reard (1946); the feat achieved by Major Edward White when he became the first U.S. astronaut to walk in space (1971); and the ordination of the first female rabbi in the United States, Sally Priesand (1972).

JUNE 4

Those with June 4 birthdays are driven by their fascination with acquiring knowledge and then taking the learning process a step further, expanding upon the information they have garnered and developing new approaches in their own, original fashion. While their attention is primarily absorbed by the conceptual realm of ideas, they are people-oriented to the extent that they feel the urge to impart to others their enthusiasm for whatever it is that most excites them. Anxious to inform and guide their friends, family members and coworkers, they yearn to influence the world at large. All June 4 individuals have great innovational potential, and although some are motivated in their work by humanitarian concerns and may perhaps become social workers or caregivers, others choose to apply their considerable intellectual talents to the realm of research. Most have a pronounced artistic streak that suits them admirably for careers as writers or actors if they are self-confident enough to capitalize on their creative capabilities. Although typically quite single-minded when inspired by a stimulating project, these people become easily bored when their intellects are restricted, particularly if they were also born in the Chinese year of the rat.

Whether unwittingly or consciously, many of those born on this day place their personal relationships in a subordinate position to their work. Their considerable charm, kindness and highly developed interpersonal skills draw others to them. Despite the great affection they genuinely feel for those closest to them, these people often may inadvertently hurt others when their profession rather than social commitments are regarded as paramount.

VIRTUES: Those born on June 4 will work with rare determination and ingenuity to achieve progress and to realize their visions. Their great personal charisma and verbal prowess make them popular and often influential figures.
VICES: These individuals are self-contained self-starters, who find their inspiration in abstract concepts. This orientation can cause them to disregard their personal obligations and shut themselves off from potentially rewarding relationships. They may even perceive love and friendship as "unnecessary" distractions from their work.
VERDICT: June 4 people should recognize that they will often achieve greater all-round satisfaction—and ultimately greater empowerment—if they accord more time and attention to their private lives. They should temper their typically over arching commitment toward their interests and career goals with greater consideration for others'—and their own—feelings.

On This Day

Famous Births: King George III of England (1738); Stephen Foster (1826); Bob Fitzsimmons (1862); Carl von Mannerheim (1867); Mabel Lucie Attwell (1879); Rosalind Russell (1908); Christopher Cockerell (1910); Gene Barry (1922); Dennis Weaver (1924); Geoffrey Palmer (1927); Dr. Ruth Westheimer (1928); Bruce Dern (1936); Freddy Fender (1937); Bob Champion (1948); Parker Stevenson (1952); Noah Wyle (1971).

Significant Events and Anniversaries: This is a day on which innovation is starred, and June 4 marks the anniversary of the staging of Britain's first Trooping of the Colour ceremony at London's Horse Guards Parade (1805); and the introduction at the Standard Supermarket in Oklahoma of the world's first shopping carts (1937). In many respects the combined characteristics of June 4 indicate leadership potential, and on this day the German Prince Leopard was installed as the first king of the Belgians (1831); King Napoleon III led the French Army to victory against the Austrians at the Battle of Magenta (1859); and Juan Péron became president of Argentina (1946). Single-minded commitment in pursuit of an inspirational cause is a further important feature of this day, on which suffragette Emily Davison threw herself under King George V's horse, Anmer, at the Epsom Derby to protest against British women's disenfranchisement, an action that cost her her life (1913). On this day that is governed by the element of air, a tragic accident at the Paris Airshow occurred when the Soviet supersonic aircraft, *Concordski*, exploded, causing the deaths of thirty-three people (1973).

Planetary Influences
Ruling planet: Mercury.
Second decan: Personal planet is Venus.

Sacred and Cultural Significance
In Christianity, Whitsunday.
Saints' day: Ninnoc (dates unknown); Petroc (6th century AD); Edfrith (d. 721).

Highlighting the commitment and follow-through—combined with leadership potential—common to June 4, construction of the White House was completed on this day in 1800.

Planetary Influences
Ruling planet: Mercury.
Second decan: Personal planet is Venus.

Sacred and Cultural Significance
Sacred Corn Dance, San Ildefonso Pueblo celebration; national day of Denmark.
Saint's day: Boniface (c.675–754).

The Sacred Corn Dance of the San Ildefonso Pueblo people—celebrated on June 5—is a festival that honors the importance and the sacredness of corn. Here Zuni women clean corn, a traditional staple central to the culture of American southwestern tribes.

JUNE 5

June 5 people have the capacity to generate such innovative ideas that others may at best admire them greatly, regarding them as geniuses, and at worse dismiss them as crackpots. Indeed, their vision and soaring imaginative powers seem unlimited in scope, for these far-sighted individuals refuse to be fettered by conventional truths, recognizing that nothing can be taken for granted. Extremely perceptive, possessed of intellectual curiosity and apparently unlimited energy when it comes to developing and researching the topics that absorb them, those born on this day have the potential to flourish in a variety of professions. The key to their success often lies simply in the extent to which they can communicate effectively with others. Despite their considerable verbal and literary skills, the task of explaining their idiosyncratic ideas often proves difficult. Both the artistic and scientific realms allow these people's talents to flourish: the first requires the suspension of belief, making their visions more likely to be acceptable, while the latter calls for rational enquiry and method, so that their theories may be proven unequivocally.

Those born on June 5 are hypersensitive within their personal relationships, for the numerous disappointments they experience due to the skepticism or ridicule of others undermine their self-confidence. They are needy and deeply appreciative of the unquestioning love and support of their close companions, while empathetic toward those who express their individuality. In this latter respect they make supportive, loving parents, who will typically encourage their children as well as delighting in the fresh approach children bring to life.

VIRTUES: June 5 people are blessed with intellectual gifts including boundless imagination, an aptitude for technical expertise and the steadfastness of focus necessary to develop and realize novel ideas. They are kind, empathetic, nonjudgemental and interested in others.
VICES: The sensitivity of June 5 people can be both a blessing and a burden, for although their profound intuition can work to their advantage, they are easily discouraged and deeply hurt when the ideas they put forward are misunderstood or rejected by others. They may as a result abandon their interests, cling to others because of a lack of self-esteem, or isolate themselves, seeing potential detractors everywhere.
VERDICT: While holding onto the dreams that inspire them, those born on this day should recognize that they may be perceived as unrealistic, and should therefore strive to withstand criticism. They should also work on communicating their ideas effectively.

On This Day
Famous Births: Adam Smith (1723); Alexey Fyodorovich L'vov (1798); John Couch Adams (1819); Francisco Pancho Villa (1878); John Maynard Keynes (1883); Ivy Compton-Burnett (1884); Kurt Hahn (1886); Federico García Lorca (1898); Sheila Sim (1922); Bill Hayes (1926); Tony Richardson (1928); Bill Moyers (1934); Roy Higgins (1938); Margaret Drabble (1939); David Hare (1947); Ken Follett (1949); Mark Walburg (1971); Chad Allen (1974).

Significant Events and Anniversaries: The innovative potential of June 5 was illustrated when the Montgolfier brothers made the world's first ascent in a hot-air balloon in France (1783). The determination indicated by June 5 promises success (sometimes against overwhelming odds), as was achieved when the French town of Benouville became the first continental town to be liberated from German control by Allied forces during World War II (1944); when U.S. Secretary of State George Marshall unveiled his economic recovery program to assist war-devastated Europe (1947); when the Suez Canal was reopened following its occupation by Israeli troops (1975); and when the democratic Solidarity Party won Poland's first free elections since the institution of communist rule in the aftermath of World War II (1989). The ideological conviction inherent in this day has frequently resulted in confrontation, as when Israeli forces attacked Arab lands, precipitating the Six-Day War with Egypt, Syria and Jordan (1967); and when U.S. presidential candidate Robert Kennedy was mortally injured by the anti-Zionist, Jordanian-born immigrant Sirhan Bisharc Sirhan (1968).

JUNE 6

Many of those born on June 6 hide their true nature behind deceptively ordinary and mild-mannered masks. They learn through bitter experience that the uninhibited expression of the sometimes radical visions that inspire them will not generally meet with widespread acceptance, so they present themselves in a deliberately conventional manner. These are, however, imaginative individuals, who disdain the ordinary in favor of the extraordinary: their mercurial intellects, inquisitiveness and flair for innovation typically lead them into uncharted realms. Because they are sharp as well as attracted to the unorthodox, they have little difficulty in accepting new ideas and rising to intellectual challenges. In those professions where they can work independently toward their aims—artistic and outdoor pursuits are particularly well starred—they have the potential to startle and delight others with their originality and capacity for lateral thinking. If constrained by the strictures of large corporations, they will work diligently, but may harbor subversive feelings which could ultimately cause them to rebel.

Although they will often take a brave and solitary stand to promote their visions, those born on this day need to feel that others believe in them, particularly their nearest and dearest. Since so much of their time and energy must be devoted to persuading work colleagues of the potential success of their unusual approach, it is vital to their emotional health that they can count on the unquestioning support of those closest to them, a requirement that is even more pronounced if they were born in the Chinese year of the goat.

VIRTUES: June 6 individuals possess original intellectual powers, and have the ability both to accept and create different strategies. Because they are sometimes insecure, sensitive to the feelings of others and understand that their ideas may appear unfeasibly outlandish, they increase their potential for success by tailoring the presentation of their visions to the characteristics of their audiences.

VICES: Although these people instinctively understand the importance of adapting their eccentricities to conform with society's norms, they are often prone to taking this strategy too far and trying to pretend to be something that they are not—a tendency which can eventually become emotionally damaging.

VERDICT: June 6 people must strike a balance between their intellectual and emotional needs. On the one hand, they must ground themselves in stable domestic relationships to add stability while on their idealistic quests; on the other they must not allow the demands of others to stifle their capacity for independence of thought.

Planetary Influences
Ruling planet: Mercury.
Second decan: Personal planet is Venus.

Sacred and Cultural Significance
National day of Sweden; in Thrace, the Bendida festival.
Saints' day: Primus and Felician (d. c.297); Gudwal (6th century AD); Jarlath (d. c.550); Norbert (c.1080–1134).

On This Day
Famous Births: Diego Velázquez (1599); Pierre Corneille (1606); Nathan Hale (1755); Aleksandr Sergeyevich Pushkin (1799); Henry Newbolt (1862); Robert Falcon Scott (1868); Thomas Mann (1875); Ninette de Valois (1898); Sukarno (1901); Aram Ilyich Khatchaturian (1903); Eugene John Carr (1904); Billie Whitelaw (1932); Asif Iqbal Razvi (1943); Robert Englund (1948); Sandra Bernhard (1955); Bjorn Borg (1956); Mike Gatting (1957).

Significant Events and Anniversaries: June 6 promises pioneering and progressive achievements, and this day marks the anniversary of a number of "firsts": the founding of the Ashmolean, the world's first public museum, in Oxford, England, by Elias Ashmole (1683); the inauguration of the first YMCA hostel, by George Williams in London (1844); the staging of the first official baseball game, between the Knickerbocker Club and the New York Nine in Hoboken, New Jersey (1844); the launching of the first detergent, Persil, by the German company Henkel et Cie (1907); and the opening of the first drive-in movie theater, at Camden, New York (1933). Ideological action is a related feature of this day—D-Day—on which Allied troops began the invasion of "fortress Europe" by landing on the Normandy beaches (1944); while the provocative protest of Sikh militants at their holy site, the Golden Temple at Amritsar, caused their forcible eviction by Indian troops, leaving over three hundred dead (1984).

Demonstrating the day's penchant for strategic thinking and ideologically motivated action, Allied troops invaded Normandy on D-Day—June 6, 1944.

Planetary Influences
Ruling planet: Mercury.
Second decan: Personal planet is Venus.

Sacred and Cultural Significance
In ancient Rome, the Vestalia festival.
Saints' day: Meriasek (6th century AD),
patron saint of Camborne, Cornwall,
England; Robert of Newminster (c.1100–59);
Antonio Gianelli (1789–1846).

Paul Gauguin painted The Artist at His
Easel *in 1885. Born on June 7 in 1848, Gauguin
began painting as a sideline during a
stockbroker career. The success of his creative
vision and technique, perhaps aided by the
single-mindedness starred by his birthday, took
Gauguin's unconventional thinking and daring
curiosity to new levels when he moved
to Tahiti and developed a unique style
embracing the primitive.*

JUNE 7

In common with other mercurially minded people born under the sign of Gemini, June 7 individuals are on a constant quest for stimulation, seeking to experience novel sensations and to acquire new knowledge. Such is the depth of this urge that while they can demonstrate remarkably single-minded focus, concentration and analytical skills when absorbed by a stimulating task or concept, if bored or uninterested they tend to flit speedily from subject to subject in search of intellectual satisfaction. Many of those born on this day profess wide-ranging interests and may find it hard to choose from among them in making an initial career choice. Although they may be successful in a variety of professions, they will rarely gain true fulfillment unless they can follow their own creative path. Their creative talents and social inclinations provide for good personal interaction, thus suiting them well to the performing arts and such commercial activities as marketing or advertising.

Their pronounced originality, self-confidence and vigor endows these gregarious people with great powers of attraction, making them popular figures, and they enjoy the variety and fun inherent in a large circle of friends and acquaintances. Committing themselves to a single life partner does not come easily to June 7 people, who are often concerned that their independence of action will be thereby curtailed. It is not that they lack the capacity to be deeply affectionate—as they typically demonstrate within their relationships with their parents, siblings or children—it is simply that these free-spirited individuals are afraid that the demands of partnership or marriage will ultimately stifle them.

VIRTUES: The primary characteristic that drives June 7 people is their strong intellectual curiosity, which may lead them not only to sample and accumulate a myriad of experiences but also to focus on those that are particularly absorbing and investigate and develop them with remarkable tenacity.
VICES: When taken to its extreme, the restless inquisitiveness to which these individuals are prone carries an inherent danger that they will never explore any intellectual interest or emotional relationship in sufficient depth to obtain ultimate satisfaction.
VERDICT: It is important that those born on this day learn to control their impulse to respond to every novel interest or stranger that beckons alluringly to them. By applying their undoubted capacity to develop, and fully explore, an interest or relationship, they will gain more profound and fulfilling rewards than by succumbing to the temptation of indulging in intellectual or physical promiscuity.

On This Day
Famous Births: Pope Gregory XIII (1502); John Rennie (1761); "Beau" Brummell (1778); Richard Doddridge Blackmore (1825); Paul Gauguin (1848); Knud Rasmussen (1879); Imre Nagy (1896); Elizabeth Bowen (1899); Jessica Tandy (1909); Pietro Annigoni (1910); James Ivory (1928); Virginia McKenna (1931); Tom Jones (1940); Liam Neeson (1952); The Artist formerly known as Prince (1958); Larisa Oleynik (1981).

Significant Events and Anniversaries: Independence in all its forms is strongly highlighted by this day, on which Norway proclaimed its independence from Sweden (1905), and Italy recognized the Lateran Treaty, by which the pope's sovereignty over the Vatican City State in Rome was declared (1929); while during World War II's Battle of Midway the U.S. Navy sank two Japanese aircraft carriers, in a significant step toward suppressing Japan's militaristic expansionism (1942). The innovative artistic potential inherent in June 7 is reflected by two operatic premieres held on this day: that of *The Seven Deadly Sins*, a collaboration between Bertold Brecht, Kurt Weill and George Balanchine, starring Lotte Lenya (1933); and that of *Peter Grimes*, by Benjamin Britten (1945). This day's predilection for personal interaction is variously reflected on the world stage: for example, when Willy Brandt, the West German chancellor, began a sensitive visit to Israel (1973), and when Britain inaugurated a series of popular celebrations to commemorate the Silver Jubilee of Queen Elizabeth II (1977).

JUNE 8

Fundamental to those born on June 8 is their driving need to experience constant intellectual stimulation; being bored is their greatest fear and they typically go to enormous lengths to avoid any situation that they suspect will smother them with feelings of tedium. This strong aversion to anything that they perceive as being dull bestows upon them a tendency to make snap judgements as to the potential level of interest inherent in any person, project or pursuit they encounter, leading to either a speedy dismissal or an enthusiastic taking-up of the subject concerned. Their actions and interests are motivated by their formidable curiosity, their alertness and their desire to actively test themselves against challenges. Their highly developed powers of analysis and their urge to effect progress make June 8 people especially well equipped for science-related careers, but artistic and design-related endeavors are also starred. Whatever profession they choose, however, it is of paramount importance that they should retain a degree of personal autonomy.

Within those personal relationships that are of their own making, those born on this day make charming, enlivening and loyal friends and partners. When they feel obligated to behave in a manner that is alien to their natures, or that their freedom of action is being limited by familial demands, however, their frustration can mount inexorably to the point of rebellion, a propensity that is especially marked when they are much younger than their parents or other authority figures. In such cases they may employ their incisive powers of perception in being cuttingly critical, thus incurring greater hurt than they perhaps intended.

VIRTUES: Intelligent, highly enthusiastic, imaginative and also sensation-seeking, June 8 people are blessed with enormous intellectual talent and vigor, as well as strong innovative inclinations, which, in their most auspicious conjunction, enables them to blaze pioneering trails through life and build a wide social circle.

VICES: These individuals' biggest enemy is their low boredom threshold, which may lead them to dismiss situations, subjects—or even people—after only a cursory assessment as being uninteresting. They may thus unwittingly miss out on a variety of experiences that, if explored initially in greater depth, could have proved surprisingly rewarding.

VERDICT: Although they value individuality—especially their own—those born on this day should beware of becoming overly judgemental with regard to the perceived shortcomings of others. Developing empathy and a greater tolerance toward the expression of others' personalities—no matter how much out of tune with their own preferences—will help widen both their intellectual and emotional horizons.

Planetary Influences
Ruling planet: Mercury.
Second decan: Personal planet is Venus.

Sacred and Cultural Significance
In Japan, an ancient rice festival; Grain in Ear festival celebrated in China.
Saints' day: Médard (c.470–c.560), patron saint of toothache sufferers; William of York (d. 1154).

Frank Lloyd Wright, creative genius of American architecture, was born on June 8, 1867. His seventy-year career was marked by the high level of energy, enthusiasm and imagination characteristic of June 8 people, and he left an indelible mark upon modern architecture and design, inspiring a generation of young builders who studied and worked with him from the early 1930s until his death in 1959.

On This Day
Famous Births: William Dampier (1652); John Smeaton (1724); Robert Schumann (1810); John Everett Millais (1829); Frank Lloyd Wright (1869); Francis Crick (1916); Robert Preston (1918); Barbara Bush (1925); Jerry Stiller (1929); Ray Illingworth (1932); Joan Rivers (1933); Millicent Martin (1934); James Darren (1936); Nancy Sinatra (1940); Boz Scaggs (1944); Derek Underwood (1947); Griffin Dunne (1955).

Significant Events and Anniversaries: Devastatingly effective wit is a pronounced feature of this day, on which the comic play *Hay Fever*, by British playwright Noël Coward, had its premiere (1925). The innovative potential promised by this day is reflected in the achievements of two female pioneers on June 8: of the politician Margaret Bondfield, who became Britain's first female cabinet member on her appointment as minister of labor by prime minister Ramsay MacDonald (1929); and of British yachtswoman Naomi James, who became the first woman to sail round the world single-handed (1978). The determined and active promotion of ideological convictions that is indicated by June 8 was mirrored in the realm of national politics when Japanese aircraft bombed the Australian cities of Sydney and Newcastle during World War II (1942); and when Spain closed its border with the British dependency of Gibraltar, over which it claimed sovereignty (1969).

JUNE 9

✱✱

Planetary Influences
Ruling planet: Mercury.
Second decan: Personal planet is Venus.

Sacred and Cultural Significance
Saints' day: Ephrem of Syria (c.306–73); Columba of Iona (c.521–97), patron saint of poets.

The main guiding principle according to which those born on June 9 conduct their lives is to remain true to their beliefs. Whatever form or orientation these beliefs take—whether they are the ethical tenets adhered to within their interpersonal relationships, or the visions that inform and motivate their work—these people will tenaciously maintain and propagate them as striking a profound chord with their inner selves. Together with this core characteristic, these individuals possess a restless, lively form of intelligence that bestows upon them the irresistible compulsion to explore any new and fascinating concept that presents itself. This urge to discover previously hidden or unknown areas of interest, as well as their marked fascination with the potential inherent in technology, endows them with a strong progressive inclination which, when developed, gives them the rare capacity to effect real advances. Reflecting the multifaceted nature of their talents and inclinations, they may find satisfaction and success in a multitude of professions, ranging from the literary, musical or dramatic arts, to the more sober fields of medical research or computers, but they generally prefer active, hands-on involvement to managerial or administrative roles.

Their high personal standards and ambitious ideological aims, however laudable, may give June 9 people some severe problems with interpersonal relationships. Because they are both highly discriminating with regard to choosing friends and partners, and also tend to give priority to their intellectual pursuits, they may inadvertently impose near-impossible demands on those closest to them. Futhermore, despite the quiet affection that they manifest toward those who offer them unconditional support—especially June 9 women—they may unwittingly fail to reciprocate the level of support that they themselves demand of others.

VIRTUES: Blessed with an apparently inexhaustible interest in understanding and exploring novel concepts, June 9 people are extremely versatile in their interests and talents and, when their attention is truly absorbed, also remarkably tenacious in working toward the attainment of their visions.
VICES: Although those born on this day insist on their own independence of thought and deed, they may find it difficult to accept that such freedom should apply to others, may therefore become judgemental and disapproving of behavior that does not conform to their beliefs and expectations.
VERDICT: In order to avoid isolating themselves from the comfort and support of honest, open and tolerant personal relationships, it is crucial that these people relax their idealistic—and often unrealistic—expectations of others, instead accepting and embracing the rich diversity that is inherent in humans and their relationships.

On This Day
Famous Births: Czar Peter the Great of Russia (1672); George Stephenson (1781); Otto Nicolai (1810); Elizabeth Garrett Anderson (1836); Walter Weedon Grossmith (1854); Carl Nielsen (1865); Grace Cook (1892); Cole Porter (1893); Robert Cummings (1910); Patrick Steptoe (1913); Jackie Mason (1934); Dick Vitale (1940); Charles Saatchi (1943); Bonnie Tyler (1951); Michael J. Fox (1961); Johnny Depp (1963); Natalie Portman (1981).

Significant Events and Anniversaries: This day indicates a fascination with effecting technological advances, and on June 9 the first self-service laundry—the automat—was opened in Philadelphia (1902); the crew of the stricken British submarine *Poseidon* off China successfully used the Davis escape mechanism for the first time (1931); John Logie Baird unveiled his high-definition television broadcast system (1933); the first nuclear submarine to carry Polaris missiles, the U.S. vessel *George Washington*, was launched (1959); and, for the first time, a live parliamentary debate was televised from the British House of Commons (1975). The progressive nature of the day was apparent when King Edward VII visited Czar Nicholas II on the royal yacht, the first official meeting between a British king and a Russian czar (1908).

A British railway engineer and inventor who constructed his first locomotive in 1814, George Stephenson went on to build the Rocket *in 1829, which provided the first mainline passenger service. His career demonstrates the propensities inherent in his June 9 birthday: fascination with technology, intellectual tenacity and progressive vision.*

JUNE 10

The most striking characteristic manifested by June 10 people, and one that makes an immediate impression on coming into contact with them for the first time, is their driving energy which, when coupled with their propensity to express their strongly held views bluntly, can be both awesome and intimidating. To the casual observer, it may seem that those born on this day lack sensitivity, but, while they may be somewhat intolerant of those whom they perceive to be lethargic or indecisive, these people possess imagination and perspicacity, dual qualities which arouse in them both compassionate feelings and strong protective instincts toward others. While they may wish to play a useful humanitarian role, their actions are prompted more by their inherent urge to take positive action and thereby achieve concrete results than by their desire to spend time in considering the theoretical aspects of a situation. In most problematic situations they are furthermore blessed with the enviable capacity swiftly to identify what needs to be done, their quick minds helping them to formulate the most appropriate response. June 10 people will thrive especially in those fields in which they can achieve tangible progress, and their vigor suits them particularly for such professions as the military or police forces, but also for theatrical careers.

The bright public personae assumed by many born on this day often hides a more negative, depressive facet of their personalities—another product of their great powers of observation and imagination, which may lead them to envisage darkly nihilistic impending scenarios. Indeed, it may be that the active lifestyles that these people generally adopt is a conscious or unconscious strategy to seek an escape from the fears that haunt them during more introspective moments. And while they typically yearn for the comfort to be found in strong personal relationships, they may find it difficult to commit themselves to friends and partners, perhaps feeling that it would be dangerous to expose their emotional vulnerability.

VIRTUES: Blessed with keen intellectual talents, endowed with prodigious energy, and possessing strong convictions, those born on this day are natural leaders, whose unlimited imagination and driving sense of purpose give them real innovative and inspirational potential.
VICES: Because they are in any case active and progressively thinking individuals, June 10 people tend to throw themselves wholeheartedly into projects, shutting out other issues lest these become addictive: this is especially true when difficult truths are involved.
VERDICT: In the interests of safeguarding their ultimate emotional well-being, it is crucial that these undoubtedly courageous people confront and overcome the worries that plague their peace of mind, rather than seeking temporary diversion in other areas or pursuits. Problems can be solved if faced squarely, but will fester and deepen if they are ignored.

On This Day

Famous Births: James Stuart, the "Old Pretender" (1688); John Dollond (1706); Gustave Courbet (1819); Carl Hagenbeck (1844); André Derain (1880); Frederick Loewe and Eric Maschwitz (1901); Terence Rattigan (1911); Saul Bellow (1915); Prince Philip, Duke of Edinburgh (1921); Judy Garland (1922); Robert Maxwell (1923); June Haver (1926); Maurice Sendak (1928); F. Lee Bailey (1933); Elizabeth Hurley (1966); Tara Lipinski (1982).

Significant Events and Anniversaries: This day highlights the active promotion of innovative visions, and marks the anniversary of a variety of events that reflects this propensity: including the opening of France's Jardin des Plantes in Paris, the world's first public zoological gardens (1793); the transmission of the first S.O.S. call by the S.S. *Slavonia* after she ran into difficulties off the Azores (1909); the patenting of the first ballpoint pen by the Hungarian Lazlo Biró (1943); and the first operation to unblock heart valves, undertaken at Guy's Hospital in London, England (1948). Strong convictions—often political or patriotic ideologies—are a further feature of June 10, on which the Italian socialist leader Giacomo Matteotti was murdered by Fascist assassins (1924); and Conservative leader Margaret Thatcher was elected to serve a second term as Britain's prime minister (1983).

Planetary Influences
Ruling planet: Mercury.
Second decan: Personal planet is Venus.

Sacred and Cultural Significance
Time Observance day in Japan.
Saint's day: Ithamar (d. c.660).

An accused "witch" is arrested in Salem, Massachusetts. In an unfortunate confluence of the day's tendencies toward strong convictions and intolerance, June 10 was the date that the first Salem "witch" was hanged, in 1692.

Planetary Influences
Ruling planet: Mercury.
Third decan: Personal planets are Saturn and Uranus.

Sacred and Cultural Significance
Saints' day: Barnabas (d. 1st century AD).

The focus and determination, as well as personal charm, of the typical June 11 personality proved a winning combination for John G. Diefenbaker, whose 1955 electoral victory brought to an end twenty-two years of liberal rule in Canada.

JUNE 11

✶✶

Although they share the same quality of restless curiosity with many of their Gemini fellows, the thirst for knowledge of those born on June 11 takes a less wide-ranging form, for once they have found a subject that truly absorbs them (and this may occur in childhood), they typically concentrate their attention and energy upon it almost exclusively. Indeed, they have an enviable facility totally to immerse themselves in their work, allowing nothing to distract them from their quest, their objective being to learn as much as they possibly can as a prelude to attempting a pioneering breakthrough. Their strong focus, determination and energy give them the outstanding potential to achieve their goals, whether they be in the realms of scientific research, artistic innovation or sporting pursuits—all areas to which June 11 people are naturally attracted. They will flourish best when operating as independent agents, however, for they will usually feel unbearably stifled by the procedures and constraints of conventional organizations.

Although they possess great personal charm, and have a profound desire both to protect their loved ones and bring them fun and enjoyment, those born on this day may find it difficult to sustain a settled family life. It is not that they lack genuine care and concern for those closest to them, but rather that the lure of outside interests may prove irresistible, leading to a neglect of family affairs. This propensity is particularly marked in the case of June 11 men, especially those who are in any case not enamored of domestic chores and responsibilities.

VIRTUES: Those born on this day possess great strength of purpose, their inspiration being rarely of the materialistic kind, but rather fueled by the desire to master their subject matter and effect real progress. To this end they combine their outstanding qualities of focus and vigor with their incisive intellectual skills, rarely allowing themselves to become discouraged by setbacks or the criticism of others.
VICES: Although their capacity for single-minded concentration and their stubborn determination augurs well for career success, these may prove incompatible with forming and maintaining personal relationships, thereby exposing these people to the risk of becoming emotionally isolated.
VERDICT: It is vital that June 11 people recognize the damaging effect that their often obsessive tendencies can have—on themselves as much as on other people. They should remember that great rewards are achieved when all areas of life are harmonized, and should therefore not sacrifice their personal lives to their intellectual missions.

On This Day
Famous Births: Ben Jonson (1572); John Constable (1776); Richard Strauss (1864); E.V. Lucas (1868); Jacques Cousteau (1910); Ruth Montgomery (1912); Richard Todd (1919); Beryl Grey (1927); Athol Fugard (1932); Gene Wilder (1935); Chad Everett (1936); Jackie Stewart (1939); Adrienne Barbeau (1945); Joe Montana (1956); Frances Ann Read (1960).

Significant Events and Anniversaries: This day indicates a determination to push the bounds of human knowledge and endeavor forward—sometimes in spite of the consequences—as was tragically illustrated when, on June 11, the British explorer John Franklin died in the Arctic while attempting to discover the route of the Northwest Passage (1847); and, in the sporting world, when three cars crashed during the Le Mans race in France, causing the deaths of eighty onlookers (1955). The often visionary sense of purpose that is a strong feature of June 11 was reflected when Benito Mussolini, Italy's Fascist leader, declared war on the Allies, who were already engaged in hostilities with Nazi Germany (1940); and, more positively, albeit also sadly involving loss of life, when Dutch marines liberated the hostages being held on a train at Assen by South Moluccan terrorists, eight of whom were killed (1977). Sporting pursuits are often starred on June 11, and on this day Sir Barton became the first racehorse to win the Triple Crown (1919) and Harry Vardon won his fourth British Open golf championship at Prestwick (1903).

JUNE 12

Those born on June 12 give the impression of being remarkably self-contained individuals, whose boundless energy, enthusiasm for embarking on unusual ventures, and quick intelligence bestow upon them the capacity not only to keep themselves occupied, but also to be pioneers in many aspects of their lives. They cannot bear inertia in any form—be it intellectual or physical—and will push themselves to their limits even during periods of so-called relaxation, filling their time away from work with hobbies, or devising entertainments for their friends and family members. Their approach to challenges—indeed, to life itself—is typically characterized by a combination of optimism and curiosity, and while they may throw themselves wholeheartedly into the pursuit of projects that capture their interest, they rarely lose sight of the larger picture. And, although their outlook is informed by rational rather than intuitive observation, their sensitivity endows them with great empathy for those who are less able to help themselves.

Their quest to achieve progress, backed by their strong organizational powers, suits them to a wide range of professions, from outdoor, physical work to administrative jobs, whether corporate or humanitarian; they often make inspirational team leaders. They may lack patience, however, with coworkers or family members having less vigor and commitment than themselves, and in such cases have a propensity either to dismiss the objects of their irritation as hopeless causes, or to attempt to "improve" them by resorting to dictatorial tactics, a tendency that is particularly pronounced if they were also born in the Chinese year of the dragon.

VIRTUES: June 12 individuals combine a mercurial, perceptive and progressive turn of mind with an urge to take action, resulting in a goal-oriented approach typically undertaken in a direct and positive manner. Their enthusiasm is infectious and others are attracted by their dynamism.
VICES: Such is their single-minded desire to realize their aims, that these disciplined, vigorous individuals may react negatively to those who are slow to fall into line with their visions and operational methods and, in their frustration, may sometimes resort to hostile or even bullying tactics.
VERDICT: In order to avoid losing the goodwill of others, it is important that these people develop a more profound acceptance of different approaches and opinions, and that they do not try to coerce others to agree with them. Evolving greater patience and tolerance will bring not only emotional rewards, but also intellectual enrichment.

On This Day

Famous Births: Charles Kingsley (1819); Rikard Nordraak (1842); Anthony Eden and Leon Goossens (1897); Norman Hartnell (1901); George Bush (1924); Vic Damone (1928); Brigid Brophy and Anne Frank (1929); Jim Nabors (1932); Chick Corea (1941); Pat Jennings (1945); Jenilee Harrison (1959); Ally Sheedy (1962).

Significant Events and Anniversaries: The successes that can result from the conjunction of aspirational intellectual qualities and determination that is strongly underlined by this day were highlighted in a number of diverse areas on June 12: when, for example, a fifteen-year-old French boy was the first patient to survive a blood-transfusion operation (using lamb's blood), administered by Jean-Baptiste Denys at Montpellier University (1667); when the U.S. sporting visionary Abner Doubleday of Cooperstown, New York, devised the game of baseball (1839); when three British climbers, including Leigh Mallory, climbed to the then highest altitude ever attained without the help of oxygen on Mount Everest (1922); when the American Bryan Allen pioneered the first crossing of the English Channel in an aircraft powered only by foot pedals (1979); and when Margaret Thatcher became Britain's prime minister for her third successive term (1987). The desire to take action was seen in the sentencing of David Berkowitz, "Son of Sam," when he received a life sentence for each of the six murders of which he had been convicted (1978).

Planetary Influences
Ruling planet: Mercury.
Third decan: Personal planets are Saturn and Uranus.

Sacred and Cultural Significance
Zeus honored in ancient Greece; in Korea, rice farmers wash their hair in a stream to ensure a plentiful harvest.
Saints' day: Basilides (dates unknown); Leo III (d. 816); Odulf (d. 855); Eskil (d. c.1080).

Poignantly demonstrating many of the virtues of her June 12 birthday in her brief life, Anne Frank chronicled the persecution and suffering inflicted on her Jewish family by the Nazis. Being born in the Chinese year of the snake reinforced her natural love of books, wise outlook and loyalty to family. Although she died in a concentration camp in 1945, her diary survived—revealing her courageous spirit.

Planetary Influences
Ruling planet: Mercury.
Third decan: Personal planets are Saturn and Uranus.

Sacred and Cultural Significance
Saints' day: Antony of Padua (c.1193–1231), patron saint of lost articles, the poor and the starving.

Signaling the beginning of a new era in transportation, Queen Victoria traveled by train for the first time on June 13—a day indicating progressive, innovative and active tendencies—in 1842.

JUNE 13

✶✶

June 13 individuals typically reject the conventional truths and behavioral norms accepted by less imaginative members of society, intuitively aware that there is more to life and human understanding than has yet been discovered. In many of those born on this day, the desire to uncover hidden knowledge manifests itself in a pronounced otherworldly streak which may inspire some to explore the abstract realms of spirituality or metaphysics and others the boundaries of scientific exploration or artistic innovation. In whichever field these people choose to make their professions—and their wide-ranging interests, openness to change, and strongly developed qualities of both perception and organization equips them well for many—they display a relish for confronting and overcoming challenges, as well as a refreshingly innovative approach that motivates others. Indeed, despite their predilection for testing their own limitations, those born on this day prefer to work as part of a team (naturally gravitating toward leadership) rather than in lonely solitude, especially if they are women.

In many respects, these individuals' quest to bring about progress is fueled by an often unconscious wish to benefit the human community as a whole, for the combination of their soaring imaginative powers and clear-sighted perspicacity cannot help but arouse profoundly empathetic feelings within them. In the personal sphere, they express this concern by striving to provide their loved ones with both emotional and material support, and enriching all their relationships with a sense of fun and magnanimous acceptance of others' foibles.

VIRTUES: Those born on June 13 are blessed with the dual qualities of profound intellectual curiosity and prodigious energy which, when combined with their innate certainty that there are many universal truths that have yet to be revealed, gives them outstanding innovative potential. They make stimulating and thoughtful friends.
VICES: Inherent in their fascination with acquiring knowledge, coupled with their propensity for throwing themselves single-mindedly into challenging situations, is the danger that these people may go to extremes, thereby inadvertently cutting themselves off from reality.
VERDICT: Although these individuals are strongly oriented toward human relationships, instinctively recognizing the importance of grounding themselves within stable and supportive emotional bonds, they should ensure that their natural predilection toward exploring the concepts that fascinate them does not lead them to become isolated from others within a parallel dimension of their own making.

On This Day
Famous Births: Fanny Burney (1752); Thomas Arnold (1795); W.B. Yeats (1865); Gerald Gardner (1884); Elisabeth Schumann (1885); Basil Rathbone (1892); Dorothy L. Sayers (1893); Paavo Nurmi (1897); Mary Whitehouse (1910); Don Budge (1915); Slim Dusty (1927); Christo (1935); Malcolm McDowell (1943); Richard Thomas (1951); Tim Allen (1953); Peter Scudamore (1958); Jamie Walters (1969); Mary-Kate and Ashley Olsen (1986).

Significant Events and Anniversaries: The innovative inclinations that are highlighted by June 13 may result in radical actions, as is illustrated when, on this day, Wat Tyler led English peasants in a revolt against the imposition of a poll tax (1381); when Chinese nationalists began their siege of Beijing's foreign embassies which heralded the Boxer Rebellion (1900); and when Hitler launched the first V-1 flying bomb, the "doodlebug," against Britain, causing the deaths of three people in Southampton (1944). This day's progressive and active tendencies were mirrored in the sporting arena by the holding of the first women's golfing championship at Royal Lytham, in England (1893), and the culmination of soccer's first European Cup, staged in Paris (1956); tragically, however, British land- and water-speed champion Sir Henry Segrave's relish for pitting himself against self-imposed challenges cost him his life when his speedboat capsized at Lake Windermere in England (1930).

JUNE 14

June 14 individuals have a strong urge to take charge, whether it be of those who surround them—their colleagues, friends or family members—or of projects that demand active responses. This instinctive propensity for supervision stems from their impressive ability to swiftly sum up the inherent components and potential outcome of a given situation (the result of their all-encompassing perspicacity), then to incisively decide upon the best course to follow. Once they have settled upon their preferred strategy, these people will follow it with fierce tenacity, pragmatically amending minor details as necessary, but rarely conceding defeat. Their confidence in their convictions is born of their strong self-belief, and it is this quality—as well as their aversion to standing idly on the sidelines—that endows these energetic people with their enthusiasm for leadership. While this dynamic outlook may indeed inspire less decisive individuals, others may be alienated by what may be perceived to be the arrogant certainty and abrupt manner of those born on this day.

The manifestation of their strong wills may prove both a blessing and a handicap, for although their single-mindedness and forcefulness augurs well for the successful attainment of their aims, their confrontational approach will almost inevitably cause havoc with their interpersonal relationships. This is particularly the case within their personal liaisons, within which—with the most laudable of motivations—they often cannot help but adopt a somewhat dictatorial approach; this is especially the case for men born on this day. This predilection is therefore best confined to the workplace, where they typically become gifted corporate leaders with a special affinity for business, although they also have the potential to make outstanding contributions in whatever field they choose.

VIRTUES: Typically possessed of clear cut, strongly held opinions, and blessed with prodigious energy, those born on this day are governed by a compulsion to take uncompromisingly direct action in the quest to achieve their far-sighted visions.

VICES: The desire to realize their ambitions often governs June 14 people to the exclusion of all other considerations, including the sensibilities of those who oppose them, as well as of those for whom they are responsible, especially their coworkers and members of their families.

VERDICT: June 14 people should make a concerted effort to anticipate the reactions that their forcefulness arouses in others, which will frequently not be positive. Adjusting their approach to include a greater awareness and consideration of others' feelings will ultimately not only bring them emotional satisfaction, but will also assist them in attaining their goals.

On This Day

Famous Births: Harriet Beecher Stowe (1811); John McCormack (1884); Heddle Nash (1896); Margaret Bourke-White (1906); Kathleen Raine (1908); Burl Ives (1909); Sam Wanamaker (1919); Pierre Salinger (1925); Che Guevara (1928); Marla Gibbs (1931); Jerzy Kosinski (1933); Donald Trump (1946); Boy George (1961); Grant Kenny (1963); Steffi Graf (1969).

Significant Events and Anniversaries: The unyielding sense of purpose that is inherent in this day, combined with a strong propensity for action, is reflected in the realm of warfare, and June 14 marks the anniversary of the Battle of Naseby during the English Civil War, when the Parliamentarian New Model Army under the command of Cromwell and Fairfax defeated the Royalist forces under Charles I and Prince Rupert (1645); the victory of the French Army over its Austrian enemy at the Battle of Marengo in Italy during the French Revolutionary War (1800); the bombing of London by the German Luftwaffe during World War I, killing about a hundred civilians (1917); the triumphant entry of the German Army into Paris during World War II (1940); and the surrender of Argentinian troops to the forces of the British Army to bring the Falklands War to an end (1982). National and political concerns are also highlighted by this day, on which Congress voted to adopt the "Stars and Stripes" as the U.S.A.'s official flag (1777); and, in Afrikaner-dominated, apartheid South Africa, the A.N.C. leader Nelson Mandela was sentenced to imprisonment for life (1964).

Planetary Influences
Ruling planet: Mercury.
Third decan: Personal planets are Saturn and Uranus.

Sacred and Cultural Significance
Saints' day: Dogmael (d. 6th century AD).

Born on June 14, 1906, Margaret Bourke-White built a remarkable career as a prolific and adventurous photojournalist. Drawing on her energetic, strong-willed and artistic birthday traits, Bourke-White was the first woman photographer to be attached to the U.S. armed forces, during World War II. Being born in the Chinese year of the horse enhanced her natural flair for leadership, love of travel and independent spirit as she became an official United Nations war correspondent during the Korean War.

Planetary Influences
Ruling planet: Mercury.
Third decan: Personal planets are Saturn and Uranus.

Sacred and Cultural Significance
Saints' day: Vitus, patron saint of dancers and epileptics, Modestus and Crescentia (d. c.303); Trillo (5th century AD).

Ben Franklin's famous 1752 experiment of flying a metal-framed kite in an electrical storm took place on June 15, a day governed by the element of air and reinforcing the qualities of curiosity and progressive thinking.

Although those born on this day exhibit the same wide-ranging curiosity as others who share their mercurial star sign, this characteristic is manifested more by their intense interest in other people than by their attraction to abstract concepts. This is not to say that they are not inspired by intellectual or physical challenges—on the contrary, June 15 people are naturally oriented toward making active progress—but rather that they are motivated by human rather than technical or philosophical concerns. Whether or not the professions that they choose fall within the humanitarian field (and the medical and social work spheres are particularly well starred), these individuals will only thrive when they are surrounded by a closely knit team of coworkers, for interpersonal interaction is a fundamental requirement for their success and ultimate satisfaction. Many of those born on June 15 will find fulfillment in artistic careers, when their performances can bring enjoyment to others, thus also giving them the reciprocal acclaim that is vital to their self-esteem. Others will employ talents and inclinations to great effect in advertising, marketing or the retail trade.

Given their interest in others, it is not surprising that June 15 people are gregarious types, who place enormous value on the strong bonds that they typically forge with friends and family members and strive to ensure their well-being. This desire to please as well as support others is particularly pronounced in the women born on this day, as well as in those born in the Chinese year of the pig. One danger inherent in the good will radiated by these people, however, is that unscrupulous types may take advantage of their generosity.

VIRTUES: These people are primarily driven by their insatiable interest in the human condition, and in seeking to understand what makes others tick they typically utilize their considerable powers of intuition and perspicacity. Their sensitivity and desire to be the beneficial instruments of progress are supplemented by their compassion and kindness.
VICES: The actions and attitudes of those born on June 15 may be unconsciously conditioned by a somewhat insecure need to feel loved and valued by others. This may make them susceptible to flattery, resulting in an inflated sense of vanity.
VERDICT: It is important that these individuals occasionally make time for periods of introspection in order honestly to examine the motives that underlie both their own actions and those of people who make demands on them. In this way they will not only be better able to direct their energies more effectively, but will learn to discriminate between their true friends and those who seek to manipulate them.

On This Day
Famous Births: Edward, the Black Prince (1330); Josiah Henson (1789); Hablot Knight Browne (1815); Edvard Hagerup Grieg (1843); Harry Philmore Langdon (1884); Ernest Urban Trevor Huddleston (1913); Yuri Andropov (1914); Erroll Louis Garner (1923); Mario Cuomo (1932); Waylon Jennings (1937); Harry Nilsson (1941); Nicola Pagett (1945); Simon Callow (1949); Jim Belushi (1954); Helen Hunt (1963); Courtney Cox (1964).

Significant Events and Anniversaries: June 15 is a day that highlights human concerns—both individual and societal—as was reflected when England's King John signed the Magna Carta at Runnymede guaranteeing political and personal rights against monarchic abuses of power (1215); when Florence Nightingale inaugurated her training school for nurses in London (1860); when the German chancellor Otto von Bismarck introduced the world's first health-insurance scheme (1883); and when the Union of Democratic Center Party, led by Adolfo Suarez, won the first free elections held in Spain since 1936 (1977). This day is governed by the element of air, and marks the anniversary of Benjamin Franklin's famous electrical experiment when, by flying a metal-framed kite during a thunderstorm, he proved that lightning is attracted to metal (1752), as well as the pioneering achievement of British aviators John Alcock and Arthur Whitten-Brown, who completed the first nonstop flight across the Atlantic, from Newfoundland to Ireland (1919).

JUNE 16

T hose born on June 16 combine within their characters an unusual blend of adventurousness and caution, qualities born on the one hand of their great imaginative and innovative inclinations, and on the other of their perspicacity and astuteness. This conjunction generally means that they will take short-term risks in the interest of achieving their longer-term goals, and their willingness to be flexible without losing their sense of purpose, is a strategy that has the potential to bring them success. In the world of business, for example, it may be manifested by backing an entrepreneurial endeavor with solid organizational support, or by judiciously speculating on the stock market to build a larger portfolio; while in the artistic and scientific realms it may be demonstrated by controlled experimentation. Yet despite the financial fruits that may be reaped by following this approach, June 16 people are motivated more by a profound desire to bring about progress.

These are serious and somewhat introverted people, who derive comfort and satisfaction from such nonmaterialistic pleasures as strong emotional relationships, or the beauty inherent in nature and the arts. They typically abide by a strongly humanitarian ethical code, which endows them with genuine concern for other people—especially those in need of help—and a innate horror of abuses of power. Thus while they are remarkably loyal and steadfastly affectionate to those closest to them, they find it hard to tolerate cynical or inconsiderate behavior.

VIRTUES: June 16 individuals are innately attracted to original and pioneering concepts, but ground their flights of imagination within a supportive framework based upon reality, a combination of innovation and pragmatism that augurs well for professional success. In all their ventures, they maintain the importance of humanitarian and moral values.
VICES: Their gift of far-sighted vision endows those born on this day with the capacity to foresee a range of possible scenarios, not all of which are positive, and they may therefore suppress their risk-taking tendencies in order to steer safe courses, a policy which may cause them to become intellectually and emotionally stagnant.
VERDICT: Although they generally balance their enterprising and prudent qualities extremely well, these people must ensure that they do not disrupt this synergy by allowing one or other to gain the upper hand, thereby becoming either too impulsive or too cautious.

On This Day

Famous Births: John Cheke (1514); Julius Plücker (1801); King Gustav V of Sweden (1858); George James Frampton (1860); Stan Laurel (1890); Lupino Lane (1892); Enoch Powell (1912); Tom Graveney (1927); Erich Segal (1937); Crash Craddock (1940); Joan Van Ark (1946); Peter Sterling (1960); Tupac Shakur (1971).

Significant Events and Anniversaries: The effective promotion of innovative ideas is an inherent feature of June 16, as was reflected when Henry Ford founded his pioneering automobile company, and the Pepsi-Cola beverage company officially registered its name—both of which were to become world famous businesses (1903); and when the U.S. Congress approved President F.D. Roosevelt's "New Deal" package of reforms designed to alleviate the pernicious effects of the Depression (1935). Humanitarian and democratic principles are highlighted by this day, on which the former prime minister of Hungary, Imre Nagy, was executed for his role in the 1956 revolution engendered by the Soviet domination of his country (1958); the Soviet ballet dancer Rudolf Nureyev defected to the West in order to enjoy increased personal liberty (1961); and about one thousand people were killed by government forces during a demonstration in the South African township of Soweto against the compulsory teaching of Afrikaans in schools (1976). On this air-governed day, the Soviet cosmonaut Valentina Tereshkova became the first woman to travel in space, in *Vostok 6* (1963); while "Space Invaders," an electronic game, was introduced to the world by Japan's Taito Corporation (1978). This day was immortalized by Irish novelist James Joyce, who based the entire action of his book *Ulysses* on June 16, 1904.

Planetary Influences
Ruling planet: Mercury.
Third decan: Personal planets are Saturn and Uranus.

Sacred and Cultural Significance
Soweto day in South Africa; Silver Chalice Day, a Pagan celebration.
Saints' day: Cyricus and Julitta (d. c.304); Ismael (6th century AD).

Soviet cosmonaut Valentina Tereshkova became the first woman to travel in space, in Vostok 6, *on June 16, 1963. Appropriately, the day is governed by the element of air, favors pioneering qualities and bodes well for innovative ideas.*

Planetary Influences
Ruling planet: Mercury.
Third decan: Personal planets are Saturn and Uranus.

Sacred and Cultural Significance
In Nara, Japan, a purification ritual is performed; Eurydice honored in ancient Greece.
Saints' day: Alban (3rd century AD); Nectan (6th century AD); Adulf and Botulf (d. 680); Moling (d. 697); Briavel (dates unknown), patron of St. Briavels, Gloucestershire, England; Rainier of Pisa (1117–61).

National and political ventures are favored by June 17, the day on which, in 1775, English troops and American colonists engaged in the Battle of Bunker Hill during the American Revolutionary War.

JUNE 17

Many of the characteristics manifested by those born on this day appear to be curiously paradoxical. Thus although they are geared toward benefiting human society and yearn to establish caring and committed personal relationships, they may have difficulty in becoming intimate with others; and while they possess highly developed organizational skills their behavior may appear radical or impulsive in the extreme. These apparent contradictions are the result of, on the one hand, their mercurial and profoundly imaginative minds causing them to be attracted to concepts that are out of the ordinary and, on the other, their saturnine tendencies that provide a grounding—yet somewhat negative—influence upon their actions. When they are successful in reconciling these characteristics, June 17 people make remarkably effective agents of progress, but the task proves impossible for many. Perhaps their primary motivation is their urge to realize the unusual visions that they have for improving human society; these may take the form of political or religious ideologies or of original forms of artistic endeavor. Although they make inspirational leaders when their often revolutionary ideas receive acceptance, other times they may find themselves plowing a lonely furrow.

Despite their considerable powers of persuasion, the forceful—often domineering—approach that these individuals usually adopt may meet with variable success, sometimes causing them to resort to more unorthodox—even unethical—methods. Because they may often experience disappointment in their professional ventures, June 17 people find profound solace in the unquestioning support and affection of their nearest and dearest, and reciprocate with loyalty and love the belief that their long-standing family members and friends show in them. Their tendency to distrust the motivations of more recent acquaintances, however, may hinder the development of new relationships.

VIRTUES: These imaginative and progressive individuals are fired by ideals that are often far ahead of their times, developing them by means of their sound investigative and organizational skills. They promote their beliefs with rare tenacity and strength of purpose.
VICES: Those born on this day may inadvertently obstruct their own progress by alienating more cautious types with the forceful promotion of their visions. When frustrated they have a propensity to lash out at their detractors rather than persisting with the persuasive methods that they employ so successfully on other occasions.
VERDICT: June 17 people should try to adopt a more realistic view of the effect that their intense approach may have on those who do not know them well. Evolving a more easygoing and tolerant acceptance of human differences will give them a better chance of achieving their desired ends, and will furthermore bring them greater emotional fulfillment.

On This Day
Famous Births: King Edward I of England (1239); John Wesley (1703); William Parsons (1800); Charles François Gounod (1818); William Crookes (1832); Igor Fyodorovich Stravinsky (1882); Ralph Bellamy (1904); Dean Martin (1917); Beryl Reid (1920); John Brian Statham (1930); Derek Ibbotson (1932); Ken Loach (1936); Newt Gingrich (1943); Barry Manilow (1946); Joe Piscopo (1951); Mark Linn-Baker (1953).

Significant Events and Anniversaries: Innovations of all kinds are highlighted by this day, which marks the anniversary of the patenting of a waterproof fabric lined with rubber by the Scottish chemist Charles Macintosh (1823); the first use of an antiseptic (carbolic acid) during a surgical operation, carried out by Joseph Lister at Scotland's Glasgow Infirmary (1867); the pioneering kidney-transplant operation performed by surgeons in Chicago (1950); and the patenting of the Polaroid camera by U.S. inventor Edwin Land (1970). National and political ventures are also features of this day, on which English explorer Francis Drake arrived in the *Golden Hind* at San Francisco Bay, which he named "New Albion" in honor of his country (1579); English troops engaged the American colonists at the Battle of Bunker Hill during the U.S. War of Independence (1775); and Iceland became a republic independent of Denmark (1944).

JUNE 18

Their great *joie de vivre*, their relish of new ideas, their typically positive and energetic approach to everything that they undertake, as well as the responsible attitude that they manifest toward their family members, friends and colleagues, all combine to make those born on June 18 attractive and popular personalities to whom others naturally gravitate. They are particularly valued for the generous encouragement and support that they offer to those closest to them, and for the enlivening and quirky sense of fun that they inject into their interpersonal relationships, a tendency that is redoubled if they were also born in the Chinese year of the horse. June 18 people are imaginative individuals, whose restless curiosity can lead them to explore previously untapped areas, often with remarkably original results. They have the potential to make an especial mark in the performing arts, for which most have a natural affinity, but they may also blaze trails as scientific researchers or business entrepreneurs. Whatever career they choose, they prefer to work as part of a team rather than in an individual capacity, for they are greatly stimulated by personal contact.

Although their propensity to enjoy life to the fullest and their gregariousness may mean that those born on this day take some time to commit themselves to a life partner, once domestically settled they are typically deeply affectionate and considerate toward their loved ones. They usually make gifted parents, although they may find it hard to resist attempting to control their offsprings' lives, a tendency that may ultimately cause resentment.

VIRTUES: June 18 people temper their adventurous, explorative streak with a profound need to ground themselves within the strong bonds that they form with their close acquaintances, combining their urge to effect progress with their humanitarian concerns. Positive and extremely good company, their relationships are characterized by mutual affection.
VICES: Although the apparently boundless concern and goodwill that those born on this day manifest toward their nearest and dearest is one of their most endearing qualities, it may also cause them to become overly protective and not allow the objects of their love to enjoy the same degree of independence that they cherish for themselves.
VERDICT: These individuals usually steer a balanced course through life, maintaining a steady equilibrium between their flightier and more stolid tendencies, as well as between their professional and personal concerns. They should, however, occasionally engage in periods of introspection to ensure that they remain true to their inner needs rather than always complying with the priorities of others.

On This Day

Famous Births: Robert Stewart, Viscount Castlereagh (1769); Edouard Daladier (1884); Jeanette MacDonald (1901); Bud Collyer (1908); Sammy Cahn (1913); E.G. Marshall (1914); Ian Carmichael (1920); Paul Eddington (1927); Roger Ebert and Paul McCartney (1942); Carol Kane and Isabella Rossellini (1952); Alison Moyet (1961); Nathan Morris (1971).

Significant Events and Anniversaries: June 18 is a day that highlights effective teamwork, and marks the anniversary of the Battle of Waterloo in Belgium, when Napoleon's numerically superior French Army was defeated by a combined German, Dutch, Belgian and British force under the command of the Duke of Wellington (1815). A further feature of this day concerns the enhancement and protection of human life, a propensity that is reflected in various events that occurred on June 18, such as when, during the Cold War, U.S. President Carter and Soviet premier Brezhnev signed the Strategic Arms Limitation Treaty (S.A.L.T.), aimed at reducing the potentially devastating build-up of nuclear armaments (1979). On a day governed by the element of air, the eponymous pioneer of the Immelmann maneuver, the German pilot Max Immelmann, was killed in action during World War I (1916); U.S. aviator Amelia Earhart touched down in Wales, thus becoming the first woman to fly across the Atlantic (1928); and the Norwegian explorer Roald Amundson died when his airplane crashed over the Arctic Ocean (1928).

Planetary Influences
Ruling planets: Mercury and the Moon.
Third decan: Personal planets are Saturn and Uranus.
Second cusp: Gemini with Cancer tendencies.

Sacred and Cultural Significance
Annual Dragon Boat Festival in China; Ana honored in ancient Rome.
Saints' day: Mark and Marcellian (d. c.290); Gregorio Barbarigo (1625–97).

Statesman Edouard Daladier served as France's prime minister during the World War II years, before he was deported by the puppet Vichy government in 1942. Returning to serve in the National Assembly from 1946 to 1958, he continued a political career that epitomized the qualities favored by his June 18 birthday— guided by progressive, humanitarian concerns and favoring a team orientation.

Planetary Influences
Ruling planets: Mercury and the Moon.
Third decan: Personal planets are Saturn and Uranus.
Second cusp: Gemini with Cancer tendencies.

Sacred and Cultural Significance
Feast of the Holy Ghost in Brazil;
in ancient Rome, the Day of all Heras.
Saints' day: Gervase and Protase (dates unknown); Romuald of Ravenna (c.950–1027); Juliana Falcoieri (1270–1341).

The French mathematician, physicist and theologian Blaise Pascal was born on June 19, 1623. Conducting pioneering work in probability, barometric pressure and development of the calculus, he is best known for Pascal's Law, which formed the basis for hydraulics. The desire to effect progress and the analytical powers favored by his birthday perhaps enhanced his natural intellectual and intuitive gifts.

JUNE 19

Perhaps the most outstanding characteristic of those people born on June 19 is their self-certainty—a quality that arouses both admiration and irritation in others: admiration because they are rarely beset by the feelings of doubt that often bedevil less focused types, and irritation on account of what may be seen as an arrogant unwillingness to compromise. Yet their steadfastness of purpose and single-minded determination in the pursuit of their visions is not the result of blinkered obstinacy, but rather of a profound confidence engendered by the knowledge that they have evaluated each alternative approach to the best of their ability and have arrived at their chosen strategy by means of logical deduction. And, indeed, June 19 people are blessed with intellectual inquisitiveness, incisive analytical talents, and a pronounced intuitive streak—qualities which in such a combination endow them with a rare gift for understanding. Whatever their preferred career choice—and their innate gifts suit them for many—they usually feel compelled to guide and improve the lives of others, and may thus find fulfillment as teachers, counselors or consultants.

Their desire to influence those around them is fueled by the best of intentions, but their typically forceful manner—although ideal for confrontational situations—may not be well received by those whom they are seeking to assist. For, however selfless their motivations, others (especially their partners or children, and even more so if they are men) may resent the imposition of what they may regard as dictatorial or controlling tactics. Cultivating a more diplomatic, less upfront approach may therefore benefit June 19 people immensely.

VIRTUES: These strong-willed people are blessed with a sense of purpose, which they will typically express forcefully. Their propensity to promote their progressive ambitions with enormous energy augurs well for success, as does their stubborn refusal to be dissuaded from their aims, even though they are good listeners.
VICES: Because they are so convinced as to the veracity of their outlook, June 19 people may not realize that others do not immediately concur with their viewpoints; they may therefore unwittingly alienate the very individuals whose best interests they have at heart.
VERDICT: If they are to retain the affection of those around them, while achieving their intellectual goals, it is important that those born on this day should apply their undoubtedly highly developed powers of perception to anticipating the effect that their actions may have on others. No matter how well meaning their intentions, a more tactful, less direct manner may reap greater rewards than their often somewhat autocratic approach.

On This Day
Famous Births: King James I of England and Scotland (1566); Blaise Pascal (1623); Douglas Haig (1861); William Ashbee Tritton (1875); Charles Coburn (1877); Wallis Simpson, Duchess of Windsor (1896); Lou Gehrig and Walter Reginald Hammond (1903); Ernst Boris Chain (1906); Joshua Nkomo (1917); Thelma Barlow (1933); Gena Rowlands (1934); Salman Rushdie (1947); Phylicia Rashad (1948); Kathleen Turner (1954); Mark Debarge (1959); Paula Abdul (1962).

Significant Events and Anniversaries: A concern with human welfare is strongly featured by this day, on which Sir Robert Peel, the British home secretary, founded the London Metropolitan police force—the predecessor of modern law-enforcement bodies whose members in Britain became popularly known as "bobbies" or "peelers" in honor of their founder (1829). The inherent characteristics of June 19 are in many ways paternalistic, and it is therefore appropriate that this day commemorates the institution of Father's Day, the brainchild of Mrs. John Bruce Dodd, of Spokane, Washington (1910). An innate danger of the influences that govern this day is that well-meaning motivations may become subject to condemnation, as is reflected when the inherently harmless Archduke Maximilian of Austria, who had been installed as the emperor of Mexico by Napoleon III, was executed by his anti-imperialistic enemies (1867); and when Ethel and Julius Rosenberg were put to death in the U.S.A. for allegedly spying for the Soviet Union (1953).

JUNE 20

The dominant character trait of people born on June 20 is that of insatiable curiosity which, when coupled with their idealism and quick-thinking minds, results in a wide-ranging spectrum of interests and concerns. With their marked enthusiasm for exploring alternative angles and their willingness to instigate or accept change, they make excellent and inspiring members of a working team. This outstanding ability to think on their feet and to adapt to shifting circumstances well equips them for careers in the fast-moving world of the investigative media, to which their searching intellectual qualities and stimulating ideas are ideally suited. Yet despite their outgoing and exuberant natures, people born on this day also possess a profound intuitive streak—a quality that endows them with unusual sensitivity in their relationships (especially if they are women) and which proves an invaluable asset when it comes to problem-solving at work.

Because they grasp intellectual concepts with enviable ease, there is an inevitable risk that June 20 people may become bored with a project once they have mastered it, and will feel tempted to move on to a new challenge. An awareness of this tendency, or the influence of a patient partner or vigilant parent, tempers this mercurial tendency and instills the discipline necessary to see a project through. Blessed with charming and magnetic personalities, June 20 people experience no difficulty in attracting others, while their lunar gift of empathy causes people to turn to them for emotional support as well as for their sparkling company, especially if they were born in the Chinese year of the horse.

VIRTUES: June 20 people exhibit incisive intellectual powers and an invaluable receptiveness to new ideas. Their open, yet sympathetic, natures make them extremely popular personalities, while their gift of insight also draws others to them.
VICES: These people have a tendency to discard carelessly the friendship of others or to lose interest in projects before they have considered them beyond a superficial level. Since they possess highly developed capacities in both rational and emotional realms, they tend to be plagued with inner conflict and self-doubt, resulting in fickle and indecisive traits.
VERDICT: In all areas of life, people born on this day should temper their restlessness and thirst for stimulation with a streak of self-discipline and realism; this will help them to find personal fulfillment and to transform their sometimes fanciful dreams into reality. They should also try to balance their intellect and emotions, seeking to build on their convictions and minimize their inconstancy.

On This Day
Famous Births: Jacques Offenbach (1819); Kurt Schwitters (1887); Catherine Cookson (1906); Errol Flynn (1909); Chet Atkins (1924); Danny Aiello (1933); Martin Landau (1934); Brian Wilson (1942); Anne Murray (1945); Lionel Richie (1949); John Goodman (1952); Cyndi Lauper (1953); Allan Lamb (1954); Nicole Kidman (1967).

Significant Events and Anniversaries: Demonstrating the restlessness and the striving toward the unexplored inherent in June 20, Norse explorer Leif Eriksson departed on his epic voyage from Greenland, via Norway, to North America (c.998–1000). Nationalism and idealism are qualities starred by this day, and on June 20 the British defenders of Calcutta were punished—by incarceration in the Black Hole by the Nawab of Bengal—for demonstrating these very traits (1756). Mirroring this day's adventurous indications, the steamship *Savannah* was the first to cross the Atlantic from the U.S.A. to Britain (1819). Marking the beginning of a period in Britain of renewed energy and innovations—traits reinforced by June 20—Queen Victoria ascended the throne on this date at the age of eighteen (1837). Under the influence of Mercury, and perhaps influenced by the adaptability and problem-solving skills favored by June 20, during a tense period in the Cold War the White House and the Kremlin demonstrated a new willingness to communicate with each other by means of a telephone hot-line (1963).

Planetary Influences
Ruling planets: Mercury and the Moon.
Third decan: Personal planets are Saturn and Uranus.
Second cusp: Gemini with Cancer tendencies.

Sacred and Cultural Significance
Day of Cerridwen, the ancient Celtic fertility goddess, celebrated by Pagans.
Saints' day: Alban (3rd century AD); Edward the Martyr (c. 962–79); Govan (6th century AD); Adalbert of Magdeburg (d. 981).

Golden Globe–winning actress Nicole Kidman demonstrates in her screen performances the insight and interest in people that are June 20 characteristics and is also blessed with the magnetic charm promised by her birthdate. Born on this day in 1967, her career has been notable for her emotional range and depth, and she is a committed mother to the children she adopted with her husband, Tom Cruise; those characteristics are consistent with the sensitivity, creativity and family loyalty suggested by her Chinese influences as a fire goat. With Mars in Libra and Venus in Leo, an acting career is strongly indicated by her stars.

Planetary Influences
Ruling planets: Mercury and the Moon.
Third decan: Personal planets are Saturn and Uranus.
Second cusp: Gemini with Cancer tendencies.

Sacred and Cultural Significance
Often the date of the summer solstice and the date on which it is most commonly celebrated; in Russia, the fertility goddess Kupala honored.
Saints' day: Aloysius Gonzaga (1568–91), patron of youth; Leufred (d. 738); Mewan (6th century AD).

Stonehenge draws British participants for the traditional Druidic summer solstice celebration, which dates back at least to early Celtic times. The solstice often occurs on June 21 and is usually celebrated on this day.

JUNE 21

Like most Geminis, the gregarious personalities and sociable natures of June 21 people mean that they do not enjoy solitude, instead finding stimulation and fulfillment in the company of others. They therefore relish lifestyles and careers that offer plenty of scope to satisfy their craving for variety, travel and human contact, as well as those in which their communication skills will be fully used—in the media or sales, for example. They manifest their love of the arts from an early age, their artistic temperaments complemented by such curious and inquiring minds that they often feel compelled to attempt to seek out the truth or to stick by their principles doggedly, however unpopular their obstinacy makes them. Their enthusiasm and idealism make them inspirational—even revolutionary—leaders, yet these very qualities also generate such high standards that others find it hard to live up to them. These qualities of persistence, as well as their inherently logical, precise and practical outlooks, are doubly reinforced if they were born in the Chinese year of the rat, the sign of tenacity.

Thanks to their formidable analytical talents, people born on this day frequently prove successful in the financial sector, provided, that is, that they are given the liberty to engage their imaginative and creative powers to the fullest. As free as the air that is their element, their independent attitudes provide these people with plenty of scope for adventure, thus making them compatible partners for like-minded Sagittarians. Their love of liberty may give more possessive people, like Scorpios and Pisceans, grounds for jealousy, however, and this caveat applies particularly to June 21 men, to whom the security of domestic life is less important than to women born on this day. Their lunar-influenced, intuitive qualities may temper any flighty tendencies or cerebral idealism with a rare level of sensitivity toward the feelings of others, however.

VIRTUES: Their inexhaustible quest for adventure and external stimuli make these people not only interested, but also inherently interesting. Blessed with the charisma and charm of the extrovert, they possess the more introspective gifts of empathy and understanding, too, thus drawing others to them. Their capacity for original thought gives them genius potential.
VICES: June 21 people sometimes allow their extreme need for independence—both in their thoughts and actions—to alienate them from the grounding influence of home and family. They may exhibit impatience with those who do not share their visions and certainties, and they tend not to always respect the opinions of others.
VERDICT: In all their ventures, June 21 people should remember that although their capacity for independent thought is laudable, greater success and satisfaction may often be achieved through cooperation with others. They should also ensure that they nurture their emotional needs rather than sacrificing them to their careers, and that they do not become obsessive about the things that excite them.

On This Day
Famous Births: Pope Leo IX (1002); Enrico Cechetti (1850); Claude Auchinleck (1884); Jean-Paul Sartre (1905); Jane Russell (1921); Maureen Stapleton (1925); Bernie Kopell (1933); Françoise Sagan (1935); John Edrich (1937); Mariette Hartley (1940); Maurice Saatchi (1946); Meredith Baxter-Birney and Michael Gross (1947); Benazir Bhutto (1953); Juliet Lewis (1973); Prince William of Great Britain (1982).

Significant Events and Anniversaries: Reflecting this day's propensity for idealistic patriotism, New Hampshire joined the Union (1789) and the German fleet scuttled itself at Scapa Flow (1919) rather than surrender to the victors of World War I. The fortuitous combination of idealism, innovation and artistic sensibility favored by June 21 was illustrated when *Die Meistersinger von Nürnberg* by Richard Wagner, was first performed on this day (1868), when long-playing records were launched by Columbia Records (1948) and when Andrew Lloyd Webber and Tim Rice's musical *Evita*, which dramatized revolutionary politics in Argentina, was first performed (1978).

CANCER

June 22 to July 22
Ruling planet: The Moon   **Element:** Cardinal water
Symbol: A crab   **Polarity:** Negative (feminine)
Physical correspondence: The stomach and breasts
Stones: Pearl, moonstone, peridot
Flowers: Lily, lily of the valley, water lily, white rose
Colors: Cream, white, silver-blue, smoky gray

Nearly every astrological tradition equates the constellation of Cancer with a crab, named Karkinos by the ancient Greeks; Kalakang by the Persians; Al-Lul or Bulug by the Babylonians; and Karkata by Hindu astrologers. Only the ancient Egyptians differed from this personification, envisaging the constellation as a scarab beetle, the symbol of regeneration, although both the Egyptians and Greeks sometimes also referred to it as a turtle or tortoise, and the Babylonians as a crayfish. The reason for the near-universal identification of this zodiacal sign with a crab, or similar creature, can be explained by the movement of the Sun during the period of Cancer's ascendancy, for it appears to mimic the crustacean's distinctive sideways, scuttling movement on its southern descent. The Greco-Roman myth that justifies the crab's position in the stars tells of how the mother goddess Hera (Juno) sent a crab to the aid of the nine-headed Hydra of Lerna in its struggle against Herakles (Hercules); Hera placed it in the heavens as a reward for its efforts. The summer solstice occurs under this sign, and Cancer is therefore known as the "gate of men," *Janus inferni*, for it was said that the solstice marked the primordial occasion when the breath of heaven—the soul—animated the collective entity of humankind. Cancer also has enormous cosmic significance, for the universe came into being when the planets were aligned within this sign, and some hold that the world will end when a similar conjunction is effected.

Cancer is ruled by the Moon, the preserve of the goddess—the creator and destroyer—which regulates the ebb and flow of water, the habitat of the crab and the element that governs Cancer. The sign's dual lunar-watery influence confers loyalty, sensitivity, intuition and emotional receptiveness, as well as the procreative, nurturing and protective qualities associated with the feminine principle. Like the crab, those born under this sign are said to possess tenacity, but are also subject to the tendency to withdraw into their shells when threatened by others or inundated with emotion.

CANCER

Planetary Influences
Ruling planets: The Moon and Mercury.
First decan: Personal planet is the Moon.
First cusp: Cancer with Gemini tendencies.

Sacred and Cultural Significance
Saints' day: Acacius (dates unknown);
Paulinus of Nola (d. 431); John Fisher
(1469–1535) and Thomas More (1478–1535).

On June 22, a day that bodes well for the realization of goals aspired to and the fulfillment of visions cherished and worked toward, Joe Lewis won the world heavyweight boxing title, beating James J. Braddock, in 1937.

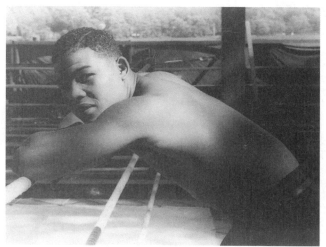

JUNE 22

Whether or not they are conscious of the quest that drives them, those born on June 22 are engaged in a constant search for their own personal idyll, be it an enduring romantic partnership, a perfect lifestyle, a Utopian environment or a combination of all three. These people yearn for personal happiness, an ideal state which ultimately depends on them winning a soul mate rather than professional success, for such is the value they place on strong emotional ties that they feel with the love and support of a caring and concerned partner they can weather any of life's storms or disappointments. It is not that other aspects of their lives lack significance in their eyes, just that finding true and lasting love is of paramount importance to their emotional well-being. Some June 22 people will indeed be lucky in their search, but others will inevitably remain unsatisfied, their visions of a fantasy mate proving unrealistic, or the intensity of their emotions and demands frightening off potential partners unwilling to live up to the idealized personality projected upon them.

Thus while these individuals typically demonstrate profound affection and loyalty toward their friends and family members, reciprocating the support and comfort that this gives them, they may be doomed to disappointment in their love lives. However, such is their zestful enjoyment of the world and their enthusiasm for intellectual and sensory stimulation, that they will not stay down for long, and may find great consolation in their professional interests. Their sensitivity suits them extremely well for careers within the arts, a sphere within which they can live out their personal fantasies as, for example, novelists, musicians or actors.

VIRTUES: These nonmaterialistic and emotionally driven people are primarily fueled by their deep-rooted urge to realize their romanticized dreams, especially with regard to love. Extremely imaginative, sensitive and empathetic, they also desire to bring happiness to those around them, as well as to the world at large.
VICES: When circumstances thwart their aspirations, those born on this day may become profoundly disillusioned and prone to periods of depression. Alternatively, they may become almost manically determined to attain their ideals, swiftly moving from person to person in their quest, sometimes crediting others with qualities that they may not possess.
VERDICT: June 22 individuals should attempt to develop a more pragmatic view of their sometimes unrealistic demands, and of what is truly required to bring them happiness. After periods of honest reflection, they may find that ultimate fulfillment lies within their own powers.

On This Day
Famous Births: George Vancouver (1757); Giuseppe Mazzini (1805); Theodor Leschetizky (1830); Henry Rider Haggard (1856); Julian Sorell Huxley (1887); Erich Maria Remarque (1898); Billy Wilder (1906); Joe Loss and Michael Todd (1909); John Hunt and Peter Neville Luard Pears (1910); Prunella Scales (1932); Kris Kristofferson (1936); Meryl Streep and Lindsay Wagner (1949).

Significant Events and Anniversaries: This day indicates the highest of aspirations and ideals which, unfortunately, will often prove unrealizable, and on June 22 John Fisher, the bishop of Rochester, was executed for his refusal to swear an oath stating his belief in King Henry VIII's supremacy over the pope (1535); the voyage of English explorer Henry Hudson was abruptly curtailed when he was set adrift by his mutinous crew, to die in the bay that was later named after him (1611); and at the Battle of Bothwell Bridge the Duke of Monmouth crushed the rebellion of the Presbyterian Scottish Covenanters (1679). Some visions were, however, effected on this day, which marks the anniversary of Richard II's accession to the throne of England (1377); the winning of the world heavyweight boxing title by Joe Louis ("the Brown Bomber"), who beat James J. Braddock in Chicago (1937); and the first Virgin Atlantic flight from Gatwick Airport in England to New York (1984).

JUNE 23

In common with many of their fellows born under the lunar-directed sign of Cancer, June 23 individuals yearn to make the world a beautiful place, not only in environmental terms but also by enriching the lives of others through artistic ventures and seeking to effect peace and harmony within human relationships. And, with this idealized vision blazing beaconlike before them, they typically devote their considerable practical and intellectual energies toward the attainment of their dreams, using their highly developed intuitive and mental perspicacity to identify areas requiring improvement and the remedial approaches that should be followed. Such is their interest in other people, and their concurrent desire to lighten their personal and professional workloads, that they cannot help but offer their assistance to coworkers, friends, family members or even to humanity as a whole. Their innate skills and natural orientation suit them admirably to careers in which they can work with other people in contributing toward human welfare—for example as nurses, doctors or social workers—or through artistic pursuits such as painting, the performing arts or poetry.

Unsurprisingly, those born on June 23 place enormous value on their own interpersonal relationships—an orientation that is even more pronounced in women born on this day—and treat their loved ones with great tenderness, consideration and affection. Finding and supporting unquestionably a life partner who will fulfill their desire for romance is one of their primary goals: once settled in such a close one-to-one liaison, these individuals will prove unwaveringly loyal, but run the concomitant risk of stifling the object of their affection with the jealous intensity of their love.

VIRTUES: June 23 people yearn both to effect their own emotional fulfillment and to ensure the happiness of all whom they encounter. They employ their dual skills of intellectual clarity and deep intuition in attempting to realize their visions, and are as practical as they are sensitive and loving.
VICES: The active concern with the happiness of others that is manifested by those born on this day is inspired by the best of intentions, but when their efforts are regarded as interfering or controlling they may irritate or alienate those they meant to benefit.
VERDICT: These people should not allow their compulsion to implement their somewhat romantic ideals regarding human behavior and relationships to cause them to project their wishes—however well-meaning—onto those who would prefer to act independently.

On This Day
Famous Births: John Fell (1625); Empress Josephine of France (1763); Edward, Duke of Windsor (formerly King Edward VIII of Britain) and Alfred Charles Kinsey (1894); Jean-Marie-Lucien-Pierre Anouilh and Ted Tinling (1910); Alan Turing (1912); William Pierce Rogers (1913); Leonard Hutton (1916); Bob Fosse (1927); June Carter Cash (1929); Adam Faith (1940); Ted Shackleford (1946).

Significant Events and Anniversaries: This day is influenced by the desire to act in others' best interests (a tendency that may have ambiguous results), as was reflected when: General Clive's imperialist British forces won a victory over the Nawab of Bengal's supporters at the Battle of Plassey (1757); English Quaker William Penn signed a treaty of friendship with members of the Lenni Lenape tribe in Shakamaxon, Philadelphia (1683); and General Gamal Nasser became president of Egypt—having been the only candidate for election (1956). Demonstrating the danger inherent in June 23 of idealism veering into extremism as it becomes divorced from reality, Sikh terrorists drew attention to their quest for independence by blowing up an airborne Air India airplane, causing the deaths of over three hundred people (1985). Mirroring the artistic potential highlighted by this day, the saxophone was patented by Belgian instrument-maker Adolphe Sax (1848).

Planetary Influences
Ruling planets: The Moon and Mercury.
First decan: Personal planet is the Moon.
First cusp: Cancer with Gemini tendencies.

Sacred and Cultural Significance
Day of Cu Chulainn, a Pagan celebration; in Western tradition, often Midsummer's Eve.
Saints' day: Etheldreda (d. 679); Joseph Cafasso (1811–60).

In 1683 William Penn signed a treaty of friendship with the Lenni Lenape tribe in the fledgling colony of Philadelphia on June 23, a day indicating a desire to act in the best interest of others, and the ambiguous results that may ensue—tragically illustrated when the Lenapes were later betrayed.

CANCER

Planetary Influences
Ruling planets: The Moon and Mercury.
First decan: Personal planet is the Moon.
First cusp: Cancer with Gemini tendencies.

Sacred and Cultural Significance
In Egypt, the Burning of the Lamps
is celebrated; Fortuna celebrated in
ancient Rome.
Saints' day: The birthday of John the
Baptist (d. c.30), patron saint of monks;
Bartholomew of Farne (d. 1193).

*John the Baptist, the prophetic New Testament
figure and saint who prefigured Christ, was
born, appropriately, on a day signifying
compassion, vision, inspiration and leadership.
He is depicted in this 1535 painting by Venetian
Renaissance artist Titian.*

JUNE 24

Despite the quietly profound affection and unquestionable commitment that characterizes their approach to their nearest and dearest, the attention of June 24 people is typically less absorbed by their personal liaisons than by their professional activities, which frequently have a humanitarian slant. Although their sensitivity endows them with genuine empathy with those who are less fortunate than themselves, their compassion is manifested less by passive sympathy than by their urge actively to formulate and initiate strategies with which to achieve progress. And, because they are blessed with keen intellectual talents, as well as with innovative imaginations, their visions may be extremely original, although rarely unrealistic, for these are simultaneously down-to-earth individuals, who possess highly developed technical and practical skills. Despite the often inspirational effect that they have on others—who may elevate them to positions of leadership—these responsible people generally perform best when undistracted by the demands of others, although they recognize that they cannot always attain their aims single-handedly.

Professionally, June 24 individuals have a special aptitude for those fields in which they can combine their talent for analysis and theoretics with the opportunity to set the results of their research in motion. Careers as scientific or technical researchers and management consultants are thus especially highlighted, as are sporting and artistic pursuits (if not followed professionally the last two areas will often be among these people's hobbies). Reflecting their vigor, those born on this day need periods of privacy in which to indulge in periods of inner reflection and to recharge their mental batteries.

VIRTUES: Those born on this day are energetic and driven individuals, whose thoughts and actions are fueled by the desire to achieve their visions of progress. Blessed with equally strong intellectual and practical talents, as well as great intuition, their capacity to focus on their aims with single-minded determination gives them enormous potential to succeed.
VICES: Although June 24 people harbor strong feelings for their family members and friends, they do not always make their emotions explicit enough. This tendency, combined with their preoccupation with work and their occasional withdrawal into solitude, may cause their loved ones to feel neglected.
VERDICT: It is important that these individuals (especially if they are also men) curtail their urge for independence, and apply their undoubted empathy toward those who share their domestic lives.

On This Day
Famous Births: John Churchill, Duke of Marlborough (1650); W. H. Smith (1825); Ambrose Gwinnett Bierce (1842); Horatio Herbert Kitchener (1850); Jack Dempsey (1895); Phil Harris (1904); Juan Manuel Fangio (1911); Brian Alexander Johnston (1912); Fred Hoyle (1915); Jack Carter (1923); Claude Chabrol (1930); Michele Lee (1942); Jeff Beck (1944); Mick Fleetwood (1947); Nancy Allen (1949); Janet Farrar (1950).

Significant Events and Anniversaries: June 24 is a day that highlights the desire to act for communal or global interests, and marks the anniversary of the defeat of the English force led by King Edward II at the hands of the troops of the Scottish king, Robert the Bruce, at the Battle of Bannockburn (1314); and also of the start of the Berlin Airlift operation during the Cold War, in which the Allies flew in essential supplies to West Berlin which had been isolated from the West by the Soviets (1948–49). A further demonstration of the strong humanitarian concern of this day was seen when, after the carnage that he witnessed on the battlefield of Solferino, his compassion with the French and Austrian wounded caused Jean Henri Dunant to form the organization that later became known as the International Red Cross (1859). Reflecting the day's capacity for advanced technology, Sally Ride became the first American woman in space (1983), and nine unidentifiable objects were tracked on radar over Washington, D.C. (1947).

JUNE 25

The personalities of those born on June 25 may be defined by two apparently contradictory characteristics: their sense of purpose in pursuit of lofty ideals, and their often vacillating or changeable behavior. Yet these seemingly conflicting tendencies are not really so paradoxical when one understands the nature of their enormous sensitivity which, when informed by their mercurial intellects, leads them to draw clear-sighted conclusions, and, when influenced by their highly developed intuitive powers, causes their hearts to rule their heads. When they are able successfully to reconcile their mental and emotional responses, those born on these day have the ability to make remarkably effective instruments of progress, but, when these qualities are imbalanced, one or the other may manifest itself more strongly, or they may coexist uneasily, resulting in confusion or inconsistency of motivations.

In many respects, the realization of the potential of those born on June 25 depends upon the interests and concerns of those to whom they are emotionally closest, or whose opinion they most respect—for whatever reason. For, despite their original turn of mind and boundless imagination, these people are somewhat reliant on the encouragement and approval of others—a propensity that is especially pronounced if they were also born in the Chinese year of the rat. This sensitivity toward others' responses, as well as their natural affinity for artistic pursuits, augurs well for their success as designers and commercial artists.

VIRTUES: June 25 people are inspired by idealized visions—be they of aesthetic beauty, human happiness and equality, or of technical perfection. Their multifaceted intellectual talents, as well as their prodigiously intuitive responses, bestow upon them the potential to act as effective and compassionate forces for good.
VICES: Such is the all-encompassing nature of their sensitivity, that these individuals appear to soak up "hard" information and "soft" emotions in a spongelike, indiscriminate manner. This capacity to absorb a variety of sometimes contradictory messages and data may cause them to become overwhelmed by confusion as to the course of action that should best be taken.
VERDICT: In order to help them steer a direct course through life, it is important that those born on this day develop their capacity for objectivity and setting priorities. This does not mean that they should suppress their sensitivity toward others (which would in any case be nearly impossible), but that they should cultivate a greater sense of realism as to what is really important in life and also achievable.

On This Day

Famous Births: Gustave Charpentier (1860); Robert Erskine Childers (1870); Louis, Earl Mountbatten of Burma (1900); George Orwell (1903); Roger Livesey (1906); Sidney Lumet (1924); June Lockhart (1925); Carly Simon (1945); Phyllis George and Jimmy Walker (1949); George Michael (1963).

Significant Events and Anniversaries: This day promises the potential realization of ideas that may initially be derided by less imaginative types, a tendency that may be reflected in various fields, as when, for example, barbed wire was patented by Lucien B. Smith of Ohio (1867); and when the Polish-born scientific researcher Marie Curie announced her discovery of radium (1903). Further manifestations of the idealist commitment highlighted by June 25—sometimes with inconsistent results—were demonstrated when Virginia became the tenth state to join the U.S. (1788); when Colonel George Armstrong Custer and nearly 265 members of the 7th U.S. Cavalry made their doomed last stand against a hostile Sioux enemy at the Battle of Little Bighorn in Montana (1876); and when communist North Korean forces crossed the 38th Parallel to invade South Korea, thus initiating the Korean War (1950).

Planetary Influences
Ruling planets: The Moon and Mercury.
First decan: Personal planet is the Moon.
First cusp: Cancer with Gemini tendencies.

Sacred and Cultural Significance
Parvati honored in India.
Saints' day: Maximus of Turin (c.350–c.415); Cyniburg of Gloucester (dates unknown); Adalbert of Egmond (d. c.710); William of Montevergine (1085–1142).

Custer's Last Stand at the Battle of Little Bighorn in Montana dramatically demonstrated the variable outcome of qualities starred by the day on which it occurred; June 25 is associated with idealistic commitment to a fixed purpose.

Planetary Influences
Ruling planet: The Moon.
First decan: Personal planet is the Moon.

Sacred and Cultural Significance
Native Americans honor Salavi, Kachinas and Corn Mothers.
Saints' day: John and Paul (d. 4th century AD); Salvius (7th century AD).

Personifying ancestral spirits or representing Pueblo gods, Kachina dolls such as this have traditionally been used in Hopi and Zuni rituals to intercede and communicate between human beings and gods. June 26 is the day on which some Native American tribes traditionally honor Kachinas, Salavi and Corn Mothers.

JUNE 26

Despite their strong ideological beliefs and often extremely imaginative inspirational vision, those born on this day are usually less geared toward the single-minded pursuit of intellectual goals than toward the people that surround them and the circumstances that impinge upon them. These are truly empathetic individuals, whose responsiveness to the feelings and situations of others arouses their highly developed protective instincts and their urge to guide and shield those for whom they feel concern. Although this tendency is especially pronounced with regard to their relations—and their children in particular if they are parents—they will generally also assume a mentoring role with regard to their work colleagues and choose careers that have a humanitarian slant. They will typically find fulfillment in those professions in which they can make an active and practical contribution toward the common good, and may employ their considerable organizational skills in such diverse functions as corporate executives, technicians and researchers, or writers and performers.

Whatever profession they pursue, these people will always be happiest when working as part of a team rather than as individuals and, within their personal lives, they similarly cherish the close bonds that characterize their liaisons with friends and family members. Their strong social orientation is perhaps their defining quality, but this may bring them both pleasure and pain for, inevitably, others will not always welcome their advice, perceiving it as an attempt to control their independence of action.

VIRTUES: Energetic, vitally interested in understanding and improving the lives of others, and blessed with enormous practical and organizational talents, these individuals are strongly committed to furthering the societal or communal welfare, and, being dynamic and self-confident people, are endowed with great potential to succeed.
VICES: Although stemming from the best of motives, these people have a propensity to be overprotective, of others close to them, and hence their positive intentions may have a somewhat negative, restricting influence on those they are seeking to assist.
VERDICT: It is important that those born on June 26 control their tendency to project their own dreams and aspirations onto other people, for not only may they alienate others by their directional tendencies, but they may also thereby suppress their own profound emotional needs, which ultimately they alone can satisfy.

On This Day
Famous Births: Charles Messier (1710); George Morland (1763); Patrick Branwell Brontë (1817); William Thomson, Baron Kelvin (1824); George Molyneux, Earl of Carnarvon (1866); Pearl S. Buck (1892); Willy Messerschmitt (1898); Peter Lorre (1904); "Colonel" Tom Parker (1910); Laurie Lee (1914); Colin Wilson (1931); Claudio Abbado (1933); Georgie Fame (1943); Greg LeMond (1961); Harriet Wheeler (1963); Chris O'Donnell (1970).

Significant Events and Anniversaries: This day highlights action usually on behalf of the communal good, but sometimes the result of personal interests, both qualities reflected in various events that occurred on June 26, when, for example, the Roman emperor Julian the Apostate died of his wounds after leading his army against the Persian enemy (363); when the Spanish adventurer and conqueror of Peru, Francisco Pizarro, was murdered by rival conquistadors (1541); when Queen Victoria rewarded the bravery of veterans of the Crimean War by investing them as first recipients of the Victoria Cross (1857); and when the first American troops landed in France to fight against the German Army during World War I (1917). Progress of all kinds is indicated by this day, which marks the anniversary of the first grand-prix race at Le Mans in France (1906); the opening of the Victoria and Albert Museum in London by King Edward VII (1909); and—especially appropriately on a day governed by the element of water—the official opening of the St. Lawrence Seaway by U.S. President Eisenhower and Queen Elizabeth II, creating the U.S./Canadian inland waterway connecting the Great Lakes with the Atlantic Ocean (1959).

JUNE 27

CANCER

Perhaps the most marked characteristic inherent in those born on June 27 is their sense of responsibility toward others, be they family members and friends, work colleagues, or the human community at a variety of levels. For not only are these people blessed with highly developed intuitive responses, which inform their convictions and actions with a sense of justice, but they are also extremely strong-willed types who in many respects feel that they have a duty to guide—or, if necessary, compel—others to follow the same uncompromisingly moral code to which they themselves adhere. The feelings of profound empathy that they experience toward the plight of the downtrodden and exploited arouse their fiercely protective instincts and instill in them a burning determination to bring about societal improvement. When thus inspired, little can either shake their belief in the veracity of their cause or divert them from their mission. They may manifest such humanitarian concerns in a range of appropriate careers, including nursing, therapy or charitable organizations—even in the evangelical religious sphere—or they may choose to propagate their message in the less overt media offered by the arts.

Their relationships with those closest to them are similarly defined by their urge to protect and further the interests of those with whom they have forged deep emotional ties, but within their personal, as well as their professional, liaisons their well-meaning efforts may prove less than welcome. Part of the problem is that their often sternly uncompromising approach may be perceived—and resented—by others as an autocratic attempt to control and direct them.

VIRTUES: The profound orientation and sense of obligation toward humanity that is an overriding feature of June 27 people's personalities stems from their innate recognition of behavioral and ethical rights and wrongs. Both protective and progressive in their inclinations, they typically devote their considerable energy and imagination toward serving others.
VICES: Once they have determined upon a particular set of beliefs, those born on this day will promote them with a rare degree of obstinacy. While this propensity is not only positive but also promises potential success, it does run the risk of causing these people to become unresponsive to alternative convictions, however valid.
VERDICT: The emotional fulfillment of those born on this day depends on their ability to exert their influence over others. To achieve their aims, it is crucial that they remain open-minded in the debates that their actions will inevitably engender, accepting that others are entitled to conflicting views and pragmatically accommodating expressions of dissent.

On This Day
Famous Births: King Louis XII of France (1462); King Charles IX of France (1550); James Smithson (1765); Samuel, Viscount Hood (1816); Charles S. Parnell (1846); Helen Keller (1880); Antoinette Perry and Guilhermina Suggia (1888); Bob Keeshan (1927); H. Ross Perot (1930); Julia Duffy (1951); Isabelle Adjani (1955); Scott Cunningham (1956); Malcolm Lowry (1957).

Significant Events and Anniversaries: Inherent in June 27 is a strong urge to effect an improvement in human affairs, and this predilection is reflected in a number of diverse events that occurred on this day, including the inauguration of the first transatlantic passenger flights on Pan Am's flying boats (1939), and the opening of the world's first nuclear-power station, in Obninsk in the Soviet Union (1954). The urge to direct the actions of others that is highlighted by June 27 may inevitably result in conflict, as was mirrored on this day when King George II of Britain led his English, Austrian and Hanoverian army to victory over the French at the Battle of Dettingen (1743); when the founder of the Church of Jesus Christ of Latter Day Saints, Joseph Smith, was murdered by an anti-Mormon mob (1844); and when Palestinian terrorists hijacked an Air France aircraft at Athens, forcing its diversion to Entebbe (1976). Appropriately, on the anniversary of Helen Adams Keller's birth, two visually impaired British mountaineers, Dave Hurst and Alan Matthews, demonstrated their determination in the face of adversity when they reached the summit of Mont Blanc (1988).

Planetary Influences
Ruling planet: The Moon.
First decan: Personal planet is the Moon.

Sacred and Cultural Significance
Sun Dance ritual of the Plains tribes.
Saints' day: Zoilus (d. c.304); Cyril of Alexandria (c.376–444).

Born on June 27 in 1800, Helen Keller lost her sight and hearing after an illness as a toddler. After being taught by Anne Sullivan to sign, read, write and eventually to speak, Helen Keller went on to write her inspirational autobiography, The Story of My Life *(1902), to earn a college degree, and to become an advocate for the disabled and a distinguished lecturer. Her natural abilities were perhaps enhanced by attributes favored by her birthday, including intuition, empathy and altruistic, humanitarian concerns.*

CANCER

Planetary Influences
Ruling planet: The Moon.
First decan: Personal planet is the Moon.

Sacred and Cultural Significance
In ancient Greece, the birthday of Hemera.
Saints' day: Potamiaena and Basilides (d. c.208); Irenaeus of Lyons (c.130–200); Austell (6th century AD).

Austrian Crown Prince Franz Ferdinand and his wife, pictured moments before they were assassinated by a Serbian terrorist in Sarajevo on June 28, 1914. Leading to World War I, the assassination occurred on a day on which tendencies toward extremism and impulsiveness converged to rationalize the nationalistic act of terrorism.

JUNE 28

★ ★

Those who are seeking to understand what exactly it is that motivates and defines those born on this day may often believe that they have found the key and then be thrown into confusion by the apparently contradictory behavior of the subjects of their analysis. For while June 28 individuals may at one moment present an extroverted and optimistic face, encouraging and entertaining others, at the next they may eschew company and withdraw into a bleakly pessimistic, introverted world of their own making. Such extreme tendencies are a result of their profoundly intuitive, and hence emotional, responses to the circumstances within which they find themselves, coupled with their innate intellectual capacity to rationalize the reasons behind their strong identification with those who excite their interest and empathy. Their actions and convictions are thus to a large extent conditioned by the situations and individuals that—for whatever reason—exert a strong influence upon their imaginations and feelings. The combination of such people-oriented sensitivity with their urge to be instruments of progress naturally equips them with a propensity toward making careers in the caring professions or other humanitarian fields, although they may sometimes choose to utilize their talents in other fields where personal interaction is a key element.

Their often irresistible tendency to follow their hearts rather than their heads can lead June 28 people to misjudge the motivations or desires of other individuals, especially when it comes to choosing a life partner. Yet once settled within a committed one-to-one relationship—as with long-standing friends and family members—they are typically steadfastly supportive and affectionate, for they sense the importance of profound emotional bonds in grounding their wilder inclinations within a stable framework.

VIRTUES: Such is their strongly empathetic orientation toward other people, which is usually manifested in a desire to please or bring about direct improvements, that those born on this day typically gain profound satisfaction from directing their prodigious energies and imaginative talents toward lightening others' lives.
VICES: Their interest in others, as well as their innate—and often uncontrollable—compulsion to act upon the messages that they intuitively receive from others, can frequently lead June 28 people to react swiftly and unthinkingly to their emotional responses, without considering the potential consequences of their behavior.
VERDICT: To protect themselves from the possibly negative repercussions of their instinctive reactions, these individuals should employ their unquestionably highly developed intellectual skills in considering their motivations and the consequences carefully before embroiling themselves in situations that may ultimately prove disastrous.

On This Day
Famous Births: King Henry VIII of England (1491); Jean Jacques Rousseau (1712); Luigi Pirandello (1867); Luisa Tetrazzini (1871); Alexis Carrel (1873); Pierre Laval (1883); Richard Rodgers (1902); Eric Ambler (1909); Stuart Farrar (1916); Mel Brooks (1926); Stan Barstow (1928); Pat Morita (1930); Gilda Radner (1946); Kathy Bates (1948); John Elway (1960); Danielle Briseboise (1969).

Significant Events and Anniversaries: This is a day that indicates action in the cause of what is perceived to be the wider interest of others, as is reflected when, on June 28, Queen Victoria demonstrated her intention to dedicate her life to her subjects when she was crowned Queen of England at Westminster Abbey in London (1838); when Gavrilo Princep, an associate of the Serbian terrorist organization the Black Hand, assassinated the heir to the throne of Austria, Archduke Franz Ferdinand, along with his wife, in Sarajevo (1914); and when representatives of the defeated Germany agreed to the terms of the Treaty of Versailles that concluded (albeit ultimately unsatisfactorily) the negotiations to reach a political settlement following World War I—a conflict that had been precipitated by Princip's action (1919).

JUNE 29

To those who do not know them well, those born on June 29 present something of an enigma, for while their love of fun, quirky sense of humor and great imaginative powers place them in the "extroverted" category, their formidable organizational powers, steadfast—and often stubborn—tenacity, and tendency to keep their deeper emotions to themselves endow them also with introverted characteristics. These are indeed complicated personalities, whose *joie de vivre*, particularly when in the company of others, often masks their need for periods of solitude in which they can explore the abstract world of concepts and dreams which exerts such a strong hold over them. When they are successful in reconciling the diverse facets of themselves, June 29 people can achieve considerable material success. Reflecting also their relish for interpersonal contact and their need for personal autonomy, they are, in many respects, best suited for careers in the fluid realm of arts and design, an affinity that is even more pronounced if they were also born in the Chinese year of the dog.

Despite their social orientation, it can be difficult to get to know these people, for when they are in the company of casual acquaintances they generally hold back the essence of their real selves. This propensity is the result of their great sensitivity, which may cause them to become beset with feelings of insecurity, and they typically hide their emotional vulnerability behind a misleading façade of bravado. Yet within their established relationships (ie. with those whom they have come to trust) those born on June 29 usually display enormous commitment, affection and loyalty.

VIRTUES: These people have two distinct sides to their characters, being simultaneously stimulated by the company of others yet also deeply introspective. Blessed with great powers of empathy, imagination and intuition, they are also prodigiously clear-sighted and practical in the pursuit of the realization of their original visions.
VICES: The enormous sensitivity of June 29 people leads them to envisage a variety of—not always positive—scenarios: this may deter them from exposing the true nature of their inner selves to others lest they thereby lay themselves open to potential hurt.
VERDICT: Those born on this day should recognize that strong emotional bonds of intimacy, so important to their feelings of self-worth and security, cannot be forged unless they open themselves up to others. They should therefore try not to automatically distrust the motivations of those who seek to become more intimate with them.

On This Day

Famous Births: Peter Paul Rubens (1577); Giacomo Leopardi (1798); George Washington Goethals (1858); William James Mayo (1861); Robert Schuman (1886); Antoine de Saint-Exupéry (1900); Nelson Eddy (1901); Leroy Anderson (1908); Frank Loesser (1910); Prince Bernhard of the Netherlands (1911); Rafael Kubelik (1914); Ruth Warrick (1915); Ian Bannen (1928); Ken Done (1940); Gary Busey (1944); Fred Grandy (1948).

Significant Events and Anniversaries: June 29 indicates the strong determination to implement ideological visions—a tendency that may be reflected in a diversity of areas—and the rewards of this approach were reflected when, on this day, Julius Caesar was victorious over Pompey at Pharsalus during the Roman Civil War (48 BC); Samuel Crowther was consecrated the bishop of Niger, thus becoming the first African Anglican bishop (1864); Norwegian women were granted the electoral vote (1913); Isabel Perón was inaugurated as president of Argentina following the death of her husband, Juan (1974); and Iceland elected its first female president, Vigdis Finnbogadottir (1980). Organizational skills are highlighted by this day, on which Britain's first population census was taken (1801); the *Daily Telegraph* newspaper was first published in London; and Carter G. Woodson, founder of the Association for the Study of Negro Life and History, was awarded the Spingarn Medal for pioneering work in African American history by the National Association for the Advancement of Colored People (NAACP) (1926).

Planetary Influences
Ruling planet: The Moon.
First decan: Personal planet is the Moon.

Sacred and Cultural Significance
In England, Bawming the Thorn ritual; Papa Legba honored in Voodoo.
Saints' day: Peter (d. c.64), patron saint of fishermen and popes, and Paul (d. c.65), patron saint of missionary bishops; Elwin (7th century AD); Judith and Salome (9th century AD).

The Three Graces *was created by one of the greatest Baroque painters, Flemish artist Peter Paul Rubens. Prolific and renowned for his exuberant and sensuous style, Rubens was born on June 29—a day favoring artistic qualities of intuition and imagination.*

Planetary Influences
Ruling planet: The Moon.
First decan: Personal planet is the Moon.

Sacred and Cultural Significance
In ancient Rome, Aestas honored.
Saints' day: The Martyrs of Rome (d. 1st century AD); George the Hagiorite (1009–65); Theobald of Provins (d. 1066).

The intuitive qualities of Lena Horne's June 30 birthdate gave her an aptitude for a stage career. Born in Brooklyn, New York, she began as a dancer at Harlem's Cotton Club at the age of sixteen, moving on to become an actress and singer. Her signature song, "Stormy Weather," revealed her depth and lunar, emotional personality, while her elegance and passion may be partly attributed to her Chinese influences as a fire snake. Outspoken in her opposition to racism, she was blacklisted in the 1950s for her association with Paul Robeson's anti-discrimination campaign.

JUNE 30

★★★

Those born on June 30 are extremely sensitive to the responses that they arouse in others, and will therefore tailor their verbal expressions and physical actions and reactions toward their audiences, hoping to receive the acceptance and acclaim that they desire. This predilection frequently stems as much from a sense of insecurity within themselves as from their innate ability to empathize with those around them, and bestows upon them a deep-rooted wish to please and thereby feel valued and loved. And, indeed, their intuitive perspicacity and inherent ability to anticipate the needs of those around them makes them popular figures, whose endearingly gratifying company is sought after by others, who furthermore appreciate the aura of optimism and fun that they exude. Their orientation toward people, combined with their enormous sensitivity and highly developed practical skills, suits those born on this day extremely well to careers as artistic performers of all kinds (but they will usually flourish in spheres in which they can interact with their coworkers). The intellectual foresight and technical skills signified by this day also bode well for their professional success.

It is ironic that, despite their gregarious natures, their loyalty to their friends and family and their need for satisfying interpersonal relationships, these people may find it hard to form enduring one-to-one liaisons. The problem lies in the very talent that draws others to them: their chameleonlike ability to reflect others' moods may cause them to suppress their own emotions and make their true selves difficult for others to know, a tendency that is especially strong in June 30 men.

VIRTUES: These individuals are defined by their strong orientation toward other people, a propensity that derives from their great sensitivity and which may be expressed in self-negating behavior calculated to bring pleasure to those around them. Positive, energetic and imaginative, as well as remarkably practical, they have outstanding potential to achieve professional recognition.
VICES: Their tendency to ignore their own needs in favor of promoting those of others carries the inevitable risk that those born on this day may remain unfulfilled, causing them to become emotionally unbalanced and temperamental.
VERDICT: It is important that June 30 people learn to appreciate that genuine happiness is achievable only when they remain true to their own emotions and aspirations rather than always seeking to satisfy those of other individuals. Making time for periods of honest introspection, and learning to prioritize their desires and responses, will help them in this task.

On This Day
Famous Births: John Gay (1685); Stanley Spencer (1891); James Gunn, Harold Laski and Walter Ulbricht (1893); Ruskin Spear (1911); Lena Horne and Buddy Rich (1917); Susan Hayward (1918); Frank Marcus (1928); Harry Blackstone, Jr. (1934); Tony Hatch (1939); Yunupingu Gallarrwuy (1948); Mike Tyson (1966); Brian Bloom (1970).

Significant Events and Anniversaries: June 30 highlights a strong orientation toward, and naive belief in, other people, a tendency that may result in disaster, as was reflected when the last Aztec emperor, Montezuma II, paid for his trust in the Spanish conquistador Cortés' motives with his life (1520); and when a number of Hitler's loyal henchmen, including Kurt Schleicher and Ernst Röhm, were assassinated at the paranoid dictator's orders during the Night of the Long Knives (1934). This day also promises the implementation of unusually imaginative personal aspirations, as when the French tightrope artist Charles Blondin walked over a line strung above the Niagara Falls, a feat that took eight minutes (1859); Margaret Mitchell published her epic classic *Gone with the Wind* (1936); and Alfred Hitchcock's seminal movie *Psycho* had its first screening (1960). The technical talents that are a strong feature of this day were demonstrated when the transistor was unveiled by John Barden and Walter Brittain at New York's Bell Telephone Laboratories (1948).

JULY 1

Although many of the personal qualities manifested by July 1 people—their deep sensitivity, their capacity for profound thought and their propensity for introspection, for example— may identify them as introverted types, they are also endowed with extroverted tendencies, as evidenced by their strong wish to please others and marked enjoyment of social occasions. Despite their natural orientation toward exploring the realm of abstract themes, their innate priority is to understand every aspect of the human condition, a predilection that may lead them not only to explore such areas as spirituality and alternative philosophies, but also to actively immerse themselves in humanitarian work. For many, the defining quality that inspires their actions is an often overwhelming empathy with others—especially those whom they perceive as having been forgotten or abused by society. And, although they are essentially gentle individuals, when their protective instincts are aroused they will throw themselves bravely into their campaign to reverse such transgressions. Their inclinations and intuitive talents may lead them into careers devoted toward helping others or pushing society forward— for example as social workers, or as artists of all kinds.

To all their endeavors, be they of a professional or private nature, those born on this day bring their deeply empathetic and generous, but also imaginative and prescient, qualities. Yet despite—or perhaps because of—the prodigious emotional and physical energy that they typically devote to others, be they the disadvantaged or their friends and relations, July 1 people generally have a tendency to suppress their own emotional requirements, possibly as a result of a misplaced sense of insecurity; indeed, it is as if they need the recognition of others to validate their worth.

VIRTUES: These extraordinarily sensitive people cannot help but act upon their highly developed intuitive responses to others' emotions, which instill in them a burning desire to rectify wrongs and alleviate suffering. When engaged in the humanitarian work to which they are irresistibly drawn, they furthermore draw upon their unusually imaginative talents, vigor and determination.
VICES: When unable to reconcile their own desires with their urge to address those of others, July 1 individuals may see themselves as martyrs, gaining a certain inverted thrill from sacrificing themselves to others rather than dealing with their own grievances.
VERDICT: It is vital that those born on this day should turn the spotlight of their empathy upon themselves more often, recognizing that many of their actions ultimately stem from a need to bolster their feelings of self-worth, and occasionally directing their talents internally, rather than externally. They should bear in mind that the judicious use of selfishness is sometimes more productive than selflessness.

On This Day

Famous Births: King Frederick II of Denmark (1534); George Sand (1804); Louis Blériot (1872); Charles Laughton (1899); William Wyler (1902); Amy Johnson (1903); Olivia de Havilland (1916); Hans W. Henze (1926); Leslie Caron (1931); Jean Marsh and Sydney Pollack (1934); Twyla Tharp (1941); John Farnham (1949); Dan Ackroyd (1952); David Gulpili (1953); Diana, Princess of Wales and Carl Lewis (1961); Pamela Anderson (1967); Liv Tyler (1977).

Significant Events and Anniversaries: July 1 is a day that highlights committed action in the cause of the perceived greater good and, in the martial sphere, it marks the anniversary of the Battle of the Boyne in Ireland, when the Protestant King William III of Great Britain defeated the ousted Catholic James II (1690); the start of the Battle of Gettysburg during the American Civil War, between General Robert E. Lee's Confederate forces and General George Meade's Union troops (1863); and the beginning of the Battle of the Somme during World War I, which was to cause over 21,000 Allied casualties (1916). In Britain, Prince Charles was identified with a common cause when he was invested as prince of Wales at Caernarvon Castle (on the occasion of his future wife's eighth birthday) (1969).

Planetary Influences
Ruling planet: The Moon.
Second decan: Personal planet is Mars.

Sacred and Cultural Significance
National day of Canada; Naga Panchami festival, devoted to the Snake Gods, in Nepal; goddess Fuji honored in Japan.
Saints' day: Julius and Aaron (d. c.304); Serf (6th century AD); Oliver Plunket (1629–81).

Highly sensitive and empathetic, Princess Diana's compassionate nature was characteristic of her birthdate, and the planet Mercury in Capricorn at her birth reinforced her sympathetic qualities. Known to the world as the "Queen of Hearts," Diana will be remembered as a loving mother and for her commitment to the "constituency of the rejected," in the moving words of her brother as he paid tribute to her life.

CANCER

Planetary Influences
Ruling planet: The Moon.
Second decan: Personal planet is Mars.

Sacred and Cultural Significance
Feast of Expectant Mothers celebrated
in ancient Rome.
Saints' day: The Visitation of the Blessed
Virgin Mary (d. 1st century AD), patron
saint of mothers, nuns and virgins; Processus
and Martinian (dates unknown);
Oudoceus (d. c.615).

*July 2 is the day on which the Visitation of the
Virgin Mary with her cousin Elizabeth, the
mother of St. John the Baptist, is
commemorated. The two women, both heavy
with child, are depicted below embracing in*
The Visitation *(1530), by Potormo.*

JULY 2

Despite their incisive clarity of vision when it comes to identifying perceived societal wrongs, and their marked determination to remedy any such abuses, those born on July 2 are generally less able to direct their considerable powers of perspicacity inward, toward analyzing and resolving the issues that often trouble their own psyches. Yet this internal confusion stems from the same source as their extremely oriented talents: their extraordinary sensitivity, which renders them on the one hand responsive and empathetic to the needs of others and, on the other, overwhelmed by the conflicting emotional messages and urges that they, as well as those around them, generate. Since they furthermore tend to prioritize the demands of other over their own needs—in part a result of their innate tendency to favor the common over the personal good—they may unknowingly bury themselves in their careers as a means of escaping their own personal demons.

Indeed, when employed in professional situations—and their talents equip them especially well for psychiatry and similar branches of medicine (especially if they were also born in the Chinese year of the snake), as well as to the arts—their formidable practical skills, energetic determination and imaginative approach come to the fore, inspiring and motivating others. Within their personal lives, too, these individuals demonstrate a selfless concern for those closest to them, and they are also gifted home-makers. Yet while the love of those closest to them may temper their inherent feelings of insecurity, they will remain unfulfilled until they address their own deepest needs.

VIRTUES: Those born on July 2 are defined by their sensitivity, a quality that leads them to empathize profoundly with those around them—especially the downtrodden—and which arouses their strong feelings of natural justice which they often feel impelled to champion. When working in the service of others, they have the ability to utilize their organizational talents and tenacity to great effect.
VICES: In many respects, these people's overwhelming identification with less fortunate individuals is caused by the conflicts and insecurities that beset their inner selves. Thus while they are devoting their energies toward others, they are tending to ignore their own, potentially destructive, emotions.
VERDICT: While never seeking to suppress their intuitive responses or their urge to help other people, it is crucial for their well-being that these individuals should examine their motivations honestly and carefully to ensure that they are not repressing any potentially pernicious internal problems.

On This Day
Famous Births: Thomas Cranmer (1489); Christoph Willibald von Gluck (1714); William Henry Bragg (1862); Hermann Hesse (1877); Jack Hylton (1892); Alec Douglas-Home and King Olaf V of Norway (1903); Thurgood Marshall (1908); Dan Rowan (1922); Imelda Marcos (1931); David Owen (1938); Cheryl Ladd (1951); Jerry Hall (1960); Jimmy McNichol (1961).

Significant Events and Anniversaries: This is a day that highlights the desire to actively rectify any perceived social abuses, a propensity that was demonstrated on July 2 when, during the English Civil War, Oliver Cromwell's antimonarchical New Model Army defeated Prince Rupert's Royalist forces at the Battle of Marston Moor (1644); when the British evangelist and social campaigner William Booth founded his Christian Mission—later renamed the Salvation Army—in London (1865); and when President Lyndon B. Johnson signed the Civil Rights Bill designed to end racial discrimination in the U.S.A. (1964). The emotional turmoil indicated by this day was illustrated by two tragic events when: Charles Guiteau shot and fatally wounded the U.S. president, James Garfield (1881); philosopher and writer Jean-Jacques Rousseau died as an insane man (1771); and U.S. novelist Ernest Hemingway took his own life (1961). That this day is ruled by the element of water was evidenced when the worst floods in U.S. history left 41 dead and 200,000 homeless in Kansas and Missouri (1951).

JULY 3

While all of those born under the sign of Cancer have a strong and intuitive sensitivity toward other people, in July 3 individuals this usually takes more of an intellectual than an emotional form. This is not to say that these people are not moved by the plight of those in need, but rather that the feelings that arise in their hearts are filtered through their heads before being given expression. Despite their intense interest in other people, their easy charm and their urge to effect progress, those born on this day may sometimes appear to others to be somewhat remote. In part, this may be because they have learned that if they expose their emotions, they are vulnerable to being hurt: but it also indicates that many of these remarkably perspicacious individuals prefer not to become actively involved with people or situations until they have observed and analyzed them and thereby built up a detailed store of information to give them command of all of the available facts. Such inclinations and talents, as well as their soaring imaginative powers, augur especially well for their success as artists, but also equip them admirably for careers as psychologists, psychiatrists and physicians.

Within their personal liaisons, July 3 people demonstrate their tireless involvement and loyalty toward those with whom they have formed deep emotional bonds. Their natural propensity for analyzing the human personality may, however, make it difficult for them to commit themselves to a life partner, for their perspicacity may lead them to envisage numerous potential problems in the relationship under consideration. Similarly, until they learn to couch their critical comments in more diplomatic terms, they may be misperceived by others as being censorious types.

VIRTUES: The rich complexities of the human psyche are of endless fascination to those born on this day, who are drawn toward the study of the characters of those who surround them, as well as of humanity as a whole. They are aided in their analysis by their great intuitive and intellectual sensitivity, and have the potential to become effective instruments of progress.
VICES: These people should take care that their natural observational inclinations do not lead them to become bystanders on the boundaries of human relationships, remaining emotionally isolated from, rather than actively participating in, social interaction and the pleasure that can result from it.
VERDICT: July 3 people should recognize that those around them may be uncomfortable with the feeling that their every move is being critically examined, and should therefore strive to temper this analytical propensity within their personal and professional relationships. They will also find that they will gain greater emotional satisfaction from being involved with others as players rather than as referees.

Planetary Influences
Ruling planet: The Moon.
Second decan: Personal planet is Mars.

Sacred and Cultural Significance
Seminole Tribe in Florida celebrates New Year's Day with the Green Corn Dance; Athena honored in ancient Greece.
Saints' day: Thomas the Apostle (d. 1st century AD), patron saint of architects and blind people; Germanus of Man (c.410–c.475).

On This Day
Famous Births: Robert Adam (1728); John Singleton Copley (1737); Leos Janáček (1854); William Wallace (1860); W.H. Davies (1871); George M. Cohan (1878); Franz Kafka (1883); Ken Russell (1927); Pete Fountain (1930); Tom Stoppard (1937); Judith Durham (1943); Richard Hadlee (1951); Alan Autry (1952); Laura Branigan (1957); Tom Cruise (1962).

Significant Events and Anniversaries: That this day is ruled by the element of water was confirmed when: the French explorer Samuel de Champlain founded the port of Québec on the St. Lawrence River (1608); Joshua Slocom, in his boat *Spray*, became the first person to circumnavigate the world single-handedly (1898); and, tragically, when: Rolling Stones member Brian Jones drowned in his swimming-pool in England (1969); and the U.S. vessel *Vincennes*, in the Gulf of Persia shot down an Iranian airplane, thus killing 290 persons (1988). This day indicates determined action, as was reflected when: Russian soldiers restored civil order in Odessa following a general strike, at the cost of the lives of 6,000 protesters (1905); the French president Charles de Gaulle confirmed the independence of the former colony of Algeria (1962); and Israeli commandos freed 103 hostages held by Palestinian terrorists on a hijacked airplane at Uganda's Entebbe airport (1976).

July 3 is ruled by the element of water and is the anniversary of a number of progressive events, including the founding of the French-Canadian port of Québec in 1608.

JULY 4

Planetary Influences
Ruling planet: The Moon.
Second decan: Personal planet is Mars.

Sacred and Cultural Significance
Independence Day celebrated in the United States; in ancient Rome, the Day of Pax; annual Sun Dance performed by Ute tribe; the Mescalero Apache Gahan Ceremonial honors mountain spirits.
Saints' day: Andrew of Crete (c.660–740); Elizabeth of Portugal (1271–1336).

Independence Day in the United States commemorates the adoption of the Declaration of Independence on this day in 1776, and is distinguished by a strong concern for the collective interest of the nation's citizens and a pronounced desire to effect social and humanitarian progress—qualities strongly highlighted on July 4. Here, Ben Franklin, a dedicated advocate of self-determination, is shown signing the original document.

Perhaps the most defining characteristic of July 4 people, and one that both inspires their intellectual actions and sustains their emotional needs, is their strong communal identification, be it with their families, their coworkers, their local community, their country—or indeed, with humanity as a whole. Their relationship with whatever societal group it is that especially absorbs their interest is a symbiotic one, for while their prodigious organizational skills, their fierce loyalty and their natural willingness to defend the wider interest all serve to benefit the common good, in return they receive a comforting sense of security by grounding themselves in the profound human bonds forged by shared concerns and goals. The dreams and visions of July 4 people are therefore generally concerned with furthering human progress. Despite the fact that, initially, these ideals may appear to be unfeasibly radical to others, they will often prove to be startlingly successful, especially when backed by their originators' practical talents, tenacity and determination.

Whatever career they choose, those born on this day will clearly be unhappy unless surrounded by a like-minded team of colleagues working together toward a mutual aim. If not involved in politics in whatever form, many will be found in such professions as medicine, the military or law-enforcement agencies; they may also direct their energies toward the arts, hoping to unite others in the pleasure that their skills may arouse. Ironically, given their human orientation, they are rather private individuals—especially if they are also men—preferring to keep their innermost emotions to themselves; opening up their hearts to potential partners may therefore initially prove difficult.

VIRTUES: July 4 people have an emotional propensity to immerse themselves in the frameworks of wider societal groupings, devoting their considerable imaginative and practical talents to the good of the common cause with remarkable vigor, loyalty and fixity of purpose. **VICES:** Such is the intensity with which those born on this day embrace the identity and aspirations of the social group with which they most strongly identify, that in times of crisis they may be unable to be objective when faced with conflicts of interest or dissident opinions. **VERDICT:** Although these people gain enormous satisfaction from their work, which is typically devoted to the service of others, they must remember that they—as well as their families, friends and colleagues—have emotional needs that communal bodies cannot satisfy. It is therefore vital that they do not allow their individuality or personal lives to be suppressed in the perceived interests of the greater good of humanity.

On This Day
Famous Births: Jean Pierre Blanchard (1753); George Everest (1790); Nathaniel Hawthorne (1804); Giuseppe Garibaldi (1807); Stephen Collins Foster (1826); Thomas Barnardo (1845); Calvin Coolidge (1872); Louis B. Mayer (1885); Louis Armstrong (1900); Gertrude Lawrence (1898); George Murphy (1902); Mitch Miller (1911); Abigail Van Buren and Ann Landers (1918); Gina Lollobrigida and Neil Simon (1927); George Steinbrenner (1930); Geraldo Rivera (1943).

Significant Events and Anniversaries: July 4 highlights an overriding concern with the communal best interest—a predilection that may be manifested in the political or national sphere—as was reflected on this day when: Karl Marx and Friedrich Engels published their seminal and hugely influential work, the *Communist Manifesto* (1848); Keir Hardie was elected to the British parliament as its first Socialist representative (1904); and the Philippines was granted its independence from the United States on the U.S.'s own Independence Day (1846). That this day is governed by the element of water was evidenced when work was initiated to construct the Erie Canal in North America (1817) and the Panama Canal in Central America (1904).

JULY 5

As with the majority of those born under the sign of the crab, July 5 people are profoundly sensitive and intuitive types, who invest their inspirational visions with great emotional significance. Yet by comparison with their Cancerian fellows, they are less oriented toward satisfying the demands of others than toward attaining their own emotional fulfillment— although they are nevertheless anxious to please those who surround them. It is this latter quest that typically informs many of the—often somewhat erratic—actions of July 5 people, who find it difficult to resist following the lure of a new and exciting person, subject or venture to which they may feel innately drawn as well as intellectually attracted. When they alight upon a subject that truly absorbs their interest, they will explore it with acute perception, great energy and keen imagination and, when action is required, utilize their strong planning and organizational skills. While they have the potential to make gifted innovators in any sphere where they can follow their instincts unhindered by the restrictions of others, they are especially suited to the freedom offered by creative careers, perhaps in design.

The combination of their original approach, charm and energy makes them extremely magnetic and popular figures, who are able to, apparently effortlessly, attract hordes of admirers. But while they are outstanding performers and entertainers in the broader context of social circumstances, they may often shy away from committing themselves to one-to-one relationships (a tendency that is especially pronounced if they were also born in the Chinese year of the horse), fearing, perhaps, that too intimate a relationship might prove stifling. Indeed, although their love for and loyalty to their friends and family members are never in doubt, they need freedom to pursue their personal dreams.

VIRTUES: Keenly sensitive, extraordinarily imaginative, vigorous and charming, these vibrant personalities are driven by their strong desire to realize their emotion-fueled visions. When focused on the fulfillment of their goals, they will typically support their visionary sense of purpose with remarkably effective practical skills.
VICES: Governed as they are by an irresistible urge to seek out pleasurable emotional and sensual experiences, there is a danger that those born on this day will never ground themselves within stable and settled emotional relationships or intellectual pursuits.
VERDICT: July 5 people should recognize that the ultimate satisfaction for which they yearn may be literally be found closer to home than expected: that is, within their private liaisons and the simple pleasures of a settled domestic life. They should therefore make a concerted effort to devote as much attention to nurturing the bonds that tie them to their nearest and dearest as they do to their external interests.

On This Day

Famous Births: Etienne de Silhouette (1709); Luke Hansard (1752); Sarah Siddons (1755); Thomas Stamford Raffles (1781); Phineas Taylor Barnum (1810); Cecil Rhodes (1853); Dwight Filley Davis (1879); Jean Cocteau (1889); Gordon Jacob (1895); Georges Pompidou (1911); Katherine Helmond (1934); Shirley Knight (1936); Julie Nixon Eisenhower (1948); Huey Lewis (1951); Elizabeth Emmanuel (1953).

Significant Events and Anniversaries: This day highlights the vigorous promotion of visions of all kinds, and on July 5 the Labour Party achieved its ambition to be elected to govern Britain (1945); and the U.S. tennis player Arthur Ashe won the men's singles championship at Wimbledon, becoming the first African-American holder of the title (1975). July 5 is cogoverned by the planet Mars, as was reflected in two events with martial associations that occurred on this day, when: Israeli troops reoccupied the disputed Palestinian-populated Gaza Strip (1967); and a military coup led by the Punjabi Army's chief of staff, General Zia ul-Haq, deposed and imprisoned the Prime Minister of Pakistan, Zulfikar Ali Bhutto (1977).

Planetary Influences
Ruling planet: The Moon.
Second decan: Personal planet is Mars.

Sacred and Cultural Significance
National day of Venezuela; the Aphelion of the Earth occurs (point when the Earth is farthest from the Sun); the goddess Maat honored in ancient Egypt.
Saints' day: Morwenna (6th century AD), patron saint of Morwenstow, Cornwall, England; Modwenna (7th century AD); Athanasius the Athonite (c.925–1003); Antony Zaccaria (1502–39).

Born on July 5, 1810, Phineas Taylor Barnum, the cofounder of the world-famous Barnum & Bailey Circus, embodied the day's capacity for originality of vision and colorful imagination.

CANCER

Planetary Influences
Ruling planet: The Moon.
Second decan: Personal planet is Mars.

Sacred and Cultural Significance
Pagans honor all horned goddesses.
Saints' day: Newlyn (dates unknown);
Monenna (d. c.518); Sexburga
(7th century AD); Godeliva (d. 1070);
Maria Goretti (1890–1902).

July 6 is characterized by the ability to realize one's visions, and on this day in 1885, Louis Pasteur successfully tested a vaccine for rabies.

JULY 6

✦✦✦✦✦✦✦✦✦✦✦✦✦✦✦✦✦✦✦✦✦✦✦✦✦✦✦✦✦✦✦✦✦✦✦

More than anything else, those born on this day yearn to realize their personal idyll, be it finding enduring love, the perfect career, a fulfilling lifestyle, or a Utopian humanitarian or spiritual vision. Whether their quest is motivated by a conscious or unconscious urge to achieve their ideal, it will nevertheless inform many of their actions and—despite the many setbacks and disappointments that they will inevitably experience—will usually remain a beacon of inspiration lighting their path through life. They usually focus on a single vision and the vibrant optimism, infectious energy and dedicated enthusiasm with which they typically imbue its pursuit may also fire the interest of others, especially if directed toward a global goal or if manifested in the realm of the arts to which, in any case, they have a natural affinity. And, when their magnetism, kindness and charm (born both of their strong wills and their desire to please others) are added to the equation, the sum of the components results in popular personalities who are both enthused and enthusing.

Because their enormous sensitivity toward those who surround them endows them with feelings of empathy and a sincere desire to lighten the lives of others, July 6 individuals make inherently loyal and affectionate friends, relations and especially parents. Forging a lasting one-on-one partnership that fully satisfies their emotional demands may prove difficult, however, unless they are prepared to compromise the often highly idealized standards that they have set for their soul mate.

VIRTUES: July 6 individuals are driven by the urge to see the vision that inspires them— be it a personal, professional or humanitarian aim—transformed into reality. To this end they deploy their manifold talents, including especially their optimism and energy, often recruiting others to their mission by means of their remarkable charisma.
VICES: Many of those born on this day become so obsessed with the pursuit of their (frequently unrealizable) personal dreams that they may close their minds to the potential fulfillment to be gained from other areas of their lives.
VERDICT: It is vital that these people should at least consider the possibility that they may never realize the objectives to which their lives are geared. They should therefore try to develop a realistic intellectual appreciation of what is feasible, as well as greater pragmatism.

On This Day
Famous Births: John Paul Jones (1747); John Flaxman (1755); Maximilian, Archduke of Austria and Emperor of Mexico (1832); Laverne Andrews (1915); Nancy Reagan (1921); Ruth Cracknell, Merv Griffin and Bill Haley (1925); Janet Leigh (1927); Della Reese (1931); the Fourteenth Dalai Lama (1935); Dave Allen (1936); Vladimir Ashkénazy and Ned Beatty (1937); Mary Peters (1939); Sylvester Stallone (1946); Allyce Beasley (1954); Tia and Tamera Mowry (1978).

Significant Events and Anniversaries: July 6 is a day that highlights single-minded loyalty to personal convictions, and marks the anniversary of the deaths of two individuals who were prepared to pay the ultimate price for their beliefs: the Bohemian religious reformer John Huss, who was burned at the stake for his rejection of papal authority (1415); and the English lord chancellor Sir Thomas More, who refused to acknowledge King Henry VIII's (rather than the pope's) claim to religious supremacy (1535; although he did not die on this day, the execution of the illegitimate son of Charles II, James, Duke of Monmouth, was heralded by his defeat at the Battle of Sedgemoor by the troops of James II (1685). Others, however, achieved their aims on this day, including: Dadabhai Naoraji, who was elected as Britain's first non-white member of parliament (1892); and U.S. tennis player Althea Gibson, who became the first African-American woman to win the women's singles final at Wimbledon (1957). Other visions realized on this day include the opening of the world's first dedicated motor-racing arena, at Brooklands, in England (1907); and the first crossing of the Atlantic by an airship, the British R34 (1919). This day's involvement with the element of water was tragically reflected when 167 workers were killed by an explosion on the Piper Alpha oil rig in the North Sea (1988).

JULY 7

* *

Those born on this day are characterized by their somewhat dualistic natures, manifested on the one hand by their extraordinarily original dreams, and on the other by their fierce drive and determination. These are the type of individuals whose soaring imaginations will cause them to espouse what may appear to others to be utterly unrealistic and fanciful projects, and then to further confound their detractors by successfully implementing the very visions previously dismissed as being unfeasible. When their various personal qualities—including their idealism, energy and practicality—are in harmony with one another, they have the potential to effect truly remarkable innovations, and they should thus strive to retain their self-belief despite being inevitably subjected to the discouragement of less progressive minds. These are pragmatic people who draw on their sensitivity toward others to tailor their approach to the form that they expect to be best received by their audiences—their vision and vigor also proving inspirational.

Their career choices will depend, of course, on the specific areas of interest that motivate them as individuals, but they are usually naturally drawn to the sphere of artistic expression—be it as musicians, painters or actors—and may furthermore have the capacity to employ their intuition and energy extremely effectively within the business world. Despite their charisma, these are somewhat private people, who cherish the close bonds of kinship and friendship that define their relationships with their nearest and dearest, from whom they gain as much as they give in terms of emotional support.

VIRTUES: These people are blessed with exceptionally wide-ranging imaginative powers, which endow them with the capacity to generate highly original ambitions. They seek to realize their goals by employing their strong intuition, determined fixity of purpose, well-developed organizational skills and vibrant energy.

VICES: When—as frequently happens—their visionary ideas are dismissed as unworkable, these people have a propensity to react strongly, sometimes resorting to extremes. This may involve persisting uncompromisingly with their plans when they would be better off modifying them to take account of the points made by their skeptics, or taking a defeatist attitude, becoming disillusioned and abandoning their plans.

VERDICT: While July 7 people should never suppress their dreams, they should learn to assess their potential success with a more realistic sense of objectivity. Listening to the views of others and evolving a more pragmatic approach will help them to be more objective, as well as to enlist the support of others.

On This Day

Famous Births: Joseph Marie Jacquard (1752); Gustav Mahler (1860); Marc Chagall (1887); George Cukor (1899); Vittorio de Sica (1901); Gian-Carlo Menotti (1911); John Pertwee (1919); Pierre Cardin (1922); Doc Severinsen (1927); Ringo Starr (1940); Bill Oddie (1941); Tony Jacklin (1944); Joe Spano (1946); Shelley Duval (1949); Jessica Hahn (1959); Fred Savage (1976); Michelle Kwan (1980).

Significant Events and Anniversaries: This day promises the achievement of pioneering goals, provided that they are pursued with tenacity and pragmatism, as was evidenced when: U.S. naval officer Matthew Perry's expedition arrived in Uraga, Japan, thus heralding negotiations that would end Japan's 250 years of isolation and open up lucrative trading opportunities (1853); round-the-world yachtsman Francis Chichester was knighted by Queen Elizabeth II, who symbolically used the sword of Sir Francis Drake for this purpose (1967); and perhaps the most important pop-music event ever staged, the Live Aid concert was held simultaneously in Britain and the United States to raise funds to alleviate starvation in Ethiopia (1985)—Queen Elizabeth II would later bestow an honary knighthood upon its originator, Irish musician Bob Geldof. Reflecting its artistic potential, this was the day on which the historical novel *Waverley*, by Sir Walter Scott, was first published (1814).

Planetary Influences
Ruling planet: The Moon.
Second decan: Personal planet is Mars.

Sacred and Cultural Significance
Running of the Bulls held in Spain; Tanabata festival celebrated in Japan; in China, the annual Feast of the Milky Way.
Saints' day: Sunniva (dates unknown); Merryn (dates unknown), patron saint of St. Merryn, Cornwall, England; Palladius (5th century AD); Erkengota (d. c.660); Boisil (d. c.661); Ethelburga of Faremoutier (d. 664); Hedda of Winchester (d. 705); Willibald (d. 786/87); Maelruain (d. 792); the translation of Thomas of Canterbury (1118–70).

Those born on July 7 are often well suited for artistic pursuits: one notable example is Marc Chagall, whose highly original and imaginative works of art gave the Surrealist movement its name.

Planetary Influences
Ruling planet: The Moon.
Second decan: Personal planet is Mars.

Sacred and Cultural Significance
In ancient Rome, the nature festival Nonae Caprotinae celebrated in honor of Juno.
Saints' day: Urith of Chittlehampton (dates unknown); Kilian (d. c.689); Grimbald (c.825–901).

July 8 is a day on which determination in pursuit of an ambitious goal is often manifested. Below, Fred J. Perry is shown winning a match at Wimbledon on this day in 1934, when he won the first of his three consecutive men's singles championships at the revered lawn tennis club.

JULY 8

Others generally admire those born on this day for their dynamism, fixity of purpose, prodigious energy and impressive practical skills, but the respect that they generate is of the awed, somewhat intimidated, variety rather than born of affection. For such is their strength of will, self-belief and uncompromising determination to achieve their aims that their tenacity can often take the form of ruthlessness. In many respects it is the organizational aspects of a task that interest them most: they have an overriding urge to realize their progressive visions by implementing a soundly supportive framework of actions, comparable to the setting in motion of a smoothly running machine. They may be found making their mark in any professional field where their imaginative visions can be imbued with the potential to achieve tangible results: their inclinations and talents equip them for commercial or scientific ventures as well as for those artistic pursuits which require detailed background research and development.

Their interpersonal relationships are typically characterized by their urge to direct the activities of those around them. Yet they usually combine the intellectual clarity of vision which informs the majority of their actions, with a sensitivity toward the feelings of others. Thus, although they have a propensity to take charge, they will rarely ride roughshod over others in their quest to achieve progress, possibly also instinctively recognizing that they will achieve more by enlisting the support of others. This pragmatic approach also stands them in good stead within their more intimate liaisons, particularly if they are men.

VIRTUES: July 8 individuals are strong-willed types who are motivated by the urge to implement their progressive aims. While their ideals may be ambitious, they are rarely unfeasible, especially since they are backed by their highly practical or technical abilities, as well as their outstanding vigor, sense of purpose and pragmatic approach.
VICES: Their goal orientation may be so all-encompassing that those born on this day may not appreciate that others—especially their family members—do not always share their priorities. They may therefore cause hurt by unwittingly giving preference to their own driving interests rather than to the concerns of those closest to them.
VERDICT: Although these are inherently intuitive people, they should consider the effect that their forceful actions (however well intended) may have on others, particularly those who are not involved in their professional projects. They should also learn to appreciate the simple pleasures that are an important part of social—and particularly familial—life, and devote more time to relaxation.

On This Day
Famous Births: Jean de la Fontaine (1621); Tom Cribb (1781); Joseph Chamberlain (1836); Count Ferdinand von Zeppelin (1838); John D. Rockefeller (1839); Arthur Evans (1851); Percy Grainger (1882); Gwendolyn Bennett (1902); Nelson Aldrich Rockefeller (1908); Billy Eckstine (1914); Steve Lawrence (1935); Cynthia Gregory (1946); Anjelica Huston (1951); Kevin Bacon (1958); Mal Mennga (1960); Kathleen Robertson (1973).

Significant Events and Anniversaries: This day indicates determined and practical action in the pursuit of an inspirational aim, as was reflected when: the Portuguese navigator Vasco da Gama embarked from Lisbon on his (ultimately successful) expedition to discover a sea route to India (1497); and the popular and elaborate show *Ziegfeld's Follies of 1907* opened in the United States (1907). This day is cogoverned by the planet Mars, and its pugilistic influence was mirrored by three events that occurred on July 8, when: Peter the Great's Russian troops defeated the army of Charles XII of Sweden at the Battle of Poltava in the Ukraine, thereby heralding the demise of the Swedish empire (1709); the last official bare-knuckle world heavyweight boxing match was staged in Richburg, Mississippi (1889); and the Gestapo executed Jean Moulin ("Max"), a leading figure of the French Resistance, during World War II (1943). The element of water rules this day, as was tragically illustrated when the English lyric poet Percy Bysshe Shelley was drowned when his boat capsized off Leghorn in Italy (1822).

JULY 9

Their questing imagination and enthusiasm for thoroughly investigating the unusual and wide-ranging interests to which they are naturally attracted, bestow upon July 9 people the potential to blaze truly innovative trails through life. Indeed, such is their innate conviction that there is more to life than has yet been discovered that they are often irresistibly drawn to explore concepts that less open-minded types might dismiss as being fanciful or as having no future—pioneering scientific or artistic theories, for example, or even psychic phenomena, mysticism and spirituality. Despite the originality of the visions that inspire them, however, those born on this day are rarely unrealistic about the possibility of success, for they supplement their great intellectual and intuitive perspicacity with remarkably effective resourceful and practical skills. Add to this combination of personal qualities great optimism and energy, and the resulting individuals are attractive and popular people.

Although their actions may be motivated by the very personal visions that inspire them, they generally prefer to work toward their realization as part of a coordinated team rather than in solitary isolation. Not only are they stimulated by the company and ideas of others, but developing strong and supportive working relationships is of vital importance to their emotional equilibrium. Similarly, within their private lives, they appreciate and value the unquestioning love of those closest to them and they typically make caring and empathetic family members, especially if they were also born in the Chinese year of the monkey.

VIRTUES: Their enduring interest in pushing the boundaries of human knowledge forward is as much the result of their intuitive acceptance of the existence of hidden truths as of their intellectual curiosity. To their progressive endeavors they bring their enormous sensitivity, energy, organizational proficiency and optimism.

VICES: Although these are inherently positive and tenacious individuals, should their progress become implacably blocked by the skepticism of others, they may become subject to overwhelming feelings of frustration, which may be manifested by displays of temper or by withdrawal into their private world of dreams.

VERDICT: While it is vital that those born on this day should not allow themselves to become depressed and discouraged by the negative responses that their advanced ideas will inevitably elicit, at the same time they should ensure that they do not sabotage their own efforts by stubbornly promoting a vision—however theoretically feasible—that others will not accept.

On This Day

Famous Births: Elias Howe (1819); Nikola Tesla (1856); Ottorino Respighi (1879); Bruce Bairnsfather (1888); Barbara Cartland (1901); Elisabeth Lutyens (1906); Edward Heath (1916); John Heath-Stubbs (1918); Ed Ames (1927); Michael Williams (1935); David Hockney (1937); Brian Dennehy (1940); O.J. Simpson (1947); John Tesh (1952); Tom Hanks (1956); Kelly McGillis (1959); Jimmy Smits (1959); Courtney Love (1964).

Significant Events and Anniversaries: A day that highlights the promotion of profoundly original visions, July 9 marks the anniversary of the staging of the first Wimbledon tennis championships in England (1877); the granting of the royal assent for Australia to become an independent sovereign nation within the British Commonwealth rather than a British colony (1900); and the first successful birth of a rhinoceros calf in captivity (1969). The influences inherent in July 9, however, indicate that many ambitions may prove unacceptable to others, and although Lady Jane Grey was proclaimed Queen of England on this day, she would be deposed by Mary I ten days later (1553). On a day that is governed by the element of water, U.S. swimmer Johnny Weismuller set a world record when he swam the 100-meter length in less than a minute (1922). July 9 indicates a marked sympathy with paranormal events, and on this day lightning struck York Minster in England, an event that some Christians interpreted as a manifestation of divine displeasure with the unorthodox comments made by the archbishop of York regarding the veracity of the Virgin birth (1984).

Planetary Influences
Ruling planet: The Moon.
Second decan: Personal planet is Mars.

Sacred and Cultural Significance
National day of Argentina; first day of the Panathenae festival honoring Athena in ancient Greece; Pagans celebrate the birthdays of Dionysus and Rhea.
Saints' day: Everild (d. c.700); the Martyrs of Gorkum (d. 1572); Veronica Giuliani (1660–1717).

Resourceful action is often a feature of this day, as was seen in England when, to protect against enemy action in World War II, gas masks were first issued to civilians in 1939.

CANCER

Planetary Influences
Ruling planet: The Moon.
Second decan: Personal planet is Mars.

Sacred and Cultural Significance
Day of Holda, Anglo-Saxon and Norse goddess of the Underworld.
Saints' day: The Seven Brothers (2nd century AD); Alexander (3rd century AD).

Blessed with his birthdate's gift of determination to achieve visions, Camille Pissarro, the leading early Impressionist, helped found one of the best-loved movements in the history of Western art. Born in 1830, his Neige à Lower Norwood *(1870, detail below) reveals his clarity of observation and sensitivity of character.*

JULY 10

Those born on this day are vitally interested in all aspects of the human condition—ranging from the psyches of those who surround them to the behavior of humanity as a whole and, such is the profound and all-encompassing nature of their perspicacity, that little passes them by. Their forte is observation, rather than action, which is not to say that they lack strong opinions and ambitions, or the determination to implement these when they feel impelled to effect progress, it is rather that detailed information-gathering is a crucial prerequisite to the formulation and promotion of their strategies. In fact, their gentle, unassuming demeanor typically masks a keen and powerful intellect, the incisive expression of which may startle those who do not know them well and may have misjudged them as being passive and dull. But once they have secured the background data that they need for the best chance of success, these individuals will embark upon the quest to realize their visions with remarkable fixity of purpose and tenacity, drawing from their armory of talents upon their prodigious organizational skills.

July 10 people are naturally attracted to nonmaterialistic pursuits, and their inclinations and skills augur especially well for their success as insightful psychologists and psychiatrists, artists, writers and musicians, as well as dedicated athletes—in fact, in any field where a "corporate ethos" would not restrict their independence of thought and action. They are generally extremely discriminating in their choice of friends and life partners, but once they have committed their affections these sensitive and loyal individuals will stick to their nearest and dearest through thick and thin.

VIRTUES: Profoundly sensitive to every nuance of human behavior, July 10 people have a strong fascination with observing and analyzing the actions and motivations of others, an approach that they also adopt with regard to any subject that arouses their interest. When fueled by an overwhelming desire to effect progress, they apply to the results of their research their practical talents and clarity of vision.
VICES: Their innate predilection toward observing others, as well as their tendency to delay acting until they have thoroughly understood their subject, may cause these people to remain perpetual bystanders on the periphery of life, looking on, but never participating.
VERDICT: In order to avoid becoming isolated from others—particularly within their personal lives—those born on this day should occasionally throw caution to the wind and join in the fun that is inherent in interpersonal relationships, regardless of the consequences (which, they will usually find informative, as well as liberating).

On This Day
Famous Births: John Calvin (1509); Pierre Joseph Redouté (1759); Frederick Marryat (1792); Robert Chambers (1802); Camille Pissaro (1830); James Abbott McNeill Whistler (1834); Marcel Proust (1871); Giorgio de Chiroco (1888); Jimmy McHugh (1894); Carl Orff (1895); Saul Bellow (1915); David Brinkley (1920); Jake LaMotta (1921); Fred Gwynne (1926); Arthur Ashe (1943); Virginia Wade (1945); Arlo Guthrie (1947); Sunil Gavaskar (1949).

Significant Events and Anniversaries: Observational characteristics are strongly highlighted by this day, as was reflected on July 10 when the U.S. launched *Telstar I* from Cape Canaveral in Florida, a communications satellite that would enable European viewers to enjoy U.S. television programs (1962); and the *Rainbow Warrior*, a ship used by Greenpeace to monitor environmental abuses at sea, was severely damaged in Auckland harbor, Australia, by a bomb planted by French intelligence agents to prevent its observation of French atmospheric nuclear testing—tragically, one crew member died (1985). This day indicates that communal action is sometimes preferable to solitary pursuits in achieving the greater good, and the recognition of the benefits that can result from such an approach were illustrated when Wyoming joined the union of United States (1890); and the Parisian underground public railway system, the Metro, was officially opened in France (1900).

JULY 11

* *

Whether they are conscious of their overriding predilection or not, those born on this day are defined by the intensity of their interest in their interpersonal relationships. Thus, although their enthusiasm may be fired by abstract, intellectual concepts, or by personal ambition or vision, this will almost always involve the participation of others, be they friends, relations, coworkers or even audiences. And, indeed, July 11 individuals—who in any case have a natural affinity with the arts and will often make dramatic or musical pursuits their careers—are in many respects natural performers, who not only relish the attention that is lavished upon them by others, but are also almost hypersensitive to the responses that they arouse. Since they are inherently charming and empathetic people who enjoy pleasing and entertaining others (both for reasons of human concern and because their confidence is boosted when they can bask in the goodwill that is thereby engendered), they will generally put the maximum possible effort into creating mutually rewarding liaisons, be they of the personal or professional variety.

Most July 11 people are innately geared toward achieving tangible success—in part a result of their driving energy and their urge to take practical action, and in part because of the acclaim that they will thus receive—and will often be found making their mark in the worlds of commercial enterprise, politics or sports. Within their private lives, too, they typically strive to bring happiness to their nearest and dearest, enlivening their relationships with their imagination and *joie de vivre,* but also offering more profound emotional support, particularly if they are women.

VIRTUES: Those born on this day are extremely sensitive to other people's reactions to their behavior and, because they are both optimistic and empathetic, have a tendency to temper their actions positively to reflect the "vibrations" that they pick up from others. These are energetic, intellectually perceptive and remarkably resourceful individuals, who possess outstanding potential to fulfill their personal ambitions.
VICES: Because of their natural propensity to seek the approval or applause of those around them, they may become susceptible to flattery when such plaudits are received and thus become prone to unobjective feelings of vanity and conceit.
VERDICT: Although it is vital that July 11 individuals should never repress their direct and positive orientation toward others, it is important that they should keep their feet on the ground and their minds focused, and not get carried away with the heady synergetic excitement that typically characterizes their interpersonal relationships.

Planetary Influences
Ruling planet: The Moon.
Second decan: Personal planet is Mars.

Sacred and Cultural Significance
Saints' day: Benedict (c.480–c.550), patron saint of monks and speleologists; Drostan (d. 7th century AD); Olga (c.879–969); Thurketyl (10th century AD).

U.S. statesman and sixth president, John Quincy Adams, who was born on July 11, 1867, manifested many of the day's personality tendencies through his natural intellect, charisma and aptitude for a political career.

On This Day
Famous Births: Robert the Bruce, King of Scotland (1274); Frederick I of Prussia (1657); Thomas Bowdler (1754); John Quincy Adams (1767); Liza Lehmann (1862); E.B. White (1899); Yul Brynner (1915); Edward Gough Whitlam (1916); Nicolai Gedda (1925); Tab Hunter (1931); Giorgio Armani (1934); Peter de Savary (1944); Deborah Harry (1945); Leon Spinks (1953); Suzanne Vega (1959).

Significant Events and Anniversaries: Dramatic action and sensation are indicated for this day on which the Roman emperor Nero is said to have committed suicide (68 BC); the Marquis de Lafayette introduced the draft of the revolutionary tract *Rights of Man and the Citizen* to the French National Assembly (1789); Aaron Burr, the U.S. vice president, challenged his implacable political enemy, the former secretary of the treasury Alexander Hamilton, to a duel, fatally wounding him (1804); and archaeologists excavating in Xian, China, discovered the "terracotta army," comprising over 6000 life-sized models of soldiers intended to protect the Emperor Qin in the afterlife (1975). And, on a day ruled by the element of water, this day marks the anniversary of English naval explorer Captain James Cook's embarkation on his third and final expedition to discover the Northwest Passage (1776). The potential to realize ambitions was evidenced when baseball legend Babe Ruth made his Major League debut (1914).

CANCER

Planetary Influences
Ruling planet: The Moon.
Third decan: Personal planets are Jupiter and Neptune.

Sacred and Cultural Significance
In Tibet, the Buddhist god of death and the Underworld, Yama, is honored with the Old Dances festival.
Saint's day: John Gualbert (c.995–1073).

The artistic sphere is often starred for those born on this day, as exemplified by Modernist Amedeo Modigliani, who was born on July 12, 1884. His Self Portrait *(1919) is shown below.*

JULY 12

There are two aspects to the personalities of those born on July 12: on the one hand they are "soft," profoundly empathetic and sympathetic individuals who are keenly attuned to the emotions exuded by others; and on the other hand they are "hard," having a compelling urge to direct the actions of those around them. Although these twin propensities may seem paradoxical, they are readily explained and reconciled by the strong orientation of these individuals toward others, which is typically manifested in a desire to set those around them on what they perceive to be the optimum path for achieving success. This instinct is the result of not only their inherent sensitivity but also their intellectual strengths—of clarity of vision, logical deduction, independence of thought and organizational powers. Their concern for others (which is redoubled if they were born in the Chinese year of the goat) may be manifested at the personal, professional or even humanitarian level.

Because they naturally engender respect, July 12 people will often be elevated to positions of leadership, and, indeed, their integrity and resistance to following the herd suits them for working autonomously. Apart from national and civic politics or social work, optimum careers include especially the artistic sphere, in which they may exert their benevolent influence on others. These people are typically sought after for the sound and carefully considered advice that they offer to those who solicit their opinions, particularly since they are rarely patronizing. And, within their personal relationships, their desire to protect and guide their nearest and dearest is even more pronounced: they are well aware that when differences have to be resolved confrontation or coercion is less effective than a more subtle and rational approach.

VIRTUES: The enormous sensitivity of those born on this day is directed toward ensuring the welfare of others, although it also serves as a valuable intellectual tool when informing their opinions. Their highly developed interpersonal skills are supplemented with formidably effective practical and analytical talents.
VICES: These people have an irresistible—although well-meaning—compulsion to control the thoughts, behavior and actions of those around them, choosing for them a route and guiding them along it. In their personal liaisons, however, the subjects of their concern may grow to resent what they may understandably perceive to be a manipulative and interfering manner.
VERDICT: If they are ultimately not to alienate others who may regard them as obsessively interfering, it is vital that July 12 individuals should occasionally judiciously desist from their propensity to offer advice, however selfless. They need to remember that sometimes it is better that people should be allowed to make mistakes in order to aid their personal development.

On This Day
Famous Births: Gaius Julius Caesar (100 BC); Josiah Wedgwood (1730); Henry David Thoreau (1817); George Eastman (1854); George Washington Carver (1864); Amedeo Modigliani (1884); George Butterworth (1885); Kirsten Flagstad and Oscar Hammerstein II (1895); Milton Berle (1908); Andrew Wyeth (1917); Alistair Burnet (1928); Bill Cosby (1937); Richard Simmons (1948); Kristi Yamaguchi (1971).

Significant Events and Anniversaries: On a day that indicates action on behalf of what is perceived to be the common good—a propensity that can have various manifestations—the English naval hero Horatio Nelson, a protagonist during the French Revolutionary Wars, lost the sight of his right eye during the siege of Calvi in Corsica (1794); the *Pas de Quatre* (a balletic divertissement) "amused" Queen Victoria and other spectators on its first performance (1845); Turkey ceded the administration of Cyprus to Britain (1878); the first racially integrated All-Star baseball game was played (1949); and U.S. president Woodrow Wilson opened the Panama Canal, connecting the Pacific and Atlantic oceans and thus facilitating the movement of naval traffic (1920). The day's emphasis on leadership was seen when Dwight D. Eisenhower retired from the U.S. Army to begin his presidential campaign (1952).

JULY 13

Their inherent preference to play an active part in life, rather than experience it passively, endows July 13 individuals with the irresistible urge to make progress and achieve the tangible targets that they typically set for themselves. And, when their highly developed intellectual and emotional perspicacity is added to this personal equation, it results in an outstanding capacity to recognize a potentially advantageous opportunity (whose merits may not be immediately obvious to less sensitive types), seize the moment and act incisively. To all their ventures—be they within their professional or their private lives—they bring their natural qualities of originality, inventiveness and vigor and, because they are so responsive to the emotions of others and are innately kind-hearted, also the desire to build supportive and close-knit teams to assist them in their endeavors. The same concern for other people naturally equips those born on this day for careers where they can work toward the welfare of humanity—as social scientists, perhaps—although their talents may suit them equally well to becoming commercial entrepreneurs or artists.

July 13 people's personal relationships are usually characterized by the deep affection and protectiveness that they manifest toward their nearest and dearest (especially if they are also women). The value that they place upon the emotional bonds that they form with others may stem from feelings of *angst*, or "otherness"—another result of their far-reaching perspicacity—which has the capacity to be enriching if positively channeled, but which may also cause them to become overly anxious with regard to what they perceive to be the fate that lies in store for them.

VIRTUES: Primarily influenced by their all-encompassing sensitivity, these people possess multifaceted imaginative talents that bestow upon them both enormous intuition and empathy in their relationships with others, as well as keenly innovative intellectual abilities. These characteristics bestow upon them the enviable capacity to achieve material success while also maintaining long-lasting personal liaisons.
VICES: Their profoundly receptive qualities, which enable them to soak up all manner of data like sponges, may result in these individuals feeling that they are being bombarded with an overload of information demanding action which, unless they analyze and prioritize it, may result in chaotic or depressed emotions.
VERDICT: Those born on this day must strive to remain focused on positive issues and aims, rather than allowing themselves to become confused by the manifold messages that they intuitively receive, which may either paralyze them into inactivity or cause them to become beset by overwhelming feelings of pessimism.

On This Day

Famous Births: John Dee (1527); William Hedley (1779); John Clare (1793); George Gilbert Scott (1811); Sidney James Webb (1859); Eric Williams (1911); David Storey (1933); Patrick Stewart (1940); Harrison Ford (1942); Cheech Marin (1946).

Significant Events and Anniversaries: July 13 is a day that highlights a compulsion for seizing opportunities, and marks the anniversary of: the stabbing of the Jacobin leader Jean Paul Marat by the Girondin adherent Charlotte Corday, who surprised him in his bath (1793); the last execution of a woman in Britain, the nightclub hostess Ruth Ellis, who had murdered her lover when in the throes of jealous anger (1955); and the ending of the Everly Brothers' musical partnership, when they impulsively and acrimoniously split up on stage while performing in California (1973). The outstanding promise that is indicated by the active and artistic influences that are inherent in this day was apparently confirmed when: the first soccer World Cup competition opened in Montevideo, Uruguay (1930); and singer Frank Sinatra cut his first record with the Harry James Band, entitled "From the Bottom of My Heart" (1939).

Planetary Influences
Ruling planet: The Moon.
Third decan: Personal planets are Jupiter and Neptune.

Sacred and Cultural Significance
The birthday of Osiris celebrated by Egyptian Wiccans; Bon festival celebrated in Japan.
Saints' day: Silas (1st century AD); Mildred (d. c.700); Henry (II) the Emperor (973–1024).

On this day of natural vitality, Wiccans celebrate the rebirth of the Egyptian fertility god Osiris, whose cycle of annual death and rebirth represents the rejuvenation of nature.

CANCER

Planetary Influences
Ruling planet: The Moon.
Third decan: Personal planets are Jupiter and Neptune.

Sacred and Cultural Significance
Bastille Day, the national day of France; the national day of Iraq; Wiccans of the Egyptian tradition celebrate the birthday of Horus.
Saints' day: Phocas of Sinope (4th century AD), patron saint of agricultural workers, gardeners and sailors; Deusdedit (7th century AD); Boniface of Savoy (1243–70); Camillus of Lellis (1550–1614), patron saint of hospitals, nurses and sick people.

July 14 is characterized both by an affinity with the natural world and the realization of ambitious dreams, and on this day in 1865 the Matterhorn was first scaled, by Edward Whymper. Exactly a century later, Mlle. Vaucher became the first woman to achieve the same feat. The third highest Alpine peak, the Matterhorn is considered the most challenging and has claimed more lives than any other mountain in the range.

JULY 14

★★

Those born on this day have the enviable ability to attract the affection and admiration of others—even when, at moments of extreme passion, they may stridently attempt to communicate the humanitarian messages that are inspired by their profound empathy with the disadvantaged. Rather than being alienated by others for their vehement stance in such inherently confrontational situations, they are often regarded with indulgence. Indulgence, however, is not usually the response that is sought, for these individuals are typically possessed of an urgent desire to bring about progress in human society, to harmonize interpersonal relationships and to right perceived wrongs, a compulsion that is the result of not only their all-encompassing sensitivity, but also their intellectual clarity and fixity of purpose. While these people will often be found in professions that are concerned with achieving humanitarian goals—as politicians or social campaigners, for instance—many will devote their talents to improving the quality of life of others by becoming artistic performers, especially if they were also born in the Chinese year of the goat.

While their enormous empathy is perhaps their greatest quality, at the same time it is also one of their most pernicious attributes. For while they cannot help but offer sympathy and advice to those whom they intuitively sense are in need of assistance, they sometimes have an overriding tendency to suppress their own identities and needs when acting on behalf of others. They manifest this strong orientation toward others in all of their liaisons, particularly their personal relationships: when they find time for introspection, their optimistic veneer may be replaced by feelings of unspecific, yet overwhelming, sadness.

VIRTUES: July 14 people have the capacity to reconcile their emotionally driven, instinctive empathy with others with their intellectual clarity and highly developed organizational talents. Such is the depth of their responsiveness that little passes them by, and this, combined with their determination to effect progress, gives them great potential for success.
VICES: There is a danger that the altruistic inclinations of these individuals may lead them to live their lives either in the service of others, or else vicariously in so far as they denigrate the importance of their own emotional fulfillment by devoting so much time and energy to trying to improve the circumstances of others.
VERDICT: Although admirable, the often pronounced propensity of those born on this day to whole-heartedly direct their attention toward other people may have destructive consequences as regards to their holistic well-being, for it may sap both their physical and emotional energies. It is vital therefore that they should make time to focus upon their own needs, and selfishly indulge themselves once in a while.

On This Day
Famous Births: Cardinal Jules Mazarin (1602); Emmeline Pankhurst (1858); William Leefe Robinson (1895); Irving Stone (1903); Terry Thomas (1911); Woody Guthrie (1912); Gerald Rudolph Ford (1913); Ingmar Bergman and Arthur Laurents (1918); Dale Robertson (1923); Harry Dean Stanton (1926); Polly Bergen (1930); Robert Stephens (1931); Roosevelt Grier (1932); Ian Stewart (1944); Sue Lawley (1946).

Significant Events and Anniversaries: This day indicates concerted action in the pursuit of humanitarian visions, as was evidenced when the people of Paris stormed the state prison, the Bastille, to commence the French Revolution (1789). The aspirational aims and fascination with natural phenomena that are features of this day were reflected when the English mountaineer Edward Whymper became the first person to scale the Alpine peak, the Matterhorn (1865), and also when, a hundred years later, Mademoiselle Vaucher became the first woman to achieve the same feat (1965). Confirming the intellectual talents bestowed by this day, the scientist Alfred Nobel presented the explosive results of his experiments with dynamite on July 14 (1867); while, this day—one that is governed by water—also marks the launching of the world's first nuclear warship, the U.S.S. *Long Beach* (1959).

JULY 15

July 15 people manage to combine their highly developed powers of imagination—which may often tend toward the mystical or the spiritual—with a more concrete awareness of, and affinity toward, their immediate surroundings, including not only their environment, but also the individuals who surround them as friends and kin, professional associates or even as part of a more global scenario. Both characteristics stem from their profound sensitivity, which typically manifests itself in the form of equal parts of intellectual perspicacity and as emotional empathy. Thus while those born on this day have the ability to arrive at astute impersonal analytical conclusions regarding a situation under consideration, their observations are given human depth by their intuitive ability to assess the input of, and the impact on, the people who are touched by it. In many respects this is a remarkable gift, which, when combined with their urge to effect progress, endows them with the potential to bring about considerable change for the good, enriching the lives of others.

Although July 15 people possess skills that are generally suited to the world of business and commerce, they typically lack the ruthlessness that is the mark of the tycoon. It is perhaps in the artistic realm that their talent to reach out and inspire others with their idiosyncratic and innovative views is most effective, especially if they are also men. And, while they appreciate the material fruits of their success as a means of generously providing for and indulging those closest to them, it is the dream of achieving perfection in the metaphysical sphere that underlies their more introspective visions.

VIRTUES: These individuals are blessed with strong powers of imagination, as well as the technical and organizational talents to promote and support their innovative ideals. Their prodigious sensitivity encompasses the emotional responses of others, bestowing upon them the desire to be beneficial instruments of humanitarian progress.

VICES: Those born on this day must guard against a tendency to set themselves unfeasible aims, the achievement of which, although sanctioned by imaginative dreams, may ultimately prove to be limited by their own abilities or the lack of cooperation of others.

VERDICT: In order to help them realize their aims as fully as possible, and thereby achieve emotional fulfillment, it is important that July 15 people focus upon the ideals that are most important to them, rather than allowing themselves to become confused by the multitude of messages to which their enormous receptiveness subjects them. Developing a greater sense of pragmatism and realism will assist them in this.

On This Day

Famous Births: Inigo Jones (1573); Rembrandt Harmenszoon van Rijn (1606); Clement Carke Moore (1779); Alfred Harmsworth (1865); Noël Gay (1898); Hammond Innes (1913); Iris Murdoch (1919); Julian Bream (1933); Harrison Birtwhistle (1934); Alex Karras (1935); Jan-Michael Vincent (1945); Linda Ronstadt (1946); Brian Austin Green (1973).

Significant Events and Anniversaries: July 15 is a day that highlights action in the furtherance of a spiritual or national ideal, and marks the date on which: the Christian forces of the First Crusade, led by Godfrey and Robert of Flanders and Tancred of Normandy, recaptured the holy city of Jerusalem from the Muslims (1099); the Duke of Monmouth was executed for his rebellious actions in attempting to wreste the English throne from his uncle, King James II (1685); Rouget de Lisle's rousing revolutionary marching song, the *Marseillaise*, was adopted as the French national anthem (1795); and during the Indian Mutiny, British troops and their families were murdered during the second massacre of Cawnpore (1857). The determined pursuit of personal visions that is also a feature of this day was reflected when: the French chemist Hippolyte Mège-Mouries patented margarine as a butter substitute (1889); William Boeing launched his Pacific Aero Products company (1916); U.S. pilot Wiley Post, in *Winnie Mae*, set off on the first successful attempt to fly round the world single-handedly (1933); and the maiden flight took place of the Boeing 707 jetliner (1954).

Planetary Influences
Ruling planet: The Moon.
Third decan: Personal planets are Jupiter and Neptune.

Sacred and Cultural Significance
In England, St. Swithin's Day; Set's birthday celebrated by Wiccans of the Egyptian tradition; in China, Ti-Tsang honored with the Annual Festival of the Dead.
Saints' day: Donald (d. 8th century AD); Swithin (d. 862); Vladimir (955–1015); David of Sweden (d. c.1080); Bonaventure (c.1218–74).

Regarded during his lifetime as the greatest portraitist in the Netherlands, a talent seen in the Anatomy Lesson of Dr. Nicolaes Tulp *(1632, detail below), Rembrandt embodied his birthdate's propensity for artistic abilities. However, a natural predilection for material trappings—another July 15 characteristic—caused the artist to declare bankruptcy.*

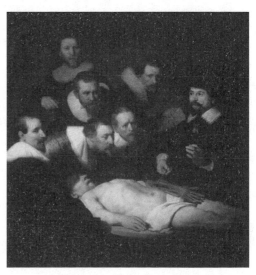

CANCER

Planetary Influences
Ruling planet: The Moon.
Third decan: Personal planets are Jupiter and Neptune.

Sacred and Cultural Significance
In Islam, the *hegira* ("flight"), the traditional starting day of the Islamic era in 622; first day of annual pilgrimage by Haitians to the Saut d'Eau waterfall.
Saints' day: Helier (6th century AD); Tenenan (7th century AD); Plechelm (8th century AD); Stephen Harding (d. 1134).

The pursuit of ideals—a characteristic of July 16—can lead to sudden acts of violence, and on this day in 1918 Bolshevik revolutionaries, believing that "the end justifies the means," executed Russia's Czar Nicholas II and his family, seen here in captivity.

JULY 16

★★★

Those born on this day are on a constant quest to realize an ideal—be it to find their soul mate, to create the perfect work of art, or to implement a faultless technical process or, indeed, a revolutionary social system. And, although their desire is primarily driven by their emotions, they typically marshal their highly developed intellectual powers of perception and analysis, as well as their formidable capacity for organization, in the pursuit of their aims. However personal the vision that fuels July 16 individuals, it rarely has a selfish purpose, for they combine their remarkable ability to identify abuses of power, or indeed any inherent failings in prevalent situations, with their profound feelings of empathy for those suffering the ill-effects. Thus their yearning to employ their energies as significant agents for change is usually ultimately directed toward bringing improved circumstances and happiness to the lives of others. Their talents and inclinations suit them particularly to the arts—where they hope their innovative work will provide spiritual inspiration and solace to a wider audience—but they may also choose to help others by becoming social or religious campaigners.

Unfortunately, their Utopian ideals may doom them to continued disappointment, with the result that they will often adopt a misleading façade of emotional robustness to protect their vulnerability and propensity for becoming depressed or frustrated by deeply felt setbacks. The emotional ties that they form with those nearest and dearest to them are therefore especially valued for the unquestioning support and belief that they offer. It may, however, take them some time to find a life partner—the result of their tendency to project a romantic ideal onto those who may not wish to be cast in such a role.

VIRTUES: The dreams and actions of July 16 individuals are fueled by their desire to effect the humanitarian, technical or artistic visions with which, they believe, they can make a positive—if not transforming—contribution to bettering the lives of others. In seeking to fulfill their missions, they draw upon their considerable intellectual and practical talents, as well as their deeply intuitive awareness of the emotions and needs of others.
VICES: Because they are so sensitive to the responses of those around them, these people may become profoundly discouraged if others are apathetic to, or critical of, their beliefs and methods. When they are thus wounded, they may either become frustrated and embittered or abandon the cherished dreams by whose expression they have incurred such devastating hurt.
VERDICT: In order to protect their emotional well-being, it is vital that those born on this day neither plow a lonely, obsessive furrow nor discard their visions. Instead, they should seek to develop more pragmatic and realistic methods of enlisting the support of others.

On This Day

Famous Births: Andrea del Sarto (1486); Joshua Reynolds (1723); Jean Baptiste Camille Corot (1796); Mary Baker Eddy (1821); Eugène Ysaye (1858); Roald Amundsen (1872); Bela Schick (1877); Trygve Lie (1896); Orville Redenbacher and Barbara Stanwyck (1907); Ginger Rogers (1911); Bess Myerson (1924); Anita Brookner (1938); Pinchas Zuckerman (1948); Stewart Copeland (1952); Barry Sanders (1968).

Significant Events and Anniversaries: July 16 indicates the pursuit of profoundly idealistic visions, and commemorates two such instances, when: Muhammad, the prophet of Islam, fled persecution in Mecca and sought refuge in Medina (622); and Bolshevik revolutionaries executed the last Russian czar, Nicholas II, and his family in Ekaterinburg (Sverdlovsk) (1918). Practical progress is also highlighted by this day, on which: the French scientist Louis Pasteur became the first physician to successfully treat a patient who had contracted rabies (1885); Oklahoma City became the first metropolis to install parking meters, the invention of Carlton Magee (1935); and the world's first atomic bomb, developed by Robert Oppenheimer and other Los Alamos scientists, was exploded in New Mexico (1945). And, on this lunar-influenced day, U.S. astronauts Neil Armstrong, Edwin "Buzz" Aldrin and Michael Collins blasted off in their spacecraft *Apollo 11*, to commence their successful mission to the Moon (1969).

JULY 17

****

The steely ambition of those born on this day is often marked by the easy-going friendliness and sociability that usually characterize their approach to their interpersonal relationships. This latter quality may manifest itself in the realm of the arts—to which their great sensitivity in any case renders them inherently sympathetic—or in the business or commercial world, to which their innovative ideas and practical skills suit them. And although some strong-willed July 17 individuals are motivated by the desire to achieve personal success and thereby win admiration and acclaim, others are more focused upon bringing about improvements for the societal group to which they have the closest affinity (their families or countries, for example) or, indeed, for humanity as a whole. In all their endeavors they prefer to surround themselves with like-minded teams rather than acting as sole agents (despite their marked independence of thought and innovative individuality). When enlisting the assistance of other people, they typically make good use of their intuitive ability to pick up on their emotions and thus adjust their approach accordingly.

Although their professional fixity of purpose may lead July 17 people to adopt a somewhat manipulative stance toward their coworkers, within their personal lives they are generally relaxed and deeply affectionate toward their nearest and dearest—this is particularly true of the men born on this day. Indeed, it is when the pressure to achieve is off that their humor and talent to entertain come to the fore, for these individuals derive genuine pleasure from their ability to bring happiness to those they love with their *joie de vivre* and generosity.

VIRTUES: Their profound intuition is one of these people's greatest talents, and they use it to remarkable effect in both their personal and professional dealings with others. Blessed also with apparently effortless intellectual perspicacity and practical skills, as well as with prodigious tenacity and determination, they have the potential to achieve success.
VICES: Because they are so goal oriented, and furthermore have the inherent capacity to tune into the minds and emotions of others, those born on this day have a propensity to use their empathetic gift in a somewhat cold and calculated fashion by deliberately molding the opinions of those around them to suit their own ends.
VERDICT: If they are to attain the targets that they set for themselves without forfeiting the goodwill of others, it is vital that July 17 people occasionally honestly examine the motives that underlie their actions, to evaluate whether these ultimately outweigh the importance of allowing others their inherent right to express conflicting convictions.

On This Day

Famous Births: Isaac Watts (1674); Donald Tovey (1875); Maxim Litvinov (1876); Erle Stanley Gardner (1889); James Cagney (1899); Hardy Amies (1909); Art Linkletter (1912); Phyllis Diller (1917); Ray Galton (1931); Donald Sutherland (1934); Diahann Carroll (1935); Wayne Sleep (1948); Lucie Arnaz (1951); David Hasselhoff and Phoebe Snow (1952).

Significant Events and Anniversaries: July 17 indicates a strong desire to achieve deeply held ambitions, a tendency that may be pursued regardless of the cost to others, and on this day: the French Army defeated its English foe at the Battle of Castillon, thereby bringing the Hundred Years War to a close (1453); and Czar Peter III of Russia was asphyxiated by nobles sympathetic to his wife, who then ascended the throne as Catherine II (1762). Also inherent in this day is a willingness to adopt a pragmatic approach to achieve a desired end, as was evidenced when: the British royal family, worried by accusations that it was sympathetic to the enemy during World War I, changed its name from the German Saxe-Coburg-Gotha to the more English-sounding Windsor (1917); the victorious Allied leaders U.S. President Truman, the Soviet Premier Stalin and British Prime Minister Attlee opened the Potsdam Conference in war-devastated Berlin to determine the future of Europe (1945); and, during the Cold War period, U.S. and Soviet astronauts demonstrated a brief rapprochement in the interests of science and humanity when they shook hands in space (1975).

Planetary Influences
Ruling planet: The Moon.
Third decan: Personal planets are Jupiter and Neptune.

Sacred and Cultural Significance
The Japanese goddess Amaterasu honored with Amaterasu-Omikami procession.
Saints' day: Alexis of Rome (dates unknown); the Martyrs of Scillium (d. 180); Kenelm (d. 812/21).

July 17 is marked by concern for the greater good of humanity and the determination to achieve goals through rational approaches. Both these qualities were demonstrated on this day in 1945, when U.S. President Truman, Britain's Prime Minister Attlee and Soviet Premier Stalin opened the Potsdam Conference to determine the future of postwar Europe.

CANCER

Planetary Influences
Ruling planet: The Moon.
Third decan: Personal planets are Jupiter and Neptune.

Sacred and Cultural Significance
National day of Spain; the birthday of Lu Pan celebrated in Hong Kong; in ancient Egypt, the birthday of Nephthys.
Saints' day: Arnulf (d. 643); Edburga of Bicester (d. c.650); translation of Edburga of Winchester (d. 960).

Awarded a Nobel Peace Prize for his dedication to dismantling apartheid in South Africa, Nelson Mandela embodies the strength of commitment to a humanitarian cause that is associated with his birthdate. Mandela's extraordinary energetic drive and leadership skills, which he maintained throughout twenty-six years as a political prisoner, are augmented by his being born in the Chinese year of the horse.

JULY 18

The visions and goals that fuel the imaginations and actions of those born on July 18 are generally bound up with furthering the communal good rather than seeking personal success and recognition. The reasons for this approach are manifold, and include the strong feelings of empathy that these individuals have with those who surround them—and with whom they typically come to identify—as well as their somewhat insecure need to ground themselves in the fraternal bonds of camaraderie that result from serving a common cause, and the recognition that they may thereby receive. Indeed, such is the overwhelming sensitivity and soaringly imaginative powers of these people that the uneasy sense of "otherness" that they often experience can lead them to seek the affection and solace that arise from manifesting solidarity with others in the pursuit of mutual interests. They may identify themselves with any of a number of societal groups—sporting, artistic or political associations, their families, their local communities, their nations or even humanity as a whole—but whichever one claims their loyalty will receive their exclusive devotion, often at the expense of their ability to be objective when it comes to a conflict of interest.

July 18 individuals will clearly be unhappy unless working as part of a close-knit team—a tendency that is even more pronounced if they were also born in the Chinese year of the ox. Although they are blessed with remarkably independent and innovative intellectual gifts, their use of these is typically tempered by the boundaries set by the common consensus. They should therefore beware of becoming somewhat narrow-minded, of losing their appreciation of healthy expressions of individuality—even if they are those of dissent—and should attempt to appreciate and embrace diversity.

VIRTUES: July 18 individuals are inspired by common goals and have a strong predilection for enthusiastically and whole-heartedly investing their considerable energies, intellectual talents and emotions in the pursuit of the realization of shared aims. They combine their enormous sensitivity with remarkable mental clarity and tenacity of purpose, and thus make powerful forces in the communal armory.
VICES: These people's propensity to identify themselves completely with social groupings is an emotional response which, however laudable, may have a negative effect if it leads to suppression of their more personal requirement for autonomy of thought and action.
VERDICT: It is crucial that those born on this day recognize that the needs of the individual and the community are not necessarily incompatible and, indeed, that a variety of viewpoints and personalities can prove communally enriching. They should therefore make more time for the pursuit of their own interests.

On This Day
Famous Births: Robert Hooke (1635); Gilbert White (1720); William Makepeace Thackeray (1811); W.G. Grace (1848); Hendrik Antoon Lorentz (1853); Vidkun Quisling (1887); Red Skelton (1913); Nelson Mandela (1918); John Glenn (1921); Yevegeny Aleksandrovich Yevtushenko (1933); Edward Bond (1934); Hunter S. Thompson (1939); Martha Reeves (1941); David Hemery (1948); Dennis Lillee (1949); Richard Branson (1950); Nick Faldo (1957).

Significant Events and Anniversaries: In many respects the influences of this day indicate the suppression of individuality in favor of the wider communal vision, and July 18 commemorates the Roman Catholic Vatican Council's proclamation of the dogma of papal infallibility (1870); and the publication of Adolf Hitler's *Mein Kampf*, setting out the author's Fascist ideology (1925). Similarly, concerted action on behalf of what is perceived to be the common good was manifested on this day when: Thomas Edison first recorded the human voice (1877); Edward Lutyen's Cenotaph, a monument honoring the British soldiers who fell during World War I, was unveiled in London (1919); the Spanish Army chiefs revolted under the leadership of the Fascist General Franco, thus initiating the Spanish Civil War (1936); and the Disneyland theme park was opened at Anaheim in California (1969).

JULY 19

Others often admire July 19 individuals for their intellectual perspicacity and profound empathy, qualities that reflect their all-encompassing sensitivity to the circumstances and company that surrounds them, and upon which they draw when offering their carefully considered advice. And, indeed, those born on this day typically not only care deeply for their nearest and dearest, seeking to ensure their happiness and success, but also are furthermore imbued with a more global desire to improve the lot of humanity. Although they are quick to identify social abuses or failings, and also to formulate strategies for humanitarian progress, they may be frustrated by their inability to communicate their visions to less imaginative people—a tendency that is not a personal failing, but lies with the unwillingness of less enlightened types to accept the idea of change. Thus, although July 19 people may prefer to act as politicians or social campaigners in their professional lives, they will often be more effective agents of progress when broadcasting their message through the more subtle and insidious medium of the arts to which, in any case, they are naturally drawn.

These are energetic individuals—physically and intellectually—who need to keep their minds and bodies engaged in progressive activities. They may often display a talent for sporting pursuits, but their vigorous nature may equally be expressed in their mastery of artistic or technical pursuits. They bring to both their professional and personal liaisons their interest and concern for others—as well as a strong sense of humor—but may nevertheless appear to be somewhat solitary individuals, whose high ideals, profundity of thought and commitment to the visions that inspire them may be difficult for others to live up to or match.

VIRTUES: Those born on this day are fueled by the deeply felt desire to help humanity to progress—be it in the social, technical or ideological field—a propensity that is the result of both their empathy with others and natural sense of justice, and their intellectual clear-sightedness. Their considerable talents and energy give them the potential to achieve their aims.
VICES: Inherent in July 19 people's ability to conceive far-sighted remedies to any area that they believe is in need of improvement, and their concomitant determination to realize their visions, is the danger that those who are comfortable with the status quo may become alarmed by their perceived radicality and oppose their ambitions. In such situations these individuals have a tendency to be deeply wounded and become embittered.
VERDICT: In order to protect themselves from their emotional vulnerability to criticism, those born on this day should strive to develop a greater ability to be pragmatic when adversity strikes. Employing their already highly developed sense of humor will help them in this, as well as evolving their capacity for realistic assessment.

On This Day
Famous Births: Samuel Colt (1814); Edgar Degas (1834); Lizzie Andrew Borden (1860); Charles Horace Mayo (1865); A.J. Cronin (1896); Louis Philip Kentner (1905); Hubert Gregg (1916); George Stanley McGovern (1922); Pat Hingle (1923); John Bratby (1928); Vicki Carr (1941); Ilie Nastase (1946); Evelyn Glennie (1965).

Significant Events and Anniversaries: The sporting prowess that is strongly featured on this day was reflected when: the first Wimbledon men's singles tennis championship was staged and won by Spencer Gore (1877); and the first Tour de France bicycle race was won by Maurice Garin (1903). An earlier sporting innovation had occured on this day when the early U.S. feminist Amelia Bloomer introduced the eponymous garment that at last allowed nineteenth-century women greater freedom of movement (1848). This is a day that is governed by the element of water, the domain in which three significant events occurred on July 19, when: just as it prepared to counter the French Navy in the Solent, the *Mary Rose*, the prized flagship of King Henry VIII of England sank, along with its seven-hundred-strong crew (1545); and British engineer Isambard Kingdom Brunel's launched two ships: the innovative steamship, the *Great Western* (1837); and the world's first all-metal liner the *Great Britain* (1843).

Planetary Influences
Ruling planets: The Moon and the Sun.
Third decan: Personal planets are Jupiter and Neptune.
Second cusp: Cancer with Leo tendencies.

Sacred and Cultural Significance
The birthday of Isis observed by Wiccans of the Egyptian tradition.
Saint's day: Macrina the Younger (c.327–79).

Those born on July 19 are people-oriented and are especially suited for artistic pursuits, where their natural sensitivity and vivid imaginations can be freely expressed. Edgar Degas, born on this day in 1834, was a leading Impressionist whose primary subject was the human figure, as seen below in Young Dancers.

CANCER

Planetary Influences
Ruling planets: The Moon and the Sun.
Third decan: Personal planets are Jupiter and Neptune.
Second cusp: Cancer with Leo tendencies.

Sacred and Cultural Significance
The Binding of the Wreaths, a lover's festival celebrated in Lithuania.
Saints' day: Arild (dates unknown); Margaret of Antioch (dates unknown), patron saint of pregnant women and women in childbirth; Wilgefortis (dates unknown), patron saint of unhappily married women; Wulmar (d. c.700).

Winston Churchill signals the "V" for victory, which, using Morse code and the opening notes of Beethoven's Fifth Symphony, *was transmitted throughout occupied Europe on this day in 1941 to signal the end of World War II. This event combined the day's capacity for organized and disciplined action with its artistic tendencies.*

JULY 20

★★★★★★★★★★★★★★★★★★★★★★★★★★★★★★★★★★★★★★

Perhaps the most striking personal feature of those born on July 20 is their energy which, like the water that is associated with their crustaceous natal sign, may meander in every direction, exploring the boundaries that contain it, or may surge irresistibly forward, rarely remaining static. Their vigor is not only of the physical variety (and many are sporting types, some even becoming professional athletes), but also defines their intellectual approach, which typically is questingly curious and constantly searching for knowledge and novel experiences. Unsurprisingly, the all-encompassing nature of their inquisitive perspicacity results in their espousal of a wide range of interests, as well as a profound empathy with others. Professionally, they will usually flourish in any field where they can combine their enjoyment of working as part of a team with their technical and practical talents, while at the same time retaining a certain autonomy of action by satisfying their need to stimulate their intellects. They are thus especially suited for the variety of opportunities that the creative or artistic sphere embraces.

Their natural exuberance and infectious optimism draws others to July 20 people, who relish taking the initiative and organizing group activities or entertaining social events, a predilection that is particularly pronounced if they were also born in the Chinese year of the dragon. Their *joie de vivre* and highly developed sense of humor makes them popular with their coworkers and friends, who feel that they can be relied upon to provide loyal and constructive support during times of crisis. Similarly, they make concerned, but also enlivening, partners and parents, who care as much about the happiness of their loved ones as they do about their material success.

VIRTUES: Blessed with enormous physical energy and vibrant intellectual vitality, these inherently cheerful individuals direct their prodigious talents and vigor toward furthering their knowledge of all that the world has to offer, as well as enriching the quality of the lives of those around them.
VICES: Such is the diffuse nature of July 20 people's interests that they sometimes have a tendency to move swiftly from subject to subject without stopping long enough to delve beyond the superficial level, a propensity that may ultimately prove unsatisfying.
VERDICT: Those born on this day should try to develop a greater sense of focus with regard to determining what exactly it is that will provide them with the greatest emotional fulfillment: once this has been done, they should ensure that they do not allow their attention to become diverted from working toward its achievement.

On This Day
Famous Births: Francesco Petrarch (1304); John Douglas, Marquis of Queensberry (1844); Alberto Santos-Dumont (1873); John Reith (1889); Jimmy Kennedy and Dilys Powell (1902); Edmund Hillary (1919); Chuck Daly (1933); Diana Rigg and Natalie Wood (1938); Kim Carnes (1946); Carlos Santana (1947); Donna Dixon (1957).

Significant Events and Anniversaries: This is a day that indicates artistic prowess, as well as strong organizational skills, both qualities that were reflected when: the B.B.C. first used the opening bars of Beethoven's *Fifth Symphony* to denote, through the Morse code, the message "V for Victory" in broadcasts to occupied Europe during World War II (1941); and the U.S. magazine *Billboard* published the first singles charts indicating the most popular musical recordings (1940). Highlighted by this day is a desire to act on behalf of others, a propensity that may result in confrontation, as was mirrored when: Count Claus von Stauffenberg attempted to assassinate Adolf Hitler at Rastenburg (and was shot on the same day in Berlin) (1944); King Abdullah of Jordan was assassinated by an Arab nationalist (1951); and two British soldiers were killed by an I.R.A. terrorist bomb in London (1982). The exploratory nature of the day was evidenced when Charles Sturt became the first European to enter Australia's Simpon's Desert (1845). On a day governed by lunar forces, U.S. spacecraft *Viking* touched down on Mars to begin transmitting television pictures of the planet's surface to Earth (1976).

JULY 21

✱✱✱

The characters of those born on this day often pose something of an enigma to those who do not know them well, for at times they manifest the exhibitionist qualities that are the mark of the extrovert, and at others they reveal their more introverted capacity for profound and considered intellectual deliberation. And, indeed, there are often two pronounced sides to their characters: the side that enjoys observing other people and, aided by their remarkable perspicacity, analyzing what makes them tick; and the side that utilizes this talent to provoke strong reactions from those who are being observed—in many cases, the more confrontational the better. Both propensities are born of their pronounced orientation toward others, a predilection that is less the product of a need to solicit the emotional support inherent in interpersonal liaisons than of the stimulation that they derive from surveying the complexities of human interaction. Such inclinations suit July 21 individuals admirably for research-based careers as psychologists or philosophers, but their great organizational skills, as well as their urge to exert a beneficial influence over others, also indicates potential success as teachers or artists.

Despite their intellectual independence and the somewhat clinical predilection for analyzing human behavior that often defines their professional relationships, those born on this day are typically extremely generous, loyal and supportive—even protective—when it comes to their nearest and dearest. Yet because they themselves adhere to a firm moral code (springing from their sense of natural justice), they find it hard to condone transgressions in others—even on the part of those closest to them.

VIRTUES: July 21 people are primarily motivated by their intense interest in human nature and in what inspires the actions of others. Blessed with great perspicacity and vigor, these are strong-willed types who are stimulated by the cut-and-thrust of intellectual debate, which they perceive as a way of encouraging independent thought.
VICES: Because they are generally themselves emotionally robust, those born on this day may not realize that their confrontational approach, as well as their highly individual expressions of humor, may upset those who are more sensitive or less certain of their intellectual ground.
VERDICT: Although they should never suppress their compulsion to force more complacent or unimaginative people into adopting more progressive modes of thought, it is vital that those born on July 21 should recognize that there are some who will be alienated by their direct approach, however well-meaning. Cultivating their latent empathetic powers will prove both emotionally and intellectually worthwhile.

On This Day

Famous Births: Jean Piccard (1620); Thomas Pelham-Holles (1693); Paul Julius von Reuter (1816); C. Aubrey Smith (1863); Jacques Feyder (1888); Hart Crane and Ernest Hemingway (1899); Marshall McLuhan (1911); Isaac Stern (1920); Kay Starr (1922); Don Knotts (1924); Norman Jewison and Karel Reisz (1926); Jonathan Miller (1934); Yusuf Islam (Cat Stevens) (1948); Robin Williams (1952); Jon Lovitz (1957).

Significant Events and Anniversaries: The confrontational approach highlighted by this day is paralleled by a number of commemorated martial anniversaries: the Battle of Shrewsbury, when King Henry IV of England put down a revolt led by "Hotspur," Sir Henry Percy (1403); the Battle of the Pyramids in Egypt, when Napoleon was victorious over the Marmelukes (1798); and the First Battle of Bull Run in Virginia, when the forces of the Confederacy under General Robert E. Lee defeated the Union Army during the American Civil War (1861). The desire for independence that is strongly featured by this day was illustrated when Belgium broke away from the Netherlands, proclaiming itself a sovereign kingdom (1831). July 21 promises progress, and this ambition was reflected in: the opening of London's Tate Gallery (1897); the breaking of the speed record of 100 m.p.h., by a Gobron-Brillie automobile, and the completion of the Trans-Siberian Railway (1904); and the election of the world's first woman premier, Mrs. Sirimavo Bandaranaike of Sri Lanka (Ceylon) (1960).

Planetary Influences
Ruling planets: The Moon and the Sun.
Third decan: Personal planets are Jupiter and Neptune.
Second cusp: Cancer with Leo tendencies.

Sacred and Cultural Significance
National day of Belgium; Mayan New Year celebrated in South America.
Saints' day: Praxedes (1st–2nd century AD); Victor (d. c.290); Laurence of Brindisi (1559–1619).

July 21 is governed by the Moon and highlights important human progress. On this day in 1969 Neil Armstrong declared, "That's one small step for a man, one giant leap for mankind," as he and Edwin "Buzz" Aldrin became the first to walk on the surface of the Moon.

CANCER

Planetary Influences
Ruling planets: The Moon and the Sun.
Third decan: Personal planets are Jupiter and Neptune.
Second cusp: Cancer with Leo tendencies.

Sacred and Cultural Significance
National day of Poland.
Saints' day: Mary Magdalen (d. 1st century AD), patron saint of ladies' hairdressers, penitents and repentant prostitutes; Wandrille (c.600–68).

Born on this day in 1822, Austrian monk and botanist Gregor Johann Mendel laid the basis for the study of genetics. He combined patient, dedicated empirical testing with his visionary theoretical approach during his years of research, thereby fulfilling his birthdate's potential for reconciling diverse talents that are rarely found in one person.

JULY 22

The passive, emotionally-oriented, lunar forces and the active solar energies that govern the personalities of those born on this day stand in direct opposition to each other and may be difficult to reconcile. Thus while July 22 people possess not only great sensitivity but are also fueled by often remarkably idealistic visions, they may unwittingly sabotage their efforts by their somewhat impatient tendency for taking immediate action without having fully thought through the potential consequences. Conversely, their strong compulsion to make direct progress may be hindered and confused by the often conflicting messages that that they intuitively receive. When, however, these qualities are in harmony, these individuals make remarkably effective instruments of innovation, drawing upon their intellectual perspicacity and physical and emotional energy in pursuing their single-minded quest to realize their ambitions. Their varied gifts give them the potential to succeed in a range of professions, but their inherent creativity makes them especially suited to those artistic or technical pursuits in which they can act as inspirational leaders of their fields.

Although these are empathetic types who cherish their close attachments to their friends and kin, they may find it hard to commit themselves to a life partner or to maintain enduring liaisons of this type. For many, the problem lies with both their diversity of interests and their emotional restlessness, which are difficult to contain within a monogamous relationship. Those closest to them should therefore attempt to set flexible boundaries for their liaisons, within which July 22 people can maintain a certain freedom of action while simultaneously remaining securely anchored by bonds of affection.

VIRTUES: On the one hand profoundly sensitive, visionary and caring, and on the other possessing a predilection for actively making progress, these individuals are endowed with a rare combination of personal qualities, which, when productively integrated, endow them with enormous promise.
VICES: Inherent in the natures of July 22 people are a number of potentially conflicting inclinations and characteristics, which, unless harmonized, may cause them to lack clarity of purpose and be confused as to whether to follow their heart or their head.
VERDICT: It is important that those born on this day should take time to be introspective, to examine the motivations that underlie their actions and ambitions, to focus upon exactly what it is that they truly desire from life, and then to concentrate on adhering to this vision rather than allowing themselves to be diverted from working toward its attainment.

On This Day

Famous Births: King Philip I of Spain (1478); Friedrich Wilhelm Bessel (1784); Thomas Stevenson (1818); Gregor Johann Mendel (1822); William Archibald Spooner (1844); Alfred Percival Graves (1846); Gwen John (1876); Selman Abraham Waksman (1888); Rose Kennedy (1890); Stephen Vincent Benet (1898); Oscar de la Renta (1932); Terence Stamp (1939); Alex Trebek (1940); Albert Brooks, Danny Glover and Don Henley (1947); Alan Menken (1949); Willem Dafoe (1955).

Significant Events and Anniversaries: July 22 indicates leadership qualities and on this day not only did the Pied Piper in German legend enchant and abduct the children of Hamelin (1284), but also Alexandr Kerensky became the premier of the revolutionary Russian provisional government following the murder of Czar Nicholas II (1917). The technical promise that is strongly featured by this day was illustrated by the first use of wireless telegraphy to aid police forces, when the captain of the liner S.S. *Montrose*, on course for Canada, alerted English detectives to the presence on board his ship of Dr. Hawley Harvey Crippen and his mistress Ethel Le Neve, who were wanted for the murder of Mrs. Crippen (1910). The justice indicated by this day was also evidenced when another notorious criminal, the U.S. bankrobber John Dillinger, was entrapped and shot dead by F.B.I. agents outside Chicago's Biograph movie theatre (1934).

LEO

♌

July 23 to August 22

Ruling planet: The Sun   **Element:** Fixed fire
Symbol: A lion   **Polarity:** Positive (masculine)
Physical correspondence: The spine, back and heart
Stones: Ruby, yellow topaz, tiger's eye, amber, cat's eye
Flowers: Sunflower, chamomile, marigold, celandine
Colors: Golden yellow, orange

The zodiacal sign of Leo governs the period when the Northern Hemisphere's summer is at its height, when the heat of the Sun, the "planet" that rules Leo, is at its fiercest, and this manifestation of solar power is probably the reason why so many Middle Eastern astrological traditions equated the constellation with the lion, the king of beasts, whose golden mane was said by classical poets to resemble the rays of the Sun. The ancient Egyptians venerated the lion because the life-giving waters of the River Nile began to rise when the Sun was in Leo, while the ancient Greeks and Persians, who called this sign Leon and Set respectively, also unequivocally personified the constellation as a lion, as did Hindu astrologers, who termed it Simha. The Babylonians, too, envisaged a leonine creature presiding over the sign, but in this case it was a lioness or dog, maybe because many of the powerful goddesses of the Mesopotamian tradition were strongly associated with these animals. Perhaps the most familiar and enduring myth associated with Leo is that of the slaying of the Nemean lion by the Greco-Roman hero Herakles (Hercules). The first of Herakles' labors was the flaying of the impermeable skin of this apparently invincible creature, which was engaged on a campaign of terror on the Nemean Plain. After many fruitless attempts Herakles finally strangled the lion while it was sleeping and skinned it with its own claws; thereafter he cloaked himself in its invulnerable pelt and wore its head as his helmet, while Zeus placed the essence of the original owner in the heavens.

The combination of the related influences that cogovern Leo—the brightly burning Sun and element of fire that gives life but can also destroy, as well as the magnificent majesty of the lion—is therefore said to endow those born under this constellation with sunny natures, creative powers, exuberance, enthusiasm, energy, generosity, courage and strength—all qualities that signify leadership potential. Conversely, however, the intellectual independence and pride that are further Leonine characteristics can result in egotism, vanity and self-indulgence.

LEO

Planetary Influences
Ruling planets: The Sun and the Moon.
First decan: Personal planet is the Sun.
First cusp: Leo with Cancer tendencies.

Sacred and Cultural Significance
National days of Ethiopia and the United Arab Republic; in ancient Rome, Neptune honored.
Saints' day: The Magi (d. 1st century AD), patron saints of travelers; Apollinaris (dates unknown); Apollonius (d. 183); Cassian (c.360–433); Bridget of Sweden (1303–73), patron saint of Sweden.

Neptune, the god of the oceans and rivers, was honored in ancient Rome on July 23.

JULY 23

Along with their sense of fun and enjoyment of the good things in life, the determinedly optimistic and cheerful face that July 23 people typically present to the world draws others to them and, indeed, they derive great stimulation from social interaction, being inherently curious about other people. These are not passive bystanders, however, for they prefer to be in the midst of their professional and social circles, contributing their strongly held opinions and exerting their influence over those around them. For despite their easygoing manner, those born on this day are often propelled by a strong desire to help others progress—be it professionally, materially or spiritually—and are prepared to devote their considerable energies to this cause. Inherently traditionalist, their intellectual beliefs and moral values will usually have been instilled in them in childhood and, once formed, will be adhered to with remarkable tenacity. Their strength of conviction, vigor and orientation toward others augurs especially well for their success as military or political leaders, but may also be effectively expressed within the varied realms encompassed by the arts.

Despite their being generous and loyal friends and relatives, who place great value upon the strong bonds of affection and support that characterize their relationships with their nearest and dearest, these people's strong wills and natural gregariousness may preclude them from forming close one-on-one relationships. They may also approach others with a sense of apprehension that they might be required to give more than they receive, thus stifling their inclination to become emotionally involved.

VIRTUES: Those born on this day are sociable individuals, who are strongly oriented toward other people, on a more superficial level relishing the stimulation and fun that they receive from the company of others, and, more profoundly, also wishing to impress their deeply held convictions on those whom they regard as requiring assistance.
VICES: The well-meaning and sincere desire of those born on this day to mold the viewpoints and guide the lives of others in the direction that they perceive to be the best may lead them to close their minds to alternative opinions, and thus to become both overly authoritarian and dogmatic in their approach.
VERDICT: Although their motivations are generally of the most benevolent variety, it is important that July 23 individuals appreciate that others will not always welcome their interventionist manner. They should therefore strive to adopt a more tolerant and pragmatic attitude toward other people's opinions—even if they strongly disagree with them.

On This Day
Famous Births: Coventry Patmore (1823); Alan Brooke (1883); Arthur Whitten-Brown (1886); Raymond Thorton Chandler (1888); Ras Tafari Makonnen, Haile Selassie (1892); Michael Wilding (1912); Michael Mackintosh Foot (1913); Gloria De Haven (1925); Victor Korchnoi (1931); Richard Rogers (1933); Bert Convy and Don Drysdale (1936); Bert Newton (1938); Don Imus (1940); David Essex (1947); Graham Gooch (1953); Woody Harrelson (1961); Stephanie Seymour (1968).

Significant Events and Anniversaries: This is a day on which traditionalist beliefs are strongly featured, and July 23 marks the anniversary of the wedding, amid much pomp and ceremony, of Prince Andrew, Queen Elizabeth II's second son, to Sarah Ferguson at London's Westminster Abbey; sadly, the marriage was not to last (1986). Reflecting the day's propensity to enact progress, William Booth founded the Salvation Army, a humanitarian organization dedicated to improving the quality of life for the homeless and poor (1865); the British Oath of Allegiance was modified to allow Jewish people to sit in Parliament (1858); and Britain's Local Defence Volunteers were renamed the Home Guard by Winston Churchill (1940).

JULY 24

That these individuals are extroverted types is undeniable: their enthusiastic espousal of the unusual and the outstanding, as well as the strong vocal or visual expression of their beliefs (which is—consciously or unconsciously—designed to attract others' attention and acclaim) is testimony to that. Yet the personalities of those born on this day cannot be defined so baldly or simplistically, for underlying the often brash and highly self-confident veneer that they typically adopt is a more reflective and sensitive core that enables them intuitively to absorb the finer details of a situation, or the intangible emotions transmitted by others. When these two sides to their characters exist in harmony, the resultant combination makes July 24 individuals formidably effective instruments of progress, who typically support their energetic quest for recognition with remarkable perspicacity, and often even empathy for those whose worth society generally discounts. When their protective instincts are aroused, those born on this day will bravely champion the cause of the downtrodden or abused, but in less extreme circumstances their ambitions are usually concerned with their personal desires: for fame, financial rewards and material comforts.

Thus, although July 24 people may pursue humanitarian careers, they may equally be found assiduously furthering their own interests as commercial entrepreneurs. Their talents suit them to a variety of professions, with the proviso that they must be allowed either to assume a leadership role, or else act as independent agents—as artists, for instance—if they are to flourish. Inevitably, their strong wills arouse similarly strong responses in others, but even when negative they will usually accept constructive criticism with grace. And, when assured of the love of those closest to them, they reciprocate such support with great generosity, loyalty and affection.

VIRTUES: Those born on this day are extraordinarily energetic types, who combine their driving urge to innovate and make tangible progress with their quieter, but no less effective, gift of sensitivity. Their primary compulsion is to inspire others—either by supporting the causes that motivate them, or by admiring their talents and achievements.
VICES: Inherent in their self-belief and the confident expression of their convictions is the danger that July 24 individuals may become carried away by what they assume to be the strength of their own argument, promoting their cause with uncompromising determination regardless of the consequences.
VERDICT: It is vital—for both their potential success and their emotional well-being—that these people do not suppress their capacity for introspection and objective consideration when drawn by the tempting allure of action in furthering the interests that excite them, instead they must learn to utilize these talents to add depth and focus to their activities.

On This Day

Famous Births: Eugène François Vidocq (1775); Simón Bolívar (1783); Alexandre Dumas *père* (1802); Franz Wedekind (1864); Ernest Bloch (1880); Robert Graves (1895); Amelia Earhart (1898); Robert Farnon (1917); Adnan Kashoggi (1925); Peter Yates (1929); Ruth Buzzi (1936); Sam Behrens (1950); Lynda Carter (1951); Kadeem Hardison (1965); Anna Paquin (1982).

Significant Events and Anniversaries: The unusually innovative leadership potential of this day was highlighted when: French-born fur-trapper, Antoine de la Mothe Cadillac, founded a trading post named Fort-Pontchartain du Detroit, later to become the automobile-manufacturing city of Detroit, Michigan (also known as Motown) (1701); the English Navy, under the inspirational command of Admiral George Rooke, captured Gibraltar from Spain (1704); and the English naval hero Horatio Nelson sustained a debilitating wound to his right arm when engaged in attacking Santa Cruz de Tenerife during the French Revolutionary Wars (1797). The democratic and humanitarian principles that are features of this day were illustrated when: the first public-opinion poll—canvassing those eligible to vote in the U.S presidential election—was undertaken in Wilmington, Delaware (1824); and the hormone insulin was first used successfully as a treatment for diabetes on patient Patricia Cheeseman at London's Guy's Hospital (1925).

Planetary Influences
Ruling planets: The Sun and the Moon.
First decan: Personal planet is the Sun.
First cusp: Leo with Cancer tendencies.

Sacred and Cultural Significance
Saints' day: Christina (4th century AD); Wulfhad and Ruffin (dates unknown); Lewinna (d. c.685); Boris and Gleb (d. 1015).

Determination, self belief and the strength to achieve goals are characteristic of this day—qualities that were rewarded when a group of persecuted Mormons reached the safety of Salt Lake City, Utah, in 1847, after an arduous journey. Shown below is the city's famous Tabernacle.

Planetary Influences
Ruling planets: The Sun and the Moon.
First decan: Personal planet is the Sun.
First cusp: Leo with Cancer tendencies.

Sacred and Cultural Significance
Festival of Paper Dolls, a protective
ceremony, held in Osaka, Japan.
Saints' day: James the Great (d. 44), patron
saint of knights, pilgrims, rheumatism
sufferers and soldiers; Christopher
(3rd century AD), patron saint of travelers.

*Innovative technical achievements and the
realization of ambitious visions are both starred
on July 25, as was evidenced in 1909 when
Louis Bleriot became the first to fly across the
English Channel.*

JULY 25

Those born on this day are motivated by the desire to realize their remarkably progressive visions, ambitions which may be dismissed by others—rightly or wrongly—as being unfeasible fantasies, but from which July 25 individuals will rarely be dissuaded. Indeed, these people are typically defined by their driving determination to effect their dreams, and in the promotion of their convictions they draw upon their prodigious physical and intellectual vigor and clarity of purpose, as well as their capacity for brave persistence in the face of dissent. Many are motivated by purely personal aims—professional recognition, or the accumulation of monetary wealth—but such is their sensitivity toward others (even when working toward their self-aggrandizement) that their actions are conditioned by a strongly ethical code of conduct which prohibits them from making progress by taking unfair advantage of others. Some may make a humanitarian or ideological cause their mission; either way, they support their professional activities with both highly developed technical and organizational skills and a more intangible talent for inspiring and motivating others with the infectious nature of their dynamic enthusiasm.

Because they are often disappointed by the criticism of their detractors, July 25 people place enormous value on the support of those who believe in them, and they demonstrate their gratitude to those who profess unquestioning confidence in their ability to achieve their aims by rewarding them with their fierce and unwavering affection and devotion. They should, however, beware of accepting false praise: it may well bolster their confidence, temporarily, but will ultimately prove unhelpful.

VIRTUES: Those born on this day are inspired by visions that are often so innovative that they tend toward the radical. Rather than be discouraged by the inevitable skepticism of others, they are energized to prove the veracity of their convictions, drawing upon their considerable resources of energy, practical talents and determination in the process.
VICES: Although their devotion to the causes that fuel their interest is admirable—and may ultimately vindicate them—July 25 people have a tendency to lose sight of reality in the pursuit of their aims, and are especially susceptible to flattery and sycophancy.
VERDICT: While they need never abandon their dreams, these individuals should beware of falling prey to a tendency to respond to challenge for challenge's sake, and also of losing their sense of objectivity, when evaluating both the probable chances of success and the motivations of those who applaud their actions.

On This Day
Famous Births: Arthur Balfour (1848); Walter Brennan and Gavrilo Princip (1894); Johnny "Rabbit" Hodges (1907); Estelle Getty (1923); Annie Ross (1930); Barbara Harris (1935); Walter Payton (1954); Iman (1955).

Significant Events and Anniversaries: This is a day that highlights the determined promotion of ambitious visions which, when combined with the technical prowess that is a feature of July 25, may ultimately prove successful, as was demonstrated when: the French pioneer of aviation, Louis Blériot, became the first person to fly across the English Channel (1909); the same body of water was crossed by English engineer Christopher Cockerell's brainchild, the S.R.N.I. hovercraft (1959); and Louise Joy Brown, the world's first "test-tube" baby, was delivered in Oldham, England (1978). The danger of the development of delusionary tendencies that is indicated by this day was reflected when Queen Mary I of England married King Philip II of Spain, mistakenly believing that she was making a love match rather than one born of national expediency (1554); and the Italian dictator Mussolini was deposed by his "creature," the Fascist Grand Council of Italy, in the vain hope that this action would reverse the disastrous consequences of his alliance with Hitler's Germany (1943).

JULY 26

****

July 26 people have the potential to blaze a fiery trail through life, for their strong will-power, unusual independence of thought and action and predilection for idiosyncratic expressions of individuality mark them out as commanding and influential personalities. The success of those born on this day is largely determined by the responses that they arouse in others, who they will use to evaluate the effectiveness of their often radical theories through the responses that they elicit by their declarations. They may thus attract admiration or ridicule in equal measure, but since in many respects the primary motivating factor behind their actions is to draw attention to themselves, they typically accept the love or loathing that they provoke with equanimity, knowing that they have accomplished their aim of publicizing themselves or their beliefs. Natural performers, July 26 people are especially suited to careers in the arts, or else in such creative commercial professions as the media or advertising.

The energetic and extroverted face that these individuals present to the world often masks their deeper, more introspective side that enables them to plot a clearly delineated course through life, which they then follow with remarkable fixity of purpose and tenacity. Their professional and private personae may be so different as to seem schizophrenic—especially if they are women—for when out of the public spotlight they guard their privacy jealously and ground themselves in a closely knit circle of friends and family members, of whom they are fiercely protective and on whom they lavish enormous affection.

VIRTUES: Underlying the powerfully energetic personalities of those born on this day are acute intellectual gifts of perception and logic, which enable them to formulate highly effective strategies for success. They bring their talents and ambitions to the notice of the wider world by means of actions that are pragmatically calculated to arouse strong responses in others.
VICES: These individuals thoroughly enjoy the often outraged reactions that their directly confrontational tactics evoke, and should recognize that, because this sensation-seeking propensity may become addictive, it should be controlled and used sparingly and judiciously if it is to be productive.
VERDICT: Although July 26 people generally strike a healthy balance between their professional and personal lives and relationships, they should beware of allowing the provocative measures that they use to such startling effect as public players to stray into their private liaisons, which would prove destructive.

On This Day

Famous Births: John Field (1782); George Bernard Shaw (1856); Serge Koussevitsky (1874); Carl Gustav Jung (1875); André Maurois (1885); Georg Grosz (1893); Aldous Huxley (1894); Paul Gallico (1897); Gracie Allen (1906); Vivian Vance (1912); Blake Edwards and Jason Robards (1922); Stanley Kubrick and Bernice Rubens (1928); Peter Doyle (1932); John Howard (1939); Mick Jagger (1943); Helen Mirren (1946); Susan George (1950); Dorothy Hamill (1956); Kevin Spacey (1959); Sandra Bullock (1965).

Significant Events and Anniversaries: This is a day that highlights expressions of independence, and it is therefore appropriate that it should commemorate: Liberia's proclamation of independence from the American Colonization Society, making it the first African colony to gain its autonomy (1847); the abdication of King Farouk of Egypt, an action forced by the pro-Republican General Neguib (1952); the nationalization of the Suez Canal, which had previously been under international administration, by President Gamal Nasser of Egypt (1956); and also the ending of the martial rule of "the Colonels" in Greece, when political parties were legalized (1974). Pragmatic and practical qualities are further features of this day, on which: the state of New York joined the U.S. Union (1788); and the U.S. federal-law-enforcement agency, the Federal Bureau of Investigation (F.B.I.), was established (1908). July 26 is a day that indicates provocative actions, as was reflected when the first recorded all-female cricket match was staged in Surrey, England, thereby breaching the male monopoly of the game (1745).

Planetary Influences
Ruling planet: The Sun.
First decan: Personal planet is the Sun.

Sacred and Cultural Significance
National day of Liberia; Kachina ceremony celebrated by Hopi.
Saints' day: Joachim and Anne (d. 1st century AD).

Psychologist Carl Jung, who was born on July 26, 1875, manifested the capacity for intellectual analysis and original thinking that are often found in people born on this day. His most important contribution to the field was to identify the concepts of the collective unconscious and universal archetypal images. Self-confident and strong-willed, his belief in his own work caused him to sever ties with his former friend and colleague Sigmund Freud.

Planetary Influences
Ruling planet: The Sun.
First decan: Personal planet is the Sun.

Sacred and Cultural Significance
Day of Hatshepsut, Egyptian queen who ruled as pharoah; in Belgium, the Procession of the Witches is held.
Saints' day: The Seven Sleepers of Ephesus (dates unknown); Pantaleon (d. c.305), patron saint of midwives; the Seven Apostles of Bulgaria (9th-10th century AD).

Successful dancer and choreographer and the London Festival Ballet's first artistic director, Anton Dolin embodied his birthdate's flair for the creative arts. Born on this day in 1904, he was a wood dragon, emphasizing his sense of drama and imaginative expression.

JULY 27

Those born on this day are blessed with prodigious energy, passion and commitment, as well as highly developed practical and organizational skills—a formidably effective combination of characteristics that July 27 people utilize to the full. These are dynamic individuals who rarely do things by halves, throwing themselves into the active pursuit of their professional and private visions with single-minded determination and dedication, fueled by the desire to make tangible progress. Although their choice of career clearly depends upon their individual preferences, most will thrive in any profession in which they can work directly toward the achievement of their goals, supervising a well-ordered team and implementing their soundly considered promotional strategies in the process. Such inclinations and talents augur particularly well for their success as corporate players, but their natural flamboyance and creativity, adventurousness and vigor furthermore equip these individuals with outstanding artistic potential—and especially so if they were also born in the Chinese year of the dragon.

Within the domestic sphere, those born on July 27 will usually assume the role of the familial linch pin around whom others revolve. Typically extraordinarily affectionate toward their nearest and dearest, they do their utmost to safeguard the well-being and happiness of those closest to them—particularly their children—while at the same time injecting an enlivening sense of fun into their relationships. It is important, however, that they should judiciously moderate their desire to exert their benevolent influence over those to whom they are most strongly attached, and allow them to make, and thus learn from, their own mistakes.

VIRTUES: Those born on this day are forceful and positive personalities, who are motivated by their compulsion to realize their progressive ambitions. Possessed of great intellectual clarity and fixity of purpose, they are capable of marshalling their considerable energy, organizational skills and unwavering tenacity in the pursuit of their visions, and are therefore blessed with enormous potential.
VICES: Especially within their personal relationships, July 27 people should beware of becoming overly controlling of others; their motives may be entirely sincere and well meaning, but they may thereby inadvertently stifle the freedom of individual expression of those whom they desire to protect and guide.
VERDICT: In order to enrich their interpersonal liaisons, these individuals should make themselves aware of the sometimes overwhelming effect that their strength of character has on others—less emotionally robust types in particular—and should recognize that a subtler approach will often prove more effective.

On This Day
Famous Births: Alexandre Dumas *fils* (1824); Enrique Granados (1867); Joseph Hilaire Pierre Belloc (1870); Ernö von Dohnányi (1877); Geoffrey de Havilland (1882); Anton Dolin (1904); Norman Lear (1922); Jack Higgins (1929); Jerry van Dyke (1931); Bobbie Gentry (1944); Betty Thomas (1947); Peggy Gale Fleming (1948); Maureen McGovern (1949); Allan Border (1955); Chistopher Dean (1958).

Significant Events and Anniversaries: The active and determined pursuit of clear-cut visions that is strongly featured by this day was illustrated by a number of events of varying success: in the martial realm, when the French and British navies engaged in the first (inconclusive) Battle of Ushant during the wars of the American Revolution (1778); in the field of scientific research, when Frederick Banting and Charles Best isolated the hormone insulin, the first successful treatment for diabetes, at the University of Toronto in Canada (1921); in the technical sphere, when the world's first jet airliner, the de Havilland Comet, made its maiden flight (1949); and in the diplomatic domain, when the armistice that finally spelled an end to the Korean War was signed at Panmunjom (1953).

JULY 28

The personalities of July 28 individuals are defined above all by their competitiveness, a burning compulsion that may be manifested as either a personal or a professional ambition and that instills in them the urge to "win" at all costs. This dominating characteristic can be the result of a variety of causes, including these people's unwavering self-belief and concomitant wish to convince others of the veracity of their convictions. They also relish testing themselves against demanding challenges and like to enjoy the material rewards of success, including basking in the recognition and acclaim of others. And, when working toward their goal, those born on this day draw upon their considerable resources and talents, including their enormous physical and intellectual energy, their ability to formulate a formidable organizational and technical framework to support their driving quest, and, most significantly, their determined refusal to be deflected from their aims or to concede defeat. These people are thus admirably equipped for professions in which confrontational tactics play an important part, such as politics, the military and commercial enterprises, and also the sporting and artistic spheres.

Many July 28 individuals believe that the admiration that their achievements may arouse will be sufficient to provide the affection that they crave from other people. Unfortunately, however, this will rarely be the case, for their single-minded and combative approach is more likely to alienate those whom they are seeking to impress, who may perceive them as being selfishly lacking in consideration for the sensibilities of others. Thus, although they are genuinely emotionally attached to their nearest and dearest, they should realize that they may be regarded more ambivalently by the objects of their affection.

VIRTUES: The thoughts and actions of July 28 people are governed by their determination to be the best at everything they set out to accomplish. In mounting their campaign for achievement they will draw upon their considerable armory of talents, including their intellectual clarity of vision and strategic organizational skills, as well as their enormous vigor and indomitable tenacity.
VICES: The excessive promotion of these individuals' urge to attain their goals at any cost is incompatible with their desire to arouse the warm affection or love of others, especially when, in their upward quest, they trample upon those who stand in their way.
VERDICT: It is vital that those born on this day should honestly reflect upon whether it is material and professional success or emotional fulfillment that they truly desire from life. They should then consider the effects that the forceful expression of their ambition has on others and temper their approach accordingly.

On This Day

Famous Births: Hudson Lowe (1769); Gerard Manley Hopkins (1844); Beatrix Potter (1866); Marcel Duchamp (1887); Rudy Vallee (1901); Karl Popper and Richard Rogers (1902); Malcolm Lowry (1909); John Stonehouse (1925); Jacqueline Kennedy Onassis (1929); Garfield Sobers (1936); Robert Hughes (1938); Phil Proctor (1940); Riccardo Muti (1941); Jim Davis (1945); Sally Struthers (1948); Albert Namatjira (1959).

Significant Events and Anniversaries: July 28 highlights the determined promotion of strongly held ambitions—often at the expense of others—as was illustrated when: on the day that King Henry VIII of England married his fifth wife, Catherine Howard, his former chancellor, Thomas Cromwell (who had been instrumental in arranging the king's disastrous fourth marriage to Anne of Cleves) was executed on the monarch's orders, condemned on trumped-up charges of treason (1540); Maximilien de Robespierre and Louis de Saint-Just, along with nineteen other Jacobins, were guillotined for their allegedly instrumental role in the Reign of Terror (1794); nationalist troops, under the leadership of José de San Martín, liberated Peru from Spanish rule (1821); and Austria-Hungary declared war on Serbia, thus heralding the outbreak of World War I (1914).

Planetary Influences
Ruling planet: The Sun.
First decan: Personal planet is the Sun.

Sacred and Cultural Significance
The national day of Peru; in Pagan Europe, Thor is celebrated.
Saints' day: Samson (d. 565); Botvid (d. 1100).

The thirty-second first lady of the United States, Jackie Kennedy Onassis was born on July 28, 1929, and fulfilled the promise of her birthdate by succeeding in her ambitions for public life and universal admiration. Her graceful elegance, affinity for cultural institutions and private nature were qualities associated with her Chinese year, the snake.

Planetary Influences
Ruling planet: The Sun.
First decan: Personal planet is the Sun.

Sacred and Cultural Significance
Tarasque festival held in Tarascon, France.
Saints' day: Martha (d. 1st century AD),
patron saint of cooks, hoteliers, homemakers
and lay-sisters; Simplicius, Faustinus and
Beatrice (d. c.304); Lupus of Troyes (d. 478);
Sulian (6th century AD); Olaf (995–1030),
king and patron saint of Norway.

*July 29 is a day of communal activities and
social responsibility, and on this day in 1907,
the Boy Scouts organization was established
by Robert Baden Powell (pictured below).
The scouting movement is now the leading
international association dedicated to fostering
self-reliance and community awareness in
young people.*

JULY 29

In common with the majority of their leonine fellows, those born on July 29 are positive and energetic types, whose natural inclination is toward controlling the actions of those around them, a predilection that is redoubled if they were also born in the Chinese year of the dragon. Yet unlike many others born under the sign of Leo, their ambitions are directed less toward achieving personal success and acclaim (although they are not averse to receiving the applause of others) than toward furthering the interests of the social group with which they primarily identify—for example, their family, their local community, their country or even humanity as a whole. They may thus typically be found working as politicians or social campaigners—or even as athletes or artists—indeed, in any profession in which there is an inherent sense of team spirit. Within such environments those born on this day typically gravitate toward leadership positions, others deferring to their strong wills, clear-cut goals, and organizational talents, as well as to their gifts of motivation and inspiration.

Their willingness to protect and assume responsibility for those around them—and this is especially true if they are males—as well as the generosity and loyalty that these leonine characters display toward the members of their "pride," is generally reciprocated by the objects of their concern. Although their personal liaisons are similarly characterized by mutually profound feelings of affection, the overridingly communal orientation of July 29 people may leave them with little time to spare for their nearest and dearest—or indeed, for the pursuit of any independent individual interests.

VIRTUES: These people are usually strongly connected to social groupings, whose interests they will assume and promote with remarkable solidarity and determination. The conjunction of their multifaceted intellectual talents and their apparently inexhaustible physical vigor bodes well for their effectiveness as inspirational leaders.
VICES: Those born on this day have such an overwhelming compulsion to identify themselves with collective entities that they run the risk of suppressing their individuality, regarding their personal needs and ambitions as less important than those of the community. Although laudable, this propensity may result in emotional problems—both for themselves and for their families and friends.
VERDICT: It is of great importance for their emotional well-being that July 29 people occasionally make time for themselves. Indulging in periods of quiet introspection, pursuing a hobby or just enjoying the company of their kith and kin will help them to recharge their physical and mental batteries and will enrich their lives as individuals.

On This Day
Famous Births: George Bradshaw (1801); Alexis de Tocqueville (1805); Armauer Gerhard Henrik Hansen (1841); Newton Booth Tarkington (1869); Benito Mussolini (1883); Sigmund Romberg (1887); Dag Hammarskjold (1905); Melvin Belli (1907); Jo Grimmond (1913); Mikis Theodorakis (1925); Elizabeth Dole (1936); Peter Jennings (1938); Michael Spinks (1956); Wil Wheaton (1972); Wanya Morris (1973).

Significant Events and Anniversaries: This day indicates a personal identification with, and consequent sense of responsibility toward, the communal interest, as was reflected when: Mary, Queen of Scots married Lord Henry Darnley, a match calculated to strengthen the Catholic cause against the domination of the Protestant Lords of the Congregation (1565); the English sailor Sir Francis Drake interrupted his game of bowls at Plymouth Hoe to protect his country against the threat of the Spanish Armada (1588); the anarchist Angelo Bresci, convinced that he was acting in his compatriots' best interests, assassinated King Umberto I of Italy (1900); Lord Robert Baden-Powell formed the Boy Scouts, a movement intended to instill qualities of citizenship and social responsibility in young men (1907); and when Charles, Prince of Wales, conscious of the need to beget an heir to the British throne, married Lady Diana Spencer at St. Paul's Cathedral in London (1981).

JULY 30

Those born on July 30 are firmly rooted in the physical world, their ambitions being primarily concerned with gaining personal status and monetary resources, or with making tangible progress of any kind, and their approach is typically of the extremely energetic variety. These individuals are blessed with the ability to think in a logical, linear fashion, and because they have a heightened sense of awareness of their surroundings, or of the inherent components of a proposal under consideration, they have the capacity to assess a situation astutely and devise a comprehensive strategy in response. They will then implement their plan with remarkable fixity of purpose and tenacity, utilizing their considerable organizational skills and gift for directing others in the process. Within their personal lives, too, they typically conduct their relationships with steadfast equanimity, displaying a profound concern for the physical and emotional well-being of their friends and family.

Their practical and interpersonal talents, when also combined with their strong goal orientation, equip July 30 people especially well for potentially glittering corporate careers in the financial and commercial realm, as well as for fame and acclaim in the sporting arena. Their highly developed sensuality also augurs well for their success as artists—painters, musicians, writers or actors, for example—although the majority of those born on this day will instead settle for surrounding themselves with objects of beauty (which, given their financial acumen, may often also represent lucrative investments).

VIRTUES: These extraordinarily vigorous individuals are motivated by the desire to make concrete progress in life and to move onward and upward, thereby gaining not only professional recognition but also the means to finance a comfortable lifestyle for themselves and those closest to them. Their clarity of vision, determination and redoubtable practical skills bestow upon them great potential to succeed.
VICES: These people's target-oriented ambitions, as well as their protective concern for their nearest and dearest, may cause them to become somewhat blinkered and narrow-minded in their approach, and therefore to dismiss wider social issues or obligations as being of relative unimportance to their lives.
VERDICT: Those born on this day typically balance their intellectual and emotional concerns well, but may nevertheless find that by broadening their interests beyond the immediate demands of their personal and professional environments they will gain a stimulating and enriching dimension to their lives.

On This Day

Famous Births: Giorgi Vasari (1511); Samuel Rogers (1763); Emily Brontë (1818); Henry Ford (1863); Casey Stengel (1891); Henry Moore (1898); Gerald Moore (1899); Cyril Northcote Parkinson (1909); Thomas Sowell (1930); Ed "Kookie" Bynes (1933); Peter Bogdanovich (1939); Clive Sinclair (1940); Paul Anka (1941); Arnold Schwarzenegger (1947); Ken Olin (1954); Delta Burke (1956); Kate Bush and Daley Thompson (1958).

Significant Events and Anniversaries: The sporting prowess that is such a strong characteristic of this day was confirmed when: Uruguay defeated Argentina in the final of soccer's first truly international tournament, the World Cup (1930); and England, in a nail-biting final, triumphed over West Germany in the same soccer showcase (1966). The dual artistic and commercial potential that is highlighted by this day was reflected when the first book to appear under the Penguin imprint, André Maurois's *Ariel*, was published (1935). The resourceful talents, as well as the personal interests, that are indicated by this day were demonstrated when the British spy Kim Philby ("the Third Man") eluded capture by the British authorities and fled to Moscow (1963). Physical well-being is a further concern of this day, on which the eleven-day-old English baby Holly Roffey became the youngest patient ever to undergo a heart-transplant operation (1984).

Planetary Influences
Ruling planet: The Sun.
First decan: Personal planet is the Sun.

Sacred and Cultural Significance
In Novia Scotia, sacred day of the Micmac tribe.
Saints' day: Abdon and Sennen (d. c.303); Peter Chrysologus (d. c.450); Tatwin (8th century AD).

Determination, initiative and personal ambition are defining characteristics of those born on July 30, including automobile engineer Henry Ford, the legendary industrialist who founded the Ford Motor Company and revolutionized production by pioneering his modern assembly line. Blessed with a clear, strongly held vision, he directed the production of 15 million Model-T cars between 1908 and 1928. Ford is pictured below with his first and 10-millionth automobile.

LEO

Planetary Influences
Ruling planet: The Sun.
First decan: Personal planet is the Sun.

Sacred and Cultural Significance
Oidhche Lughnasa celebrated by Celts.
Saints' day: Joseph of Arimathea
(d. 1st century AD), patron saint of funeral
directors; Germanus of Auxerre (d. 446);
Neot (d. c.877); Helen of Skovde (d. c.1160);
Ignatius Loyola (1491–1556), patron saint
of retreatants; Justin de Jacobis (1800–60).

*Actor Wesley Snipes embodies the characteristic
drive and voracious enthusiasm for life of the
July 31 personality. An ambitious go-getter from
the Bronx, he has showcased his martial arts
training as well as his extraordinary emotional
range in his movie performances, which include
roles in Spike Lee's* Mo' Better Blues *and*
Jungle Fever; Waiting to Exhale; *and* U.S.
Marshals. *A true dynamo, he has five planets
in Leo, and his Chinese sign, the tiger, reinforces
his hard-working, outgoing and magnetic sides.*

JULY 31

✳✴✳✴✳✴✳✴✳✴✳✴✳✴✳✴✳✴✳✴✳✴✳✴✳✴✳✴✳✴✳✴✳✴✳✴✳

The quest for discovery is extremely strong in many July 31 people. Although they are primarily fueled by an urge to further their own learning and understanding, any progress made by these individuals will usually also contribute significantly to the store of human knowledge since the topics that especially interest them are typically global in their scope—human psychology, for example, abstract political or economic theories, or even the as yet unrevealed secrets of the cosmos. Indeed, these are not the types to isolate themselves in the ivory towers of academia—they much prefer active modes of investigation, such as directing the activities of teams of researchers, and, once they have achieved a breakthrough, will rush to share their triumphs with the wider world (often with as much accompanying razzmatazz as possible). This highly developed concern for exploring every facet of human existence, combined with their extremely logical train of thought and their tenacity, suits those born on this day for investigative careers of all types—as academic researchers, scientists or journalists, for instance—but also as teachers, for they possess a powerful desire to utilize their findings to help others.

Despite the deep devotion and magnanimous tolerance that characterizes the nature of July 31 people's affection for those closest to them, they may not always enjoy the stable and harmonious personal lives that they crave. Part of the problem may result from their tendency to throw themselves whole-heartedly into their work, which—despite their prodigious physical vigor—may leave them with little time to spare for their friends and families.

VIRTUES: July 31 people are fascinated by the influences that affect the human condition as a whole, and are therefore motivated by their progressive desire to employ the fruits of their discoveries for the benefit of others. In all their endeavors they draw upon their considerable resources of energy, determination and clarity of thought.
VICES: While concentrating on the wider human concerns that typically excite their interest, those born on this day may inadvertently neglect the no-less-important demands of their nearest and dearest, either by spreading their time and energy too thinly, or by giving precedence to their professional activities.
VERDICT: If they are to become emotionally fulfilled, it is vital that these people consider their priorities. They should recognize that cherishing their kith and kin by paying as much attention to their emotional needs as they do to their physical well-being—and to their nonfamilial interests—will reap immeasurable rewards.

On This Day
Famous Births: John Canton (1718); Friedrich Wohler (1800); John Ericsson (1803); George Henry Thomas (1816); Helena Petrovna Blavatsky (1831); George "Gubby" Allen (1902); Milton Friedman (1912); Norman Del Mar (1919); Whitney More Young, Jr. (1921); Peter Nichols (1927); Lynne Reid Banks and Don Murray (1929); Geraldine Chaplin and Jonathan Dimbleby (1944); Evonne Goolagong Cawley (1951); Ernie Dingo (1956); Wally Kurth (1958); Wesley Snipes (1962); Dean Cain (1966).

Significant Events and Anniversaries: The urge to further human knowledge is a pronounced feature of this day, on which: explorer Christopher Columbus, during his final voyage of discovery of the coast of South America, plotted a course that would lead him to Trinidad (1498); the U.S. spacecraft *Ranger 7* transmitted the first close-up images of the Moon's surface to the Earth (1964); and millions of television viewers watched U.S. astronauts David Scott and James Irwin traverse the Moon's terrain in a lunar buggy (1971). This day indicates personal and collective action on behalf of wider human interests—a propensity that may be reflected in the national and political arena—and commemorates the British offensive against entrenched German troops that marked the start of the third Battle of Ypres (Passchendaele) during World War I (1917); and the establishment of the Weimar Republic in Germany, intended to replace imperial rule with constitutional government (1919).

AUGUST 1

✦✦

Those born on this day are self-sufficient individuals who present something of a paradox—even to their nearest and dearest. For on the one hand they can be genuinely empathetic toward the plight of the disadvantaged (responding to their natural sense of justice), yet on the other they will jealously reserve their own right to privacy and autonomy. Their approach to life is typically underlined with two main personal qualities: their imaginative powers, which enable them to identify with the emotions and circumstances of others and be stimulated by their company; and their propensity to think in a linear and logical fashion. Ultimately it is the realm of abstract concepts—particularly artistic theories and expression—that most strongly interests them, and their frequent withdrawal into solitude is often necessitated by their predilection for intellectual exploration. Such is the value that they place on independence of thought and action that they are generally unsuited to working as cogs in the corporate wheel (unless they are themselves driving the mechanism). They are inherently better equipped for self-employment or for working in those professional areas where their research can be transformed into products—for example as scientists or writers.

Although August 1 people are not amenable to others' regulations (and even less so if they were born in the Chinese year of the dragon), they manifest prodigious discipline when it comes to their own affairs—both personal and private—a tendency that results more from their desire to keep their lives running smoothly and efficiently than from any wish to exert control over others. Thus, despite the deep affection and magnanimous tolerance they display toward those closest to them, they will often conduct their relationships within strict boundaries, the limits of which they set for themselves.

VIRTUES: Those born on this day are drawn to the realm of thoughts and ideas, an interest fueled by both their imaginative talents and their more direct desire to bring about progress through their own prodigious efforts. Despite their innate need for independence, they employ their great organizational powers to create supportive operational frameworks.
VICES: So deep-rooted is the self-sufficiency of these individuals and their horror of submitting to the authority of others that they may—consciously or unconsciously—cut themselves off from other people, a propensity that may both leave them emotionally isolated and wound those who wish to offer their help and affection.
VERDICT: It is important in terms of their ultimate well-being that August 1 people should attempt to moderate their preference for privacy and devote as much time to social interaction as they do to their personal intellectual interests. They will usually find that they gain more than they sacrifice from adopting a more sociable approach.

On This Day

Famous Births: Claudius I (10 BC); Jean Baptiste de Monet Lamark (1744); Francis Scott Key (1779); Richard Henry Dana (1815); Herman Melville (1819); Jules Leotard (1838); Jack Kramer (1921); Frank Worrell (1924); Lionel Bart and Geoffrey Holder (1930); Dom DeLuise (1933); Yves St. Laurent (1936); Jerry Garcia (1942); Rob Camilletti (1964); Tempestt Bledsoe (1973).

Significant Events and Anniversaries: This day indicates innovative achievements of all types and is the anniversary of: English chemist Joseph Priestley's discovery of oxygen (1774); the completion of San Francisco's cable-car network, the Clay Street Hill Railroad (1873); and the staging of the first European Soccer Cupwinner's Cup in Berlin, Germany (1960). The artistic prowess indicated by August 1 was reflected when Glenn Miller recorded the seminal big-band hit "In the Mood" (1939). The propensity for direct and progressive action of this day was paralleled in the realm of politics when: the German elector of Hanover, George Louis, became king of England (1714); English naval commander Horatio Nelson defeated the French fleet at the Battle of the Nile in Aboukir Bay (1798); the German Kaiser, Wilhelm II, declared war on Russia (1914); and Western and Soviet powers signed the Helsinki Agreement guaranteeing the upholding of human rights (1975).

Planetary Influences
Ruling planet: The Sun.
Second decan: Personal planet is Jupiter.

Sacred and Cultural Significance
National day of Switzerland; Lammas Sabbat (First Festival of Harvest), a Pagan celebration; in Macedonia, the Day of the Dryads nature festival.
Saints' day: The Maccabees (c.168 BC); Kyned (6th century AD); Ethelwold (c.912–84); Alphonsus Liguori (1696–1787).

Jerry Garcia, iconoclastic singer–songwriter and lead guitarist of the legendary folk–rock band the Grateful Dead, exemplified the spirit of independence, imagination and creativity characteristic of those born on August 1. Consistent with the spirit of this day, Garcia showed unwavering dedication to his artistic vision and deep commitment to his fans, thus influencing generations of musicians and loyal followers in true Leonine style.

LEO

Planetary Influences
Ruling planet: The Sun.
Second decan: Personal planet is Jupiter.

Sacred and Cultural Significance
Feast of Anahita in ancient Persia; in England, Lady Godiva Day celebrated.
Saints' day: Stephen I (d. 257); Eusebius of Vercelli (d. 371); Sidwell (dates unknown); Etheldritha (d. c.835); Plegmund (d. 914); Thomas of Hales (of Dover) (d.1295).

Born on this day of extreme clarity of vision coupled with the drive to effect change and progress, James Baldwin made his indelible mark on the literary establishment with his first book, Go Tell it on the Mountain. *Also influenced by the Chinese year of the rat, Baldwin combined an active imagination and compassionate nature with incisive and often devastating social commentary.*

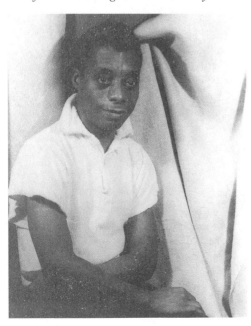

AUGUST 2

The ambitions that motivate those born on August 2 are generally of the briskly progressive rather than the more nebulously idealistic type. These are straightforward people and their incisive clarity of vision makes it easy for them to identify their goals and then, aided by their directly logical approach and exceptional organizational abilities, work single-mindedly toward their realization. The nature of the aims that fire their enormous energy and determination inevitably vary according to their specific personal interests, but their great imaginative powers and sensuality typically propel them toward such artistic careers as acting, writing, painting or composing. Their intellectual curiosity furthermore promises potential success as scientists or even inventors. In all their professional endeavors they are rarely afraid to take a brave lone stand when convinced of the correctness of their convictions, and their self-knowledge and confidence is such that they will often prove their detractors wrong. Indeed, many August 2 people will eventually set up their own businesses rather than conform to a corporate ethos.

While their professional relationships are frequently characterized by confrontation—the result of a conflict between their driving urge to promote their ideas and the demurral of their colleagues or competitors—their personal liaisons are generally far more harmonious. August 2 people cherish the strongly supportive bonds they enjoy with their kith and kin, to whom they manifest their capacity for unwavering loyalty. Fiercely protective of those closest to them, they not only desire the physical and material well-being of their loved ones—especially their children if they are parents—but also their happiness.

VIRTUES: Those born on this day are blessed with not only penetrating intellectual qualities—such as logical analysis, practicality and far-sighted fixity of purpose—but also with energy, determination and tenacity. Because they will rarely allow themselves to be deflected from their chosen path, their success often seems assured.
VICES: Such is their overwhelming drive to effect progress, that August 2 people may pursue their ambitions regardless of the cost to others—or to themselves. Thus they may on the one hand expect of their coworkers the same prodigiously high commitment and standards as they demand of themselves and, on the other, arouse the enmity of others with their impatience.
VERDICT: Although these individuals innately understand the importance of family life in terms of maintaining their emotional equilibrium, they should nevertheless beware of giving way to their strong compulsion to devote their full attention to their work, a propensity that may both sap their health and quality of life.

On This Day
Famous Births: John Tyndall (1820); Elisha Gray (1835); Ernest Dowson (1867); Berta Ruck (1878); Ethel Dell (1881); Arthur Bliss (1891); Myrna Loy (1905); James Arthur Baldwin and Carroll O'Connor (1924); Betsy Bloomingdale (1926); Peter O'Toole (1932); Lance Ito (1950); Sammy McIlroy (1954); Victoria Jackson (1959).

Significant Events and Anniversaries: August 2 indicates a predilection for taking direct action in pursuit of an aim, a tendency that may be manifested in ruthlessness toward others, as was demonstrated when: unpopular King William II (Rufus), of England was murdered while hunting by an arrow allegedly fired by Walter Tirrel (1100); U.S. law enforcer "Wild Bill" Hickok was fatally shot in the back while playing poker by Jack McCall (1876); Adolf Hitler, upon the death of President Paul von Hindenburg, proclaimed himself to be Germany's "*Führer*" (1934); members of an Italian right-wing terrorist group planted a bomb in Bologna's railway station, thereby killing eighty-four people (1973); and Saddam Hussein's Iraqi troops invaded Kuwait (1990). The artistic talents—as well as the love of children—that are highlighted this day were illustrated when Lewis Carroll's classic book *Alice's Adventures in Wonderland* was published (1865). Finally, on this day governed by the element of fire, a conflagration at Summerlands, a vacation center on the Isle of Man, cost the lives of thirty people (1973).

AUGUST 3

Those born on August 3 are energetic people, primarily driven by their inherent need for excitement, an overriding urge that can stem from many underlying psychological causes, including their low boredom thresholds, the stimulation they gain from pitting their talents against testing challenges, or even their yearning to receive the acclaim of others by succeeding in their ventures. This adventurous compulsion may inevitably lead them to behave impulsively, to seize an alluring opportunity before it vanishes into the past; but such is their ability to realistically assess the limits of their own potential that they will rarely embark upon a project that is utterly unfeasible (although it may often appear so to onlookers). And if they should fail, they will typically learn from their experience before moving on to address the next challenge that presents itself. Their personal bravery, vigor, self-discipline and single-minded determination to achieve their ambitions augurs especially well for their success in competitive situations, perhaps as business entrepreneurs, or wherever courage is essential, particularly in the emergency services. Whatever career they choose, however, it is vital that their freedom of action and thought remain largely unrestricted.

Although their professional activities may unavoidably generate confrontation and rivalry—particularly if they are men—in common with most of those born under the sign of Leo, their personal relationships are defined by the strong affection, loyalty and protectiveness they direct toward those closest to them. In all their interpersonal liaisons, however, they should beware of allowing their susceptibility to praise and flattery to lead to excessively egotistical feelings, which may isolate them from both others and reality.

VIRTUES: August 3 people combine their quest to experience exciting situations with their remarkable intellectual focus, dual qualities which endow them with real pioneering potential. They support their innovative and progressive urges with soundly practical and disciplined *modi operandi*, as well as with determined tenacity and almost reckless courage.
VICES: The sensation-seeking, goal-driven approach of these individuals may often bring them success (and with it the danger of vanity), but its inherent addictiveness may equally doom them to a life of constant restlessness and ultimate dissatisfaction.
VERDICT: It is important that those born on this day should take the time to carefully and honestly consider their motives before embarking upon a novel campaign, as well as the possible consequences of their actions.

On This Day

Famous Births: Joseph Paxton (1801); Elisha Graves Otis (1811); Stanley Baldwin of Bewdley (1867); King Haakon VII of Norway (1872); Rupert Chawner Brooke (1887); Clifford Donald Simak (1904); Lawrence Brown (1907); P.D. James (1920); Richard Adler (1921); Leon Uris (1924); Tony Bennett (1926); Terry Wogan (1938); Martin Sheen (1940); Martha Stewart (1941); John Landis (1950); Jay North (1952); Osvaldo Ardiles (1953).

Significant Events and Anniversaries: The confrontational and courageous—but also logistical—qualities highlighted by this day are closely paralleled in the realm of warfare, as was evidenced when: at the Battle of Cannae, the Carthaginian general Hannibal defeated the Roman Army (216 BC); English forces defeated the besieging Scots at Roxburgh Castle and killed King James II of Scotland (1460); and Germany declared war on France (1914). The adventurous nature of this day was demonstrated when Christopher Columbus embarked from Spain for the New World at the start of his first voyage of discovery (1492). And, on a day that promises pioneering achievements and innovations, August 3 commemorates: the inauguration of Milan's La Scala opera house (1778); African-American athlete Jesse Owens's triumph in winning his first Olympic gold medal at Munich (1936); and the first performance of the Irish dramatist Samuel Beckett's seminal Theater of the Absurd piece, *En attendant Godot* [*Waiting for Godot*] (1955).

Planetary Influences
Ruling planet: The Sun.
Second decan: Personal planet is Jupiter.

☉ ♃

Sacred and Cultural Significance
In Japan, Aomori Nebuta harvest festival.
Saints' day: Manaccus (dates unknown); Waldef (c.1100–60).

The qualities of innovation and pioneering achievement inherent in this day were evident in 1926 when the first traffic lights were installed in London's Piccadilly Circus— a practical yet ground-breaking event that eventually transformed traffic patterns in every city throughout the world.

LEO

Planetary Influences
Ruling planet: The Sun.
Second decan: Personal planet is Jupiter.

Sacred and Cultural Significance
Saints' day: Sithney (dates unknown), patron saint of mad dogs and Sithney, Cornwall, England; Molua (d. c.609); Jean-Baptiste Vianney (1786–1859), patron saint of parish priests.

Embodying this day's spirit of influence, autonomy and unflagging courage in the face of adversity, the Red Cross—the organization most symbolic of diligent, far-reaching and compassionate humanitarian service— was founded in Britain in 1870.

AUGUST 4

Those born on this day are strong-willed characters whose personal autonomy of thought and action is of the utmost importance to them. Although they may, paradoxically, seek to influence others, they fiercely claim the right of independence for themselves. Their need for freedom is as much the product of their constant quest for knowledge as of their incisive and perceptive intellects, which lead them to gather as much information as possible before deciding upon a fixed goal or course of action from which they will rarely waver. But while their natural sense of justice may lead them to champion the disadvantaged as a whole— thus naturally equipping them as social campaigners or politicians—they may disregard the right of others to profess conflicting opinions, instead employing aggressively confrontational techniques in their quest to implement what they regard as being unquestionably the correct method of proceeding. This propensity may occasionally lead them to behave somewhat perversely, rebelling against authority figures simply because of their strong antipathy for being restrained, as well as of their more general dislike of complacency and the unthinking acceptance of the status quo. They are probably most suited for artistic, educational or sporting careers, in which their inclinations and talents can best be used to inspire others.

So averse are August 4 individuals to submitting to the perceived control of others that—even from childhood—they may reject entirely well-meaning attempts to assist them, fearing that more sinister, dominating motives lurk behind the helping hand, a propensity that can lead them to become rather isolated figures. When they channel their energies positively, they typically enliven their personal relationships greatly; those closest to them should be careful, however, never to restrain, or to appear to challenge, these people's independence.

VIRTUES: Their keen intelligence, restless curiosity and desire to employ their considerable energies and practical abilities in achieving tangible progress endow these dynamic individuals with often radical convictions and approaches. Their resistance to accepting the norms and constraints of others, and their personal bravery in championing nonconformist views, blesses them with pioneering potential.
VICES: Those born on this day are driven by the urge to act independently in everything that they do—even if this results in them making mistakes. They may thus make life unnecessarily difficult for themselves (and for those around them) and may furthermore alienate those who genuinely desire their best interests.
VERDICT: It is important that August 4 people control their inherent propensity to indiscriminately regard the motives of others with suspicion, for they may thereby be unwittingly sabotaging their own potential to be successful, as well as their ability to form supportive emotional attachments.

On This Day
Famous Births: Edward Irving and Percy Bysshe Shelley (1792); Walter Horatio Pater (1839); William Henry Hudson (1841); Harry MacLennan Lauder (1870); Queen Elizabeth, the Queen Mother (1900); Louis Armstrong (1901); Osbert Lancaster (1908); Raoul Wallenberg (1912); Yasser Arafat (1929); David Russell Lange (1942); Richard Belzer (1944); Mary Decker Slaney (1958); Roger Clemens (1962); Jeff Gordon (1971).

Significant Events and Anniversaries: This day highlights courageous resistance to perceived injustices, as was evidenced when: Simon de Montfort, Earl of Leicester, leader of the baronial revolt against monarchical abuses, was killed at the Battle of Evesham by the forces of the future King Edward I of England (1265); and Germany invaded Belgium, causing Britain in turn to declare war on Germany (1914). The strong urge to shake up the status quo that is a further feature of this day was demonstrated when Beatles' member John Lennon, in a discussion on a U.S. radio station, outraged some Christians by suggesting that his group was more popular than Jesus Christ (1966).

AUGUST 5

LEO

The focused approach and steely determination manifested by those born on this day instills in others a sense of admiration, if not awe, for once they have resolved upon their chosen course of action they will typically pursue it until their goal has been achieved with almost superhuman tenacity, compelled by their resolute sense of purpose. August 5 people rarely simply accept conventional truths, preferring instead to independently investigate a subject thoroughly before evaluating the data they have collected and then making an informed decision as to how best to proceed. When engaged in assessment exercises they utilize their talent for clear-sighted analysis and their remarkable powers of perception, while the nature of their decision-making is characterized by their reliance on logical thought processes. Once satisfied with the soundness of their convictions, they promote their progressive aims and opinions by means of direct and energetic action. Inevitably, their fixity of purpose often arouses the antagonism of others, but these people are energized rather than discouraged by opposition and confrontation, which spurs them on still farther.

August 5 individuals have the potential to achieve success in any sphere that holds their interest, but their need to act autonomously with tangible targets suits them especially well for such artistic careers as movie-making or musicianship, as well as to become scientific, social or even philosophical innovators. Their impressive self-discipline with regard to everything they undertake masks strong emotions which, if they are crossed in any way, may break free and explode in dramatic displays of temper. And, although their feelings of affection, generosity and protectiveness for those closest to them are similarly profound, the combination of their controlling and volatile tendencies may have an unsettling effect on those around them.

VIRTUES: These individuals are blessed with the ability to think in a logical, linear and forward-looking fashion, an approach that enables them to work tenaciously toward the achievement of their progressive visions. The combination of their intellectual talents, their considerable energy and courage, and their fierce determination, makes these people potentially formidable agents of change.
VICES: So incisive is their clarity of thought, and so urgent their drive to realize their ambitions, that those born on this day lack patience with any obstacle that hinders their progress. In such situations their frustration may be expressed by means of furious and uncontrolled outbursts of rage, a tendency that may drive away potential allies.
VERDICT: In order to help attain their goals more easily and to reconcile rather than alienate others, it is crucial that August 5 individuals should moderate their tempers. Recognizing the sometimes overwhelming effect that they have upon others, learning to be more tolerant of different views—however contradictory they may be—and cultivating a willingness to compromise, will benefit them immensely.

On This Day

Famous Births: Edward John Eyre (1815); Guy de Maupassant (1850); Louis Wain (1860); Joan Hickson and John Marcellus Huston (1906); Harold Edward Holt (1908); Jacquetta Hawkes (1910); Robert Taylor (1911); Geraldine Stutz (1924); Neil Alden Armstrong (1930); Loni Anderson (1946); Patrick Ewing (1962), Amy Foster (1975).

Significant Events and Anniversaries: August 5 highlights progressive innovations of all kinds, as was illustrated when: the laying of the first transatlantic cable was completed by Cyrus Field, an event marked by an inaugural conversation between President Buchanan in the U.S.A. and Queen Victoria in Britain (1858); first use of an American Express traveler's check (1891); and the world's first electrically operated traffic lights were used in Cleveland, Ohio (1914). This day furthermore indicates that emotional turmoil may be seething beneath a sanguine exterior, as was apparently the case when the body of American actress Marilyn Monroe was discovered following her suicide (1962).

Planetary Influences
Ruling planet: The Sun.
Second decan: Personal planet is Jupiter.

Sacred and Cultural Significance
Saints' day: Cassyon of Autun (4th century AD); Oswald of Northumbria (d. 642).

Trusting one's own judgement and powers of perception, perhaps at the expense of conventional wisdom, is often the motivating power behind August 5 events, as illustrated by Captain James Howard's conviction that what he saw on this day in 1963 was indeed a UFO.

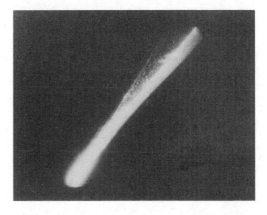

Planetary Influences
Ruling planet: The Sun.
Second decan: Personal planet is Jupiter.

Sacred and Cultural Significance
National day of Bolivia; Cherokee Earth-Goddess Elihino and Sun-Goddess Igaehindro honored.
Saint's day: Sixtus II (d. 258).

Radical social change is associated with this day, as seen in the devastating Spanish Civil War. On August 6, 1936, government troops surrendered to the insurgents at Somosierra, in northern Spain, after suffering fatal casualties at the hands of militiamen.

AUGUST 6

Blessed as they are with great personal charm, the extraordinarily strong wills and uncompromising convictions that occasionally emerge from behind the normally mild-mannered façade of those born on this day often surprise those who do not know them well. Yet despite their pragmatic recognition of the need to recruit rather than alienate others, it is precisely these beliefs—arrived at after exhaustive and rigorous investigation and evaluation—that inform their actions and ambitions, in effect providing them with a blueprint to which they conduct their lives accordingly. And although their visions may also encompass short-term or minor goals, these individuals are generally concerned with the wider picture (especially if they were also born in the Chinese year of the dragon), with making global social, scientific or political improvements, for example, or with pushing the bounds of human endeavor forward as artists or athletes. Provided that they are allowed to retain decision-making powers and the fundamental autonomy that is so vital to them, their perceptive intellects, propensity for taking direct action and unwavering determination augurs well for their success in whatever professional field they choose to apply their considerable energies.

In their personal lives, too, August 6 individuals are often guided by their moral values, which generally instill in them an appreciation of the grounding importance of secure bonds of friendship and kinship. Yet their overriding commitment to their work, when combined with their strong sense of responsibility for those closest to them, may cause those born on this day to overstretch themselves by attempting to devote equal time to their professional and private concerns.

VIRTUES: Those born on this day are driven by their desire to benefit others by implementing the soundly considered convictions and values to which they themselves adhere within a broader social context. Drawing upon their highly developed intellectual powers of perception and organization, they promote their visions with steadfast tenacity, while displaying a willingness to compromise when necessary.

VICES: August 6 individuals recognize the importance of maintaining a healthy equilibrium in terms of their working and personal lives, and they wish to play a significant role within each without detriment to the other. This often results in a tendency to push themselves to their physical limits, a propensity that may ultimately have destructive consequences for their health and happiness.

VERDICT: In terms of their overall well-being, it is vital that these people accept that their urge to participate fully in every area of their lives may sap their physical energy and thereby lessen their intellectual effectiveness. Learning to prioritize the demands made on their time and ensuring that they incorporate periods of relaxation into their busy schedules should help them ensure that they do not exhaust themselves.

On This Day
Famous Births: Matthew Parker (1504); Daniel O'Connell (1775); Alfred, Lord Tennyson (1809); Paul Claudel (1868); Frederick Jane (1870); Alexander Fleming (1881); Charles Crichton (1910); Lucille Ball (1911); Dom Mintoff (1916); Robert Mitchum (1917); Freddie Laker (1922); Jack Parnell (1923); Frank Finlay (1926); Andy Warhol (1928); Chris Bonington (1934); Barbara Windsor (1937); Daryl Somers (1952); Geri Estelle Halliwell (1972).

Significant Events and Anniversaries: On a day that indicates the active pursuit of inspirational visions, the U.S. athlete Gertrude Ederle achieved the feat of becoming the first woman to swim across the English Channel (1926). The concern with promoting or upholding a strong set of social values—be they political or national—highlighted by this day gives it a somewhat judicial and confrontational aspect, and August 6 marks the anniversary of: the death of William Kemmler, at Auburn Prison in New York, the first person to be executed in Harold P. Brown's recently invented electric chair (1890); and the first detonation of an atomic bomb, dropped on Hiroshima in Japan by the U.S. Boeing B-29, the *Enola Gay* (1945).

AUGUST 7

LEO

Those born on this day combine their searching curiosity and quest for knowledge with their progressive urge to employ the fruits of their research in benefiting others—no matter whether individuals, or humanity as a whole. Innately predisposed toward investigating all available data objectively before drawing their own firm conclusions, these people are not content with accepting those conventional beliefs and societal norms that go unquestioned by less independently minded types, until they have satisfied themselves as to their veracity. This deep-rooted tendency to explore and test, on the one hand, may make August 7 people uncomfortable to work or live with, but on the other may yield startlingly innovative—even revolutionary—results, for once they have decided upon a course of action or a set of convictions they will promote it with all of the considerable personal resources available to them, including their intellectual and physical vigor, their highly developed practical skills and their obstinate tenacity. And although the frequently unconventional nature of their opinions may inevitably arouse antagonism in others, they possess the courage to press forward despite the personal consequences.

Yet although these individuals respond to challenge—and are indeed stimulated by the cut and thrust of intellectual debate—their ultimate intention is not to act as devil's advocate simply for the sake of disrupting the status quo, but rather to embark on a personal journey of discovery. Their inclinations and talents suit them especially to careers in which they can express themselves freely, unrestricted by others. Because they are usually extrovert characters, they are often at the center of attention. Their sense of social responsibility is reflected in the protectiveness and deep affection that they offer their loved ones, while their unconventionality provides an invigorating element to their relationships.

VIRTUES: Their keen powers of perception, independent intellect and related propensity to form their convictions on the basis of their own research endow people born on August 7 with the potential to make a radical mark on society. Blessed with a remarkable fixity of purpose, especially in the face of adversity, they promote their views with compelling vigor, determination and practicality.

VICES: Not only are these individuals inherently compelled to challenge accepted beliefs, but their confrontational approach when doing so—and the strong reaction that this frequently provokes—may become an almost addictive form of behavior, causing them to forfeit the goodwill of others.

VERDICT: There is a danger that these people's somewhat combative attitude may cause them to sabotage their own best efforts. They should therefore recognize the profound effect that they have on others and, if this is negative, judiciously adjust their approach to make it more palatable to others, especially those who are in a position to assist them.

On This Day

Famous Births: Frederick Farrar (1831); Granville Bantock (1868); Margaretha Zelle ("Mata Hari") (1876); Billie Burke and Dornford Yates (1885); Louis Leakey (1903); Ralph Bunche (1904); Stan Freberg (1926); Roland Kirk (1936); Helen Caldicott (1938); Garrison Keillor and B.J. Thomas (1942); Lana Cantrell (1943); Greg Chappell (1948); Alexei Sayle (1952); David Duchovny (1960); Walter Swinburn (1961); Charlotte Lewis (1967).

Significant Events and Anniversaries: August 7 is a day that highlights the brave challenging of accepted conventions, a predilection that can be expressed in a diversity of areas, and on this day the British parliament, following extensive investigation into the practice, abolished the previously legitimate employment of young boys as chimney sweeps (1840); while in possible confirmation of the belief indicated by this day that more universal truths exist than have yet been discovered, an unidentified flying object appeared over the Swiss city of Basel (Basle), an event captured in a woodcut illustration (1556).

Planetary Influences
Ruling planet: The Sun.
Second decan: Personal planet is Jupiter.

☉ ♃

Sacred and Cultural Significance
In Egypt, the Breaking of the Nile festival held; in ancient Greece, the Adonia mourning festival observed.
Saint's day: Cajetan (1480–1547).

This Swiss woodcut, depicting the wonder and awe of the inhabitants of a town in Switzerland upon the appearance of a UFO, on August 7, 1556, suggests the heightened perceptions associated with this day, as well as the zest for exploration and desire to challenge conventional beliefs to reach the underlying truth.

Planetary Influences
Ruling planet: The Sun.
Second decan: Personal planet is Jupiter.

Sacred and Cultural Significance
In Christianity, the birth of the Virgin Mary observed; Festival of Venus celebrated in ancient Rome.
Saints' day: Lide (dates unknown); Dominic (c.1170–1221), patron saint of astronomers.

Perhaps the most renowned Olympic games of the twentieth century opened in Berlin on this day in 1936 and have come to exemplify the vigorous determination, courage and often heroic achievement of the many athletes who competed here under the shadow of Nazi Germany.

AUGUST 8

There are two especially pronounced sides to the characters of those born on this day: their desire for stimulation, which may take the form of intellectual exploration or of testing themselves against a variety of challenges; and their clarity of purpose, a quality which may be manifested in their pursuit of specifically goal-oriented projects or as a set of firmly defined intellectual or ethical values. And although these dual propensities might initially seem to be incompatible, they are in fact effectively reconciled within August 8 people's personalities, the latter providing a stable framework within which the former may be given its free expression. Thus, for example, if they pursue artistic or sporting careers (and these curious, imaginative and energetic people have a natural affinity for both), their experimental and innovative activities will typically be contained within the technical parameters of their chosen field. Similarly, whether or not they become political activists, their views and activities will be typically governed by a strong ethical code of whose veracity they will seek to convince others, regardless of the confrontation they may thereby engender.

Although their relish of competition and occasional combativeness may be directed toward others, these individuals are not really interested in scoring victories solely for the sake of winning, but rather are motivated by their urge to bring about progress or protect that which they hold dear. Indeed, they are devoted to their friends and family members, desiring above all to ensure their physical and emotional well-being, but also contributing their capacity for adding love and humor to their personal liaisons.

VIRTUES: Those born on this day are strong-willed, vigorous characters who not only possess a strong sense of social responsibility, but also have the courage and determination to attempt to change the world for the better. Although they adhere tenaciously to their personal values, their quest for knowledge and relish of challenge affords them wide-ranging interests.
VICES: Their self-confidence and conviction may lead them to fiercely promote or defend their deeply held beliefs and ambitions, despite the potential cost to themselves or those around them: a less confrontational manner might prove more successful.
VERDICT: Although the actions of August 8 people are usually fueled by the best of intentions, their uncompromisingly direct methods may reduce their ultimate effectiveness. Before embarking on a typically determined course of action they would be well advised to compare its potential outcome with those of alternative approaches.

On This Day
Famous Births: Thomas Anstey Guthrie (1856); Matthew Henson (1866); Frank Richards (1876); Marjorie Kinnan Rawlings (1896); Victor Young (1900); Ernest Orlando Lawrence (1901); Benny Carter (1907); Dino de Laurentis (1919); Rory Calhoun and Esther Williams (1923); Carl Switzer (1927); Joan Mondale (1930); Mel Tillis (1932); Dustin Hoffman (1937); Keith Carradine (1949); Donny Most and Nigel Mansell (1953); Princess Beatrice of Britain (1988).

Significant Events and Anniversaries: This day highlights the determined defense of social values, a propensity that has clear parallels in the realm of national politics, and August 8 commemorates: the defeat of the Spanish Armada off Gravelines by the defending English naval forces (1588); the start of the German Luftwaffe's bombing campaign against the British Isles (1940); the execution of five senior German Army officers for their attempt to murder Hitler and overthrow the Nazi regime (1944); the Soviet Union's declaration of war on Japan (1945); and also the signing of the Test Ban Treaty by the Soviet Union, the United States and Britain (1963). In line with this day's moral and judicial aspect, Richard Nixon resigned the office of U.S. president to avoid impeachment over his role in the Watergate affair (1974). The urge to achieve progress, also a feature of this day, was demonstrated when: Tycho Brahe initiated the construction of the world's first astronomical observatory, at Uraniborg in Denmark (1576); and when French climbers Michel Gabriel Piccard and Jacques Balmat became the first to reach the Alps' highest peak, Mont Blanc (1786).

AUGUST 9

The combination of their capacity for keenly incisive thought and strong orientation toward their fellow beings endows those born on this day with a fierce desire to help others to identify and then follow an optimum course through life. Blessed with powerfully perceptive skills, as well as the ability to marshal the information that they amass into a structured and constructive strategy for achieving progress, they have an apparently effortless talent both for analysis and for transforming the results of their researches into clear and direct plans of action. Those around them solicit their carefully considered advice, especially since they have a gift for communicating their genuine concern for others in an optimistic, kindly and encouraging manner. Natural leaders, these individuals are therefore well suited to professions in which they can devote themselves to guiding and benefiting others; careers as teachers, counselors or human resources specialists—are particularly well starred.

The personal relationships of those born on this day are similarly characterized by their profoundly protective attitude to those closest to them—especially their children, if they are parents. Desiring their emotional happiness as well as their material well-being, these individuals' typical approach (and one that is even more pronounced if they are women) is to gently steer their loved ones into what they perceive as being the best direction. Although this benevolent exertion of control is entirely unselfish, they should anticipate potential rebellion on the part of the subjects of their concern, who may resent such attempts to direct their actions.

VIRTUES: These positive individuals are driven by their urge to devote their considerable talents—especially their clarity of thought and ability to communicate the fruits of their knowledge concisely—to the service of other people. By employing encouraging and nonconfrontational techniques, they enhance not only their effectiveness, but also their potential to inspire.

VICES: In many respects August 9 people may be compared to sheepdogs who are governed by the urge to shepherd those in their charge. Their constant vigilance may, however, irritate those whom they are seeking to help, who may misinterpret their well-meaning intentions as attempts to dominate them and restrict their freedom.

VERDICT: In order to avoid being hurt when others reject their proffered assistance, those born on this day should strive to develop a more pragmatic acceptance of the possibility that some people may prefer to make their own decisions—even if they inevitably make mistakes in the process—and recognize that such expressions of autonomy are also valuable aids to personal development.

On This Day

Famous Births: King Henry V of England (1387); Izaak Walton (1593); John Dryden (1631); Thomas Telford (1757); Leonide Massine and Jean Piaget (1896); Solomon Cutner (1902); Elizabeth Lane (1905); Robert Aldrich (1918); Philip Larkin (1922); Rod Laver (1938); David Steinberg (1942); Sam Elliott (1944); Melanie Griffith (1957); Whitney Houston and Lonnie Quinn (1963); Deion Sanders (1967); Gillian Anderson (1968).

Significant Events and Anniversaries: This day indicates a strong sense of responsibility toward others, and marks the anniversary of: the conclusion of the Battle of Thermopylae, when King Leonidas of Sparta and his force of a thousand men perished in their brave attempt to protect the pass of Thermopylae against an invading Persian army (480 BC); and the official recognition of two national leaders: King Edward VII of Britain, who was crowned on this day (1902), and Gerald Ford, who became the first non-elected U.S. president when he was inaugurated following Richard Nixon's resignation (1974). Highlighting this day's evocation of positive, progressive action, the incomparable Jesse Owens was awarded four gold medals at the Berlin Olympics (1936).

Planetary Influences
Ruling planet: The Sun.
Second decan: Personal planet is Jupiter.

Sacred and Cultural Significance
Feast of the Fire Spirits, a Wiccan celebration.
Saint's day: Romanus (d. 258).

Convinced of the moral dominance of the United States and profoundly protective of its citizens and allies, President Truman gave the order to detonate the second atomic bomb on Nagasaki on this day of well-intentioned, but often misguided, even tragic action. Paradoxically, his decision had the dual effect of cruelly decimating Nagasaki and its inhabitants while forcing Emperor Hirohito to surrender to the Allies, thus avoiding further destruction.

LEO

Planetary Influences
Ruling planet: The Sun.
Second decan: Personal planet is Jupiter.

Sacred and Cultural Significance
Ghanta Karna Day celebrated in Nepal.
Saints' day: Laurence (d. 258), patron saint of cooks, deacons and firefighters; Bettelin of Ilam (dates unknown).

Faithful to the August 10 spirit of knowledge in the service of humanity, the venerable Smithsonian Institution was founded in 1846 in Washington, D.C., including in its charter the dedication to promoting science, human endeavor and the quest for knowledge.

AUGUST 10

Possessed of firm opinions and strongly oriented toward others, August 10 individuals seek to communicate their ideas and beliefs to as wide an audience as possible by means of direct interpersonal action. It is their ability to think incisively and logically (especially if they are men), as well as their highly developed intellectual perspicacity, that leads them to form clear-cut and powerful views, which are usually of a positive and progressive nature and are intended to bring benefit to others—either in material or social terms, or in the less tangible emotional arena. And, once those born on this day have convinced themselves of the veracity of their beliefs, they typically seek to influence others accordingly. Indeed, these individuals are hard to ignore: possessed of remarkable self-assurance and a pronounced independent streak, they are unafraid of making a determined stand when promoting their visions—the main thing, as far as they are concerned, is that they should make their voices heard and thereby draw others' attention to what they have to say.

The specific issues that may move August 10 people vary according to the individual, but their natural sense of justice and desire to improve the lives of others have clear parallels in the realm of political or social campaigning. Their considerable creativity, when combined with their great communication skills, also augurs well for careers as writers, artists or actors. Their inherent optimism and infectious enthusiasm furthermore gives them the capacity to inspire others, as well as making them valued friends and relations.

VIRTUES: Those born on this day possess the enviable ability to identify areas where progress can be made and then formulate effective remedial strategies, which they promote with steadfast determination. They understand the importance of converting others to their mission, and exert their persuasive influence by utilizing their verbal, visual and literary skills.
VICES: August 10 people are typically so certain of the correctness of their convictions, and so intent on transmitting their message to others, that they are often unwilling to accept alternative viewpoints or approaches, a dismissive tendency that may ultimately hinder their progress.
VERDICT: These individuals would do well to make the time for periods of honest introspection, in order to objectively examine their motives along with those of whom they believe occupy a contrary stance, and question whether any differences are indeed so contradictory. Ideological tolerance and cooperation may often prove effective instruments of progress.

On This Day
Famous Births: Camillo Benso di Cavour (1810); Charles Keene (1823); William Willett (1856); Alexander Konstantinovich Glazunov (1865); Laurence Binyon (1869); Herbert Hoover (1874); Jane Wyatt (1912); Rhonda Fleming (1923); Jimmy Dean and Eddie Fisher (1928); Rocky Colavito (1933); Anita Lonsborough (1941); Ian Anderson (1947); Rosanna Arquette (1959); Antonio Banderas (1960).

Significant Events and Anniversaries: Intellectual perspicacity and a desire to help humanity progress are dual characteristics of this day, on which: King Charles II laid the foundation stone of England's Royal Observatory at Greenwich to aid astronomical study (1675); the Smithsonian Institution in Washington, D.C., was founded to promote scientific research (1846); and the U.S.A. launched its first moon satellite, *Orbiter I* (1966). These tendencies were furthermore reflected on a more practical level when: English glass-worker Dan Rylands patented the screw bottle-top (1889); and engineers at Germany's Krupps plant tested Dr. Rudolf Diesel's eponymous engine (1893). The artistic potential inherent in this day, as well as its strong popular appeal, was demonstrated when Wolfgang Amadeus Mozart finished his lyrical composition *Eine kleine Nachtmusik* (1787); and English composer Sir Henry Wood inaugurated his Promenade concerts, then staged at the Queen's Hall in London (1895).

AUGUST 11

Those born on August 11 have a strong desire to uncover essential truths and then communicate their discoveries to others in order to enlighten them and thus enable humanity to progress—either as individuals or as a whole. This overriding propensity usually takes the form of either long-term research into abstract, theoretical concepts, or the investigation of more immediate concerns. Thus on the one hand they may make careers within such academic disciplines as science or philosophy, for example, or on the other be found working as law-enforcement agents, journalists or critics. To whatever profession these tenacious individuals devote their energies, however, they typically contribute their talents of clear-sighted observation, their capacity for organized and logical thought, and their resourcefulness, courage and determination. And these last qualities are of particular importance, since their propensity to debunk conventional beliefs and expose hypocrisy will inevitably lead them into confrontation with those wishing to maintain the status quo.

Their marked intellectual autonomy suits these people best for working independently—at least while carrying out the research-based aspects of their work—although they recognize the importance of recruiting supporters when seeking to broadcast their conclusions, and employ their prodigiously persuasive skills in doing so. Yet despite their general concern for others, their personal lives may be beset with difficulty, for their predilection for analyzing the motivations of others, and their tendency to criticize, can make even their nearest and dearest wary of incurring their censure.

VIRTUES: Motivated by the desire to benefit others by means of their findings, August 11 people are fueled by the urge to strip away layers of obfuscation and thereby uncover the core of truth underlying any subject of investigation, in the process employing their formidable intellectual powers of logical analysis and unwavering tenacity.
VICES: Although their naturally critical inclinations may serve them exceptionally well within their professional activities, this is not necessarily the case within their personal liaisons, where their painfully honest observations usually prove fatally hurtful to building and maintaining solid and enduring relationships.
VERDICT: If those born on this day are to avoid becoming emotionally isolated, it is important that they should learn to moderate their propensity for brutal honesty and deprecation with regard to their nearest and dearest. Developing greater tolerance of others' personal foibles and imperfections will help them retain the affection of those closest to them.

On This Day

Famous Births: Richard Meade (1673); Charlotte Mary Yonge (1823); Bertram Mills (1873); Mary Roberts Rinehart (1876); Hugh MacDiarmid (1892); Marie Goossens (1894); Enid Blyton (1897); Anne Josephine Haney (1906); Cyril Smith (1909); Angus Wilson (1913); Alex Haley (1921); Mike Douglas (1925); Arlene Dahl (1928); Alun Hoddinott (1929); Jerry Falwell (1933); Anna Massey (1937); Steve Wozniak (1950); Terry "Hulk" Hogan (1953).

Significant Events and Anniversaries: Highlighted by this day is the determination to express perceived truths, even in the face of opposition, and August 11 commemorates: the premiere performance of the *Leningrad*, the Seventh Symphony of Dmitri Shostakovich, a composer whose works did not always find favor with Soviet officialdom (1942); the proclamation of Hussein ibn Talal as king of Jordan following the acknowledgement of his schizophrenic father, Talal's incapacity to rule (1952); the tragic death in a car accident of the abstract expressionist painter Jackson Pollock, whose work often outraged the artistic establishment (1960); and the acknowledgement by Herbert Hoover, despite outspoken opposition, that prohibition had encouraged more crime than it deterred, leading to the repeal of prohibition (1932). The desire for autonomy inherent in this day was reflected when the North African country of Chad obtained its independence from France (1960). As befitting this day whose patroness is Saint Clare, patron saint of television, the first color broadcast—of a baseball game—was aired (1951).

Planetary Influences
Ruling planet: The Sun.
Third decan: Personal planet is Mars.

Sacred and Cultural Significance
In Ireland, Puck Fair fertility festival celebrated; Odduda honored in Santeria religion.
Saints' day: Tiburtius and Susanna (3rd century AD); Blane (6th century AD); Clare (1194–1253), patron saint of television.

On this day in 1960 the African nation of Chad declared its independence from France after nearly 150 years of European influence and 40 years of French colonization, finally regaining the autonomy and independence indicated by the aspects of August 11.

Planetary Influences
Ruling planet: The Sun.
Third decan: Personal planet is Mars.

Sacred and Cultural Significance
Lychnapsia (Festival of the Lights of Isis) in Egypt; the "Glorious Twelfth" in Britain.
Saints' day: Murtagh (6th century AD); Jambert (d. 792).

Nearly exterminated by white hunters in the nineteenth century, the sad fate of the South African quagga zebra was sealed forever on this day in 1883 when the last surviving quagga died in an Amsterdam zoo. August 12 is associated with certainty—even absolutism—and commemorates many beginnings and endings.

AUGUST 12

★★★★★★★★★★★★★★★★★★★★★★★★★★★★★★★★★★★★★★★

Like Janus, the Roman deity of doorways, those born on August 12 have an intellectual propensity to simultaneously look forward and backward. Although their primary urge is to make progress by leading others along an innovative path, before striking out in a new direction they will thoroughly examine and assess existing knowledge and conventions, retaining those concepts they regard as being valid and discarding those they consider to be false or inappropriate. In many respects they resemble historians or scientists (and some may indeed devote their careers to these disciplines) in that they typically amass as much relevant information as possible, subject it to a logical and objective evaluation, and then reach incisive conclusions as to the optimum method of proceeding. When promoting their aims they draw deeply upon their reserves of resourcefulness, single-mindedness and tenacity, impressing others with their clarity of purpose. Although they are independently minded, their overriding purpose is to benefit humankind as a whole; their work may involve the smallest of details, but it is upon the wider picture that they are ultimately focused.

The knowledge that they have thoroughly investigated every aspect of their beliefs endows August 12 people with unshakeable self-certainty, as well as the confidence to attempt to persuade others of the veracity of their views. Despite the potential professional success that such an uncompromising approach promises, however, it may arouse the resentment of the very people whom those born on this day are seeking to influence and guide—especially those closest to them—who may perceive August 12 individuals to be overly arrogant and authoritarian (especially if they were also born in the Chinese year of the ox).

VIRTUES: Those born on this day are responsible individuals who are fueled by the compulsion to make a positive and progressive contribution to human knowledge and society, and who recognize the importance of mastering their chosen field of interest before moving forward in their typically direct and determined fashion.
VICES: Rightly or wrongly, these individuals are typically convinced of the correctness of their viewpoints and rarely allow their self-belief to be shaken by the objections of others, a tendency which may not only lose them potential allies, but also ultimately incite others to rebel against them.
VERDICT: While never abandoning their values or convictions, it is important that August 12 individuals assess the potentially negative reactions of others to their forceful approach. Developing greater patience, tolerance and pragmatism with regard to any expression of dissent will not only help them achieve their aims more effectively, but may bestow an additional dimension on their lives.

On This Day
Famous Births: Thomas Bewick (1753); King George IV of England (1762); Robert Southey (1774); Cecil B. DeMille (1881); Frank Swinnerton (1884); Guy Penrose Gibson (1918); Mohammad Zia ul-Haq (1924); Norris and Ross McWhirter (1925); John Derek (1926); Mstislav Leopoldovich Rostropovich (1927); Buck Owens (1929); Porter Wagoner (1930); William Goldman (1931); George Hamilton (1939); Mark Knopfler (1949).

Significant Events and Anniversaries: This is a day that indicates the capacity to refer to the past when formulating strategies for the future—a propensity that is particularly valuable in the scientific, technical and engineering realms—as was demonstrated when: Thomas Alva Edison, reciting a nursery rhyme, made the world's first sound recording on his Edisonphone (1887); Henry Ford's factory produced the first Model T automobile (1908); P.L.U.T.O., the Pipe Line Under The Ocean, began transmitting petrol from the Isle of Wright to the Allied forces in France during World War II (1944); the U.S.A. launched *Echo I*, the first communications satellite (1960); and, coincidentally, on the same day as the world's last quagga (a species of zebra) died in an Amsterdam Zoo (1883), and the first giant panda was born in captivity in a Mexican zoo (1980).

AUGUST 13

LEO

Individuals born on this day are typically unconventional and guided by visions that are so unusual, or so ambitious—introducing a revolutionary technical invention or a radically novel social system, for example—that others may regard them as being unrealistically fanciful, even ridiculous. Despite the deeply wounding criticism or mockery to which their detractors may subject them, August 13 people generally remain faithful to their beliefs. For not only are these of an inspirational variety, but their originators rest secure in the knowledge that their visions have been rigorously investigated and tested before being revealed to the wider world. Indeed, the innovative theories advanced by those born on this day will typically be supported by sound evidence, for their extraordinary imaginations are supplemented by strong analytical and organizational skills. Fueled by the desire to benefit others with the fruits of their labors, these people are especially drawn to those political, scientific and artistic pursuits which enable them to make a tangible contribution to society.

Despite the courage of their convictions, and their enduring optimism in the face of opposition from others, August 13 people are nevertheless sensitive types who must learn to develop effective self-defensive strategies with which to protect their sensibilities. While preferring to work as leaders of closely knit and highly motivated teams, they will more usually find themselves working in isolation (until the event of their recognition by others). They therefore place enormous value on receiving the unquestioning affection and support of their friends and relations, rewarding the belief of their loved ones with loyalty and generosity.

VIRTUES: Although inspired by highly original visions, these individuals are prodigiously practical and technically proficient. They back their innovative ambitions with solid research undertaken with faultlessly logical precision and when convinced of their veracity, adhere to them with unwavering clear-sightedness and tenacity.
VICES: The strong—and frequently negative—responses aroused by the expression of their dreams inevitably inflict emotional scars upon August 13 people, who may shield themselves from further hurt by either cutting themselves off from others in an attempt to preempt critical comment or by abandoning their visions altogether.
VERDICT: August 13 people are adept at coping with adversity, but must ensure that they do not cause themselves emotional damage by either promoting their aims at any cost in terms of interpersonal relationships or else suppressing the ambitions that are so vitally important to them. Working on their undoubted ability to be pragmatic and realistic will help them steer an effective middle course.

On This Day

Famous Births: Phoebe Anne Moses ("Annie Oakley") (1860); John Logie Baird (1888); Bert Lahr (1895); Jean Borotra (1898); Alfred Hitchcock (1899); Felix Wankel (1902); Basil Spence (1907); Ben Hogan (1912); Melvin Frank and Archbishop Makarios III (1913); George Shearing (1919); Fidel Castro (1927); Pat Harrington (1929); Don Ho (1930); Dan Fogelberg (1951); Betsy King (1954); Quinn Cummings (1967).

Significant Events and Anniversaries: A day on which the pursuit of ambitious goals is strongly featured, August 13 commemorates: the spectacular victory of the forces of the English Duke of Marlborough and the Austrian Prince Eugène over Marshal Tallard's French and Bavarian troops at the Battle of Blenheim during the War of the Spanish Succession (1704); Britain's purchase of the Cape of Good Hope from The Netherlands, having occupied the territory for nearly twenty years (1814); the first staging of Richard Wagner's complete *Ring Cycle, Der Ring des Nibelungen* (1876). Sadly, however, circumstances may prevent the attainment of cherished dreams, as seen fatally when: on the second anniversary of the initiation of the Berlin Wall's erection, East German border guards shot would-be escapee Peter Fechter (1962); and when two hot-air balloons collided above Alice Springs, Australia, causing thirteen deaths (1989).

Planetary Influences
Ruling planet: The Sun.
Third decan: Personal planet is Mars.

Sacred and Cultural Significance
Saints' day: Hippolytus, patron saint of horses (d. 235); Radegund (518–87); Maximus the Confessor (c.580–662); Wigbert (d. c.738); Benild (1805–62).

Annie Oakley, born Phoebe Anne Moses on this day in 1860, flouted social convention to become the first female rodeo star and sharpshooter of her time, demonstrating the unconventional vision and tenacity of purpose characteristic of August 13 people.

Planetary Influences
Ruling planet: The Sun.
Third decan: Personal planet is Mars.

Sacred and Cultural Significance
Saint's day: Maximilian Kolbe (1894–1941).

Born in the Chinese year of the monkey— a sign with affinity for being in the public eye—the lovely and talented Halle Berry transformed her successful modeling career into a stellar career as an actress. This also shows the August 14 individuals' gift of insight into the motivations of others and desire to express their conclusions, thus exerting their influence over a wider audience.

AUGUST 14

Those born on this day are perceptive individuals who are extremely interested in the workings of society and in the quirks and foibles of the human condition: their primary orientation is toward the people that surround them and the various circumstances within which they live their lives. Blessed with acute clarity of vision and prodigious analytical talents, August 14 individuals have a remarkable gift for astutely assessing not only the motivations of other people, but also the influences and impulses that govern their behavior. Because they feel compelled to share their findings with as wide a public as possible, and, indeed, possess a pronounced talent for expressing their conclusions in a direct (albeit sometimes brutally honest) fashion that is often made more palatable by the judicious use of humor, their observations are rarely ignored. In voicing their opinions they are generally fueled by the well-meaning intention of helping others to recognize their shortcomings and thereby to progress, although their success depends largely on how accurately they have assessed the receptiveness of their audience and how sensitively they present their views.

The professions to which those born on this day are especially suited are therefore those where they can exert an effective and positive influence by means of their social or political commentary: such literary fields as journalism, or dramatic or cinematic pursuits, for example. Yet ironically it is their very fascination with others' behavioral patterns that may preclude them from forming strong personal relationships, for others—and particularly those closest to them—will inevitably be uncomfortable with such close scrutiny.

VIRTUES: August 14 people find the observation of people and personal interaction a source of endless interest and are stimulated by the challenge of attempting to unravel the strands that make up the fabric of both individual characters and society as a whole. Their thinking is remarkably incisive, and because they are strong-willed and outgoing, their potential influence over others is therefore extremely powerful.
VICES: If they are not to become emotionally isolated and thereby ultimately unfulfilled, these individuals must beware of allowing their propensity to stand on the outside looking in to prevail over their full participation in the richly rewarding game of human relationships.
VERDICT: Those born on this day should recognize that although their talent for entertaining or informing the wider world with the often biting accuracy of their comments may bring short-term success and acclaim, in the long run it may make people wary of exposing their emotions to them lest their vulnerability be exploited.

On This Day
Famous Births: Hans Christian Oersted (1777); Samuel S. Wesley (1810); Richard von Krafft-Ebing (1840); John Galsworthy (1867); Ernest Everett Just (1883); Kaikhosru Sorabji (1892); John Ringling North (1903); H. Montgomery Hyde (1907); Pierre Schaeffer (1910); Fred Davis (1913); Sydney Wooderson (1914); Russell Baker (1925); Frederic Raphael (1931); David Crosby (1941); Steve Martin (1945); Susan Saint James (1946); Danielle Steel (1947); Ervin "Magic" Johnson (1959); Sarah Brightman (1961); Halle Berry (1968); Keiren Perkins (1973).

Significant Events and Anniversaries: A predilection for identification and classification is indicated by this day, on which: France introduced the world's first driving licenses and registration plates for owners of automobiles (1893); and the first international beauty pageant was staged in the English town of Folkestone (1908). A further feature of this day is the desire to provide information for the benefit of a wider audience, and on August 14 New York's W.R.N.Y. station broadcast the first scheduled television programs (1928). Autonomy is another quality highlighted by this day, on which: Pakistan became an independent state following its partition from India (1947). And, on a day that is governed by the martial planet of Mars: the Allies forced Japan to surrender unconditionally, thereby ending World War II (1945); and the British government deployed troops to restore order in Northern Ireland, beset by sectarian strife (1969).

AUGUST 15

✦✦

Those born on this day are highly ambitious individuals, whose burning desire to realize their visions is the main factor underlying the majority of their actions. The nature of the dreams that inspire them varies according to their personal predilections and circumstances; some may yearn to achieve social recognition and material gains, while others may cherish less immediately selfish aims regarding the betterment of society as a whole. Whatever their guiding purpose in life, however, their approach is typically characterized by its extreme directness and refusal to be deflected from following the path of progress. They formulate their far-sighted strategies with the help of their strong talent for logical thought and practical organizational skills, which they put to good use in delegating details to, and orchestrating, others. These extroverted, confident people are above all oriented toward leadership, and will flourish in any profession where they have the freedom to not only implement plans of their own devising, but also take charge of a team.

Within their domestic lives, too, August 15 individuals assume a commanding role in their quest to ensure the emotional happiness and physical well-being of their nearest and dearest. And although these pleasure-loving people demonstrate extreme magnanimity and open affection toward their loved ones, they generally expect the members of their pride to toe the line that they, the leonine leaders, have laid down, demanding the same high standards to which they themselves adhere—a tendency that is even more pronounced in women born on this day, or in those who were also born in the Chinese year of the dragon.

VIRTUES: Not only do August 15 people have a talent for envisaging the wider picture rather than focusing on a narrower component, they are also strongly motivated toward transforming their visions into reality. In working toward their goals, they demonstrate remarkable tenacity and determination, as well as the capacity to lead and inspire others.
VICES: So compelling is their urge to attain the aims on which their sights are firmly fixed, that these individuals will often disregard the finer sensibilities—or even the valid objections—of others when in the grip of their ambition. This tendency, along with their innate bossiness, can cause others to regard them as authoritarian and unfeeling figures.
VERDICT: It is important, if they are not to alienate others and thereby become emotionally isolated, that those born on this day moderate the confrontational and commanding approach that often defines their interpersonal relationships. They should try to develop a greater sense of empathy with others, and recognize that the right to personal autonomy is not their sole preserve.

On This Day
Famous Births: Napoleon Bonaparte (1769); Walter Scott (1771); Thomas de Quincey (1785); James Keir Hardie (1856); Samuel Coleridge-Taylor (1875); Ethel Barrymore (1879); Edna Ferber (1887); T.E. Lawrence (1888); Jacques Ibert (1890); Tom Mboya (1903); Julia Child and Wendy Hiller (1912); Huntz Hall (1919); Robert Bolt and Phylis Schlafly (1924); Mike Conners, Rose Marie and Oscar Peterson (1925); Jimmy Webb (1946); Princess Anne of Britain (1950).

Significant Events and Anniversaries: This day is cogoverned by the warlike planet of Mars, and commemorates the anniversary of: the death of King Macbeth of Scotland at Lumphanan at the hands of Malcolm, son of King Duncan I, whose crown Macbeth had usurped in 1040 (1057); and the race riots that broke out at Watts, Los Angeles, during which twenty-eight people died (1965). August 15 furthermore indicates the potential success of ambitious long-term plans, and this was the day on which: the citizens of the victorious Allied countries rejoiced on V. J. (Victory over Japan) Day, which marked the end of World War II (1945); and India celebrated its independence from Britain (1947). Sensual appreciation and a love of entertainment—often on a grand scale—is also highlighted by this day, on which: Denmark's Tivoli Pleasure Gardens were opened in Copenhagen (1843); and the now-legendary Woodstock open-air music and arts festival commenced in upstate New York (1969).

Planetary Influences
Ruling planet: The Sun.
Third decan: Personal planet is Mars.

Sacred and Cultural Significance
In ancient Rome, the Festival of Vesta.
Saints' day: the Blessed Virgin Mary (d. 1st century AD), patron saint of mothers, nuns and virgins; Tarsicius (3rd to 4th century AD), patron saint of altar-servers; Arnulf (d. 1087).

Lasting several days and costing thirty-five lives, the Watts race riots, which broke out on August 15, 1965, in Los Angeles were the tragic culmination of the day's warlike aspect and the tendency to take authority into one's own hands if the powerful need to achieve a larger vision is thwarted. Although gained at great cost, these riots did lead to greater participation in local politics and government subsidies for African American-owned businesses.

Planetary Influences
Ruling planet: The Sun.
Third decan: Personal planet is Mars.

Sacred and Cultural Significance
Salem Heritage Day in Massachusetts.
Saints' day: Armel (d. c.552); Stephen of Hungary (c.975–1038); Laurence Loricatus (c.1190–1243); Roch (c.1350–c.1380), patron saint of invalids and prisoners.

Media-savvy star Madonna made her meteoric rise to fame largely by scandalizing the nation (as with her book Sex*), but this only represents one half of the dual nature of those born today. A formidable drive, ambition and outspoken honesty underscore the more tempestuous side of these highly creative people, especially those born, like Madonna, in the Chinese year of the dog.*

AUGUST 16

No shrinking violets these, August 16 people are driven by the compulsion to turn the spotlight upon themselves and, thus illuminated, to broadcast their strong convictions to the widest possible audience. It is sometimes difficult to tell what motivates these dynamic characters more: the urge to share their message or the means by which they draw others' attention to themselves. Certainly the majority of those born on this day are extroverted individuals who bask in acclaim but regard even a hostile reception with equal equanimity— their main priority being to attract notice. Yet behind the often brash and confrontational façades that these people typically adopt as their public personae lies a more serious self, an essential core that is often completely contrary to the personal image that they choose to project. In theatrical terms, it is as if these people are simultaneously actor and director, the former interpreting the commands of the latter and presenting them in the most attention-grabbing manner, while following an ambitious game plan with remarkable focus and tenacity. Indeed, some August 16 people will find professional success as artistic performers or producers, although they are well equipped for any field—politics or teaching, for example—in which they can inspire and direct others.

The more profound ambitions of many of those born on this day are geared toward the attainment of personal happiness rather than material riches (although they recognize that financial wealth will clearly be of help in building a secure future). They typically guard their private lives jealously, for this is the one arena in which they feel they can take off their masks and be themselves. Similarly, they value those who love them for what they actually are rather than what they seem to be, and in turn offer their nearest and dearest their fierce affection, protection and loyalty.

VIRTUES: There are two pronounced sides to these individuals' characters: one that is exuberant, extroverted and attention-seeking, and the other that is more level-headed, calculating, practical and focused. When reconciled, these qualities endow those born on this day with the remarkable capacity to inspire and lead others in the pursuit of the progressive visions that drive them.
VICES: An inherent danger in the dual nature of August 16 people's personalities is that they may veer to behavioral extremes, either overpromoting themselves by means of outrageous and confrontational actions, or else becoming overly manipulative and emotionally disconnected.
VERDICT: Those born on this day generally strike a healthy balance between their professional and personal lives, but in the interests of maintaining their emotional equilibrium they should nevertheless ensure that they take the time to relax, to enjoy the simple pleasures of life, and thereby remain grounded in reality.

On This Day
Famous Births: Jean de la Bruyère (1645); Frederick Augustus, Duke of York (1763); Lady Nairne (1766); Georgette Heyer (1902); Menachem Begin (1913); Charles Bukowski (1920); Fess Parker (1925); Ann Blyth (1928); Robert Culp and Frank Gifford (1930); Eydie Gorme (1932); Lesley Ann Warren (1946); Kathie Lee Gifford (1953); James Cameron (1954); Dominic Erbani (1956); Madonna Ciccone (1958); Timothy Hutton (1960); Nigel Redman (1964).

Significant Events and Anniversaries: Confrontational behavior is indicated by this day on which: English troops led by King Henry VII defeated the French Army at the Battle of the Spurs in Guinegatte in France (1513); and, during the "Peterloo massacre," the British yeomanry caused the deaths of eleven people when they broke up an open-air meeting held at St. Peter's Field in Manchester to debate parliamentary reform (1819). Inherent in this day is a desire for freedom of action, and on August 16 Cyprus gained its independence from Britain (1960). The artistry that is strongly featured by this day was demonstrated in the sphere of popular music when: Ringo Starr became the Beatles' drummer (1962); and Phil Collins graduated from the position of drummer to lead singer within the group Genesis (1975).

AUGUST 17

M any of those born on this day are larger-than-life personalities, who attract the admiration of others by means of their flamboyance, dynamism and self-sufficient disregard for petty convention. These are independent types, whose great energy, imagination, determination not to be fettered by others' rules, and capacity for focusing single-mindedly on their progressive goals bestow upon them outstanding potential for blazing inimitably idiosyncratic trails through life. They have a strong orientation toward other people and are usually unhappy unless they can test themselves and measure their success by the reactions that their often unconventional behavior arouses in others. And, because they are the strong-willed professors of firm convictions, the responses that they engender will typically be extreme, either winning them devoted fans or creating implacable enemies. Convinced of the veracity of their views, these people prefer to recruit others to their cause and then control their actions: when their powerful influence fails, they are prepared to adopt confrontational tactics.

Their determination to live life on their own terms means that these individuals will fare best when engaged in careers where they can carve out their own path or make an impact on others, and many will thus find success in the public eye, undaunted by pressure. Although they are fiercely protective and generous friends and family members, their personal relationships may occasionally be explosive: when, for example, those closest to them fail to fall in with their wishes, or when their innate authoritarianism drives their loved ones (especially their children, if they are parents) to rebel against them.

VIRTUES: Blessed with remarkably original and innovative minds, as well as enormous vigor, fixity of purpose and self-confidence, these commanding individuals are driven by their desire to promote their ambitious visions unhindered by any social constraints, and in doing so to recruit others to their cause.
VICES: Because those born on this day possess a steely certainty of conviction and are furthermore undeterred by opposition—some even thrive on it—they will rarely accept advice from others, however well-meaning, soundly considered, or even potentially helpful—a tendency that may ultimately prove damaging.
VERDICT: If they are to achieve the success that they crave, and also enjoy fulfilling emotional relationships, it is important that August 17 people should make the effort to objectively listen to, and genuinely consider, the opinions of others—especially if these are in conflict with their own firm views—rather than rejecting them out of hand.

On This Day

Famous Births: Davy Crockett (1786); Monty Woolley (1888); Mae West (1892); Maureen O'Hara (1920); George Melly (1926); Ted Hughes (1930); V.S. Naipaul (1932); Robert De Niro (1943); Alan Minter (1951); Noni Hazelhurst (1953); Robin Cousins (1957); Belinda Carlisle (1958); Sean Penn (1960); Donnie Wahlberg (1969); Jim Courier (1970).

Significant Events and Anniversaries: August 17 highlights the determination to promote ambitious visions—whatever the inherent dangers or conflicts—a quality that may be reflected in many ventures, as was demonstrated when: Napoleon's invading forces defeated the retreating Russian Army at the Battle of Smolensk (1812); the Canadian steamship the *Royal William* became the first powered vessel to cross the Atlantic (1833); the Pulitzer Prize was established by Joseph Pulitzer (1903); a Soviet vessel, the nuclear-powered icebreaker the *Artika*, became the first to reach the North Pole (1977); and an American-crewed hot-air balloon succeeded in its pioneering quest to cross the Atlantic (1978). The desire for autonomy that is strongly featured by this day was illustrated when Indonesia, newly liberated from Japanese occupation, proclaimed its independence from The Netherlands (1945). And, on a day that is governed by the Sun, traditionally symbolized by the color and metal gold, significant deposits of this metal were discovered in Canada at Bonanza Creek, in the Yukon Territory (1896).

Planetary Influences
Ruling planet: The Sun.
Third decan: Personal planet is Mars.

Sacred and Cultural Significance
National day of Indonesia; Festival of Diana is celebrated in ancient Rome.
Saints' day: Hyacinth of Cracow (1185–1257); Clare of Montefalco (d. 1308).

Today marks the anniversary of the ancient Roman Festival of Diana, goddess of the hunt, symbolizing vigor, self-confidence and sense of purpose, characteristics of those born on this day. The illustration below shows a contemporary Dianic figure, with two of her attributes, mistletoe and a scythe. She is also frequently depicted with bow and arrows.

Planetary Influences
Ruling planet: The Sun.
Third decan: Personal planet is Mars.

Sacred and Cultural Significance
In China, the Festival of Hungry Ghosts.
Saints' day: Agapitus (dates unknown);
Helena (c.250–33).

Actor and Oscar-winning director Robert Redford, acclaimed for his progressive vision not only in his films but also in his personal endeavors, founded the Sundance Film Festival to provide a venue for young, aspiring filmmakers. His profound dedication to nurturing others' visions and, indeed, his own commitment to furthering humanitarian causes mark him as an exemplary August 18 person.

AUGUST 18

The propensity for independence of thought and action professed by those born on this day, along with their innovative yet logical mindset, gives them the potential to be masters of their chosen fields. Their steadfast conviction of belief and determination to directly improve the lives of others instills in them the urge to direct others along their chosen path. Indeed, many make inspirational leaders, whose genuine concern for those under their wing—be they coworkers or more intimate associates—arouses loyalty and affection. Such inclinations and qualities, when also combined with their organizational powers and tenacity, augur well for their professional success—especially in the realms of law enforcement or social work, but also in the artistic world with which August 18 people have a strong affinity. Although many of those born on this day will have to work hard to realize their ambitions and will encounter many obstacles in their paths (including the resistance of others to their attempts to spread their powerful influence), they possess the resilience and resourcefulness—as well as the clarity of vision—to continue to promote their aims.

Because the emotional and professional fulfillment of the majority of August 18 people depends on their ability to persuade others of the correctness of their approach, it follows that their interpersonal relationships are of great significance to them. And despite the disappointment that they may experience when they fail to win professional allies, they typically retain their positive orientation toward others. The unquestioning support and love of those closest to them sustains their self-belief, and they reciprocate by manifesting profound protectiveness, generosity and tolerance toward their friends and family.

VIRTUES: August 18 people possess remarkable determination in the pursuit of their far-sighted, progressive and human-oriented ambitions, and they will rarely be dissuaded from working steadily toward their aims. Because they feel a pronounced sense of responsibility toward others, their urge to benevolently guide and protect those under their aegis is strong.
VICES: Although they generally seek to rise above the setbacks and hindrances that strew the paths of those born on this day, the difficulty of their quest will often prove discouraging to these individuals, who in such cases have a propensity to replace their initial optimism with grim determination.
VERDICT: In order to safeguard their emotional well-being, these people should try to take regular breaks from their endeavors—to spend time with their kith and kin, for example. Creating a more even balance between their professional and private concerns will not only prove refreshing, but will also give them an extra dimension to life.

On This Day
Famous Births: Virginia Dare (1587); Antonio Salieri (1750); Meriwether Lewis (1774); Emperor Franz Josef I of Austria-Hungary (1830); Marshall Field (1834); Edgar Fauré (1908); Henry Cornelius (1913); Caspar Weinberger (1917); Alain Robbe-Grillet and Shelley Winters (1922); Rosalyn Carter (1927); Roman Polanski (1933); Robert Redford (1937); Martin Mull (1943); Patrick Swayze (1954); Malcom-Jamal Warner (1970).

Significant Events and Anniversaries: August 18 indicates the steadfast promotion of collective visions, even in the face of adversity, as was demonstrated on this Mars-governed day when: under the command of Admiral Boscawen, the British fleet was victorious over its French enemy, led by Commander de la Clue, at the Battle of Lagos Bay (1759); and Prussian troops forced the retreat of the French invaders at the Battle of Gravelotte (1870). This visionary and progressive quality was also variously reflected in other events that occurred on this day: in the artistic arena when the movie *The Wizard of Oz* was premiered in New York (1939); in the technical sphere when the Sydney Bridge in Australia was completed (1930); in the medical world when an oral contraceptive first went on sale, in the U.S.A. (1960); and in the political realm when the Olympic Committee prohibited South Africa from taking part in future Olympic Games until it abandoned its racist policies (1964).

AUGUST 19

LEO

Working steadfastly behind the deceptively easy and open façade that an August 19 person typically presents to the world is an altogether more serious persona—one that has a definite agenda and will press ahead determinedly until this has been achieved. The visions that inspire those born on this day will often have been astutely identified early on in life—a desire to change society based on the noting of perceived abuses, for example, or a gap in the commercial market that might be profitably filled—but although these individuals will typically adhere tenaciously to their convictions and ambitions, they are also extremely realistic types, who recognize that innovation and change cannot be effected without careful prior preparation. Once their game plan has been set, they will devote their considerable energies toward amassing an armory of information, expertise and contacts, and not until they feel that they are properly equipped and that the circumstances are right will they launch themselves on their mission. Such intellectual dedication, resourcefulness and fixity of purpose augurs well for their success in any profession that particularly holds their interest, provided, that is, that they can act without undue restriction.

Indeed, such is their outgoing nature, personal charm and talent for inspiring enthusiasm that others tend to follow wherever August 19 people lead. And in turn these individuals generally manifest great affection and concern for the well-being of those who place their trust in them. There is a risk, however, that the acclaim that they engender may go to their heads, and that they may therefore become prey to delusions of invincibility; thus while they may be grandly magnanimous to those who admire them, they may display enmity to those who—despite their efforts to enlist their support—nevertheless continue to express dissent.

VIRTUES: Those dynamic individuals born on this day are fueled by the urge to realize the long-term, all-encompassing visions that inspire them, and toward whose fulfillment they work with remarkable focus. Blessed with incisive intellectual powers, as well as great practical and organizational capabilities, their talent for attracting and motivating others furthermore endows them with enormous potential.

VICES: Although they are rarely unrealistic when it comes to assessing concrete facts, their predilection for concealing their plans from others until they are ready to act, and the additional danger that they may succumb to their own propaganda in the event of their success, may lead these people to isolate themselves from the grounding influence of personal relationships.

VERDICT: Because those born on this day instinctively understand the importance of making friends rather than foes when engaged in their professional work, they have a tendency to cultivate a persona that is not necessarily true to their inner selves. It therefore is important that they do not lose sight of their core values, and that their close relationships are honest.

On This Day

Famous Births: John Flamsteed (1646); James Nasmyth (1808); Charles Montague Doughty (1843); Orville Wright (1871); Gabrielle "Coco" Chanel (1883); Ogden Nash (1902); James Gould Cozzens (1903); Malcolm Forbes (1919); William Shoemaker (1931); Ginger Baker (1940); Bill Clinton (1945); Tipper Gore (1948); John Deacon (1951); Adam Arkin (1956); Ron Darling (1960); John Stamos (1963); Kevin Dillon (1965); Christian Slater (1969).

Significant Events and Anniversaries: This is a day that highlights the dogged promotion of inspirational ideals, and on August 19 Poland at last broke free of its Soviet-dominated, one-party political system when, following the electoral success of Solidarity, Tadeuz Mazowiecki became the country's premier (1989). That this day is cogoverned by the planet of Mars was reflected when British and Canadian troops launched a daring (but ultimately disastrous) raid on the German-occupied French town of Dieppe during World War II (1942). The potential for implacable enmity that is indicated by this day was demonstrated when, after having been made to dig his own grave, the Spanish playwright and poet Frederico García Lorca was shot by Falangists during the Spanish Civil War (1936).

Planetary Influences
Ruling planets: The Sun and Mercury.
Third decan: Personal planet is Mars.
Second cusp: Leo with Virgo tendencies.

Sacred and Cultural Significance
In ancient Rome, Vinalia Rustica wine-harvest festival.
Saints' day: Mochta (5th century AD); Credan (8th century AD); Louis of Toulouse (1274–97); John Eudes (1601–80).

Charismatic U.S. president Bill Clinton, born on this day in 1945, scored consistently high ratings in the popularity polls not only due to his affability and eagerness to please, but also his dedication to formulating real solutions to long-standing humanitarian issues and the ability to implement his programs, an auspicious characteristic often found in people born today. With several planets in Leo, including Venus and Mars, he has an unusually powerful and persuasive personality.

LEO

Planetary Influences
Ruling planets: The Sun and Mercury.
Third decan: Personal planet is Mars.
Second cusp: Leo with Virgo tendencies.

Sacred and Cultural Significance
Saints' day: Oswin (d. 651); Philibert (c.608–c.685); Bernard of Clairvaux (c.1090–1153), patron saint of bee-keepers; Rognvald (d. 1158/59).

Fearlessly independent 23rd U.S. president Benjamin Harrison, true to those born today, was as revered for his empathy and humanism as for his intelligence and strong sense of justice. But his austerity (also common in the August 20 personality) sometimes led to misunderstanding by all but those closest to him; thus he is often remembered as a greater man than president.

AUGUST 20

Those born on August 20 are complex, self-contained individuals who, despite their pronounced orientation toward others, may be difficult to understand. The reason for their essential elusiveness generally lies in their fiercely guarded private lives: and in their need for occasional periods of solitude where they may not only escape the demands made upon them by other people, but also be themselves, and concentrate on the intellectual pursuits that interest them most. These people are blessed with prodigiously logical minds and a clarity of vision that makes it easy for them to identify areas ripe for improvement and then formulate effective remedial strategies that they implement with determination and great practical skills. Because the concepts that typically absorb the attention of these empathetic types are typically geared toward improving the lot of humanity, they are drawn toward guiding other people along what they perceive to be the optimum route, while others are in turn drawn to them by the aura of capability and security that they generate. They thus have the potential to make gifted academic researchers—especially in the field of science—as well as counselors, but many also use their talents to great acclaim as artists, writers or musicians.

Their highly developed sense of social responsibility and genuine concern for the well-being of those who surround them (tendencies that are especially pronounced if they are also women) means that August 20 individuals rarely ignore a cry for help and will work in the interests of others with unwavering dedication. The danger inherent in such an approach, however, is that they will neglect their own needs and may ultimately be left feeling resentful and unfulfilled. The mutual support to be found in strong and honest personal relationships is therefore extremely important to them.

VIRTUES: Endowed with incisively analytical and organizational intellectual talents, those born on this day are adept at problem-solving and at devising progressive but also practical programs with which to effect improvement. Their empathy with, and interest in, others makes them much sought-after for their soundly considered advice.
VICES: Such is their empathetic responsiveness to those whom they perceive to be in need of their assistance, that August 20 people are innately predisposed toward putting the demands of others above their own, a potentially destructive propensity that may cause them to become emotionally frustrated.
VERDICT: It is important that these individuals examine their priorities and try to work out exactly what it is that will bring them genuine happiness. On occasion they should take the conscious decision to be selfish and to indulge their own desires rather than sacrificing them on the altar of the welfare of others.

On This Day
Famous Births: Jacopo Peri (1561); Benjamin Harrison (1833); Raymond Poincaré (1860); H.P. Lovecraft (1890); Salvatore Quasimodo (1901); Jack Teagarden (1905); Bunny Austin (1906); Jacqueline Susann (1921); Jim Reeves (1924); Isaac Hayes (1942); Rajiv Gandhi (1944); Connie Chung (1946); Robert Plant (1948); John Emburey (1952); Courtney Gibbs (1967).

Significant Events and Anniversaries: August 20 is a day that indicates the implementation of innovative visions designed to benefit the wider world, as was variously reflected when: Harry Brearley, of Sheffield, England, first produced stainless steel (1913); and Adolphe Pégond demonstrated the first successful use of the parachute when he baled out of an airplane above Buc in France (1913). A number of events that occurred on this day confirms the martial planet Mars' governorship of August 20, as when: Ramon Mercader (acting, it is believed, on the orders of Stalin) fatally wounded Leon Trotsky with an icepick in Mexico (1940); at the height of the Battle of Britain during World War II, British premier Winston Churchill made his inspiring "Never in the field of human conflict" speech (1940); and Soviet troops invaded Czechoslovakia to restore the primacy of Communism (1968).

AUGUST 21

The public personae that August 21 people adopt are sometimes totally at odds with the personal core that they shield from the attention of others. For such is the originality—even radicality—of the visions that inspire them that many have learned through experience that others may be disturbed by their unvarnished expression and therefore recognize the importance of modifying their approach in order to maximize the chances of acceptance. Although those born on this day would clearly prefer not to have to compromise themselves in this manner, they are pragmatic and realistic enough to accept that such a course is necessary if they are to succeed in attaining their ambitions—and what innovative ambitions they are. Driven by the compulsion to effect tangible progress, these imaginative individuals utilize their prodigiously perceptive and rigorously logical intellectual skills in both identifying potential areas for improvement and then working with steadfast determination to implement their aims. Whatever profession they choose, they will generally be spurred by the desire to bring about positive global changes—be this in the artistic sphere with which most have a strong affinity, for example, or in the realms of science or government.

Their innately inward-looking preoccupation with their interests and aims means that August 21 individuals will typically flourish best when acting as independent operators unconstrained by the less daring imaginations of others, presenting their conclusions only when they are ready. Often somewhat solitary figures within their professional spheres, those born on this day place enormous value on the belief, love and loyalty demonstrated by those closest to them, and reciprocate such sentiments with profound dedication.

VIRTUES: Extraordinarily imaginative, yet blessed with formidably resourceful practical and organizational skills with which to support and develop their visions, these people have real trailblazing potential. They furthermore accept the importance of pragmatically "selling" their innovative ideas to others, thereby giving them a greater chance of success.
VICES: Although those born on this day generally do not allow the criticism of others to deflect them from their ambitions, they do have a tendency to conceal the aims that drive them from others, a propensity that, if taken to its extreme, may cause them to become emotionally isolated.
VERDICT: August 21 individuals are generally clear-sighted and realistic, particularly when it comes to estimating the reactions of others to their dreams. They should, however, beware of suppressing their deepest emotions in the interests of success, and should instead try to find effective ways of expressing, and thereby sharing, the ideals and aspirations that inspire them.

On This Day

Famous Births: William Murdoch (1754); King William IV of Britain (1765); Aubrey Vincent Beardsley (1872); Claude Grahame-White (1879); Albert Ball (1896); William "Count" Basie (1904); Chris Schenkel (1923); Jack Weston (1924); Chris William Brasher (1928); Princess Margaret of Britain (1930); Melvin Van Peebles (1932); Janet Abbott Baker and Barry Norman (1933); Wilt Norman Chamberlain (1936); Nyoongah Mudrooroo and Kenny Rogers (1938); Peter Weir (1944); Anne Hobbs and Jim McMahon (1959).

Significant Events and Anniversaries: This is a day that indicates the potential attainment of remarkably original visions, as was reflected when: Sam Browne, the British commander of the 2nd Punjab Cavalry in India, devised his eponymous belt to compensate for the loss of one of his arms in battle (1858); the Cadillac automobile company was founded in Detroit (1901); and a performance of Shakespeare's *Two Gentlemen of Verona* marked the triumphant reconstruction of the seventeenth-century Globe Theatre in London, the ambitious brainchild of American actor Sam Wanamaker (1996). One of the planets that influences this day is Mars, and August 21 commemorates the anniversary of the Battle of Vimiero, the first conflict of the Peninsular War, when British forces under the Duke of Wellington scored a victory over their French opponents commanded by General Junot (1808).

Planetary Influences
Ruling planets: The Sun and Mercury.
Third decan: Personal planet is Mars.
Second cusp: Leo with Virgo tendencies.

Sacred and Cultural Significance
Consualia harvest festial held and Hercules honored in ancient Rome.
Saint's day: Pius X (1835–1914).

The Cadillac Motor Company has remained synonymous with luxury and excellence since its founding on this day in 1921. Although the company's expansive vision has given it an undeniable edge, its longevity has much to do with the ability to adapt to the changing needs of the consumer—both qualities common to endeavors consummated on this day.

LEO

Planetary Influences
Ruling planets: The Sun and Mercury.
Third decan: Personal planet is Mars.
Second cusp: Leo with Virgo tendencies.

Sacred and Cultural Significance
Nu Kwa honored in China.
Saints' day: Alexander (d. c.250); Arnulf (dates unknown); Sigfrid (d. 688).

This day highlights the quality of extreme resourcefulness, which was turned to bad account in 1911, when Leonardo da Vinci's immortal Mona Lisa was stolen from the Louvre. Fortunately, the priceless painting—one of the few extant by the Renaissance master—was later recovered.

AUGUST 22

Those born on this day are stimulated by the company of others, and because they are blessed with great personal charm and provide an enlivening influence with their infectious optimism and vitality, others are effortlessly drawn to them. Yet they are rarely as uncomplicated and straightforward as their easy-going approach might suggest, for at the core of their personalities lies a strong-willed, opinionated kernel that fuels them with the urge to have their own way—sometimes regardless of the potential cost to others or, indeed, to themselves. The visions that motivate their actions are frequently grandiose ones, the product of their innate capacity to note the shortcomings of existing circumstances and then, assisted by their powerful practical ability, to formulate resourceful and direct strategies for improvement. Such is their all-encompassing curiosity (and courage) that they are especially attracted to careers in the public service, although their inclinations and talents may lead them to become leaders and managers, inspiring others with their originality and ambition.

Many August 22 people are thus impelled to blaze an initial trail and subsequently direct the thoughts and actions of those who follow them. They manifest their strong leadership qualities in every sphere of their lives, both professional and personal. Because these pragmatic individuals understand the efficacy of persuading rather than forcing others to comply with their convictions, they generally consciously employ their charismatic powers to enlist the support of others. If obstructed, however, their natural combativeness comes to the fore and they will not hesitate to seek to impose their wishes by forceful methods.

VIRTUES: August 22 individuals are driven by the urge to implement their far-seeing and carefully constructed game plans for realizing ambitious and progressive visions, developed through their capacity for logical thought. Practical as well as imaginative, they furthermore draw upon their considerable resources of determination, tenacity and courage in seeking to realize their aims.
VICES: Such is their certainty of belief and confidence in their convictions and abilities that those born on this day have a tendency not to listen objectively to any sustained expressions of dissent, taking the monochromatic view that those who are not for them are against them. This sometimes destructive propensity may not only lose them allies, but may destroy their potential to be successful.
VERDICT: If they are not to become isolated figures, especially in terms of their private liaisons, it is vital that those born on this day—particularly if they are men—modify their self-righteous and sometimes overbearing approach, take on board the opinions of others, and become willing to compromise if necessary.

On This Day
Famous Births: Jean François de la Pérouse (1741); Joseph Strauss (1827); Alexander Mackenzie (1847); Claude Debussy (1862); Jacques Lipchitz (1891); Percy Fender (1892); Dorothy Parker (1893); Leni Riefenstahl (1902); Deng Xiaoping (1904); Henri Cartier-Bresson (1908); John Lee Hooker (1917); Ray Bradbury (1920); Honor Blackman (1926); Karlheinz Stockhausen (1928); Norman Schwarzkopf (1934); Carl Yastrzemski (1939); Valerie Harper (1940); Cindy Williams (1947); Steve Davis (1957); Tori Amos (1963); and Howie Dorough (1973).

Significant Events and Anniversaries: This Mars-influenced day indicates the willingness to employ confrontational tactics when seeking to implement driving visions, as was demonstrated when: Henry Tudor (subsequently King Henry VII) led his troops to a decisive victory over the army of the Plantagenet King Richard III at the Battle of Bosworth Field, thereby ending the War of the Roses (1485); King Charles I heralded the outbreak of the English Civil War by raising his standard before his Royalist supporters in Nottingham (1642); and the Irish nationalist leader Michael Collins was murdered in a Republican ambush (1922). This day is governed by the element of fire, as was sadly reflected when a British Boeing 737 ignited at Manchester Airport, causing the deaths of fifty-five people (1985).

VIRGO

♍

August 23 to September 22

Ruling planet: Mercury   **Element:** Mutable earth
Symbol: A virginal woman   **Polarity:** Negative (feminine)
Physical correspondence: The intestines, abdomen and spleen
Stones: Sapphire, amethyst, carnelian, peridot
Flowers: Jasmine, wintergreen, sage, narcissus, cornflower
Colors: Indigo, navy blue

The astrologers of most traditions identified the constellation of Virgo as a female figure who presided over the harvest season. The most ancient personifications of this divine woman, however, emphasized her fecundity and, by extension, the fruitfulness of the Earth. Like many other peoples, the ancient Egyptians, depicted her (like Isis) holding an ear of corn; to the Romans she was Ceres, the goddess of corn; and to the Babylonians she was Ab-Sin ("the furrow"), Nidaba or Shala, the grain goddess. Her virginal aspect was signified by the names that the Persians (Khusak), Greeks (Parthenos) and Hindus (Kanya) gave her, all of which denote a maiden or virgin. That an earth goddess should be so closely linked with a virginal deity may seem paradoxical, but in ancient tradition the universal Goddess was believed to encompass sexual inviolability and maturity (that is, motherhood), and thus simultaneously embodied both states. There are two Greco-Roman myths that tell of the creation of the constellation Virgo: the first concerns the female vintner Erigone, who hanged herself in despair at the death of her father Icarus. In recognition of her devotion, Zeus immortalized Erigone as Virgo. The second tale associates Virgo with the Greek goddess Astraea ("the starry one"), a deity of justice who lived upon Earth during humanity's Golden Age but who retreated to the heavens when humankind became increasingly corrupt: she became Virgo, and her scales of justice became Libra. Virgo is also associated with the Virgin Mary, the star-adorned "queen of heaven."

The personal characteristics bestowed by Virgo reflect apparently conflicting influences. The element of earth, as well as the constellation's ancient links with the mother goddess, endow Virgoans with stability, orderliness, conscientiousness, practical skills and the potential to reap the fruits of material success. Virginal demureness is paralleled by modesty, idealism and highly developed analytical capacities. The influence of the sign's ruling planet of Mercury denotes quick minds and intellectual curiosity. On the negative side, Virgoans are sometimes narrow-minded, overly critical and unimaginative.

Planetary Influences
Ruling planets: Mercury and the Sun.
First decan: Personal planet is Mercury.
First cusp: Virgo with Leo tendencies.

Sacred and Cultural Significance
Nemesis celebrated in ancient Greece, Volcanalia festival held in ancient Rome.
Saints' day: Timothy, Hippolytus and Symphorian (3rd to 4th century AD); Tydfil (d. 480?), patron saint of Merthyr Tydfil, Wales; Philip Benizi (1233–85); Rose of Lima (1586–1617), patron saint of florists.

Under the influence of this day of paradoxes, Alexander Godunov, faced with the impossible choice between duty and freedom, defected to the United States in 1979, thereby placing his commitment to his own personal vision above his passionate dedication to the Bolshoi Ballet.

AUGUST 23

The multihued strands that make up the complex fabric of the personalities of those born on August 23 may in many respects seem paradoxical. On the one hand, for example, these people are empathetic toward the plight of those in unfortunate circumstances, yet on the other their preoccupation with their personal goals can make them seem selfish and self-obsessed. Although some of these individuals are indeed exclusively focused on the exploration and ultimate attainment of the ambitions that drive them, the majority are able to accord their potentially conflicting characteristics by reconciling their interests with those of a wider social grouping. Endowed with strong perceptiveness, marked technical abilities and a remarkable level of flexibility, as well as resourcefulness and tenacity, August 23 people have the potential to achieve their visions, whatever form these may take: practical, humanitarian or academic. Despite their strong self-reliance and intellectual focus, their concern with others enables them to work as team players, provided, that is, that they retain the autonomy of thought and action that is so vital to them.

Their inherent kindness and desire to lend assistance to those in need makes these individuals valued and respected colleagues, friends and family members. Yet despite their orientation toward those who manifestly require support, the primary commitment of many August 23 individuals remains their fascination with the work or visions that absorb their interest. Thus although their affection and loyalty to their loved ones is never in doubt, they may inadvertently neglect less pressing—but equally important—aspects of their personal relationships when responding to the siren call of other preoccupations.

VIRTUES: Those born on this day are irresistibly drawn to problem-solving and progress-making activities, a predilection that is born of their objective thinking, logical rigorousness and determination. Their urge to act as agents of improvement is frequently manifested in their adherence to pursuits intended to bring benefit to other people.
VICES: August 23 people have such a strong tendency to immerse themselves in the solitary pursuit of their intellectual concerns that they often stand on the periphery of their private liaisons and may thus act to the detriment of their own emotional well-being.
VERDICT: In the interests of fulfilling the emotional needs of those closest to them—and therefore also their own—it is vital that these individuals do not abandon their more mundane personal obligations in favor of more enticing abstract interests, and that they devote sufficient time and attention to their kith and kin.

On This Day
Famous Births: King Louis XVI of France (1754); Arnold Joseph Toynbee (1852); Edgar Lee Masters (1869); Constant Lambert (1905); Carl Dolmetsch (1911); Gene Kelly (1912); Peter Thomson (1929); Vera Miles (1930); Mark Russell (1932); Barbara Eden (1934); Keith Moon and Willy Martin Russell (1947); Geoff Capes, Shelley Long and Rick Springfield (1949); Gerry Cooney (1956); River Phoenix (1970).

Significant Events and Anniversaries: This day highlights the determined pursuit of aims that (although sometimes of a dubious nature) are regarded as justified by being beneficial to the wider interest, a propensity that has clear parallels in national and international politics, as was indicated when: Visigoth warriors, inspired by the desire to enrich their people, sacked Rome (410); Scottish patriot Sir William Wallace, who had led a rebellion against the English, was executed by hanging, drawing and quartering at the orders of King Edward I (1305); the British Expeditionary Force engaged in its first battle of World War I at Mons, on the same day as Japan declared war on Germany (1914); two suspected anarchists, Nicola Saccho and Bartolomeo Vanzetti, were (erroneously) electrocuted in the U.S.A. for their alleged part in a robbery (1927); Hitler and Stalin signed a non-aggression pact on behalf of Germany and the Soviet Union (1940); and German bombers began "blitzing" London with night raids during World War II (1940).

AUGUST 24

Such is the all-encompassing nature of their intellectual curiosity that no detail is too small to escape the clear-sighted scrutiny of those born on this day. Possessed with an irresistible compulsion to understand every issue that excites their attention, they leave no stone unturned and no avenue unexplored in their quest to further their knowledge. Although this tendency is present in every activity they undertake, or with regard to every individual with whom they come into contact, most will channel their intellectual inquisitiveness into a specific professional interest—often academic. And August 24 people are naturally drawn to the endless possibilities for exploration and experimentation that are inherent in artistic pursuits—painting, writing and music, for example—and the products of their quests will frequently delight their audiences with their originality and vision. The realm of human relationships and social systems are similarly ever-changing subjects of fascination, and thus these individuals may make gifted and astute psychologists, therapists and commentators on human behavior—be this of an individual or a communal nature.

Despite their (often somewhat clinical) interest in others, those born on this day are frequently loners—especially if they were also born in the Chinese year of the snake—who prefer to observe others' activities rather than play an active part within them. Although their affection to those closest to them is never in doubt, these are not the sort of people whose relationships are characterized by unquestioning devotion, and their nearest and dearest may sometimes be wounded by the devastatingly critical—if accurate—expression of their observations, however well meant.

VIRTUES: These individuals are driven by their quest for knowledge and understanding, a fundamental quality that they support by means of their formidable clarity of vision and restless intellectual energy. Their innovative talents and progressive inclinations endow them with the potential to enrich the lives of others with the fruits of their observations.
VICES: The all-absorbing nature of their interests, as well as their impartial curiosity, means that those born on this day can be solitary figures who are more concerned with adding to their store of information by standing on the sidelines looking on than by actively participating in interpersonal relationships.
VERDICT: Although they should never suppress their urge for discovery, it is vital that August 24 people recognize that their predilection for observing and analyzing—and critically commenting upon—the behavior of others should be moderated within their personal liaisons if they are to retain the trust and affection of their nearest and dearest that is so important to their emotional well-being.

On This Day

Famous Births: Robert Herrick (1591); George Stubbs (1724); William Wilberforce (1759); James Wedell (1787); Max Beerbohm (1872); Jorge Luis Borges (1899); Graham Sutherland (1903); Durward Kirby (1912); Charles Causley (1917); Antonia S. Byatt (1936); Sam Torrance (1953); Steve Guttenberg (1958); Cal Ripken, Jr. (1960); Marlee Matlin (1965).

Significant Events and Anniversaries: Exploratory inclinations are highlighted by this day, on which: Job Charnock, an agent of the East India Company, founded a trading post at the small settlement of Kalikata (Calcutta), West Bengal (1690); and the first successful attempt of Howard Florey and Ernst Chain to purify penicillin was reported by the British medical journal the *Lancet* (1940). Inherent in the tendencies indicated by August 24 is the determined pursuit of driving ambitions, often excessively and regardless of the potential human consequences, and this was reflected in various disparate events that occurred on this day when: on the order of the Catholic King Charles IX (influenced by his mother, Catherine de Medici), about fifty thousand Protestant Huguenots were murdered in Paris, in what became known as the St. Bartholomew's Day Massacre (1572); and British soldiers rampaged through Washington, D.C. and burned the White House and the Capitol (1814).

Planetary Influences
Ruling planets: Mercury and the Sun.
First decan: Personal planet is Mercury.
First cusp: Virgo with Leo tendencies.

Sacred and Cultural Significance
Saints' day: Bartholomew (1st century AD), patron saint of shoemakers and tanners; Ouen (c.600–84).

With more determination than regard for the human cost—a danger to beware of on this day—the British stormed Washington, D.C., in 1814, burning it to the ground in a brutal act of retaliation during the War of 1812.

Planetary Influences
Ruling planets: Mercury and the Sun.
First decan: Personal planet is Mercury.
First cusp: Virgo with Leo tendencies.

Sacred and Cultural Significance
National day of Uruguay; Opiconsiva festival
celebrated in ancient Rome.
Saints' day: Genesius of Arles (d. c.303),
patron saint of actors and secretaries; Ebbe
(d. 683); Louis IX of France (1214–70),
patron saint of France and kings; Joseph
Calasanz (1556–1648).

*Regarded as the most famous flapper of the Jazz
Age, actress Clara Bow was born on August 25,
1905. Reflecting the day's extroverted qualities,
she became a symbol of the emancipated
American woman and, in 1928, was voted the
most popular female movie star in America. As
a wood snake, she had a natural inclination for
acting and indulging her more hedonistic side.
Her many films include* Mantrap *(1926),* It
(1927) and Dangerous Curves *(1929).*

AUGUST 25

Whether they are introverted or—as is often the case—extroverted types, those born on this day are strongly oriented toward other people. Their deep sensitivity to the feelings expressed by others, be they covert emotions or more overt messages, compels them to respond actively and positively. This propensity may even cause August 25 individuals to make a career working for the benefit of distressed individuals or communal groupings—within the legal or political spheres, for example, or the social, medical or caring services. Thus impelled to offer their assistance as a result of their all-encompassing interest in others, these people relish the challenge of pitting their intellects and talents against thorny problems, and are aided in their task by their imaginative yet logical thought processes, as well as their enormous vigor and determination. When their individual preferences lean less toward altruistic professional pursuits, those born on this day nevertheless have the potential to exert a powerful influence over others as managers, team leaders, through the media or in any other role where they can summarize and express the conclusions of their observations in their own, inimitable "voice."

Despite the powerfully inspirational effect that their originality and humanitarian concern frequently has on others, and the acclaim that they may thereby generate, August 25 people are in many respects beset by insecurity. In this regard their enormous sensitivity may be as much a handicap as a blessing, firstly because the mass of data they pick up may have a confusing effect; and secondly because they may tend to measure their feelings of self-worth by means of the reactions they provoke in others. Rooting themselves in the grounding bonds of secure friendships and loving family relationships will help them gain a greater sense of confidence, perspective and priority.

VIRTUES: Those born on this day are endowed with deeply perceptive powers when it comes to their assessment of other people, and also with respect to more abstract concepts. Vigorous, determined and resourceful individuals, they have a pronounced talent for translating the information that they innately absorb into innovative and effective strategies.
VICES: Because they are naturally so strongly geared toward receiving the messages transmitted by others, there is an inherent danger that August 25 people may sometimes act impulsively, responding to individuals and situations as they encounter them instead of following a fixed set of personal principles.
VERDICT: Rather than following a somewhat indiscriminate and erratic path through life, many of these people will gain a more fulfilling sense of purpose by taking time to consider and identify, and then focus upon those values and ambitions that are truly important to their emotional well-being.

On This Day
Famous Births: Czar Ivan IV, "the Terrible" (1530); Allan Pinkerton (1819); Bret Harte (1836); Robert Stolz (1880); Clara Bow (1905); Ruby Keeler (1909); Van Johnson (1916); Mel Ferrer (1917); Leonard Bernstein (1918); George Wallace (1919); Monty Hall (1923); Sean Connery (1930); Regis Philbin (1934); Frederick Forsyth (1938); Rollie Fingers (1946); Martin Amis and Gene Simmons (1949); Elvis Costello (1954); Billy Ray Cyrus (1961); Blair Underwood (1964).

Significant Events and Anniversaries: The conjunction of many aspects highlighted by this day indicate the pursuit of unusually imaginative and ultimately pioneering visions, aims that may be manifested in many different spheres, such as when: British rider Alicia Meynell, competing at a race meeting in York, became the world's first official female jockey (1804); Londoner Henry William Crawford patented his method for galvanizing iron (1837); three graduates of the Oberlin Collegiate Institute of Ohio became the first female bachelors of arts (1841); English seafarer "Captain" Matthew Webb became the first person to swim across the English Channel (1875); and photographs sent back to Earth by the U.S. spacecraft *Voyager* revealed new images of three of Neptune's moons, including Triton (1989).

AUGUST 26

Although the visions that inspire these people's actions may be soaringly ambitious ones, they are rarely fueled by the selfish desire for personal aggrandizement, but are instead more generally concerned with pushing forward the bounds of their experience and horizons. Endowed with markedly mercurial talents, such as intellectual curiosity and a predilection for testing conventional limits—whatever form these might take, be they academic, societal, technical or artistic—as well as the necessary supportive discipline and tenacity required to pursue their aims with remarkable concentration, August 26 individuals have the potential to devise and then implement original and effective strategies with which to benefit the wider world, within whatever professional sphere they choose to operate. Because they are geared toward making tangible progress rather than winning acclaim and glory (though they welcome the recognition of others for their attainments), their goal orientation makes them committed team members who welcome the input of others just as their coworkers appreciate their fair and democratic manner.

Those born on this day typically demonstrate their interest and concern for those who surround them in both their professional and private relationships. And although their protective instincts are especially aroused by those who are experiencing difficulties—particularly if they were also born in the Chinese year of the goat—they treat most people with tolerance and respect for their individuality. Such qualities endear them especially to their nearest and dearest, who appreciate their willingness to offer advice and assistance without seeking to control and dominate their actions.

VIRTUES: Those born on this day are blessed with prodigious intellectual powers, including independence of thought, the capacity to generate imaginative and innovative ideas, and a logical approach. They complement their progressive urge with strong determination, and recognize the importance of working closely with others, making them steady, reliable companions and good team players.

VICES: Despite their general lack of interest in being crowned with laurels and showered with material rewards as accolades for their work, their self-effacing approach may encourage others to ignore their efforts and achievements, which may eventually cause them to become disillusioned and embittered.

VERDICT: Although August 26 people are not shy about promoting a concept about which they feel particularly strongly, they are less willing to draw attention to their own personal need for recognition, believing that their actions and attainments will speak for themselves. This will not always be the case, however, and in the interests of their emotional well-being these individuals should develop strategies to ensure that their contributions are not overlooked by others.

On This Day

Famous Births: Robert Walpole (1676); Joseph Michel Montgolfier (1740); Antoine Laurent Lavoisier (1743); Prince Albert of Saxe-Coburg-Gotha (1819); Lee De Forest (1873); John Buchan (1875); Guillaume Apollinaire (1880); Christopher Isherwood (1904); Ben Bradlee (1921); Geraldine Ferraro (1935); Malcolm Pyrah (1941); Valerie Simpson (1948); Branford Marsalis (1960); Macaulay Culkin (1980).

Significant Events and Anniversaries: On a day that highlights the determined and resourceful pursuit of visionary aims: Edward III's English archers were instrumental in defeating the forces of Philip VI of France at the Battle of Crécy, the first conflict of the Hundred Years' War over England's claim to France (1346); the revolutionary French Assembly approved the Declaration of the Rights of Man and the Citizen granting equal rights to the French citizenship (1789); American women received the right to vote as a result of the Nineteenth Amendment of the U.S. Constitution (1920); the British Royal Air Force (R.A.F.) carried out the first bombing raid on the German capital of Berlin during World War II (1940); and U.S. swimmer Lynne Cox became the first person to swim across the Siberian Lake Baikal (1988).

Planetary Influences
Ruling planets: Mercury and the Sun.
First decan: Personal planet is Mercury.
First cusp: Virgo with Leo tendencies.

Sacred and Cultural Significance
In Hinduism, the rebirth of Krishna celebrated; Feast Day of Ilmatar in Finland.
Saints' day: Zephyrinus (d. 217); Ninian (5th century AD); Bregowine (d. 764); Pandonia (d. c.904).

Largely due to the monumental efforts of woman suffrage leaders such as Harriet Easton Stanton Blatch (pictured below), in 1921, on this day of progressive action and the urge to effect change by working closely with others, U.S. women proudly won the right to vote.

Planetary Influences
Ruling planet: Mercury.
First decan: Personal planet is Mercury.

Sacred and Cultural Significance
Saints' day: Decumen (6th century AD); Monica (332–87); Caesarius of Aries (c. 470–542); Rufus (dates unknown). Often the date when Harvest Festival is celebrated in the Northern Hemisphere.

Mother Teresa, Nobel Peace Prize-winning Catholic nun, devoted her life to assuaging the suffering of the poor and sick, benevolent qualities often bestowed upon those born in the Chinese year of the dog. Like many born on this day, she combined a practical earthiness with the highest standard of service to whatever endeavor she undertook.

AUGUST 27

★★★

Rational and intellectual, as well as inventive and curious, those born on August 27 boast the capacity for genius. They are very practical and grounded—an earthy quality—and possess the discipline to work extremely hard to unusually high standards, often making them dazzling successes in their chosen fields. These people especially excel in careers in which their formidable intellectual capacities, as well as their analytical and methodical gifts, can be utilized fully; they are particularly successful in the fields of science and medicine, financial planning and accountancy, or investigative journalism. Although keen lovers of the arts, they are nevertheless drawn to those practical and intellectual pursuits that satisfy their realistic and rational natures, qualities that make them refreshingly straightforward as friends and colleagues.

The powerful combination of incisive wit and fluent powers of communication possessed by August 27 people, as well as the coolly analytical Virgoan approach, means that, as well as fascinating their audiences, they have the power to wound (even devastate) more sensitive people's feelings. They should therefore remember to choose their words with tact—this particularly applies to those born in the Chinese year of the rooster, who have a frequently irresistible tendency to speak their minds. Studious and diligent, people born on this day often find satisfaction by burying themselves in their work, but the endearing shyness and modesty that many exhibit may mask an unjustified lack of self-confidence. Parents and partners should therefore bolster August 27 people's egos, providing the sense of security and self-esteem necessary for their formidable talents to flourish. In adult life, generous and appreciative partners, especially Leos, may similarly provide a stable relationship within which their gifts can thrive.

VIRTUES: These people exhibit highly developed powers of lateral thinking, which cut straight to the heart of intellectual problems. Determination, tenacity and articulacy are further qualities that contribute to their success and personal appeal.
VICES: There is a danger that these people may concentrate on cerebral pursuits to the detriment of personal relationships and their emotional well-being. They tend to forget that not everyone can, or indeed should, live up to their own lofty ideals.
VERDICT: In general, August 27 people should beware of allowing their perfectionist tendencies to dominate other areas of their lives, lest they suffer the inevitable consequences of isolation, disappointment and disillusionment. They should ensure that they allocate time to rest and relaxation, as well as to their family and friends, in order to help them achieve inner contentment.

On This Day
Famous Births: Confucius (c. 551 BC); Theodore Dreiser (1871); Charles Stewart Rolls (1877); Samuel Goldwyn (1882); C.S. Forester (1899); Sir Donald Bradman and Lyndon Baines Johnson (1908); Mother Teresa of Calcutta (1910); Tony Crombie (1925); Lady Antonia Fraser (1932); Michael Holroyd (1935); Barbara Bach (1947); Pee-Wee Herman (1952); John Lloyd and Derek Warwick (1954); Bernard Langer (1957); Gerhard Berger (1959).

Significant Events and Anniversaries: Consistent with the inventiveness signified by this day, the Montgolfier brothers and Jacques Alexandre César Charles launched the first hydrogen balloon (1783). Edwin Drake drilled the world's first oil well at Titusville, Pennsylvania (1859), thus tapping into the earth's natural resources. And reflecting this inherent capacity for genius sometimes culminating in enormous success or even fame, rock and roll giants Elvis Presley and the Beatles first met on this day (1965). The volcano Krakatoa erupted on Pulau (1883), paralleling the fact that even earth signs can explode if negative conditions prevail. One of the world's most influential modern scientists in the field of communication, Thomas Edison, demonstrated sound movie projection (1910). The determined senior yachtsman Francis Chichester launched his solo round-the-world trip on Gypsy Moth IV (1966).

AUGUST 28

People born on August 28 are blessed with the potential for exceptionally well-developed intellectual success because of their mental independence and creativity. Their ceaseless search for knowledge and understanding often provides the driving force behind their actions. The desire to transcend the bounds of accepted wisdom in order to discover new insights means that these people have the originality and ability to excel in their careers, but their stubborn resistance to following the crowd can be taken too far and lead to isolation. Their birthdate indicates idealism, but any mercurial tendencies are counterbalanced by a practical and steady approach, thus producing a rare combination of imagination and groundedness. People born on this day are therefore especially suited to careers in academia—especially science—or in the literary arts, where their simultaneously creative and analytical talents, as well as their impressive articulacy, can be given full reign and can also benefit others.

Parents of August 28 children should encourage their interests from a young age—however quirky they may seem—for, if pursued, an enthusiasm conceived early on may lead to outstanding success in later life. In their relationships, too, people born on this day find happiness with people who value their creativity and single-mindedness, and who allow them the necessary freedom to grow and flourish: easy-going Leos, for example, or those who share August 28 people's demanding values, are especially tolerant of these basic needs. They should also cherish their friendships and personal relationships (particularly if they are men) so that they receive the stable emotional support that will both add a rewarding dimension to their lives and provide a secure framework within which they can realize their full potential.

VIRTUES: Incisive, communicative and determined, August 28 people are often in great demand as advisers because of their ability to offer new perspectives and brilliant solutions to thorny problems. Their imagination, idealism and original thinking usually earn them professional success and the respect of others.

VICES: An overriding absorption with cerebral pursuits to the exclusion of all else may leave these people socially isolated. They sometimes develop arrogance and an attitude of superiority, forgetting that other's opinions—especially if different from their own—are nevertheless valuable.

VERDICT: August 28 people should ensure that they do not lose patience with the conventions of others, whom they often regard as limited or resistant to change. They should try to respect other's beliefs and cooperate with them, and remember to accept people as they are. They should consciously devote time to their personal relationships, which are often neglected.

On This Day

Famous Births: Johann Wolfgang von Goethe (1749); Leo Tolstoy (1828); Peter Fraiser (1884); Charles Boyer (1899); Lindsay Hassett (1913); Godfrey Hounsfield (1919); Donald O'Connor (1925); Ben Gazzara and Windsor Davis (1930); Elizabeth Seal (1933); Lou Piniella (1943); David Soul (1944); Emlyn Hughes (1947); Ron Guidry (1950); Daniel Stern (1957); Emma Samms (1960).

Significant Events and Anniversaries: Reflecting the influence of Mercury—the sign of communication—the first telegraph cable was laid under the Channel, thus linking England and France (1850). The opera Lohengrin was premiered at Weimar (1850); its idiosyncratic composer, Richard Wagner, was both celebrated for his genius and reviled for his radical racial philosophy. Dr. Martin Luther King, Jr., the dedicated, yet realistic, battler for civil rights, made his famous "I have a dream" speech at the Lincoln Memorial, Washington, D.C. (1963). Three high-flying Italian airplanes crashed at an airshow in Ramstein, West Germany, killing more than thirty people (1988).

Planetary Influences
Ruling planet: Mercury.
First decan: Personal planet is Mercury.

Sacred and Cultural Significance
Saints' day: Augustine of Hippo (354–430); Hermes (3rd century AD); Julian of Brioude (3rd century AD).

August 28, a day noted for idealism and communication, marks the anniversary of Martin Luther King Jr.'s legendary 1963 "I have a dream" address in Washington, D.C. Noted for his passionate convictions, he used his formidable oratorical gifts to counter aggression and hatred with his message of peace.

Planetary Influences
Ruling planet: Mercury.
First decan: Personal planet is Mercury.

Sacred and Cultural Significance
Ancient Egyptian New Year; the Gelede celebrated by the Yoruba in Nigeria.
Saints' day: The beheading of John the Baptist (d. c.30), patron saint of monks; Sebbi (7th century AD); Edwold of Cerne (9th century AD).

After a long yet peaceful occupation by sheepherders, John Batman, a consortium leader, purchased 60,000 acres from the government of New South Wales to found the city of Melbourne, thus achieving the aims of many and reflecting the idealism and a love of autonomy characteristic of August 29 people and events.

AUGUST 29

Two distinct sides may be perceived to the nature of August 29 people: on the one hand they are relentlessly drawn to understanding and formalizing abstract concepts and issues, while on the other they are somewhat romantic and idealistic individuals whose emotions may be less rigorously ordered. Yet these characteristics are neither discrete nor incompatible, stemming as they do primarily from these individuals' all-encompassing curiosity and interest in exploring and experiencing all that life has to offer and then sharing their ideas with others. In their intellectual pursuits their inquisitiveness and desire to make sense of the often disparate data they identify by means of their close scrutiny can lead those born on this day to become talented analysts. They utilize their qualities of imagination, insight and technical or organizational skills to present the fruits of their researches in innovative and inspiring reinterpretations. Depending on their personal inclinations, their energies may be devoted to a variety of professional fields, but the technology, computing and design spheres, in which they can operate relatively unhindered, augur particularly well for their potential success.

Despite their typical desire to benefit others when it comes to their work, those born on this day may be somewhat solitary figures who are admired from afar. It may be that their radical aims or marked independence of mind intimidates others, or that they expect too much of their closest associates while at the same time jealously insisting on their own right to personal autonomy (a tendency that is especially pronounced if they are men). Thus while their affection for their nearest and dearest is considerable, those closest to them may have to be particularly indulgent and tolerant if their relationships are to flourish.

VIRTUES: Blessed with the gifts of intellectual curiosity, wisdom and independence, those born on this day are reluctant to be confined by the limits set by accepted convention, and instead prefer to gather and analyze existing information, reappraise it and then present their findings in a new and original manner.
VICES: Although their typically nonconformist approach may well bring them professional success, such disregard for convention may not only cause them to become estranged from general society, but may also have negative implications with regard to their private lives.
VERDICT: In order to safeguard their emotional well-being, it is crucial that these individuals recognize the importance of grounding themselves within strongly supportive personal relationships. They should therefore make every effort to nurture their bonds with those closest to them, moderating their occasional predilection for extreme behavior and making compromises where necessary.

On This Day
Famous Births: Jean-Baptiste Colbert (1619); John Locke (1632); Jean Auguste Dominique Ingres (1780); Oliver Wendell Holmes (1809); Maurice Maeterlinck (1862); Preston Sturges (1898); Ingrid Bergman (1915); Isabel Sanford (1917); Charlie Christopher Parker (1920); Richard Samuel Attenborough (1923); Charles Gray and Dick O'Neill (1928); Thom William Gunn (1929); Elliott Gould (1938); William Friedkin (1939); Robin Leach (1941); James Hunt (1947); Lenny Henry and Michael Jackson (1958).

Significant Events and Anniversaries: The analytical and catalytic influences inherent in this day promise pioneering breakthroughs in a variety of areas, as was illustrated when: English physicist Michael Faraday unveiled his electrical transformer at London's Royal Institute (1831); after intensive negotiations on the part of British diplomats, China ceded Hong Kong to Britain by signing the Treaty of Nanking, thereby concluding the First Opium War (1842); and German engineer Gottfried Daimler patented the world's first motorcycle (1885). That this is also a day of the determined pursuit of unusual visions was demonstrated when: John Batman, the leader of a consortium, purchased 60,000 acres of land north of Australia's Port Phillip Bay from their Aboriginal owners to found Melbourne (1835); and the Australian cricket team defeated England on her home territory for the first time (1885).

AUGUST 30

I n common with the majority of their fellow Virgoans, those born on August 30 are blessed with mercurial minds, a gift that not only bestows on them marked curiosity with regard to the functioning of any system, be it academic, practical, technical or social, but also the desire to impose order upon any area that impinges upon their lives. And these individuals are talented organizers, who put their highly developed analytical powers to use by astutely identifying subjects with scope for improvement and then employing their logical intellects in formulating effective strategies with which to realize their perfectionist aims. Despite their recognition of the need to address every inherent detail—however small—in order to incorporate it into a smoothly running whole, those born on this day always retain a clear view of the wider picture, and this determined fixity of purpose, as well as their highly developed capacity for self-discipline, augurs well for their success. Yet these are not usually unbendingly rigid types, for, being both pragmatic and geared toward achieving tangible results, they appreciate the need for adaptability and compromise when the occasion demands.

Their progressive inclinations and organizational skills endow those born on this day with the potential to succeed in any career that especially excites their interest, although commercial ventures, scientific pursuits (especially pharmacy and the medical field), sports and teaching may prove especially fruitful. As a result of the emphasis that they innately place upon building supportive frameworks, they naturally gravitate toward forging close-knit teams, a propensity that applies as much to their private as their professional lives. They do, however, prefer to play a leading role within their relationships and this predilection may occasionally cause friction with those of their nearest and dearest—especially their children—who would prefer more personal freedom.

VIRTUES: Although the aims that inspire August 30 people are progressive and ambitious, they are usually attainable, particularly since they back their realistic powers of perception with their considerable determination, strong organizational powers and ability to communicate their visions directly to others, and thus inspire those with whom they work.
VICES: Because these are self-reliant types, who are themselves strongly focused upon the achievement of their goals, they have a rather authoritarian tendency to demand a similar level of commitment and devotion to their cause from other people, regardless of their inclinations.
VERDICT: Those born on this day should recognize that their sometimes overbearing tendency to seek to control the actions of others—particularly those closest to them—may cause resentment and ultimately mutinous behavior from those whom they wish to influence. When circumstances permit, they should therefore relax the expectations and demands that they impose on other people and allow them a measure of personal autonomy.

On This Day
Famous Births: Jacques Louis David (1748); Mary Wollstonecraft Shelley (1797); Ernest Rutherford of Nelson (1871); Raymond Hart Massey (1896); John Gunther (1901); Shirley Booth (1907); Fred MacMurray (1908); Denis Winston Healey (1917); Regina Resnik (1924); Elizabeth Ashley (1941); Jean Claude Killey (1943); Peggy Lipton (1947); Timothy Bottoms (1951); Robert Parish (1953); Cameron Diaz (1972).

Significant Events and Anniversaries: This day highlights prodigious organizational and directional powers in the pursuit of concrete visions, as was reflected when: General Thomas "Stonewall" Jackson masterminded the victory of his Confederate troops over their Unionist opponents at the Second Battle of Bull Run in Virginia (1862); the large-scale evacuation of British city children to the relative safety of the countryside was inaugurated during World War II to remove them from danger of anticipated German bombing raids (1939); and the German army began its siege of Leningrad (1941). Clear-sighted realism is a further feature of August 30, on which day it is believed that Cleopatra, the queen of Egypt, recognizing that the war against Rome was lost, committed suicide by encouraging an asp to bite her (30 BC).

Planetary Influences
Ruling planet: Mercury.
First decan: Personal planet is Mercury.

Sacred and Cultural Significance
Saints' day: Felix and Adauctus (d. c.304); Rumon (6th century AD); Fiacre (d. c.670), patron saint of gardeners, horticulturists, syphilis-sufferers and taxi-drivers.

Jacques Louis David (1748), Parisian painter and creator of the masterpiece The Rape of the Sabines, *devoted his considerable artistic gift to the glorification of the Bonaparte empire. His predilection for perfectionism and attention to minute detail, combined with the ability for deep personal commitment typified by the August 30 person, are evident in his work and his life.*

Planetary Influences
Ruling planet: Mercury.
First decan: Personal planet is Mercury.

Sacred and Cultural Significance
Saints' day: Eanswyth (d. c.640); Aidan (d. 651); Cuthberga (d. c.725); Quenburga (d. c.735); Waldef (d. 1076); Raymund Nonnatus (1204–40).

The primary motivation behind events of this day is the achievement of goals by inspiring others. Marcus Garvey, black nationalist leader who believed that African Americans must restore self-respect through pride in a glorious heritage, was elected provisional president of the Republic of Africa on this day in 1920.

AUGUST 31

Others admire those born on this day for the apparently effortless way in which they carry out their endeavors with both efficiency and remarkable personal charm. Indeed, although August 31 people are strongly committed to achieving their professional goals, unless exasperated by perceived inefficiency or lack of interest on the part of those with whom they are working, they typically manage to remain courteous and considerate in their dealings with their colleagues. Such a balanced approach reflects both their pragmatic recognition of the benefits of making allies rather than foes and the empathy that is born of their prodigious powers of perception (a quality that is even more pronounced if they are women); it is furthermore a particularly effective *modus operandi*. Yet their primary overall motivation is the achievement of their aims, to which they devote their independence of thought, highly developed organizational skills, technical expertise and tenacity, as well as their ability to inspire others. Friendships are also very important to these people.

The goals that fuel August 31 people's actions are typically progressive and directed toward benefiting the social group with which they are most closely identified—their coworkers, their community, or even humanity as a whole. They are well equipped to succeed in any number of professions, with the proviso that they should have influence and direct others. Yet they are also personally ambitious (not so much with regard to winning material rewards but more in terms of their individual development and fulfillment) and are, furthermore, vitally concerned with the well-being and happiness of their nearest and dearest, whose actions they have a propensity to control (albeit with the best of intentions).

VIRTUES: Those born on this day manage to retain a genuinely sensitive interest in, and concern for, those around them, while still remaining focused on the achievement of their ambitions. Motivated by the desire to effect progress, their capacity to draw upon their remarkable levels of energy, as well as their practical and organizational skills, gives them outstanding potential for success.
VICES: In their determined efforts to attain their goals, and to set those for whom they care on what they perceive to be the correct track, August 31 people may neglect their own needs, especially for relaxed relationships conducted on equal terms.
VERDICT: Although they are blessed with a clear-sighted sense of perspective when it comes to taking action, their desire to help others or accomplish given tasks may cause them to give priority to the immediate and short-term demands of others, to the detriment of both their physical energy and emotional resources. They should therefore consciously make time for relaxation in order to recharge their batteries and remain in touch with their inner selves.

On This Day
Famous Births: Caligula, Emperor of Rome (12); Emperor Jahangir of the Moguls (1569); Théophile Gautier (1811); Herman von Helmholtz (1821); Maria Montessori (1870); Queen Wilhelmina of the Netherlands (1880); DuBose Heyward (1885); Arthur Godfrey (1903); William Saroyan (1908); Alan Jay Lerner (1918); Buddy Hacket (1924); James Coburn (1928); Raymond Buckland (1934); Eldridge Cleaver (1935); Isao Aoki (1942); Clive Lloyd (1944); Van Morrison and Itzhak Perlman (1945); Richard Gere (1949); Edwin Moses (1955); Debbie Gibson (1970).

Significant Events and Anniversaries: August 31 highlights a talent for instituting practical strategies in the pursuit of guiding visions, as was variously reflected when: the British VIII Army under General Bernard Montgomery halted the previously inexorable advance of General Erwin Rommel's German troops at the Battle of Alam al-Halfa during World War II (1942); and U.S. swimmer Mark Spitz achieved the remarkable feat of winning five of his seven gold medals during one day at the Munich Olympics (1972). An autonomous approach motivated by the desire to bring benefit to others is a further feature of this day, on which two dependencies gained their independence from Britain: Malaya, redesignated as Malaysia (1957), and Trinidad and Tobago (1962).

SEPTEMBER 1

T heir overriding ambition and concomitantly single-minded focus in striving to achieve the visions that guide them are perhaps the most striking characteristics of those born on this day. The aims that propel them on their determinedly direct paths through life may be concerned with their personal betterment or with bringing about wide-ranging improvements for the benefit of others, but all their ventures are defined by their astuteness of perception, their enviable ability to formulate a practical progressive strategy, and their steadfast tenacity in implementing their plans of action. They also possess remarkable self-knowledge, a gift that endows them with the confidence to stand their ground in the face of adversity. Yet because they are sensitive and blessed with immense personal appeal, when it comes to dealing with doubters, they typically prefer to charm them with regard to their visions with silver-tongued words than to have to resort to the combative approach of which they are well capable.

The highly developed capacity of September 1 people verbally to influence others augurs especially well for their success in advertising, marketing, sales and retail careers, or as powerful writers or performers of any type. Their goal orientation and independence may, however, lead them to neglect their private lives—a tendency that is particularly pronounced in the men born on this day—despite the enormous value that they place on the support offered by the bonds of strong and honest emotional relationships.

VIRTUES: Those born on this day manifest an extraordinary fixity of purpose in the pursuit of their clearly defined aims. They augment this visionary quality with their powerfully effective organizational abilities, the practical strengths born of their keen judgement and the persuasive talents with which they enlist the support of others.
VICES: Such is their overwhelming compulsion to realize the ambitions that drive them that September 1 individuals have a propensity to exclusively devote their considerable energies to their quests, a tendency that may ultimately cause them not only to overextend themselves, but also to pay insufficient attention to the needs of those closest to them.
VERDICT: In terms of their all-round fulfillment, it is important that these people learn to appreciate that nurturing their interpersonal liaisons, as well as their own physical and emotional well-being, is at least as significant as the attainment of their intellectual targets. They should therefore take time both to relax and to spend more time with their friends and families.

On This Day

Famous Births: Amilcare Ponchielli (1834); Engelbert Humperdinck (1854); Roger Casement (1864); James "Gentleman Jim" Corbett (1866); Edgar Rice Burroughs (1875); Marilyn Miller (1898); Mary Padula (1905); Yvonne DeCarlo (1922); Rocky Marciano (1923); Cecil Parkinson (1931); George Maharis and Conway Twitty (1933); Seiji Ozawa (1935); Lily Tomlin (1939); Barry Gibb (1946); Peter Gibb (1947); Gloria Estefan (1957).

Significant Events and Anniversaries: On a day that highlights a strong commitment to progressive visions: the profoundly visually and aurally impaired U.S. scholar Helen Keller graduated from Radcliffe College (1904); English writer H.G. Well's prophetic work *The Shape of Things to Come* was published (1933); and Bobby Fischer was victorious over Boris Spassky at Reykjavik in Iceland, thereby becoming the first American to win the chess world's highest title (1972). Reflecting the controlling and practical urges that are strong features of this day—ones that are inherent in nationalist foreign policies—September 1 marks the anniversary of: the start of France's League of Nations' mandate to administer the eastern Mediterranean state of Lebanon (1920); the invasion of Poland by Hitler's troops, thus making the outbreak of World War II a certainty (1939); and the overthrow of King Idris I of Libya by a group of army officers led by Muammar al-Qadhafi (1969). Paralleling the destructive effects that may result from the suppression of emotions—a danger indicated by this day—a volcanic eruption in Japan caused the deaths of over 300,000 people in Tokyo and Yokohama (1923).

Planetary Influences
Ruling planet: Mercury.
Second decan: Personal planet is Saturn.

Sacred and Cultural Significance
National day of Libya.
Saints' day: Priscus of Capua (dates unknown); Drithelm (d. c.700); Giles (d. c.710), patron saint of mothers, crippled people, hermits, lepers and horses.

Deprived by severe illness of her sight and hearing at the age of 19 months, and thus the capacity to learn to speak, the education and writing career of Helen Keller represent an extraordinary and inspiring accomplishment. Reflecting this day's strong commitment to progressive visions, it was on September 1, 1904, that she graduated cum laude *from Radcliffe College and embarked on a life dedicated to publicly aiding the deaf and the blind.*

Planetary Influences
Ruling planet: Mercury.
Second decan: Personal planet is Saturn.

Sacred and Cultural Significance
In ancient Athens, the Grape Vine Festival held in honor of Ariadne and Dionysus.
Saint's day: William of Roskilde (d. 1070).

Caravaggio's depiction of Dionysus, youngest of the major gods of Olympus, who created the wine that became a sacred pleasure to the Greeks and Romans, and in whose honor as the God of wine, and that of Ariadne, the Grape Vine Festival was held on this day in ancient Athens.

SEPTEMBER 2

★★

The straightforward face that September 2 people present to the world is no façade: with those born on this day, what you see is what you get—a formidably direct and focused personalized package of determination and energy. Such is their urgent desire to realize their ambitions as efficiently as possible that these individuals have no patience with subterfuge or prevarication, regarding game-playing or indecision as irritating obstacles on the path to success. And indeed, when obstructed in any way, these usually controlled people may explode with frustration, the uncharacteristically violent expression of their seething annoyance startling those who have not experienced it before. Yet despite such occasional flare-ups they are otherwise organized, practical and disciplined in the pursuit of their goals. While the concerns and interest manifested by those born on this day may vary according to the individual, a common feature is their progressive nature and their wish to exert a beneficial influence on others—in the public services, perhaps, or as administrators.

These people are scrupulously fair in their dealings with others—a quality that results from their critical discernment and their empathy with those who are unhappy or the victims of perceived abuses. And in such instances, as in all their endeavors, their independence of thought and predilection for devising remedial strategies come to the fore. Yet in devoting themselves to resolving the problems of others, September 2 people may neglect their own needs. Furthermore, despite their profound—if understated—affection for those closest to them, unless they are in real trouble they may expect the same level of self-reliance to be demonstrated by their nearest and dearest as they exhibit themselves.

VIRTUES: Those born on this day favor an unequivocally direct approach to everything that they undertake, a propensity that is born of their perceptiveness in identifying areas ripe for improvement and their fixity of purpose.
VICES: A potentially ambivalent effect of the goal-oriented urge of September 2 people is that they react negatively when their progress is blocked. In addition, their tendency to single-mindedly concentrate on the task at hand may preclude them from addressing their emotional needs, as well as those of their kith and kin.
VERDICT: In order to gain ultimate, holistic fulfillment, these individuals should attempt to develop a wider perspective on their lives so as to balance their intellectual aims with their emotional requirements. They would therefore be well advised to cultivate mutually supportive personal relationships, and to find time to indulge in enriching social pursuits.

On This Day
Famous Births: John Howard (1726); Wilhelm Ostwald (1853); Frederick Soddy (1877); George Brown (1914); Russ Conway (1925); Francis Matthews (1931); Peter Ueberroth (1937); Michael Hastings (1938); Christa McAuliffe (1948); Mark Harmon (1951); Jimmy Connors (1952); Linda Purl (1955); Keanu Reeves (1964).

Significant Events and Anniversaries: The influences that prevail on September 2 indicate the uncompromising implementation of ambitious visions, often on behalf of the perceived interests of a communal group, and this day commemorates: the defeat of the Sudanese Khalifa, or Mahdi, who had revolted against Egyptian rule, by British forces at the Battle of Omdurman (1898); the holding of the first democratic elections of the Irish Free State (1923); the destruction of the anti-Nazi Ghetto in Warsaw, Poland, by S.S. troops (with the loss of around 50,000 lives) (1942); the surrender of Japan aboard the U.S. aircraft carrier *Missouri* in Tokyo Bay (1945); and appointment of the Vietminh leader Ho Chi Minh as president of the newly communist North Vietnam Republic (1954). The same quality of active determination in the pursuit of a visionary aim was demonstrated when Norwegian explorer Roald Amundson became the first person to navigate the Northwest Passage (1906). Reflecting the potential for emotional pyrotechnics inherent in September 2, this day marks the outbreak of the Great Fire of London, its source a bakery in Pudding Lane (1666).

SEPTEMBER 3

Those born on this day are remarkably determined individuals, a quality that those who do not know them well may not recognize until particular situations arise in which they demonstrate their readiness to adopt combative methods. Generally, however, they prefer a conciliatory and affable manner, believing that more will be achieved by communication than by confrontation: this personal style, however effective, may lead others to misjudge their strength of purpose. Blessed with mercurial and independent minds, a highly developed sense of natural justice and empathy for the downtrodden, and enormous technical and organizational talents, September 3 people are especially interested in finding practical solutions to the problems that beset humanity. They may thus gravitate toward professions where they can help others to make tangible progress, or at least live their lives more happily, and careers as engineers, scientific researchers, artists and in sports are particularly well starred.

Those born on this day bring to all their endeavors their astute perceptiveness, tolerance, patience and tenacity, as well as their desire to set everything—or everyone—that they encounter on a smoothly running path. This propensity is especially pronounced within their personal lives (and even more so if they are women), and their friends and family members appreciate the support and understanding that they readily offer. Yet despite their typically quiet and understated manner, these people are no pushovers, a caveat that applies as much to their private as to their professional liaisons.

VIRTUES: Endowed with inquisitive and questing intellects, as well as the capacity to patiently develop soundly organized strategies with which to bring about progress, these perceptive individuals are interested in not only ensuring the welfare of others, but also acting of agents as advancement and assistance.
VICES: Since these people's primary concern is to realize their ambitions as quickly and efficiently as possible, their approach is often a nonconfrontational one intended to maximize their chances of success. They may, however, thereby fail to communicate the urgency of their cause, and thus mislead others as to strength of their wills.
VERDICT: Those born on September 3 are well-balanced individuals who seek to achieve their aims with the minimum of fuss. Yet they may render themselves still more effective if they can develop their communication skills and make their intentions clearer to others.

On This Day
Famous Births: Matthew Boulton (1728); Cecil Parker (1897); Frank Macfarlane Burnet (1899); Alan Ladd (1913); Kitty Carlisle-Hart (1914); Irene Pappas (1926); Eileen Brennan (1935); Pauline Collins and Brian Lochore (1940); Valerie Perrine (1943); Charlie Sheen (1965).

Significant Events and Anniversaries: This is a day that highlights pragmatic and reconciliatory qualities, as was reflected when Britain recognized the independence of the United States of America, thus concluding the American War of Independence (1783). Despite the diplomatic tendencies inherent in this day, the influences governing September 3 indicate a preparedness to employ uncompromising methods when all else has failed, as was demonstrated when: the British pilot Captain Leefe Robinson became the first person to shoot down a German Zeppelin in World War I, over London (1916); World War II commenced when Britain, Australia, New Zealand and France declared war on Germany on the same day that a German U-boat torpedoed a passenger ship, the *Athenia*, that was ferrying women and children from Britain to the safety of the U.S.A.—112 people died (1939); and the English General Oliver Cromwell's forces twice defeated their aggressive Scottish foe, at the Second Battle of Dunbar (1650) and at the Second Battle of Worcester (1651). Coincidentally, Cromwell was also to die on this day (1658). Marked determination in the pursuit of guiding visions is further featured by this day, on which: French aviators Diedonne Coste and Maurice Bellonte completed the first nonstop transatlantic flight (1930); and British seamen John Ridgway and Chay Blyth realized their dream of crossing the Atlantic in a rowing boat (1966).

Planetary Influences
Ruling planet: Mercury.
Second decan: Personal planet is Saturn.

Sacred and Cultural Significance
In Ghana, the Akan people celebrate Akwambo, the Path Clearing Festival; the Maidens of the Four Directions honored by women of the Hopi tribe.
Saints' day: Macanisius (d. c.514); Gregory the Great (c.540–604), patron saint of musicians, popes and singers.

Kitty Carlisle-Hart, the accomplished actress and singer with a long record of achievement in both the arts and public service, was born on September 3, 1914. Displaying the technical and organizational talents that are characteristic of those born on this day, she served with distinction as, inter alia, *Chair of the New York State Council of the Arts. Her Chinese birth influence as a wood tiger enhanced both her artistic creativity and her desire for recognition: in 1991 she was awarded the U.S. National Medal of Arts.*

Planetary Influences
Ruling planet: Mercury.
Second decan: Personal planet is Saturn.

Sacred and Cultural Significance
The Changing Woman Ceremony held by members of the Apache tribe.
Saint's day: Ultan of Ardbraccan (d. 657).

A grandchild of slaves, Richard Wright was born on a plantation in Mississippi on September 4, 1908. In his career as a novelist, short-story writer and critic, he demonstrated the inspirational and perceptive qualities that are typical of those born on this day. Best known for his autobiographical novel Black Boy *(1945), Wright's Chinese influences under his sign of the monkey gave him a serious, intellectual demeanor and a talent with words.*

Those born on this day may present something of an enigma to those who do not know them well, for on the one hand they are gifted problem-solvers who are stimulated by challenge—be it physical or intellectual—yet on the other are impatient when forced to deal with the petty details that form part of the routine of business practices. The answer to this apparent conundrum of character lies in their mercurial minds, which endow them with marked curiosity and a relish for new experiences. Indeed, when frustrated by circumstances outside their control, these usually pragmatic and self-disciplined types are prone to explode in startling displays of temper. Generally, however, September 4 individuals are good-natured people, who make cooperative—sometimes inspirational—team members, with the provision that they are able to retain autonomy of thought and action. They are, moreover, rarely ambitious for personal glory, being instead motivated by the desire to realize more impersonal progressive aims.

Because their skills usually assume more of an intellectual than a technical aspect, and in view of their innate urge to achieve tangible results through their own vigorous and focused efforts, these individuals are frequently best suited for acting as independent agents of change. Their talents and inclinations equip them for potential success in a wide variety of professions, but the freedom inherent in artistic and academic pursuits may prove especially attractive to September 4 individuals. They retain a similarly independent stance within their personal relationships, and, although they have a deep affection for those closest to them, they are not interested in embroiling themselves in the minutiae of domestic life.

VIRTUES: Blessed with quick-witted perspicacity, a progressive predilection for seeking out and building upon the knowledge that they uncover, as well as enormous energy and clarity of vision, these are strongly independent individuals who are stimulated by challenge.
VICES: Despite the great appeal that their infectious enthusiasm exerts upon others, those born on this day are extremely self-reliant people, who typically prefer to pursue their interests independently rather than grounding themselves within solid friendships.
VERDICT: In terms of maintaining a healthy balance between their intellectual and emotional needs, September 4 people should strive to recognize the supportive benefits that are inherent in human relationships: they should try to moderate their urge for independence.

On This Day
Famous Births: Robert Raikes (1736); François René de Chateaubriand (1768); Anton Bruckner (1824); Darius Milhaud (1892); Antonin Artaud (1896); Mary Renault (1905); Edward Dmytryk and Richard Wright (1908); Henry Ford II (1917); Paul Harvey (1918); Mitzi Gaynor (1930); Dinsdale Lansden (1932); Dawn Fraser (1937); Tom Watson (1949); Judith Ivey (1951); William Kennedy Smith (1959); Peter Virgile (1960); John Preston (1968); Ione Skye (1970).

Significant Events and Anniversaries: This is a day that highlights the determined promotion of progressive—even revolutionary—ambitions, as was demonstrated when: following France's defeat by Prussia during the Franco-Prussian War, French Emperor Napoleon III was ousted and the Third Republic proclaimed (1870); Canada and South Africa entered World War II (1939); Queen Wilhelmina of the Netherlands abdicated to make way for her daughter Juliana (1948); and nine African-American students attempted to assert their civil rights by taking the places assigned for them at the previously all-white Central High School in Arkansas, prompting the state's governor to call out the National Guard (1957). The insistence on personal autonomy that is such a pronounced feature of this day was reflected when the Soviet ballerina Natalia Makarova defected to the West while touring with the Kirov Ballet (1970). The artistic talent promised by September 4 was confirmed when: English writer and illustrator Beatrix Potter wrote to five-year-old Noel Moore, illustrating her letter with the first-known images of Peter Rabbit, Flopsy, Mopsy, Cottontail, and Squirrel Nutkin (1893); and the Beatles held their first recording session, at London's Abbey Road studios (1962).

SEPTEMBER 5

These magnetic people are fueled by a desire to realize their own idiosyncratic visions of Utopia, yet while their dreams are highly individual, they rarely encompass selfish ambitions alone, instead being concerned with building a happier and more enlightened world for others. In common with the majority of those born under the planet of Mercury, these are inquisitive and perceptive types, who have little difficulty in quickly and astutely identifying areas that are ripe for improvement, and who are furthermore fired with the burning determination to be the agents of change. Despite the practical skills that they bring to their missions, in their righteous enthusiasm to set the world to rights they may fail to assess realistically their chance of success and thereby inadvertently sabotage their best efforts. The form that their ambitions take will vary according to the September 5 individual, but most will espouse professions that enable them to exert their influence over others in some positive way: possibly as social campaigners, for example, but more likely as artistic performers who can impart their messages in inspirational fashion.

Their pronounced concern about the welfare of others permeates every aspect of their lives, and, in turn, others are drawn to them because of their easy charm, infectious optimism and enormous generosity. These are individuals who like to encourage those around them, and—particularly if they were also born in the Chinese year of the dog—they usually expend tremendous energy in bolstering the confidence of those of whom they are fond. Occasionally, however, their magnanimity may cause them to neglect their own emotional needs.

VIRTUES: The astute discernment and empathy possessed by September 5 individuals, combined with their energetic and progressive disposition, motivates them to formulate remarkably imaginative strategies for improvement, which they promote with great determination and invigorating enthusiasm.
VICES: The sometimes unfeasible nature of their ambitions may lead these individuals to become profoundly discouraged when their determined efforts consistently fail. Their energetic and generous promotion of the interests of others may furthermore lead them to put the needs of others before their own.
VERDICT: In order to maintain their emotional equilibrium, when it comes to implementing their aims those born on this day should concentrate on developing their ability to evaluate realistically the eventual chances of their success before wholeheartedly embarking on a new venture. They should also strive to devote as much time to their inner selves as they do to helping others.

Planetary Influences
Ruling planet: Mercury.
Second decan: Personal planet is Saturn.

Sacred and Cultural Significance
In ancient Rome, the Roman Games, honoring Jupiter, began; the Hindu god Ganesh honored in India.
Saints' day: Bertin (d. 698); Laurence Giustiniani (1381–1455).

Often described as the greatest monarch of his age, King Louis XIV of France, known as the Sun King, was born on September 5, 1638. Fired with the burning determination to be an agent of change that is starred for this day, on assuming the throne at the age of 23 he pursued aggressive foreign and commercial policies and established the guidelines for successful absolutism.

On This Day
Famous Births: King Louis XIV of France (1638); Johann Christian Bach (1735); John Wisden (1826); Victorien Sardou (1831); Jesse James (1847); Arthur Koestler and Winnifred Gladys Horrocks Thomas (1905); John Cage (1912); Frank Yerby (1916); Bob Newhart (1929); Carol Lawrence (1934); Dick Clement and William Devane (1937); Raquel Welch (1940); Freddy Mercury (1946); Cathy Guisewaite (1950); Dweezil Zappa (1969).

Significant Events and Anniversaries: On a day that highlights the pursuit of soaringly ambitious goals, September 5 commemorates the anniversary of: U.S. pilot James Doolittle's pioneering feat in becoming the first person to fly across the U.S.A. from coast to coast (1922); and—especially appropriately since this is a day governed by the element of earth—the official opening of the ten-mile-long St. Gotthard road tunnel under the Swiss Alps, linking Goschenen and Airolo (1980). A tragic manifestation of the active promotion of visionary ideals indicated by September 5 occurred on this day when Palestinian members of the P.L.O. splinter group, the Black September guerrilla movement, attacked the Israeli accommodation block at the Olympic Village in Munich, Germany, killing two people and capturing eight athletes; subsequently all of the hostages, terrorists and a German policeman were killed during a failed rescue attempt at Munich airport (1972).

✶✶

Planetary Influences
Ruling planet: Mercury.
Second decan: Personal planet is Saturn.

Sacred and Cultural Significance
Situa, an ancient Inca blood festival.
Saints' day: Bee (7th century AD)

The assassination of President McKinley by Leon Czolgosz in Buffalo, New York, on September 6, 1901, is indicative of the strong force of conviction and radical, sometimes violent, action associated with this day.

September 6 people are complex characters whom others may find difficult to get to know or understand fully. On the one hand their perspicacity and natural sense of justice endow them with profound sensitivity—particularly toward the less fortunate—and concern for the well-being of others, yet on the other, these are also strong-willed types whose force of conviction and independence of mind often belies their mild, somewhat stoic, manner. However, their desire for intellectual autonomy and their orientation toward others are not necessarily incompatible—indeed, those born on this day may frequently combine these personal traits to great effect in their professional lives as doctors, lawyers or social campaigners, for example. For above all these individuals are compelled by the urge to bring about progressive advances that will benefit the wider world (they are usually unconcerned with attaining personal gains), especially if they were also born in the Chinese year of the dragon. And, when engaged upon their quest, they draw upon their considerable resources of energy, determination and integrity, as well as their strong organizational talents.

Despite their interest in others and generally reluctantly assumed leadership qualities, September 6 people may sometimes appear to be somewhat solitary figures, who prefer to follow their inquisitive instincts independently rather than allow themselves to be bound by the ties inherent in human relationships, perhaps fearing that to do so would compromise their need for freedom. As is the case with their liaisons with family and friends, when they eventually commit themselves to equal one-on-one partnerships, they typically demonstrate their innate capacity to be loyal, affectionate and supportive.

VIRTUES: The thoughts and actions of those born on this day are governed by their overriding intellectual curiosity and urge to explore the uncharted waters of knowledge in the hope of revealing and instituting innovative measures with which to further the progress of humanity. They support all their endeavors with their highly developed organizational skills, clarity of vision and unwavering tenacity.
VICES: In their desire to indulge their inquisitiveness and thereby also to benefit others with the fruits of their discoveries, September 6 people may inadvertently neglect their physical requirements for relaxation and their often unacknowledged need to ground themselves in stable emotional relationships.
VERDICT: In order to maintain a healthy emotional/intellectual equilibrium, these people should beware of suppressing the more fundamental prerequisites that are common to us all, and should occasionally yield to the lure of simple and undemanding pursuits, including the enjoyment of sociable interaction with others.

On This Day
Famous Births: Marquis de Lafayette (1757); John Dalton (1766); John James Richard Macleod (1876); Joseph Kennedy (1888); Edward Appleton (1892); Billy Rose (1899); Franz Josef Strauss (1915); Bernie Winters (1932); Jo Anne Worley (1937); Jackie Trent (1940); Monica Mason (1941); Britt Ekland (1942); Swoosie Kurtz (1944); Jane Curtin and Roger Waters (1947).

Significant Events and Anniversaries: On a day that highlights both progressive and adventurous qualities: the *Vittoria*, the only surviving ship of Ferdinand Magellan's expedition to circumnavigate the world, arrived at Spain's San Lucar harbor after three years at sea (1522); and the British transatlantic liner the *Lusitania* embarked on her maiden voyage to New York (1907). Also indicated on this day is determined—often violent—action on the perceived behalf of the greater good, as was reflected when: the anarchist Leon Czolgosz assassinated U.S. President William McKinley (1901); a white parliamentary messenger, Dmitri Tsafendas, stabbed to death the South African premier Hendrik Verwoerd, in Cape Town (1966); Palestinian terrorists hijacked three commercial airliners, forcing them to fly to Jordan in order to draw attention to their cause (1970); and the U.S.S.R. shot down a Korean passenger airplane that had flown into Soviet airspace, causing the deaths of 269 people (1983).

SEPTEMBER 7

Those born on this day are tenacious individuals whose actions are primarily motivated by a desire to push the bounds of human knowledge and endeavor forward. This is not to say that they do not welcome the acclaim or financial rewards that their actions may reap—to the contrary—but rather that their questing natures and intellectual dynamism are more compelling factors in their behavior than is mere personal ambition. And should they find themselves masters of their fields (which is often very likely, given their independent drive and strength of purpose), they will rarely bask in the glory that others reflect on them, but harness the support thereby garnered toward the attainment of their aims. For as well as being blessed with the highly developed qualities of perspicacity and resourcefulness, enabling them to formulate imaginative and yet profoundly practical strategies, their organizational skills and innately pragmatic approach equips them as naturally gifted leaders.

September 7 people gravitate toward any profession (and their multifaceted skills equip them admirably for many) where they can achieve tangible results and exert their progressive influence over others. Since they also demand complete autonomy, in many respects they are particularly well suited to those academic, artistic, literary or musical careers where they can work relatively unhindered. Although they demand the same level of freedom within their personal relationships, they may paradoxically seek to control their nearest and dearest—albeit with the best of intentions—a predilection that may arouse the resentment of their loved ones, especially, if they are parents, within their children.

VIRTUES: Energetic, determined and blessed with incisive intellectual capabilities, September 7 people are spurred on in their efforts by their urge to effect the innovative ambitions that inspire them. They are assisted in their quests by their considerable tenacity, practical skills and, when necessary, combativeness, thus further endowing them with great potential.
VICES: The sensitivity of these individuals typically assumes the form of intellectual perspicacity rather than of human-oriented empathy, and in their impatient urge to realize their far-reaching goals, they may disregard the feelings or opinions of others, perceiving them as being irrelevant or obstructive.
VERDICT: It is important that those born on this day recognize that the price for the success on which they are so strongly focused may be a high one in terms of their emotional well-being. While never abandoning their aims, they should take greater account of others—particularly those closest to them—and should learn the value of compromise.

On This Day

Famous Births: Queen Elizabeth I of England (1533); Thomas Coutts (1735); Henry Campbell-Bannerman (1836); Anna Mary "Grandma" Moses (1860); Edith Sitwell (1887); Elia Kazan (1909); Anthony Quayle (1913); James Alfred Van Allen (1914); Leonard Cheshire (1917); Peter Lawford (1923); King Baudouin I of the Belgians (1930); Malcolm Bradbury and John Paul Getty, Jr. (1932); Buddy Holly (1936); Richard Roundtree (1942); Julie Kavner (1951); Chrissie Hynde (1952); Corbin Bernsen (1954; Devon Sawa (1978).

Significant Events and Anniversaries: This is a day that indicates fixity of purpose, originality and resourcefulness, qualities that were variously demonstrated when: during the American War of Independence, *The American Turtle*, the first submarine to be deployed for war-faring purposes, tried (but failed) to attach a mine to the British flagship H.M.S. *Eagle* in New York's harbor (1776); Napoleon's French forces defeated Prince Mikhail Kutuzov's troops on Russian soil at the Battle of Borodino (1812); British lighthouse-keeper's daughter Grace Darling rowed to the rescue of five passengers whose steamer, the *Forfarshire*, had been wrecked off the Farne Islands (1838); the Allies forced Italy to surrender unconditionally during World War II (1943); and Desmond Tutu was ordained as archbishop of Cape Town, thus becoming the first African Anglican primate (1986). The desire for autonomy that is a feature of this day was reflected when Brazil proclaimed its independence from Portugal (1822).

Planetary Influences
Ruling planet: Mercury.
Second decan: Personal planet is Saturn.

Sacred and Cultural Significance
National day of Brazil; Healer's Day;
in India, Deana honored.
Saints' day: Evurtius (4th century AD);
Tilbert (8th century AD).

Queen Elizabeth I of England was born on September 7, 1533. Determined, ambitious, tenacious and a natural leader, all characteristics starred by this day, she was to lead England as an emergent world power, establishing effective dominance over the seas.

Planetary Influences
Ruling planet: Mercury.
Second decan: Personal planet is Saturn.

Sacred and Cultural Significance
Saints' day: The nativity of the Blessed Virgin Mary (d. 1st century AD), patron saint of mothers, nuns and virgins; Kinemark (5th century AD); Ethelburga (d. 647); Disibod (7th century AD).

Originally intended to adorn the façade of the Cathedral of Florence, but instead placed inside the main entrance to Palazzo Vecchio, Michelangelo's David, *a symbol of Florence's independence, was unveiled on September 8, 1504. The thirteen-foot marble statue took three years to complete, and its unveiling highlighted the personal commitment and tenacity that are features of this day.*

SEPTEMBER 8

Their remarkable strength of conviction and fierce determination to set others on the path that they regard as being the correct one endow those born on this day with pronounced leadership potential. They are usually respected (although not necessarily regarded with affection) for both their dynamism and their fixity of purpose. While these individuals may be fueled by the desire to maintain or protect the status quo, they may be equally fired by the urge to implement innovative progressive systems. Either way, they will have first evaluated the existing situation thoroughly, drawing upon their capacity for objective analysis in the process, and then utilized their great organizational and practical skills either to bring about improvement by modification, or to formulate an alternative. Once they have decided upon their preferred course of action, they typically promote it with uncompromising tenacity, often demonstrating their powerful talent for communication in their quest to convince others. Such inclinations have a clear parallel with the political sphere, and many of those born on this day may become career politicians; others choosing to spread their message through artistic media, which they do with great success.

Despite their perspicacity, clarity of vision and persistence—qualities which augur well for their professional success—when it comes to their intellectual interests many of those born on this day may experience troubled personal relationships, particularly if they are men. The problem is that others may not concur with their opinions and can become alienated by, and resistant to, their often stubborn attempts to persuade them otherwise; bitter confrontation is usually inevitable.

VIRTUES: Those born on this day are possessed by the desire to direct the actions of others in accordance with their own strongly held beliefs, which are formed as a result of their incisive intellectual powers and are adhered to and promoted with their characteristic energy and determination.
VICES: September 8 individuals are typically so firmly convinced of the superior merits of their convictions that they will not only strive to impose them on others, but they will also tend to dismiss any conflicting viewpoints out of hand, a propensity that is likely to make them more enemies than friends, and may also cause them to become narrow minded.
VERDICT: In terms of their emotional well-being in particular, it is vital that these people learn to appreciate the often negative effect that their uncompromising approach may have on others—even those whose interests they have most strongly at heart. They should therefore moderate their forceful manner and pay more attention to the opinions expressed by others, however much they disagree with them.

On This Day
Famous Births: King Richard I of England (1157); Ludovico Ariosto (1474); Frédéric Mistral (1830); Antonin Dvorak (1841); Siegfried Sassoon (1886); Claude Pepper (1900); Hendrik Verwoerd (1901); Jean-Louis Barrault (1910); Harry Secombe (1921); Sid Caesar and Lyndon LaRouche (1922); Peter Sellers (1925); Jack Rosenthal (1931); Patsy Cline (1932); Michael Frayn (1933); Peter Maxwell Davies (1934); Jonathon Taylor-Thomas (1981).

Significant Events and Anniversaries: This is a day that highlights the powerful promotion of often inflexible aims, as was demonstrated when: the English navy forced the surrender of the Dutch colony of New Amsterdam, renaming it New York (1664); controversial Democratic U.S. senator Huey Long was shot and mortally injured (1935); during World War II, the first German "flying bomb," the V2 long-range rocket, was launched from the Netherlands and landed in Chiswick, London, killing three people (1944); and, in an attempt to remain true to his principles of nonsurrender and avoid standing trial for war crimes, Japanese General Hideki Tojo attempted suicide (but failed) (1945). A further tendency featured by September 8 is that of institutional change, as was reflected when, on this day, the city of Johannesburg was founded in South Africa, following the discovery of gold (1886).

SEPTEMBER 9

✱✱✱✱✱✱✱✱✱✱✱✱✱✱✱✱✱✱✱✱✱✱✱✱✱✱✱✱✱✱✱✱✱✱✱✱✱✱

Those born on September 9 are serious individuals, who are not only absorbed by abstract concepts but also feel a strong sense of responsibility toward those around them. Like the majority of those born under the mercurial sign of Virgo, their birthright includes a markedly independent and inquisitive turn of mind, with the result that they have a predilection both for intellectual exploration and for seeking to implement progressive innovations. Thus, having examined an issue from all angles with incisive judgement, they will typically draw an original conclusion as to the best course of action and then dip deep into their considerable reserves of resourcefulness and organizational skills to promote their aims with steadfast tenacity. These are sensitive individuals who will seek to enlist the support of others; their determination should not be underestimated, however, when this is not possible to arrange, they will battle on alone if necessary. Such is their concern with the well-being of others that their inclinations and talents may lead them into pursuing humanitarian careers, or at least those where their work can be of wider benefit—as scientific researchers or educators, for example.

Despite their interest in the welfare of others, September 9 people may appear somewhat solitary individuals, who will readily participate in team or social pursuits but nevertheless seem to stand apart from the crowd. This propensity may be partly explained by their innate preference for independent observation, but may also be a product of their great sensitivity which may, in some instances, cause them to be beset by—usually unjustified—feelings of insecurity (a tendency which is even more pronounced if they are women). Receiving the unconditional love and support of their nearest and dearest is therefore of great importance to them, and they reciprocate such emotional bolstering with quiet but unwavering loyalty.

VIRTUES: September 9 individuals possess inquisitive, independent and ingenious intellects, but are also fueled by the urge to make a positive contribution to the lives of their fellows. In all their endeavors they combine their progressive and benevolent inclinations with their practical, tenacious and original approach.
VICES: Such is their concern for the greater good, and their urge to be responsible agents for improvement, that those born on this day may suppress what they consider to be their trivial desires to occasionally just have fun.
VERDICT: In order to safeguard their happiness, it is vital that these people should acknowledge their right to uninhibited enjoyment every so often. They already understand the importance of nurturing their personal relationships, and they would benefit from directing toward their inner selves some of the concern that they extend to others.

On This Day

Famous Births: Cardinal Richelieu (1585); Luigi Galvani (1737); William Bligh (1754); Leo Nikolaevich Tolstoy (1828); Max Reinhardt (1873); James Agate (1877); James Hilton (1900); Cesare Pavese (1908); Michael Aldridge (1920); Cliff Robertson (1925); Chaim Topol (1935); Richard Sharpe (1938); Otis Redding (1941); Billy Preston (1946); John Curry (1949); Michael Keaton (1951); Angela Cartwright (1952); Hugh Grant (1960); Henry Thomas (1971).

Significant Events and Anniversaries: This is a day that indicates a certain willingness for self-sacrifice in a wider cause, as was variously demonstrated when: King James IV of Scotland lost his life while fighting the English at the Battle of Flodden Field (1513); after having claimed the territory known as Newfoundland, the English navigator Sir Humphrey Gilbert drowned on his return journey, off the Azores (1583); California joined the Union of the United States (1850); combined French and British troops forced Germany's retreat at the First Battle of the Marne during World War I (1914); and, during World War II, Allied forces disembarked at Salerno in Italy and engaged in fierce combat with the occupying German troops (1943). The strong desire for autonomy that is a further feature of September 9 was reflected when: North Korea proclaimed itself a "people's republic" (1948); and Czechoslovakian tennis player Martina Navratilova defected to the West (1975).

Planetary Influences
Ruling planet: Mercury.
Second decan: Personal planet is Saturn.

Sacred and Cultural Significance
Tao Yuan-Ming honored in China with the drinking of chrysanthemum wine.
Saints' day: Gorgonius (dates unknown); Ciaran of Clonmacnoise (c.512–c.545); Omer (d. c.699); Bettelin (8th century AD); Wulfhilda (d. c.1000); Peter Claver (1580–1654), patron saint of people of African origin and race relations.

Born on September 9, 1585, as Armand Jean du Plessis, Cardinal Richelieu had a predilection both for intellectual exploration and for seeking to implement progressive innovations, typical characteristics of those born on this day. These traits were evidenced by his effective rule as First Minister of France and his founding of the French Academy.

Planetary Influences
Ruling planet: Mercury.
Second decan: Personal planet is Saturn.

Sacred and Cultural Significance
Saints' day: Finnian of Moville (d. 579);
Frithestan (d. c.932); Nicholas of Tolentino
(1245–1305).

*Golfer Arnold Palmer was born on this day
in 1929. Demonstrating the practical skills
and focused approach that are starred for
those born on this day, he has had a long
and successful golfing career, winning, inter
alia, the U.S. Masters four times within
a period of seven years (1958–1964).
He is generally credited with changing golf
from an exclusive sport to a popular pastime.*

SEPTEMBER 10

The aura that surrounds September 10 people is that of capability, and indeed these are focused, resourceful and thoughtful individuals who prefer steering a steady and controlled path through life rather than acting impulsively. Motivated by the urge to bring order and implement progress where before there was chaos and unproductiveness, their attention is drawn to those subjects and situations where they adjudge improvements, thereby hoping that through their efforts they will make a real contribution to the welfare of others. Their typical approach is to draw on their clear-sighted perspicacity to make an objective and realistic assessment of the existing scenario, and then, utilizing their practical and organizational talents, construct a watertight strategy designed to facilitate advancement through the support of a stable, supportive system. Their dealings with others are similarly characterized by their predilection for creating and directing effective interpersonal frameworks, and they thus make responsible team captains who, as well as being goal oriented, manifest genuine concern for those under their aegis.

Although those born on this day favor a sensible and considered approach, this does not mean that they are dull and unimaginative individuals—far from it: being intellectually inquisitive types, they are fascinated by unusual and innovative topics and people, and even if they do not make a career of exploring such subjects—as writers, artists or academics, for instance—they will still be attracted to boldly individualistic characters. Indeed, being defined by mutual tolerance and respect, any relationships that they may form with such polar opposites will often be remarkably successful.

VIRTUES: September 10 individuals have a love of creating orderly structures and strategies with which to bring about direct progress intended to be of wider benefit to others. Blessed with incisive far-seeing intellect, practical skills and the gift of patient determination, they have outstanding potential to achieve their aims.
VICES: Their marked orientation toward ensuring the welfare of others, as well as their propensity to divide their energies equally between their work and their personal relationships, may ultimately prove physically—and, more importantly—emotionally debilitating, for those born on this day may tend to place their own needs last.
VERDICT: Although these people understand the importance of maintaining an even balance between their professional and private lives, their tendency to direct their attention and efforts externally may cause them to neglect their own well-being. They should therefore allow themselves more time to relax and be themselves.

On This Day
Famous Births: Thomas Sydenham (1624); Giovanni Domenico Tiepolo (1727); John Soane (1753); Mungo Park (1771); Robert Koldewey (1855); Prince Ranjitsinhji (1872); Cyril Connolly (1903); Terence O'Neill and Robert Wise (1914); Beryl Cook (1926); Arnold Palmer (1929); Charles Kuralt and Roger Maris (1934); José Feliciano (1945); Amy Irving (1953).

Significant Events and Anniversaries: This is a day that highlights concerted practical action in pursuit of what is regarded as the common good, as was evidenced when: the English troops of Edward Seymour, Duke of Somerset—motivated by his desire to unite England and Scotland through the proposed marriage of Edward VI to Mary, Queen of Scots—defeated their Scottish enemy at the Battle of Pinkie (1547); the British Royal Air Force, the R.A.F., dropped over 100,000 bombs on the town of Düsseldorf hoping to inflict crippling damage on Germany's industrial infrastructure and thereby end World War II (1942); and Hungary opened its western frontier, thus allowing thousands of East German refugees access to the West (1989). This is also a day that indicates the deployment of great organizational skills in the quest for progress, as was reflected when the Treaty of St. Germain was signed, giving the Habsburg Empire's non-Austrian former territories to Czechoslovakia, Yugoslavia, Poland and Romania (1919).

SEPTEMBER 11

In common with the majority of their Virgo fellows, those born on this day have the ability to think clearly and independently. The empathy of many September 11 people is aroused by their observation of the plight of the disadvantaged, resulting in a fraternal feeling that instills in them the determination to improve their circumstances by whatever means they can. And, indeed, they have a veritable armory of weapons at their disposal, including their pronounced gift for communication—both verbal and literary—and their highly developed organizational skills, as well as the courage of their convictions, which compels them to battle on, even in the face of stiff opposition. Such inclinations and talents augur especially well for their potential success as politicians, lawyers or social campaigners, although many September 11 individuals may choose to exert their influence by less direct—though no less powerful—artistic means, as writers, for example, a propensity that is even more marked if they were also born in the Chinese year of the goat.

Their urge to help those around them may thus take a somewhat radical form, but may equally be manifested in the determined defense of existing social systems. For in many respects those born on this day are traditionalists, whose love of order may lead them to lend their support to tried-and-tested conventions. Certainly, September 11 people believe in the virtues of stable familial relationships for the mutual support that they offer, and typically make concerned friends, partners and parents, although their forceful opinions and moral rectitude may cause conflict with their children.

VIRTUES: Those born on this day are remarkably perceptive types who employ their observational powers to identify areas in need of improvement and then formulate clear-sighted and practical strategies for change.

VICES: These people have a tendency to tenaciously—even stubbornly—adhere to their opinions regardless of the antagonism that they may thereby engender. Although this propensity is generally laudable, it may not always be appropriate, particularly within personal relationships.

VERDICT: Although their intentions are usually of the best, September 11 people should try to ensure that they do not alienate their nearest and dearest—and thus end up emotionally isolated—by insisting that they conform to beliefs and behavioral patterns with which they may not agree: instead, they should allow them to develop their own criteria for living their lives.

On This Day

Famous Births: Pierre de Ronsard (1524); James Thomson (1700); William Sidney Porter ("O. Henry") (1862); James Jeans (1877); D.H. Lawrence (1885); Herbert Lom, Ferdinand Marcos and Jessica Mitford (1917); Brian DePalma (1940); Lola Falana (1946); Roger Uttley (1949); Barry Sheene (1950); Virginia Madsen (1961); Kristy McNichol (1962); Harry Connick, Jr. (1967).

Significant Events and Anniversaries: The influences that govern September 11 indicate a strong determination to defend or promote strongly held collective social, political or national values, and this day marks the anniversary of: the trouncing of Edward I's invading English army at the hands of Scottish patriots under William Wallace at the Battle of Stirling (1297); the victory of the combined forces of the English Duke of Marlborough and the Austrian Prince Eugène over their French foe, led by Marshal Villars, at the Battle of Malplaquet during the War of the Spanish Succession (1709); the defeat of George Washington's American troops by the British army led by General Howe at the Battle of Brandywine Creek during the American War of Independence (1777); the deposition of the democratically elected government of Chile's President Salvador Allende by a military junta led by General Augusto Pinochet (1973); and the murder of the defector Georgi Markov in London by a Bulgarian secret agent wielding a poison-tipped umbrella (1978). There is also artistic potential inherent in this day, as was demonstrated when U.S. musician W. C. Handy published the "St. Louis Blues" (1914); and Igor Stravinsky's *The Rake's Progress* was premiered (1951).

Planetary Influences
Ruling planet: Mercury.
Second decan: Personal planet is Saturn.

Sacred and Cultural Significance
In Egypt, the Day of Queens honors Hatshepsut, Nefertiti and Cleopatra.
Saints' day: Protus and Hyacinth (dates unknown); Deiniol (d. c.584).

Honored in Egypt on this Day of Queens, Cleopatra was born in 69 BC, the third daughter of King Ptolemy XII. Ascending the throne at the age of eighteen and remembered for dramatically taking her own life (through an asp bite) at the age of thirty-nine, her story has been so romanticized by later writers that it is hard to recover the historical perspective behind the myth.

VIRGO

Planetary Influences
Ruling planet: Mercury.
Third decan: Personal planet is Venus.

Sacred and Cultural Significance
Saint's day: Ailbe (6th century AD).

Born on September 12, 1913, James Cleveland Owens, popularly known as Jesse Owens, was to dominate athletics during the mid 1930s, setting five world records in 1935 and winning four gold medals at the Berlin Olympics. His determination and driving motivation are characteristic of those born on this day, and were strongly augmented by his birth in the Chinese year of the ox.

SEPTEMBER 12

Never the types to indulge in subterfuge, manipulation or power games, those born on this day are straightforward and direct, their primary motivation being to attain their aims and to do so as effectively as possible. Stimulated by their quest for knowledge and, being of an independent turn of mind, they prefer to seek out facts for themselves and then draw their own conclusions rather than unquestioningly to accept conventional truths. Their intellectual approach is typically characterized by their incisive ability to grasp abstract concepts, their perceptiveness and their capacity to marshal their findings into logically constructed strategies for progress. And, once these have been reached, they will not only adhere to their conclusions with single-minded tenacity, but also seek to persuade others of their veracity—often with considerable success, since September 12 people have a marked facility with words, and because others cannot help but respect their sincerity. Their social concern and desire to instruct and thereby assist others suits them particularly well to careers as educators, for example, or in the public service.

Despite their genuine urge to exert their influence over those around them—or society as a whole—these are somewhat solitary individuals, who have a strong need for periods of privacy in which they can be alone with their thoughts, undisturbed by the demands of others. Yet they are also loyal and supportive friends, partners and family members, who, moreover, respect the individuality of their nearest and dearest and will rarely attempt to impose their opinions on those closest to them if this would be hurtful.

VIRTUES: September 12 people are perhaps defined by the dual nature of their characters: on the one hand, their need for personal autonomy and, on the other, their desire to pass on the beneficial fruits of their discoveries to others. Endowed with objective and rational intellects, as well as with communication skills, they are also good motivators.
VICES: Going hand-in-hand with their prerequisite for intellectual freedom is their need for privacy, for occasions when they can pursue their interests without distraction or disruption. Their highly developed social responsibility may, however, lead them to neglect this fundamental requirement, to the ultimate detriment of their emotional well-being.
VERDICT: Those born on this day often find it hard to turn down either overt or covert requests for help, but it is nevertheless vital that they do not allow themselves to become overwhelmed by the demands of others. They should therefore learn to prioritize their own needs, and, when necessary, encourage others to address their problems independently.

On This Day
Famous Births: Richard Marsh Hoe (1812); Richard Gordon Gatling (1818); Herbert Asquith (1852); H.L. Mencken (1880); Maurice Chevalier (1888); Irène Joliot-Curie (1897); Ben Blue (1901); Margaret Hamilton (1902); Louis MacNeice (1907); Jesse Owens (1913); Han Suyin (1917); Ian Holm and George Jones (1931); Wesley Hall (1937); Linda Gray (1940); Maria Muldaur (1943); Barry White (1944); Peter Scolari (1954); Richard Ward (1957).

Significant Events and Anniversaries: A day that highlights inspirational verbal talents, September 12 commemorates the anniversary of the British navy's attack on Fort McHenry near Baltimore, an event that caused Francis Scott Key to pen the words of "The Star-spangled Banner" (1814). September 12 also indicates the urge to direct others along what is perceived to be the optimum progressive path, a propensity that is paralleled in the realm of both social innovation and national politics and which was variously demonstrated on this day when: the world's first female police officer, Alice Stebbins, was hired by the Los Angeles Police Department (1910); Nikita Khruschev became First Secretary of the Soviet Communist Party (1953); two British trawlers were sunk by Icelandic gunboats, during the "Cod War" over fishing rights in the North Sea (1972); Ethiopian emperor Haile Selassie was deposed by a military coup (1974); and South African civil rights' campaigner Steve Biko was made to pay the price for his anti-apartheid principles when he died while in police detention (1977).

SEPTEMBER 13

T̲hose born on September 13 are remarkably self-sufficient individuals who, despite their somewhat abstract interest in humanity as a global entity, may appear to others to be remote, even standoffish figures. This is not an entirely fair assessment, however, for these people are sensitive and may be deeply moved by their strong feelings of empathy with those who are miserable or in trouble. It is just that they would prefer to be able to pursue their intellectual interests (and thereby contribute to human knowledge) undisturbed by the trivia of everyday existence. In many respects, those born on this day may often be characterized as workaholics and, although otherwise generally positive and good-humored, grow restless and tetchy if circumstances prevent them from immersing themselves in a particularly absorbing undertaking. Blessed with keen concentration and application, they will rarely abandon a project or problem until they have completed or solved it to their own satisfaction.

These individuals will thrive in any professional field where they are both constantly challenged and allowed total autonomy; their problem-solving talents make them especially suited to scientific or business careers, although their original and imaginative approach also augurs well for writing and research. And, if they do work as part of a team, they are only happy if they can direct others; hard task-masters, they lead by example and expect the same level of vigor, dedication and goal-orientation from others as they themselves demonstrate. This is also true of their personal relationships (even more so if they are men), within which they have a tendency to claim their own right of freedom while seeking to control the lives of those closest to them.

VIRTUES: Those born on this day are irresistibly attracted to challenging situations and subjects where they can test their intellectual talents and ultimately achieve pioneering breakthroughs. When their interest is stimulated, they display their strong determination, originality and acute perception in their drive to realize their visions.
VICES: Their self-reliance and all-absorbing fascination with their professional and intellectual concerns can lead these individuals to neglect their own prerequisite for the relaxing benefits of a rich personal life and—perhaps more pertinently—the more profound needs of those closest to them in terms of their time and attention.
VERDICT: If they are not to become isolated and socially out of touch, it is crucial that September 13 people recognize the importance of maintaining an even balance between their professional and personal lives. They should learn occasionally to resist the urge to respond to an intellectual siren call in favor of nurturing their relationships with their nearest and dearest, thus reaping immeasurable emotional rewards.

On This Day

Famous Births: Oliver Evans (1735); Clara Schumann (1819); Walter Reed (1851); Milton S. Hershey (1857); John Pershing (1860); Arthur Henderson (1863); Arnold Schoenberg (1874); Sherwood Anderson (1876); Robert Robinson (1886); J.B. Priestley (1894); Claudette Colbert (1903); Roald Dahl and Dick Haymes (1916); Mel Torme (1925); Bela Karolyi (1942); Jacqueline Bisset and Midget Farrelly (1944); Nell Carter (1948); Ben Savage (1980).

Significant Events and Anniversaries: September 13 highlights staying power, as was demonstrated in the realm of warfare when: at the Battle of Marathon, Greek forces repelled the invasion of the Persian army under King Darius I (490 BC); and the British army, commanded by General James Wolfe, defeated the defending French forces under the Marquis de Montcalm on the Plains of Abraham in Canada, capturing Quebec (1759). Also a day of progressive inclinations, September 13 marks the anniversary of: New York's (short-lived) elevation to the status of the U.S.A.'s federal capital (1788); and the establishment of the world's first official baseball club, New York's Knickerbocker Club (1845). And, confirming the day's artistic potential, this was the day on which: Austrian composer Oscar Straus's operetta *The Chocolate Soldier* was first staged (1909); and Little Richard recorded his seminal hit "Tutti Frutti" (1955).

Planetary Influences
Ruling planet: Mercury.
Third decan: Personal planet is Venus.

Sacred and Cultural Significance
The ceremony of the Lighting of the Fire held in Egypt to commemorate All Souls' Day.
Saint's day: John Chrysostom (347–407), patron saint of preachers.

Writer and World War II fighter pilot Roald Dahl was born on September 13, 1916. His original and imaginative approach, typical of those born on this day, was demonstrated in the bizarre elements of his children's stories James and the Giant Peach *(1961) and* Charlie and the Chocolate Factory *(1964). A Chinese dragon, Dahl was naturally witty and independent.*

SEPTEMBER 14

✦✦

Planetary Influences
Ruling planet: Mercury.
Third decan: Personal planet is Venus.

Sacred and Cultural Significance
In ancient Rome, the Feast of the Holy Cross.
Saints' day: The exaltation of the Holy Cross; Cornelius (d. 253) and Cyprian (c.200–58).

Illustrator and cartoonist Charles Dana Gibson was born on this day in 1867. Possessed of the acutely critical eye that characterizes September 14 people, he drew society cartoons for such periodicals as Life, Scribner's *and* Harper's *and, through his celebrated Gibson Girl drawings (depicted below), he created an idealized image of the American woman.*

Perhaps the primary preoccupation of those born on this day is with bringing order to any system (or person) that they suspect is not realizing its maximum potential. Possessed of an acutely critical eye—the result of both their incisive intellects and their observant natures—they find it easy to identify areas in which the component parts are imbalanced or deficient in some way. Because their urge to plan, organize, control and thereby institute and maintain smoothly running and effective programs is so strong—and even more so if they were born in the Chinese year of the ox—they are able to take charge of situations quickly, work out optimum strategies for success and then direct the actions of others. September 14 individuals are thus natural leaders who pursue their goals with a determined sense of purpose (and expect others to do the same), and will flourish in any career where they can harmonize discord and bring about tangible results—the scientific, political and legal professions are particularly well starred, as are city planning and the building trades.

Yet these individuals are not totally geared toward intellectual or professional pursuits: to the contrary, they innately understand the importance of counterbalancing the pressures of work with a full personal life. Many of them are somewhat sensuous types, who appreciate beauty in all its manifold forms and possess a lively sense of fun. Responsible friends and family members (and totally devoted, if at times controlling, parents), they are also good conversationalists and sociable types, who enjoy surrounding themselves with people and hosting well-organized social entertainments.

VIRTUES: These energetic people typically have two sides to their natures: on the one hand they are disciplined, orderly and efficiency oriented, and on the other they are gregarious and pleasure-loving. They bring their perceptive, practical and steadfast qualities to bear on all their activities, and are remarkably talented organizers.
VICES: Although their strongly critical faculties are usually extremely effective when employed in professional pursuits, their inherent tendency to find fault with the behavior, opinions or methods of others—however positive the intention—can wreak havoc upon their relationships with those closest to them.
VERDICT: September 14 people appreciate the importance of balancing their intellectual and emotional needs, as well as their professional and private lives. They should, however, beware of adopting an overly controlling and critical approach toward their nearest and dearest, a propensity that may cause them to be regarded with resentment and result in their closest relationships eroding through the loss of spontaneous warmth.

On This Day
Famous Births: Agrippa von Nettesheim (1486); Michael Haydn (1737); Luigi Cherubini (1760); Alexander von Humboldt (1769); Ivan Pavlov (1849); Charles Dana Gibson (1867); Margaret Sanger (1883); Jan Masaryk (1886); Peter Scott (1909); Jack Hawkins (1910); Clayton Moore (1914); Zoe Caldwell and Harvey Presnell (1933); Nicol Williamson (1938); Joey Heatherton (1944); Sam Neill (1947); Joe Penny (1956); Faith Ford (1964).

Significant Events and Anniversaries: The institution of well-organized systems is highlighted by this day, on which: Miguel Primo de Rivera took charge of the Spanish government, thereby becoming virtual dictator of Spain (1923); after years of careful research and preparation, the Soviet space probe *Lunik II* became the first spacecraft to land on the moon (1959); and Pope Paul VI created the first American saint, Elizabeth Bayley Seton, in recognition of the work carried out by the American Sisters of Charity that she had founded (1975). Conversely, this day also indicates that success cannot usually be attained without order, as was demonstrated when, upon reaching Moscow, Napoleon discovered that its citizens had burned the city to the ground, rendering his feat a bitter victory (1812). September 14 is governed by the element of earth, which perhaps favored golfer Tom Morris when he achieved the first recorded hole-in-one shot at Prestwick in Scotland (1868).

SEPTEMBER 15

* *

In many respects those born on this day can be characterized as specialists, for they are drawn to a single area of interest (their choice often having been made in childhood) and seek to become masters of their field. The subjects that typically fascinate September 15 individuals are those where the scope for exploration is boundless and where their quest for discovery can therefore lead them into previously uncharted territories. Even though they are intellectually curious, these are rarely restless or roving types. Once they have alighted upon a topic that absorbs their attention they will devote their energies exclusively to its study, probing, testing and amassing a wealth of information. Their inclinations and simultaneously imaginative and organized methods suit September 15 people for a variety of professions, from scientific research to the arts. They are gifted directors of others, who never lose sight of the wider picture or, indeed, surrender their own inherent requirement for autonomy of thought and action.

Others admire their technical expertise, as well as their determination and clarity of vision, but may be somewhat intimidated by their refusal to compromise their convictions or integrity. Although they may appear to be somewhat solitary figures, they are by no means solely oriented to their work, for they value the strong emotional bonds that they form with their family and friends. As sensual individuals, they are moved by music, the beauty of art and the flavors of gourmet cuisine. And it is primarily in order to indulge such tastes, as well to support their families, that those born on this day appreciate the material rewards that their professional success brings them.

VIRTUES: September 15 people possess independent and investigative minds, and complement their relish for originality with organization, discipline and tenacity, with the result that they have the potential to make a truly innovative and substantial mark on the world. They are also pleasure-loving and affectionate types.

VICES: The combination of their wide-ranging interests, dedication to their visions, and determination to live a full and varied life may cause those born on this day to overstretch themselves—both emotionally and physically—a tendency that may be aggravated by their perfectionism and high expectations.

VERDICT: Although these individuals appreciate the importance of maintaining a balanced range of interests, if they are not to become obsessive or stale, they should recognize that they are not superhuman and may not be able to devote their energies to every area of their lives without becoming exhausted.

On This Day

Famous Births: Trajan (53); Titus Oates (1649); James Fenimore Cooper (1789); William H. Taft (1857); Bruno Walter (1876); Hans Arp (1887); Robert Benchley (1889); Agatha Christie (1890): Jean Renoir (1894); Umberto II of Italy (1904); Fay Wray (1907); Margaret Lockwood (1916); Jackie Cooper (1922); Brian Henderson (1931); Jessye Norman (1945); Tommy Lee Jones and Oliver Stone (1946); Dan Marino (1961); Prince Henry of Britain (1984).

Significant Events and Anniversaries: This is a day that highlights technical innovations, as was evidenced when: the Liverpool and Manchester railroad was inaugurated in England; unfortunately William Huskisson, chief of the Board of Trade, was struck by the *Rocket* locomotive, giving him the dubious distinction of being the first person to be killed by a train (1830); the first tanks (designed by Ernest Swinton) to be used in warfare went into action for the British Army during World War I's Battle of the Somme (1916); German bombers subjected British cities to their most devastating bombardment during World War II's Battle of Britain (1940); and the world's largest museum dedicated to movie-making, the Museum of the Moving Image, was opened in London, England (1988). September 15 also indicates the uncompromising promotion of ideological convictions, as was demonstrated when: Alexander Kerensky pronounced Russia a Communist republic (1917); and hostility between Beirut's Christian and Muslim factions erupted into civil war (1975).

Planetary Influences
Ruling planet: Mercury.
Third decan: Personal planet is Venus.

Sacred and Cultural Significance
Saints' day: Nicomedes (dates unknown); Mirin (7th century AD); Adam of Caithness (11th–12th centuries); Catherine of Genoa (1447–1510).

Undoubtedly a master of her genre, writer Agatha Christie was born on September 15, 1890. Complementing her originality with a pronounced streak of discipline and tenacity, a combination strongly featured for those born on this day, she wrote over seventy detective novels.

Planetary Influences
Ruling planet: Mercury.
Third decan: Personal planet is Venus.

Sacred and Cultural Significance
National day of Mexico.
Saints' day: Geminianus (dates unknown);
Cornelius (d. 253) and Cyprian (c.200–58);
Edith (961–84).

Reflecting the innovative vision and strong desire for autonomy starred for this day, the Pilgrim Fathers set sail in the Mayflower *from Plymouth, England, on September 16, 1620.*

SEPTEMBER 16

Exuberant and energetic, positive and progressive, September 16 people are physical and intellectual live-wires who are fueled by the urge to push the boundaries of human knowledge forward and thereby blaze an innovatory trail to light the way for others. Their questing compulsion is in part due to their humanitarian principles and desire to assist others, but is also the result of their mercurial inquisitiveness and relish for discovering and experiencing novel concepts and situations. Their urge to make progress is a forceful one, and once they have settled upon a subject that absorbs their interest (and this may not be immediately evident, given their wide range of interests), they will typically harness their considerable vigor and talents—including their originality, objectiveness and organizational skills—in their tenacious drive to effect a breakthrough. Achieving concrete results is of great importance to them—as is receiving recognition for their efforts—and they are therefore particularly suited to financial planning, scientific or artistic pursuits, or manufacturing trades where they can not only demonstrate the fruits of their labors, but also inspire or benefit others and make a name for themselves.

Although their intellectual independence and refusal to be bound by convention augurs well for their ability to work autonomously, those born on this day are strongly oriented toward others, wishing both to share their knowledge and to derive pleasure from the stimulation of social interaction. The same is true of their personal liaisons, where they assume mentoring roles (especially if they are women), and enliven their relationships with an infectious *joie de vivre*.

VIRTUES: Those born on this day are optimistic and vigorous people whose actions are driven by their sense of adventure and desire for achievement. Their aims are rarely selfish, but are instead motivated by their desire to make a positive contribution to humanity. They are independent and well organized, and their positive, upbeat natures make them popular as friends and colleagues.
VICES: The inherent risk in these individuals' searching approach and appetite for novelty is that their attention may be too widely spread, thus preventing them from concentrating on specific areas of interest. Unless their intellects are stimulated, boredom and restlessness may also become potential problems.
VERDICT: September 16 people must ensure that they moderate their propensity to be attracted to the exploration of any exciting new concept that hoves into view. They would benefit from examining their priorities and then concentrating their prodigious energies upon the subjects that will bring them the greatest satisfaction.

On This Day
Famous Births: King Henry V of England (1387); Thomas Barnes (1785); Edward Marshall Hall and Andrew Bonar Law (1858); Nadia Boulanger (1887); Karl Doenitz (1891); Alexander Korda (1893); Joe Venuti (1905); Allen Funt (1914); Lee Kuan Yew (1923); Lauren Bacall (1924); Charlie Byrd, Charles James Haughey and B.B. King (1925); Peter Falk (1927); Ed Begley, Jr. (1949); Robin Yount (1955); David Copperfield.

Significant Events and Anniversaries: A day that indicates a strong desire for autonomy, September 16 marks Malaya's achievement of independence from Britain and the proclamation of its new status as the Federation of Malaysia (1963). September 16 also highlights innovative visions supported by practical and technical expertise, and on this day: General Motors, the giant American automobile company, was formed as a result of the merger of the Buick and Oldsmobile operations (1908); the widescreen CinemaScope film process was demonstrated for the first time by 20th Century Fox when it screened the movie *The Robe* (1953); and, in apartheid-dominated South Africa, John Khani became the first African actor to take the leading role in Shakespeare's *Othello*, in a brave production directed by Janet Suzman (1987).

SEPTEMBER 17

Such is their focus and drive that those born on this day frequently appear to be powerfully single-minded individuals who will allow nothing or no one to stand in the way of their progress. In many respects this assessment is an accurate one, for these people are not only remarkably goal oriented, but they also combine their capacity for concentration, logical thought and intellectual and physical vigor with their somewhat stubborn tenacity to generate an almost irresistible force. Yet the personalities of those born on this day are not as straightforward as they may appear on superficial examination, for as well as being linear thinkers, their intellectual curiosity also endows them with the ability to think laterally, while they are also blessed with sensitivity and perceptiveness, qualities that make them extremely empathetic toward others. The combination of their humanitarian instincts and organizational talents may lead them to pursue professions where they can assist or enlighten others, possibly through creative endeavors. They also make gifted and generous team leaders.

Similar feelings of concern and responsibility for the well-being of others characterize their relationships with their nearest and dearest, toward whom September 17 people typically assume a protective stance. Although they rarely express their emotions openly, they demonstrate their affection for those closest to them through nurturing and practical action. Although initially shy, many are lively companions, who are stimulated by artistic pursuits (to which some choose to devote their careers) and also have an infectious sense of fun.

VIRTUES: September 17 people are blessed with a decisive sense of purpose, and when working toward the realization of their ambitions employ their acutely perceptive intelligence and their talents for organizing and motivating others. Their actions are typically fueled by the desire to bring about concrete progress with which to benefit others.
VICES: Because they are somewhat private and self-disciplined types, those born on this day are not given to broadcasting their profounder emotions freely. By adopting such a controlled approach, however, they may bottle up their negative feelings until frustration causes them to be released in a dramatically destructive fashion.
VERDICT: In order to avoid both physical exhaustion and emotional stress, it is vital that those born on this day learn not only to relax but also to share their thoughts and feelings with their loved ones to a greater degree.

On This Day
Famous Births: William Carlos Williams (1883); Isaac Wolfson (1897); Francis Chichester (1901); Frederick Ashton (1904); Junius Jaywardene (1906); Chaim Herzog (1918); Roddy MacDowell (1928); Stirling Moss (1929); Anne Bancroft (1931); Dorothy Loudon (1933); Maureen Connolly (1934); Ken Kesey (1935); Billy Bonds (1946); Lol Creme (1947); John Ritter (1948); Cassandra "Elvira" Peterson (1951); Yunupingu Djarrtjuntjun (1956).

Significant Events and Anniversaries: On a day that indicates progress toward the greater good, September 17 commemorates the approval of the draft U.S. Constitution by members of the Constitution Convention (1787). This day also highlights a willingness to employ forceful action for change, a propensity that was demonstrated when: Union General George McClellan, repulsed the invasion of Confederate troops under General Robert E. Lee at Antietam, during the American Civil War (1862); British paratroopers landed at Arnhem, in The Netherlands, at the start of Operation Market Garden during World War II (1944); members of the Fighters for the Freedom of Israel guerrilla movement, a Jewish Zionist group also known as the Stern Gang, assassinated the Swedish United Nations' mediator, Count Folke Bernadotte, in Palestine (1948); and Turkish prime minister, Adnan Menderes, was executed on the orders of General Cemal Gursel, the leader of the military coup that had ousted him (1961). The artistic and technical affinities that are featured by this day were reflected when R.C.A.-Victor revealed to the world its development of long-playing records (1931).

Planetary Influences
Ruling planet: Mercury.
Third decan: Personal planet is Venus.

Sacred and Cultural Significance
Demeter honored in ancient Greece with a festival of secret rites.
Saints' day: Lambert (c.635–c.705), patron saint of children and Liège, Belgium; Hildegard (1098–1179); Robert Bellarmarmine (1542–1621).

Honored in ancient Greece on this day, Demeter, goddess of fertility and the harvest, was revered as guardian of the crops.

Planetary Influences
Ruling planet: Mercury.
Third decan: Personal planet is Venus.

Sacred and Cultural Significance
National day of Chile; in Berkshire,
England, the Scouring of the White Horse.
Saint's day: Joseph of Copertino (1603–63),
patron saint of astronauts, air passengers
and aviators.

*Born Greta Lovisa Gustafsson in Stockholm,
Sweden, on September 18, 1905, and famed
for her often-repeated statement that "I want
to be alone," actress Greta Garbo's reclusive
nature provides a somewhat extreme example
of the deeply private nature and introspection
of those born on this day. As a Chinese snake,
her discretion and reserve were reinforced, but
her sensitivity and creative talents were evident
throughout her career.*

SEPTEMBER 18

★ ★

Those born on this day are deeply private and introspective individuals, who nevertheless feel compelled occasionally to emerge from their self-imposed solitude in order to share the fruits of their labors with others. The planets that govern their day of birth exert a particularly powerful influence on their psyches, Mercury endowing them with a strong urge for intellectual exploration and discovery, and Venus blessing them with profound sensuality and a highly developed appreciation of beauty. And when these two inclinations achieve their highest level of harmonious interaction, September 18 people have the potential to initiate truly innovative and inspirational advances that will excite the admiration of others and may even influence generations to come. Their natural affinity with all things artistic augurs especially well for their success as writers, musicians, artists or movie-makers, while their equally strong attraction to the acquisition of technical knowledge suits them also for scientific pursuits. Although the focus of their professional endeavors fully absorbs their attention, their ultimate aims are typically to benefit humanity as a whole.

It is this dual propensity to help others advance while at the same time concentrating upon the concepts that fascinate them that may cause September 18 people's personal lives to be troubled. Because they exude genuinely empathetic concern, and are such attractive and interesting individuals, others are drawn to them. Yet in many respects the interest that they show in other individuals assumes a somewhat abstract rather than direct form (a tendency that is even more pronounced if they are men) and they therefore shy away from having to assume responsibility for the happiness of others, particularly if this would mean having to divert their attention from their intellectual quests.

VIRTUES: Sensitive and artistically inclined, intellectually inquisitive and progressive, September 18 individuals are fueled by an almost irresistible desire to immerse themselves in their private world of discovery, hoping to contribute new knowledge to the world.
VICES: These people have a predilection for devoting their exclusive attention to the study of those abstract concepts and pursuits that fascinate them so greatly, a tendency that inevitably causes them voluntarily to isolate themselves from others, and one that can be hard on the emotional needs of those closest to them.
VERDICT: In order to fulfill their fundamental requirement for emotional support from their nearest and dearest, those born on this day should recognize that they may frequently adopt potentially damaging exclusionary tactics toward others: they should therefore strive to moderate their approach and participate more actively in their interpersonal relationships.

On This Day
Famous Births: Samuel Johnson (1709); J.B.L. Foucault (1819); Arthur Benjamin (1893); Fay Compton (1894); John George Diefenbaker (1895); Greta Garbo (1905); Edwin M. McMillan (1907); Kwame Nkrumah (1909); Jack Cardiff (1914); Jack Warden (1920); Bob Dylan (1933); Robert Blake (1934); John Spencer (1935); Frankie Avalon (1939); Peter Shilton (1949).

Significant Events and Anniversaries: This is a day that indicates the desire to impart knowledge to a wider audience, as was demonstrated when: the first issue of the *New York Times* was published (1851); and Irish Nazi sympathizer William Joyce, soon to be known as "Lord Haw-Haw," made the first of a series of what the British authorities regarded as dangerously subversive broadcasts to its citizens shortly after the outbreak of World War II (1939). September 18 also highlights strong humanitarian and democratic concerns, and this day commemorates: the anniversary of the British king George V's granting of his assent to the Irish Home Rule bill (1914); and France's abolition of the guillotine as a method of capital punishment (1981). Tragically, this was also the day on which Dag Hammarskjold, secretary-general of the United Nations—an organization dedicated to enforcing international peace and cooperation—was killed along with 130 other passengers when their airplane crashed in what was then North Rhodesia (Zambia) (1961).

SEPTEMBER 19

September 19 individuals are vitally interested in everything that crosses their paths, their mercurial minds latching onto every novel concept that presents itself. Their keen eye for beauty and warm sensuality endow them with a more aesthetic—and frequently also rather earthy—disposition. They are not content to sit quietly on the sidelines of the game of life; instead they throw themselves enthusiastically into the stimulating pursuit of new experiences, indulging their taste for the unusual and original (and particularly so if they were also born in the Chinese year of the horse). Yet despite their versatile interests, those born on this day are rarely flighty types, for they are also gripped by the desire to transcend the superficial and move into more serious, progressive realms, thereby hoping to add to their own lexicon of knowledge and to benefit the wider world by means of their efforts. Innately humanitarian, as well as being blessed with the potential to make a significant impact as ingenious scientists or artists working in a variety of areas, these are multitalented individuals who will flourish in any profession they choose, provided that their attention and interest are constantly occupied.

A similar combination of concern for others, sociability and *joie de vivre* characterizes their interpersonal relationships, and their dynamic and lively personalities in turn typically draw others into their magnetic orbit. Despite their gregariousness, however, September 19 people manage to devote special attention to those closest to them, maintaining easy and relaxed relationships, while at the same time protecting their own interests.

VIRTUES: Such is their wide-ranging curiosity and relish for searching out knowledge and new experiences, that there is very little that escapes the attention and investigation of those energetic individuals born on this day. As well as being anxious to add to their personal understanding, they enjoy helping others.
VICES: Inherent in their all-encompassing inquisitiveness is the danger that these people may spread their energies too thinly, thereby becoming exhausted and frustrated.
VERDICT: While their generally positive and active orientation toward every concept, situation or person they encounter is one of the greatest strengths of those born on this day, at the same time it may ultimately sabotage their effectiveness. They should try to develop a more focused sense of priority as to whatever it is that will bring them all-round fulfillment, and ensure that their attention is not diverted from this ambition.

On This Day

Famous Births: Lajos Kossuth (1802); George Cadbury (1839); William H. Lever (1851); William Golding (1911); Emil Zatopek (1922); Penelope Mortimer (1928); Derek Nimmo (1932); David McCallum (1933); Brian Epstein (1934); Zandra Rhodes and Paul Williams (1940); "Mama" Cass Elliot (1943); Randolph Mantooth (1945); Rosie Casals and Jeremy Irons (1948); "Twiggy" (1949); Joan Lunden (1950); Kevin Hooks (1958); Jim Abbott (1967).

Significant Events and Anniversaries: September 19 is a day that highlights the investigation and often realization of highly original aims, and marks the anniversary of two events that confirmed this promise: the first ascent of a hot-air balloon carrying passengers: the French Montgolfier brothers, a rooster, a duck and a sheep (1783); and the patenting of the carpet-sweeper by U.S. inventor Melville Bissell (1876). This day also indicates a willingness to take action on behalf of the perceived benefit of others, as was demonstrated when: during the Hundred Years War fought between England and France over the ownership of French territory, the English army under Edward, the Black Prince, won a notable victory over the French at the Battle of Poitiers, taking the French king, Jean II, captive (1356); New Zealand took a pioneering constitutional step by granting its female citizens the right to vote (1893); and Argentinian dictator Juan Perón was deposed as a result of military coup (1955). The exuberance and artistic potential indicated by this day were reflected when U.S. musician Chubby Checker's single "The Twist" spiraled into the U.S. pop charts (1960).

Planetary Influences
Ruling planets: Mercury and Venus.
Third decan: Personal planet is Venus.
Second cusp: Virgo with Libran tendencies.

Sacred and Cultural Significance
In ancient Babylonia, the goddess of birth, Gula, honored.
Saints' day: Januarius (d. c.305?); Theodore of Canterbury (d. 690).

The multitalented individualism and concern for others that are typical of those born on this day were both demonstrated by George Cadbury. Born in Birmingham, England, on September 19, 1839, he successfully expanded the chocolate business established by his father and was proprietor of a daily newspaper. A devout Quaker, he placed great importance on the welfare of his employees.

Planetary Influences

Ruling planets: Mercury and Venus.
Third decan: Personal planet is Venus.
Second cusp: Virgo with Libran tendencies.

Sacred and Cultural Significance

The birthday of Quetzalcoatl celebrated
in South America.
Saints' day: Eustace (dates unknown), patron
saint of hunters; Martyrs of Korea (d. 1839).

*Reflecting this day's emphasis on the potential
of teamwork, Salisbury Cathedral, a landmark
of early English Gothic architecture that took
forty laborious years to construct, was
consecrated on September 20, 1258.*

SEPTEMBER 20

Those born on this day generally possess two defining characteristics: an almost irresistible urge to take control of situations and people; and a desire to win the genuine affection and admiration of those around them. Their perceptive and mercurial dispositions propel them to seek the best way to organize both themselves and others. Although the visions that fuel their actions are frequently highly individualistic, their concerns are usually intended to benefit or inform a wider audience, and they favor teamwork over individual action. While they feel compelled to exert their benevolent influence over others, they seek to do so by employing persuasive rather than coercive methods, thereby hoping to inspire others to cooperate enthusiastically in the pursuit of a common mission. They are endowed with the potential to attain success in a variety of professions, but many often have a special attraction to the innovative possibilities inherent in the arts or the media.

Their wish to build harmonious relationships with others pervades every aspect of the lives of those born on this day, and reflects their urge to achieve their aims as smoothly and quickly as possible, as well as their innate—and sometimes unacknowledged—desire to win the love and respect of those with whom they come into contact. However, their self-assurance and their confidence in the veracity of their convictions may cause the resentment of others (particularly those closest to them) for what may be perceived to be a manipulative approach, no mater how charmingly it is presented.

VIRTUES: The ambitions and actions of September 20 people are fueled by their desire to lead others into new and progressive fields of interest. These are independently minded, inquisitive and resourceful people, who are also highly sociable.
VICES: Those born on this day are rarely subject to feelings of self-doubt. They often believe themselves justified in employing whatever tactics it takes to bring others into line with their beliefs—a propensity that will frequently alienate rather than reconcile other people.
VERDICT: Although winning others round to their point of view is important, these individuals should recognize that retaining goodwill is equally vital, and that these two requirements may sometimes be fundamentally incompatible. They would be well advised to moderate their interpersonal approach carefully.

On This Day

Famous Births: James Dewar (1842); George Robey (1869); Upton Sinclair (1878); "Jelly Roll" Morton (1885); Stevie Smith (1902); Kenneth More (1914); John Dankworth and Rachel Roberts (1927); Dr. Joyce Brothers (1928); Anne Meara (1929); Sophia Loren (1934); Pia Lindstrom (1938); Gary Cole (1957).

Significant Events and Anniversaries: This is a day that emphasizes the success that may be achieved by concerted team efforts, as was variously reflected when: nearly forty years after building work commenced, Salisbury Cathedral, England, was consecrated (1258); during the Wars of the French Revolution, French forces defeated German troops at the Battle of Valmy (1792); during the Crimean War, a combined British, French and Turkish force trounced its Russian foe at the Battle of Alma (1854); and Britain's monarch launched the liner named after her, the *Queen Elizabeth II*, at Clydebank, Scotland (1967). A danger inherent in this day is that passionately held aims and methods may only be achieved at the expense of the well-being of others, a propensity that was mirrored when: Mussolini's Fascist delegates took control of Italy's Chamber of Deputies, the country's primary legislative body (1928); and an Islamic suicide bomber devastated the U.S. Embassy in war-torn Beirut, killing forty people (1984). September 20 indicates the determined pursuit of innovative ambitions, as was demonstrated when: Portuguese navigator Ferdinand Magellan embarked from Seville, Spain, on his pioneering quest to reach the East Indies by taking a westerly course (1519); and Argentinian swimmer Antonio Albertondo began his attempt to become the first person to swim nonstop across the English Channel and back (1961).

SEPTEMBER 21

The stellar influences that subtly govern the dispositions of those born on this day endow September 21 individuals with an unusual and complex combination of personal characteristics and tendencies. On the one hand these intellectually progressive people are fascinated with the unusual and innovative, and are therefore drawn to the exploration of novel or bizarre subjects at which more unimaginative or conventional types might balk. On the other hand they are sensuous types, who possess a highly developed aesthetic sense, as well as receptiveness to others. Not only do they feel compelled to seek out new experiences, but their appreciation of the potency of artistic media as powerful means of expression bestows upon them the potential to make their highly original mark on the world as pioneering writers, composers, artists or movie-makers. They are aided in their quest to realize their extremely original ambitions by their strong practical and organizational skills, qualities that also equip them well for more technical or administrative careers.

Although their overriding preoccupation with their private visions inevitably sets September 21 people apart from the crowd, their ultimate aim is to share their discoveries or viewpoints with others. This concern often takes a spiritual or intellectual slant, so that while they may communicate their ideas simply, their messages are often extremely profound (and even more so if they were born in the Chinese year of the pig). Nevertheless, they are frequently misunderstood, causing them either to withdraw further into their solitary world or to become discouraged and depressed. The unconditional love and support of those closest to them is therefore of great importance in bolstering their self-confidence.

VIRTUES: Those born on this day possess an irresistible attraction to new and different concepts, a predilection that is the result of both their intellectual curiosity and their desire to be instruments of human advancement. Yet, although their spiritual or aesthetic visions may be remarkably original, they innately understand the importance of presenting them in such a way as to allow others to share their ideas.
VICES: September 21 people's typical absorption in their intellectual concerns—and, indeed, their frequently unusual and profound natures—may have a somewhat isolating effect in terms of their interpersonal liaisons. They may, moreover become frustrated and embittered if others do not share their interests, and consequently descend into introspection.
VERDICT: In order to safeguard their emotional well-being, it is crucial that these people ground themselves within close-knit and stable personal relationships. Receiving the vital encouragement of their nearest and dearest will not only strengthen them, but also help them to maintain a healthy intellectual and emotional balance.

On This Day

Famous Births: Girolamo Savonarola (1452); John Loudon McAdam (1756); H.G. Wells (1866); Gustav Holst (1874); Juan de la Cierva (1895); Learie Constantine and Allen Lane (1902); Chico Hamilton (1921); Larry Hagman (1931); Shirley Conran (1932); Leonard Cohen (1934); Henry Gibson (1935); Stephen King (1947); Bill Murray (1950); Rob Morrow (1962); Ricki Lake (1968); Joseph Mazzello (1983).

Significant Events and Anniversaries: September 21 is a day that highlights the effective deployment of a variety of media with which to impart intellectual information and messages, as was illustrated when: the inaugural issue of *The Pennsylvania Packet and General Advertiser,* the first enduring U.S. daily newspaper, was published (1784); and what is believed to be the first movie of the Western genre, *Kit Carson,* had its premiere (1903). This is also a day that indicates the pursuit of aims that may not accord with the maintenance of the status quo, as was reflected when: England's king, Edward II, was murdered (by means of a red-hot poker) at Berkeley Castle on the orders of his wife, Isabella (1327); and Jacobite troops led by the Stuart "pretender" to the British throne, Bonnie Prince Charlie, scored a notable victory over English forces loyal to George II at the Battle of Prestonpans in Scotland (1745)

Planetary Influences
Ruling planets: Mercury and Venus.
Third decan: Personal planet is Venus.
Second cusp: Virgo with Libran tendencies.

Sacred and Cultural Significance
National day of Malta; in ancient Greece, the birthday of Athena celebrated.
Saint's day: Matthew (d. 1st century AD), patron saint of accountants, bankers, book-keepers and tax-collectors.

St. Matthew, patron saint of this day, as depicted by Caravaggio in The Inspiration of St. Matthew *(below). One of the twelve disciples of Jesus, St. Matthew, who had previously been a tax collector and is generally credited with writing the first Gospel of the New Testament, went on to become a missionary in Judaea, Ethiopia and Persia, before dying as a martyr.*

Planetary Influences
Ruling planets: Mercury and Venus.
Third decan: Personal planet is Venus.
Second cusp: Virgo with Libran tendencies.

Sacred and Cultural Significance
Wiccan initiation ceremonies traditionally performed.
Saints' day: Maurice, patron saint of dyers, weavers and soldiers (d. c.287); Laudus (6th century AD); Thomas of Villanova (1486–1555).

Chemist, physicist and philosopher Michael Faraday was born in England on September 22, 1791. With the intellectual curiousity, prodigious energy and the urge to contribute to human progress that are starred for people born on this day, he made remarkable advances in the fields of electricity, electro-chemistry and electromagnetism.

SEPTEMBER 22

Those born on September 22 are typically motivated by two fundamental desires: to satisfy their intellectual thirst for stimulation and exploration; and to devote their energy to helping others. They may often combine these dual inclinations to form a single, remarkably progressive, vision, which they will promote with fierce determination. Blessed with deeply perceptive and mercurial intellects, these individuals are particularly adept at identifying social abuses, and devising imaginative and effective strategies with which to redress the situation. Not only are they drawn to innovative concepts and theories, but they also have a highly developed sense of justice that often compels them to work for the common good. Clearly suited to scientific, public service or humanitarian work, they may also seek to enlighten others by means of writing or research.

Despite their general concern for the welfare of others, their typically forthright manner and uncompromising promotion of their beliefs will inevitably alienate some people: those born on this day will therefore often be reluctantly forced to assume a confrontational stance in their desire to achieve their visions. They therefore rely on the unquestioning support of their personal relationships, and they reciprocate the affection of those closest to them wholeheartedly, especially if they are women.

VIRTUES: September 22 people want to make an active and positive contribution to society, and enjoy exploring innovative intellectual concepts. They have the potential to blaze a truly progressive trail through life.
VICES: Their determined adherence to often extremely unconventional beliefs and visions will typically condemn those born on this day to struggle for the acceptance of others, causing them to adopt emotionally defensive strategies for coping with the disappointments that may be experienced. In protecting themselves in this manner, they run the risk of damaging their psychological well-being.
VERDICT: It is important that those born on this day should honestly consider whether the pursuit of their intellectual ambitions justifies the emotional price they may be forced to pay. They should try to nurture their mutually supportive relationships with their friends and family members, wherein they will find much comfort and joy.

On This Day
Famous Births: Anne of Cleves (1515); Michael Faraday (1791); Christabel Pankhurst (1880); Paul Muni and Erich von Stroheim (1885); John Houseman (1902); Dannie Abse (1923); Tommy Lasorda (1927); Fay Weldon (1931); Dale Spender (1943); Mark Phillips (1948); Shari Belafonte-Harper (1954); Debby Boone (1956); Nick Cave (1957); Joan Jett (1961); Scott Baio, Catherine Oxenburg and Eric Stoltz (1961).

Significant Events and Anniversaries: This is a day that indicates tough strategies to promote strongly held beliefs, as was demonstrated when: Shaka, the Zulu leader, was murdered by two of his half-brothers (1828); a British submarine attacked and disabled the German battleship *Tirpitz* in a Norwegian fjord during World War II (1943); and Lech Walesa formed the Solidarity trade-union movement to oppose the Communist policies of the Polish government (1980). September 22 also emphasizes the high price of communal ideals, as seen when: the patriot Nathan Hale was hanged by the British for alleged espionage during the American War of Independence (1776); three British naval cruisers, H.M.S.s *Hogue, Cressy* and *Aboukir* were sunk by a German submarine during World War I (1914); and a bomb attack by I.R.A. terrorists cost the lives of ten Royal Marine musicians at Deal, England (1989). This is a day that also highlights concern with humanity's advancement, as was manifested when: Joseph Smith revealed the existence of the *Book of Mormon* (1827); and when surgeons at England's Harefield Hospital carried out a heart-and-lung transplant on a two-and-a-half-month old baby, then the youngest patient to undergo such an operation (1986).

LIBRA

September 23 to October 22
Ruling planet: Venus   **Element:** Cardinal air
Symbol: The scales   **Polarity:** Positive (masculine)
Physical correspondence: The kidneys
Stones: Quartz, opal, jade, emerald, sapphire
Flowers: Rose, pansy, foxglove, daisy, hydrangea
Colors: Pink, blue, lavender

The balance or scales that represent the zodiacal sign of Libra are universal to the various astrological traditions: the Persian called the constellation Tarazuk; the Babylonians Zibanitu; and the Hindus Tula—all names that signify scales. The only notable exception was the symbol used by the ancient Greek astrologers, to whom Libra was Zugos, "the yoke." The constellation's resemblance to, and association with, a balance (or a primitive yoke with which oxen were harnessed), is persuasively explained by the fact that Libra dominates the period when night and day are of approximately equal length. Yet the image of the scales also has a more spiritual significance, for this instrument is symbolically related to ancient Egyptian lore, in which a balance was used in Osiris's hall of judgement to weigh the hearts of the recently deceased against the feather of Ma'at, the goddess of truth. This jurisdictive symbolism was also associated with the Carthaginian goddess of Tanit—alternatively known as Astoarche ("lady of the stars")—and in Greek mythology, the judicial scales of Astraea were incorporated in the heavens as Libra. Some scholars postulate that the ancient Egyptian hieroglyphic that symbolized Libra—which resembles the sign's modern sigil—represents the Sun (embodying masculinity and spirituality) setting over the Earth (signifying femininity and materiality), an analogy that is compatible with both the post-mortem weighing of souls and the balancing of opposing principles.

The Romans sometimes considered their deity of metal-working and measurement, Vulcan, to be present in this constellation, and his consort Venus (known as the morning star) is the planetary ruler of Libra. She endows those born under this sign with charm, a love of beauty and a desire to bring harmony, while the element of air that further exerts its influence over Libra signifies intellectual affinities, as well as a desire for freedom. The zodiacal scales signify a strong sense of natural justice and steady psychological equilibrium, but may equally imply flightiness and emotional or intellectual indecisiveness.

LIBRA

Planetary Influences
Ruling planets: Mercury and Venus.
First decan: Personal planet is Venus.
First cusp: Libra with Virgo tendencies.

Sacred and Cultural Significance
National day of Saudi Arabia.
Saints' day: Thecla of Iconium (1st century AD); Adomnan (627–704).

Born in Albany, Georgia, on September 23, 1930, and blind from the age of seven, entertainer Ray Charles has demonstrated throughout his career the inspirational creative talents and empathy with others that are featured for those born on this day. With his Moon in Libra, he is sociable and charming, and as a Chinese metal horse, he is independent and intuitive, making him as popular as he is successful—he has received eight Grammy Awards.

thers are drawn to September 23 individuals for a variety of reasons, including their unassuming personal charm, genuine kindness, integrity and reliability. Despite the potentially conflicting qualities that are bestowed by the planets that rule their day of birth—sensory indulgence and intellectual inquisitiveness—they are generally able to reconcile these characteristics, with the result that they are not only balanced, but also versatile. Thus while they are inspired by progressive visions, and typically display considerable energy and resourcefulness in pursuing them, their ambition is rarely at the expense of others. Those born on this day usually enjoy harmonious and mutually respectful working relationships, and many may choose to devote their careers to the service of others, perhaps—and particularly if they are women—within the caring professions.

September 23 people are also blessed with a sensitive appreciation of beauty, a gift that endows them with a profound affinity for the myriad forms of subtle expression encompassed by the artistic realm, and some may therefore choose to share their talents with a wider audience as writers, artists, movie-makers or musicians. Their pronounced empathy with, and orientation toward, other people characterizes all of their interpersonal relationships, and in turn they are regarded with deep affection by everyone with whom they come into contact. Their desire to please is genuine, and they typically treat others, especially those closest to them, with consideration, generosity and loyalty.

VIRTUES: September 23 people are not only resourceful and multitalented types whose interest is stimulated by a wide variety of subjects, but they are also endowed with real concern for the well-being of others. They are thus highly popular and deservedly command the respect of their peers.
VICES: Because they are innately kind-hearted souls who prefer conciliation to confrontation, there is a danger that these individuals may either fail to communicate their strength of conviction or, in more extreme instances, abandon their personal ambitions if they believe that to pursue them would cause others unhappiness.
VERDICT: Those born on this day generally maintain a healthy equilibrium between their emotional and intellectual concerns and their professional and private lives. They should, however, beware of becoming overly compliant within their interpersonal relationships, particularly if, by making concessions, they are sacrificing cherished dreams.

On This Day
Famous Births: Gaius Octavius Caesar (63 BC); Armand Hyppolyte Louis (1819); Baroness Orczy (1865); John Boyd Orr (1880); Walter Lippman (1889); Mickey Rooney (1920); John Coltrane (1926); Ray Charles (1930); Julio Iglesias (1943); Paul Peterson (1945); Mary Kay Place (1947); Bruce Springsteen (1949); Jeff Squire (1951); Jason Alexander (1959).

Significant Events and Anniversaries: Although the influences inherent in this day generally highlight peace, once all other methods have failed, more combative methods have been resorted to on behalf of the common good, as was demonstrated when: during the American War of Independence, U.S. and French ships mounted a successful attack on the British vessels *Serapis* and *Countess of Scarborough* off Flamborough Head in the North Sea (1779); during the same conflict, the British major John André, who had secretly arranged the surrender of West Point with Benedict Arnold, was intercepted—and hanged—by the Americans (1780); and British troops under Arthur Wellesley (later the Duke of Wellington) were victorious over their Maratha foes under Doulut Rao Sindhia at the Battle of Assaye in India (1803). The talent for popular entertainment inherent in September 23 was reflected by two premieres held on this day: Mack Sennet's first Keystone Cops movie, *Cohen Collects a Debt* (1912); and *Fiddler on the Roof,* with Zero Mostel taking the leading role (1964). On a day also governed by the element of air, September 23 marks the anniversary of German astronomer Johann Gottfried Galle's discovery of the planet Neptune (1846).

SEPTEMBER 24

For those individuals born on September 24, the balance that symbolizes their astrological sign of Libra often appears somewhat weighted in favor of Venus and all that she represents, for not only are these people sensual and pleasure-loving, they also have a deep desire to love and be loved. Yet the presence of Mercury at the other end of their personality scale endows them with keenly curious intellectual qualities, adding a progressive and inquiring streak to their natures. While the dispositions of those born on this day vary from one individual to another, these two astrological influences generally combine to create people who are not only considerate, sensitive and empathetic, but are also oriented toward helping others through their resourceful and imaginative efforts. Some may be inclined to devote their careers to social, humanitarian or political issues, while other September 24 people may harness their affinity for all things artistic to their quest for enlightening or entertaining others, a propensity that is doubly pronounced if they were also born in the Chinese year of the goat.

The liaisons formed by those born on this day—be they professional or personal—are typically defined by these individuals' intuitive ability to detect unhappiness in others, and their urge to relieve such feelings of distress through positive and supportive gestures. Despite their sociability and concern for others' well-being, they do, however, have an inherent need both for periods of solitude, in which they can indulge in the pursuits that particularly interest them, and for intellectual and sensory stimulation. Unless these needs are fully respected by those closest to them, they may sometimes result in discord within their most intimate relationships.

VIRTUES: The conjunction of such "soft" qualities as a love of beauty, a desire to bring harmony to the lives of others, and great empathy and intuition, with their "harder" urge to realize their progressive visions by means of direct action, results in those born on this day being versatile people, who manifest both human concern and shrewd intellects.
VICES: The aura of emotional warmth that they exude draws others to these people, and they in turn have a strong need for the affection and support inherent in close emotional bonds. There is a danger that their prerequisite for intellectual freedom and novel experiences may either be stifled by their altruism, or that they may wound those closest to them by withdrawing into a private world away from their demands.
VERDICT: September 24 people generally manage to reconcile their predilection for intellectual and sensory exploration with their genuine sympathy for others, but should nevertheless ensure that they do not mislead others about their determination to achieve their personal goals, even if this means placing their own interests over less selfish concerns.

On This Day
Famous Births: Horace Walpole (1717); A.P. Herbert (1890); F. Scott Fitzgerald (1896); Howard Florey (1898); Konstantin Chernenko (1911); Richard Hoggart (1918); Jim McKay (1921); Sheila MacRae (1924); Anthony Newley (1931); Svetlana Beriosova (1932); Jim Henson (1936); Linda McCartney (1941); Gerry Marsden (1942); Phil Hartman (1948).

Significant Events and Anniversaries: September 24 highlights outstanding artistic talent, and on this day British wit and playwright Noël Coward's play *Private Lives* had its first performance (1930). This day also indicates the desire to achieve progressive ambitions, as was reflected when: Britain's St. Leger horse race was staged for the first time, at Doncaster, England (1776); and the first successful attempt to scale Mount Everest via its challenging southwest face was completed by British mountaineers Doug Scott and Dougal Haston (1975). On a day governed by the element of air: French engineer Henri Giffard made the first-ever flight in a hydrogen airship powered by a steam engine (1852); and the world's first nuclear-powered aircraft carrier, U.S.S. *Enterprise*, embarked from Newport, Virginia, on its maiden voyage (1960).

Planetary Influences
Ruling planets: Mercury and Venus.
First decan: Personal planet is Venus.
First cusp: Libra with Virgo tendencies.

Sacred and Cultural Significance
In ancient Egypt, the annual rebirth of Osiris celebrated; Obatala honored in West Africa.
Saints' day: Gerard Sagredo (d. 1046); Robert of Knaresborough (1160–1218).

Francis Scott Key Fitzgerald, who was born on September 24, 1896, is widely recognized as one of the greatest novelists of the twentieth century. Displaying in his writing the deep sensitivity and empathetic qualities that are typical of those born on this day, his personal life was often unhappy and he sometimes withdrew into a private, troubled world. He nevertheless overcame his periods of emotional difficulties and created literary classics including The Beautiful and the Damned *(1922),* The Great Gatsby *(1925) and* Tender is the Night *(1934).*

LIBRA

Planetary Influences
Ruling planets: Mercury and Venus.
First decan: Personal planet is Venus.
First cusp: Libra with Virgo tendencies.

Sacred and Cultural Significance
Saints' day: Firmin (4th century AD);
Cadoc (5th–6th century AD); Finbar
(c.560–c.610), patron saint of Cork, Ireland,
and Barra, Outer Hebrides; Ceolfrith
(d. 716); translation of Wivina (d. 1170);
Albert of Jerusalem (c.1150–1214);
Sergius of Radonezh (1315–92);
Vincent Strambi (1745–1824).

*Born in Mississippi on September 25, 1897,
William Faulkner was one of the South's
greatest writers. A perceptive observer
of people and society, characteristics shared by
those born on this day, he was an avid reader
who traveled widely before returning to his
home state to further his writing career. Always
experimenting with new styles, Faulkner's
works, including* The Sound and the Fury
(1929) and As I Lay Dying *(1930), earned
him the Nobel Prize for Literature in 1949.*

SEPTEMBER 25

★★★

September 25 people are complex individuals whose primary personal characteristics can be somewhat contradictory. Their sympathetic and empathetic qualities lead them to identify with others, while their keen perception and independence of mind may cause them to stand apart from the crowd, noting and criticizing everything they observe. Ultimately, however, those born on this day often have noble aims, although their methods may not always make this clear. They enjoy exploring their intellectual interests, be they scientific theories, modes of artistic expression, or societal structures and conventions, as well as sharing their knowledge with a wider audience. And because these are honest people who are not afraid of articulating the truth—however uncomfortable—and who possess an innate sense of natural justice, they have the potential to make effective political and social campaigners, although many may choose to communicate their ideas by means of journalism or artistic media.

In many respects their humanitarian orientation generally assumes a rather abstract form (especially if they are men), a tendency which, when combined with their need for personal autonomy of thought and action, may cause difficulties within their interpersonal relationships. For despite their genuine affection for those closest to them, and their relish for the comforts of domestic life, their judgemental propensities and need for independence may result in emotional isolation.

VIRTUES: Their incisive and objective intellects, along with their sensitivity for perceived injustices, endow those born on this day with strongly defined critical abilities. In sharing their often acerbic—but always accurate—conclusions with others, they demonstrate a desire to act as agents of progress.
VICES: Although their actions and words are inspired by their wish to move society forward, the direct and often brutally frank modes of expression that September 25 people typically employ may not be appreciated by others, and may prove particularly wounding when directed toward their nearest and dearest.
VERDICT: If they are not to alienate those whose interests they have at heart, it is important that these individuals take account of the emotional sensibilities of others. By adopting a more subtle and compromising attitude and manner, they will often enhance their potential for success, and attract the affection of others.

On This Day
Famous Births: Jean-Philippe Rameau (1683); Felicia D. Hemans (1793); Melvyn R. Bissell (1843); John French (1852); William Faulkner (1897); Mark Rothko (1903); Dmitri Shostakovich (1906); Robert Muldoon (1921); Colin Davis (1927); Barbara Walters (1931); Glen Gould (1932); Adolfo Suarez (1933); Juliet Prowse (1936); Michael Douglas (1944); Mark Hamill (1951); Christopher Reeve (1952); Heather Locklear (1961); Scottie Pippen (1965); Will Smith (1968).

Significant Events and Anniversaries: On a day that indicates humanitarian concerns: the first blood-transfusion operation to use human blood was performed in London, England (1818); and, in Little Rock, Arkansas, national guardsmen escorted nine African-American children in their successful attempt to enter the previously all-white Central High School (1957). The desire for independence that is inherent in September 25 was reflected when the Catalonian region of Spain was granted its autonomy (1932). A day that also highlights communication, September 25 marks the anniversary of the publication of North America's first newspaper, Boston's *Publick Occurrences, Both Foreign and Domestic* (1690). Finally, this day emphasizes a propensity to take action for the common good, as was demonstrated when: King Harold II of England defeated the invading army of King Harold III (Hardrada) of Norway at the Battle of Stamford Bridge (1066); and British and French troops attacked their German foe at the Battle of Loos in World War I (1915).

SEPTEMBER 26

Others often regard September 26 individuals as perfectionists, whose tenacity in their desire to achieve their elevated visions is the subject of awed—if somewhat baffled—admiration. And indeed, when enthralled by an inspirational ambition, the determination, self-discipline and absorption manifested by those born on this day can become obsessive. Since they are also blessed with great imagination and an uncompromisingly logical turn of mind, their career potential is therefore of the highest order. Many September 26 people are attracted by the progressive opportunities inherent in science and (especially) the arts, but all desire to make a positive contribution to humanity by means of their discoveries or guiding influence prompting some to academic careers.

Despite their intellectual independence and fascination—indeed, compulsion—for experimentation, the love and support those closest to them is of profound value to those born on this day, who innately recognize the importance of maintaining a grounding emotional counterbalance to their cerebral interests. Typically affectionate and loyal to those who believe in them, as well as interesting and enlivening companions, they may nevertheless unwittingly neglect their emotional needs, or those of their loved ones, when their attention is irresistibly occupied by a work-related challenge (a tendency that is even more pronounced if they are men).

VIRTUES: Despite the variety of talents with which they are blessed, those born on this day are usually drawn to studying a specific area of interest, hoping that they can benefit others with the products of their research. To all their ventures they bring both tenacity and resourcefulness, while never losing their fellow-feeling.

VICES: These people's typical approach toward the topics that hold their attention is so totally focused that in many respects it can be characterized as compulsive. This propensity augurs well for their professional success, but may cause them to ignore not only their own emotional requirements, but also those of their nearest and dearest.

VERDICT: Although September 26 individuals are instinctively aware of the significance of maintaining strong emotional ties, they should nevertheless strive to moderate their obsession with their work to ensure that they actively nurture their relationships and find time for enjoyable and relaxing communal pursuits.

On This Day

Famous Births: Jean Louis André Théodore Géricault (1791); Alfred Cortot (1877); Barnes Neville Wallis (1887); T.S. Eliot (1888); George Raft (1895); Pope Paul VI (1897); George Gershwin (1898); Leonard Sachs (1909); Jack LaLanne (1914); Julie London (1926); Ian Michael Chappell (1943); Bryan Ferry (1945); Lynn Anderson (1947); Mary Beth Hurt and Olivia Newton-John (1948); Shawn Stockman (1972).

Significant Events and Anniversaries: This is a day that highlights total commitment to ambitious aims, as was demonstrated when: the English seaman Francis Drake returned to Plymouth having circumnavigated the world in the *Golden Hind* (1580); Britain's Queen Mary launched the Cunard-White Star liner named after her (1934); and Alan Bond's yacht *Australia II* won the Americas Cup trophy, ending a line of American victories that stretched back for 132 years (1983). The outstanding artistic and technical potential inherent in this day was confirmed when: Emile Berliner patented his "Gramophone" (1887); the musical *West Side Story* had its premiere (1957); and U.S. musician Bob Dylan performed in public for the first time, at a folk club in Greenwich Village, New York (1961). Independence and communal spirit are emphasized on this day, on which: a Korean patriot assassinated the Japanese resident-general Hirobumi Ito (1909); and New Zealand was granted dominion (self-governing) status within the British Empire (1907). And on a day ruled by air, September 26 marks the anniversary of the inauguration of Freddie Laker's pioneering Skytrain passenger air service between England and the United States (1977).

Planetary Influences

Ruling planets: Mercury and Venus.
First decan: Personal planet is Venus.
First cusp: Libra with Virgo tendencies.

Sacred and Cultural Significance

Theseus honored in ancient Greece.
Saints' day: Cosmas and Damian (dates unknown), patron saints of doctors, barbers and surgeons; Cyprian and Justina (d. c.300); Nilus of Rossano (c.910–1005).

The commitment to a cause that characterizes this day was demonstrated on September 26, 1687, when the Parthenon (below) in the Acropolis at Athens, Greece, was severely damaged in an attack by the Venetian Army on Turkish forces encamped there.

LIBRA

Planetary Influences
Ruling planet: Venus.
First decan: Personal planet is Venus.

Sacred and Cultural Significance
In China, the Moon Festival held.
Saints' day: Florentius (dates unknown);
Barry (6th century AD); Vincent
de Paul (1581–1660), patron saint
of charitable societies.

*American revolutionary politician Samuel
Adams—second cousin of President John
Quincy Adams—was born in Boston,
Massachusetts, on September 27, 1722.
Throughout his long political career, in which
he led the opposition to the hated Stamp Act
and was a prime mover in the Boston Tea
Party, he demonstrated the ambitious vision,
tenacity and strong sense of fairness that are
so typical of those born on this day.*

SEPTEMBER 27

Those born on this day are determined and vigorous individuals who are driven by their ambitions, however obstacle-strewn the path to success. Indeed, in many respects they are stimulated by adversity, leading others to wonder why they so often appear to focus on such difficult and demanding aims instead of opting for those that offer an easier route to success. There are no easy answers to this question, for these are complex people, whose motivations vary from individual to individual. Imbued with a strong sense of fairness, which causes them to seek to reverse social injustices (a predilection guaranteed to bring them into conflict with those who wish to maintain the status quo), many feel compelled to engage in a personal struggle of strength by testing their abilities against the most unpromising of challenges. Yet because these are objective and realistic types, their aims are rarely unfeasible, and September 27 people's courage, tenacity and perfectionism augur well for their attainment.

Despite their pronounced individualistic stance, their critical and progressive faculties are usually oriented toward humanitarian aims, and they may therefore choose to employ their talents as either political, social or legal campaigners, or else artistic, technical or design pioneers whose efforts are intended to inspire or enhance others' lives. In terms of their interpersonal liaisons, they operate well as team captains (but not as small and unquestioning cogs in a larger social wheel) and they prefer to lead by example, demanding the same level of commitment from others as they themselves demonstrate. Despite their profound concern and affection for their loved ones, their judgemental and perfectionist tendencies may make for explosive personal relationships.

VIRTUES: Those born on this day are blessed with acutely perceptive, objective and determined intellects, qualities that, when also combined with their fearless championing of moral rectitude and humanitarian principles, enable them to see the potential for advancement through the most unlikely of approaches.
VICES: Although the actions of these individuals are motivated by their elevated and benevolent interest in the well-being of others, their typically outspoken and direct *modi operandi*, as well as their somewhat perfectionist attitudes, frequently make them difficult to work and live with, and they may be particularly resented by those closest to them.
VERDICT: September 27 greatly value the love and support of their friends and family members, but should recognize that their propensity for criticism and the high demands that they make on others—however well meant—may have the effect of emotionally exhausting, and ultimately alienating, those who are most important to them.

On This Day
Famous Births: Samuel Adams (1722); George Cruikshank (1792); Louis Botha (1862); Cyril Scott (1879); Jacques Thibaud (1880); Vincent Youmans (1898); William Empson (1906); Bernard Miles (1907); William Conrad (1920); Arthur Penn (1922); Jayne Meadows (1926); Sada Thompson (1929); Wilford Brimley and Greg Morris (1934); Josephine Barstow (1940); Alvin Stardust (1942); Meatloaf and Cheryl Tiegs (1947); Barbara Dickson (1948); Mike Schmidt (1949); Shaun Cassidy and Paul Grabowsky (1958).

Significant Events and Anniversaries: This is a day that highlights the promotion of ambitious projects aimed at benefiting the greater good, as was variously reflected in the engineering and national spheres on September 27 when: the world's first public railroad system, built by the steam-engine pioneer George Stephenson and operating between the English towns of Stockton and Darlington, was officially opened (1825); and King Constantine I of Greece was deposed following his army's defeat by Turkey (1922). The energetic determination inherent in sporting prowess that is strongly featured by this day was confirmed when: U.S. golfer Bobby Jones won the sport's first grand slam as a result of his triumph in the U.S. National Amateur Championships (1930); and members of the European Ryder Cup golf team beat their American hosts for the first time (1987).

SEPTEMBER 28

September 28 people are particularly susceptible to the potent influence of the planet of Venus that governs their day of birth, and, like the eponymous Roman goddess of love, many seek personal fulfillment through affairs of the heart, indulgence of the senses, or the pursuit of beauty in all its forms. They are also, however, imaginative and empathetic types who wish to bring progress and harmony to the world, even while they have a special affinity with the less tangible spiritual and artistic concerns that arouse strong emotional responses in them. Their intellectual independence and compulsion to explore the world of emotions and senses cause those born on this day to place a far greater value on nonmaterialistic achievements than on those that offer rewards of wealth and status. The hard-nosed realm of commerce is therefore anathema to them, and they will generally flourish only when they can satisfy their natural inclinations and inspire others in the process, as artists, writers, graphic designers or actors, for example, or even as athletes.

Others are drawn to these magnetic people for the interesting and enlivening aura that they exude, and they in turn are not only stimulated by personal interaction, but manifest a benevolent concern for the happiness of those with whom they come into contact. Yet ironically their relationships with their nearest and dearest may not be of the smoothest, for despite their love for those closest to them, their innate nonconformity (which is even more pronounced if they were born in the Chinese year of the horse) and urge to further their personal progress by means of individual experience precludes their capacity to sacrifice their independence to the altar of familial harmony. Their romantic idealism may furthermore set an impossibly high standard for their partners.

VIRTUES: Those born on this day are highly individualistic types, who are irresistibly attracted to beauty, whether physical, aesthetic or intellectual—and who therefore feel especially compelled to explore the realms of ideas and artistry in their quest to achieve the ideals that are strongly linked to their emotional fulfillment.
VICES: As well as being one of their greatest strengths, the discriminating brand of perfectionism manifested by September 28 people is potentially very damaging, for there is a danger that not only will they remain unsatisfied, but that they may also project unfair demands onto those around them.
VERDICT: While they should never abandon the visions that are so fundamental to their natures, it is important that these individuals recognize that their soaring, and sometimes unrealistic, expectations—of themselves and of those closest to them—may ultimately have an emotionally destructive effect. They would therefore be well advised to work on adopting a more relaxed and accepting approach.

On This Day

Famous Births: Caravaggio (1573); "Gentleman John" Jackson (1769); Richard Bright (1789); Prosper Mérimée (1803); Georges Clemenceau (1841); Kate Wiggin (1856); "Sapper" (Herman Cyril McNeile) (1888); Ed Sullivan (1902); Max Schmeling (1905); Al Capp (1909); Peter Finch (1916); Michael Soames (1917); Marcello Mastroianni (1924); Arnold Stang (1925); Jeremy Isaacs (1932); Brigitte Bardot (1934); Joel Higgins (1946); Janeane Garofalo (1964); Moon Unit Zappa (1967); Gwyneth Paltrow (1973).

Significant Events and Anniversaries: A day that emphasizes intellectual idealism, September 28 commemorates the formation of the First International, or International Working Men's Association, by Karl Marx at a public meeting in London (1864). A close affinity with all things artistic, as well as a desire to inspire others, are further features of this day, on which: the powerfully patriotic song "God Save the King" (later adopted as the British national anthem) was first sung by an audience, at London's Drury Lane Theatre, during an era when the Stuart "young pretender," Bonnie Prince Charlie, was threatening the position of the Hanoverian king, George II (1745); and the first entirely Lapp-made movie had its premiere (1987).

Planetary Influences
Ruling planet: Venus.
First decan: Personal planet is Venus.

Sacred and Cultural Significance
In ancient Athens, the Thesmophoria festival celebrated.
Saints' day: Machan (6th century AD); Lioba (d. 782); Wenceslas (907–29), patron saint of Czechoslovakia.

Depicted below in his Self Portrait, *Baroque master painter Caravaggio was born in the town of that name, in Italy, as Michelangelo Merisi on September 28, 1573. Like many born on this day, he was dedicated to his art: aside from portraits, his works include altarpieces and religious paintings, and are noteworthy for their dramatic contrasts of light and dark.*

LIBRA

Planetary Influences
Ruling planet: Venus.
First decan: Personal planet is Venus.

Sacred and Cultural Significance
In England, Michaelmas.
Saints' day: Michael (and all Angels), patron saint of grocers and sick people; Gabriel, patron saint of broadcasters, diplomats and telecommunications; and Raphael.

Perhaps reflecting the highly imaginative nature of this day, as well as the influence of the element of air, this unidentified flying object was photographed hovering over Ontario, Canada, on September 29, 1967.

SEPTEMBER 29

There are often two distinct sides to the characters of those born this day, for on the one hand they have a predilection for bringing about harmonious solutions to unbalanced situations and circumstances through orderly systems, yet on the other they are highly imaginative, sensitive and idealistic individuals, whose instinctive emotional responses may create the same chaos within their personal lives as they devote their professional energies to trying to resolve. Maintaining their intellectual and emotional balance may therefore be a constant struggle, for September 29 people possess a strong sense of social responsibility and often feel compelled to suppress their personal desires and needs in order to concentrate their efforts on helping those individuals with whom they most strongly identify. These are thus multifaceted people, who promote their ideas with remarkable determination, vigor and practical or technical skill, yet never lose their sensitivity and feelings of empathy toward others—despite the demands involved.

The combination of their tenacity and originality, along with their positive orientation toward others, endows September 29 people with the ability to inspire others, whether in the pursuit of a tangible common quest or in the more intangible arena of artistry, with which in any case they have a strong affinity. Yet many find that personal happiness is an elusive commodity—perhaps because their active concern with the well-being of others may obscure their recognition of what is most important for their own emotional fulfillment. Thus, while they manifest both genuine affection and loyalty to their nearest and dearest, their tendency to sublimate selfish desires in favor of more altruistic behavior (a trait that is especially pronounced in the women born on this day) may leave them feeling dissatisfied, restless or frustrated.

VIRTUES: September 29 people are extremely sensitive and perceptive individuals, whose strong identification with a common cause drives them to make an active contribution to society. Blessed with great ingenuity as well as highly developed practical skills, they have the potential to make inspirational leaders and talented organizers.
VICES: Although their altruistic compulsion to be of service to others is an admirable one, their propensity to regard their personal needs as less important—and therefore to ignore or underplay them—is one that will inevitably condemn them to remaining unsatisfied, however great their professional achievements.
VERDICT: It is important that September 29 people strive to maintain a more even balance between their external orientation and their emotional well-being, even if this occasionally involves a decision to pursue a personal interest instead of a communal one. By following such a path, they will usually benefit all round.

On This Day
Famous Births: Pompey the Great (106 BC); Tintoretto (1518); Miguel de Cervantes (1547); Robert Clive (1725); Horatio Nelson (1758); Elizabeth Gaskell (1810); Enrico Fermi (1901); Gene Autry (1907); Greer Garson (1908); Stanley Kramer (1913); Trevor Howard (1916); Richard Bonynge (1930); Anita Ekberg (1931); Jerry Lee Lewis (1935); Madeline Kahn (1942); Lech Walesa (1943); Bryant Gumbel (1948); Sebastian Coe (1956).

Significant Events and Anniversaries: In many respects September 29 highlights individual sacrifice on behalf of the perceived greater good, as was demonstrated when: the absolutist English monarch Richard II was forced to abdicate as the result of a revolt against his rule led by his cousin, Henry Bolingbroke, who subsequently became King Henry IV (1399); and Irish dramatist George Bernard Shaw refused the offer of a British peerage, thereby remaining true to his socialist principles (1930). This was also the day on which the American founder of Standard Oil, John D. Rockefeller, a socially concerned entrepreneur who poured much of his great wealth into his philanthropic Rockefeller Foundation, officially became the world's first billionaire (1916).

SEPTEMBER 30

Those born on this day are focused individuals, who can perhaps best be characterized as champions of the truth, for they have an acute eye for identifying what they believe to be social or intellectual wrongs. They are driven by the desire to convince others of the veracity of their judgements and thereby effect change. Because they are especially sensitive to social injustice, and are extraordinarily empathetic toward the victims of such abuse, September 30 people are strongly drawn to those professions where they can devote their energy and talents to rectifying the situation. And in working toward their humanitarian aims they typically utilize their organizational skills, uncompromisingly logical intellectual approach and meticulous attention to detail in building dynamic force for progress. Because they recognize that their efforts will often be met with opposition, they strive to create a veritable armory of weapons, which they employ with courage and resourcefulness. There is a danger, however, that their heightened sense of justice may lead them to employ an overly aggressive approach toward those—especially their nearest and dearest—whose behavior does not live up to their high moral standards.

Their inclinations clearly suit these individuals for careers where they can make tangible advances, for example as social campaigners, lawyers or members of the caring professions. But those born on this day also have a sensual affinity with the beauty inherent in the arts, and many will therefore seek both to help others and to provide inspiration through literature, music, or visual forms of artistic expression.

VIRTUES: The combination of their acute sensitivity and uncompromising sense of fairness arouses their urge to redress the wrongs they identify by means of concerted intellectual and practical action. They characteristically work toward the achievement of their visionary aims with close attention to detail and fearless tenacity.

VICES: Reflecting their highly developed critical faculties and fierce promotion of the behavior and principles they believe to be ethically correct, September 30 people tend to pounce on perceived transgressions, and to expose and punish them with merciless vigor. There is a risk, however, that such judgemental tendencies will alienate their loved ones who, ironically, may regard themselves as being unfairly treated.

VERDICT: If they are to retain their unquestioning affection and support, it is vital that these individuals recognize that their propensity for pointing out the failings of those closest to them can have a negative and emotionally damaging effect on all concerned. They should therefore not only moderate their unduly critical approach, but also try to be tolerant of more harmless human foibles.

On This Day

Famous Births: Lord FitzRoy Raglan (1788); Lord Frederick Roberts (1832); Charles Villiers Stanford (1852); Reinhard von Scheer (1863); Hans Geiger (1882); Lewis Milestone (1895); Michael Powell (1905); Michael Innes (1906); David Oistrakh (1908); Deborah Kerr (1921); Donald Swann (1923); Truman Capote (1924); Angie Dickinson (1931); Johnny Mathis (1935); Marilyn McCoo (1943); Victoria Tennant (1950); Martina Higgins (1980).

Significant Events and Anniversaries: September 30 is a day that indicates outstanding artistic potential, as was confirmed by the staging of two musical premieres on this day: Wolfgang Amadeus Mozart's opera *Die Zauberflöte* (*The Magic Flute*) (1791); and George Gershwin's *Porgy and Bess* (1935). Dynamic political change is also highlighted by this day, which marks the anniversary of the Munich Agreement—signed by French premier Edouard Daladier, British Prime Minister Neville Chamberlain, Italian dictator Benito Mussolini, and German *Führer* Adolf Hitler—which upheld Germany's claim to the Sudetenland, the German-speaking region of Czechoslovakia (1938). And, on a day governed by the element of air, the world's first rocket-propelled aircraft, the invention of German engineer Franz von Opel, made its maiden excursion into the skies (1929).

Planetary Influences
Ruling planet: Venus.
First decan: Personal planet is Venus.

Sacred and Cultural Significance
National day of Botswana; Meditrinalia festival held in Rome; in ancient Greece, the Epitaphia observed.
Saints' day: Jerome (c.341–420), patron saint of archaeologists, librarians and scholars, Honorius (d. 653); Tancred, Torthred and Tova (d. 870).

September 30 marks the anniversary of the 1938 Munich Agreement, which upheld Germany's claim to the German-speaking region of Czechoslovakia. This was an illustration of the day's political character: Hitler (temporarily) furthered his territorial ambitions, while the other signatories believed they had achieved "peace in our time," in the words of Neville Chamberlain.

LIBRA

Planetary Influences
Ruling planet: Venus.
Second decan: Personal planet is Saturn.

Sacred and Cultural Significance
National days of China and Nigeria.
Saints' day: Mylor (dates unknown);
translation of Remigius (d. 533); Bavo
(d. c.655); Theresa of Lisieux (1873–97),
patron saint of missionaries.

*On a day that emphasizes a driving concern
with effecting social change, General Francisco
Franco (pictured below) assumed the leadership
of the Spanish Nationalist government
at Burgos on October 1, 1936, heralding
the outbreak of the Spanish civil war.*

OCTOBER 1

Those born on this day are focused individuals, the majority of whom are unquestionably ambitious. However, their goals rarely have to do with personal glory or self-aggrandizement (although most appreciate the security and comfort that comes with the attainment of financial rewards), being instead concerned with the achievement of more intellectually significant matters. By working toward their inspirational visions, they hope to not only satisfy their desire to progress as far as possible as individuals, but also to leave a lasting legacy that will benefit their peers and, perhaps, even future generations. Some may thus seek to aid human advancement by devoting their energies to political or humanitarian pursuits; some will capitalize on their precision and natural aptitude for the innovative possibilities offered by the scientific or technical fields; and some will be attracted to exploring and pushing forward the more subtle boundaries of artistic expression, with which all of those born on this day have a strong affinity. To all these endeavors they bring their dedication, tenacity and no-nonsense approach to getting the job done.

October 1 people may find themselves elevated to leadership positions, but while they will discharge their responsibilities to others with integrity, they may nevertheless resent being distracted from their work. A similar duality often prevails in their personal relationships, for although they draw strength from the affection they receive from their loved ones, their preoccupation with intellectual concerns may preclude their ability to reciprocate in kind.

VIRTUES: Personally stimulated by the challenge of transforming raw and disparate materials into orderly and progressive systems, October 1 people are imbued with the desire to make a positive contribution to the wider world through their efforts and, moreover, possess the intellectual originality, steadfastness and discipline with which to do so.
VICES: Not only are those born on this day perfectionist types, but, when taken to its extreme, their all-absorbing focus on their visions may be characterized as obsessive. As a result, they may have little attention or time to spare for nurturing of their more intimate liaisons, and thus become emotionally isolated.
VERDICT: Although the depth of their love for their nearest and dearest is never in doubt, their propensity to concentrate on their own interests to the exclusion of all else is potentially damaging, to their own emotional equilibrium and that of those closest to them. They should therefore try to spend more time relaxing in the company of friends and relations.

On This Day
Famous Births: King Henry III of England (1207); Alessandro Stradella (1644); Robert Smirke (1781); Henry Clay Work (1832); Annie Besant (1847); Paul Abraham Dukas (1865); Stanley Holloway (1890); Vladimir Horowitz (1904); Walter Matthau (1920); James Whitmore (1921); James Earl Carter (1924); Charlie Brown (1926); Tom Bosley (1927); Laurence Harvey and George Peppard (1928); Randy Quaid (1950); Jay Underwood (1968); Richard Harris (1932); Julie Andrews (1935); Gary Ablett (1961).

Significant Events and Anniversaries: This is a day that emphasizes progress intended to benefit the general good, as was reflected in the fields of transport and technology when: London's St. Pancras railroad station was opened in Britain (1868); the Edison Lamp Works company began its production of the world's first electric lightbulbs for domestic use in New Jersey (1880); and the British Broadcasting Corporation (B.B.C.) began transmitting regular television programs from London's Alexandra Palace (1936). This strong desire to advance a common cause was also variously demonstrated in the realm of politics when: during the Arab revolt against Turkey, Emir Faisal's troops, with the aid of British Army officer T. E. Lawrence, captured Damascus (1918); General Francisco Franco assumed the leadership of the Spanish Nationalist government, heralding the outbreak of civil war (1936); German troops marched into the Sudetenland in Czechoslovakia to annex this German-speaking region to Hitler's Fourth Reich (1938); and the U.S.A., Britain and the U.S.S.R. signed the Nuclear Test Ban Treaty (1963).

OCTOBER 2

The infectiously invigorating aura of vitality and *joie de vivre* of those born on October 2 attracts others to them, and these gregarious, pleasure-loving types in turn relish the stimulation of social interaction. Whatever career they choose to pursue, their strong orientation toward others invariably plays an integral part—whether it be in the nature of their work (often in the service industries or sales) or in the interpersonal professional relationships that they form. In all their ventures, their favored approach is typically a direct one aimed at attaining their goals as swiftly and effectively as possible. Because they have a propensity for making instant decisions and then promoting them with determination, October 2 people have little patience with those who manifest uncertainty or prevaricate, and will seek to influence them to adopt the course that they believe to be the correct one. Their self-certainty and predilection for action thus endows them with leadership potential (which is doubly pronounced if they were also born in the Chinese year of the dragon).

Despite their genuinely well-intentioned desire to guide others—and particularly those closest to them—those born on this day may have difficulty persuading others of the veracity of their viewpoints. The problem frequently stems from their propensity to analyze every issue that holds their attention in black-and-white terms—a tendency that may lead them to ignore the subtleties in between. And, since they are straightforwardly direct and have the courage of their convictions, the unvarnishedly honest expression of their beliefs may alienate the very individuals whom they are trying to help.

VIRTUES: Those born on this day are bright individuals who possess a talent for astute intellectual analysis: they are thus gifted decision-makers and strategists. They promote their beliefs and visions with single-minded determination and energy, fueled by the urge to enlist and direct others in the collective pursuit of their cause.

VICES: Such is their strength of self-belief and compulsion to realize their ambitions by the most direct means possible that October 2 individuals may unwittingly sabotage their own efforts. They tend to adopt an overly confrontational approach toward potential allies when more persuasive and tolerant tactics would often stand a better chance of success.

VERDICT: Realizing their ambitions yet also retaining the goodwill of those around them are of equal importance to the emotional fulfillment of these people, yet in working uncompromisingly toward the former, there is a danger that they may forfeit the latter. They should therefore take the time to consider the potentially negative effect of their words and actions, and also try to develop a more *laissez-faire* attitude toward others.

On This Day

Famous Births: King Richard III of England (1452); Edward Burnett Tylor (1832); Paul von Hindenburg (1847); Ferdinand Foch (1851); William Ramsay (1852); Patrick Geddes (1854); Mahatma Gandhi (1869); Cordell Hull (1871); Groucho Marx (1890); Bud Abbott (1896); Graham Greene and Shri Lal Banadur Shastri (1904); Alexander Todd (1907); Robert Runcie (1921); Rex Reed (1937); Don McLean (1945); Donna Karan (1948); Sting (1951); Tiffany (1971).

Significant Events and Anniversaries: This is a day that emphasizes the unyielding promotion of unequivocal aims, and October 2 marks the anniversary of: Jerusalem's recapture from its Christian occupiers by the Muslim forces of Saladin (1187); the invasion of Abyssinia (Ethiopia) by Italian troops (1935); and the sinking of a British vessel, *The Empress of Britain*, carrying children to the safety of Canada during World War II, by a German submarine (1940). The propensity for head-on confrontation that is also strongly featured by this day was demonstrated when: the first rugby-football match, between Richmond and Harlequins, was staged at England's Twickenham ground (1909); and two British ships, the cruiser *Curacao* and liner *Queen Mary*, collided off Ireland, causing the deaths of 338 people (1942). The strongly focused qualities endowed by this day were reflected when the Dutch spectacle-maker Hans Lippershey revealed his telescope—believed to be the world's first (1608).

Planetary Influences
Ruling planet: Venus.
Second decan: Personal planet is Saturn.

Sacred and Cultural Significance
Saints' day: Guardian angels; Leger (c.616–79); Thomas of Hereford (1218–82).

October 2 is Guardian Angel's day. In this detail from a painting by Dante Gabriel Rossetti, God's angelic messenger consoles and protects a troubled soul.

LIBRA

Planetary Influences
Ruling planet: Venus.
Second decan: Personal planet is Saturn.

♀ ♄

Sacred and Cultural Significance
Day of Reunification in Germany.
Saints' day: Hewald the Black (d. c.695)
and Hewald the White (d. c.695).

*The progressive urge that is featured for this
day was manifested in 1863 when President
Abraham Lincoln designated the last Thursday
in November as Thanksgiving Day,
a national holiday.*

OCTOBER 3

★★

The streak of perfectionism that is manifested by the majority of those born under the astrological sign of Libra is particularly pronounced in October 3 individuals, who are constantly striving to achieve the very best—both in terms of their personal activities and within the more global realm of human endeavor. Blessed with incisive perspicacity, a direct and logical intellectual approach, as well as remarkable resourcefulness in overcoming obstacles, these are people who find it easy to identify areas that are flawed or ripe for improvement and then to formulate imaginative and straightforward strategies to bring about progress. Their natural inclinations and talents equip them for professions where they can benefit others by initiating tangible advances, giving them the potential to make particularly innovative scientists or engineers, inspirational and ground-breaking artists or, indeed, pioneering figures in such socially oriented realms as government.

While October 3 people are to be admired for their energy and dedication, others may wonder why they are so unwilling to delegate tasks to others or to take satisfaction from their own achievements. The answer lies in both their active natures and their predilection for critical evaluation, which they apply as objectively to themselves as to others. Their desire to exert a benevolent influence on the lives of those around them pervades all their interpersonal relationships, although the importance they accord their work may result in them spending less quality time with their family and friends than they would under ideal circumstances (especially if they are men).

VIRTUES: Those born on this day are strong-willed and clear-sighted types, who pursue their progressive and innovative aims with tenacity and vigor. Although their actions are guided by ambitious inspirational visions, they display a remarkable attention to detail and adopt a practical, hands-on approach to all their ventures.
VICES: October 3 people have a marked tendency to totally immerse themselves in every aspect of the projects that fire their interest: while this augurs well for their potential success it may also sap their intellectual and physical energies and leave them with little to spare when it comes to participating fully in their personal relationships.
VERDICT: In order to safeguard their own well-being, and enable them to devote more attention to the emotional needs of their kith and kin, it is vital that these individuals recognize that perfection is not only rarely achievable but that its pursuit may exact an unacceptably high price. They should therefore try to relax the demands they make of themselves.

On This Day
Famous Births: Samuel Browne (1824); Eleanora Duse (1859); Pierre Bonnard (1867); Henri Alain-Fournier (1886); Thomas Wolfe (1900); Michael Horden (1911); James Herriott (1916); Ray Lindwall (1921); Gore Vidal (1925); Shridath Surendranath "Sonny" Ramphal (1928); Eddie Cochran (1938); Chubby Checker (1941); Al Sharpton and Stevie Ray Caughan (1954); Jack Wagner (1959); Tommy Lee (1962); Kevin Richardson (1972); Neve Campbell (1973).

Significant Events and Anniversaries: October 3 indicates innovatory potential, especially in the realms of science and technology, as was reflected when: U.S inventor J.S. Thurman patented a motor-powered vacuum cleaner (1899); "S.O.S.," the Morse-code signal for "Save our Souls," was officially adopted as the international distress signal (1906); U.S. telecommunications pioneer C.F. Jenkins transmitted the first fax image (1922). The artistic talents highlighted by this day were confirmed with the staging of three notable premiers: the light comic opera *The Yeoman of the Guard*, by British collaborators W. S. Gilbert and Arthur Sullivan (1888); British composer Edward Elgar's oratorio *The Dream of Gerontius* (1900); and the movie *The Maltese Falcon* (1941). The progressive urge of the day was emphasized in national politics when: Rebecca L. Fulton became the first woman to be elected to the U.S. Senate (1922); and the reunification of West and East Germany—separate countries following World War II—was formally celebrated (1990).

OCTOBER 4

LIBRA

Not only do most October 4 individuals seem remarkably at ease with themselves, but they also have a pronounced gift for getting along harmoniously with other people. In many respects their relaxed attitude to life is the product of their astutely perceptive way of looking at the world, which endows them with a strong sense of realism as to the nature of what is possible and what is simply unfeasible. This is not to say that they do not harbor firm opinions or inspirational visions and, when convinced that these are ultimately attainable, work toward their realization with clear-sighted determination, but rather that they instinctively prefer not to waste their energy trying to effect impossible changes. For this reason they are often drawn to professions where they can not only achieve tangible goals but also make a significant and positive contribution to the lives of others. Thus careers are indicated as social workers, doctors, lawyers or judges, for example, or as engineers or scientists.

Those born on this day manifest their genuine interest for others within all their interpersonal relationships, and the subjects of their concern in turn appreciate their good-humored and tolerant acceptance of human quirks and foibles and respect their integrity. And, since October 4 people are also sensual types who are blessed with an infectious sense of fun, they have a talent for enlivening even their most serious ventures. A similar combination of invigorating *joie de vivre* and steady and benevolent protectiveness characterizes their more personal liaisons, especially if they are men or if they were also born in the Chinese year of the dog.

VIRTUES: These are remarkably level-headed individuals, whose logical turn of mind and capacity for objective assessment leads them to set their sights on realistic, although nevertheless ambitious, targets with which to advance humanity's knowledge or capabilities. Their gregariousness, sensuality and relish for the good things in life make them popular with others.

VICES: Their varied interests and external orientation may result in those born on this day spreading their energies too thinly across the range of attractions that hold their attention. In seeking to address every demand made of them or enjoying every benefit inherent in their professional and personal pursuits and relationships they may become too distracted.

VERDICT: While October 4 individuals generally maintain a healthy equilibrium when balancing their intellectual and emotional concerns and predilections, they should ensure that they avoid creating any imbalance and thus any potential personal stasis by either overextending themselves or indulging in one particular fascination too greatly.

On This Day

Famous Births: Richard Cromwell (1626); Giovanni Battista Piranesi (1720); Jean-François Millet (1814); Rutherford Birchard Hayes (1822); Fred E. Weatherly (1848); Damon Runyon (1884); Henri Gaudier-Brzeska (1891); Engelbert Dollfuss (1892); Buster Keaton (1895); Charlton Heston (1924); Alvin Toffler (1928); Terence Conran (1930); Basil d'Oliviera (1931); Anne Rice (1941); Patti LaBelle (1944); Clifton Davis (1945); Susan Sarandon (1946); Armand Assante (1949); Alicia Silverstone (1976).

Significant Events and Anniversaries: This day highlights the promotion of concrete goals intended to advance humanity, as was reflected: in the literary sphere, when English Protestant priest Miles Coverdale published the first printed English-language version of the Bible (1535); and U.S. newspaper the *New York Herald* printed its first European edition, in Paris (1887). On a day governed by the element of air, three significant events confirmed this association: U.S. aviation pioneer Orville Wright became the first pilot to fly for longer than thirty-three minutes (1905); the U.S.S.R. launched the first space satellite to successfully orbit the Earth, *Sputnik I* (1957); and Soviet spacecraft *Lunik III* blasted off on its mission to photograph the Moon (1959).

Planetary Influences
Ruling planet: Venus.
Second decan: Personal planet is Saturn.

Sacred and Cultural Significance
Jejunium Cereris, a day of fasting in honor of Ceres, observed in ancient Rome.
Saint's day: Francis of Assisi (1181–1226), patron saint of animals, birds and ecologists.

October 4 is the feast day of Francis of Assisi, patron saint of animals, birds and ecologists, depicted below in St. Francis in Ecstasy *(1437), by Sassetta. Born in Assisi, Italy, as Giovanni Bernardone, he abandoned his worldly life to live as a hermit, devoting himself to the care of the poor and the sick and founding the Franciscan Order. He was canonized in 1229, three years after his death.*

LIBRA

OCTOBER 5

Planetary Influences
Ruling planet: Venus.
Second decan: Personal planet is Saturn.

Sacred and Cultural Significance
Festival of the Old Woman celebrated in Lithuania; in Romania, the Dionysiad wine festival honors Ariadne, Dionysus and the Maenads.
Saints' day: Maurus (6th century AD) and Placid (6th century AD).

On October 5, 1983, a day associated with reversing perceived social and moral abuses, Polish citizen Lech Walesa received the Nobel Peace Prize. Former leader of the independent trade union, Solidarity, Walesa became president of Poland in 1990, launching innovative programs of social reform.

In common with many fellow-Librans, two predominant characteristics influence those born on this day: their highly developed sense of justice and their sensuality. Some may thus feel compelled to devote their professional energies to reversing perceived social or moral abuses—perhaps as social campaigners or judges—while others may make successful careers within such artistic specialties as drama or music. Yet in whatever field they choose, they will typically display both a marked humanitarian concern and a predilection for sensory indulgence, thus making them not only deeply empathetic and supportive to those in need, but also charming, sociable and fun-loving. Despite their independence of thought, those born on this day are natural team leaders rather than solitary operators, who are blessed with an impressive talent for motivating others in the determined pursuit of a common cause, and are admired by others for these qualities.

Ideally, many would prefer to explore their intellectual or artistic interests without distraction, but such is the importance that they attach to the just treatment of others that, in this imperfect world, their sense of ethical responsibility often propels them to assume a champion's mantle and vigorously defend those who they believe to be victims of injustice. In such instances they draw upon their courage and resourcefulness (frequently surprising others with their vehement forcefulness), but, when carried away with the urgency of their mission, they may nevertheless sabotage their own efforts by failing to adopt a more pragmatic and diplomatic approach. It goes without saying that October 5 people are loyal, loving and lively friends and family members, and particularly gifted parents.

VIRTUES: Extremely sensitive individuals, those born on this day are not only especially receptive to artistic stimuli, but also empathetic to those whose circumstances are palpably unhappy or unjust. To all of their ventures they bring their concern for others, their ingenuity and optimistic determination, characteristics that frequently excite the admiration of others and make them valued by their friends as pillars of emotional support.
VICES: These people possess both the courage of their moral convictions and the willingness to take action to redress any perceived abuses of power, which may lead them to throw themselves into the passionate defense of those whose situations they wish to ameliorate without giving sufficient consideration to the consequences of their methods. They can at times become carried away and lose their sense of perspective.
VERDICT: It is important that October 5 people try to moderate their somewhat righteous propensity to become impatient and even enraged by the—perhaps reasonable—objections of those who do not share their viewpoints. While they should never abandon their visions, they should work on developing a more palatable manner.

On This Day
Famous Births: Mary of Modena (1658); Charles "Chevalier" d'Eon (1728); Chester Alan Arthur (1830); Louis Jean Lumière (1864); Larry Fine and Ray Kroc (1902); Joshua Logan (1908); Donald Pleasance (1919); Glynis Johns (1923); Barbara Kelly (1924); Vaclav Havel (1936); Karen Allen (1951); Roy Laidlaw (1953); Bob Geldof (1954); Mario Lemieux (1965); Grant Hill (1972); Kate Winslet (1975).

Significant Events and Anniversaries: On a day that emphasizes humanitarian fairness: Bulgaria proclaimed its independence from the Ottoman Empire (1908); during the Depression era, newly unemployed workers from Palmer's Shipyard set off from Jarrow on their march to London to present a petition to the British government delineating their plight (1936); and in Londonderry, Northern Ireland, a demonstration by Catholics demanding equal civil rights with Protestants erupted in violence (1968). The talent for artistic entertainment inherent in this day was confirmed when: the first episode of the comic television program "Monty Python's Flying Circus" was broadcast in Britain (1969); and the famous Parisian nightclub, the Moulin Rouge, celebrated its centenary (1989).

OCTOBER 6

LIBRA

Perhaps the defining characteristic of those born on October 6 is their adventurous zest for living, a propensity that endows them with an irresistible urge to savor and be stimulated by the multitude of experiences and sensations that life has to offer. Their strong exploratory predilection is evident in everything they encounter or undertake, and whenever a novel person, situation or intellectual concept enters their personal orbit they will typically waste little time in enthusiastically garnering as much information as they can about it—their task assisted by their intuition, as well as their talent for swift analysis and judgement. Although their need to satisfy their intellectual curiosity is a compulsive one, October 6 people are rarely motivated by selfish urges, for their empathetic identification with others fills them with the desire to benefit those around them—and even humanity as a global entity—by means of their discoveries.

These multitalented and resourceful people will flourish in a variety of professions—provided, that is, that they can retain autonomy of thought and action—but they are especially well suited for careers where they can satisfy their progressive urges and influence others. Blessed with pioneering potential, the engineering, building and scientific realms have a fascinating allure for those born on this day, but perhaps the field that offers them the greatest opportunity for experimentation and expression is art and design, with which these undoubted sensualists have a naturally strong affinity. Interesting, positive and enlivening companions, partners and family members, October 6 individuals value the grounding bonds of kinship as a counterbalance to their somewhat restless intellectual tendencies.

VIRTUES: Those born on this day are versatile in terms of both their interests and their practical talents and are fueled in all their endeavors by their desire to make an inspirational contribution to the wider world. Their optimism in the pursuit of their progressive visions and typical *joie de vivre* exert a magnetic attraction on those around them.
VICES: There is a danger that their inherent relish for stimulation of all kinds may cause October 6 people to actively respond to everything they encounter, thereby diminishing their ability to devote their full attention to a single topic and limiting their potential for success, as well as for their ultimate emotional fulfillment.
VERDICT: Their intellectual curiosity is among the most interesting and promising personal features of these individuals, but if they are to achieve their imaginative visions it is vital that they should apply a focused and exclusive approach to their promotion, and do not let themselves be distracted by the siren lure of novelty.

On This Day

Famous Births: Matteo Ricci (1552); Nevil Maskelyne (1732); Louis Philippe of France (1773); Jenny Lind (1820); George Westinghouse (1846); Karol Szymanowski (1883); Charles Jeanneret, "Le Corbusier" (1887); Ernest Walton (1903); Helen Wills Moody (1905); Janet Gaynor (1906); Carole Lombard (1909); Barbara Castle (1910); Thor Heyerdahl (1914); Tommy Lawton (1919); Richie Benaud (1930); Melvyn Bragg (1939); Britt Ekland (1942); Tony Greig (1946); Elisabeth Shue (1963); Amy Jo Johnson (1970).

Significant Events and Anniversaries: This is a day that highlights the implementation of imaginative innovations intended to advance the common good, as was reflected: in the sphere of engineering, when the African railroad linking Cape Town in southern Africa with Beira in Mozambique, southeastern Africa, was completed (1902); and in the film world, when the first "talkie," Warner Brothers' *The Jazz Singer*, starring Al Jolson, had its premier (1927). October 6 also indicates the tenacious adherence to strong convictions, as was demonstrated when: English Christian reformer William Tyndale, who offended Catholic sensibilities by translating the New Testament into English, was punished by being asphyxiated and burned as a heretic at Vilvorde, Flanders (1536); and, outraged by his conciliatory approach to Israel, Egyptian president Anwar Sadat was assassinated by Muslim fundamentalists, on the eighth anniversary of the Arab-Israeli War (1987).

Planetary Influences
Ruling planet: Venus.
Second decan: Personal planet is Saturn.

Sacred and Cultural Significance
First day of nine-day festival honoring Hindi God Vishnu in Nepal.
Saints' day: Faith (3rd century AD); Bruno (c.1032–1101).

Reflecting the dedication, enthusiasm and energy of this day, American golfer Bobby Jones won the Amateur Golf Cup on October 6, 1928.

LIBRA

Planetary Influences
Ruling planet: Venus.
Second decan: Personal planet is Saturn.

Sacred and Cultural Significance
Saints' day: Justina of Padua (d. c.300);
Helen of Cornwall (dates unknown);
Osith (d. c.700).

U.S. retired military officer Oliver North was born on October 7, 1943, and thus also in the Chinese year of the goat. Reflecting the vigorous approach, strong opinions and determined—often confrontational—adherence to guiding principles that characterize this day, he had a brilliant but latterly controversial career as a National Security Council officer in the Reagan administration.

OCTOBER 7

Those born on this day are vigorous and strongly opinionated individuals, and whether they be admirers or detractors, the majority of those who come into contact with them are impressed by their determined promotion of the ideals that motivate them. Indeed, October 7 people often engender love and loathing in equal measure and—although they are sensitive and apparently intuitively pick up the emotions exuded by others—they seem to accept the extremes of reactions that they provoke with equanimity, perhaps strengthened by their acceptance that progress cannot be achieved without alienating the more conventional upholders of the status quo. Thus while they would prefer to win allies rather than to make enemies, their strength of belief endows them with the courage to battle when necessary for the realization of their visions. Their profound orientation toward others and their all-encompassing curiosity typically compels those born on this day to strive to effect the advances they believe are justified.

The nature of their progressive urge varies according to the October 7 individual, and while many will choose to channel their energies in the furtherance of social or spiritual ideals, others will try to exert their influence on others through technical, creative or artistic pursuits. And, despite their radical messages, all employ their considerable personal charm, humor and ingenious and imaginative powers in the propagation of their aims. Within their personal relationships (which they often prefer to keep strictly separate from their intellectual or professional work), such gentler qualities come to the fore, especially with regard to those who arouse their protective instincts—their closest friends, partners and children in particular.

VIRTUES: Their sensitivity toward others and driving urge to bring about improvements in those areas that they have identified as being unsatisfactory endow October 7 people with pioneering potential. Despite the combative approach that is sometimes manifested in pursuit of their visions, they remain magnetic and socially concerned types.
VICES: Those born on this day must beware of being carried away by the momentum generated by their evangelizing stance, a tendency that may cause them to become not only as intransigent as those they castigate, but also too self-righteous and perhaps blind to the validity of alternative viewpoints.
VERDICT: Although they should never abandon their quest to bring about improvement, it is vital that these individuals retain as clear-sighted a sense of objectivity with regard to their own motives and methods as they apply to external issues. Employing such an internal monitoring system will enable them to enhance their focus and effectiveness, and to remain open-minded, to achieve personal growth and become more accepting of the struggles and weaknesses of others.

On This Day
Famous Births: William Laud (1573); William Still (1821); James W. Riley (1849); Niels Bohr (1885); Heinrich Himmler (1900); Andy Devine (1905); Arnold Crowther (1909); Shura Cherkassy (1911); Joseph Cooper (1912); June Allyson (1917); R.D. Laing and Al Martino (1927); Desmond Tutu (1931); Thomas Keneally (1935); Clive James (1939); Oliver North (1943); John Cougar Mellencamp (1951); Yo Yo Ma (1955); Jayne Torvill (1957); Judy Landers (1961).

Significant Events and Anniversaries: This day emphasizes a determined adherence to guiding principles, as was reflected in the realm of international politics when: the naval Battle of Lepanto was fought in the Gulf of Corinth between the Muslim Ottoman Turks and a victorious combined Venetian, Genoese, Spanish and Papal State Christian force under the command of Don John of Austria (1571); and Palestinian terrorists hijacked the Italian cruise ship the *Achille Lauro* to draw attention to their anti-Israeli cause (1985). The importance of objectivity is highlighted by this day, on which the first issue of the supposedly nonpartisan British newspaper the *Independent* was published (1986).

OCTOBER 8

In many respects those born on this day are defined by the lofty idealism of their desire to reach beyond the bounds of existing circumstances or knowledge and thereby attain an elevated state which will enlighten them and humanity as a whole. The visions that inspire them are often so ambitious that others may regard them as unfeasible and their originators as eccentrics at best, and as crackpots at worst. But even those who seriously doubt their motives or abilities will often succumb to sneaking feelings of admiration for their optimism and enthusiasm. Despite the mockery or even downright hostility that October 8 people often seem to engender, they typically remain true to their dreams, not least because these are intellectually sharp and logical types who have thought through their beliefs carefully and can envisage no potential bar to their progress save the limitations of the imaginations of others. Those born on this day are multitalented individuals, whose ingenuity, originality and progressive inclinations bestow on them the potential to make their marks in such varied professional spheres as commercial entrepreneurship, the financial world, technical and scientific pursuits, and sporting and artistic ventures.

Despite their great charm, the combination of their innate perfectionism and unceasing compulsion to attain their soaring visions may cause those born on this day to be somewhat demanding and remote with regard to their personal relationships, not only in their intellectual pursuits, but also when searching for a romantic idyll. Their ideal soul mate may prove elusive, with the result that October 8 people—and even more so if they are men—may find it hard to commit themselves to a potential life partner.

VIRTUES: Those born on this day are unfailingly optimistic with regard to the potential success of their extremely advanced goals, targets that not only reflect personal ambition but are also intended to benefit others. The combination of their clarity of vision, driving determination and considerable resourcefulness augur well for their potential success.

VICES: October 8 individuals must beware of allowing their tendency to pursue their idealistic dreams regardless of the objections of others to develop into an obsession. There is a danger that they may not only remove themselves from reality, but may isolate themselves from the grounding and emotional rewards inherent in strong and honest relationships with their spouses, family and friends.

VERDICT: If they are to achieve their aims and also retain the love and support of those closest to them, it is important that these individuals moderate their propensity to immerse themselves in their intellectual interests to the exclusion of all else. They should instead ensure that they devote sufficient time and attention to those whose unquestioning belief and affection is so vital to their emotional well-being.

On This Day

Famous Births: John Milton Hay and Montagu Lowry-Corry (1838); John Cowper Powys (1872); Alfred Munnings (1878); Eddie Rickenbacker (1890); Juan Perón (1895); Rouben Mamoulian (1898); Cesar Milstein (1927); Neil Harvey (1928); Betty Boothroyd (1929); Ray Reardon (1932); Rona Barrett (1936); Merle Park (1937); Paul Hogan (1939); Jesse Jackson (1941); Chevy Chase (1943); Sarah Purcell (1948); Sigourney Weaver (1949); Stephanie Zimbalist (1956); James DePaiva (1957); Matt Damon (1970).

Significant Events and Anniversaries: On a day that indicates the pursuit of the highest of ideals, this propensity was given concrete expression: in the realm of ecclesiastical architecture, with the consecration of St. Mark's Cathedral in Venice (1085). The idealism that is so strongly emphasized by October 8 was further demonstrated when Serbia, Greece and Montenegro declared war on Turkey, their common Ottoman ruler, thus inaugurating the First Balkan War (1912). Indeed, collision is in many respects inherent in the combination of influences that govern this day, as was tragically reflected when a three train accident in Harrow, England, resulted in the deaths of 112 individuals (1952).

Planetary Influences
Ruling planet: Venus.
Second decan: Personal planet is Saturn.

Sacred and Cultural Significance
Cheng Yeung Dan (Festival of High Places), an annual good luck festival, celebrated in China.
Saints' day: Triduana (dates unknown); Pelagia (5th century AD); Keyne (6th century AD), patron saint of St. Keyne, Cornwall, England; Iwi (7th century AD).

The Chicago fire of 1871 was considered one of the most devastating in American history, resulting in the loss of 90,000 homes and destroying four square miles of the city. But rebuilding began almost immediately, demonstrating idealism and the ability to transcend adverse circumstances to benefit humanity, true to the spirit of this day.

LIBRA

Planetary Influences
Ruling planet: Venus.
Second decan: Personal planet is Saturn.

Sacred and Cultural Significance
National day of Uganda; Day of Felicitas celebrated in ancient Rome.
Saints' day: Denys (d. c.250), patron saint of France; Luis Bertran (1526–81); John Leonardi (c.1542–1609).

Venerable and esteemed Yale University, founded on this day in 1701, remains one of the oldest and finest institutions of higher learning in the U.S. Consistent with the progressive ideals, independent and original thought and service to humanity common to this day, it has attracted the best and the brightest in all academic endeavors.

OCTOBER 9

Those born on October 9 are acutely observant individuals and very little escapes their attention, particularly in the realm of human and societal behavior and systems, with which they are often strongly fascinated. Blessed with remarkably developed powers of perception—both intellectual and intuitive—as well as a logically progressive mindset, these people are talented analysts who possess not only the ability easily to identify the nub of problems but also the ingenuity to devise strategies for improvement. Once they have determined the optimum method for effecting the advances that appear necessary, they will promote it with vigorous zeal and unwavering tenacity. Such a focused and determined approach augurs well for their potential success in whichever professional field holds their interest, but since the majority are oriented toward enlightening those around them, many will choose to direct their energies toward helping others—perhaps in mentoring roles as academics, psychiatrists, judges, social workers or even spiritual guides, or in those spheres where they can inspire by example, for instance as athletes or artists.

Although the independently minded individuals born on this day are natural leaders whose strength of conviction enables them to push bravely forward regardless of the opposition that their determined stance may provoke, they do not relish conflict for conflict's sake. They would far prefer to make friends rather than foes (especially if they are women). Their goodwill toward others is evident within all of their interpersonal relationships—particularly with regard to their nearest and dearest—although their tendency to criticize and direct, albeit with the best of motivations, may not always be taken in the spirit that it is intended.

VIRTUES: October 9 people are astute observers, analyzers and strategists, whose sensitivity to others and desire to effect improvement by means of soundly considered, positive and direct forms of action makes them gifted problem-solvers.
VICES: Their clear-sighted ability to pinpoint perceived failings in existing systems or behavioral patterns and then formulate imaginative solutions are undoubted talents, but may nevertheless also run the risk of causing those born on this day to be overly critical and judgemental in their assessment of others' methods and approaches, a propensity that could provoke resentment, particularly from those closest to them.
VERDICT: If they are not to alienate those whose best interests they have at heart by their well-meaning urge to provide positive direction, these individuals should occasionally turn the focus of their objectivity upon themselves, both to examine their motives and to consider whether the possibly negative effect of their incisive words justifies the cause at their root.

On This Day
Famous Births: Camille Saint-Saëns (1835); Alfred Dreyfus (1859); Aimee Semple McPherson (1890); Bruce Catton (1899); Alaistair Sim (1900); Jacques Tati (1908); Donald Sinden (1923); Donald McCullin (1935); Brian Blessed (1937); John Lennon (1940); Peter Tosh (1944); Jackson Browne (1948); Robert Wuhl (1951); Steve Ovett (1955); Michael Pare (1959); Sean Lennon (1975); Zachery Ty Bryan (1981).

Significant Events and Anniversaries: This is a day that highlights the desire to instruct and illuminate others, as was reflected in two events that occurred on October 9: the dedication of a temple on Rome's Palatine Hill to the Roman deity Apollo to provide a spiritual focus for the god's worship (28 BC); and the granting of a founding charter to Yale College in New Haven, Connecticut, to educate U.S. students (1701). October 9 furthermore emphasizes a willingness to take direct action in the promotion of firmly held—often collective—beliefs, and this day marks the anniversary of: the murder of King Alexander I, the effective dictator of Yugoslavia, by, it is variously believed, either a Croatian, Macedonian or Italian Fascist assassin (1934); and the capture and execution of the Argentinean Marxist Ernesto "Che" Guevara in Bolivia, where he was attempting to encourage an uprising against the military government, by Bolivian forces loyal to the establishment (1967).

OCTOBER 10

Those born on this day are sensible individuals who typically abhor disorder, regarding chaos as a hindrance to the progress that they are so intent on achieving. Indeed, blessed as they are with logical and perceptive intellects, they are able to identify the existing flaws in any situation they encounter and suggest constructive solutions. They positively itch to actively throw themselves into the absorbing task of bringing order and harmony to unproductive or otherwise unsatisfactory situations. In many respects they take as much pleasure in instituting and maintaining effectively functioning systems as they do in reaping the rewards of their labors, a predilection that is more pronounced if they were also born in the Chinese year of the rooster. Their inclinations and talents suit them to a wide variety of careers, and their no-nonsense, hands-on approach, self-discipline and realistic clarity of purpose augurs especially well for their success as supervisors, team leaders and business executives.

Many October 10 people display the same love of order within their personal lives, running smoothly functioning households and giving steady support—both emotional and financial—to their loved ones. Yet beneath the rational and balanced exterior they present to the wider world lies a more sensual and emotional core that not only endows those born on this day with a relish for indulging in the good things in life but also makes them susceptible to romance of all kinds. Thus when these two sides to their personalities are in harmony, others are drawn to them for their charming, as well as their reliable, qualities.

VIRTUES: October 10 people are blessed with remarkably perceptive and rational intellects, and are therefore quick to identify and seek to rectify any disorder they encounter by instituting practical and straightforward countermeasures. As well as being interested in detail, they never lose sight of their ultimate vision.

VICES: The disciplined and orderly methodology that characterizes their approach to their professional ventures—and often their personal affairs—is effective in attaining concrete results, but may also cause those born on this day to suppress their "softer" emotions, with the risk that these will eventually find a negative—even destructive—outlet.

VERDICT: It is vital that these individuals do not neglect their emotional well-being in their quest to achieve their intellectual ambitions. They should therefore ensure that they maintain a healthy balance between the pursuit of their professional interests and their profound need to both give and receive affection, to enjoy the restorative benefits of relaxation, and to indulge in spiritually nurturing, nonmaterial activities.

On This Day

Famous Births: Jean A. Watteau (1684); Henry Cavendish (1731); Benjamin West (1738); Giuseppe Verdi (1813); Paul Kruger (1825); Fridtjof Nansen (1861); William Morris (1877); Helen Hayes (1900); Vladimir Dukelsky (1903); Thelonius Monk (1920); James Clavell and Edward D. Wood, Jr. (1924); Harold Pinter (1930); Daniel Massey (1933); Charles Dance and Ben Vereen (1946); David Lee Roth (1955); Tanya Tucker (1958); Brett Favre (1969).

Significant Events and Anniversaries: October 10 highlights strong organizational capabilities in the pursuit of visionary aims, as was reflected on this day when the English suffragette Emmeline Pankhurst founded the Women's Social and Political Union as an instrument with which to agitate for English women's right to vote (1903). A similar preference for the use of direct action is strongly emphasized by this day, as was demonstrated when, during World War II, a German bombing raid destroyed the high altar of London's St. Paul's Cathedral (1940). The influences governing this day warn of the explosive dangers inherent in the suppression of emotions, and this threat was paralleled on October 10 when a radiation leak at the English nuclear-power station of Windscale (since renamed Sellafield) threatened the surrounding area of Cumbria and beyond (1957). On a day governed by the element of air, the giant Transcontinental and Western Airlines (T.W.A.) company was formed as a result of the merger of three U.S. airlines (1930).

Planetary Influences
Ruling planet: Venus.
Second decan: Personal planet is Saturn.

Sacred and Cultural Significance
In Brazil, the Festival of Lights.
Saints' day: Gereon, patron saint of headache-sufferers, and Companions (d. 304?); Paulinus of York (d. 644); Francis Borgia (1510–72).

Founded on this day in 1845, the United States Naval Academy still stands today as a symbol not only for martial activities, but as a monument to leadership, progress and a love of order—qualities desirable in an institution of its stature and in keeping with the character of this day.

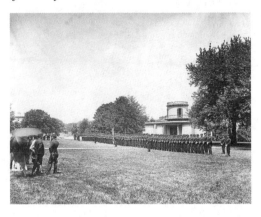

LIBRA

Planetary Influences
Ruling planet: Venus.
Second decan: Personal planet is Saturn.

Sacred and Cultural Significance
The Old Lady of the Elder Trees honored by Pagans in Denmark and Germany.
Saints' day: Canice (c.525–c.600); Ethelburga (d. 675); Alexander Sauli (1534–92).

With outstanding grace, humanity and intellect, the birthright of those born today, Eleanor Roosevelt earned the love of her nation. But figurehead she was not; as diplomat and humanitarian she proved an invaluable advisor to her husband, Franklin D. Roosevelt, throughout his presidency, served the United Nations in several capacities and hosted her own press conferences, a practice unprecedented in U.S. history.

OCTOBER 11

Those born on this day are positive individuals, who in many respects may be characterized as social idealists, for they are fueled by their desire to effect not only their own emotional happiness, but also that of others—be it those with whom they come into contact, wider communal groupings, or humanity as a global entity. Indeed, these twin aims are often inextricably linked, for such is the strong sense of natural justice possessed by these people, and their profound empathy with those whom they believe are being unfairly treated, that even if their own circumstances are harmonious they may nevertheless feel compelled to campaign on the behalf of the less fortunate. A similarly benevolent concern for others defines their personal and professional relationships, yet although they generally favor conciliation and cooperation over aggression and confrontation, their urge to reverse perceived injustices should not be underestimated (although it frequently is by those who misjudge their easy-going approach for weakness of will).

Balancing their altruism and clear-sighted perspicacity are the markedly more self-indulgent personal characteristics possessed by October 11 individuals. Their highly developed response to emotional and sensual stimuli bestows on them the tendency to immerse themselves with willing abandon in the pleasures of the senses. Given such extreme inclinations, those born on this day have the potential to flourish across a wide spectrum of professions—as writers, musicians, athletes, philanthropists or social reformers, for example.

VIRTUES: Reflecting their engaging *joie de vivre* and empathy for others, those born on this day are interesting and attractive personalities who attract others to them. Yet despite their typical kindness and love of life, these are no intellectual lightweights, for when motivated by the urge to effect progress they show remarkable resourcefulness, dedication and determination in the pursuit of their goals.
VICES: October 11 individuals have a propensity to go to extremes, either when defending or promoting a cherished cause or principle, or—and even more so if they were born in the Chinese year of the horse—when they give themselves over to their strong predilection for succumbing to the enticing allure of sensual indulgence.
VERDICT: Keeping their emotional, sensual and intellectual inclinations in equilibrium is of crucial importance if these people are to achieve the all-round fulfillment that they crave. They would therefore be advised to occasionally take time for honest introspection in order to identify what will bring them the greatest satisfaction in life, and then remain focused on working toward this aim, regardless of the seductive distractions that may present themselves.

On This Day
Famous Births: Arthur Phillip (1738); George Williams (1821); H.J. Heinz (1844); Friedrich Bergius and Eleanor Roosevelt (1884); François Mauriac (1885); Leff Pouishhonoff (1891); Danie Craven (1910); Jerome Robbins (1918); Art Blakey (1919); Elmore Leonard (1925); Toney Kinsey (1927); Ennio Morricone (1928); Roy Scheider (1935); Bobby Charlton (1937); Maria Bueno (1939); Alan Pascoe (1947); Daryl Hall (1949); Joan Cusack (1962); Luke Perry (1966).

Significant Events and Anniversaries: One characteristic propensity indicated by this day is that of great strength of purpose in the promotion of communal ideals, as was demonstrated when: King Henry VIII of England was rewarded for his defense of Catholicism and attack on the Protestantism of Martin Luther by Pope Leo X's bestowal upon him of the title "Defender of the Faith" (1521); Swiss religious reformer Ulrich Zwingli was killed at the Battle of Kappel while attempting to impose his form of Protestantism on nonconformist Swiss cantons (1531); and Peter the Great, the emperor who was determined to modernize his country, became czar of Russia (1689). October 11 is governed by the element of air, as was reflected when: British astronomer Bernard Lowell's radio telescope was used for the first time (1957); U.S. *Apollo 7* space mission was launched (1968); and Soviet spacecraft *Salyut 6* landed on Earth, having spent a then-record 185 days in space (1980).

OCTOBER 12

The astrological influences that govern October 12 endow those born on this day with complex characters: on the one hand pleasure-loving and sensual, these individuals are also independently minded, intellectually curious and resourceful types who demand autonomy while being simultaneously strongly oriented toward others. Such a combination of personal characteristics may manifest themselves in various ways, depending on the individual. Some may sublimate their self-indulgent side in their dedication to serving their communities in an imaginative yet traditional fashion; while others may appear to be more maverick, nonconformist types, who forge their own, inimitable paths through life. All, however, cherish the inherent desire—and, indeed, possess the potential—to lead or inspire others by example. Whatever career those born on this day choose to pursue, their ultimate aim is to make a concrete contribution to the advancement of humanity (perhaps as educators, or maybe as visionary researchers or academics) by instituting truly pioneering innovations.

Despite their prerequisite for independence, the actions of those born on this day are fueled by their selfless, humanitarian concern with improving the welfare of others. That is not to say that they do not appreciate the acclaim and rewards that may accompany their own success—to the contrary, they long to receive the recognition of their peers, and they welcome the security and comfort that money can buy—but rather that their goals are generally of the globally beneficial rather than personally ambitious variety. And, as long as their need for freedom is respected, they are generous and affectionate to those closest to them.

VIRTUES: October 12 individuals are strong-willed individuals, whose intellectual inquisitiveness and propensity to challenge conventional truths endow them with a decidedly independent turn of mind. The combination of their powers of imagination with their technical and organizational skills, as well as their interest in others, furthermore blesses them with the potential to bring about wide-ranging advances in the realm of human knowledge.
VICES: There is a danger that their individualistic approach and readiness to counter any opposition that their convictions or methods may, and often do, arouse, may lead these people to become addicted to the attention—be it outrage or acclaim—that the idiosyncratic expression of their viewpoints may provoke, causing them to merely seek a reaction from others.
VERDICT: If they are to attain the visionary and original ideals that mean so much to them, it is important that those born on this day should retain their sense of focus, and not permit themselves to become distracted by the sheer enjoyment of acting independently (and frequently provocatively) for the sake of inciting a strong response in others.

On This Day

Famous Births: King Edward VI of England (1537); Isaac Newton Lewis (1858); Elmer Ambrose Sperry (1860); Ramsay MacDonald (1866); Ralph Vaughan Williams (1872); Aleister Crowley (1875); Jaroslav Drobny (1921); Jean Nidetch (1923); Magnus Magnusson (1929); Dick Gregory (1932); Luciano Pavarotti (1935); Chris Wallace (1947); Susan Anton (1951); Kirk Cameron (1970).

Significant Events and Anniversaries: This is a day that highlights questingly pioneering capabilities, and October 12 commemorates the anniversary of: Italian explorer Christopher Columbus's first sighting of the New World, the territory believed to be what is now called San Salvador Island (1492); the first transatlantic flight of a dirigible, the German Z3 Zeppelin which landed in Lakenhurst, New Jersey, having set off from Friedrichshafen (1924); and the first successful use of the "iron-lung" artificial respiratory system, at the Boston Children's Hospital in Massachusetts (1928). October 12 is also a day on which courageous adherence to humanitarian principles is indicated, as was reflected when: English Red Cross nurse, Edith Cavell, was executed by the Germans during World War I for assisting the escape of Allied so New Zealand parliament abolished the death penalty (1961).

Planetary Influences
Ruling planet: Venus.
Third decan: Personal planets are Uranus and Mercury.

Sacred and Cultural Significance
Columbus Day in Spain and the U.S.A.
Saints' day: Edwin (584–633); Wilfred (c.633–709).

Loyal to the Spanish crown yet fiercely determined to follow his own inquisitive nature, Christopher Columbus and his crew first sighted what was to be called the "New World" in 1492 on this day of pioneering innovation. Columbus Day is celebrated in the United States and Spain to commemorate this day's spirit of independence, resourcefulness and conquest.

LIBRA

Planetary Influences
Ruling planet: Venus.
Third decan: Personal planets are Uranus and Mercury.

Sacred and Cultural Significance
Saints' day: Comgan (8th century AD); Gerald of Aurillac (855–909); translation of Edward the Confessor (1003–66), patron saint of kings.

Margaret Thatcher, nicknamed "the Iron Lady" and leader of Britain's Conservative party for twenty years (the longest reign of any premier of the 20th century), was born on this day, auspicious for social change and influence on a global scale. The further influence of the Chinese year of the ox brings the qualities of articulacy and uncompromising vigor-sometimes to the point of stubbornness-excellent qualities for those politically ambitious people born on October 13.

OCTOBER 13

Their strength of conviction and total focus on the attainment of their often radically pioneering ideals inevitably arouses equally strong and unambiguous responses—be they of devoted admiration or intense antipathy—to those born on this day. Indeed, October 13 people recognize that their clear-cut visions and uncompromisingly direct methods have an energizing tendency to shock the generally apathetic out of their lethargy and thereby at least win recognition for their cause. In many cases, however, they are naturally combative types who enjoy the cut and thrust of confrontational debate, not least because they secretly relish drawing the spotlight upon themselves. Apart from any attention-seeking motivations, these are intellectually progressive individuals, who possess strong feelings of social responsibility. Not only are they inherently critical types who cannot help but identify perceived societal failings or injustices, but also their logical turn of mind endows them with the propensity to formulate practical—and often ingenious—strategies with which they can bring about positive advances for the benefit of others. Natural leaders, their strong communication skills suit October 13 people especially well for advertising and marketing careers, although they may equally excel as ground-breaking, if controversial, politicians.

Despite their typically well-intentioned humanitarian orientation, the concern that those born on this day manifest toward others often assumes an abstract rather than a personal form. Thus, although their fierce affection, support and ambition for their nearest and dearest is never in doubt, their innate perfectionism and personal standards may cause them to make near-impossible demands upon those closest to them, without consideration for personal predilections or talents, a tendency that is even more pronounced if they were also born in the Chinese year of the rooster.

VIRTUES: Those born on this day are fueled by their desire to assist others to progress. Blessed with highly developed analytical and critical faculties, they feel compelled to take direct action to ameliorate those human situations that they regard as being unsatisfactory. Focused, tenacious, and also original and resourceful, they possess outstanding courage in the pursuit of their convictions.
VICES: Such is their driving urge to bring about advances intended to be of concrete benefit to the common good, that October 13 individuals have a propensity to sublimate to the altar of their lofty ideals not only their own, more personal (but no less significant) urges, but also the individual desires of their nearest and dearest.
VERDICT: Although the attainment of their visions, and their wish to make a tangible contribution to society is inextricably bound up with their emotional happiness, it is important that these people recognize the importance of maintaining honest and relaxed personal liaisons for their own emotionally enriching benefits, and to retain a balanced and tolerant attitude toward the foibles of others.

On This Day
Famous Births: Rudolf Virchow (1821); Lillie Langtry (1852); Art Tatum (1910); Cornel Wilde (1915); Yves Montand (1921); Lenny Bruce and Nipsey Russell (1924); Margaret Thatcher (1925); Paul Simon (1941); Art Garfunkel (1942); Edwina Currie (1946); Sammy Hagar (1947); Marie Osmond (1959); Jerry Rice (1962); Nancy Kerrigan (1969).

Significant Events and Anniversaries: On a day that highlights outstanding leadership qualities: a scion of the house of Lancaster, Henry Bolingbroke was crowned Henry IV of England (1399); and the U.S.A.'s first president, George Washington, laid the foundation stone of the Executive Mansion (later to be renamed the White House) (1792). Selfless action in pursuit of the perceived common good is a further feature of this day, on which British commander Sir Isaac Brock lost his life at the Battle of Queenston but nevertheless prevented the American invading force from penetrating further into Canada (1812). The intellectual pioneering promised was reflected when Austrian psychiatrist Sigmund Freud published *The Interpretation of Dreams* (1904).

OCTOBER 14

The personalities of many of those born on this day typically manifest a curious combination of a marked propensity for excessive behavior and a striving for order and harmony. While some October 14 people are able to maintain their personal equilibrium—albeit with a struggle—others are not, particularly when such behavioral extremes are more pronounced. Blessed with enormous intellectual curiosity, which endows them with a strong sense of adventure—and these individuals are keen travelers—those born on this day are undoubtedly independently minded. Yet they also appreciate the importance of remaining grounded within the social conventions that bind society together, and therefore recognize the need to moderate, or at least channel, their more questing tendencies and self-indulgent cravings. When they are successful, they have the potential to make imaginative and inspirational leaders, perhaps most obviously as social or political figureheads, but also as gifted and original teachers, painters, actors or designers.

To all their endeavors they bring their enthusiasm, good humor and unusual perspective on the world, making them attractive individuals who are popular with others. In turn October 14 people often identify strongly with the social group with which they have the strongest affinity, and they will work hard to promote or protect its interests. Although their preferred approach is to be easy-going, tolerant and noncombative, their readiness to protect those closest to them from any threat should not be underestimated.

VIRTUES: Those born on this day are extraordinarily receptive to sensory or emotional stimuli, and furthermore possess inquisitive minds that attract them to exploration of all kinds. Yet because they also have a highly developed sense of social responsibility and feel profound concern for the well-being of others, they are committed team-players as well as strong individualists.

VICES: Since these people are naturally drawn to extremes, they may allow their behavior to become imbalanced, perhaps completely giving themselves over to self-indulgence and neglecting the needs of those around them, or, at the other end of the scale, sublimating their more selfish urges by placing themselves unreservedly at the service of others.

VERDICT: October 14 individuals instinctively understand the value of steering a balanced course through life, if they are to safeguard their emotional well-being and satisfy their dual urge to promote their own interests along with those they care for. They should nevertheless ensure that they do not thereby suppress their individuality in their attempts to conform.

On This Day

Famous Births: Peter Lely (1618); King James II of Britain (1633); William Penn (1644); George Grenville (1712); Eamon de Valera (1882); Katherine Mansfield (1888); Dwight D. Eisenhower (1890); Lillian Gish (1893); e e cummings (1894); Bud Flanagan (1896); John Wooden (1910); Roger Moore (1927); Shirley Maureen Cunliffe (1934); Ralph Lauren (1939); Cliff Richard (1940); Justin Hayward (1946); Harry Anderson (1952); Arleen Sorkin (1956); Steve Cram (1960).

Significant Events and Anniversaries: Highlighted on October 14 is a strong commitment to promoting communal interests—a quality that is clearly mirrored in warfare—as was demonstrated on this day when: at the Battle of Hastings in England fought on Senlac Hill, William, Duke of Normandy, defeated the defending English army under King Harold II (who was killed) and earned the nickname of "William the Conqueror" (1066); a German submarine torpedoed and destroyed the British battleship *Royal Oak* at Scapa Flow, off the Orkney Islands, with the loss of 810 crew members' lives during World War II (1939); and on the Jewish Day of Atonement, Yom Kippur, a combined Egyptian and Syrian force invaded Israel, thereby initiating the Fourth Arab-Israeli, or October, War (1973). A less combative desire to help human advancement was variously reflected on October 14 when: U.S. inventor George Eastman patented his pioneering photographic film (1884); and the U.S. test pilot Chuck Yeager, flying in his Bell X-1 rocket airplane, became the first person to break the sound barrier (1947).

Planetary Influences
Ruling planet: Venus.
Third decan: Personal planets are Uranus and Mercury.

Sacred and Cultural Significance
The planets of the Milky Way galaxy celebrated by Interplanetary Confederation Day; in Bangladesh, Durga, the mother goddess, honored with Durga Duja festival.
Saints' day: Callistus (d. 222); Manacca (5th–6th century AD); Selevan (6th century AD), patron saint of St. Levan, Cornwall, England; Burchard (d. 754).

The striking, if paradoxical qualities of a love of order and a strict sense of social responsibility combined with a tendency toward excessive behavior common to those born today, were justly manifested in the presidency of Dwight D. Eisenhower, 34th U.S. President. Although a champion of civil rights, he was avidly opposed to those social philosophies he found contrary to his own, as evidenced in his crusade against Communism at home and abroad.

OCTOBER 15

✦✦

Planetary Influences
Ruling planet: Venus.
Third decan: Personal planets are Uranus and Mercury.

Sacred and Cultural Significance
In ancient Rome, sacred harvest festival of Mars celebrated with a chariot race.
Saints' day: Tecla (d. c.790); Theresa of Avila (1515–82).

Warrior god Mars, first child of Hera and Zeus, was honored on this day by the ancient Romans. Although endowed with the seductive qualities of power and great physical beauty, his terrible lust for war and conflict made him most feared and least loved of the pantheon.

Although October 15 individuals possess resolutely independent wills and cannot bear to have their investigative intellects constrained in any way, they are also sociable types who are strongly connected to all those around them. Thus even though they are strong individualists, they are also socially concerned and responsible people whose actions are often motivated by their desire to make a significant contribution to the world, or to redress instances of injustice. Indeed, their mercurial minds and highly developed powers of perception and analysis, along with their relish of discovery and novelty, bestow upon them the potential to become pioneers in their specific field of interest, while their predilection for creating orderly and efficient systems gives them the ability to capitalize on their innovative visions by supporting them with soundly structured operational frameworks. Their natural talents, progressive inclinations and positive orientation toward others equip them admirably for a wide variety of careers, but they need to be able to retain autonomy of thought and action as well as interacting with others.

Despite their deep-rooted (but frequently rather abstract) concern for other people, the relationships that those born on this day form with others may sometimes be tempestuous, for although their affection for those closest to them is profound, their need for freedom is so strong that any perceived attempts to tie them down or make them conform to societal norms may arouse negative feelings of resistance (especially if they are men). As long as their nearest and dearest understand their innate desire for independence, however, they typically prove enlivening and generous partners and friends.

VIRTUES: Not only are those born on this day blessed with extraordinarily adventurous intellects, they also have the necessary analytical and organizational skills to present the fruits of their discoveries to others in a faultlessly ordered package. Although personally stimulated by their intellectual interests, their actions are fueled by their wish to inform or educate others.
VICES: Despite their desire to guide others along what they adjudge to be the best route, October 15 individuals are extremely jealous of their own personal autonomy, and may react badly if they feel that others are attempting to restrict their intellectual, emotional or even physical freedom, a tendency that is particularly pronounced in their relationships with their partners or parents.
VERDICT: In order to benefit from the grounding and supportive rewards of close personal liaisons, it is vital that these individuals appreciate that the maintenance of strong emotional bonds does not constitute a threat to their freedom. They should therefore try to moderate their urge to constantly act as independent agents and learn the value of compromise.

On This Day
Famous Births: Virgil (70 BC); Evangelista Torricelli (1608); Friedrich Nietzsche (1844); John L. Sullivan (1858); Marie Stopes (1880); P.G. Wodehouse (1881); Mervyn Leroy (1900); C.P. Snow (1905); J.K. Galbraith and Godfrey Winn (1908); Arthur Schlesinger, Jr. (1917); Mario Puzo (1920); Lee Iacocca (1924); Linda Lavin (1937); Penny Marshall (1942); Jim Palmer (1945); Richard Carpenter (1946); Sarah Ferguson (1959).

Significant Events and Anniversaries: October 15 is a day that highlights boldly adventurous qualities, as was demonstrated when the mountaineers Vera Komakova and Irene Miller succeeded in their attempt to become the first women climbers to scale the Himalayan peak of Annapurna One (1978). A markedly humanitarian—even judicial—concern is strongly featured on this day, which marks the anniversary of: the beginning of Napoleon Bonaparte's enforced exile on the island of St. Helena following his defeat at the Battle of Waterloo (1815); the executions of: the pro-German Dutch spy Mata Hari by a French firing squad during World War I (1917) and of Pierre Laval, vice-premier of the French Vichy government that had collaborated with the country's German occupiers during World War II (1946); and the foundation of the human-rights organization Amnesty International (1962).

OCTOBER 16

LIBRA

Perhaps the primary characteristics that define the personalities of those born on this day are their remarkable intellectual curiosity and their highly developed critical faculties. Irresistibly drawn to analyzing and rationalizing everything they encounter, October 16 people are especially fascinated observers of individual or societal human behavior, a mine of endlessly rich variety. Because they have a talent for cutting incisively through layers of obfuscation, exposing existing failings, and presenting their findings with objective honesty, many of these natural critics are suited to such professional pursuits as literary commentary, social or political campaigning and most scientific or medical specialties. In sharing their conclusions with a wider audience, these individuals are motivated by their genuine desire to help those around them, but such is the uncomfortable accuracy of their observations, as well as their often devastatingly frank mode of expression, that those whom they wish to educate may become defensive and accuse them of being overly judgemental.

Others admire those born on this day for their stimulating wit, integrity and independence of mind, but often choose to do so from a distance, safely removed from the line of fire. And unless those closest to them have extra thick skins or are extremely forgiving, the dual propensity of October 16 people to criticize others while reserving the right to behave as they wish can make them difficult to live with. But despite their tendency to speak their minds, their intentions are rarely malicious, and beneath their tough exterior lies a generous and affectionate heart.

VIRTUES: These independent individuals born on this day are blessed with acute observational and analytical intellectual talents, which they employ to remarkable effect in cutting to the core of any subject that excites their interest and then exposing the unvarnished truth to the gaze of others, hoping thereby to instigate improvement.
VICES: Knowing they have subjected the objects of their analysis to rigorously logical and objective examination, October 16 people possess profound confidence in their convictions and also the courage to express them openly. Unfortunately others may feel threatened by their brutal honesty, and either mount a counterattack or retreat to a position of safety.
VERDICT: If they are to avoid frightening their friends and partners away, it is crucial that these individuals should consider the potentially devastating effect of their words before expressing their observations candidly. In certain circumstances—particularly within their personal relationships—a discreet and tolerant silence may be preferable to criticism.

On This Day

Famous Births: Noah Webster (1758); Lord James Thomas Brudenell Cardigan (1797); Oscar Wilde (1854); Austen Chamberlain (1863); David Ben-Gurion (1886); Eugene O'Neill (1888); Michael Collins (1890); Max Bygraves (1922); Bert Kaempfert (1923); Angela Lansbury (1925); Günter Grass (1927); Simon Ward (1940); Suzanne Somers (1946); Terry Griffiths (1947); Tim Robbins (1958); Kellie Martin (1975).

Significant Events and Anniversaries: October 16 indicates strongly analytical and progressive tendencies, qualities that are inherent in the fields of science and technology, and this day marks the anniversary of the first use of an anesthetic (diethyl ether) during a surgical operation, by Dr. William T. G. Morton, of the Massachusetts General Hospital (1846); and the inauguration of the world's first birth-control clinic in New York, the brainchild of Ethyl Byrne and Margaret Sanger (1916). On a day that highlights the determined promotion or defense of convictions: English Protestant bishops Hugh Latimer and Nicholas Ridley were burned at the stake on the orders of the Catholic Queen Mary (1555); Marie Antoinette was guillotined by French revolutionaries (1793); U.S. slavery abolitionist John Brown, along with eighteen others, captured the government arsenal at Harper's Ferry, Virginia, intending to give the seized weapons to former slaves (1859); ten leading Nazi war criminals were executed at Nuremberg (1946); and the premier of Pakistan, Liaquat Ali Khan, was assassinated by a Muslim fanatic (1947).

Planetary Influences
Ruling planet: Venus.
Third decan: Personal planets are Uranus and Mercury.

♀ ♅ ☿

Sacred and Cultural Significance
In Nepal, the Festival of the Goddess of Fortune, Laleshmi Puji, celebrated.
Saints' day: Gall (d. c.630); Lul (c.710–86); Hedwig (c.1174–1243); Gerard Majella (d. 1755), patron saint of lay brothers.

With a brilliant, unconventional mind and rapier wit, Oscar Wilde, the writer, poet and philosopher born on this day in 1854, became the victim of his own elevated ideals, a danger to those gifted October 16 people. Highly principled and true to his own artistic vision, he refused to compromise when faced with those who, fearful of his revolutionary ideas, felt threatened enough to destroy him.

LIBRA

Planetary Influences
Ruling planet: Venus.
Third decan: Personal planets are Uranus and Mercury.

Sacred and Cultural Significance
Kanname-Sai, a Japanese Shinto ceremony.
Saints' day: Ignatius of Antioch (d. c.107); Rule (4th century AD); John the Dwarf (5th century AD); translation of Etheldreda, (d. 679); Ethelred and Ethelbricht (7th century AD); Nothelm (d. 739); Margaret Mary Alacoque (1647–90).

Insightful and deeply intelligent, Baroness Karen von Blixen (pen name Isak Dinesen), born on this day in 1885, won the hearts of readers worldwide with her many short stories and her autobiographical novel Out of Africa. *Overcoming obstacles with uncommon strength and courage—qualities of those born today—not only added dimension to her writing, but marked her as an uncommon woman, fascinating in her own right.*

OCTOBER 17

Inherent in the characters of those born on this day is a curious mixture of apparently conflicting qualities, for they are, on the one hand, perfectionists who seek to build and improve upon existing circumstances, and on the other, sensation-seekers who are stimulated by the lure of exploring the new. Depending on their personal make-ups, these essential characteristics may be in equilibrium or may combine to produce, at one end of the scale, staunch and judgemental traditionalists and, at the other end, intellectually and physically reckless types. Common to all, however, will be their courageous strength of conviction and desire to positively influence and guide others. Blessed with powerfully perceptive, analytical and progressive minds, those born on this day are rarely willing to accept the conventions and truths of others without question, but instead feel compelled to subject them to objective research in order to reach their own conclusions. And, once convinced, they will defend or promote their viewpoints with vigorous tenacity.

The combination of their strong social orientation and independence of thought fuels those born on this day with the urge to lead by example, particularly in the promotion of their professional interests. Thus although they may derive great personal satisfaction from their career pursuits, their ultimate intention is to further the advancement of humanity. Many are therefore suited to educational careers, while others may seek to communicate their findings by means of more subtle artistic expression, or by effecting scientific or technical innovations. Yet despite their profound desire to enlighten and instruct those around them—especially those closest to them, whose affection is so vital to their emotional balance—their nearest and dearest may either feel neglected as a result of their more global concern with others, or become the undeserving victims of their critical pronouncements.

VIRTUES: Although October 17 people are independent and objective thinkers who are stimulated by challenging accepted knowledge and conventions, their humanitarian concern anchors their more adventurous propensities firmly within society, with the result that however idiosyncratic their beliefs and actions, their ultimate aim is to help others.
VICES: Although their innately judgemental tendencies and determination to attain their visionary aims augur well for these individuals to make a significant contribution to society, they may be less effective in terms of maintaining harmonious personal liaisons, in that their honest objectivity may tend to wound the emotional sensitivity of those closest to them.
VERDICT: It is important that those born on this day appreciate the emotionally enriching and grounding benefits that can be gained from nurturing their close relationships. They should therefore ensure that they either do not allow themselves to be distracted from devoting time and attention to their loved ones, or alienate them by being unnecessarily critical.

On This Day
Famous Births: John Wilkes (1727); Georg Büchner (1813); Elinor Glyn (1864); Karen Blixen (1885); Herbert Howells (1892); Spring Byington (1893); Nathaniel West (1903); Jean Arthur (1905); Arthur Miller (1915); Rita Hayworth (1918); Montgomery Clift (1920); Tom Poston (1927); Jimmy Breslin (1928); Ann Jones (1938); Evel Knievel (1939); Margot Kidder and George Wendt (1948); Howard Rollins (1950); Vince Van Patten (1957).

Significant Events and Anniversaries: This day highlights the determined promotion of strongly held socially ideological convictions, as was reflected when: Charles Stuart—the future King Charles II of England—finally escaped to the safety of France following the defeat of his royalist followers at the hands of Oliver Cromwell's Parliamentarian troops at the Battle of Worcester (1651); and, during the American War of Independence, British forces commanded by General John Burgoyne surrendered to General Horatio Gates following the Battle of Saratoga (1777). October 17 furthermore promises technical advances intended to benefit human society, as was demonstrated on this day when British engineer Harry Bessemer patented his method of converting molten pig-iron into steel (1855).

OCTOBER 18

Self-reliant and yet socially aware, October 18 individuals typically have two prerequisites for their personal happiness: freedom to explore intellectual issues, and stimulation and opportunity to pursue the shared goals inherent in their interpersonal activities. These are on the one hand essentially selfish and, on the other, more altruistic urges, and their innate attraction to both may result in a finely balanced variety of interests or cause them to favor one or the other. Whatever their personal inclinations, however, all have analytical, progressive and resourceful qualities, as well as a highly developed sense of responsibility for safeguarding the common good and promoting the happiness of others. In the most serendipitous of professional circumstances, October 18 people will flourish in those careers where, while working toward advancing the welfare of others, they are allowed the autonomy of thought and action that is so vital to them.

When thus harnessed to their social orientation, their intellectual versatility and imaginative talents augur well for their success as teachers, although many may choose to impart their messages by developing more overtly creative means of expression—as artists, writers, actors or musicians, for example. In all their endeavors, however individualistic, their genuine benevolence and obvious sincerity engenders the respect and affection of others, while their easy-going, humorous wit draws people to them. There is a danger, however, that those born on this day may give more than they receive—particularly if they are also women—and that they may therefore become overburdened by the demands of others.

VIRTUES: The complex, though well-balanced, characters of October 18 people are both introverted and extroverted, so they feel compelled not only to further their own personal quests for knowledge, but also to transform their discoveries into tangible advances intended to benefit or inspire others.
VICES: Those born on this day have a propensity to respond strongly to the allure of a fascinating intellectual question, to the exclusion of all else, or alternatively to suppress their more selfish urges by giving priority to the needs of those around them.
VERDICT: These individuals instinctively recognize that their emotional happiness is strongly linked to the well-being of those whose interests they have at heart. But they should also remember that the pursuit of their personal interests is of equal importance in terms of their all-round fulfillment and should not be sublimated in their desire to help others.

On This Day

Famous Births: Richard "Beau" Nash (1674); Antonio Canaletto (1697); Pierre de Laclos (1741); Thomas Love Peacock (1785); Christian Friedrich Schonbein (1799); Henri Bergson (1859); Emmanuel Shinwell (1884); Lotte Lenya (1900); Pierre Trudeau (1919); Jesse Helms (1921); Melina Mercouri (1925); Chuck Berry (1926); George C. Scott (1927); Peter Boyle (1935); Mike Ditka and Lee Harvey Oswald (1939); Laura Nyro (1947); Pam Dawber (1951); Martina Navratilova (1956); Jean-Claude Van Damme (1960); Wynton Marsalis and Erin Moran (1961).

Significant Events and Anniversaries: This day indicates the desire to actively inspire or otherwise bring pleasure to others, as was reflected: in the sporting arena, when representatives from the U.S. universities of Yale, Princeton, Columbia and Princeton laid down the rules for the game of American football (1887); and in the realm of the media when the British Broadcasting Company (B.B.C.) was established (1922). On a day that highlights intellectually curious qualities while being ruled by the element of air, a Soviet *Venera* space probe made the first successful landing on Venus (1967). Collective social responsibility is also strongly featured by October 18, on which: following the end of the Spanish-American War, in which the U.S.A. had backed a revolt of Cuban revolutionaries against Spanish rule, the U.S.A. was accorded ownership of Cuba, Puerto Rico, Guam and the Philippines (1898); and specialist German antiterrorist troops freed the hostages being held captive on a Lufthansa airplane at Somalia's Mogadishu Airport, killing three Palestinian hijackers (1977).

Planetary Influences
Ruling planet: Venus.
Third decan: Personal planets are Uranus and Mercury.

Sacred and Cultural Significance
Great Horned Fair celebrated by Pagans in England.
Saints' day: Luke (d. 1st century AD), patron saint of artists, doctors and surgeons; Gwen of Cornwall (dates unknown); Justus of Beauvais (3rd century AD).

With the October 18 characteristic combination of collective social responsibility and drive to safeguard the common good, on this day in 1898, the U.S. took possession of Cuba, Puerto Rico, Guam and the Philippines from Spain at the close of the Spanish-American War.

Planetary Influences
Ruling planets: Venus and Pluto.
Third decan: Personal planets are Uranus and Mercury.
Second cusp: Libra with Scorpio tendencies.

Sacred and Cultural Significance
In Tokyo, Japan, the Bettara-Ichi fair celebrated.
Saints' day: Ptolomaeus and Lucius (d. c.150); Ethbin (6th century AD); Frideswide (c.680–727), patron saint of Oxford University, England; Peter of Alcantara (1499–1562); Jean de Brébeuf (1593–1649) and Isaac Jogues (1607–46); Paul of the Cross (1694–1775).

When British General Lord Cornwallis surrendered to the forces of George Washington at Yorktown, Virginia, on this day in 1781, the long and bloody American War for Independence was ended. The victory demonstrated this day's qualities of visionary inspiration and willingness to fight for change.

OCTOBER 19

The various astrological influences that govern their day of birth endow October 19 people with a complex set of personal characteristics which they may spend their lives struggling to reconcile. Although they are sensual individuals who seek to find happiness in the simpler things in life, such as esthetic beauty, or harmonious personal relationships, they are also intellectually inquisitive, reluctant to accept conventional truths without having first analyzed and verified them to their own satisfaction. Simultaneously peace-loving yet prepared to fight for the causes in which they strongly believe, they often feel torn between defending the status quo and battling to reverse perceived injustices or promote their visions. Perhaps the single most striking quality manifested by those born on this day, however, is their desire to benefit the social group with which they most strongly identify by means of their independent discoveries or actions. Energetic and determined individuals who do not shrink from taking a contrary stance if they believe it to be right, they are natural leaders and innovators, whose talents and inclinations equip them admirably as scientists and artistic pioneers.

Despite their social orientation and propensity for acting on behalf of the greater good, October 19 people may appear to be somewhat solitary figures. This is in part a result of their jealously upheld prerequisite for personal autonomy, and the inevitable product of their uncompromisingly direct approach, which may at best intimidate, and at worst incur the enmity of those who feel themselves threatened. Yet when they are fortunate enough to enjoy unquestioning tolerance and love, their softer, profoundly protective, affectionate and generous side emerges, particularly if they were also born in the Chinese year of the ox.

VIRTUES: Those born on this day are free-spirited people and independent thinkers, who are stimulated by the pursuit of knowledge. Blessed with enormous vigor and the courage of their convictions, they are prepared to promote their viewpoints at almost any cost.
VICES: Because they believe that they are armed with the truth, October 19 people often feel justified in adopting combative methods when faced with opposition, a tendency that may sometimes be inappropriate and even damaging—especially when directed toward those closest to them.
VERDICT: In order to attain the emotional contentment that they crave, these individuals must recognize that their predilection for criticism will not endear them to others. Before voicing their outspoken opinions, they should therefore consider the possibly negative effect of their words, and if this outweighs the benefits they would be better advised to employ greater tact.

On This Day
Famous Births: Thomas Browne (1605); James Henry Leigh Hunt (1784); Tom Taylor (1817); Adam L. Gordon (1833); August Lumière (1862); Sidonie Goossens (1899); Robert Beatty (1909); Jack Anderson (1922); David Cornwall (John Le Carré) (1931); Yakubu Gowon (1934); Peter Max (1937); Michael Gambon (1940); John Lithgow and Jeannie C. Riley (1945); Evander Holyfield (1962); Amy Carter (1967).

Significant Events and Anniversaries: October 19 highlights the promotion of strongly held convictions intended to advance or defend the wider interest, and therefore commemorates various martial anniversaries: the conclusion of the American War of Independence, when besieged British troops under Lord Charles Cornwallis surrendered to General George Washington at Yorktown, Virginia (1781); the defeat of Napoleon's French Army during the Napoleonic Wars at the hands of combined forces at Leipzig, a conflict that became known as the Battle of the Nations (1813); and the victory of General Philip Sheridan's Unionist troops over General Jubal A. Early's Confederate soldiers at the Battle of Cedar Creek during the American Civil War (1864). Exposing the truth is a vital preoccupation indicated by October 19, and in Britain, the "Guildford Four," alleged I.R.A. terrorists who had served fifteen years of their prison sentences for their supposed part in planting bombs in Guildford and Woolwich, were adjudged to have been victims of a miscarriage of justice and released (1989).

OCTOBER 20

There are typically two pronounced sides to the personalities of October 20 people: their great artistry, evident in their aesthetic appreciation, sensuality and creativity; and their harder, more judgemental qualities. Those born on this day accommodate both propensities within their daily lives, perhaps indulging their artistic tastes in relaxing pastimes and pursuing more conventional careers or, if they are especially talented, earning their livings as professional artists, writers, designers or architects. Whatever career they choose, however, their highly developed visual and analytic powers generally play an important part in their success, as do their objective and independent turn of mind and their desire to make a significant contribution to humanity. Such personal characteristics and inclinations equip these people for a wide range of professions, from scientific research to politics and social campaigning, or from sporting activities to business and commerce.

Despite their twin enthusiasms for sensory and intellectually stimulating exploration, those born on this day are rarely maverick types who give themselves completely over to self-indulgent activities; on the contrary, they possess remarkable discipline, especially when engaged in promoting the common good. Possessed of strong convictions formed jointly by their capacity for logical analysis and their progressive imaginations, these otherwise easy-going individuals can display tremendous determination—even obstinacy—when called upon to defend or promote their beliefs, and will resort to combative tactics if necessary. However, they are interesting and invigorating companions, who display genuine concern for, and enormous magnanimity toward, their nearest and dearest.

VIRTUES: Those born on this day have a particular affinity with, and talent for, all varieties of artistic expression. Complementing their emotional and sensual sensitivity are their objectivity and intellectual analysis, all of which combine to produce markedly independent, original and progressive minds.

VICES: Perhaps the greatest threat to the well-being of October 20 people is their urge to give full attention to their multitude of interests which, in conjunction with their sense of social responsibility, may lead them to spread their energies and attention too thinly, ultimately causing them to become physically and emotionally exhausted, and thus less effective.

VERDICT: If they are to avoid overtaxing their strength, it is crucial that these individuals recognize that it may be impossible for them to commit themselves fully to the pursuit of the many things that attract their interest or concern. They should therefore focus upon only those areas that bring them the greatest satisfaction and try not to let their attention be diverted from their priorities.

On This Day

Famous Births: Christopher Wren (1632); Colin Campbell (1792); Thomas Hughes (1822); Arthur Rimbaud (1854); John Dewey (1859); Charles Ives (1874); Bela Lugosi (1884); James Chadwick (1891); Anna Neagle (1904); Alfredo Campoli (1906); Art Buchwald (1925); Lord Montagu of Beaulieu (1926); Joyce Brothers (1928); Mickey Mantle (1931); William Christopher (1932); Jerry Orbach (1935); Selena Fox (1949); Tom Petty (1953).

Significant Events and Anniversaries: This is a day that promises enormous artistic potential, and marks the anniversary of the official opening of Australia's Sydney Opera House—a widely acclaimed example of avant-garde architecture—by Queen Elizabeth II (1973). October 20 furthermore indicates the readiness to promote ideological aims with the utmost determination, as was reflected in the martial and political spheres when: during the Napoleonic Wars, outmaneuvered Austrian troops who surrendered to the victorious French emperor at the Battle of Ulm (1805); Mao Zedong, leader of the Chinese Jiangxi Soviet, and his supporters completed their "Long March" from Jiangxi to Yan'an, having traveled 9,600 km (6,000 miles) (1935); and during World War II, Allied soldiers broke through the German lines and captured the German town of Aachen (Aix-la-Chapelle) (1944).

Planetary Influences
Ruling planets: Venus and Pluto.
Third decan: Personal planets are Uranus and Mercury.
Second cusp: Libra with Scorpio tendencies.

Sacred and Cultural Significance
Saints' day: Acca (d. 740); Maria Bertilla Boscardin (1888–1922).

This soaring and visionary monument to music and the human spirit has become emblematic of the city of Sydney, Australia. The famous Sydney Opera House, dedicated on this day in 1973, exemplifies the great appreciation of creativity in all its forms and the desire to collectively manifest a single vision characteristic of October 20.

LIBRA

Planetary Influences
Ruling planets: Venus and Pluto.
Third decan: Personal planets are Uranus and Mercury.
Second cusp: Libra with Scorpio tendencies.

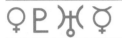

Sacred and Cultural Significance
Trafalgar Day in Britain; in the former Czechoslovakia, the Day of Ursula celebrated.
Saints' day: Hilarion (c.291–c.371), patron saint of hermits; Malchus (d. c.390); Ursula, patron saint of schoolgirls, and Companions (4th century AD); Fintan Munnu (d. 635); John of Bridlington (d. 1379).

The powerful and infectious love of life, unusual charm and courageous unconventionality characteristic of this day could be summed up in one musical moment—Bebop—a jazz genre created by jazz trumpeter and impresario, Dizzy Gillespie, born today in 1917.

OCTOBER 21

Others admire those born on this day for their magnetic charisma, as well as their physical and intellectual vigor, and are furthermore drawn into their personal orbit by their charming nature and infectious *joie de vivre*. Indeed, in an ideal world October 21 people would like nothing more than to indulge their strongly sensual and pleasure-loving propensities, sharing their enjoyment of such entertainment with like-minded individuals. But since they are extremely perceptive and somewhat critical types who wish to make a positive contribution to society, they recognize the unfeasibility of such an agreeable scenario. Because they are so concerned with effecting the well-being of others on the one hand and have such a strong affinity with artistic pursuits on the other, many of these people will combine these two interests to make careers as inspirational writers, artists, musicians and actors. Others may prefer to capitalize upon their analytical skills and progressive inclinations within the realms of science or commerce as long as their need for personal autonomy of thought and action is not compromised, a prerequisite that is especially important if they were also born in the Chinese year of the horse.

Yet despite their undoubted ability to sublimate their more selfish desires in favor of what they perceive to be the common good, they remain profoundly emotionally oriented individuals whose desire to attain their romantic ideals cannot be completely suppressed (nor, indeed, should it be). This propensity may find an outlet in social or artistic idealism, but is more often directed toward their nearest and dearest—and particularly their partners—who may find it difficult to live up to the idealized qualities that are projected upon them.

VIRTUES: October 21 people are idealists, who are fueled by the urge to satisfy both their own inherently perfectionist needs and to help those around them attain better circumstances. Their clear thinking and desire to actively effect progress characterize their typical approach to all their ventures, as do their charming manner and evident goodwill.
VICES: Although they draw heavily upon their intellectual talents in the promotion of their ideological ambitions, the actions of those born on this day are essentially motivated by powerful emotional forces which, if not given their full expression, may build up and vent themselves in potentially negative manifestations—especially toward family and friends.
VERDICT: The sense of social responsibility of these individuals and their wish to take positive action to ameliorate instances of misfortune or unhappiness are admirable qualities, but they should nevertheless ensure that they do not neglect their equally important, if more self-indulgent, needs, for such suppression may result in restless personal dissatisfaction, which may be directed toward those who are closest in the firing line: their loved ones.

On This Day
Famous Births: Katsushka Hokusai (1760); Samuel Taylor Coleridge (1772); Alfred Nobel (1833); Ernest Swinton (1868); Georg Solti (1912); "Dizzy" Gillespie (1917); Malcolm Arnold (1921); Nadia Nerina (1927); Maureen Duffy (1933); Simon Gray (1936); Manfred Mann (1940); Benjamin Netanyahu (1949); Carrie Fisher (1956); Jeremy Miller (1976).

Significant Events and Anniversaries: On a day that highlights outstanding artistic potential, October 21 marks the anniversary of: the staging of the first performance of French composer Jacques Offenbach's light opera *Orphée aux enfers [Orpheus in the Underworld]* (1858); and the publication of U.S. novelist Ernest Hemingway's novel *For Whom the Bell Tolls* (1940). Scientific and technical advances are also promised on October 21, on which: Englishman Joseph Aspdin patented his formula for Portland cement (1824); and the world's first planetarium was opened in the German town of Munich (1923). Furthermore a day that indicates the willingness to take direct action on behalf of the perceived communal good, October 21 commemorates the naval Battle of Trafalgar during the Napoleonic Wars, when the British admiral Horatio Nelson called successfully upon his men to do their duty against the combined French and Spanish force led by Admiral Pierre Villeneuve, but lost his life in the process (1805).

OCTOBER 22

LIBRA

Those born on this day are blessed with a charismatic presence that draws all eyes to them and although they are not at all averse to basking in the attention of others, they would prefer to be admired for their capabilities rather than for more superficial reasons, such as their physical appearance. And, indeed, October 22 people possess a veritable treasure chest of talents and positive qualities, including their intellectual and intuitive perspicacity, which endows them with the ability to discriminate between right and wrong, and their profound empathy with those whose circumstances are less than happy, as well as their urge to defend or promote the interests of those with whom they strongly identify. Although they are imaginative and independently minded individuals who are irresistibly attracted to seeking out and exploring novel experiences—particularly of the sensual variety—their ultimate aim is to combine their personal predilections with their desire to assist the emotional or circumstantial advancement of others.

Despite their orientation toward others, however, October 22 individuals remain resolute individualists who never lose sight of their emotional ideals, a propensity that may make them difficult to live with, in that they may become overly preoccupied with their dreams or else make unfeasible demands of their nearest and dearest. Especially perfectionist when it comes to the regulation of their own lives, they typically set their visionary sights high, and will work toward their attainment with prodigious determination. Best suited to careers where they can pursue their innovative aims freely, those born on this day will therefore especially flourish as artists working in a variety of specialties; or, with their powerful sense of justice, careers in the legal or social spheres.

VIRTUES: Markedly imaginative and original, October 22 people are stimulated by their quest to further their personal knowledge and experience and, thus enriched, to share their findings to the benefit of a wider audience. Sensitive and empathetic toward others, they are also motivated by their urge to help create a fairer world.
VICES: Although stemming from the most benevolent or idealistic of intentions, the soaringly elevated or rosy-hued demands manifested by those born on this day may prove draining—if not impossible—to meet, especially when they are made of those closest to them.
VERDICT: Although these individuals are unquestionably positively orientated toward others, desiring both to improve their lives and to spread happiness, they should recognize that the subjects of their concern—particularly their friends and relations—may feel unable or unwilling to meet their extremely high standards. They would therefore be advised to adopt a less demanding, more *laissez-faire* policy.

On This Day

Famous Births: Franz Liszt (1811); James Blond (1854); Lord Alfred "Bosie" Douglas (1870); Matthew Smith (1879); Curly Howard (1903); Joan Fontaine (1917); Doris Lessing (1919); Timothy Leary (1920); Robert Rauschenberg (1925); John Blashford-Snell (1936); Derek Jacobi and Christopher Lloyd (1938); Tony Roberts (1939); Annette Funicello (1942); Catherine Deneuve (1943); Jeff Goldblum (1952); Zac Hanson (1985).

Significant Events and Anniversaries: This is a day that highlights the pursuit of ambitious and innovative goals designed to assist others, as was demonstrated when the Trans-Australian Railway was completed, facilitating the journey from Kalgoorie to Port Augusta (1917). Artistic ventures intended to inspire a wider audience are similarly featured on October 22, on which: New York's Metropolitan Opera House was opened (1833); and the British B.B.C. Symphony Orchestra gave its first performance, at the Queen's Hall in London (1930). This is a day that is not only governed by the element of air, but which also emphasizes a strong attraction to novelty, as was reflected when: the Frenchman André-Jacques Garnerin made his pioneering parachute jump, from a hot-air balloon floating above Paris (1797); and French aviator Elise Deroche achieved the feat of becoming the first woman to fly single-handedly (1909).

Planetary Influences
Ruling planets: Venus and Pluto.
Third decan: Personal planets are Uranus and Mercury.
Second cusp: Libra with Scorpio tendencies.

Sacred and Cultural Significance
The Festival of Fire, a purification ceremony, celebrated in Japan.
Saints' day: Mellon (4th century AD); Donatus (d. 876).

October 22 people, with their innate charisma, love of attention and visionary natures, often find their true calling in the arts, as was the case with Franz Liszt, the virtuoso musician born on this day in 1811, one of the most prolific and accomplished composers of the 19th century.

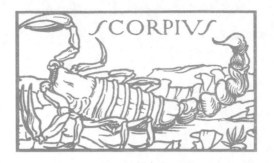

SCORPIO

October 23 to November 21

Ruling planet: Pluto   **Element:** Fixed water
Symbol: A Scorpion   **Polarity:** Negative (feminine)
Physical correspondence: The genitals and bladder
Stones: Topaz, agate, ruby, garnet, carnelian, amber
Flowers: Heather, thistle, geranium, chrysanthemum
Colors: Russet, red, maroon

With the exception of the ancient Egyptian zodiac, which depicted a scarab presiding over this sign, most astrological traditions have seen a scorpion's form in this constellation, the Babylonians naming it Gir-Tab ("the stinger"); the Persians Gazdum; the Greeks Skorpion; and the Hindus Vrischika. The various cultural myths associated with Scorpio are thus primarily concerned with protection and aggression, the Mesopotamian civilizations, for instance, believing that hybrid scorpion-men stood sentry at the "gateway of the Sun," while in Greco-Roman lore a scorpion was sent by Apollo to punish the vain hunter Orion, who had bragged that he could destroy any living creature: the constellation of Orion sets when Scorpio rises. Sacred to the god of war, Ares (Mars), the scorpion—and, by association, the characteristics it confers on those born under its sign—was said to mirror the deity's disposition, in particular his martial, combative qualities. Scorpio's association with destruction is further underlined by the ancient Egyptians' belief that their god of vegetation, Osiris, died when the Sun was in Scorpio, while the Celtic festival of Samhain (Hallowe'en), when the dread spirits of the dead roamed at large, was also celebrated when this constellation was dominant. Following the discovery of the planet Pluto (named after the Roman god of the underworld, the counterpart of the Greek Hades) in 1930, Mars' rulership of Scorpio was shared with Pluto. Yet Scorpio's connotations are not all negative, for some astrologers made a distinction between the "degenerate Scorpio," which signified decline and death, and the "regenerated Scorpio," personified by the mighty eagle and heralding rebirth.

The personal characteristics highlighted by Scorpio are complex: the disciplined aggression and intensity level of Mars, as well as his potent and passionate sexuality, are counterbalanced by the profound emotional depth signified by the element of water. Scorpio people have Plutonian, jealous natures and destructive powers. Conversely, however, they are blessed with subtlety, creative imaginations and outstanding potential to attain spiritual enlightenment, transformation and regeneration.

OCTOBER 23

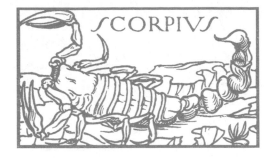

Others frequently admire October 23 people for their intellectual and physical energy, as well as their ability to make quick decisions and stick by them with remarkable determination, but sometimes secretly wonder why they appear to make life so difficult for themselves, for they seem to create a maelstrom around them whatever they do. Although there are no easy answers to this conundrum, part of the answer may lie in these individuals' inherent zest for stimulation. Easily bored, they are naturally drawn to demanding or difficult situations in which they can test their courage and talents. Furthermore blessed with incisive clarity of vision and balanced objectivity, they possess the imagination and resourcefulness to devise and implement strategies for improvement that are so ambitious that they tend toward the radical. Given such a dynamic combination, those born on this day manifest clear innovatory and leadership potential, propensities that are further underlined by their sense of fairness and humanitarian concern with helping and directing others.

October 23 people are thus suited to any professional activity where they can actively indulge their innate urge to make tangible—even ground-breaking—advances, and they may therefore be found working effectively as artists or athletes, or equally as pioneering business entrepreneurs or social campaigners. Retaining their autonomy is important to them, and they typically prefer to captain a committed team rather than to act as independent agents. A similar feeling of interest and connection characterizes their relationships with those closest to them, although, however well-meaning their intentions, their tendency to assume a commanding and controlling role within their circle may cause those who would prefer to follow their own path through life to become resentful.

VIRTUES: Those born on this day are active individuals who are not content to sit passively on the sidelines of life but instead respond instantly and decisively to any stimulating opportunity. Blessed with rational and objective minds, these are progressive and independent types, who nevertheless possess a strong desire to assist and inspire others.
VICES: October 23 people find it hard to resist taking charge of any challenging situation or project that excites their interest, a propensity that can have startlingly successful results but which may also cause them problems within their interpersonal relationships (especially their more intimate ones) if a conflict of wills is thereby aroused.
VERDICT: Although their desire to set those closest to them on what they believe to be the right track is an entirely benevolent one, these people should recognize that the subjects of their concern will not always appreciate what they may perceive to be attempts to limit their personal independence, and should therefore occasionally hold back.

On This Day

Famous Births: Pierre Larousse (1817); Robert Bridges and Louis Riel (1844); Douglas Jardine (1900): Johnny Carson (1925); Diana Dors (1931); David Nelson (1936); F. Murray Abraham (1939); Edson Arantes do Nascimento, "Pelé" (1940); Michael Crichton and Anita Roddick (1942); "Weird" Al Yankovic (1959); Doug Flutie (1962); Al Leiter (1965).

Significant Events and Anniversaries: Not only is October 23 governed by the planet Pluto, indicating upheaval and transformation, but it also highlights the determined promotion of progressive strategies, as was demonstrated in the martial realm when: Mark Antony and Octavian's army defeated the forces of Marcus Junius Brutus (Julius Caesar's assassin) and Cassius at the Battle of Philippi (42 BC); the first battle of the English Civil War, between King Charles I's Royalist Cavaliers and Oliver Cromwell's Parliamentarian Roundheads, was fought at Edgehill (1642); and General Bernard Montgomery's British VIII Army began its assault on General Erwin Rommel's German troops in North Africa, thus starting World War II's Second Battle of El Alamein (1942). A similarly confrontational spirit was displayed in the political sphere, when Hungarian citizens staged a massive demonstration in Budapest against Soviet rule, thus initiating the Hungarian Revolution (1956).

Planetary Influences
Ruling planets: Pluto and Venus.
First decan: Personal planet is Mars.
First cusp: Scorpio with Libran tendencies.

Sacred and Cultural Significance
Saints' day: Boëthius (c.475–524); Romanus (d. c.640); Ethelfleda (fl. c.960); John of Capistrano, patron saint of jurists (1386–1456).

Those born today are not content to sit life out on the sidelines. Their free-spirited love of action coupled with their innate ability to work in teams often make them excellent athletes, as was the case with Edson Arantes do Nascimento, "Pele," perhaps the greatest soccer player in the game's history, born on this day in 1940.

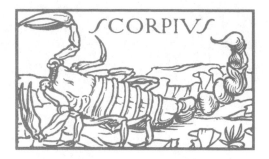

Planetary Influences
Ruling planets: Pluto and Venus.
First decan: Personal planet is Mars.
First cusp: Scorpio with Libran tendencies.

Sacred and Cultural Significance
United Nations Day; the national day of Zambia; annual Feast of the Spirits of Air celebrated by Wiccans.
Saints' day: Felix of Thibiuca (247–303); Maglorius (d. c.575); Antony Claret (1807–70).

Novelty gives way to progress on October 24, 1861, as happened when the first transcontinental telegraph made the Pony Express obsolete, thus marking the practical and ambitious technical advances possible on this day.

OCTOBER 24

Those born on this day typically possess two pronounced—and apparently contradictory—sets of personal characteristics: those related to their inherent perfectionism and those stemming from their adventurous, somewhat radical, persona. And while it is true that some October 24 people may tend toward one or other of these extremes, others are able to reconcile them with remarkable success by backing up their highly original and ambitious visions with their more grounded qualities: meticulous attention to detail, self-discipline and strong organizational talents. These are energetic types, fueled by the compulsion to effect concrete and progressive advances with which they hope both to satisfy their own questing drive and also to benefit others. Although undoubtedly independently minded, their strong social orientation leads them to seek to enlist the support of others in their cause. Because their preferred approach is hands-on, they set themselves—as well as those around them—prodigiously high standards. They typically lead by example, however, demonstrating extraordinary dedication and focus in the process.

The careers that attract those born on this day vary depending on the personal predilection of the individual, but their technical and practical talents, as well as their natural prerequisite for autonomy suit them especially well for mechanical and administrative pursuits. Despite the admiration that their commitment and imagination typically arouses in others, these very qualities—particularly when combined with their judgemental and perfectionist tendencies—may make them difficult to live with. For on the one hand, they may neglect the needs of those closest to them when preoccupied with their work (a propensity that is doubly pronounced in October 24 men) and, on the other, they may seek to direct or "improve" the behavior of their loved ones.

VIRTUES: Natural leaders and innovators, and intellectually imaginative, enterprising and progressive, those born on this day possess more solid personal qualities, such as their highly developed organizational skills, their interest in detail, and their disciplined tenacity in working toward the realization of their visions.
VICES: Because they are blessed with a remarkable sense of focus and purpose, and make such lofty demands of themselves and others, October 24 people may unwittingly place a heavy burden of expectation on those around them—especially their nearest and dearest—which they may be unwilling or, indeed, unable, to fulfill.
VERDICT: In order to ensure that their personal relationships are happy, it is important that these individuals recognize that their compulsion for controlling others' actions and often uncompromising manner may engender resentment in others. They would thus be well advised to adopt a more tolerant and relaxed approach, especially toward their loved ones.

On This Day
Famous Births: Anton van Leewenhoek (1632); Jacques Laffitte (1769); Sarah Hale (1788); Sybil Thorndike (1882); Merian C. Cooper (1893); Moss Hart (1904); Fred Pontin and Robert Sainsbury (1906); Tito Gobbi (1915); Robin Day (1923); Jack Warner (1924); John P. Richardson, "The Big Bopper" (1930); David Nelson and Bill Wyman (1936); F. Murray Abraham (1939); Phil Bennett and Kevin Kline (1948).

Significant Events and Anniversaries: This is a day that highlights ambitious visions supported by organizational and practical capabilities, as reflected on this day when: a group of Cambridge University graduates formed the world's first official soccer club in Sheffield, England (1857); construction of the first telegraph line to link the U.S.A.'s west and east coasts was completed (1861). A strongly judgemental propensity is also featured on October 24, and on this day: suffragettes Emmeline and Christabel Pankhurst were jailed for inciting a riot to agitate for British women's right to vote (1908); notorious U.S. gangster Al Capone was imprisoned in Chicago for tax evasion (1931); and U.S. television evangelist Jim Bakker was given a prison sentence for fraud (1989).

OCTOBER 25

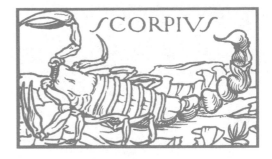

✴✴

Those born on this day are forceful and determined individuals whose actions are fueled by their urge to give concrete expression to the innovative visions that inspire them—that is, to translate their dreams into reality. Critically observant, imaginative and yet also extremely practical, they have a talent for incisively identifying perceived failings and then formulating remedial strategies, which they promote with unwavering tenacity and vigor. And because October 25 people are vitally interested in, and highly responsive to, everything that enters their personal orbit, this driving compulsion may be manifested in a wide range of areas or professions. Thus they may be seized by the desire to replace an unsatisfactory existing social or political system with a more fair and enlightened one; to develop a scientific or technical theory or instrument; to fill a gap in the commercial market; to make a company more productive; or to impart their messages to others by means of an inspirational artistic body of work. Inherent in all their aims and preferred methods is their innate perfectionism, as well as their predilection for directing the opinions or controlling the actions of others.

It perhaps goes without saying that those born on this day are socially responsible individuals who possess a burning desire to set others on what they believe to be the right path, or otherwise make a positive contribution to humanity. It is also clear, however, that their extremely critical, judgemental tendencies endow them with a profound sense of self-belief that may cause them to refute the validity of alternative viewpoints. So although they are reliable, protective, generous and affectionate friends and family members, they are typically intolerant of those who deviate from their wishes.

VIRTUES: October 25 people are blessed with acutely critical powers of perception, a gift that, in conjunction with their actively progressive inclinations, arouses their strong desire to bring about tangible improvements intended to be of benefit to the wider world. Their potential for success is enhanced by means of the soundly structured organizational systems they devise to their aims.
VICES: Because they are uncompromising perfectionists and are furthermore convinced of the veracity of their beliefs and methods, those born on this day not only set dauntingly high standards for themselves and those around them, but also have a tendency to regard negatively anyone who objects to their visions or approaches, propensities that may cause problems within their closer relationships.
VERDICT: Although their strong opinions and decisive actions generally stem from their well-meaning desire to make a positive contribution to the well-being of others, these individuals should recognize the importance of remaining tolerant and open-minded . By pursuing a more relaxed approach they will prove more effective in terms of eliciting support and also reap great intellectual and emotional rewards.

On This Day

Famous Births: Thomas Macaulay (1800); Richard Parkes Bonington (1802); Johann Strauss the Younger (1825); Georges Bizet (1838); Sarah Bernhardt (1844); Pablo Picasso (1881); Richard E. Byrd (1888); Abel Gance (1889); Leo G. Carroll (1892); Eddie Lang (1902); Minnie Pearl (1912); Billy Barty (1924); Galina Vishnevskaya (1926); Anthony Franciosa (1928); Helen Reddy (1941); Jon Anderson (1944); Tracy Nelson (1963).

Significant Events and Anniversaries: The keen desire to effect concrete advances inherent in this day was illustrated: in the realm of technology when U.S. inventor L. L. Curtis patented the airbrush (1881) and U.S. professor Lee de Forest patented his Audion three-diode amplification valve (1906); and in that of architecture when Queen Elizabeth II opened London's National Theatre, the vision of architect Denys Lasdun (1976). This day is also affected by both Mars and Pluto, as demonstrated when King Henry V and his English troops defeated their French foe at the Battle of Agincourt (1415); and during World War II, the U.S. Navy defeated the Japanese at the battles of Surigao, San Bernadino Strait, Samar and Cape Engano in Leyte Gulf (1944).

Planetary Influences
Ruling planets: Pluto and Venus.
First decan: Personal planet is Mars.
First cusp: Scorpio with Libran tendencies.

Sacred and Cultural Significance
Saints' day: Crispin and Crispinian (d. c.285), patron saints of leather-workers and shoemakers; Forty Martyrs of England and Wales (d. 1535–1679).

One of the most powerfully creative and uniquely influential artists of the 20th century, Pablo Picasso, born on this day in 1881, revolutionized not only modern art in general with his unique synthesis of the political and the avant-garde, but the vision of an entire century of artists and art appreciators. Paintings like Guernica *and* Les Desmoiselles d'Avignons *illustrate the innovation, perception and forceful determination common to those born on this day.*

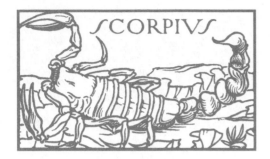

Planetary Influences
Ruling planet: Pluto.
First decan: Personal planet is Mars.

Sacred and Cultural Significance
National day of Austria; the Birthday
of the Earth celebrated.
Saints' day: Cedd (d. 664); Eata (d. 686);
Bean (11th century AD).

*A founding member of the Bolshevik party, avid
Marxist Leon Trotsky (born on this day in 1879)
was a natural leader, but the October 26
qualities that brought Trotsky to prominence —
the ability to organize others, the urge to control
and direct and passionate dedication to a
cause — also led to a power struggle within
party leadership, resulting in Trotsky's exile and
eventual assassination at Stalin's orders.*

OCTOBER 26

Perhaps the most prominent personal characteristic manifested by October 26 people is their compulsion to organize others. They harbor a conviction that concerted communal endeavors are more effective in achieving progress than the efforts of lone agents of change. With their ability to focus upon distant goals while at the same time addressing more immediate concerns, these are gifted leaders, whose decisiveness and dedication arouse respect (if not always affection). These are people who can be found planning local events and serving on committees, always involved in community affairs. They are admirably suited to careers as national or civic politicians, business executives, accountants or bankers.

Their desire to mold those around them applies as much to their personal relationships as to their professional lives, and they will typically do their utmost to persuade their kith and kin of the veracity of their viewpoints—a task usually undertaken with enthusiasm and logic rather than by passionate or combative means. Because they are natural pragmatists they will accept the demurrals of those who do not share their beliefs, but will nevertheless impress their disapproval upon others. When they and those closest to them are in agreement, their endearingly affectionate and generous qualities come to the fore.

VIRTUES: Those born on this day are natural leaders, whose orientation toward others results both from their desire to further the collective welfare of those with whom they identify and their relish for coordinating and directing others.
VICES: Their powerful predilection for forming and controlling the efforts of teams of like-minded individuals endows October 26 people with remarkable career potential: however, they may be less successful when seeking to organize and control those to whom they are linked by emotional ties, for those closest to them may resent the perceived restriction of their autonomy.
VERDICT: If they are not to become emotionally isolated—a risk that they may impose upon themselves by either suppressing their own, more selfish urges, or by making somewhat authoritarian demands of their nearest and dearest—those born on this day should try to appreciate that expressions of individuality are not necessarily incompatible with the greater good.

On This Day
Famous Births: Domenico Scarlatti (1685); Georges Jacques Danton (1759); C.P. Scott (1846); Lewis Casson (1875); Leon Trotsky (1879); Mahalia Jackson (1911); Jackie Coogan (1914); François Mitterand (1916); Shah Mohammed Reza Pahlavi of Persia (1919); Bob Hoskins (1942); Pat Sajak (1946); Hilary Rodham Clinton and Jaclyn Smith (1947); Cary Elwes (1962).

Significant Events and Anniversaries: This day is both governed by the element of water and highlights the promotion of advances toward a common good, as was reflected in the realm of transport on this day when both the Erie Canal in New York State, connecting the Niagara and Hudson rivers, and the Woolwich Tunnel under the River Thames in Britain were officially opened (1825 and 1912 respectively). The sublimation of personal interests in the pursuit of communal interests was illustrated on October 26 when: King Oscar II of Sweden and Norway reluctantly bowed to the Norwegian people's demands for independence and abdicated his Norwegian throne in favor of Prince Carl of Denmark (Haakon II) (1905); and novelist Jeffrey Archer resigned as deputy chairman of Britain's Conservative Party, in order to spare it embarrassment arising from accusations as to his alleged sexual misdemeanor (1986). Social responsibility in its wider sense was demonstrated when: during World War II, a U.S. naval carrier force under Rear Admiral Thomas Kincaid engaged its Japanese foe commanded by Admiral Nobutake Kondo at the Battle of the Santa Cruz Islands (1942); and the United Nations decided to set up the International Atomic Energy Agency (I.A.E.A.), to ensure responsible use of nuclear power (1956).

OCTOBER 27

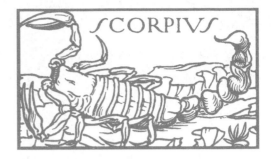

SCORPIVS

Such is the passion with which they express their emotions, and their active and immediate response to anyone or anything that they encounter, that the majority of October 27 people are impossible to ignore. Although unquestionably attention-seekers, their compulsion to attract others to them is rarely fueled by self-serving motivations or vanity but instead results from their almost irresistible urge to express their feelings and opinions freely and to influence or direct those around them. And while their convictions and actions are essentially emotion driven, they have considerable intellectual talents and practical skills at their disposal with which to work toward the realization of their goals. Thus despite their tendency to react somewhat impulsively to emotional stimuli—especially those concerned with morality or spirituality—once their interest has been aroused they manifest imagination, resourcefulness and organizational powers in support of their ambitions.

Those born on this day are perfectionists, but this quality is usually of the idealistic rather than the technical variety. Blessed with great communication skills, they will thrive in careers where they can impart their visions to others, maybe as journalists or teachers, but especially as writers, musicians and actors—professions in which their emotions and innovative dreams can simultaneously be given free rein and inspire their audiences. They are admired for their driving energy and pioneering turn of mind, but it is these very characteristics that can make them demanding—but lively and fun—colleagues, friends and family members.

VIRTUES: October 27 people are invigoratingly active and imaginative individuals who are extremely responsive to their emotions yet also possess more practical and rational personal qualities which, when reconciled, give them outstanding potential. Despite their need for personal autonomy, these natural leaders are strongly oriented toward others, desiring to play an educational, directional and inspirational role in life.
VICES: Their powerfully temperamental natures and urge to control give those born on this day the ability to excite and galvanize others, but they also run the risk of appearing provocative and aggressive if they misjudge those whom they are seeking to influence, a danger that is particularly pronounced in their dealings with those closest to them.
VERDICT: It is important that these individuals recognize that the emotional and intellectual freedom that is so vital to them is a prerequisite that is equally cherished by others: when seeking to impart their views they should therefore adopt a more tolerant and patient approach toward those who do not instantly fall in with their beliefs.

On This Day
Famous Births: James Cook (1728); Niccolò Paganini (1782); Isaac Merit Singer (1811); Theodore Roosevelt (1858); Emily Post (1872); Enid Bagnold (1889); Dylan Thomas (1914); Harry Saltzman (1915); Nanette Fabray (1920); Ruby Dee and Roy Lichtenstein (1923); David Bryant (1931); Sylvia Plath (1932); John Cleese (1939); Peter Martins and Carrie Snodgress (1946); Jayne Kennedy (1951); Glen Hoddle (1957); Simon Le Bon (1958); Marla Maples (1965).

Significant Events and Anniversaries: This is a day that highlights both visionary ideas and resourcefulness, as was demonstrated when: the New York Subway was officially opened (1904); and the Congo Republic in central Africa changed its name to the Republic of Zaire to signal a clear break from its colonial past (1971), [this would be reversed in 1997]. The leadership quality inherent in this day was confirmed when Winston Churchill became Britain's prime minister for the second time (1951). October 27 furthermore indicates the uncompromising promotion of powerful convictions, reflected when, on this day, the Spanish Anabaptist Michael Servatus was burned at the stake in Geneva, Switzerland, on the orders of the Protestant reformer John Calvin (1553). And finally, this is a day on which explosive temperaments are featured, and therefore appropriately commemorates the radical deregulation of the City of London's money markets—an event popularly known as the "Big Bang" (1986).

Planetary Influences
Ruling planet: Pluto.
First decan: Personal planet is Mars.

♇ ♂

Sacred and Cultural Significance
In England, Allan Apple Day celebrated by Pagans.
Saint's day: Odran of Iona (d. c.563).

One of the most popular presidents in U.S. history, Theodore Roosevelt (born on October 27, 1858) exhibited this day's rare combination of intelligence, inspiration, ambition and the practical ability to achieve goals. His famous "Square Deal" policy for social equity became the blueprint for subsequent reform movements.

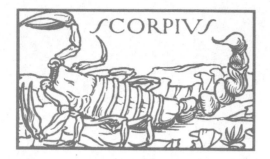

Planetary Influences
Ruling planet: Pluto.
First decan: Personal planet is Mars.

♇ ♂

Sacred and Cultural Significance
Phoenician sun-god Baal of the Heavens honored; in ancient Egypt, Autumn ceremonies honoring Isis began.
Saints' day: Simon (d. 1st century AD), patron saint of fishermen, and Jude, patron saint of hopeless causes (d. 1st century AD); Salvius (7th century AD).

On this day in 1886, one hundred years after the signing of the Declaration of Independence, France's great gift to the city of New York, the Statue of Liberty, was dedicated by President Grover Cleveland. It commemorates the spirit of independence, social justice and progress inherent in this day.

OCTOBER 28

Their work is of all-consuming importance to many of those ambitious individuals born on this day. Yet their ambition is rarely of the type to demand personal glory or spectacular financial rewards, but is instead the natural product of their perfectionism. October 28 individuals are inquisitive types who are determined to use the fruits of their discoveries to move forward into uncharted waters. Fascinated with deconstruction and reconstruction, their meticulous attention to detail and logical turn of mind give them remarkable potential to make pioneering contributions to the world. Because they are extremely tenacious and focused, they are typically absorbed in their endeavors—indeed, when others regard them as having reached the pinnacle of their success, they will remain unsatisfied, believing that their task remains uncompleted and that progress can still be made.

Their independent inclinations endow those born on this day with the capacity to break new ground in any area that excites their interest, particularly in the realms of science and technology. Although they are fueled by their desire to benefit others, and are firm but fair leaders, their concern is often of the more abstract, humanitarian variety rather than emotionally based. Their propensity to immerse themselves in their intellectual or professional interests make them rather solitary figures, whose love and loyalty is genuine: however, those closest to them may not always realize this, since they are not given to expressing their affection openly.

VIRTUES: Imaginative and ingenious, logical and organized, those born on this day are prone to investigate their interests with punctilious thoroughness. Though sometimes shy, they value their friendships and are especially committed to their families.
VICES: The combination of their focused sense of purpose, their concentration and their tenacity in the pursuit of their ambitions may cause October 28 people not only to neglect those areas of their lives that are unrelated to their work, but also to become impatient with those who do not share their commitment or maintain their high standards.
VERDICT: If they are not to become emotionally isolated, it is vital that these individuals recognize that, although important, their intellectual interests are not the be all and end all of their existence, but components that should be accommodated within a more balanced lifestyle. They should therefore ensure that they do not sublimate the emotional or relaxational needs of themselves or those around them.

On This Day
Famous Births: Cornelis Jansen (1585); Robert Liston (1794); George-Auguste Escoffier (1846); Evelyn Waugh (1903); Francis Bacon (1909); Richard Doll (1912); Jonas Salk (1914); Cleo Laine (1927); Joan Plowright (1929); Charlie Daniels and Carl Davis (1936); David Dimbleby (1938); Jane Alexander (1939); Hank Marvin (1942); Dennis Franz (1944); Dennis Taylor (1948); Bruce Jenner (1949); Annie Potts (1952); Bill Gates (1955); Jami Gertz (1965); Lauren Holly (1966); Julia Roberts (1967); Joaquin Phoenix (1974).

Significant Events and Anniversaries: Highlighted on this day are progressive and focused propensities concerned with effecting tangible advances, as was illustrated by: the foundation of the U.S.A.'s first university, Harvard, at New Towne (Cambridge), Massachusetts (1636); English physicist Michael Faraday's demonstration of his electrical dynamo (1831); U.S. inventor George Eastman's announcement of his development of a pioneering color photographic process (1914); the resolution of the U.S./Soviet stalemate during the Cuban Missile Crisis; and the decision of the British parliament to join the European Common Market (1971). Independence is a further quality emphasized by this day, on which the monumental sculpture created by Auguste Bartholdi, the Statue of Liberty—a gift of the French nation—was dedicated by President Grover Cleveland in New York, during the centenary celebrations of the signing of the Declaration of Independence (1886). And, on a day that warns of the risks of suppressing emotional needs, this threat was mirrored in the natural world when a massive earthquake all but destroyed the Peruvian cities of Lima and Callao (1746).

OCTOBER 29

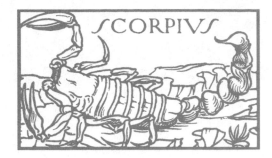
SCORPIVS

Although they possess highly independent minds and a relish for innovation, the combination of their pronounced sense of social responsibility and compulsion to organize and synchronize the actions of others makes October 29 people natural leaders. Indeed, such are their clarity of vision, logistical talents and resourcefulness, that in many respects those born on this day can be described as highly accomplished tacticians and strategists. This is not to say that they lack charisma—to the contrary, others respond instinctively to their aura of authority and strength of purpose—but rather that they prefer to research their subject rather than dashing impulsively forward with guns blazing. And just as the chess master appreciates the element of surprise, October 29 individuals are somewhat secretive types, who may keep even those closest to them in the dark regarding their true intentions.

Their progressive predilections, along with their pragmatic way of looking at the world, augur well for the success of these people in any professional sphere that they choose, although many will feel themselves drawn to those political, military or commercial pursuits where they can harness the efforts of others to promote their goals. Admired by their colleagues for their rationality, tenacity and loyalty, a completely different side to their characters emerges when they relax with their nearest and dearest (and they prefer to keep their professional and private lives separate), a side that includes their passionate affection, their fierce protectiveness, and their sensuality and love of pleasure.

VIRTUES: Those born on this day are blessed with direct, independent and progressive intellectual powers, which endow them with the ability to formulate visionary and ingenious plans of action. Their strong identification with the people with whom they are involved instills in them the desire to organize and direct those around them.
VICES: Their predilection for playing their cards close to their chests is an empowering tactic designed to strengthen their personal and strategic position, and is often useful when employed within professional scenarios. It may, however, cause deep hurt to their coworkers, friends and family members, who may feel excluded or distrusted.
VERDICT: October 29 people should try to overcome their tendency to conceal their intentions from others, bearing in mind the wounding effect that such a policy may have on their allies and loved ones. They should make an effort to open up more to others, thereby also reaping rich emotional benefits.

On This Day

Famous Births: Duke of Alba (1507); James Boswell (1740); Jean Giradoux (1882); Fanny Brice (1891); Josef Goebbels (1897); Vivian Ellis (1904); Robert Hardy (1925); Frater Zarathustra (1939); Melba Moore (1945); Richard Dreyfus (1947); Kate Jackson (1948); Winona Ryder (1971).

Significant Events and Anniversaries: October 29 is a day that highlights the extremely organized promotion of progressive communal goals, as was demonstrated when: Israeli troops under General Moshe Dayan began their invasion of the Sinai Peninsula in reprisal for Egypt's support of Muslim raids on their country and its nationalization of the Suez Canal (1956); and the recently independent African countries of Tanganyika and Zanzibar united to form the United Republic of Tanzania (1964). This is a day that warns of the possibly detrimental effects of secrecy, and marks the anniversary of "Black Tuesday," when the true status of the securities and commercial concerns in which speculators had enthusiastically invested was revealed, leading to the panic selling of shares and the crash of New York's Wall Street stock exchange, thus ushering in the Depression era (1929). On a lighter note, this is also a day on which pleasure-loving characteristics are indicated, and October 29 appropriately commemorates the premiere performance of Austrian composer Wolfgang Amadeus Mozart's opera *Don Giovanni* (1787). And finally, October 29—which is cogoverned by the planet Mars—was the day on which the Soviet archaeologist Peter Kozlov identified the tomb of the great Mongol conqueror, Genghis Khan, at Ejin Horo, Inner Mongolia (1927).

Planetary Influences
Ruling planet: Pluto.
First decan: Personal planet is Mars.

♇ ♂

Sacred and Cultural Significance
Feast of the Dead celebrated by Iroquois; national day of Turkey.
Saints' day: Colman of Kilmacduagh (d. c.632); translation of Merewenna (10th century AD).

First brought to wide public attention with her role in the film Beetlejuice *(1988), Winona Ryder, born on this day in 1971, has since become one of Hollywood's most engaging actresses, winning hearts with her sincerity and charm. Augmenting the professionally successful qualities of the October 29 person is the influence of the Chinese year of the pig, bringing her sensuality, charisma, honesty and intelligence.*

OCTOBER 30

* *

Planetary Influences
Ruling planet: Pluto.
First decan: Personal planet is Mars.

Sacred and Cultural Significance
In Mexico, the Angelitos festival celebrated.
Saints' day: Marcellus the Centurion
(d. 298); Clare of Montefalco (d. 1308);
Alphonsus Rodriguez (1533–1617).

Best known for his ethereal landscapes with large luminous skies, Alfred Sisley, impressionist painter and etcher, was born on this day in 1840 in Paris. Although his works did not find a wide audience until after his death, under the influence of this day that highlights devotion to a wider social affiliation, Sisley maintained his dedication to the Impressionist movement throughout his life and career.

October 30 people tend to immerse themselves in projects and issues that affect their communities, often volunteering to participate in, or organize, school, club or fundraising activities. Because these are active types who prefer to take charge of situations rather than stand idly by, they typically throw themselves wholeheartedly into the pursuit of common goals, in the process enlisting the support of those around them and directing their cohorts with imagination and confidence. Possessing logical and progressive intellects, those born on this day understand innately that most ventures need to be supported by meticulous preparation: thus they pay special attention to even the most mundane issues of research and organization. They are friendly, sociable and straightforward people who enjoy being with others and are rarely given to solitary pursuits. Given their socially oriented inclinations and interpersonal skills, October 30 people are particularly suited to teaching, the medical field and the service industries.

These individuals are generally unhappy when working as independent operators, far preferring to surround themselves with a supportive team of like-minded people—a predilection that applies as much to their personal as to their professional lives. Their communal commitment is total, and therefore they not only have a tendency to suppress what they may regard as selfish desires, but also to demand the same level of dedication from their colleagues, kith or kin, regardless of their personal inclinations. They come into their own as parents, devoting endless energy to encouraging their children's growth and interests.

VIRTUES: Those born on this day are rational, objective thinkers who instinctively recognize that lasting progress can often be achieved more effectively by means of collective, rather than individual, efforts. Endowed with a strong sense of responsibility for those around them, they are natural organizers and leaders of others.
VICES: These individuals have an unselfish tendency to put communal interests above their own personal prerequisites. There is a dual danger inherent in this approach: that their emotional equilibrium will become imbalanced; and that they may demand a correspondingly devoted approach from others.
VERDICT: Although their altruistic propensities are admirable, October 30 people should appreciate that expressions of individuality or nonconformity are not always incompatible with the greater good and, indeed, are generally socially enriching. Therefore, they should consciously relax their high expectations—of themselves as well as of others—and occasionally allow themselves to be self-indulgent.

On This Day
Famous Births: John Adams (1735); R.B. Sheridan (1751); Adelaide A. Procter (1825); Alfred Sisley (1840); Ezra Pound (1885); Charles Atlas (1893); Philip Heseltine (1894); Ruth Gordon (1896); Gordon Parks (1912); Louis Malle (1932); Michael Winner (1935); Claude LeLouch (1937); Grace Slick (1939); Henry Winkler (1945); Harry Hamlin (1951); Diego Maradona (1960).

Significant Events and Anniversaries: This is a day that highlights the determined pursuit of interests intended to advance the greater good, as was reflected when: following a revolutionary uprising, Czar Nicholas II of Russia agreed to the demands of the October Manifesto for limited constitutional reforms, including an elected parliament (1905); a republican revolution forced the five-year-old Qing emperor of China, P'u-i (Pu Yi), to grant constitutional concessions (1911); a new nation of Czechoslovakia was created following the post-World War I dissolution of the Austro-Hungarian Empire (1918); and King Victor Emmanuel III invited the Fascist leader Benito Mussolini to become Italy's premier in an attempt to avert civil war (1922). The strong desire to effect humanity's advancement that is emphasized by this day was also demonstrated in the technical and artistic realms when: the Scottish electrical engineer John Logie Baird succeeded in transmitting the world's first televised images (1925).

OCTOBER 31

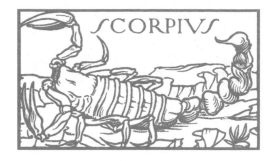

The perfectionist tendencies of October 31 people are stimulated by challenging situations of all kinds, for they are not only blessed with incisive clarity of vision but also possess the courage and integrity necessary to stand firm when promoting their strongly held beliefs. Many of those self-reliant individuals born on this day gravitate toward demanding scenarios that offer the opportunity to test themselves, a personal predilection that stems less from sensation-seeking motives, than from their desire to place themselves at the service of others. Underpinning their actions therefore are dual propensities for self-sacrifice and confrontation, both of which arise from their profound concern for and interest in the welfare of those with whom they most strongly identify—their friends and families, workmates, compatriots, or even humanity as a whole. To all their endeavors they bring their direct and logical turn of mind, their organizational skills, and the determination to realize their visions.

Their orientation toward others and their idealistic inclinations suit October 31 people to any profession where they can work toward the common good. Natural pioneers and leaders, their strength of purpose and commitment is respected by others, although those closest to them in particular may feel reluctant or, indeed, unable, to meet their standards. In their urge to lead by example, they run the risk of alienating those about whom they care the most, who may feel that their individual needs are being disregarded.

VIRTUES: October 31 individuals are blessed with perceptive, rational and determined intellects, complemented by their emotional connection with those around them. They are rarely put off by dauntingly difficult challenges.
VICES: Their profound belief in the moral or intellectual veracity of their causes, as well as their willingness to employ a combative approach if necessary, results in these people's tendency to brook no opposition when pursuing their aims, which may cause them to reject rather than accommodate any expressions of dissent, thus leading to emotional isolation.
VERDICT: Although their actions are typically informed by the best intentions, those born on this day should recognize that their single-minded devotion to their convictions may arouse the resentment of those closest to them. Remaining tolerant of individual choices is therefore of crucial importance to the well-being of those born on this day.

On This Day

Famous Births: John Evelyn (1620); Jan Vermeer (1632); John Keats (1795); Benoit Fourneyron (1802); Joseph Swan (1828); Juliette Low (1860); Cosmo Lang (1864); Marie Laurencin (1885); Chiang Kai-shek (1887); Ethel Waters (1900); Dale Evans (1912); Dick Francis (1920); Barbara Bel Geddes (1922); H.R.F. Keating (1926); Lee Grant (1927); Eddie Charlton (1929); Michael Collins (1930); Dan Rather (1931); Michael Landon (1937); David Ogden Stiers (1942); Deidre Hall (1948); John Candy and Jane Pauley (1950); Larry Mullen (1961).

Significant Events and Anniversaries: This is a day that indicates the active—and often confrontational—promotion of visionary goals with a communal purpose, when, for example: German Protestant reformer Martin Luther nailed to the door of Wittenberg's church his ninety-five theses attacking the Catholic system of selling papal indulgences (1517); U.S. scientists exploded the world's first hydrogen bomb at Eniwetok Atoll in the Pacific Ocean (1952); and a Sikh extremist working as her bodyguard assassinated the Indian premier, Indira Gandhi, in New Delhi (1984). A progressive urge was demonstrated in the realms of technology and medicine when Scottish inventor John Boyd Dunlop patented his pneumatic bicycle tires (1888); and Swedish doctor Ake Senning carried out the first operation on a patient's heart to implant a pacemaker (1958). Furthermore a day which highlights the sublimation of selfish desires in order to benefit wider, communal concerns, October 31 marks the anniversary of Princess Margaret's announcement that she had decided not to marry Peter Townsend, because his divorce made any such marriage unacceptable to the British monarchy (1955).

Planetary Influences
Ruling planet: Pluto.
First decan: Personal planet is Mars.

Sacred and Cultural Significance
Hallowe'en (All Hallow's Eve); ancient Celts celebrated New Year's Eve.
Saints' day: Quentin (dates unknown); Erc (dates unknown); Foillan (d. c.655); Begu (d. 660); Wolfgang of Regensburg (c.924–94).

Halloween—from the Celtic holiday Samhain Eve marking the cross quarter between the fall equinox and the winter solstice—is traditionally a night of revelry and bonfires celebrating the dissolution of boundaries between the physical and spiritual worlds, allowing those seeking clarity of vision (a characteristic of those born today) to enlist help from the spirits of the otherworld.

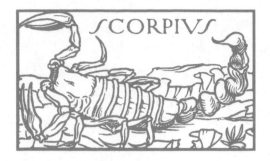

Planetary Influences
Ruling planet: Pluto.
Second decan: Personal planets are Jupiter and Neptune.

♇ ♃ ♆

Sacred and Cultural Significance
All Saint's Day; in ancient Rome, the Feast of Pomona; the Day of the Dead celebrated in Latin America and Spain; Cailleach's Reign, a Pagan festival.
Saints' day: All Saints; Benignus of Dijon (2nd century AD); Dingad (dates unknown); Gwythian (dates unknown); Cadfan (5th century AD); Vigor (d. c.537).

Painted on the ceiling of the Sistine Chapel and unveiled on November 1, 1512, Michelangelo's fresco The Creation of the Sun, Moon and Planets *(detail below) demonstrates the resourcefulness in pursuit of visions associated with this day, for which artistic ventures are also starred.*

NOVEMBER 1

Those born on this day have an absolute dread of inactivity and intellectual boredom. Typically "doers" rather than thinkers, their intellectual talents are of the progressive rather than the quietly reflective kind. Especially stimulated by pioneering—even radical—concepts, November 1 individuals throw themselves into the exploration and development of new ideas with single-minded enthusiasm, using ingenuity and resourcefulness to realize their goals. Because they are blessed with remarkable self-assurance and fearlessness in the face of adversity or opposition, these natural leaders refuse to be bound by convention and have the capacity to perform especially well in a wide range of professional areas, particularly artistic, inventive or scientific fields or as business entrepreneurs where independence of thought is an asset.

Because their urge to effect progress is so strong, and their *modi operandi* so vigorous, those born on this day have a tendency (especially notable if they were born in the Chinese year of the dragon) to focus on their aims regardless of personal consequences—to themselves or those around them. This approach can be detrimental to maintaining stable emotional relationships. Yet despite this *caveat*, November 1 people are naturally predisposed toward grounding themselves in the strong and affectionate ties of kith- and kinship and make loyal and stimulating friends and relations.

VIRTUES: Both intellectually and physically energetic November 1 individuals are drawn to unusual and challenging situations of all kinds. Their desire to extend the bounds of human knowledge and endeavor is often inspiring to others.
VICES: Their fear of stagnation may lead those born on this day to behave impulsively when tedium creeps up on them, a trait that could condemn them to eternal restlessness or disruptive behavior. Their profound self-belief and willingness to challenge the status quo may lead to delusions of superiority, even invincibility.
VERDICT: It is vital that these people safeguard their emotional equilibrium by controlling their need for excitement so that their thoughts and actions do not become unfocused. They should also be aware that a confrontational, nonconformist stance is not always productive, and they should make time for periods of honest introspection.

On This Day
Famous Births: Benvenuto Cellini (1500); Antonio Canova (1757); Spencer Perceval (1762); Stephen Crane (1871); L.S. Lowry (1887); Alexander Alekhine (1892); Edmund Blunden (1896); Naomi Mitchison (1897); Michael Denison (1915); Victoria de los Angeles (1923); Gary Player (1935); Robert Foxworth (1941); Larry Flynt (1942); Lyle Lovett (1957); Fernando Valenzuela (1960); Sharon Davies (1962); Jenny McCarthy (1972).

Significant Events and Anniversaries: November 1 is a day that promises marked leadership potential, as was apparently confirmed when, after Indira Gandhi's assassination, Rajiv Gandhi became India's premier (1984). Exploratory tendencies are emphasized by this day, on which the first of many prehistoric cave paintings was discovered in the Lascaux cave system in the Dordogne region of France (1940). On a day that highlights pioneering innovations, the American Motor League was formed—the world's first such automotive organization (1895). The actively confrontational tendencies that are featured on this day were reflected in the attempted assassination of American President Harry S. Truman by two republican Puerto Ricans (1950). And, on a day that is ruled by the element of water, November 1 commemorates the naval Battle of Coronel off the coast of South America during World War I, when a German force under Admiral Maximilian von Spee sank two British cruisers, including H.M.S. *Good Hope* (1914).

NOVEMBER 2

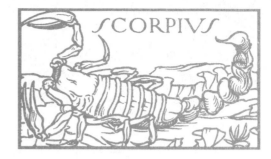

The combination of their natural predilection for taking action and their keen interest in promoting the welfare of those around them (a concern that often takes a more abstract, humanitarian form) endows those born on this day with real leadership potential. Incisive and progressive thinkers, November 2 people can identify the faults and flaws in various situations and devise solutions. Despite their willingness to adopt a combative stance if they believe that confrontation is the only available option—a policy that applies particularly when they defend humanitarian or ideological issues—their personal charm and benevolent intentions usually elicit an affectionate, if not always acquiescent, reaction from others.

Their strong and positive orientation toward other people, as well as their undoubted interpersonal talents, equip those born on this day admirably for careers as politicians or social campaigners, although some may be drawn to pursuing such artistic modes of expression as acting as a means of exerting their influence over a wider audience. Their goodwill and desire to assist others to advance is evident in all areas of their lives, and generally makes them popular figures. Their irresistible urge to offer even unsolicited advice and support and innate belief that their viewpoints are morally correct may, however, cause them to unwittingly arouse the resentment of those who would prefer to be allowed to forge their own path through life, especially their nearest and dearest.

VIRTUES: Blessed with acutely logical intellectual powers, as well as a marked sense of social connection and responsibility for their fellows, the actions of those born on this day are fueled by their urge to make a positive contribution to the welfare of others, be these the members of their immediate circle or, indeed, humanity as a whole. As good-natured as they are determined, they have great inspirational and leadership potential.

VICES: Although these may stem from the best of intentions, their keen interest in others and compulsion to devote themselves to their assistance may not always be appreciated; and may, in fact, cause them to be branded as meddlers. Their strength of conviction may furthermore cause them to be intolerant of expressions of dissent.

VERDICT: In order to avoid alienating the subjects of their concern, it is important that these individuals should recognize that not only may others not welcome their urge to intervene in their affairs, but, more importantly, that their interference may even be totally unjustified or inappropriate. Developing a more *laissez-faire* approach and a better sense of judgement should help them to target and direct their efforts more effectively.

Planetary Influences
Ruling planet: Pluto.
Second decan: Personal planets are Jupiter and Neptune.

♇ ♃ ♆

Sacred and Cultural Significance
Saints' day: All Souls.

On This Day
Famous Births: King Edward V of England (1470); Daniel Boone (1734); Queen Marie Antoinette of France (1755); James Knox Polk (1795); Warren Gamaliel Harding (1865); Aga Khan III (1877); Paul Ford (1901); Luchino Visconti (1906); Burt Lancaster (1913); Ray Walston (1924); Pat Buchanan (1938); Stefanie Powers (1942); Keith Emerson (1948); Alfre Woodard (1953); Ken Rosewall (1954); k.d. lang (1961).

Significant Events and Anniversaries: November 2 is a day on which leadership qualities are promised, as was confirmed when: Ras Tafari Makonnen was crowned Haile Selassie, emperor of Ethiopia, (1930); Prince Faisal ibn Abd al-Aziz was proclaimed King of Saudi Arabia (1964); and Democratic candidate Jimmy Carter was elected president of the United States (1976). On a day that highlights the active promotion of ambitions intended to advance the common good: the states of North and South Dakota joined the U.S. Union (1889); Boer forces besieged the British-held town of Ladysmith in Natal, during the South African Wars (1899); and British Foreign Secretary Arthur Balfour wrote to the British Zionist Lord Rothschild promising support for a proposed Jewish homeland in Palestine—a missive that became known as the "Balfour Declaration" (1917). Finally, on a day that is governed by the element of water, U.S. tycoon and pilot Howard Hughes tested his massive H.4 Hercules flying boat off California's Long Beach Harbor (1947).

The Australian tennis champion Kenneth Ronald Rosewall, born in Sydney on November 2, 1954, showed the energy and determination typical of those born on this day. He was also ambitious and competitive, reflecting his birth in the Chinese year of the horse. During a brilliant career, he won the U.S. singles title twice and the British, U.S., French and Australian doubles titles. As a professional, from 1956, he won the professional world championships in 1971 and 1972.

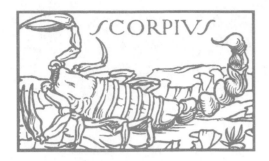

SCORPIVS

Planetary Influences

Ruling planet: Pluto.
Second decan: Personal planets are Jupiter and Neptune.

♇ ♃ ♆

Sacred and Cultural Significance

In Egypt, the final day of the Isia, the annual festival of the rebirth of Osiris through Isis.
Saints' day: Clydog (6th century AD); Rumwold (dates unknown); Wulganus (dates unknown); Winefride (7th century AD); translation of Hubert (d. 727), patron saint of dogs and hunters; Pirmin (d. 753); Malachy (1094–1148).

The completion of Nelson's Column in Trafalgar Square, London, on November 3, 1843, was consistent with the ambitious projects highlighted on this date.

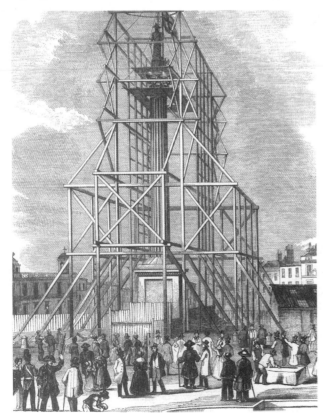

NOVEMBER 3

★★★★★★★★★★★★★★★★★★★★★★★★★★★★★★★★★★★★★★★

Perhaps the most pronounced characteristic of November 3 personalities is that of driving ambition. And because they possess a straightforward turn of mind and a remarkable talent for organization, many will have formulated their life plans as early as childhood. The nature of their goals will vary from one person to another: some may be concerned primarily with personal betterment (in terms of their social or financial status, for example); while others may seek to make a contribution to the world. Whatever their underlying motivations, all will share progressive instincts, as well as the mental and physical vigor, courage and tenacity to promote their aims regardless of the consequences (to themselves or others). These characteristics that are especially notable in those born in the Chinese year of the dragon. Indeed, they relish testing their skills and stamina against demanding challenges.

Despite the overriding importance that they place on the attainment of their self-set goals—a prerequisite that may cause them to act independently of the common consensus—November 3 people generally prefer to elicit the support of allies rather than the enmity of foes. They are often drawn to professions that provide an effective forum in which to exert their influence on those around them—as educators or entertainers, for instance. However, their forceful and uncompromising approach may have an alienating effect on those around them.

VIRTUES: Those born on this day are capable people who exploit their deep reserves of energy, as well as their intellectual and organizational talents, to transform the ambitions that drive their actions into reality. Blessed with enormous strength of purpose, they possess the necessary clarity of vision and resourcefulness to enable them to succeed.
VICES: Their unwavering fixity of purpose carries the risk that the pay-off may be costly in terms of their holistic well-being: they may not devote enough attention to their own emotional needs or to the sensibilities of others.
VERDICT: These individuals should recognize that their single-minded focus may tax the goodwill of their associates. Relaxed relationships will improve their emotional balance.

On This Day

Famous Births: Henry Ireton (1611); John Montague, Earl of Sandwich (1718); Daniel Rutherford (1749); Karl Baedecker and Vincenzo Bellini (1801); King Leopold III of the Belgians and André Georges Malraux (1901); Ludovic Henry Coverley Kennedy (1919); Charles Bronson (1922); John Barry (1933); Jeremy Brett (1935); Lulu (1948); Larry Holmes (1949); Roseanne Barr (1952); Dennis Miller (1953); Adam Ant (1954); Dolph Lundgren (1959).

Significant Events and Anniversaries: This is a day that emphasizes the determined pursuit of pioneering and progressive visions, as was demonstrated when: the U.S.S.R. sent the first living creature, a dog named Laika, into space aboard the satellite *Sputnik II* (1957); and Queen Elizabeth II officially opened the world's first underwater oil-carrying pipeline, to deliver North Sea oil to the Grangemouth Refinery on Scotland's Firth of Forth (1975). The extremely elevated nature of the ambitions highlighted by November 3 was neatly illustrated when a statue of English naval hero Horatio Nelson was pulled atop its supporting column erected in London's Trafalgar Square, named after his famous victory (1843). Inherent in this day is the willingness to utilize combative tactics in order to bring about success, as was demonstrated when: the British VIII Army under General Bernard Montgomery breached the German general Erwin Rommel's Egyptian front line during World War II (1942); and two French intelligence agents on trial in a New Zealand court admitted to having sunk the Greenpeace flagship, *Rainbow Warrior*, in Auckland Harbor (1985). The autonomous qualities featured by November 3 were reflected when Panama declared itself a republic independent of Colombia (1903).

NOVEMBER 4

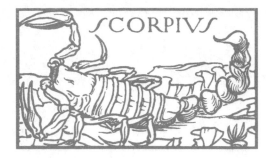

SCORPIVS

The conjunction of their logical minds and independence of thought endows those born on this day with simultaneously perceptive and progressive intellects that give them the ability both to pinpoint areas that are ripe for improvement and to formulate positive strategies for advancement. Fueled by the urge to share the conclusions that result from their analytical and conceptual skills, November 4 people are not content to keep their opinions to themselves but instead seek to make them public, hoping to thereby enlighten others and thus help them to advance. They manifest their communication skills in every area of their lives, and such is their acute talent for putting their messages across with clarity and accuracy that their intended recipients will rarely be left in the dark. Indeed, many of those born on this day are drawn to careers where they can reach the widest possible public—as actors or performers on stage and screen; writers, journalists and artists, or even as politicians or social reformers. And because their typical approach is based on a mixture of strong convictions laced with a dash of humor, others generally respond positively to them, even if their viewpoints are sometimes not very palatable.

Indeed, such is the respect and affection that November 4 individuals engender that they may often find themselves elevated to positions of leadership—somewhat to their surprise (although not necessarily their displeasure)—and because they are socially responsible types they will discharge their duties with integrity. Yet in many respects these people would prefer to be left to their own devices in order to pursue their intellectual interests free from the demands of others and to enjoy the enriching pleasures of domestic life and fulfilling interpersonal relationships, from which they derive such support and satisfaction.

VIRTUES: November 4 people are blessed with remarkable clarity of vision and extremely rational and objective powers, which enable them to identify flaws and formulate alternative strategies. As skilled communicators, they are able to present their viewpoints remarkably effectively, earning the respect of others.
VICES: Their strong urge to share their opinions with those around them stems from their social concern and desire to inform and illuminate others. As a consequence, however, they may find themselves assuming burdens of responsibility that divert their attention from personal interests.
VERDICT: Those born on this day should become aware of their potentially magnetic effect upon others. Their words and actions may place them in the public arena, with restrictive consequences for their personal lives.

Planetary Influences
Ruling planet: Pluto.
Second decan: Personal planets are Jupiter and Neptune.

♇ ♃ ♆

Sacred and Cultural Significance
The Lord of Death honored by Pagans; in England, Mischief Night.
Saints' day: Clether (6th century AD); Birstan (10th century AD); Charles Borromeo (1538–84), patron saint of bishops.

At a time when the pace of life was less hurried than it is today, racehorse Phar Lap won the 1930 Melbourne Cup on a day auspicious for success and fame.

On This Day
Famous Births: François Le Clerc du Tremblay (1577); King William III of England (1650); Augustus Montague Toplady (1740); Frank Benson (1858); Eden Phillpotts (1862); Herman Finck (1872); Will Rogers (1879); Walter Cronkite (1916); Art Carney (1918); Martin Balsam (1919); Loretta Swit (1937); Rodney Marsh (1947); Markie Post (1950); Yanni (1954); Ralph Macchio (1961); Lena Zavaroni (1963).

Significant Events and Anniversaries: This is a day that emphasizes highly developed powers of perception and the concurrent ability to take pioneering steps, as reflected when: the United Nations founded its Educational, Scientific and Cultural Organization (U.N.E.S.C.O.) to improve education worldwide (1946). Today also reflects the drive to make drastic changes as demonstrated in the realm of politics when: a Korean assassin murdered Japanese prime minister Hara Takashi (1922); anti-American followers of the Ayatollah Khomeini in the new republic of Iran stormed the U.S. embassy in Tehran, taking sixty-six people hostage (1980); and, while attending a peace rally in Tel Aviv, Israeli premier Yitzhak Rabin was shot dead by a right-wing, anti-Palestinian gunman (1995). The day's promise of leadership potential, was seen in the election of two U.S. presidents: Dwight D. Eisenhower (1952) and Ronald Reagan (1980).

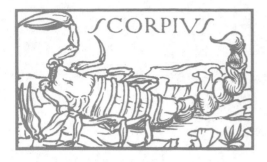

SCORPIVS

NOVEMBER 5

✦✦✦

Planetary Influences
Ruling planet: Pluto.
Second decan: Personal planets are Jupiter and Neptune.

♇ ♃ ♆

Sacred and Cultural Significance
Guy Fawkes (Bonfire) Night in Britain; in Shebbear, England, the one-ton Devil's Boulder is rotated.
Saints' day: Zachary and Elizabeth (d. 1st century AD); Kea (dates unknown); Martin de Porres (1579–1639), patron saint of the poor.

The quest for intellectual discovery associated with this day was rewarded on November 5, 1920, when British archeologist Howard Carter discovered Tutankhamen's tomb in Egypt's Valley of the Kings.

Those born on this day have two pronounced sides to their personalities: their strongly social feeling of connection with the people around them; and their private propensity for indulging their individual interests undisturbed by the demands of others. In some respects the influence of these two tendencies may cause November 5 people to feel torn between their desire actively to assist humanity—whether this be at the familial, communal, national or even global level—and their more selfish urge to shut themselves away so as to be able to concentrate on pursuits that excite their personal fascination. Many, however, are fortunate enough to be able to often find a way of reconciling these predilections, often by choosing careers where they can retain their prerequisite for autonomy of thought and action while at the same time sharing their findings with a broader audience, thereby making a positive contribution to the lives of others. The scientific and business realms, as well as such artistic specialties as writing and acting can thus be said to provide ideal professional arenas for their inclinations and skills.

November 5 individuals are intellectually curious and progressive types, who prefer to seek out knowledge for themselves rather than to be spoon-fed with it. Drawing on their highly developed powers of perception to amass a fund of information, they have the capacity to identify existing failings or abuses and then prepare logical and realistic proposals with which to bring about advancement; they thus possess real leadership ability. Yet although the honest expression of their criticism may be inherently uncomfortable to those who wish to maintain the status quo, these people's evident goodwill and earnest desire to bring about tangible advances usually make them subjects of admiration and especially valued friends, partners and parents.

VIRTUES: These cerebral people are stimulated by their driving urge to increase their personal lexicon of knowledge, to analyze and assess the data that they have discovered and then, because they are also socially concerned individuals, to reveal both their negative and positive conclusions in order to help enlighten others.
VICES: November 5 people are blessed with a strong sense of moral obligation and will rarely fail to enter the public domain when they believe that their services are required. Yet this admirable propensity may cause them to become beset by feelings of frustration if their attention becomes too thinly spread and thus hinders them from concentrating on their personal interests.
VERDICT: If they are to maintain their emotional equilibrium and physical health, it is crucial that these individuals should keep their professional and private concerns as evenly balanced as possible. By developing a greater recognition of their own priorities, they will not only enhance their ability to target their energies more effectively, but also reap prodigious rewards in terms of their emotional happiness.

On This Day
Famous Births: Ella Wheeler Wilcox (1850); James Elroy Flecker (1884); John Haldane (1892); Joel McCrea (1905); Roy Rogers (1911); Vivien Leigh (1913); John Bowen (1924); Ike Turner (1931); Lester Piggott (1935); Elke Sommer (1940); Art Garfunkel (1941); Sam Shepard (1943); Bryan Adams (1959); Andrea McArdle and Tatum O'Neal (1963).

Significant Events and Anniversaries: November 5 highlights the quest for intellectual discovery, as was illustrated on this day when British archaeologist Howard Carter discovered the fourteenth-century BC tomb of the boy pharaoh Tutankhamen at Luxor, in Egypt's Valley of the Kings (1920). The leadership potential inherent in this day was shown when F.D. Roosevelt was elected U.S. president for an unprecedented third term (1940). The willingness to expose or act upon perceived failings or injustices was demonstrated on November 5 when Guy Fawkes, a leading conspirator in the Catholic Gunpowder Plot, was executed for his effort to assassinate the Protestant king, James I, and members of Parliament (1605). Governed by the planet of change, November 5 commemorates the Battle of Inkerman during the Crimean War, when allied English and French troops defeated the Russians (1854).

NOVEMBER 6

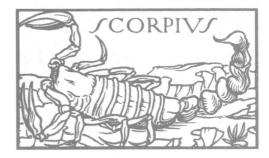

*S*uch is their propensity for action and their decidedly positive outlook on life that it often seems to others that November 6 people are blessed with limitless supplies of energy and boundless optimism. And in many respects this assessment is an accurate one, for these "can-do" individuals typically refuse to be dissuaded from pushing the visions that excite them to their ultimate conclusions, brushing aside the objections of their detractors—although in a charming and good-humored manner—in their determination to achieve their goals. Possessing not only great perceptiveness when it comes to identifying areas in which action is called for, but also logical and straightforward minds, as well as highly developed practical and technical talents, those born on this day manifest remarkable strength of conviction, self-belief and tenacity when working toward the realization of aims that are so ambitious that others might (and frequently do) brand them as unfeasible. Yet, despite the skepticism that may be engendered by the originality of their actions, the engaging enthusiasm and galvanizing vigor of November 6 people generally arouse indulgent affection rather than concerted opposition.

These individuals will thrive in any profession where their imaginative and progressive qualities are not suppressed; if they are employed within corporate structures, for example, they will do best when given the freedom to plan and implement advanced policy decisions. Naturally inspirational leaders, many are perhaps happiest working as scientists and artists of various types, simultaneously effecting innovations and exerting their influence directly over their publics. And, although they are stimulated by personal challenge, these are deeply humanitarian people who wish to benefit others through their efforts. Enlivening and generous companions, their concern for the well-being of those around them is evident in both their personal and professional relationships, particularly for the women born on this day.

VIRTUES: November 6 people are resourceful and direct individuals, who effectively harness their prodigious intellectual talents—including their rational outlook, ingenuity and organizational skills—along with their energy and practical expertise, to their dedicated quests to realize their extremely innovative visions.
VICES: The actions of those born on this day are often justified by their unwavering belief in the feasibility of their visions, as well as in their personal ability to effect them, but their tendency to disregard the concerns of others when pushing single-mindedly forward may cause them not to consider advice that could be to their advantage.
VERDICT: In order to attain the success that is so crucial to their emotional satisfaction, these individuals should recognize that those around them may have valid and useful criticisms to make about their own approaches and methodologies. They should try to remain open-minded and objective when others express their views—even if they appear to be negative.

On This Day
Famous Births: James Gregory (1638); Colley Cibber (1671); Alois Senefelder (1771); Adolphe Sax (1814); Charles Henry Dow (1851); John Philip Sousa (1854); James A. Naismith (1861); Walter Perry Johnson (1887); John Alcock (1892); Ray Coniff (1916); Donald Houston and Don Lusher (1923); Donald Churchill (1930); Mike Nichols (1931); P.J. Proby (1938); James Bowman (1941); Sally Field (1946); Glenn Frey (1948); Catherine Cryer and Gareth Williams (1954); Maria Shriver (1955); Lori Singer (1962); Peter De Luise (1966).

Significant Events and Anniversaries: This is a day on that highlights both strong leadership qualities and humanitarian instincts, as reflected by three elections on November 6: Abraham Lincoln and Herbert Hoover as presidents of the U.S.A. (1860 and 1928, respectively), and Stanley Baldwin as prime minister of Britain (1924). This day is ruled by the element of water, as illustrated when work began on construction of the Kariba Dam, on the border of the African countries of Zambia and Zimbabwe, with a view to providing both countries with hydroelectric power (1956).

Planetary Influences
Ruling planet: Pluto.
Second decan: Personal planets are Jupiter and Neptune.

♇ ♃ ♆

Sacred and Cultural Significance
The birth of Tiamat, ancient Babylonian goddess, celebrated.
Saints' day: Melaine (d. c.535), patron saint of Mullion and St. Mellyan, Cornwall, England; Illtud (d. 6th century AD); Leonard (6th century AD), patron saint of prisoners; Winnoc (d. c.717); Vietnam Martyrs (d. 1745–1862).

In 1924 the politician Stanley Baldwin was elected prime minister of Britain on November 6, a day favorable to inspirational leadership and instincts to pursue the common good.

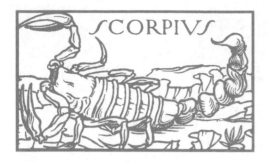

SCORPIVS

Planetary Influences
Ruling planet: Pluto.
Second decan: Personal planets are Jupiter and Neptune.

♇ ♃ ♆

Sacred and Cultural Significance
In ancient Greece, the Night of Hecate celebrated with a fire festival; Lono honored by the Hawaiian Harvest Festival.
Saints' day: Congar (dates unknown), patron of Hope, Clwyd, Wales; Willibrord (658–739).

The Polish-born physicist Marie Curie, born in Warsaw, Poland, on November 7, 1867, was acutely perceptive, logical and ingenious, as is typical of those born on this day. Devoted to advancing scientific knowledge, she worked with her husband Pierre Curie on magnetism and radioactivity and discovered radium. She shared two Nobel Prizes: for Physics, awarded in 1903, and for Chemistry, in 1911.

NOVEMBER 7

✳✳✳✳✳✳✳✳✳✳✳✳✳✳✳✳✳✳✳✳✳✳✳✳✳✳✳✳✳✳✳✳✳✳✳✳✳

Those physically and mentally active individuals born on this day are extremely responsive to challenge, stimulated not by combative instincts (although they will take a confrontational stance to defend their strongly held convictions) but by their desire to break through the existing limits of human knowledge or experience. These are curious and progressive types, who relish the opportunity to test their skills and stamina against demanding (in the eyes of others, even hopeless) challenges. Acutely perceptive, rigorously logical and ingenious in their intellectual approach, and endowed with highly developed organizational and practical skills, November 7 people have the potential and talent to become pioneers in their professions. They are also blessed with the magnetic charisma necessary to enlist the support and direct the actions of those around them. And although they are personally excited by their career ambitions or private interests, their innate humanitarianism and sense of social responsibility bestows on them the desire to work toward goals that they believe will be of concrete benefit to the wider world.

The nature of the careers chosen by November 7 people will vary. Some may seek to bring about social or spiritual changes, some to further humanity's scientific or technical knowledge; others will be drawn to the artistic or sporting spheres. However, all will lead by example, expecting a similarly high level of commitment from others. (Those born in the Chinese year of the rooster are especially single-minded in pursuit of their goals.) Although they are generally magnanimous and affectionate friends and family members, those closest to them may have difficulty living up to their expectations.

VIRTUES: November 7 people are acutely responsive to circumstances or concepts that require the utmost effort in terms of ingenuity or resourcefulness. Blessed with rational and perceptive intellectual talents, they are propelled forward by their inquisitiveness to explore the outermost parameters of existing knowledge. They inspire their friends and families with their enthusiasm and positive attitudes.
VICES: Energized by their determination to succeed, the single-minded focus that those born on this day display when in pursuit of their ambitious goals augurs well for their eventual success, but may inevitably cause them to neglect the less immediate—but no less important—personal and emotional needs of their loved ones.
VERDICT: These individuals should strive to balance their professional and private lives to ensure that their tendency to concentrate on their intellectual interests does not have a detrimental effect on the lives of those closest to them or, indeed, on their own emotional equilibrium.

On This Day
Famous Births: Marie Curie (1867); Lise Meitner (1878); Chandrasekhara Venkata Raman (1888); Herman J. Mankiewicz and Ruth Pitter (1897); Dean Jagger (1903); William Alwyn (1905); Albert Camus (1913); Helen Suzman (1917); Billy Graham (1918); Al Hirt (1922); Wolf Mankowitz (1924); Joan Sutherland (1926); Gwyneth Jones (1936); Mary Travers (1937); Helen Garner and Jean Shrimpton (1942); Joni Mitchell (1943); Lucinda Green (1953); Keith Lockhart (1959); Mark Hately (1961); John Barnes (1963); Jason and Jeremy London (1972).

Significant Events and Anniversaries: November 7 indicates pioneering achievements of all kinds, and on this day: manufacture of the world's first pocket lighter—the Erie—began at the Springfield, Massachusetts plant of the U.S. Repeating Light Company (1865); the Canadian Pacific Railway was completed (1885); and Jeanette Rankin was elected the first female member of the U.S. Congress by the state of Montana (1916). The predilection for activity in the perceived common interest was reflected when Vladimir Ilyich Lenin led Bolsheviks against Alexander Kerensky's provisional government in the so-called "October Revolution" (according to the Julian calendar then employed in Russia) (1917). Leadership potential was confirmed when Konrad Adenauer was elected chancellor of West Germany for the fourth time (1961).

NOVEMBER 8

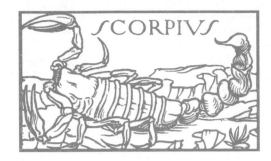

✦✦

November 8 individuals are blessed with extraordinary vitality—a quality manifested by their physical vigor, but also (and perhaps especially) by their remarkably imaginative and progressive minds. They are attracted by subjects so unusual that other, less receptive, peole may reject them as too radical or threatening to the status quo. Yet although those born on this day have original and curious turns of mind, their interests are rarely flighty or superficial. They support their search for knowledge with meticulous attention to detail. Their powers of concentration and courage pursuing their quests augur well for their success (although winning the recognition of their peers may take some time). A happy domestic life and the support of those closest to them are important to grounding them in emotional equilibrium. They are generous, tolerant and invigorating friends and family members.

Personally stimulated by intellectual discovery, November 8 people will flourish in any profession where they can meet their altruistic needs and retain autonomy of thought and action. Given the nature of their talents and inclinations, they have marked potential to become inspiring artists, writers, musicians, actors, or pioneering scientists and engineers.

VIRTUES: November 8 people are fascinated by the possibilities inherent in unconventional areas of interest, especially those they believe have not yet been fully explored. Fueled by their innate desire for discovery and eager for personal acclaim, they pursue their interests with energy, determination and resourcefulness.

VICES: Because they are rational and perceptive individuals, those born on this day do not regard their theories and convictions as being untenable or unfeasible and may therefore experience feelings of profound hurt when others disparage their efforts. In such instances they have a tendency to adopt self-defensive strategies, such as retreating into their private worlds of introspection.

VERDICT: Although they need never abandon the pursuit of their visions, these people should beware of cutting themselves off from those around them and thereby becoming emotionally isolated. While they instinctively appreciate the value of maintaining strong ties with their nearest and dearest, it is important that they should not allow their intellectual preoccupations to divert too much of their attention from their loved ones.

On This Day

Famous Births: Edmund Halley (1656); Benjamin Hall (1802); Pierre Bosquet (1810); Bram Stoker (1847); Herbert Austin (1866); Arnold Bax (1883); Steve Donaghue (1884); Margaret Mitchell (1900); June Havoc (1916); Christiaan Barnard (1922); Patti Page (1927); Morley Safer (1931); Esther Rolle (1933); Alain Delon (1935); Martin Peters (1940); Bonnie Raitt (1949); Rupert Allason (Nigel West) and Mary Hart (1951); Christie Hefner (1952); Leif Garrett (1961).

Significant Events and Anniversaries: This is a day that promises pioneering advances to benefit society, as was demonstrated when: the Louvre, the former French monarchical palace, was opened to the public as an art gallery (1793); German physicist Wilhelm Röntgen discovered X-rays while engaged in research at Würzburg University (1895); and U.S. voters elected the first African-Americans as state governor (Douglas Wilder, in Virginia) and civic mayor (David Dinkins, in New York City) (1989). A similar desire to effect perceived—and often controversial—social advancement was illustrated in the political sphere when: F.D. Roosevelt, campaigning on his "New Deal" ticket, was first elected president of the U.S.A. (1932); future German dictator Adolf Hitler made an inflammatory speech at a beer hall in Munich, proposing the overthrow of the government of the Weimar Republic (1923); and I.R.A. terrorists drew the world's horrified attention to their cause by detonating a bomb at the cenotaph of the town of Enniskillen in Northern Ireland, killing eleven people who had gathered there to honor their war dead (1987).

Planetary Influences
Ruling planet: Pluto.
Second decan: Personal planets are Jupiter and Neptune.

♇ ♃ ♆

Sacred and Cultural Significance
Fuigo Matsuri, a Shinto festival, held in Japan to honor Hettsui No Dami, the kitchen-range goddess.
Saints' day: Four Crowned Martyrs (d. 4th century AD), patron saints of stonemasons; Cybi (6th century AD); Tysilio (7th century AD); Willehad (d. 789); Gerardin (d. c.934).

The world-famous Louvre, converted from the former French monarchical palace, was opened to the public as museum of art in 1793, on a day associated with intellectual discovery, creativity and progress in the public interest.

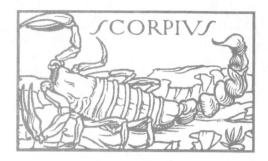

SCORPIVS

Planetary Influences
Ruling planet: Pluto
Second decan: Personal planets are Jupiter and Neptune.

♇ ♃ ♆

Sacred and Cultural Significance
Traditional wish ritual performed in Thailand.
Saint's day: Theodore (4th century AD).

Reflecting the deep humanitarian concern and sense of social responsibility that are predicted by this day, the long-awaited demolition of the divisive Berlin Wall began in Germany in 1989.

NOVEMBER 9

Those lively individuals born on this day are not the types to sit passively on the sidelines of life watching the world pass them by, which is not to say that they are not highly observant people—to the contrary, they are extremely perceptive, especially with regard to human behavior, be it individual or societal—it is simply that they prefer to do rather than view. Possessing a dread of inactivity, November 9 people feel compelled to involve themselves fully in every area of their lives—professional and personal, intellectual, emotional and sensual—so as to satisfy their innate need for individual growth and also to contribute to the lives of those around them. Extremely responsive to stimuli of all kinds, they are at the forefront of any activity, blazing a pioneering trail and directing those who follow in their wake. Yet while they manifest a keen, and somewhat impulsive, interest in any novel subject or concept they encounter, their fascination is rarely superficial, for they are fueled by their urge to explore it to its fullest extent and thereby to uncover previously undisclosed truths. Such is the wide variety of subjects that excite their attention that they have the potential to make significant contributions across the full professional spectrum, but they are especially drawn to the limitless possibilities inherent in art and design.

Although they are strong-willed and somewhat self-indulgent types (and even more so if they were also born in the Chinese year of the horse), those born on this day are profoundly oriented toward those around them. Others enjoy their enlivening companionship, and appreciate their kindness and generosity, characteristics that are particularly pronounced in their dealings with their nearest and dearest, or with those whom November 9 people believe have been dealt a raw deal in life. As well as being natural leaders, they are also instinctive humanitarians who will dip deep into their pockets to help the victims of misfortune or social abuses.

VIRTUES: Those born on this day are vital and energetic. They rarely do anything by half measures and react with enthusiasm to new concepts or experiences. Motivated by their desire to further not only their individual knowledge but that of humanity as a whole, they are interesting people who feel a strong sense of social responsibility.
VICES: Although they display considerable focus and determination in the face of an intriguing challenge, November 9 people may become easily bored and run the risk of flitting restlessly from one thing to another, leaving themselves dissatisfied.
VERDICT: These individuals have a deep-rooted need for intellectual stimulation, but as life is rarely consistently exciting, they should try to develop greater self-discipline in what they perceive as mundane activities.

On This Day
Famous Births: Ivan Sergeyevich Turgenev (1818); King Edward VII of Britain (1841); Giles Gilbert Scott (1880); Herbert Kalmus (1881); Jean Monnet (1888); Anthony Asquith (1902); Muggsy Spanier (1906); Katharine Hepburn (1909); Heddy Lamarr (1913); Spiro Agnew (1918); Hugh Leonard (1928); Ronald Harwood and Carl Sagan (1934); Mary Travers (1936); Tom Weiskopf (1942); Lou Ferrigno (1952).

Significant Events and Anniversaries: Inherent in this day is a deep humanitarian concern with improving the welfare of others, as was reflected on November 9 when: an anesthetic (chloraform) was successfully used for the first time by Dr. James Young Simpson of Edinburgh, Scotland, to alleviate the pain of childbirth (1847); and the British Army outlawed the flogging of its soldiers (1859). A more reluctant acknowledgement of social responsibility was demonstrated on this day when: German emperor Wilhelm II, who had instigated World War I, abdicated his throne and fled to The Netherlands (1918); and the communist East German government bowed to its citizens' demands and opened its borders with West Germany (1989). Outstanding leadership potential is also highlighted by this day, on which John F. Kennedy was elected to the U.S. presidency (1960).

NOVEMBER 10

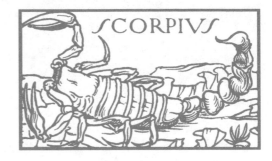

Those born on this day are highly creative individuals with the imagination, skills and focus to make a substantial contribution to the world and an unforgettable impression on everyone they encounter. Empathetic and benevolent, they are concerned with helping humanity as a whole to progress via spiritual, intellectual or material means. However, they are also introspective, and have a profound need to satisfy their desires to explore, assimilate, experiment and grow. They are often perfectionists, who set themselves high standards and are reluctant to share their findings with others until they are sure of the value of their conclusions. Inquisitiveness, ingenuity and resourcefulness mark their efforts in professions that call for independent research and development. Academia, science and the arts may attract them, as these fields also offer intermittent solitude.

Although their genuine goodwill and affection for their close associates is undoubtable, their absorption with their work may limit the attention they pay to emotional needs—a tendency that men born on this day display the most. They may even become dismissive or intolerant of those who do not share their interests and beliefs.

VIRTUES: Those born on this day are fueled by their compulsion to further their knowledge and then transform the information that they have garnered into new and progressive concepts with which they hope to enlighten, inspire or otherwise assist others. Remarkably dedicated and meticulous when it comes to pursuing their interests, they are blessed with the potential to make a significant mark on human society.

VICES: November 10 individuals may become so totally involved in their intellectual interests that they may cut themselves off from those around them in order to avoid having to divert their attention from their primary concerns. They thus not only run the risk of becoming obsessive, but also may neglect their emotional well-being, as well as that of those closest to them.

VERDICT: If they are not to become emotionally isolated, it is important that these people try to share their visions and feelings with those around them. By opening up they will not only gain an enriching perspective on life but will also find great fulfillment in the supportive bonds inherent in honest and relaxed interpersonal relationships. They should capitalize on their naturally attractive qualities to develop, rather than avoid, new friendships.

On This Day

Famous Births: Martin Luther (1483); Paracelsus (1493); François Couperin (1668); King George II of England (1683); William Hogarth (1697); Oliver Goldsmith (1728); Johann Christoph Friedrich von Schiller (1759); Vachel Lindsay (1879); Jacob Epstein (1880); Arnold Zweig (1887); Claude Rains (1889); J.P. Marquand (1893); Harry Andrews (1911); Richard Burton (1925); Roy Scheider (1935); Tim Rice (1944); Donna Fargo (1949); Ann Reinking and Jack Scalla (1950); Sinbad (1956); MacKenzie Phillips (1959).

Significant Events and Anniversaries: On a day that highlights the single-minded exploration of uncharted territory—both intellectual and physical—November 10 commemorates: U.S. journalist and explorer Henry Morton Stanley's success in finding the Scottish missionary David Livingstone at Ujiji, on Lake Tanganyika in east Africa (1871); and the identification of the location off Veracruz, Mexico, of the wreck of the U.S. vessel *Somers*, immortalized by Herman Melville in his book *Billy Budd* (1987). Pioneering achievements of all kinds are emphasized by this day, on which: Paul Daimler became the first person to ride a motorcycle, the invention of his father, the German engineer Gottlieb Daimler (1885); and Britain gained its first black mayor, John Archer, who was elected to office by the citizens of the London district of Battersea (1913). The uncompromising nature of political convictions was reflected when: Hirohito was crowned emperor of Japan (1926); and Nazi stormtroopers went on an anti-Semitic rampage of terror in Germany, destroying Jewish-owned property and hundreds of synagogues on the infamous *Kristallnacht* (1938).

Planetary Influences
Ruling planet: Pluto.
Second decan: Personal planets are Jupiter and Neptune.

♇ ♃ ♆

Sacred and Cultural Significance
In ancient Scotland, Old November Eve honored the goddess Nicnevin.
Saints' day: Leo the Great (d. 461); Aed Macbricc (d. 588); Justus (d. 627); Andrew Avellino (1521–1608).

On this day when artistic achievements are starred, Vincent van Gogh's Irises *(detail below) was sold for $53.9 million in 1989—a belated recognition of the tormented painter's invaluable contribution to modern art.*

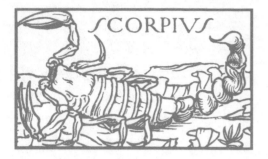

Planetary Influences
Ruling planet: Pluto.
Second decan: Personal planets are Jupiter and Neptune.

♇ ♃ ♆

Sacred and Cultural Significance
In Britain, Remembrance Day; Old November Day, in Scotland; in northern Europe, Pagans celebrated the Day of the Heroes.
Saints' day: Mennas (d. c.300), patron saint of pilgrims; Martin of Tours (c.316–97), patron saint of beggars; Theodore the Studite (759–826).

On a day strongly associated with humanitarian interests and advances for the common good, crowds outside Buckingham Palace celebrated the signature of the armistice ending World War I in 1918. Commemorated annually in Britain from that date, Armistice Day now also marks the end of World War II.

NOVEMBER 11

★★★★★★★★★★★★★★★★★★★★★★★★★★★★★★★★★★★★★

November 11 individuals are extremely complex personalities who have the capacity to surprise those around them through previously unsuspected sides of their characters. Indeed, those born on this day may themselves be unsure about the exact nature of their convictions and what they want from life. Although their multitude of interests and powerfully instinctive responses to concepts, situations and other people are undoubted strengths, they may also have a confusing effect. On the one hand these peolpe are active, straightforward and progressive types who yearn to advance toward tangible goals, while on the other they are also profound—sometimes even darkly pessimistic—thinkers, whose propensity for deep deliberation may restrict their progress. When they are able to reconcile these conflicting propensities they have the potential to do well in their careers and form lasting relationships. The nature of their chosen careers will vary from individual to individual: some may prefer work in hands-on positions in building or technical fields; others may have their interest fired by writing or research—all, however, will manifest extraordinary determination, imagination and humanitarian concern in pursuit of their professional goals.

Their desire to serve others underlies virtually everything undertaken by those born on this day. Even though they are innately independent operators, they are fueled by their compulsion to assist, direct or at least positively inspire others by example. Their colleagues typically respect them greatly, but many may feel that they do not know them fully and, indeed, November 11 people often prefer to keep their professional and private lives separate, cherishing the domestic sphere as a haven in which they can relax and be themselves.

VIRTUES: Those born on this day possess simultaneously introverted and extroverted personal characteristics. Blessed with serious and contemplative intellects, their strong orientation toward, and sense of social responsibility for, those around them instills in them the urge to actively contribute their talents and energies to the benefit of the greater good.
VICES: Torn as they frequently are between their compulsion to explore the ideas and hobbies that fascinate them and their desire to help others, November 11 people have a tendency to go to extremes, either retreating into their private worlds or sublimating their own needs.
VERDICT: It is vital that these individuals should try to balance their various traits: they should strive to moderate their selfish desires in order to avoid becoming isolated and try to control their unselfish urges to avoid becoming frustrated.

On This Day
Famous Births: Louis Antoine de Bougainville (1729); Fyodor Mikhailovich Dostoyevsky (1821); Jean Edouard Vuillard (1868); Ernest Alexandre Ansermet (1883); George Smith Patton (1885); René Clair (1898); Pat O'Brien (1899); Alger Hiss (1904); Stubby Kaye (1918); Roy Jenkins (1920); Kurt Vonnegut, Jr. (1922); June Whitfield and Jonathan Winters (1925); Bibi Andersson (1935); Daniel Ortega (1945); Rodney Marsh (1947); Demi Moore (1962); Calista Flockhart (1964); Leonardo DiCaprio (1974).

Significant Events and Anniversaries: On a day that indicates a profound desire to advance or safeguard the perceived common good, November 11 commemorates: the hanging of Australian bank-robber Ned Kelly in Melbourne for the murder of two law-enforcement officers (1880); the enlistment of Washington state into the U.S. Union (1889); the signing by Germany and Allied representatives of the armistice ending World War I, in a railroad carriage sited in the French Forest of Compiègne (1918); the Rhodesian government's issuing of its Unilateral Declaration of Independence (U.D.I.) from Britain (1965); and Portugal's granting of Angolan independence (1975). Two technical innovations associated with this day also reflect this progressive urge: U.S. automotive company Willys's launching of the Jeep (1940); and U.S. inventors John Mullin and Wayne Johnson's unveiling of their V.C.R. (video-cassette recorder) prototype (1965).

NOVEMBER 12

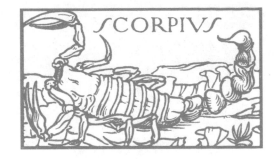

Others admire those born on this day for the controlled energy, sure sense of purpose and transforming touch that they display in all their professional ventures, but in many respects the self-assured image that November 12 people project is consciously manufactured, both to inspire such confidence and to conceal the emotional turmoil that lies beneath. For these are complex individuals who are frequently torn between their desire to achieve perfection (in every area of their lives, but particularly in terms of producing an inspiring product, service or system and thereby make a enduringly progressive or illuminating donation to the wider world) and their internal battle with the strong and sometimes confusing emotions that beset them. While on the one hand they are imaginative, straightforward and positive types, on the other they may innately feel that they will never attain the soaring visions that drive them, and they sometimes give way to feelings of frustration or even despair. And because their goals are ambitious, and they themselves so demanding, they will often only be reached after a great internally and externally oriented personal struggle.

The natural inclinations of those born on this day suit them for a wide variety of careers, but their idealistic urges will often find a particularly rewarding outlet in the realms of the arts or science, and although their audiences may venerate their achievements they will rarely be aware of the amount of hard work and worry—maybe even self-doubt—that underpin them. Given to concealing their problems from those around them, November 12 people are nevertheless extremely empathetic to the unhappiness or misfortune of others and will do their utmost to lend their practical support to those in need. Yet, despite their special concern for the well-being of their nearest and dearest, they may still need to occasionally withdraw from their loved ones in order to address their personal demons.

VIRTUES: Those born on this day are strongly influenced by visionary quests for excellence, in pursuit of which they show keen intellects, organizational skills and tenacity. Humanitarians at heart, they yearn to help others through their personal exertions.
VICES: Because November 12 people tend to keep their most deeply-rooted anxieties to themselves, others are often oblivious to the burden of angst that they bear, causing them to feel insecure and even more isolated from those around them.
VERDICT: These individuals should remember the importance of the emotional well-being that is vital to their happiness. By sharing their worries in particular with those closest to them and winning their understanding and support, they will not only receive the benefit of solace, but may gain an enlightening perspective on their circumstances and self-worth.

On This Day

Famous Births: Edward Vernon (1684); Jacques Charles (1746); Gerhard von Scharnhorst (1755); Elizabeth Cady Stanton (1815); Alexander Borodin (1833); Auguste Rodin (1840); John Rayleigh (1842); Sun Yat-sen (1866); Ben Travers (1886); Chad Varah (1911); Jo Stafford (1918); Kim Hunter (1922); Grace Kelly (1929); Charles Manson (1934); Lucia Popp (1939); Wallace Shawn (1943); Al Michaels (1944); Neil Young (1945); Nadia Comaneci (1961); David Schwimmer (1966); Tonya Harding (1970).

Significant Events and Anniversaries: November 12 highlights the pursuit of high ambitions, as demonstrated in a variety of ventures on this day, when: French circus artist Leotard premiered his flying-trapeze act—without a safety net—at the Parisian Cirque d'Eté (1859); and German pharmaceutical company Bayer patented polyurethane, a new form of plastic (1942). And, governed by the element of water, November 12 commemorates the sinking of the German battleship *Tirpitz* in Norway's Alta Fjord by British Royal Air Force bombers during World War II, with the loss of 1200 lives (1944).

Planetary Influences
Ruling planet: Pluto.
Third decan: Personal planet is the Moon.

♇ ☽

Sacred and Cultural Significance
In ancient Rome, Jupiter, Minerva and Juno honored with Epulum Jovis in Capitola festival.
Saints' day: Machar (6th century AD); Cadwaladr (d. 664); Lebuin (d. c.775); Josaphat (1580–1623), patron saint of ecumenists.

Born on this date in 1815, women's rights pioneer Elizabeth Cady Stanton showed the strength of conviction inherent in her birthdate through an arduous career directed toward improving the condition of women everywhere. She was instrumental in securing woman suffrage, female property rights and educational opportunities closed to previous generations.

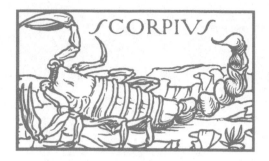

NOVEMBER 13

Planetary Influences
Ruling planet: Pluto.
Third decan: Personal planet is the Moon.

♇ ☾

Sacred and Cultural Significance
Saints' day: Brice (d. 444); Abbo of Fleury
(d. 1004); Homobonus (d. 1197), patron
saint of clothworkers, merchants and tailors;
Stanislaus Kostka (1550–68).

*On a day that highlights stubbornness and
strong opinions, British Lifeguards were
assigned to protect Trafalgar Square during
the London riots of 1887.*

Perhaps the primary characteristics manifested by November 13 people are their interst in people and their strong wills, qualities that inform their predilection for observing and opining the mores and workings of human society. Indeed, in many respects those born on this day could be compared to chemists because of their ability to absorb all manner of data, subject it to rigorous analysis and process it before transmitting it into the public arena in a converted or crystallized configuration. With their heightened powers of perception, they have the enviable capacity to draw upon their intuitive as well as their objective talents when assessing the world or people around them, yet once they have arrived at their opinions after careful deliberation they will typically adhere to them with remarkable tenacity, even in the face of opposition. Just as their interest is aroused by virtually everything they encounter, so they may be found working in a variety of professions, although they may be especially drawn to scientific or technical pursuits, as well as to those concerned with informing or enlightening their peers—such as teachers, journalists, or even as spiritual or political leaders.

Such is their urge to exert their progressive influence over those around them that November 13 individuals will often gravitate toward leadership or pioneering roles: in turn, they are respected by others for their strength of conviction and charismatic presence. Although strongly socially oriented, they may unwittingly overlook the more personal—though no less important—needs of their nearest and dearest in their quests to assist the wider human community to advance (a tendency that is even more pronounced in the men who share this birthday).

VIRTUES: Those born on this day are extremely observant and use their powers to identify flaws in existing systems or behavior. They can formulate realistic and effective strategies for advancement and they always act from good motives.
VICES: November 13 people tend to become so involved in the promotion of their professional interests that they may neglect their personal liaisons. As a result, they run the dual risk of hurting their closest associates and becoming emotionally isolated.
VERDICT: While their humanitarian concerns are admirable, they should not forget the importance of a full and committed personal life. By nurturing their close relationships, they will gain an enriching dimension to their lives and benefit from the grounding influence of strong emotional bonds.

On This Day
Famous Births: King Edward III of England (1312); John Moore (1761); Charles Frederick Worth (1825); James Clerk Maxwell (1831); Robert Louis Stevenson (1850); Louis Brandeis (1856); Ludwig Koch (1881); Eugène Ionesco (1912); Nathaniel Benchley (1915); Oskar Werner (1922); Adrienne Corri (1930); George Carey (1935); Jean Seberg (1938); Dack Rambo (1941); Whoopi Goldberg (1949); Tracy Scoggins (1958).

Significant Events and Anniversaries: On a day on which leadership potential is promised, Charles de Gaulle became head of the provisional French government that regulated France between the ending of World War II and the inauguration of the Fourth Republic (1945). November 13 emphasizes pioneering advances of all kinds, as was reflected on this day when: in the technical sphere, a telegraphic service was inaugurated to facilitate communication between London and Paris (1851), and an early form of the helicopter achieved limited lift-off in Normandy, France (1907); and, in the realm of entertainment, Walt Disney's ground-breaking movie *Fantasia* was premiered (1940), and the U.S. team won the worlds' first international bridge championship in Bermuda (1950). As well as being a day governed by the element of water and the martial planet, November 13 highlights the uncompromising promotion of strong convictions, as was demonstrated when a German U-boat torpedoed and sank the British aircraft carrier H.M.S. *Ark Royal*, off Gibraltar during World War II (1941).

NOVEMBER 14

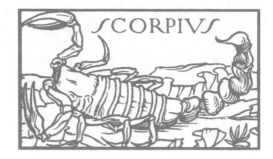

SCORPIVS

Those born on this day are serious individuals who possess a strong desire to fully understand those concepts, circumstances or people who excite their interest, a predilection that stems from not only their innate curiosity but also their urge to apply their personal knowledge and psychological growth in the effective service of others. Indeed, their sense of social responsibility—even duty—is so essential to their natures that it will typically have been evident from childhood, manifested, for example, by their profound feelings of empathy with other people's unhappiness and their endearing attempts to "make it better" by offering their support. This deep-rooted wish to assist others—practically, intellectually, emotionally or spiritually—remains a guiding principle throughout their lives (especially if they were also born in the Chinese year of the rooster), and although they are stimulated as individuals by learning, honing their expertise and refining their views, their ultimate purpose is make themselves agents of progress. November 14 people thus have a natural affinity with those professional realms that are concerned with benevolently directing, illuminating or otherwise making a positive contribution to those around them, and have the potential to become outstanding social workers, nurses, doctors and therapists.

Those born on this day place enormous value on the tight bonds that they form with their friends, partners and children, and draw real emotional support and strength from the unquestioning affection of their loved ones. Despite the typical tolerance and generosity that characterizes their relationships with those closest to them, they frown upon any instances of selfish or thoughtless behavior and will not hesitate to make their displeasure known. Inherent in their magnanimous approach, however, lies a danger that either they may neglect their own personal needs, or their goodwill may be exploited by more unscrupulous types.

VIRTUES: Clearly apparent in all of their ventures is the fundamental humanitarianism o November 14 individuals—that is, their concern with contributing positively to the greater good. Both intuitively and intellectually perceptive, and also blessed with a rational outlook and strong organizational talents, they are fueled by their determination to redress perceived injustices and instigate tangible advances by means of enlightened and practical measures.
VICES: So profound is their desire to devote their energies and talents to helping others that those born on this day may not only suppress their personal ambitions but also discourage manifestations of self-indulgence on the part of those closest to them, regarding them as selfish—a propensity that although laudable, may ultimately be emotionally damaging.
VERDICT: November 14 people should recognize that it is important that they balance their orientation toward others with their own needs, for unless they maintain a healthy emotional/intellectual equilibrium they will not only find it difficult to attain all-round fulfillment, but also will render themselves less effective professionals, as well as friends, partners and parents.

On This Day
Famous Births: Leopold Mozart (1719); Robert Fulton (1765); John Curwen (1816); Claude Monet (1840); Leo Baekeland (1863); Pandit Jawaharlal Nehru (1889); Frederick Banting (1891); Aaron Copland (1900); Harold Larwood and Dick Powell (1904); Joseph McCarthy (1909); Rosemary DeCamp (1910); Veronica Lake (1919); Brian Keith (1921); Boutros Boutros-Ghali (1922); Bart Cummings (1927); MacLean Stevenson (1929); Elizabeth Frink (1930); Bernard Hinault (1934); King Hussein of Jordan (1935); Charles, Prince of Wales (1948).

Significant Events and Anniversaries: November 14 highlights the urge to contribute significantly to human knowledge and endeavor, as was demonstrated when: the Scottish explorer James Bruce located the source of the Blue Nile River, in Ethiopia (1770); and U.S. aviator Eugene Ely became the first pilot to take off from the deck of a ship (1910). And, on a water-governed day that warns of the risks inherent in suppression, a violent underwater volcanic eruption occurred off the coast of Iceland (creating the island of Surtsey) (1963).

Planetary Influences
Ruling planet: Pluto.
Third decan: Personal planet is the Moon.

♇ ☽

Sacred and Cultural Significance
Druidic festival of the Feast of the Musicians celebrated by Wiccans; in India, children receive blessings from the Children's Goddesses, Befona, Mayavel, Rumina and Surabhi.
Saints' day: Dyfrig (d. c.550); Modan (6th century AD); Laurence O'Toole (1128–80).

French painter Claude Monet, born on this day in 1840, exhibited his seminal work Impression: Sunrise *(1872) in 1874. The Impressionist movement derived its name from this work, and Monet's intuitive nature, reflected by his birthdate, continued to influence both artists and the public in works of increasing power and originality.*

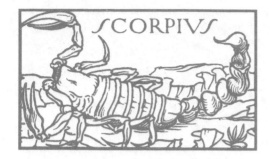

SCORPIVS

Planetary Influences
Ruling planet: Pluto.
Third decan: Personal planet is the Moon.

♇ ☽

Sacred and Cultural Significance
The goddess Ferona honored by Pagans; in Japan, Shichi-Go-San, a good-health ritual, performed in Shinto shrines.
Saints' day: Malo (6th–7th century AD); Fintan of Rheinau (d. 879); Albert the Great (1206–80), patron saint of medical technicians and scientists.

American painter Georgia O'Keefe, born on November 15, 1887, pioneered the development of abstract art in America. The perceptive qualities associated with her birthdate, combined with its potential for inner conflict, are apparent in her evocative work, especially her stark Southwestern paintings.

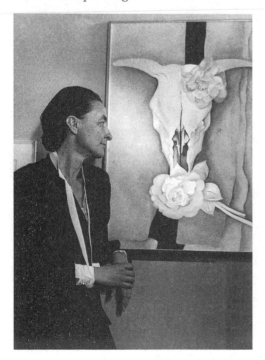

Inner conflict is often an inevitable fact of life for those people born on November 15; indeed, however calm and competent the face that they present to the world, underneath their typically composed façade lie personalities that are in turmoil. The main problem these individuals have is in reconciling their desire to devote themselves single-mindedly to the service of others (especially their colleagues or compatriots) with their personal integrity, individual convictions or emotional needs. When these interests coincide and they are able to accomplish this, they frequently become highly respected pillars of strength, who inspire, reassure and protect those with whom they identify most strongly—perhaps as civic or national politicians. Yet all too often they will initially dutifully espouse the party line, believing that social conformity is the best way in which to serve the common interest: subsequently, since they are perceptive types, they will become uncomfortably aware of its inherent failings and abuses, and incur profound feelings of doubt. In such circumstances they may reluctantly feel it necessary to rebel and oppose the system in order to remain true to themselves.

Underlying all their actions is their compulsion to make a positive contribution to those around them—even humanity as a wider entity—and some may therefore chose careers within the spheres of scientific or artistic research and development, in which their progressive urge can be fulfilled and expressed without the need to compromise their convictions. Loving and generous friends and relations, they furthermore enjoy the simple pleasures of life and thus make enlivening as well as supportive companions.

VIRTUES: Those born on this day are deeply humanitarian individuals. Their empathy with others is manifested by the urge to improve their lot by making tangible progress, and in working toward this aim they show their intellectual and physical strength and good organizational skills.
VICES: Torn as they frequently are between their external and internal orientations and concerns, November 15 people may feel themselves forced to make a choice between the two. Thus they may either sublimate their opinions and wishes to what they perceive as be the common good, or opt out altogether to follow a lonely path through life.
VERDICT: In terms of their ultimate happiness, it is important that those born on this day should identify the personal priorities that are most important to them and then remain true to them, compromising where necessary but not to the extent that they feel that they are betraying their principles. Nurturing open and stable personal relationships will help both to strengthen their sense of purpose and to give them invaluable emotional support.

On This Day
Famous Births: Catherine of Braganza (1638); William Pitt the Elder (1708); William Cowper (1731); William Herschel (1738); Gerhart Hauptmann (1862); Marianne Moore and Georgia O'Keefe (1887); Richmal Crompton (1890); Erwin Rommel (1891); Aneurin Bevan and Sacheverell Sitwell (1897); Annunzio Mantovani (1905); Claus von Stauffenberg (1907); Jade Dyer (1913); John Whiting (1917); Ed Asner (1929); J.G. Ballard and Barbara Thiering (1930); Petula Clark (1932); Sam Waterson (1940); Daniel Barenboim (1942); Frida Lyngstad (1945); Peter Phillips (1977).

Significant Events and Anniversaries: November 15 is a day that highlights pursuits to advance the common interest, as seen in the political realm when: during the Revolutionary War, delegates to the Congress of Philadelphia adopted the Articles of Confederation—the first step toward formation of the United States (1777); and, during the American Civil War, Union troops under General Sherman left Atlanta to attack the Confederate-held town of Savannah, Georgia (1864). Technological advances occurred on this day when: British teacher Isaac Pitman published his pioneering work on the use of shorthand (1837); New Yorker Miller Reese patented an electrical device to help hearing-impaired people (1901); and U.S. National Broadcasting Corporation (N.B.C.) began its transmissions (1926).

NOVEMBER 16

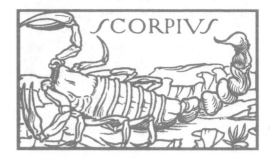

Those born on this day combine active and inquiring minds with a profound urge to understand how things work and the insight to promote their ideas to the common good. As children or young adults, their innate sense of connection to those around them may not be immediately apparent, and as their personalities form, they often challenge the status quo. But once they reach conclusions that satisfy their minds, they will not only remain true to them, but seek to convince others of their worth.

Those born on this day are especially suited for leadership roles in which they can exert influence over others. They will gravitate toward such professions as politics and teaching, although they may also be drawn to more artistic activities, in which they can inspire a broader audience. Those around them generally respect their strength of purpose (even when they do not agree with their forthright opinions or methods) and, in fact, November 16 individuals should try to use tact and tolerance in enlisting support for their aims—especially with regard to their nearest associates, whose love and support is important to their emotional well-being.

VIRTUES: Blessed with inquisitive, yet also logical and progressive, minds, the actions of those born on this day are fueled by their compulsion to explore, assess and then further the boundaries of human endeavor and knowledge. Strong-willed and tenacious, their personal charisma and highly developed organizational skills augur well for their success.
VICES: So convinced are they of the potential benefits for others that are inherent in their viewpoints, and so strong is their urge to enlighten and inspire those around them to adopt their preferred approaches, that November 16 people have a propensity to disregard any objections voiced by dissenters instead of seeking accommodation or reconciliation.
VERDICT: It is crucial that these individuals do not become obsessed with the promotion of their interests to the exclusion of all else (especially their own emotional needs and those of their loved ones). They should try to remain open-minded and to respect the right of others to hold different opinions.

On This Day

Famous Births: Tiberius Claudius Nero (42BC); Jean le Rond d'Alembert (1717); Rodolphe Kreutzer (1766); William John Thoms (1803); John Bright (1811); William Frend De Morgan (1839); William Christopher Handy (1873); George S. Kaufman (1889); Paul Hindemith (1895); Oswald Mosley (1896); Eddie Condon (1905); Burgess Meredith (1908); Daws Butler and Max Gillies (1916); Willie Carson (1942); Griff Rhys Jones (1953); Frank Bruno (1961); Dwight Gooden (1964); Lisa Bonet (1967).

Significant Events and Anniversaries: This is a day that highlights the conjunction of a strong sense of social responsibility and marked leadership abilities, as was demonstrated when: King Gustavus Adolphus of Sweden, the "Lion of the North," defeated the Austrian forces of Albrecht of Wallenstein at the Battle of Lützen in Saxony, but paid for his victory with his life (1632); and Georges Clemenceau became the prime minister of France for the second time (1917). November 16 is not only ruled by the element of water, but emphasizes progressive tendencies, as shown when: Australian explorer Hamilton Hume discovered the continent's longest river, the Murray (1824); the Suez Canal in Egypt, constructed under the supervision of French engineer Ferdinand de Lesseps, was formally opened (1869); and the Soviet Union launched its unmanned spacecraft *Venus III*, destined for the planet for which it was named (1965). Actions perceived as protective of the common good are stressed on November 16, the anniversary of: the execution of the notorious English highwayman Jack Sheppard (1724); the hanging of Louis Riel, Métis leader of the Northwest Rebellion in Canada, by the British authorities (1885); and the state of Oklahoma's admission to the U.S. Union (1907). The artistic potential inherent in this day was confirmed when: French novelist Marcel Proust's autobiographical work *A la recherche du temps perdu* (*Remembrance of Things Past*) was first published (1913).

Planetary Influences
Ruling planet: Pluto.
Third decan: Personal planet is the Moon.

Sacred and Cultural Significance
Festival of Lights celebrated in India to mark the Hindu New Year.
Saints' day: Margaret of Scotland (1046–93); Edmund of Abingdon (c.1175–1240); Gertrude (d. 1302); Giuseppe Moscati (1860–1927).

Reflecting the deep sense of social responsibility and the leadership abilities inherent in her feast day, St. Margaret of Scotland, the wife of King Malcolm, worked tirelessly for the good of her people. She was canonized in 1250 by Pope Innocent IV for her achievements as wife, mother and patron of the church and the arts.

SCORPIVS

Planetary Influences
Ruling planet: Pluto.
Third decan: Personal planet is the Moon.

♇ ☾

Sacred and Cultural Significance
Saints' day: Gregory the Wonderworker (c.213–c.70); Gregory of Tours (539–94); Hilda (614–80); Hugh of Lincoln (c.1140–1200); Elizabeth of Hungary (1207–31), patron saint of charitable societies and nurses; the Martyrs of Paraguay (d. 1628); Philippine Duchesne (1769–1852).

The desire to cooperate on behalf of the common good, a feature of November 17, was demonstrated when the Suez Canal was opened to international shipping in 1869.

NOVEMBER 17

Their perspicacity, sense of justice and orientation to the social group with which they identify most strongly endow those born on this day with the potential to make a real contribution to the world. Yet despite their benevolent urge to help others, November 17 people are autonomous: their independence of mind often causes them to stand apart even from those whose welfare they have at heart. Gifted social commentators, they use their observations to expose wrong-doings or failings and work toward correcting them. They deliver their messages with unerring accuracy and a sense of humor that fosters co-operation rather than alienation.

Those born on this day are admirably equipped to excel in any profession in which they can retain their prerequisite for freedom of thought and expression while simultaneously working toward a concrete goal, and high-tech pursuits like web design are particularly well starred. Others admire their personal magnetism, ready wit and enviable ability to elicit the cooperation of those around them, but may nevertheless feel that they do not know the essence of November 17 individuals' personalities. And, indeed, these people guard their privacy jealously (a propensity that is even more pronounced in the men born on this day) and will only open up fully to those whom they trust implicitly. Their relationships with their nearest and dearest are thus of vital importance to them as emotional havens of unquestioning affection and security.

VIRTUES: November 17 individuals are keen analysts of the societies to which they belong; acutely perceptive, coolly rational and fair-minded, they are motivated by their urge to share their astute findings and conclusions with others in order to make them aware of existing flaws and thereby assist them to progress in a positive direction.
VICES: The observational predilection of those born on this day, along with their innately benevolent desire to make those around them aware of their faults, can cause them to become overly critical or authoritarian, and therefore to unwittingly erect psychological barriers between themselves and those whose welfare they have at heart.
VERDICT: These individuals should try to become more aware of the sometimes intimidating effect that their firmly expressed opinions and observations can have on others. Although they instinctively recognize that humor is a useful tool when communicating their messages, they should thus nevertheless beware of isolating themselves and should strive to become both more tolerant and more open in their dealings with other people.

On This Day
Famous Births: King Louis XVIII of France (1755); Bernard Law Montgomery (1887); Lee Strasberg (1901); Israel Regardie (1907); Rock Hudson and Charles Mackerras (1925); Michael Freeman (1931); Peter Cook (1937); Gordon Lightfoot (1938); Auberon Waugh (1939); Martin Scorsese (1942); Lauren Hutton (1943); Danny DeVito, Lorne Michaels and Tom Seaver (1944); Ru Paul (1960); Isaac Hanson (1980).

Significant Events and Anniversaries: Highlighted for November 17 is the desire to effect progress by means of cooperation, as was demonstrated on this day when: the U.S. Congress convened its first meeting (1800); and Siberia elected to become part of the Soviet Union (1922). Inherent in this day are also somewhat judgemental and authoritarian tendencies, as was reflected when: the trial began of English naval adventurer Sir Walter Raleigh, accused of treasonous conspiracy against King James I, (1603); Turkish revolutionary leader Mustafa Kemal Pasha (later known as Kemal Atatürk) abolished the Ottoman institution of the sultanate, forcing Muhammad VI into exile (1922); and General Gamal Abdel Nasser compelled Egyptian premier Mohammed Neguib to resign and then assumed the presidential office himself (1954). Finally, on a day that is partly subject to lunar influences, November 17 commemorates the anniversary of the landing of the unmanned Soviet spacecraft *Luna 17* on the Moon (1970).

NOVEMBER 18

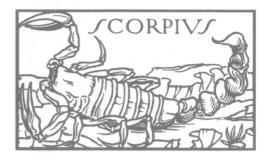

Others enjoy the company of the exuberant individuals born on this day, who enliven any social gathering with their vitality, humor and goodwill. And November 18 people are in turn stimulated by those around them—not least because they enjoy being the center of attention. Beneath the cheerful face that they present to the world, however, confusion and self-doubt may be a problem. These intuitive people are especially receptive to any unhappy "vibes" that emanate from others, and susceptible to the unsettling influence of their emotional responses. Thus they may feel directionless, a tendency that is pernicious to active individuals whose ultimate fulfillment is bound up with their desire to achieve tangible progress (on behalf of themselves, as well as others). This is why, in their search for enlightenment and focus, they are so strongly oriented to others, and also why they make such empathetic friends, colleagues and companions, for in sublimating their own problems to those of others around them they are often able to clarify their thoughts and feelings.

The conjunction of their sensitivity with their yearning to effect their own individual growth and life goals augurs particularly well for the potential success of November 18 people as artists, musicians and writers—even as spiritual guides—as well as innovators in a variety of fields, including science and technology. While they assume positive and charismatic personae when engaged in their professional endeavors, it is within their personal liaisons that their insecurity is most apparent, and they therefore place enormous value on receiving the support and affection of their loved ones (and even more so if they were also born in the Chinese year of the goat), who know and accept them as they are and thus bolster their self-esteem.

VIRTUES: The thoughts and visions of those born on this day are informed primarily by their emotional responses to the people and circumstances that surround them. Their empathetic reactions make them kind and reliable friends.
VICES: November 18 people have a tendency to become overwhelmed by their emotions: their sense of purpose may become obscured. The indecisiveness that results can thwart their innate desire to be useful, and they can sometimes suffer from depression.
VERDICT: It is vital that these people safeguard their emotional well-being through periods of honest introspection that help them identify what will bring them fulfillment. By sticking to these prerogatives despite doubts and diversions they will enhance their potential for attaining happiness and balance.

On This Day

Famous Births: Vespasian (AD 9); David Wilkie (1785); Henry Rowley Bishop and Carl Maria von Weber (1786); Louis Jacques Mandé Daguerre (1789); John Nelson Darby (1800); W.S. Gilbert (1836); Ignacy Jan Paderewski (1860); Amelita Galli-Curci (1889); George Gallup (1901); Alec Issigonis (1906); Imogene Coca (1908); Johnny Mercer (1909); Alan B. Shepard, Jr. (1923); Brenda Vaccaro (1939); David Hemmings (1941); Linda Evans (1942); Susan Sullivan (1943); Jameson Parker (1947); Kim Wilde (1960).

Significant Events and Anniversaries: On a day that highlights artistic ventures meant to inspire a wide audience: the pioneering English printer William Caxton published his first typeset book, the *Dictes or Sayengs of the Philosophres* (1477); and "Steamboat Willie," the first cartoon in which Disney's Mortimer Mouse appeared as Mickey Mouse, was shown in the U.S. in movie theaters (1928). Spiritual concerns also emphasized on November 18, which marks the anniversary of: the consecration of St. Peter's Cathedral in Rome (1626); and the mass suicide of 900 followers of the cult leader Jim Jones in Guyana, following their murder of three investigative reporters and a U.S. Congressman who had arrived to question their activities (1978). And, on a day that indicates volatility, a fire at London's King's Cross Station killed thirty travelers (1987).

Planetary Influences
Ruling planet: Pluto.
Third decan: Personal planet is the Moon.

♇ ☽

Sacred and Cultural Significance
The Mother of the Stars, Ardvi, honored with the Ardvi Sura festival.
Saints' day: Mawes (5th century AD), patron of Mawes, Cornwall, England; Mabyn (6th century AD); Odo of Cluny (879–942).

Demonstrating the inventiveness that is typical of those born on this day, French photographic pioneer Louis J.M. Daguerre invented the daguerreotype process in 1839. This type of photographic print (an early example of which is shown below) would be widely used into the twentieth century, especially for portraits.

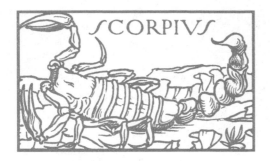

SCORPIVS

Planetary Influences
Ruling planets: Pluto and Jupiter.
Third decan: Personal planet is the Moon.
Second cusp: Scorpio with Sagittarian tendencies.

P 4 ☽

Sacred and Cultural Significance
Warlock Day.
Saints' day: Ronan (dates unknown);
Ermenburga (d. c.700).

Actress Jodie Foster, a native of the Bronx, New York, shows the vigor and enthusiasm of those born on November 19. Her capability for hard work is typical of those who were also born in the Chinese year of the tiger. She began her acting career at the age of three and had appeared in eighteen films by the time she graduated from Yale University magna cum laude in 1982. She won Oscars for her performances in The Accused *(1988) and* The Silence of the Lambs *(1991) and has also distinguished herself as a director.*

NOVEMBER 19

Those born on this day are vigorous individuals who are naturally enthusiastic participants in life; rarely content to assume a passive role, they instead itch to play a vital part in every activity that excites their interest and they hope to thereby also make a significant contribution to the world. Both intellectually perceptive and intuitive types, whose sympathies and desire to make a difference are aroused by what they perceive to be manifest failings or abuses, November 19 people are especially stimulated by addressing the various issues inherent in human society, be it within their immediate circle, their local communities, or even on a grander, humanitarian level. Whatever profession they choose to pursue—and their progressive and organized intellects, as well as their potentially outstanding technical expertise suit them to many, including scientific and creative pursuits—their ultimate purpose is thus to direct the actions of those around them according to the principles and methods that they adjudge to be the optimum ones in terms of benefiting the common good. In any event natural leaders, many will be drawn to pursuing high-flying careers.

Those born on this day are extremely self-assured people, whose confidence stems from their strength of purpose in promoting the convictions in which they believe. As a result they attract admirers and detractors in equal measure but, such is their belief in the veracity of their viewpoints and their corresponding urge to implement them that they accept both reactions with equanimity (as long as they can proceed unhindered). As committed to involving themselves as fully as possible in the lives of their nearest and dearest as they are dedicated to their professional interests, November 19 people are generally concerned and affectionate friends and relations, but nevertheless have a tendency—which is especially marked in the women born on this day—to seek to regulate the actions of those closest to them, a propensity that may not always be welcome.

VIRTUES: Both intellectually and physically energetic, these clear-sighted and socially oriented individuals are galvanized by their dual compulsion to play a prominent part on the world's stage and in so doing to also influence those around them to embrace the same progressive convictions that they themselves espouse.
VICES: November 19 people believe in leading by example, and, since practically every area of their lives excites their interest, have a propensity to throw themselves decisively and enthusiastically into their endeavors—be these connected with their professional or their private concerns. They thus run the risk of becoming physically and intellectually drained and hence less tolerant as their energy reserves become inexorably depleted.
VERDICT: If they are not to exhaust themselves and diminish their capacities, it is important that these people realize that they are not superhuman and have only limited personal resources at their disposal. They should learn to pace themselves, freeing time for simple recreational pursuits.

On This Day
Famous Births: King Charles I of England and Scotland (1600); Ferdinand de Lesseps (1805); James Abram Garfield (1831); Hiram Bingham (1875); José Raul Capablanca (1888); Clifton Webb (1891); Anton Walbrook (1900); Tommy Dorsey (1905); Indira Gandhi (1917); Larry King (1933); Dick Cavett (1936); Ted Turner (1938); Calvin Klein (1942); Kathleen Quinlan (1954); Meg Ryan (1961); Jodie Foster (1962); Kerri Strug (1977); McCaughey septuplets (1997).

Significant Events and Anniversaries: November 19 emphasizes inspirational leadership qualities, as was variously confirmed on this day by three individuals: Alfred Lord Tennyson, who was appointed Britain's poet laureate (1850); Abraham Lincoln, the U.S. president who gave his celebrated Gettysburg Address at the dedication of the national cemetery for Civil War casualties of the Battle of Gettysburg, Pennsylvania (1863); and "Pelé" (Edson Arantes do Nascimento), the Brazilian soccer player who scored his thousandth goal while a member of the Santos team (1960).

NOVEMBER 20

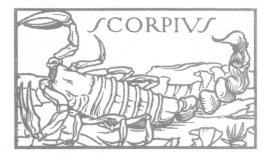

SCORPIVS

Among the primary personal characteristics of those born on this day are their active and progressive minds, plus a deep desire to promote the interests of those to whom they feel most strongly connected—families, friends or the human community. Quick-thinking and intuitive, they readily identify faults in existing concepts, systems or behavioral patterns, and produce clear-cut remedial strategies. They can show marked impatience with those who impede their progress, dismissing expressions of dissent with harsh words or spectacular displays of temper (especially those who were born in the Chinese year of the dragon). However, their usual approach is to be self-controlled and disciplined, and they would rather use their (considerable) powers of charm and persuasion than coerce others into doing what they want.

The careers to which those born on this day are attracted include politics, scientific and technical pursuits, commercial ventures, city planning and environmental issues. All throw themselves wholeheartedly into these ventures while nurturing their personal relationships as well.

VIRTUES: Perceptive and rational, but also visionary and progressive types, November 20 people are fueled by their compulsion to defend or promote the welfare of the social grouping whose interests they have most strongly at heart. Blessed with remarkable fixity of purpose, as well as enormous energy and tenacity, they have the potential to blaze a pioneering trail through life and to inspire others to follow their route.
VICES: Such is the urgency with which they advance their firmly held convictions and ambitions that those born on this day have a propensity to react with explosive fury if any obstacles are placed in their path, a tendency that may result in them sabotaging their own best efforts.
VERDICT: These individuals should recognize that their total commitment to the causes that drive their actions may have the negative effect of causing them to become so physically and mentally exhausted that they may end up operating on an unhealthily short fuse. They should therefore consciously take the time to relax and recharge their batteries, especially in the supportive company of their kith and kin.

On This Day

Famous Births: Thomas Chatterton (1752); Samuel Cunard (1787); Edwin Hubble (1889); Alexandra Danilova (1906); Alistair Cooke (1908); Wilfred Wooler (1912); Bobby Locke (1917); Dulcie Gray and Gene Tierney (1920); Robert Kennedy (1925); Kay Ballard (1926); Estelle Parsons (1927); Richard Dawson (1932); Dick Smothers (1938); Veronica Hamel (1943); Bo Derek and Mark Gastineau (1956).

Significant Events and Anniversaries: This is a day that highlights the strong desire to act in the perceived common interest, a tendency that was demonstrated when: the British Navy under Admiral Sir Edward Hawke repelled the French fleet commanded by Admiral Hubert de Conflans at the Battle of Quiberon Bay, off the coast of Brittany, and thus saved England from invasion (1759); Venezuelan revolutionary Simón Bolívar, "the Liberator," declared his country independent of Spain (1818); and the first massed formation of tanks were used by the British Army during World War I against its German enemy at the Battle of Cambrai (1917). Inherent in the sense of social responsibility that is such a pronounced feature of this day is the willingness to punish perceived transgressions against the communal welfare, as was reflected when: the trial of leading German Nazis accused of war crimes was initiated by the victorious Allied powers at Nuremberg (1945); and self-confessed pro-Soviet British spy Anthony Blunt, the former incumbent of the office of surveyor of the queen's pictures and the elusive "Fourth Man," was stripped of his knighthood (1979). Outstanding advances of all kinds are indicated by November 20, a day that commemorates: the premiere performance of Beethoven's only (but seminal) opera *Fidelio* (1805); and the foundation by Charles Steward Rolls and Frederick Henry Royce of the British automobile company Rolls-Royce (1906).

Planetary Influences
Ruling planets: Pluto and Jupiter.
Third decan: Personal planet is the Moon.
Second cusp: Scorpio with Sagittarian tendencies.

♇ ♃ ☽

Sacred and Cultural Significance
Saints' day: Colman of Dromore (6th century AD); Edmund (841–69).

Social responsibility and determination to act in the common interest are features of this day, on which the Nuremberg Trials of accused war criminals opened in 1945.

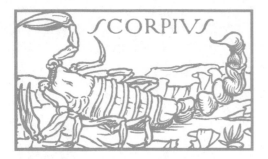

SCORPIVS

Planetary Influences
Ruling planets: Pluto and Jupiter.
Third decan: Personal planet is the Moon.
Second cusp: Scorpio with Sagittarian tendencies.

♇ ♃ ☽

Sacred and Cultural Significance
Mayans celebrate the god Kukulcan.
Saint's day: Condedus (7th century AD).

Surrealist painter René Magritte, a native of Belgium, showed the sensitivity and artistic ability typical of the November 21 person. Initially a designer and commercial artist, he became a leading member of the newly formed Belgian Surrealist group in 1924, producing dreamlike paintings including Meditation *(1937), illustrated below.*

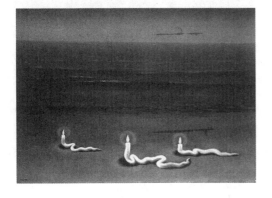

NOVEMBER 21

Good-natured, blessed with an infectious sense of fun, eager to please or assist others, November 21 individuals are usually regarded with affection—not only by those closest to them, but by their colleagues and casual acquaintances. Beneath the sunny and straightforward exterior that they present to the world, however, lie hidden depths that those who do not know them well might not suspect. Indeed, those born on this day are profoundly sensitive. Their emotional responses to the people around them are at least as influential as their intellectual concerns. And it is partly because they are especially highly attuned to any instances of unhappiness, misfortune, or even failings and abuses their intuitive antennae may detect that they make such empathetic, cheering and generous companions. Their deep concern for others— even humanity as a wider entity—does not preclude the pursuit of their more personal interests and visions, but most November 21 people will choose careers where they can combine their internal and external orientations by generating concepts or products (particularly within the realm of artistry) that they envisage will help society progress: inspirational *oeuvres* of literary, artistic, musical or dramatic work, for example, or maybe pioneering technical advances.

Such is the importance that many of those born on this day place on their emotional happiness (which is inextricably bound up with that of those around them) that even when they fulfill their professional potential and are applauded for their work they will rarely be genuinely happy unless they can share their success with a close-knit circle of family and friends. For not only do they value the strong bonds that they form with their nearest and dearest for the strengthening love and support that they receive while working for the benefit of others, but their personal relationships are perhaps the only part of their lives in which they feel they can relax, be themselves and share their worries and visions with those who understand them best.

VIRTUES: Those born on this day are deeply empathetic people. Their ambitions are influenced by their urge to exert a positive influence on those around them. Energetic and tenacious, they display a remarkable aptitude for informing, entertaining and providing support to others and as a result are popular companions.
VICES: Such is their concern with ensuring other people's well-being (both emotional and physical), that November 21 people have a tendency to suppress their personal needs. They may become exhausted and frustrated through neglecting their own prerequisites for fulfillment.
VERDICT: These people should try to maintain a healthy balance in their lives and not deny themselves self-care and relaxation in the cause of service to others.

On This Day
Famous Births: François-Marie Arouet (Voltaire) (1694); William Beaumont (1785); Leslie Ward (1851); Harold George Nicolson (1886); René Magritte (1898); Coleman Hawkins (1904); Stan Frank Musial (1920); Telly Savalas (1922); Joseph Campanella (1927); Malcolm Williamson (1931); Beryl Bainbridge (1934); Marlo Thomas (1938); Natalia Makarova (1940); Juliet Mills (1941); Harold Ramis (1944); Goldie Hawn (1945); Mariel Hemingway (1961); Nicolette Sheridan (1963); Troy Aikman (1966).

Significant Events and Anniversaries: November 21 indicates the urge to make an active and tangible contribution to society, as was reflected in various technical advances that occurred on this day when: French ballooning pioneers François de Rozier and the Marquis d'Arlandes made the world's first free-flight ascent, over Paris, in a hot-air balloon built by the Montgolfier brothers (1783); inventor Thomas Hancock patented his formula for vulcanizing rubber (1843); construction work started on Scotland's Forth Road Bridge (1858); and New York City's single-span Verrazano Narrows Bridge—then the longest such type in the world—was officially opened (1964). The potential to give pleasure to others through artistic entertainment that is highlighted by November 21 was confirmed when U.S. composer Cole Porter's musical *Anything Goes* had its premiere (1934).

SAGITTARIUS

November 22 to December 21

Ruling planet: Jupiter   **Element:** Mutable fire

Symbol: The centaur/archer   **Polarity:** Positive (masculine)

Physical correspondence: The liver, hips and thighs

Stone: Garnet, turquoise, amethyst, citrine, topaz

Flower: Wallflower, dandelion, narcissus, lime flower, carnation

Color: Blue and purple

The name "Sagittarius" is derived from the Latin word *sagitta*, "arrow," and the archer is tradition-ally associated with this sign. Although the hybrid centaur—half man and half horse—is often portrayed as this zodiacal archer (and the Persians called the constellation Nimasp, "the centaur"), some scholars believe that they represent scorpion-men rather than equine/human hybrids. The majority of astrological traditions have consistently identified this constellation with an archer, the ancient Greeks, for example, calling it Toxotes ("the archer"), and Hindu astrologers, Dhanus ("the bow"). The ancient Greeks originally personified the Sagittarian archer as a satyr (possibly Crotus), before this two-legged, pleasure-loving attendant of Dionysus (Bacchus) was displaced by the four-legged centaur. In Greco-Roman mythology centaurs were said to have lived in Thessaly, a culture area noted for outstanding horsemanship (which may have led observers to believe that the riders were seamlessly fused with their mounts). The myth that specifically explains the origins of the constellation of Sagittarius tells of the centaur Chiron of Magnesia, who acted as the mentor of such notable Greek heroes as Achilles, Pholus and Jason. After his accidental wounding by Herakles' (Hercules') poisoned arrow he was said to have volunteered to bestow his immor-tality upon Prometheus, and in recognition of his noble gesture was raised to the heavens by Zeus (Jupiter).

Paralleling the hybrid nature of the centaur, Sagittarians are said to possess the impetuous animal power of the horse and the intellectual capacity of humanity, along with the aspirational qualities and that are sig-nified by the arrow. Under the influence of the element of fire, further personal characteristics associated with Sagittarius include restlessness and emotional warmth, while the sign's ruling planet, Jupiter, bestows joviality, versatility and a sense of honor. There is a danger for those born under this sign, however, that material concerns may prevail over intellectual wisdom, and that passion, impulsive enthusiasm and impa-tience may hinder a focused approach.

Planetary Influences
Ruling planets: Jupiter and Pluto.
First decan: Personal planet is Jupiter.
First cusp: Sagittarius with Scorpio tendencies.

♃ ♇

Sacred and Cultural Significance
Saints' day: Philemon and Apphia
(d. 1st century AD; Cecilia (d. 3rd century
AD), patron saint of musicians and singers.

*The gifted British novelist Mary Ann Evans,
who wrote under the pseudonym George Eliot,
was blessed with the moral and intellectual
strength that is typical of her November 22
birthdate. Born in 1819, she wrote for, and
eventually became assistant editor of, the*
Westminster Review, *defying convention in
both her career and her personal life. Her
distinguished novels include* Silas Marner
(1861) and Middlemarch *(1871–72) and she is
memorialized in the Poet's Corner at
Westminster Abbey.*

Blessed with both physical and intellectual vigor, those born on this day seek to combine their individual goals in life with the general good. Their desire to move ever onward and upward is influenced less by the craving for personal aggrandizement than by their desire to implement idealistic programs. Astute, inquisitive and perceptive, they work to replace existing unsatisfactory systems with more effective alternatives, or to pioneer new concepts. And because they tend to be perfectionists, they set themselves (and others) high standards. Energetic, determined and also given to directing others along what they perceive to be the optimum path, November 22 people lead by example and are not afraid to adopt combative methods if they believe these to be necessary. They are thus sometimes seen as interfering or downright bossy, though they rarely bear grudges and usually win the affection of their colleagues and friends.

Their inclinations and talents equip those born on this day admirably for a wide range of careers, with the proviso that they can retain the autonomy of thought and deed that is so vital to them while simultaneously exerting their powerful influence on their coworkers, audiences or publics (prerequisites that are especially pertinent if they were also born in the Chinese year of the dragon). They may thus be found working in management or supervisory positions. In all their actions and ventures their essential humanitarianism and concern for those whose welfare they have most strongly at heart—particularly their nearest and dearest—shines through. As strong-willed as they are energetic, their urge to direct everyone around them may, however, arouse the resentment of those who value their individuality as much as they themselves do.

VIRTUES: Blessed with curious and incisive intellects, the people born on this day feel compelled to explore and assess everything that they encounter. Their strong convictions and ingenious ideas for improvement give them great potential to succeed.
VICES: Because November 22 people hold such firm opinions and are convinced of their inherent benefit to the wider world, they tend to impose these ideas on others regardless of doubt or dissent.
VERDICT: These individuals should recognize that the uncompromising promotion of their aims may alienate those around them. They would be well advised to employ persuasive rather than confrontational tactics and to remain open-minded and tolerant of those who disagree or rebel against them.

On This Day
Famous Births: Thomas Cook (1808); Mary Ann Evans (George Eliot) (1819); Cecil Sharp (1859): Charles de Gaulle (1890); Hoagy Carmichael and Wiley Post (1899); Joaquín Rodrigo (1901); Benjamin Britten (1913); Andrew Huxley (1918); Rodney Dangerfield (1921); Geraldine Page (1924); Peter Hall (1930); Robert Vaughn (1932); Terry Gilliam (1940); Tom Conti (1941); Billie-Jean King and Mushtaq Mohammad (1943); Jamie Lee Curtis (1958); Boris Becker (1967).

Significant Events and Anniversaries: On a day on which exploratory predilections are featured, the Portuguese navigator Vasco da Gama, seeking a sea route to India, sailed round the Cape of Good Hope in southern Africa (1497). November 22 highlights progressive ventures of all types, as was demonstrated on this day when: U.S. composer George Gershwin's musical *Funny Face* had its first performance (1927); and Hungarian inventor Laslo Biro's pioneering ballpoint pen was offered for sale for the first time (1946). Furthermore a day that highlights combative—even violent—propensities, this was the day on which: "Blackbeard," the English pirate Edward Teach, was killed in a skirmish off North Carolina (1718); U.S. president John F. Kennedy was shot dead in Dallas, Texas, allegedly by the Communist sympathizer Lee Harvey Oswald (1963); and U.S. boxer Mike Tyson became world heavyweight boxing champion (then the youngest person ever to win the title) when he beat Trevor Berbick (1986).

NOVEMBER 23

There are often two distinct, but not entirely unrelated, sides to the November 23 personality: one that is inspired by extremely original visions by whose implementation they believe they can make a significant and benevolent contribution to society; and another, more pugnacious, side that seems inevitably to involve them in confrontational situations. Yet those born on this day do not enjoy conflict for conflict's sake, but are nevertheless prepared to challenge views or methods that they regard are either wrong or ineffectual, particularly when they are engaged in the promotion of their inspirational aims. These are essentially fair-minded individuals, whose passions are especially aroused by any instances of perceived societal abuses, and who are consequently naturally inclined toward designing and actively advancing pioneering remedial solutions. Because they are also blessed with rational intellectual powers, as well as considerable practical expertise, their proposed strategies are typically carefully thought through from every angle; even so, the upholders of the status quo may regard them as being unfeasibly radical, and it is thus that feelings of mutual antagonism arise.

November 23 people have the potential to make their mark within many professional pursuits, but will perhaps be happiest—and most successful—when working within those spheres where the realization of their soaring fantasies is not constrained by the objections of less imaginative individuals: the many specialties encompassed by new technology and creative ventures are thus especially well starred. Because their professional relationships are so often characterized by argument, these individuals deeply value the unquestioning love and belief of their nearest and dearest, and return their support with profound affection, loyalty and generosity.

VIRTUES: Those born on this day are blessed with perceptive and intellectually questing minds, with the result that they have a propensity to question conventional truths and, if they find them wanting, to devise extremely innovative alternative options for change and betterment. Their determination to implement their visions is strengthened by the courage of their convictions, whatever the obstacles in their paths.
VICES: Inherent in the uncompromising directness that is November 23 people's preferred approach is the danger that they may undermine their own best efforts by alienating those whose support they are seeking to elicit, who may feel threatened by the forcefulness with which these individuals advance their frequently radical ambitions.
VERDICT: These people should recognize that the vehement intensity that characterizes their *modi operandi*—the product of the urgency with which they invest their aims—may be interpreted by others as aggressive and coercive attempts to force them to concur with aims that they may in any case regard as being untenable. They should therefore try to adopt a more conciliatory and palatable manner and will thus find their chances for achieving success greatly enhanced.

On This Day

Famous Births: Franklin Pierce (1804); William H. Bonney, "Billy the Kid" (1859); Valdemar Poulsen (1869); Manuel de Falla (1876); William Pratt (Boris Karloff) (1887); Harpo Marx (1888); Peter Saunders (1911); Michael Gough (1917); Lew Hoad (1934); Steve Landesberg (1955); Shane Gould (1956); Maxwell Caulfield (1960).

Significant Events and Anniversaries: On a day that highlights unusual visions that challenge the status quo, the Flemish-born pretender to the English throne, Perkin Warbeck, who claimed to be Richard, Duke of York and led a rebellion against King Henry VII, was hanged (1499). November 23 also emphasizes pioneering potential in a variety of areas, but especially in the realms of artistry and technology, as shown on this day when: French playwright Molière's work *Le bourgeois gentilhomme* was staged for the first time (1670); the world's first juke box was installed in San Francisco's Palais Royal Saloon (1889); and the World War I song that became so popular with British soldiers, "Pack Up Your Troubles in Your Old Kit Bag," was published (1915).

Planetary Influences
Ruling planets: Jupiter and Pluto.
First decan: Personal planet is Jupiter.
First cusp: Sagittarius with Scorpio tendencies.

♃ ♇

Sacred and Cultural Significance
Shinjosai Festival for Konohana-Hime honoring Amaterasu is held in Japan.
Saints' day: Clement (d. c.100), patron saint of lighthouse-keepers; Columbanus (c.543–615); Alexander Nevski (1220–63).

American statesman Franklin Pierce, born on November 23 1804, displayed the combative quality typical of his birthdate. Admitted to the bar in 1927, he served as a brigadier general in the Mexican War and was elected the fourteenth president in 1853. His controversial handling of the question of slavery in the territories and his unpopular Cuban policy led to his retirement from politics in 1857.

Planetary Influences
Ruling planets: Jupiter and Pluto.
First decan: Personal planet is Jupiter.
First cusp: Sagittarius with Scorpio tendencies.

♃ ♇

Sacred and Cultural Significance
Tori-No-Ichi held in Japan; in ancient Egypt the sacred goddesses of light and birth honored.
Saints' day: Chrysogonus (d. c.304); Colman of Cloyne (c.530Äc.606); Minver (6th century AD); Enfleda (d. c.704).

French painter and lithographer Henri de Toulouse-Lautrec was born on November 24, 1864, a day well suited to artistic pursuits, although his personal life was marred by misfortune. A frail child, he broke both legs at the age of fourteen and ceased to grow. In 1884 he settled in Montmartre, where he painted and drew the local prostitutes, barmaids and clowns as well as fashionable members of society. His numerous works include At the Moulin Rouge *(1892),* The Bar *(1898) and (below)* The Laundress *(1884).*

NOVEMBER 24

Those born on this day are deeply interested in, and orientated toward, the people around them. They try to improve conditions for them, whether family members, neighbors, or the wider society. They may find satisfaction in working as politicians, humanitarians, parents, or members of the caring professions. When their independent and sensual traits predominate, their career goals often center on creativity, leading them to become artists, writers, musicians or actors. Inspiring, enlightening and bringing pleasure to others is appealing, but they are also stimulated by the chance to expand their emotional and intellectual horizons through these artistic media. The approbation this brings is welcome, but not essential to their innate sense of self-worth.

November 24 people surprise those who do not know them well by their strength of conviction in promoting the causes they espouse. Underlying their tolerant approach toward others is an emotional core that causes them to react strongly to social abuses and faults. Although their potential to make loving, supportive and protective friends, partners and parents is second to none, they will criticize thoughtlessness or wrongdoing sharply. Those who value their fine qualities will make allowances for their occasional displays of impatience, which are not intended to wound.

VIRTUES: November 24 individuals are blessed with inquisitive minds, yet despite their independence of thought they feel such a deep sense of connection with their social and spiritual groups that they prefer to contribute their considerable talents toward advancing the greater good rather than focusing on self-centered aims.
VICES: Those born on this day have such an affinity for others that they may sublimate their personal inclinations to the common good, which carries the risk that they may remain personally unfulfilled. They should be aware of their tendency to hide their inner selves behind their dedications.
VERDICT: It is important that these people strike a healthy balance between satisfying their external orientation on the one hand, and cultivating their personal desires on the other. Imbalance creates emotional and intellectual frustration, while a well-rounded agenda that is open to growth and change will serve them well—and others with them.

On This Day
Famous Births: Baruch Spinoza (1632); Laurence Sterne (1713); Zachary Taylor (1784); Grace Darling (1815); Frances Hodgson Burnett (1849); Bat Masterson (1853); Henri de Toulouse-Lautrec (1864); Scott Joplin (1868); Dale Carnegie (1888); Herbert Sutcliffe (1894); Hans Popper (1903); Garson Kanin (1912); Geraldine Fitzgerald (1914); Howard Duff (1917); David Kossof (1919); William F. Buckley, Jr., Al Cohn and Alun Owen (1925); Billy Connolly (1942); Claudia Dreifus (1944); Steve Yeager (1948); Ian Botham (1955).

Significant Events and Anniversaries: This is a day that highlights explorative propensities, as was demonstrated when: the Dutch navigator Abel Janszoon became the first European to sight the island of Tasmania off the southern coast of Australia, which he named Van Diemen's Land in honor of his patron, the governor general of the Dutch East Indies (1642); and English scientist Charles Darwin published his seminal—and controversial—work, based on years of research in South America and the Galapagos Islands, *On the Origin of Species by Means of Natural Selection* (1859). Furthermore a day that emphasizes a profound sense of social connection and responsibility, November 24 marks the anniversary of: the murder in an underground car lot in Dallas Texas, of U.S. president John F. Kennedy's alleged assassin, Lee Harvey Oswald—then in police custody—at the hand of the outraged Jack Ruby (1963); and the resignation of the secretary of the Czechoslovakian Communist Party, Milos Jakes, who bowed to anti-Communist public opinion demonstrated during a mass civic rally in Prague, at which the former Czech premier Alexander Dubcek spoke on behalf of the politically reformist group Civic Forum (1989).

NOVEMBER 25

The focused actions of those born on this day are fueled by their desire to realize their visions, and to do so as efficiently and effectively as possible. And although the nature of their ambitions inevitably varies according to the personal makeup of the November 25 individual, all manifest their somewhat perfectionist urges in their pursuit, and, despite the stimulation that they personally derive from facing up to demanding challenges, all are ultimately concerned with inspiring, enlightening, or otherwise acting for the benefit of society as a whole. For although these are independently minded people who cherish their right to personal autonomy, they nevertheless manifest a strong sense of social responsibility with regard to the wider human community, and they will rarely feel completely satisfied in the event of their personal success unless they have also helped to advance the well-being of others. Indeed, many will combine their dual prerequisites for personal fulfillment with their externally oriented concerns within their professions, perhaps working as teachers or scientists, or even serving as political, moral or spiritual leaders.

November 25 people are blessed with astute, rational and perceptive minds, and are naturally attracted to the exploration of novel concepts. Yet despite their intellectual appreciation of the new and original, they prefer to build upon or reform existing beliefs or systems, exploring, assessing and then amending them as they believe necessary rather than espousing radically innovative causes. To some extent they are thus upholders of tradition and continuity (a propensity that is especially pronounced in the women who share this birthday) and may regard those who appear to disrupt the status quo with disapproval. And although they are deeply affectionate and supportive friends and relations who are vitally concerned with, and protective of, those closest to them, they may thus seek to suppress any behavior that deviates from the societal norm, believing that they are acting in their loved ones' ultimate best interests.

VIRTUES: Those born on this day are rational, capable and quietly progressive individuals who, when addressing any given task, are fueled by their determination not only to make, but to do so as efficiently as possible. Their endeavors are characterized by the benevolent urge to assist others.
VICES: Their fixity of purpose, self-discipline and high expectations (of themselves as well as of those around them) may not only lead November 25 people to become overly focused on the achievement on their aims, but may also cause them to become somewhat intolerant of those whose standards and values do not accord with their own.
VERDICT: If they are not to be disappointed by what they may regard as the failure of others to fall into line with their convictions and methods—perhaps an inevitable consequence of their firm views and the concomitant demands that they make of their coworkers and families in particular—these individuals must learn to accept and work with, rather than against, those who profess differences of opinion. By embracing diversity they may also gain an enriching dimension to their lives.

On This Day
Famous Births: Lope de Vega (1562); Andrew Carnegie (1835); Karl Benz (1844); Carry Nation (1846); Leonard Woolf (1880); Pope John XXIII (1881); Isaac Rosenberg (1890); Arthur Schwarz (1900); Frances Durbridge (1912); Auguste Pinochet (1915); Ricardo Montalban (1920); Dickie Jeeps (1931); Kathryn Crosby (1933); Bev Bevan (1946); John Larroquette (1947); Imran Khan Niaz (1952); John F. Kennedy, Jr. (1960).

Significant Events and Anniversaries: A day that emphasizes a belief in the virtues of traditional values, November 25 commemorates the anniversary of: the death of King Henry I of England's son, Prince William, the recognized heir to the throne, thereby heralding a bitter struggle between two rival claimants, Stephen and Matilda (1120); and the ritual suicide (*hari kiri*) of Japanese novelist Yulio Mishima, in a dramatic protest against the breakdown of traditional values within Japanese society, particularly the erosion of the samurai warrior code (1970).

Planetary Influences
Ruling planets: Jupiter and Pluto.
First decan: Personal planet is Jupiter.
First cusp: Sagittarius with Scorpio tendencies.

♃ ♇

Sacred and Cultural Significance
Windmill Blessing Day once held in older Holland.
Saint's day: Catherine of Alexandria (4th century AD), patron saint of young women, philosophers and students.

Windmill Blessing Day, long celebrated in Holland on November 25, originated in the custom whereby millers threw a handful of flour into the wind to appease the mischievous windmill spirits that threatened their livelihood. Depicted below are historic windmills that once graced the Zaanstreek on De Hemmes Peninsula, The Netherlands.

NOVEMBER 26

****

Planetary Influences
Ruling planet: Jupiter.
First decan: Personal planet is Jupiter.

♃

Sacred and Cultural Significance
Fire festival celebrated in Tibet.
Saint's day: Leonard of Port Maurice (1676–1751), patron saint of missionaries.

Musical careers are auspicious for those born on this day, as seen in the career of singer and actress Tina Turner, who was born Anna Mae Bullock on November 26, 1939. Her creativity was enhanced by her birth in the Chinese year of the rabbit. As the sensual queen of raunch rock, she starred with her husband in The Ike and Tina Turner Review, *receiving a Grammy Award in 1971. Her award-winning album* Private Dancer *(1984) sold over ten million copies, and she starred with Mel Gibson in* Mad Max Beyond Thunderdome *(1985). Inducted into the Rock Hall of Fame in 1991, she published her autobiography* I, Tina *in 1993.*

November 26 people are determined and free-thinking individualists, who are absorbed by intellectual discovery and experimentation and feel compelled to set inspiring examples to others through their actions and make concrete advances for the benefit of society. They are prodigiously organized and practical types, who manifest great technical expertise when engaged in their work, yet are also blessed with extremely active imaginations. They may thus become fixated on realizing visions that are so unusual or ambitious that those around them sometimes question whether they are actually achievable. These individuals, however, are rarely troubled by feelings of doubt when in thrall to a fascinating challenge, for since they are astute assessors of both their own abilities and the potential chances of success, they envisage no obstacles to their progress beyond those imposed by the closed minds of others. Perfectionist, tenacious and determined, they concentrate on their aims to the exclusion of all else.

These people will thrive in any career where they can pursue their quests for knowledge and innovation unhindered by outside constraints. Naturally drawn to the possibilities for advancement offered by academic research of all kinds, as well as science and the arts, those born on this day have the potential to make truly outstanding contributions to humanity. Others admire their originality and independent minds, but these very strengths may prohibit November 26 people from maintaining enduring life partnerships in particular, for they often secretly fear that by committing themselves to another person their freedom of thought and action may be restricted (a propensity that is even more pronounced in the men born on this day). Despite this caveat, however, they typically make enlivening, loyal and affectionate friends and family members.

VIRTUES: Intellectually curious, vigorous and progressive, those born on this day are seized by the irresistible desire to investigate, learn and then push forward the bounds of human understanding and endeavor. Blessed with great powers of focus and concentration, as well as highly developed technical capabilities, they have the courage and determination to achieve their aims, however fantastic they may seem to others.
VICES: Inherent in these people's all-encompassing dedication to their intellectual interests is the danger that they may neglect their emotional needs, for the priority that they accord their careers often leaves them with little time or attention to devote to nurturing their relationships with their nearest and dearest, or simply to relax and indulge themselves.
VERDICT: Although they should never abandon or compromise the visions that are so important to them, November 26 people should recognize that the typically single-minded and active pursuit of their goals may cause them to risk physical, intellectual and emotional burnout. They should therefore consciously strive to introduce an element of balance into their lives, and should especially appreciate the emotional rewards that may be reaped from interpersonal relationships.

On This Day
Famous Births: William Cowper (1731); William Armstrong (1810); George Emlyn Williams (1905); Charles Forte (1908); Cyril Cusack (1910); Eugene Ionesco and Eric Severeid (1912); Charles Monroe Schulz (1922); Robert Goulet (1933); Rich Little (1938); Art Themen and Tina Turner (1939); Jim Mullen (1945).

Significant Events and Anniversaries: This is a day that promises pioneering technical innovations, as shown when: the first trams—developed by John Mason—began running in New York City, between Prince and 14th streets (1832); and the world's first tidal power station was inaugurated by President Charles de Gaulle in Brittany, France (1966). Exploratory propensities are featured on November 26, the anniversary of the opening of Pharaoh Tutankhamun's 3000-year-old tomb in Luxor's Valley of the Kings by the English archaeologist Howard Carter and his sponsor, the Earl of Carnarvon (1922).

NOVEMBER 27

Those born on this day are complex people who are fiercely individualistic types. On the one hand they react negatively to any perceived attempts to limit their personal autonomy, and on the other, they are positively oriented to those around them. Some November 27 people are able to successfully reconcile these two potentially conflicting propensities within their professional careers, for example by working independently to formulate a new product or concept and then sharing the fruits of their labors with a wider audience. These are mentally active and remarkably technically minded individuals, who have the potential to research, develop and then pioneer advances that are intended—and certainly have the potential—to enlighten, inspire or otherwise assist others. In many respects their concern for those around them is the result of their highly developed natural sense of justice and instinctive dislike of authoritarianism, as well as their more emotional response to the plight of those whom they perceive to be unhappy or suffering. Although personally stimulated by the pursuit of their interests, the motivations underlying their work often stem from their desire to lighten the lives of others. They may become politicians (usually of the democratic type), artists or scientists.

Their relationships—both professional and personal—with those around them are typically characterized by mutual respect and goodwill; that having been said, however, they will not hesitate to make their feelings forcefully known if they detect any transgressions. Predisposed toward forming and maintaining open and relaxed relationships with their nearest and dearest—provided, that is, that their loved ones understand and accommodate their need for a certain level of freedom, a prerequisite that is all the more important if they were also born in the Chinese year of the tiger—November 27 people make deeply supportive, generous and enlivening partners and companions, and especially gifted parents.

VIRTUES: Those born on this day possess markedly independent turns of minds; never ones to conform to societal norms unquestioningly, they prefer to seek out knowledge and truth for themselves and then formulate and adhere to their own opinions and visions. Nevertheless profoundly concerned with the welfare of others, they seek to utilize their talents and convictions to advance the common good.
VICES: Although generally tolerant types, such is their innate resistance to what they may regard as attempts to impose controls or restrictions upon them that many November 27 individuals have a tendency to be oversensitive regarding their perceptions of the behavior and attitudes of others—especially those in positions of authority—one that may lead them to react with (perhaps unjustified) hostility.
VERDICT: In the interests of enlisting the cooperation and support of those around them, these people should try to moderate their propensity to rebel against any perceived attempts to repress their individuality, and should instead try to acknowledge that those who hold different viewpoints are entitled to express their beliefs, and are not necessarily seeking to impose their opinions and methods upon them.

On This Day

Famous Births: Anders Celsius (1701); Mary Robinson (1758); Fanny Kemble (1809); Chaim Weizmann (1874); William Orpen (1878); Konosuke Matsushita (1894); James Agee (1909); "Buffalo" Bob Smith (1917); Alexander Dubcek (1921); Ernie Wise (1925); Alan Simpson (1929); Bruce Lee and John Alderton (1940); Eddie Rabbitt (1941); Jimi Hendrix (1942); Caroline Kennedy (1957); Robin Givens (1964); Jaleel White (1976).

Significant Events and Anniversaries: This is a day on which independent action and resistance to submitting to authority are highlighted, as was demonstrated when the French Navy scuttled its vessels at Toulon harbor during World War II to prevent them from falling into the hands of the invading German Army (1942). November 27 governed by the element of fire is the day when explosives stored in a cave in Staffordshire, England, during World War II accidentally ignited, killing sixty-eight people (1944).

Planetary Influences
Ruling planet: Jupiter.
First decan: Personal planet is Jupiter.

Sacred and Cultural Significance
Gujeswari honored by Buddhists and Hindus in Nepal; Parvati-Devi held in India.
Saints' day: Congar (6th century AD); Fergus (8th century AD); Virgil (d. 784).

The religious festival of Parvati-Devi, held in India on November 27, honors the goddess known as the Mother of the Universe, whose three aspects are Sarasvati (Maiden), Lakshmi (Mother) and Parvati (Crone). Pictured below with her mount, the peacock, her all-encompassing vision is signified by the many "eyes" of its fanlike tail feathers.

****

Planetary Influences
Ruling planet: Jupiter.
First decan: Personal planet is Jupiter.

Sacred and Cultural Significance
Pagans celebrate the ancient Greek goddess Sophia.
Saints' day: Juthwara (dates unknown); Gregory III (d. 741); James of the Marches (1394–1476); Catherine Labouré (1806–76).

Poet, painter, engraver and mystic William Blake was born on this day in 1757, highly gifted with its visionary qualities. His freedom of imagination is clear in his mysterious works, which include: Songs of Innocence *(1789),* Songs of Experience *(1794) and* The Marriage of Heaven and Hell *(1789). Pictured below is his* The Ancient of Days *(1794).*

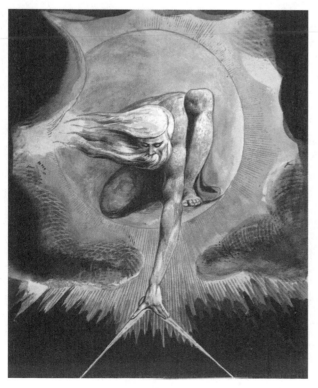

Those born on this day are astute and critical observers, not only of others, but of group dynamics as a whole. Blessed with sensitive powers of intuition, they test their conclusions analytically before sharing them with a wider audience. Their independence of mind fosters skepticism in the face of prejudice and convention. Because they have an innate sense of fairness, November 28 people are natural debunkers, but their intentions are not destructive. They rarely offer criticisms without proposing viable alternatives attuned to the needs of those around them.

Their interest in the workings of society and in human behavior suit November 28 individuals especially well for careers as social reformers, politicians and journalists. Professions in the artistic or scientific spheres may also attract them, especially as venues for personal and social enlightenment. Given their critical propensity, the people with whom they live and work tend to admire and respect them but inevitably feel uncomfortable lest they become the next target of their censure. This is an unfortunate (if understandable) reaction, since November 28 people are ultimately motivated by the most well-meaning of intentions and, furthermore, crave the affection and security that result from profound bonds of friend- and kinship.

VIRTUES: Those born on this day are astute observers of individuals and society; blessed with enormous intuition, as well as highly developed analytical faculties. They cut to the core of any issue to inform others and engender positive change.
VICES: The propensity of November 28 individuals to be uncompromisingly frank when expressing their opinions is entirely in accordance with their distaste for hypocrisy and their predilection for revealing the true state of affairs. Although this approach can have remarkable results, it also has a tendency to cause others to distance themselves so as to avoid criticism, which may cause November 28 people to become emotionally isolated.
VERDICT: It is vital that these people recognize that their friends, partners or relations may often be intimidated by their honesty and that they themselves may be unwittingly alienating those for whom they feel nothing but affection and concern. They should therefore moderate their predilection for criticism, or at least try to employ tact and diplomacy.

On This Day
Famous Births: Jean Baptiste Lully (1632); William Blake (1757); George Manby (1765); Friedrich Engels (1820); John Wesley Hyatt (1837); Brooks Atkinson (1894); José Iturbi (1895); Nancy Mitford (1904); Alberto Moravia (1907); Claude Lévi-Strauss (1908); Keith Miller (1919); Berry Gordy, Jr. (1929); Hope Lange (1931); Gary Hart (1936); Randy Newman (1943); Joe Donte (1946); Alexander Godunov and Paul Shaffer (1949); Ed Harris (1950); Judd Nelson and Stephen Roche (1959); Jane Sibbet (1961); Jon Stewart (1963); Anna Nicole Smith (1967).

Significant Events and Anniversaries: Highlighted on November 28 is a strong desire to further the quest for human knowledge and truth, as was reflected on this day when: the Royal Society was founded in London, England, an institution dedicated to scientific research (1660); and Australian anthropologist Raymond Dart announced his discovery of a fossilized human skull that he identified as the "southern African ape," *Australopithecus africanus,* which became more popularly known as the "missing link" (1924). Also inherent in this day is the urge to replace perceived societal abuses with more enlightened systems of change and reform, as was demonstrated in the realm of politics when: the women of New Zealand became the first females to vote in a general election (1893); Irish journalist Arthur Griffith founded the political organization Sinn Fein, with the intention of reviving Irish culture (1905); and American-born Nancy, Viscountess Astor (née Nancy Witcher Langhorne), became the first woman to be elected a British member of parliament (1919).

NOVEMBER 29

Those born on this day are dynamic individuals, stimulated by challenge. Even during periods of relaxation they remain busy, perhaps pursuing sporting activities or adding to their knowledge by reading and observation. Imbued with the desire to move forward in terms of personal growth, career goals, or the common good, they are "can-do" types, who can assess a given situation and formulate innovative strategies. They are also pragmatic realists, who will rarely focus their energies on a venture unless they believe it stands a good chance of success. They also expect others to fall in with their views and may become impatient if the beliefs they espouse are slow to gain acceptance.

November 29 individuals are usually drawn to careers that can satisfy their pioneering and progressive urges and make a contribution to others. Despite their independence of mind, they have a strong sense of social responsibility and may gravitate toward political or scientific ventures, teaching, or humanitarian causes. A similarly profound concern for the well-being of their loved ones defines their personal relationships, and they in turn are deeply valued for their enlivening influence and loyalty. However, their tendency to direct those closest to them may not always be taken in the spirit in which it was intended.

VIRTUES: Those born on this day are invigorating people, who manifest their energy and urge to make progress—on others' behalf as well as their own—in everything that they undertake. Blessed with questing and perceptive minds, they support their aims with practical methodologies.
VICES: Not only do November 29 people set themselves high standards and display remarkable focus and commitment in the pursuits: they expect others to shares their convictions and be similarly dedicated. This tendency may alienate those who are just as convinced of an alternative viewpoint.
VERDICT: In the interests of retaining the goodwill of others and protecting themselves from disappointment, these individuals should recognize that not everyone share their enthusiasms. A more tolerant attitude to expressions of dissent will help them to enlist cooperation and form more lasting friendships.

On This Day

Famous Births: Gaetano Donizetti (1797); Christian Johann Doppler (1803); Louisa May Alcott (1832); Tz'u-shi, the Dowager Empress of China (1834); Francis Cowley Burnand (1836); Gertrude Jekyll (1843); John Fleming (1849); Busby Berkeley (1895); C.S. Lewis (1898); Adam Clayton Powell, Jr. (1908); Billy Strayhorn (1915); Madeline L'Engle (1918); Vin Scully (1927); Berry Gordy, Jr. (1929); Jacques Chirac and Diane Ladd (1932); John Mayall (1933); Tony Coe (1934); Peter Bergman (1939); Chuck Mangione (1940); Suzy Chaffee (1946); Gary Shandling (1949); Dusty Hare (1952); Howie Mandel (1955); Jeff Fahey (1956); Charles Grant (1959); Cathy Moriarty (1960); Jon Knight (1968).

Significant Events and Anniversaries: On a day that features independent propensities, Josip Tito proclaimed the former monarchy of Yugoslavia a socialist federal republic (1945). The pursuit of aims intended to promote national power—however misguided—marks this as the tragic anniversary of the annihilation of some 400 peaceful Cheyenne and Apache at the hands of "Colonel" John M. Chivington and his militia at Sand Creek, Colorado (1864). This day also highlights the pursuit of pioneering goals, as demonstrated when the U.S. explorer Richard Byrd, with aviator Bernt Balchen, became the first people to fly over the South Pole (1929). The talent for entertaining that is emphasized by this day was reflected when U.S. composer Cole Porter's show *The Gay Divorcee* was first staged (1932).

Planetary Influences
Ruling planet: Jupiter.
First decan: Personal planet is Jupiter.

Sacred and Cultural Significance
Feast of Hathor as Sekhmet held in ancient Egypt.
Saint's day: Brendan of Birr (d. 573).

At the Teheran Conference, held in Iran from November 28 to December 1, 1943, President F.D. Roosevelt, Prime Minister Winston Churchill and Premier Joseph Stalin planned the World War II Allied invasion of western Europe. Under the auspices of promoting the common good, it was agreed that an eastern offensive would be launched to coincide with invasions of German-occupied France—a strategy that would prove successful in bringing an end to the war.

NOVEMBER 30

Planetary Influences
Ruling planet: Jupiter.
First decan: Personal planet is Jupiter.

♃

Sacred and Cultural Significance
Saint's day: Andrew (d. c.60), patron saint of fishermen, Scotland and Russia.

Writer, journalist and lecturer Mark Twain was born Samuel Langhorne Clemens on November 30, 1835. He showed the intellect, energy and imagination typical of this birthdate in The Innocents Abroad *(1869),* The Adventures of Tom Sawyer *(1876),* The Adventures of Huckleberry Finn *(1884) and other works of deep humorous insight into American life and culture.*

The typically mild-mannered and good-humored face that those born on this day present to the world often masks an incisive mind that is hard at work analyzing people and circumstances. These astute individuals often harbor a plan for life whose ambition would surprise those who take their rather laid-back image at face value. This is not to say that these people are not genuinely charming and benevolent, but they understand the importance of reserve until they are ready to act. Perfectionistic by nature, they use their resources to maximize their potential for success.

Organizational skills and a talent for communication make them natural leaders. Concerned with helping others to advance, they may defend or promote political, social or national interests. Their preparation, self-control, and fixity elicits the admiration of others, but may become detrimental in their personal lives, if those closest to them resent their propensity for taking charge or friends see them as unfeeling.

VIRTUES: Those born on this day are physically and intellectually active individuals who are blessed with great mental clarity and perspicacity and who operate tenaciously and determinedly according to carefully thought-out strategies. Their affability, along with their ability to motivate and organize those around them in the pursuit of a common ideal, engenders respect and affection.

VICES: While their focused and controlled manner, as well as their propensity for playing their cards close to their chests, augurs exceptionally well for their professional success, such an approach may prove less appropriate when applied to in their dealings with their loved ones, who may feel both excluded by their perceived secrecy and irritated by their attempts to direct their actions.

VERDICT: With respect to their relationships with their close circle of friends and family, it is important that those born on this day open up rather more, sharing their visions and feelings and concomitantly adopting a tolerant, *laissez-faire* approach to the dreams and expressions of individuality of others.

On This Day
Famous Births: Andrea Palladio (1508); Philip Sidney (1554); Jonathan Swift (1667); Frederick Temple (1821); Samuel Langhorne Clemens (Mark Twain) (1835); Angela Brazil (1868); Nils Gustaf Dalen (1869); Winston Churchill and Lucy Maud Montgomery (1874); Geoffrey Household (1900); Virginia Mayo (1920); Efrem Zimbalist, Jr. (1923); Richard Crenna (1926); Dick Clark (1929); G. Gordon Liddy (1930); Abbie Hoffman (1936); Robert Guillaume (1937); Otter Zell (1942); David Mamet (1947); Mandy Patinkin (1952); Shuggie Otis (1953); Billy Idol (1955); Gary Lineker (1960); Bo Jackson (1962).

Significant Events and Anniversaries: On a day that highlights outstanding leadership qualities, the remains of the former French revolutionary general and emperor Napoleon Bonaparte, who had died in exile, were returned from the island of St. Helena to Paris, to be reinterred with pomp and ceremony at the Hôtel des Invalides (1840). Further emphasized on November 30 are pioneering advances of all kinds, as was demonstrated in the artistic sphere when British actor Charlie Chaplin's first movie, *Making a Living*, was screened (1913); and in the realm of science and technology when Japanese naval vessel *Hosho*, the world's first dedicated aircraft carrier, was unveiled (1922). This day is governed by the element of fire, as was sadly reflected when the Crystal Palace, the glass and iron building designed by British architect Joseph Paxton to house the Great Exhibition of 1851, burned to the ground in London's Sydenham Hill (1936).

DECEMBER 1

Those born on December 1 are extremely energetic individuals fueled by a driving ambition, yet such is their charm and their astute use of humor that others are seduced into applauding actions that they might otherwise consider ruthless. Some have a clear idea as to what they are aiming for in life: perhaps the achievement of excellence, the acclaim of their peers and concomitant financial rewards; others may be less focused, but nevertheless feel the urge to manifest their individuality unfettered by the constraints of opinion. All express themselves freely and will react particularly badly to any perceived attempts to restrict their autonomy of thought and action—in fact, any disapproval or dissent on the part of others frequently has the effect of spurring them on along their idiosyncratic path with renewed vigor and determination. Yet although they will defend or promote the freedom they cherish so greatly, sometimes to the point of defiance, these are not individuals who generally employ combative strategies for the sake of confrontation: they prefer to win others over by the sheer force of their personalities.

December 1 people will flourish in any profession where they can act independently and make an original contribution. They can work well as part of a team, but they are better suited to being leaders than followers. Given their predilections, they have the potential to make outstanding performers and entertainers, particularly in the sporting or artistic fields. Others admire their driving energy and good humor, and those born on this day revel in the attention they excite, yet also take real pleasure in pleasing those around them. Indeed, they are also genuinely concerned and affectionate friends and relations, valued for their enlivening company and optimistic, "can-do" attitude.

VIRTUES: Those born on this day are positive, exuberant and active individuals, who seek to fulfill themselves and relate to others unhindered by convention, blazing their own, original trail through life. Gregarious and invigorating, they bring pleasure and enlightenment to their friends and acquaintences.

VICES: December 1 people are so averse to suppressing their individuality and conforming to what they may perceive as dull authoritarian systems that they tend to move to the other extreme, leading lifestyles and professing opinions that often seem outrageously radical to those around them.

VERDICT: It is important in terms of their emotional well-being that these individuals try to strike a healthy balance between their need for autonomy and their equally strong orientation to others, for by acting as obstinately independent agents they may lose the essential support, affection and mutual regard of relaxed interpersonal relationships.

On This Day

Famous Births: (Madame) Marie Tussaud (1761); Queen Alexandra of England (1844); Henry Williamson (1895); Cyril Ritchard (1897); Alicia Markova (1910); Mary Martin (1913); Matt Monro (1930); Woody Allen (1935); Lou Rawls (1936); Lee Trevino (1939); Richard Pryor (1940); Bette Midler (1945); Gilbert O'Sullivan (1946); Bob Fulton (1947); Jaco Pastorius and Treat Williams (1951); Stephen Poliakoff (1952); Charlene Tilton (1958).

Significant Events and Anniversaries: This is a day that highlights the desire for autonomy, seen in the Portuguese proclamation of independence from Spain (1640). Freedom of thought is similarly emphasized on this day, when the English Jesuit Edmund Campion was martyred in London, accused of espionage and treason by the Protestant government (1581). The original and progressive qualities inherent in December 1 were demonstrated by: the foundation of Britain's Royal Academy of Arts by King George III (1768); the world's first ascent in a hydrogen balloon by the French scientist J.A.C. Charles (1783); and inauguration of the first dedicated movie theater, the Cinema Omnia Pathé, in Paris (1906). The day's artistic potential was shown by the premieres of the movie *Gone With the Wind* (1939) and British composer Benjamin Britten's opera *Billy Budd* (1951).

Planetary Influences
Ruling planet: Jupiter.
Second decan: Personal planet is Mars.

Sacred and Cultural Significance
World AIDS Day observed.
Saints' day: Tudwal (6th century AD);
Eloi (c.588–660), patron saint of blacksmiths, farriers, goldsmiths and jewelers.

Born on this day in 1910, Briton Lilian Alicia Marks (known as Alicia Markova) combined the artistic and athletic promise of her birthdate in her career as a prima ballerina (with the Ballet Russes and Ballet Rambert), a director (for her Markova-Dolin Company and the Metropolitan Opera Ballet) and a professor of ballet. Like many December 1 people, she found her own niche in life; she also demonstrated the perfectionism typical of people born in the Chinese year of the dog.

Planetary Influences
Ruling planet: Jupiter.
Second decan: Personal planet is Mars.

Sacred and Cultural Significance
In Bodh Gaya, India, the world's oldest tree honored by Tibetan Buddhists; Hari Kugo, an annual women's festival, takes place in Tokyo.
Saints' day: Bibiana (Viviana) of Rome (d. 363).

Born on this day of originality and imagination, French artist Georges Pierre Seurat initiated a new style of painting, known as Pointillism, of which Sunday Afternoon on the Grand-Jatte *(1885, detail below) is one of the leading examples. Although Seurat was not a prolific artist, he was fascinated by the principles of color vision and perception, and he experimented widely with new techniques, ultimately making a unique and significant contribution to the art world.*

DECEMBER 2

Many of those born on this day feel constantly torn between their desire to forge their own, determinedly individualistic path through life and their profound sense of responsibility for others—be they their families, friends, colleagues, compatriots or even the fellowship of humanity. Blessed with extremely imaginative, innovative and curious minds, on the one hand these vigorous individuals feel compelled to pursue the interests and visions that excite them, while on the other their innate fair-mindedness and empathy with those whom they perceive to be victims of injustice urges them to champion the oppressed. When these tendencies are imbalanced, December 2 people may experience profound frustration—indeed, they have quick tempers when crossed or obstructed in any way, particularly if they were also born in the Chinese year of the dragon. If they can reconcile their need for independence with their concern for safeguarding or promoting the welfare of others, they have the potential not only to attain personal satisfaction, but to make contributions to society, perhaps as pioneering scientists or inspirational artists.

Those around them respect the strength of character of December 2 people and may often elevate them to positions of leadership—a responsibility that those born on this day may view ambivalently. Although they have an enviable gift for organization and motivation and would far rather command than obey, they may feel that their leadership duties preclude them from pursuing their own ambitions. A similarly ambiguous attitude characterizes their relationships with their nearest and dearest (which is even more pronounced in the women who share this birthdate), for while they manifest deep affection and protectiveness for their loved ones, they may sometimes feel stifled by their (often self-imposed) duties of caretaking.

VIRTUES: Those born on this day are charismatic people, both individualistic and socially concerned, and driven by a profound urge to place their talents at the service of their fellows. Blessed with a strong sense of natural justice, as well as imaginative and resourceful intellects, they have the potential to make an inspirational mark on the world.
VICES: Their strongly dualistic urge, both to indulge their personal quests for knowledge and progress and to make a significant contribution to those with whom they most identify, carries the risk that in their attempts to fulfill their desires and obligations, December 2 people may spread their energies too thinly and become exhausted and emotionally frustrated.
VERDICT: Balance and moderation are the keys to the happiness and well-being of these individuals. They need to forge an effective accommodation between their selfless and personal instincts and activities, neither promoting one set of inclinations to the detriment of the other, nor running themselves ragged trying to satisfy both.

On This Day
Famous Births: Joseph Bell (1837); Georges Seurat (1859); Ruth Draper (1884); Harriet Cohen (1895); Georgi Konstantinovich Zhukov (1896); John Barbirolli (1899); Peter Carl Goldmark (1906); Adolf Geren (1915); Maria Callas (1923); Julie Harris (1925); Cathy Lee Crosby (1948); Tracy Austin (1962); Monica Seles (1973).

Significant Events and Anniversaries: December 2 is a day on which outstanding leadership qualities are indicated, as seen by: Napoleon Bonaparte's coronation as emperor of France (1804), and the new emperor's defeat of a combined Austro-Russian army at the Battle of Austerlitz (1805). A desire to promote the communal interest was highlighted when U.S. President James Monroe proclaimed his eponymous doctrine that further European colonization in the Western hemisphere was inimical to American security (1823). This day also emphasizes technical and scientific capabilities, as was demonstrated when: English architect Sir Christopher Wren's remodeled St. Paul's Cathedral was officially opened in London (1697); U.S. physicists Enrico Fermi and Arthur Compton effected the world's first nuclear chain reaction, at the University of Chicago (1942); and Dr. Barney B. Clark became the first person to receive an artificial heart, at Salt Lake City's Utah Medical Center (1982).

DECEMBER 3

Intricate systems and abstract concepts exert tremendous fascination upon those individuals born on this day. Blessed with investigative and at the same time determinedly progressive minds, the attention of these people is irresistibly drawn to exploring complex issues, gathering data, identifying any inherent flaws and then, using this knowledge to devise and formulate original strategies with which to bring about advancement. Despite the unusual—even radical—ideas that they typically espouse, and the soaringly ambitious nature of their visions, these are profoundly rational and meticulous types who prefer not to make their theories public until they are convinced of their feasibility; their proposals are can thus rarely be likened to castles built on shifting sand, as the have the most stable of foundations. Add to this solid basis their organizational and technical skills, as well as their tenacity, and the result is a formidably effective instrument of progress. Indeed, December 3 people can be said to possess pioneering promise, and will especially excel in those professional fields where they can combine their innovative inclinations and practical expertise and thus lead by example—perhaps as scientists or engineers, or else within the more fluid realms of artistry and athletics.

While others respect their vigor, focus and drive, they may feel that these individuals have thrown up an invisible shield around them, making it difficult (if not impossible) to penetrate to the core of their personalities. And it is true that those born on this day prefer to keep their emotions private—sometimes even concealing them from their nearest and dearest—perhaps believing that their expression would distract from intellectual pursuits. Many of their visions are driven by the desire to assist society, and they make caring, responsible and generous friends and family members, even when their professional interests take a higher priority.

VIRTUES: Those born on this day seek to make improvements or advances in the spheres that excite their interest. Possessing analytical and rational intellects, with the determination to develop their technical talents fully, their attention to detail combined with clear-sightedness in the pursuit of their aims augurs well for their success.

VICES: Not only are many December 3 individuals totally focused on their professional or intellectual goals, but their single-minded quests foster the tendency to disregard their own emotional needs, and those of others. This may lead them to become detached from both the rewards and the demands inherent in human relationships.

VERDICT: It is vital that these people learn to balance their intellectual aspirations and the emotional prerequisites for happiness, for they tend to sublimate the latter to the former. They need to become more open to those around them and participate more fully and freely in their relationships.

On This Day

Famous Births: Niccolo Amati (1596); Samuel Crompton (1753); Rowland Hill (1795); Joseph Conrad (1857); Thomas Beecham (1879); Anton von Webern (1883); Lesley Ames (1905); Trevor Bailey (1923); Jean-Luc Godard and Andy Williams (1930); Ozzy Osbourne (1948); Mel Smith (1952); Katarina Witt (1965); Anna Chlumsky (1980).

Significant Events and Anniversaries: A day that indicates great innovative potential, December 3 marks the anniversary of: the unveiling of a prototype form of neon lighting at the Paris motor show, the brainchild of the French scientist George Claude (1910); and the carrying out of the first human-to-human heart transplant operation, performed by Dr. Christiaan Barnard at Cape Town's Groote Schuur Hospital in South Africa (1967). The decisive promotion of progressive visions highlighted by this day was variously reflected in two events that occurred on December 3: the defeat of the Austrian army under Archduke John by General Jean Victor Marie Moreau's French troops at the Battle of Hohenlinden during the Napoleonic Wars (1800); and the state of Illinois' admission to the Union (1818).

Planetary Influences
Ruling planet: Jupiter.
Second decan: Personal planet is Mars.

♃ ♂

Sacred and Cultural Significance
Secret women's rituals performed in ancient Rome; Rhea and Cybele honored in ancient Greece.
Saints' day: Birinus (d. 650); Francis Xavier (1506–51), patron saint of missionaries.

On this progressive, proactive day in 1847, abolitionist Frederick Douglass (pictured below) founded the North Star *newspaper in Rochester, New York. With the slogan "Right is of no sex—Truth is of no color—God is the father of us all, and all we are Brethren," the first editorial promised: "We solemnly dedicate the* North Star *to the cause of our long oppressed and plundered fellow countrymen."*

Planetary Influences
Ruling planet: Jupiter.
Second decan: Personal planet is Mars.

Sacred and Cultural Significance
In ancient Rome, Minerva honored with
an annual festival; the Yoruba god Chango
honored in West Africa.
Saints' day: Barbara (dates unknown), patron
saint of architects, gunners, miners and the
dying; John Damascene (c.657–c.749);
Osmund (d. 1099), patron saint of paralyzed
people and toothache sufferers.

*Showing the resourceful and socially observant
characteristics highlighted on his birthdate,
Scottish man of letters Thomas Carlyle wrote
with an informed, independent stance
on current affairs and history, promoting
his considered viewpoint with acuity.*

DECEMBER 4

It is a curious dichotomy of December 4 people's characters that although they cherish their
individuality jealously, innately refusing to submit to the rules and conventions of others,
they typically feel compelled to impose their convictions upon those around them. They may
not be consciously aware of the first predilection and therefore see no contradiction in seeking
to control the thoughts and actions of others while at the same time reserving their own right
to total personal autonomy, and, in any case, their directional urges usually stem from the
best of intentions. For those born on this day are both thoughtful and socially responsible
individuals, whose guiding visions are generally concerned with advancing the greater good
rather than any more selfish ambitions. Their sense of natural justice and balanced objectivity
in particular propel them toward activities that are intended to bring about a more enlightened
or better regulated society, and they may hence often be found promoting a clear-cut set of
ideological or political beliefs, either as politicians or social campaigners, or else through the
more subtle, but no less effective media encompassed by the artistic disciplines.

December 4 people back their strongly held opinions and ambitions with resourcefulness,
energy and vigor, and—since they are additionally practical and organized types—with
carefully devised and impeccably executed plans of action. Stimulated by challenge, they
relish taking risks and facing obstacles squarely—a strategy that often has remarkable results
but which may equally cause them to explode with frustration when they find their progress
blocked. Others regard their determined and confrontational approach with awe, but sometimes
prefer to give them a wide berth lest they find themselves in the firing line. Those closest to
them see the gentler, more affectionate side to their characters.

VIRTUES: Energetically active mentally and physically, those born on this day have independent
intellects that lead them to evaluate and sometimes to reject societal conventions in favor of
their own visions. They show highly developed powers of organization and technical expertise.
VICES: Such is their need to act with total freedom, and their urgency in pursuing their
ambitions, that December 4 individuals may act without regarding the possibility of negative
emotional consequences—for themselves or others.
VERDICT: These people should develop a greater awareness of the effect that their certainty
of conviction and drivingly assertive approach typically has on those whose welfare they have
at heart. Others resent their perceived unwillingness to listen tolerantly to alternative viewpoints,
as well as their undoubted urge to compel them to fall in line with their beliefs and methods.
Developing a more *laissez-faire* attitude should help them to both achieve their goals more
easily and retain the affection of those around them in the process.

On This Day
Famous Births: Thomas Carlyle (1795); Samuel Butler (1835); Lillian Russell (1861); Edith
Cavell (1865); Wassily Kandinsky (1866); Rainer Maria Rilke and Edgar Wallace (1875);
Hamilton Harty (1879); Francisco Franco (1892); Herbert Read (1893); A.L. Rowse (1903);
Jimmy Jewel (1912); Deanna Durbin (1921); Ronnie Corbett (1930); Richard Meade (1938);
Yvonne Minton (1943); Dennis Wilson (1944); Jeff Bridges (1949); Pamela Stephenson (1950);
Josef Sabovcik (1963); Marisa Tomei (1964); Tyra Banks (1973).

Significant Events and Anniversaries: This is a day that highlights leadership qualities, as
was demonstrated when Nicholas Breakspear became the first (and only) Englishman to be
elected pope (Adrian IV, 1154). The potential to make innovations is also emphasized by this
day, on which: the first edition of Britain's oldest enduring Sunday newspaper, the *Observer*,
was published (1791); and U.S. playwright Tennessee Williams's *A Streetcar Named Desire* had
its premiere on Broadway (1947). The urge to act with total autonomy that is a feature of this
day is inherent in the case of U.S. comedian "Fatty" Arbuckle, who was brought to trial for
his alleged involvement in a sex and murder scandal. Although he was subsequently acquitted,
his career never recovered (1921).

DECEMBER 5

Being actively engaged in a potentially rewarding endeavor is a prerequisite for the happiness of those born on this day. Both intellectually and physically energetic, with a deep-rooted need to stimulate their minds and bodies in the pursuit of progress and knowledge, their attention is quickly captured by the pioneering possibilities inherent in challenging concepts or situations. Indeed, they respond to ideas and visions that would be dismissed by more conservative and cautious individuals. Yet such are their powers of imagination, and their optimistic approach to the most daunting tasks, that December 5 people rarely allow themselves to be dissuaded from an exciting new venture. This sometimes leads them to make serious errors of judgement, but may equally result in remarkable innovations—and those around them admire their indomitable spirit and enthusiasm. They are regarded with affection and tolerance by their coworkers, friends and relations (feelings that they reciprocate), but in many respects their primary concern is with their intellectual ambitions.

The majority of those born on this day are concerned with making a real contribution to those with whom they identify, whether their families, compatriots or even humanity as a whole, and may be drawn to political or social pursuits. They supplement their clarity of purpose by drawing upon their resourcefulness, technical and organizational skills. They will thrive in any career where their interest remains actively engaged, but perhaps will derive the greatest satisfaction as artists, writers, musicians or movie-makers.

VIRTUES: Stimulated as their active and imaginative minds are by the possibilities inherent in the novel and original, those born on this day are enthusiastic proponents of innovative—and often ingenious—concepts intended to benefit the greater good, toward whose realization they direct their determination, vigor, as well as their practical talents.
VICES: Because the ambitions that excite the interest of December 5 people are frequently of a somewhat radical or unusual nature, they typically, of necessity, become used to brushing off the doubts of others and proceeding along their preferred path regardless of the admonitions of those around them. In consequence, they deny themselves potentially valuable advice and frequently alienate people.
VERDICT: If they are to attain the aims that are so important to their all-round fulfillment, is it crucial that these individuals should take heed of the (usually well-meant) comments and suggestions of others regarding the nature of their visions or their approaches. By listening to a variety of viewpoints, and maybe adopting or adapting salient points, their chances for success are likely to be enhanced, and they will thereby also enlist the cooperation of those who might otherwise feel excluded from their activities. They should spend more time nurturing their bonds with those closest to them.

On This Day

Famous Births: Martin Van Buren (1782); Christina Rossetti (1830); George Armstrong Custer (1839); John Jellicoe (1859); Fritz Lang (1890); Walt Disney (1901); Emeric Pressburger (1902); Otto Preminger (1906); James Cleveland (1931); Little Richard (Penniman) (1935); José Carreras (1946); Jim Messina (1947); Morgan Brittany (1951); Carrie Hamilton (1963).

Significant Events and Anniversaries: December 5 emphasizes the pursuit of original ambitions, as was demonstrated when the British founder of the eponymous auctioneering house, James Christie, conducted his first auction (1766). This day is also governed by the element of fire, as shown when Japanese naval firepower destroyed the Russian fleet at Port Arthur (Lushun), off the northeastern coast of China (1904). And, on a day that highlights a fascination with the unusual, two mysterious events occurred on December 5 that captured the public imagination: the U.S. trading ship *Marie Celeste* was discovered drifting off the Azores in the Atlantic Ocean, its captain, his family and seven crew members having apparently vanished from the face of the Earth (1872); and five U.S. Navy airplanes disappeared while flying over the area known as the "Bermuda Triangle" (1945).

Planetary Influences
Ruling planet: Jupiter.
Second decan: Personal planet is Mars.

Sacred and Cultural Significance
Poseidon honored with annual seaside festival in ancient Greece; in Italy, the First Feast of Saint Lucia held.
Saints' day: Crispina of Tagora (d. 304); Justinian (6th century AD); Christina of Markyate (c.1097–c.1161); Galgano (c.1140–81).

Flamboyant and daring, George Armstrong Custer was a headstrong U.S. Army general, known to the Sioux as "Son of the Morning Star" because of his deadly surprise dawn raids. Epitomizing both the virtues and vices of the December 5 personality, Custer was excitable, original and sometimes brilliant, but refused to heed advice—ultimately, at the 1876 Battle of Little Bighorn, at the expense of his own life, and many of his soldiers'.

Planetary Influences
Ruling planet: Jupiter.
Second decan: Personal planet is Mars.

♃ ♂

Sacred and Cultural Significance
National day of Finland.
Saint's day: Nicholas (4th century AD), patron saint of children, apothecaries, fishermen, merchants, pawnbrokers, perfumiers and sailors.

Independent and unconventional, Susanna Moodie, who was born in England in 1803, lived in Canada for most of her adult life as a pioneer and writer whose literary and personal influence resonates strongly today. Like many who share her birthdate, she spurned convention and went her own way, channeling her intellectual abilities with great focus. Her personality and outlook enliven the pages of her best-known work, the autobiographical Roughing It in the Bush: or, Life in Canada *(1852).*

DECEMBER 6

Perhaps the primary personal characteristics manifested by those born on this day are their concurrently perceptive and rational ways of looking at the world. In many respects they may be compared to scientists (which, indeed, many may decide to become), for they assume a somewhat clinical approach to collecting available data, assessing it objectively, and then identifying areas that are in need of improvement or change before formulating original theories for advancement. This talent for impartial evaluation and forward-planning is not only applicable to the scientific sphere, but may also be employed to great effect in many other professions, including those related to commerce, as well as to political, sporting and even artistic ventures, in which imaginative reinterpretations of existing conventions can have startlingly successful results. Because they are themselves convinced of the veracity of their convictions, having submitted them to exhaustive examination before reaching their conclusions, December 6 individuals typically seek to enlist the support of those around them in their promotion, and, as gifted organizers, have the potential to spearhead highly motivated and smoothly operating teams.

Others regard their solid commitment to their often extremely unusual—perhaps, in the eyes of more conventional types, even radical—causes with awed admiration. Yet since the ultimate goal of those born on this day is to achieve concrete results, and because they are furthermore not above employing coercive tactics if they feel that their progress is being willfully hindered (and particularly so for the men born on this day), they may not always inspire feelings of affection—even if their aims are intended to benefit others. Their preoccupation with their intellectual interests, along with their well-meaning propensity for pointing out any perceived failings on the part of others, may lead them to stand somewhat apart from those around them, a tendency that—despite their genuine concern for their loved ones—may not always augur well for domestic harmony.

VIRTUES: Blessed with highly developed intellectual qualities of clear thinking, objectivity and progressiveness, those born on this day are adept at evaluating concepts and systems and devising strategies for improving them. Natural leaders, their energy and determination contribute to their successes.
VICES: December 6 people tend to brook no argument or obstacles to their progress, which may cause them to disregard the finer feelings or doubts of others. This focused approach may be useful in attaining their goals, but costly to the goodwill of those around them.
VERDICT: In order to avoid alienating others, these individuals would be advised to weigh their aggressive approach against the danger of engendering animosity. Developing more tact and consideration should help them to achieve better balance.

On This Day
Famous Births: King Henry VI of England (1421); George Monck, Duke of Albemarle (1608); Warren Hastings (1732); Joseph Louis Gay-Lussac (1778); Susanna Moodie (1803); John Brown (1816); Charles Martin Hall (1863); William S. Hart (1870); Joyce Kilmer (1886); Will Hay (1888); Dion Fortune (1890); Osbert Sitwell (1892); Ira Gershwin (1896); Agnes Moorehead (1906); Cyril Washbrook (1914); Dave Brubeck (1920); Wally Cox (1924); Don King (1932); David Ossman (1936); Tom Hulce and Will Shriner (1953); Steven Wright (1955).

Significant Events and Anniversaries: December 6 is a day auspicious for pioneering, as seen when: Genoese navigator Christopher Columbus became the first European to discover Hispaniola (now Haiti and the Dominican Republic) (1492); and U.S. scientist Thomas Alva Edison made the first recording of a human voice (1877). Also a day that highlights the promotion of new causes, December 6 commemorates the Austrian government's unprecedented action in introducing a state educational system (1774); Finland's declaration of independence from Russia, then also in the throes of revolution (1917); and the twenty-six southern Irish counties self-government and dominion status from Britain (1921).

DECEMBER 7

December 7 people are especially notable for daring to be different, a propensity that is due not to attention-seeking (although this usually inevitably follows) but to their great originality and enjoyment of adventurous forays into the unknown. These individuals seek knowledge and experience beyond society's conventional norms, a predisposition that is influenced by their ability to absorb and assess information and to uncover truths that are as yet obscure. With the Sagittarian qualities of intellectual curiosity and an original turn of mind, they possess pioneering—even leadership—potential. Maintaining their freedom of thought and action is vital to their well-being: they feel intellectually and emotionally stifled if forced to conform to others' mores. They are well suited to professions in which they can act independently, including science and the arts.

Despite their tendency to stand apart from the crowd, those born on this day are not true loners, for they feel a strong sense of responsibility for, those around them, a propensity that is even more pronounced in the women born on this day. Their questing outlook on the world instills tolerance, but they will stand up for their strongest convictions—humanitarian principles, for instance. While their inherent restlessness leads them to investigate new issues, people and places with great enthusiasm, they are reliable and loyal people and are devoted to their friends, partners and families, who in turn cherish them for their benevolent and affectionate qualities.

VIRTUES: December 7 people are inquisitive and unconventional types. Attracted by the original and unusual, they have the insight, energy and courage to pursue their interests and visions despite the doubts expressed by less imaginative detractors. They also manifest sincere concern for the welfare of others.
VICES: Their lively curiosity and innate resistance to conforming may cause these individuals to live on the fringes of society, single-mindedly investigating their interests to the exclusion of "mundane" concerns, often becoming emotionally isolated.
VERDICT: Those born on this day should moderate their tendency to cut themselves off from the "real world" by grounding themselves in the emotional bonds that are vital to their happiness. Mutually enriching relationships will help them to realize their full potential and bring them greater fulfillment.

On This Day

Famous Births: Gian Lorenzo Bernini (1598); Theodor Schwann (1810); Pietro Mascagni (1863); Willa Sibert Cather (1876); Joyce Cary (1888); Eli Wallach (1915); Ted Knight (1923); Mario Soares (1924); Noam Chomsky (1928); Ellen Burstyn (1932); Harry Chapin (1942); Gregg Allman and Johnny Bench (1947); Priscilla Barnes and Larry Bird (1956); Ed Hall (1958).

Significant Events and Anniversaries: This is a day that highlights innovative achievements, as was reflected in theatrical settings when: the Theatre Royal, Britain's first opera house, opened in London (1732); and British collaborators W.S. Gilbert and Arthur Sullivan's comic opera *The Gondoliers* was first staged (1889). Leadership qualities are also indicated on December 7, when: twenty-four-year-old Tory politician William Pitt the Younger became Britain's youngest prime minister (1783); and British prime minister Herbert Asquith was replaced by the more dynamic David Lloyd George as the head of a wartime coalition government (1916). December 7 also emphasizes unusual strength of conviction, even in the face of stiff opposition, as was demonstrated on this day when: pro-Octavian Roman orator Cicero was executed for his attacks on Mark Antony (43 BC); and French marshal Michael Ney was executed for treason for failing to arrest Napoleon on the latter's return from Elba and fighting with him at the Battle of Waterloo (1815). And, on a day that is cogoverned by the martial planet, Japanese bombers destroyed much of the U.S. Pacific fleet at Pearl Harbor, Hawaii, killing over 2,000 U.S. servicemen and precipitating the nation's entry into World War II (1941).

Planetary Influences
Ruling planet: Jupiter.
Second decan: Personal planet is Mars.

Sacred and Cultural Significance
Haloia of Demeter honored in ancient Greece.
Saints' day: Ambrose (339–97), patron saint of bee-keepers and bishops; Diuma (d. 658).

Gian Lorenzo Bernini, whose exquisite Daphne *(1622–24) is pictured below, was an outstanding Baroque sculptor, architect and painter. The son of Florentine sculptor Pietro Bernini, he was born on December 7, 1598, and true to his birth influences, developed a style quite distinct from his father's—and any previous sculptor's. His sculpture is notable for its realistic detail and passionate expression, as seen in his most famous work,* The Ecstasy of St. Teresa *(1645–52), while his architectural works include the piazza of St. Peter's Basilica, Rome.*

DECEMBER 8

Planetary Influences
Ruling planet: Jupiter.
Second decan: Personal planet is Mars.

Sacred and Cultural Significance
Amaterasu honored at Shinto temples in Japan; the Festival of Neith celebrated in Egypt to honor the Earth goddess Delta.
Saints' day: The Immaculate Conception of the Blessed Virgin Mary (d. 1st century AD), patron saint of mothers, nuns and virgins; Budoc (6th century AD), patron saint of Budock and Budoc Vean, Cornwall, and St. Budeaux, Devon, England.

With the warlike influence of the planet Mars at the fore, December 8 marks the anniversary of President Franklin D. Roosevelt's 1941 declaration of war on Japan, following the previous day's devastating attack on Pearl Harbor, Hawaii.

December 8 individuals are passionate people, driven by their compulsion to live life to the full. Extraordinarily active in every respect, they often show intense emotional and sensual responses, throwing themselves wholeheartedly into any new venture or relationship that promises stimulation. Indeed, these individuals may be characterized as true idealists, engaged in a constant quest to realize their visions of perfection—intellectual, spiritual or emotional. In their search for their personal Utopia, they manifest boundless enthusiasm, determination and vigor, often inspiring others with their drive and infectious optimism. Their motives are rarely selfish, however; they have a deep-rooted desire to bring happiness to others, and many will capitalize upon their artistic affinities to become professional writers, musicians, artists and performers.

Perhaps inevitably, given their high expectations, December 8 people may never feel that they have attained their elusive goals, even when others applaud them. They may spur themselves on to even greater efforts (especially if they were born in the Chinese year of the horse), or else sink into deep depression, when disappointed with themselves or the results of their efforts. It is important that their confidence be bolstered by understanding friends and relations, whose support helps to safeguard their emotional well-being.

VIRTUES: The thoughts and actions of these vital individuals are guided by their profound desire to realize the ambitious intellectual visions that are linked with their emotional satisfaction. Imaginative, enthusiastic, driven and energetic, they immerse themselves totally in the pursuit of their ideals, inspiring and exciting the admiration of others in the process and providing lively, refreshing companionship.
VICES: Inherent in their often intangible vision of perfection is the danger that December 8 people may never find the fulfillment they seek, with the result that they may either become manic and unfocused, or grind to a metaphorical halt in stasis.
VERDICT: Maintaining a balanced outlook is crucial to the emotional well-being of those born on this day. They should try to retain a realistic perspective on their chances for success and, although they should never abandon their dreams, they should recognize that some things may not be achievable. Indulging in the simple pleasures of life, including strong relationships, will help them retain their equilibrium.

On This Day
Famous Births: Quintus Horatius Flaccus, "Horace" (65 BC); Mary, Queen of Scots (1542); Eli Whitney (1765); Bjørnstjerne Martinius Bjørnson (1832); Jean Julius Christian Sibelius (1865); Diego Rivera (1886); Bohuslav Martinu (1890); James Grover Thurber (1894); Lee J. Cobb (1911); Richard Fleischer (1916); Lucian Freud (1922); Sammy Davis Jr. (1925); Maximilian Schell (1930); Flip Wilson (1933); David Carradine (1936); James MacArthur (1937); James Galway (1939); Geoff Hurst (1941); Jim Morrison (1943); Kim Basinger (1953); Teri Hatcher (1964); Sinead O'Connor (1966).

Significant Events and Anniversaries: This day emphasizes the most elevated of visions, as shown when: Pope Pius IX proclaimed the Immaculate Conception of the Virgin Mary a Roman Catholic dogma (1854); British engineer Isambaard Kingdom Brunel's landmark Clifton Suspension Bridge, spanning the River Avon in Bristol, was officially opened (1864); and U.S and Soviet premiers Ronald Reagan and Mikhail Gorbachev signed an agreement paving the way for the I.N.F. (Intermediate-range Nuclear Forces) Treaty the following year, to eliminate the threat of nuclear weapons (1987). December 8 is subject to the influence of the planet Mars, and its confrontational tendencies were highlighted when: U.S. fighter John C. Heenan and the English pugilist Tom King contested the world's first international heavyweight boxing championship in Woodhurst, England (1863); a British naval force sank four German vessels during World War I's Battle of the Falkland Islands (1914); and John Lennon was murdered (1980).

DECEMBER 9

Whether or not they present a physically dashing figure to the world, those born on this day are gripped by the most original and ambitious of visions—dreams in which they envisage themselves making a substantial and inspirational contribution to the greater good. Blessed with soaringly imaginative minds (which are as much influenced by their emotional orientation to others as by their more abstract, intellectual propensities), as well as the more rational capacity to identify faults or failings in existing systems or concepts, December 9 people possess true pioneering potential. Utilizing both their intuition and their clear-sighted perspicacity, they have an innate ability to identify what is lacking or wrong in the lives of those around them, and a concomitant urge to remedy the situation. And in pursuing their ambitions they draw upon their prodigious vigor, organizational and technical skills, along with their unwavering fixity of purpose. The nature of their aims varies: some will advance within the political or scientific spheres, while others choose such artistic media as music, literature or drama.

Active concern also characterizes the interpersonal relationships of December 9 individuals, with colleagues, family and the larger community. They do their utmost to safeguard the emotional and physical well-being of others. Inherent in such an involved approach, however, is the tendency to control, and others may reject or resent their advice.

VIRTUES: December 9 people are fueled by an all-encompassing, albeit dualistic, urge to enlighten, motivate or otherwise assist the advancement of those around them by implementing their original and progressive visions. Fundamentally idealistic individuals, they are personally stimulated by the challenge of effecting wide-ranging improvements within human society.
VICES: Those born on this day are so intent on playing a leading role in the lives of those around them, and are, moreover, so certain of the rectitude of their opinions and approaches, that they have a tendency to disregard the right of others to profess and follow their own convictions—in short, in seeking to offer help in accordance with their principles, they may ignore manifestations of the very individuality that they themselves defend so jealously.
VERDICT: If they are to enjoy mutually open and honest relationships with their nearest and dearest, these individuals should try to moderate their propensity for firmly shepherding their loved ones in the direction that they adjudge the best. They should therefore seek to accept and understand differing viewpoints and approaches and find ways of reconciling these with their own methodologies and visions.

On This Day

Famous Births: John Milton (1608); Claude Louis Bertholet (1748); Emile Waldteufel (1837); George Grossmith (1847); Joel Chandler Harris (1848); Clarence Birdseye (1886); Beatrice Harrison (1892); Dolores Gomez Ibarruri (1895); Emmett Kelly (1898); "Rab" Butler and Margaret Hamilton (1902); Douglas Fairbanks Jr. (1909); Elisabeth Schwarzkopf (1915); Kirk Douglas (1916); Redd Foxx (1922); Dina Merrill (1925); Dick Van Patten (1928); John Cassavetes and Bob Hawke (1929); Buck Henry (1930); Judi Dench (1934); Deacon Jones (1938); Beau Bridges (1941); Billy Bremner and Dick Butkus (1942); Joan Armatrading (1950); John Malkovich (1953); Donny Osmond (1957); Jakob Dylon and Allison Smith (1969); David Kersh (1970).

Significant Events and Anniversaries: On a day that indicates inherent leadership potential, the reformist Whig politician William Gladstone became Britain's prime minister (1868). The artistic talent highlighted by this day was reflected when the German composer Richard Strauss's first opera *Salome* had its premiere (1905). The determined promotion of autonomous principles is a further feature of December 9, on which the eastern African country of Tanganyika gained its independence from Britain (1961) and, on which in the following year, it pronounced itself a republic (1962). And, finally, on a day that is cogoverned by the warring planet of Mars, Israeli soldiers launched an assault on Palestinian refugees camped at Jabaliya in the Gaza Strip; the resultant deaths heralded the anti-Israeli "intifada" movement (1987).

Planetary Influences
Ruling planet: Jupiter.
Second decan: Personal planet is Mars.

♃ ♂

Sacred and Cultural Significance
National day of Tanzania; in Mexico, the Fiesta of the Mother of Health honors the healing goddess Tonantzin.
Saint's day: Wolfeius (11th century AD).

On this day of leadership potential, when the influences of Jupiter and Mars bestow a heady dose of success and power, William Ewart Gladstone (pictured below) became prime minister of Britain in 1868.

Planetary Influences
Ruling planet: Jupiter.
Second decan: Personal planet is Mars.

♃ ♂

Sacred and Cultural Significance
Purification rites held by members
of the Inuit tribe.
Saint's day: Eulalia of Merida (d. c.304).

*On December 10, 1869, Wyoming earned
its future nickname, "Equality State," when
the territory's women became the first in the
United States to win the right to vote. This day
favors social reform and communal progress.*

DECEMBER 10

The quiet and controlled demeanor that characterizes those born on this day often masks their steadily burning determination to realize their ideals. Deep thinkers, December 10 individuals tend to be concerned with furthering human knowledge—exploring abstract, academic or spiritual concepts, instituting scientific or artistic advances, or reforming social systems. Blessed with objective and balanced intellects, they are able to make informed and soundly reasoned assessments when approaching major decisions and formulate effective plans. Indeed, their organizational skills are second to none, and they may seek careers as event managers, in politics or in other forms of community service. Others are attracted to the opportunities inherent in the academic world.

Since their endeavors are intended to result in benefits for the greater good, rather than simply to satisfy selfish ambitions, and because of their initiative and focus, those born on this day make gifted leaders. They may well be demanding, but never expect more from others than they themselves give, a propensity that is redoubled if they were also born in the Chinese year of the rat. Sometimes accused of insensitivity, they are actively concerned with the welfare of their friends, families and coworkers, but do not often express themselves. Others generally admire and respect their selfless motivations and drive, but even their nearest associates may feel excluded from sharing their inner worlds of emotions and dreams, which they tend to keep hidden (particularly if they are men) beneath their disciplined exterior.

VIRTUES: Astute observers of people and situations, with keen analytical powers, those born on this day are progressive. They utilize their knowledge and organizational skills in working toward the causes they believe in.
VICES: December 10 individuals throw all their personal resources into the single-minded pursuit of their tasks, a propensity that may lead them to sublimate their emotional needs (as well as those of others) to the drive for achievement.
VERDICT: It is important for their holistic well-being that these people maintain a healthy emotional/intellectual balance in their lives, and especially that they do not sacrifice the rewards of simple pleasures with friends, partners and children on the altar of work.

On This Day
Famous Births: Felice Orsini (1819); César Franck (1822); Emily Dickinson (1830); Melvil Dewey (1851); E.H. Shepard (1879); Harold Alexander, Earl Alexander of Tunis (1891); William Plomer (1903); Olivier Messiaen (1908); Chet Huntley (1911); Morton Gould (1913); Dorothy Lamour (1914); Michael Manley (1924); Dan Blocker (1928); Gloria Loring (1946); Susan Dey (1952); Kenneth Branagh (1960); Jahangir Khan (1963).

Significant Events and Anniversaries: On a day on which the desire to make communal progress is highlighted: the state of Mississippi joined the U.S. Union (1817); Spain ceded Cuba to the U.S.A. as part of the terms of settlement following the Spanish-American War (1898); and, following the death of the autocratic ruler Miguel Primo de Rivera, Spanish citizens were allowed to elect their president for the first time, voting Alcalá Zamora into office (1931). Also a day that promises innovative achievements intended to benefit others, December 10 marks the anniversary of: the patenting of pneumatic tires by British engineer Robert Thompson (1845); the premiere of French dramatist Alfred Jarry's play *Ubu Roi*, a prototype Theater of the Absurd piece (1896); and the opening of the Piccadilly Circus subway in London, England (1928). Reflecting the concern with pushing forward the boundaries of human endeavor that is emphasized on December 10, this was the day on which: as stipulated in the will of the Swedish chemist Alfred Nobel, the first Nobel prizes were awarded (1901); the Polish-born physicist Marie Curie became the first female recipient of such an award, which she shared with Pierre Curie and Henri Becquerel for their investigation of radioactivity (1903); and the Soviet dissident Alexandr Solzhenitsyn received his Nobel prize for literature four years after his award was announced, after his expulsion from the U.S.S.R. (1974).

DECEMBER 11

Those born on this day often feel torn between their strong sense of social responsibility and their equally profound desire to attain happiness by indulging in their personal interests. These dual propensities can create conflict in the realm of family life. While they derive great pleasure from the company of their loved ones, they are apt to be controlling. December 11 people are often drawn to professional pursuits that challenge their intellectual qualities and are directly concerned with improving the lives of those around them—even humanity as a whole. Many are interested in systems of social regulation and feel inclined to act as the champions of the downtrodden, perhaps as humanitarian activists or politicians. Others seek to make scientific advances intended to help humanity, or to work in medical or emergency services or as mechanics or engineers.

Whatever professions they pursue, all December 11 individuals are notable for their driving energy and dedication to their causes and visions. Innate perfectionists, they demand as high a level of commitment from those around them as they themselves demonstrate, and do not easily tolerate errors or poor judgement. This level of intensity may produce remarkable results but may also backfire or have an intellectually and physically exhausting effect on everyone involved. And, despite their profound affection and concern for the well-being of those closest to them (as well as the value they in turn place on receiving their unquestioning emotional support), their elevated standards and sometimes overly active promotion of the behavioral and ethical principles that they espouse may arouse the resentment of those whose interests they have most strongly at heart.

VIRTUES: December 11 people are strongly oriented to those around them, be these their immediate circle of friends and family, their coworkers or the members of their social communities. Their concern for the welfare of others fuels their beliefs and actions, and they work with remarkable vigor and focus toward the achievement of their progressive aims.
VICES: Such is their strength of conviction and urge to actively implement the visions that inspire them, that those born on this day are in danger of ignoring or neglecting their personal prerequisites for relaxation and self-indulgence, and furthermore of denying these necessities for emotional fulfillment to those around them, propensities that may cause holistic imbalance and eventual burnout.
VERDICT: It is vital that these individuals recognize the importance of regularly taking the time to switch off from their work, both in order to recharge their mental and physical batteries and to retain a more wide-ranging sense of perspective in life. Nurturing open and easy personal relationships and showing tolerance of the minor foibles of their closest associates will reap immeasurable emotional rewards.

On This Day

Famous Births: Pope Leo X (1475); Charles Wesley (1707); David Brewster (1781); Hector Berlioz (1803); Alfred de Musset (1810); Robert Koch (1843); Fiorella Henry La Guardia (1882); Gilbert Roland (1905); Carlo Ponti (1913); Alexandr Solzhenitsyn (1918); Kenneth MacMillan (1929); Rita Moreno (1931); Donna Mills (1943); Brenda Lee (1944); Teri Garr (1949); Christina Onassis (1950); Jermaine Jackson (1954); Rider Strong (1979).

Significant Events and Anniversaries: December 11 is a day that highlights a potential conflict of interests, as was demonstrated in the realm of government when: the actively pro-Catholic sympathies of King James II of England and Scotland precipitated the "Glorious Revolution" and resulted in his forced abdication in favor of his Protestant daughter, Mary, and her husband, William of Orange (1688); and King Edward VIII renounced the British throne in order to marry the U.S. divorcée Wallis Simpson (1937). This is furthermore a day that promises technical innovations intended to benefit the greater good, as was reflected when: British inventor Edward Beran patented his design for Venetian blinds (1769); and the world's first car show, showcasing the latest automotive advances, opened in Paris (1894).

Planetary Influences
Ruling planet: Jupiter.
Second decan: Personal planet is Mars.

Sacred and Cultural Significance
In Italy, Pagans celebrate the Day of Bruma.
Saints' day: Damasus (c.304–84), patron saint of archaeologists; Daniel the Stylite (409–93).

Technical and medical advances are a feature of December 11, which marks the anniversary of the world's first dental operation performed with the aid of anesthesia, in 1844.

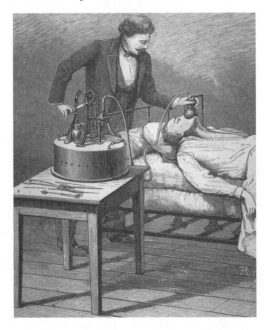

Planetary Influences
Ruling planet: Jupiter.
Third decan: Personal planet is the Sun.

♃ ☉

Sacred and Cultural Significance
National day of Kenya; Zoroastrian fire
festival held in Sada; Our Lady
of Guadelupe religious festival occurs
in Mexico.
Saints' day: Finnian of Clonard (d. 549);
Vicelin (c.1086–1154); Jane Frances
de Chantal (1572–1641).

*Combining this day's focus on communications
and new technology, Guglielmo Marconi first
demonstrated his radio on December 12, 1896.*

DECEMBER 12

★★★★★★★★★★★★★★★★★★★★★★★★★★★★★★★★★★★★★★★

Perhaps the most obvious trait of December 12 people is their tendency to express their
emotions and convictions in the public arena. Generally, they are not seeking notice for
its own sake, but in the belief that they have an important message to impart to the world—
one that will help people to progress. Highly perceptive in terms of both intellect and intuition,
their profound sense of justice causes them to react strongly to social abuses. Their attempts
to redress these are pursued with vigor and unwavering determination—even (or especially)
in the face of opposition. They make effective and popular teachers and are often successful
in marketing and sales, especially when they are promoting novel or technological products.

Although the causes that inspire December 12 people vary, all feel compelled to share them
with the world through their talent for communication, which is even more pronounced if
they were born in the Chinese year of the horse. Whether they employ verbal, literary, visual
or musical media, their ability to hold the attention of their audiences—either by shocking or
delighting—augurs well for their success. Many are aware that by opening such conduits for
discussion they will excite negative as well as positive reactions, but believe that the potential
benefits outweigh the risks, or sometimes simply cannot keep silent. The real danger, however,
is that they may forfeit their privacy—and that of others whose love and support is vital to
their emotional well-being.

VIRTUES: The thoughts and deeds of those born on this day are influenced by their strong
sense of social connection and their resultant desire to make a tangible and beneficial
contribution to the lives of others. Both intellectually and physically active, they are blessed
with the ability to identify areas in need of improvement and then communicate their remedial
visions to those around them in a truly unforgettable fashion.
VICES: Although their predilection for transmitting the essence of their beliefs and principles
to others by placing them in the public arena typically stems from the most laudable of
intentions, it may have unexpected consequences with regard to their personal lives. Once
they have converted those around them to their ideas, they may be unable to switch them
off again and may thus become frustrated by others' perceived intrusions and demands. They
may also arouse the enmity of those who disagree with them.
VERDICT: December 12 people would be well advised to carefully consider the potential
effects and repercussions of their propensity for assuming a center-stage position when seeking
to communicate their messages to a broader audience, for they may thereby—consciously
or unwittingly—open metaphorical floodgates which they may find hard to control.

On This Day
Famous Births: Samuel Hood (1724); Erasmus Darwin (1731); Carl Maria von Weber (1786);
Gustave Flaubert (1821); Edvard Munch (1863); Edward G. Robinson (1893); Fred Elizade
(1907); Frank Sinatra (1915); Joe Williams (1918); Bob Barker (1923); John Osborne (1929);
Connie Francis (1938); Dionne Warwick (1941); Cathy Rigby (1952); Sheila E. (1957); Tracy
Austin (1962); Madchen Amick (1970); Mayim Bialik (1975).

Significant Events and Anniversaries: December 12 emphasizes the desire to act in the
communal interest, as was demonstrated when: the state of Pennsylvania joined the U.S.
Union (1797); the east African country of Kenya gained its independence from Britain (1963);
and a U.S. court fined and sentenced tycoon Leona Helmsley for tax evasion (1989).
Communication skills are also highlighted on December 12, on which Italian-born physicist
Guglielmo Marconi unveiled his "wireless" (radio) to a London audience (1896), and made
the first trans-Atlantic radio communication (1901). New technology was also introduced by
German designer Hugo Junkers's innovative metal airplane on its maiden flight (1915); and
British engineer Christopher Cockerell's patent for his hovercraft design (1955). A danger
indicated by this day is that fame may turn to notoriety, as when the U.S. singer Jerry Lee
Lewis caused public outrage by marrying his thirteen-year-old cousin, Myra (1957).

DECEMBER 13

Simultaneously curious and perfectionistic, those born on this day have the potential to initiate advances notable not only for their originality, but based upon solid foundations. Their innovations utilize their highly developed powers of perception to identify gaps in knowledge and endeavor. Innately vigorous and capable of deep concentration, they seek to fill these gaps, or rectify faults that they have pinpointed. To all their ventures they bring confidence, resourcefulness and tenacity, along with meticulous attention to detail. They will thrive in any profession where their exploratory and active needs can be fulfilled, but many require a structured working environment and are especially drawn to the fields of accountancy, engineering, science and the law.

December 13 people are instinctive humanitarians, whose natural sense of justice and empathy for those in unfortunate circumstances arouse protective responses in them. Their interpersonal relationships—whether with coworkers, friends, partners or children—are also characterized by genuine interest and concern, especially in the women born on this day, although they do not tend to show their feelings openly. Dependable individuals, they usually offer carefully considered advice based on astute observations, but their desire for involvement is such that their benevolent intentions may be misinterpreted by independent loved ones as attempts to mold or control them.

VIRTUES: Those born on this day are socially responsible individuals who are naturally predisposed to contributing toward the greater good. Optimistic, brisk, rational and positive types, they draw upon their considerable personal resources, including their practical skills, to formulate and put into place ingenious, yet extremely effective, conceptual or technical advances.

VICES: December 13 people have a predilection for involving themselves fully in every aspect of their lives, both in terms of their professional activities and in their personal relationships, a tendency that carries the dual risk that they may thus run themselves ragged and neglect their need for self-care and relaxation, and that their concerted attempts to solve the problems of their nearest and dearest may be regarded as interfering.

VERDICT: It is important that these individuals moderate their tendency to apply their problem-solving abilities to the personal objectives or difficulties of those who may prefer to be left to their own devices. They should recognize that personal development (others' as well as their own) requires taking responsibility for one's own actions and acknowledging rather than suppressing emotional responses.

On This Day

Famous Births: William Hamilton (1730); Heinrich Heine (1797); Ernst Werner von Siemens (1816); Alvin Cullum York (1887); John Piper (1903); Laurens van der Post (1906); Archie Moore (1913); Alan Bullock (1914); Balthazar Johannes Vorster (1915); Dick van Dyke (1925); Christopher Plummer (1927); John Davidson (1941); Howard Brenton (1942); Ted Nugent (1948); Paula Wilcox (1949); John Francome (1952); Jim Davidson (1954).

Significant Events and Anniversaries: A day that highlights exploration, December 13 marks the anniversary of: English seaman Francis Drake's departure from Plymouth, England, in his ship the *Golden Hind,* on a trip that would culminate in his circumnavigation of the world (1577); and the first sighting of New Zealand by a European navigator, the Dutchman Abel Tasman (1642). December 13 also promises remarkably original technical innovations, as was confirmed when: inventor Percy Everitt patented the world's first weighing machine activated by coins (1884); and New Yorker Italo Marcione registered his patent for ice-cream cones (1903). The social changes emphasized on December 13 may be manifested in warfare: this was the day on which the World War II naval Battle of the River Plate began, when the British cruisers H.M.S. *Ajax, Achilles* and *Exeter* forced the German battleship *Graf Spee* to flee to the waters off Montevideo, Uruguay (1939).

Planetary Influences
Ruling planet: Jupiter.
Third decan: Personal planet is the Sun.

Sacred and Cultural Significance
St. Lucia's Day in Sweden.
Saints' day: Lucy (d. 304), patron saint of visually impaired people and eye diseases; Judoc (d. c.668); Edburga of Minster (d. 751).

On this day of exploration and resourcefulness, Sir Francis Drake embarked on his famous round-the-world voyage in 1577.

Planetary Influences
Ruling planet: Jupiter.
Third decan: Personal planet is the Sun.

♃ ☉

Sacred and Cultural Significance
Saints' day: Fingar (d. c.455); Nicasius (5th century AD); Venantius Fortunatus (c.530–c.610); Hybald (7th century AD); John of the Cross (1542–91), patron saint of mystics, mystical theologians and poets.

Norwegian Roald Amundsen (pictured below) led his team to the world's last frontier, the South Pole, becoming on December 14, 1911, the first to accomplish this remarkable achievement. Their arrival reflects the discipline and determination starred by this day, and occurred when the Sun, bestowing the day's energy, is at its strongest in Antarctica.

Others cannot help but admire the aura of controlled energy, capability and efficiency exuded by those born on this day, and, indeed, December 14 people are extremely active types who cannot bear to stand idle when there are issues to explore, things to do and progress to be made. Blessed with rational and yet imaginative intellects, mental and physical vigor, and strong organizational skills, they approach all their endeavors with enthusiasm and determination. Their decisiveness makes them natural leaders, and they have a talent for directing others with a firm but benevolent hand, frequently balancing their high expectations with a dash of humor. They will thrive in any profession where they are allowed the freedom of action to work toward their objectives unhindered by others' constraints (which is not to say that are not rigorously disciplined—to the contrary) and they are therefore especially suited to careers where research and development play an integral part—within the academic, manufacturing or pharmaceutical spheres, for example.

Although they are sociable people who display enormous goodwill toward those around them, in many respects those born on this day are self-contained and self-reliant types whose potential for fulfillment lies in their individual quests for discovery and progress. Thus although others frequently turn to them for advice and support—and are never turned away—they may feel torn between their sense of social responsibility and their profound desire to pursue their personal interests undisturbed by the demands of those around them. It is important therefore that their friends and relations respect their need for privacy and space, and that they in turn try to find a happy medium between their internal and external orientations.

VIRTUES: December 14 people are intellectually astute and imaginative individuals who are predisposed toward realizing their progressive aims as directly and efficiently as possible. Blessed with remarkable energy they work toward their goals with a sure sense of purpose and determination, their disciplined approach auguring well for their success.
VICES: Those born on this day derive personal satisfaction from addressing stimulating challenges but, because they are talented problem-solvers and inspire confidence in others through their decisive and positive approach to everything they undertake, they have a tendency to assume the burden of responsibility for addressing the dilemmas and difficulties of others. They may become frustrated by such diversions from their true interests, while others often find them intimidating.
VERDICT: It is crucial for their emotional well-being that these people find a working balance between the potentially isolating pursuit of their individual interests and their innate, and often unrelated, desire to lend their assistance to those around them. They should therefore take the time for introspection, identify the priorities that are most significant to them in terms of their eventual fulfillment, and try to concentrate on these.

On This Day
Famous Births: Michel de Nostraedame, "Nostradamus" (1503); Tycho Brahe (1546); Roger Fry (1866); John Christie (1882); King George VI of Britain (1895); Spike Jones (1911); Morey Amsterdam (1914); Shirley Jackson (1919); Clark Terry (1920); Charlie Rich (1932); Lee Remick (1935); Jeanette Scott (1938); Patty Duke, Michael Ovitz and Stan Smith (1946); James Horan (1954); Alain Loreieux (1957); Chelsea Noble (1964).

Significant Events and Anniversaries: This is a day that indicates the tenacious pursuit of unusually original visions, and marks the anniversary of: German physicist Max Planck's revelation of his quantum theory, following years of work on radiated energy (1900); the pioneering feat of four Norwegian explorers led by Roald Amundsen, who became the first people to trek to the South Pole (1911); and the transmission of the first detailed pictures of the planet Venus, sent back to Earth by the U.S. spacecraft *Mariner II* (1962). December 14 is furthermore a day that highlights a sense of communal responsibility, as was reflected when Alabama joined the U.S. Union (1819).

DECEMBER 15

Those born on this day are complex personalities: on the one hand optimistic, vital and filled with benevolent feelings for those around them, and on the other possessing somewhat uncompromising, controlling and dictatorial tendencies. Blessed both with intellectual clarity—which enables them to pinpoint perceived faults and failings—and extremely logical minds, they devise straightforward plans of action. Mentally and physically active, they do not isolate themselves in a personal vacuum, but prefer to lead from the front, enlisting the support of like-minded individuals and motivating them with the help of their great personal charm. Indeed, others are attracted to these natural leaders on account of their invigorating enthusiasm, "can-do" attitude and no-nonsense approach.

Many of those born on this day have the ability to develop real expertise in the fields that interest them, including business, new technology and corporate management. Whatever career they choose, however, their ultimate objective is concerned with enlightening, educating or making their mark on a broader public. Their intentions toward others are thus of the most positive variety, but they should nevertheless beware of seeking to control those around them at any cost, however justified they feel themselves to be. This is particularly pertinent within their personal relationships, for by trying to direct the thoughts and actions of their loved ones they may inadvertently be suppressing their need for individual autonomy, and they may lose their receptiveness to other ideas and perspectives.

VIRTUES: December 15 individuals are blessed with incisive and forward-thinking intellects, as well as prodigious energy, drive and strong practical talents. Personally stimulated by challenge, they also have the necessary charisma to persuade others as to the correctness of their viewpoints, and thus to their quests to achieve progress, whether intended to benefit the greater good or for their personal gain.
VICES: Those born on this day are not given to procrastination, indecision or inactivity, and since they possess remarkable strength of conviction, have a tendency to become impatient with, and even intolerant of, those who do not fall readily into line with their beliefs and approaches, a propensity that may cost them the goodwill of possible professional allies, as well as of those closest to them.
VERDICT: These people are both goal-oriented and desirous of exerting a positive influence upon around them, but in working toward their aims they may alienate those whom they wish to convince or assist by means of their assertive and uncompromising *modi operandi*. They should therefore try to respect and understand the viewpoints of others and strive to accommodate them rather than rejecting them out of hand.

On This Day

Famous Births: Nero (AD 37); George Romney (1734); Gustave Eiffel (1832); Antoine Henri Becquerel (1852); Lazarus Ludwig Zamenhof (1859); Rudolf von Laban (1879); Maxwell Anderson (1888); John Paul Getty (1892); Maurice Wilkins (1916); Ahmed Ben Bella (1918); Alan Freed (1922); Tim Conway (1933); Edna O'Brien (1936); Dave Clark (1942); Don Johnson (1949); Helen Slater (1965).

Significant Events and Anniversaries: This is a day that promises pioneering technical innovations, as was reflected when the commercial production of nylon thread was instituted at a Delaware plant (1939); U.S. spacecraft *Gemini 6* and *Gemini 7* effected the first space rendezvous while in orbit (1965); and a subsidiary of Philips/M.C.A., Magnavision, unveiled its revolutionary Laservision video disks (1978). The promotion of uncompromising visions is further highlighted by December 15, on which: Sioux Chief Sitting Bull was killed while resisting arrest for his alleged part in inciting tribal rebellion (1890); Boer forces under General Louis Botha defeated their British foe, led by General Redvers Buller, at the Battle of Colenso during the Boer War (1899); and French troops launched a major assault on German lines during World War I's Battle of Verdun (1916).

Planetary Influences
Ruling planet: Jupiter.
Third decan: Personal planet is the Sun.

Sacred and Cultural Significance
The Yule Child honored in Puerto Rico with the religious festival Navidades.
Saint's day: Offa of Essex (d. c.709).

A native of Lancashire, British portrait painter George Romney (pictured below) showed the decisiveness of his December 15 birthdate by moving to London, where he became famous for his studies of Lady Hamilton and other members of the British nobility.

DECEMBER 16

* *

Planetary Influences
Ruling planet: Jupiter.
Third decan: Personal planet is the Sun.

Sacred and Cultural Significance
Members of the Hopi tribe celebrate the Soyal ceremony; in Mexico, the religious festival Posadas honors the Yule Child.
Saint's day: Bean (dates unknown).

Under the favorable influences of December 16's vision, confidence and determined strength, parliamentarian general Oliver Cromwell, who had played a major role in defeating the royalists in the Civil War, was made lord protector of England, proclaiming a reforming agenda and religious tolerance.

Blessed with original imaginations and the desire to explore concepts that less visionary types would condemn as unfeasible, December 16 people are profound thinkers with the potential to make significant contributions. They are also articulate and persuasive and tend to make strong first impressions on others. Their logical and objective approach to new issues precludes any tendency to succumb to flights of fancy. While open-minded enough to consider a wide variety of opinions and possibilities, they subject the ideas that attract their interest to rigorous examination. Once convinced of the validity of their theses, they pursue their goals with vigor, concentration and tenacity, rarely deflected by the opposition they might encounter. In many respects they therefore present somewhat solitary figures, for although they possess the courage of their convictions, they may find themselves isolated from others by their need to pursue their own agenda.

Those born on this day will flourish when unconstrained by society's norms and conventions, and will almost certainly feel stifled within corporate structures. They are better suited for careers as academic or scientific researchers and innovators in such problem-solving fields as software development or production management. Their ultimate purpose is usually unselfish and they often have a social concern that may not be immediately apparent. Their deep affection for those closest to them sometimes appears compromised by their drive to achieve, but they are capable of forming loyal partnerships.

VIRTUES: Their imaginative intellectual qualities endow December 16 individuals with a deep affinity for ideas so radical that others may doubt their feasibility. But because they are logical, meticulous and determined, they may pioneer far-reaching innovations.
VICES: An inherent danger in the nature of their unusually progressive interests, and their single-minded tenacity in pursuing the visions of whose possibilities they themselves are firmly convinced, is that those born on this day may isolate themselves from others in order to satisfy their career aspirations or personal interestes undisturbed by the distractions engendered by other people's doubts or demands.
VERDICT: While they should never abandon their intellectual visions, it is crucial that these individuals should safeguard their emotional equilibrium and not cut themselves off completely from the society of those—especially their nearest and dearest—who could both encourage them in their endeavors and certainly provide them with an enriching and supportive additional dimension to their lives.

On This Day
Famous Births: Catherine of Aragon (1485); Gebhard Berecht von Blücher (1742); Ludwig van Beethoven (1770); Jane Austen (1775); Johann Wilhelm Ritter (1776); King Leopold I of the Belgians (1790); Edward Emerson Barnard (1857); Jack Hobbs and Zoltán Kodály (1882); Noël Coward (1899); V.S. Pritchett (1900); Margaret Mead (1901); Arthur C. Clarke (1917); Liv Ullmann (1938); Leslie Stahl (1941); Steven Bochco (1943); Benny Andersson (1946); Ben Cross (1947); Billy Gibbons (1949); Joel Garner (1953); William "Refrigerator" Perry and Melanie Smith (1962); Michael McCary (1971).

Significant Events and Anniversaries: The potential achievement of radical ambitions was confirmed in a variety of areas on December 16 when: Puritan Parliamentary leader Oliver Cromwell became Lord Protector—head of state—of England (1653); a party of American colonists led by Samuel Adams donned Mohican costumes and flung tea imported from Britain into Boston Harbor to protest taxation without representation, paving the way to the Revolutionary War (1773); the *Charlotte Jane*, the first British ship carrying colonists to New Zealand, arrived at Lyttleton (1850); Antonio López de Santa Anna (of Alamo fame) assumed leadership of Mexico (1853); Marthinus Pretorius pronounced a Boer republic in southern Africa's Transvaal province (1856); and Indonesian nationalist Achmed Sukarno became president of his country (1949).

DECEMBER 17

Their twin desire to effect concrete results and significant progress may be the primary characteristic of December 17 people, who are go-getters and have little patience with those who prefer to ponder interminably rather than make a decision. This is not to say that they are unthinking individuals whose urge for action leads them to throw themselves impulsively into a task without having first properly thought it through—on the contrary—rather that those born on this day are blessed with the ability quickly to sum up and assess the inherent components of a concept or situation and then rapidly to devise straightforward strategies with which to effectively move forward. Vigorous, practical and progressive types, they undertake nothing half-heartedly. This uncompromisingly direct attitude characterizes their approach to all their endeavors, and also defines their preferred stance within their interpersonal relationships, often with mixed success. Although these natural leaders have a gift for firing the enthusiasm of, directing and organizing, their colleagues, their attempts to marshal their nearest and dearest along the lines that they are convinced are the best (especially if they are men) may not always be appreciated. They may also find it difficult to embark on new relationships, as they can often appear unapproachable and are rarely demonstrative, although they are sociable, cheerful and ebullient.

Despite their somewhat abrupt manner, however, December 17 individuals feel a strong and benevolent sense of connection with, and responsibility for, their families, friends, coworkers and others. They will readily spring to the defense of their loved ones and are dependable allies. Their capacity to pinpoint faults within situations and remedy them suits them well for management careers; they may also be attracted to the business sphere or other fields in which they can make their mark on the wider world.

VIRTUES: December 17 people are vital, energetic and resolute. Their ability to identify areas in need of improvement and talent for devising plans of action gives them pioneering potential. Their magnetic personalities and orientation toward others endow them with high leadership abilities.
VICES: Because they are so decisive and active, those born on this day have a propensity for stepping in and taking charge of people or situations that they perceive to be foundering or directionless. This tendency can arouse resentment, especially in those closest to them, who may feel that their autonomy is threatened.
VERDICT: If they are to enjoy harmonious interpersonal relations, these people need to curb their well-meaning urge to control the thoughts and actions of their loved ones. Developing greater respect and tolerance for the right of others to express their individuality will contribute to mutually happy and relaxed relationships.

On This Day

Famous Births: Prince Rupert of the Rhine (1619); Domenico Cimarosa (1749); Humphry Davy (1778); Joseph Henry (1797); John Greenleaf Whittier (1807); Ford Madox Ford (1873); Mackenzie King (1874); Robertson Hare (1891); Arthur Fiedler (1894); Erskine Caldwell and Ray Noble (1903); Willard Frank Libby (1908); William Safire (1929); Bob Guccione (1930); Tommy Steele (1936); Kerry Packer (1937); Peter Snell (1938); Bob Ojeda (1957).

Significant Events and Anniversaries: Leadership qualities are highlighted on December 17, on which: People's Party leader Zulfiqar Ali Bhutto became Pakistan's first prime minister (1971); and National Reconstruction Party politician Fernando Collor was elected president of Brazil (1989). This day's link to artistic and technical achievements was demonstrated when: English author Charles Dickens's work *A Christmas Carol* was published (1843); the Russian Imperial Ballet premiered composer Pyotr Ilyich Tchaikovsky's *The Nutcracker* (1892); U.S. aviation pioneers Orville and Wilbur Wright became the first to fly a powered airplane (1903); and the U.S.-built Douglas Dakota (DC-3) made its maiden flight (1935).

Planetary Influences
Ruling planet: Jupiter.
Third decan: Personal planet is the Sun.

Sacred and Cultural Significance
In ancient Rome, Saturn honored.
Saint's day: Lazarus of Bethany (d. 1st century AD).

On this pioneering and go-getting day in 1903, Orville and Wilbur Wright made aviation history when they achieved the first powered, controlled flight, at Kill Devil Hills, North Carolina. The flight lasted 12 seconds, and another—later on the same day—lasted 59 seconds and covered a distance of 852 feet (260 meters).

Planetary Influences
Ruling planet: Jupiter.
Third decan: Personal Planet is the Sun.

Sacred and Cultural Significance
The birth of Diev and rebirth of the Sun celebrated in Latvia; the Eponalia feast held in Ancient Rome.
Saints' day: Mawnan (dates unknown); Flannan (7th century AD); Samthann (d. 739); Winnibald (d. 761).

American filmmaker Steven Spielberg exemplifies the qualities signified by this birthdate, including imagination, daring and the ability to communicate his visions, and his unconventional, free-thinking traits are reinforced by his having several planets in Sagittarius. His powerful films seize and hold an audience, as seen in Raiders of the Lost Ark *(1981),* E.T. *(1982),* Jurassic Park *(1993) and others that have been uniquely popular and successful. Born in the Chinese year of the pig, he has the rare creativity and passionate commitment of that sign.*

DECEMBER 18

Blessed with soaring imaginations, December 18 individuals are not only fascinated by conceptual visions that those of a less original turn of mind might dismiss, but are also determined to translate their dreams into reality. Even from childhood those born on this day may often have formulated a game plan for life, that revolves around the specific interests that absorb their attention. They remain resolutely focused, regardless of the vicissitudes they may experience, the tempting diversions that may present themselves, or even the doubts of those to whom they have confided their aspirations. Always keeping their ultimate objectives firmly in mind, they work meticulously toward their achievement, displaying resourcefulness, ingenuity, and practical and organizational talents in the process. And because they are rational and clear-sighted individuals, the elevated aims that inspire them are usually realistic, although concentration and sheer hard work will be required for their eventual success. These qualities inspire the admiration of those around them, and their effectiveness in terms of results cannot but win over even the most hardened of skeptics.

Those born on this day will flourish in any profession where they can retain their autonomy in the pursuit of their guiding visions and are therefore better suited to careers that allow for such independence, perhaps those encompassed by science and technology, the arts or the sporting arena. Innately resistant to toeing the corporate line, December 18 people are nevertheless charismatic leaders, a gift that, when combined with their ability to maintain a broader view, equips them admirably as politicians. Despite the respect they inspire, and their goodwill to those around them, those who seek more intimate relationships with December 18 people (men especially) may find it hard to access the emotional side of their characters.

VIRTUES: These individuals are not only visionary types who are single-mindedly focused on attaining their ambitious, long-term goals, but are also extremely practical and resourceful people who back their ideas with soundly constructed and well-organized support systems. Their technical accomplishments, vigor and tenacity further enhance their potential, while their easy confidence and sunny natures make them highly popular.
VICES: Those born on this day are so intent on realizing their aims that they will brook no distractions or opposition to their pursuit, a tendency that may promise a successful conclusion, but may have more negative emotional consequences if they deem the nurturing of strong personal liaisons to be unnecessary to their personal fulfillment.
VERDICT: It is crucial that December 18 people do not cut themselves off emotionally from those closest to them by becoming totally preoccupied with their work. Relaxation, the enjoyment of simple pleasures and receiving and returning the love and support of others will help them retain a healthy equilibrium, providing them with an enriching dimension to their lives and also making them more effective professionally.

On This Day
Famous Births: Charles Wesley (1707); Joseph Grimaldi (1779); William Frederick Yeames (1835); Joseph John Thomson (1856); Francis Thompson (1859); Edward MacDowell and Lionel Monckton (1861); Hector Hugh Monro, "Saki" (1870); Paul Klee (1879); Ty Cobb (1886); Edward Howard Armstrong (1890); Christopher Fry (1907); Celia Johnson (1908); Jules Dassin (1911); Willy Brandt (1913); Betty Grable (1916); Ossie Davis (1917); Galt MacDermot (1928); Roger Smith (1932); Keith Richards (1943); Steven Spielberg (1947); Leonard Maltin (1950); Brad Pitt (1964).

Significant Events and Anniversaries: December 18 highlights the pursuit of progressive visions, as demonstrated when the state of New Jersey joined the U.S. Union (1787), and the Thirteenth Amendment to the U.S. Constitution was ratified, making slavery illegal (1865). Taking his vision to extremes, paleontologist Charles Dawson claimed he had discovered "Piltdown man," but this was subsequently exposed as a hoax (1912).

DECEMBER 19

Uncompromisingly individualistic personalities, December 19 people are natural nonconformists who refuse to be bound by what they may regard as the petty conventions of society. They have a strong attraction for what is profound and original and an equally deep dislike—even contempt—for passivity, lack of curiosity, or stodginess. Dismissive of societal norms that do not accord with their own visionary beliefs, they are not afraid to express themselves freely, even relishing the controversy they may provoke with their outspokenness—a propensity that is heightened in those who were born in the Chinese year of the dragon. However, their purpose is not negative, but stems from their desire for stimulating debate. They promote their views with passion and commitment. Among their intellectual strengths are clarity of vision and a strong sense of justice.

December 19 people are clearly unsuited to becoming cogs in corporate wheels. Their need for autonomy and exploration bodes well for their success as pioneering artists, scientists or entrepreneurs. Because many will prefer to work alone, the unconditional love and support of those closest to them is especially important. Strong bonds of affection characterize their relationships with friends, partners and family members, who in turn cherish them for their generosity and loyalty.

VIRTUES: Those independent and vigorous souls born on this day are free and original thinkers, who have a strong resistance to accepting any idea or convention unquestioningly, instead investigating, challenging, and often themselves generating innovative alternative concepts. In doing so they are fueled by their desire to illuminate, educate or otherwise further human progress; others respect and admire them for their integrity.
VICES: Given their somewhat combative intellectual approach, December 19 people are no strangers to controversy and, indeed, much prefer to provoke others into thought and action rather than to meekly accede to the status quo. There is a danger, however, that they may become almost addicted to the stimulation of adopting a contrary stance, and that they may thus play devil's advocate for the sheer fun of being perverse.
VERDICT: If they are not to drive others away and thereby alienate potential allies or those whom they wish to enlighten, it is vital that these people moderate their somewhat aggressive propensity to challenge the beliefs that others hold dear, limiting their challenges to promoting those convictions about which they feel the most strongly and otherwise seeking to effect a working compromise.

On This Day
Famous Births: William Edward Parry (1790); Albert Abraham Michelson (1852); Carter G. Woodson (1875); Grace Mildmay (1900); Ralph Richardson (1902); Leonid Ilyich Brezhnev (1906); Jean Genet (1910); Edith Piaf (1915); David Susskind (1920); Eamonn Andrews (1922); Gordon Jackson (1923); Cicely Tyson (1933); Al Kaline (1934); Tim Reid (1944); Robert Urich (1947); Jennifer Beals (1963); Alyssa Milano (1973).

Significant Events and Anniversaries: This is a day that highlights profoundly held beliefs and a concomitant willingness to oppose those who hold a contrary viewpoint, as was demonstrated when Huguenot and Catholic forces clashed at the Battle of Dreux, thus heralding the French Wars of Religion (1562). Yet December 19 also indicates the importance of pragmatic conciliation, as was illustrated when representatives of Communist China and Conservative-governed Britain signed the Treaty of Beijing, in which Britain agreed to return Hong Kong to its "motherland" in 1997, in return for China's guarantee that it would safeguard the former colony's social and economic freedom (1984). Furthermore a day that promises technical and artistic innovations, December 19 marks the anniversary of: British inventor Frederick Walton's patenting of linoleum (1863); and American musician Carl Perkin's recording of his best-known song "Blue Suede Shoes," later to become a hit for Elvis Presley (1955).

Planetary Influences
Ruling planets: Jupiter and Saturn.
Third decan: Personal planet is the Sun.
Second cusp: Sagittarius with Capricorn tendencies.

Sacred and Cultural Significance
In ancient Rome, Sabine honored and the Opalia feast held; Pongol, a Hindu solstice celebration, honors the goddess Sankrant.
Saint's Day: Anastasius I (399–410).

Glittering Hong Kong and its remarkable harbor, the prize disputed by Great Britain and China for decades before the December 19, 1984, Treaty of Beijing—an accord that demonstrates the day's potential for conciliation. Both the major powers involved made concessions aimed at an orderly transition of government from British colonial status to reaffiliation with mainland China.

Planetary Influences
Ruling planets: Jupiter and Saturn.
Third decan: Personal planet is the Sun.
Second cusp: Sagittarius with Capricorn tendencies.

♃ ♄ ☉

Sacred and Cultural Significance
Saint's day: Dominic of Silos (c.1000–73).

Australia's Robert Menzies, born on this day in 1894, was well suited for his distinguished political career as statesman and prime minister. Endowed with a deep sense of social responsibility, he rose steadily to high office, demonstrating his decisive leadership skills while maximizing economic growth and national security through alliances with the United States.

DECEMBER 20

Those born on this day are vigorous individuals who are often concerned with helping society to progress by implementing changes that will materially assist or inform a broad public. These socially responsible people feel a profound sense of connection with those around them and are therefore determined to do their utmost to remedy any perceived failings or abuses or to implement alternative systems of political or intellectual belief, technical innovations, or in some way positively to inspire others to follow the path that they believe to be the optimum one. December 20 individuals are astute and realistic assessors of any situation, and because they are predisposed to initiating responsive action as speedily and efficaciously as possible, are gifted problem-solvers and decision-makers. They supplement their capacity for incisive and direct thought with prodigiously practical skills, and also have a marked talent for motivating and organizing others. Clearly natural leaders, their ability to transmit their benevolent intentions and strength of conviction to those whose interest they have strongly at heart ameliorates the demands inherent in their lofty expectations—of themselves as much as of their coworkers, friends or family members.

Their propensity for leading by example, mastery of technical and conceptual issues, and their social orientation suits those born on this day especially for careers where they can play a tutelary or guiding role, and they may thus be found excelling in professional fields as varied as teaching, politics, the arts or sciences. Yet it is precisely because they believe so strongly in the importance and veracity of the messages that they communicate to their pupils, compatriots, or even humanity as a global entity, that those who hold alternative viewpoints may come to regard them as overly controlling, a danger that may present especial problems for their children if they are parents, or for their spouses.

VIRTUES: December 20 individuals are blessed with simultaneously perceptive and objective intellects, and are, moreover, vitally interested in the workings of human society, with the result that they are especially drawn to identifying social issues that are in need of improvement and then working assiduously toward effecting their progressive aims. Yet they are not lone operators: instead they believe that change must be effected communally and they therefore seek to enlist the support of others for their quests.
VICES: The vital concern with the welfare of those around them, and firmly held beliefs, may cause those born on this day to disregard the doubts or objections of others as to the correctness of their principles or methods, considering them as at best unhelpful or uninformed, and at worst willfully perverse attempts to obstruct the attainment of the advances on which they are so intent—a dismissive tendency that may lose them potential converts, supporters and friends. Their interpersonal skills often need attention.
VERDICT: In order to both propagate their cherished visions and retain the goodwill of those who are themselves determined to express their individuality (especially those closest to them), it is important that these people adopt a more *laissez-faire* attitude to develop greater patience with, and tolerance to, conflicting viewpoints.

On This Day
Famous Births: Thomas Graham (1805); George Galvin, "Dan Leno" (1860); Harvey Firestone (1868); Yvonne Arnaud (1890); Robert Menzies (1894); George, Duke of Kent (1902); Irene Dunne (1904); James Leasor (1923); Errol John (1924); Noel Ferrier (1930); Uri Geller (1946); Jenny Agutter (1952); Billy Bragg (1958).

Significant Events and Anniversaries: December 20 is a day of active intervention, as illustrated when U.S. troops invaded Panama during the Bush administration and captured the alleged dictator and drug trafficker General Manuel Noriega (1989). Ideology bowed to reality on December 20 when: in the face of hopeless adversity, Australian, New Zealand and British troops were evacuated from Gallipoli during World War I (1915); and having scuttled his German battleship *Graf Spee*, Captain Hans Langsdorff committed suicide (1939).

DECEMBER 21

Those determined individuals born on December 21 are susceptible to extremes in that they are intent on having their way, no matter how high the cost in emotional repercussions—for themselves, or those who stand in their way. They can therefore project an intimidating aura, and are sometimes seen as dogmatic, authoritarian and selfish. Yet their motivation is often based upon ideological convictions with the potential for wide-ranging benefits to others. Their rational intellects and perspicacity enable them to identify systems in need of improvement, which they strive to remedy. They may use confrontation to combat opposition, but usually prefer to rely on their force of will and magnetic charm to win others over. Once people get to know these strong-willed individuals, they will admire their generosity, honor and integrity.

December 21 people may be found working in—and potentially dominating—fields as disparate as commerce, science, sports and the arts, but they are well suited for political or social reform. Their personalities often inspire respect and admiration in those around them, but their single-minded focus may alienate others. The friends and relations on whom they rely deeply (whether or not they are aware of it) for love and support, may come to resent their autocratic tendencies.

VIRTUES: Perspicacity, vigor and their desire to excel through innovative endeavors bestows pioneering and leadership potential upon December 21 individuals. Blessed with remarkable clarity of vision, as well as organizational and practical skills, they work toward their goals with resourcefulness and dedication.
VICES: Their self-confidence and passionate belief in their convictions may pose a threat to their interpersonal relationships, if they become markedly intolerant of those who profess conflicting views.
VERDICT: There is a risk that by giving no quarter in the pursuit of their ambitions, those born on this day may not only lose the potential support of those who might have helped their cause, but may become intellectually and emotionally isolated even from their loved ones. A more conciliatory approach may be desirable.

On This Day

Famous Births: Benjamin Disraeli (1804); Josef Stalin (1879); Walter Hagen and Rebecca West (1892); Anthony Powell (1905); Heinrich Böll (1917); Kurt Waldheim (1918); Paul Winchell (1922); Phil Donahue (1935); Jane Fonda (1937); Greville Starkey (1938); Frank Zappa (1940); Walter Spanghero (1943); Michael Tilson Thomas (1944); Carl Wilson (1946); Samuel L. Jackson (1948); Chris Evert (1954); Kiefer Sutherland (1967).

Significant Events and Anniversaries: This is a day that highlights the determined promotion of ideological convictions, as was demonstrated when: the Pilgrim Fathers, a group of English emigrants including Puritans searching for religious freedom, disembarked from the *Mayflower* at Plymouth Rock in Massachusetts (1620); the Isle of Man's house of representatives, the House of Keys, became the first such body to grant women the right to vote (1880); Charles de Gaulle assumed the office of president of France in response to a plea for his leadership from the national assembly (1958); and suspected Libyan terrorists blew up a U.S. jumbo jet flying over Lockerbie in Scotland, their uncompromising attempt to draw attention to their cause costing the lives of over 270 people (1988). Pioneering technical and artistic pursuits intended to educate or inspire a wide public are also promised by this day, on which: the first issue of the U.S. newspaper the Boston *Gazette* was published (1719); Norwegian playwright Henrik Ibsen's play *The Doll's House* was first staged (1879); the world's first crossword puzzle appeared in the U.S. journal the *New York World* (1913); Latvian director Sergei Eisenstein's Communist propaganda movie, *The Battleship Potemkin*, was premiered (1925); and the first feature-length animated movie in color and with sound, Walt Disney's *Snow White and the Seven Dwarfs*, had its first screening (1935).

Planetary Influences
Ruling planets: Jupiter and Saturn.
Third decan: Personal planet is the Sun.
Second cusp: Sagittarius with Capricorn tendencies.

Sacred and Cultural Significance
In the U.S.A., Forefathers' Day; Wiccans celebrate the Winter Solstice Sabbat.
Saints' day: Thomas the Apostle (d. 1st century AD), patron saint of architects, visually impaired people and Portugal; Beornwald (8th century AD); Peter Canisius (1521–97).

The formidable Charles de Gaulle brought the decisive qualities of this day to his presidency of postwar France, beginning in 1958. His determined promotion of the national interest, based on unswerving convictions, made him a powerful statesman, respected even by those he alienated with his autocratic ways.

CAPRICORN

♑

December 22 to January 19

Ruling planet: Saturn   **Element:** Cardinal earth
Symbol: The goat-fish   **Polarity:** Negative (feminine)
Physical correspondence: The bones, joints, teeth and knees
Stones: Onyx, beryl, white sapphire, black diamond, jet, amethyst
Flowers: Coltsfoot, black poppy, pansy
Colors: Indigo, gray, dark green

The name of the zodiacal sign of Capricorn is derived from its Roman appellation *capricornus* (from *caper*, "goat," and *cornu*, "horn"). While the image of a horned goat is encapsulated within this constellation, its nether parts traditionally represent a fish's tail. This unusual, hybrid corpus derives directly from a Mesopotamian deity, whom the Sumerians equated with the god Enki, and the Babylonians with Ea or Oannes, the ruler of the waters. Other astrological traditions also adopted the goat-fish imagery, the Persians naming the constellation Vahik, the sea-goat; the ancient Greeks terming it Aigokeros, "the goat-horned one"; and the Hindus bestowing on it the Sanskrit name Makara, represented by a hybrid sea creature. An ancient Greco-Roman myth identifies this constellation with Pan (Faunus), who eluded the monstrous giant Typhon by leaping into the River Nile, whereupon his legs became transformed into a fish's tail. Some scholars believe that the duality inherent in the goat-fish represents the juxtaposition of water—a symbolic metaphor for the unconscious mind—with the mountainous habitat of the ibex, symbolizing intellectual aspiration. Capricorn encompasses the Northern winter solstice within its sphere of influence (indeed, its sigil is sometimes used to represent the solstice itself). For this reason, the sign was also known in classical times as the "gateway of the gods," *Janua coeli*, or the "gate of death." Its association with death stems from winter's cold, and Capricorn's planetary ruler, Saturn, equates to the Greek god Kronos (also the Greek word for time), whose sickle popularly identifies him with "father time" or the "grim reaper."

The personal characteristics endowed by Capricorn include a desire for material security, manifested by focused ambition, tenacity and steady reliability, as well as strong loyalty and practical skills—gifts of the element of earth that influences this sign. More negative qualities include a tendency to pessimism (reflecting the influence of Capricorn's saturnine ruler), and to placing greater value on achieving career aims than on nurturing profound emotional relationships.

DECEMBER 22

Those born on this day are tenacious and ambitious people; they may act according to a long-term plan formulated as early as childhood. Financial security is important to them, but they are more intent on attaining the high standards they set for themselves, or on implementing ideological concepts that they see as beneficial to society. December 22 people will flourish in professional activities that allow them total autonomy and promise tangible results—for example, as freelancers or self-starting entrepreneurs. Pragmatic realists, they recognize that enduring progress cannot be achieved overnight or without cooperation. Thus they understand the need for meticulous preparation (especially if they were born in the Chinese year of the ox) and have the patience to bide their time, working steadily behind the scenes until they see the opportunity to put their plans into action.

Their ability to focus on visionary goals while paying attention to detail makes them effective directors of their coworkers, who generally respect their strength of purpose and capability. Yet those born on this day are generally more preoccupied with realizing their aims than with fostering congenial working relationships and may appear to stand apart from others. A similar attitude defines their family relationships, especially with their children, of whom they have the highest expectations. Their controlling tendency may stem from the desire to safeguard the welfare of their loved ones, but it often creates resentment.

VIRTUES: December 22 people typically have a clear idea of their objectives in life, and work tenaciously toward realization of their goals. Methodical, organized and practical, they have an unusual potential for success.
VICES: Their unwavering faithfulness to their aims may reap rich rewards, but those born on this day can become intolerant of conflicting viewpoints and methods, resulting in emotional imbalance and narrow-mindedness.
VERDICT: These individuals would be well advised to recognize the negative effects that may result from their exclusive focus on achievement: they may deny themselves relaxational pursuits, limit their range of interests or alienate those closest to them, who may not share their ideals.

On This Day

Famous Births: Jean Baptiste Racine (1639); John Crome (1768); John Nevil Maskelyne (1839); Frank Billings Kellogg (1856); Giacomo Puccini (1858); Edwin Arlington Robinson (1869); Alan Dudley Bush (1900); Peggy Ashcroft (1907); Patricia Hayes (1909); Claudia Alta "Lady Bird" Johnson (1912); Gene Rayburn (1917); Barbara Billingsley (1922); James Burke and Hector Elizondo (1936); Diane Sawyer (1945); Noel Edmonds (1948); Maurice and Robin Gibb (1949); Ralph Fiennes (1962).

Significant Events and Anniversaries: December 22 promises the attainment of pioneering ambitions through perseverance and dedication, as was demonstrated on this day when: Swiss scientist Raoul Pictet became the first person to produce liquid oxygen (1877); the German physicist Wilhelm Röntgen made the world's first X-ray—of his wife's hand (1895); and, after a period of searching, the first living specimen of *Latimeria chalumnae*, a coelancanth (a lobe-finned fish believed to have become extinct fifty million years previously) was captured in the Bay of Chalumna, off the coast of southern Africa (1938). This is a day that also highlights the active promotion of grandiose ideals—with varying degrees of success—as was illustrated when: "Old Pretender," James Edward Stuart, disembarked at Peterhead in Scotland with the ultimately ill-fated intention of leading a Jacobite rebellion against the British monarch, George I, thereby hoping to reclaim the throne of his father, James II's (1715); Unionist troops under General William Tecumseh Sherman captured Savannah, Georgia, during the American Civil War (1864); and terrorists affiliated with the Palestine Liberation Organization (P.L.O.), led by "Carlos the Jackal," drew the world's attention to their cause by taking seventy hostages captive at the headquarters of the Organization of Petroleum Exporting Countries (O.P.E.C.) in Vienna, Austria (1975).

Planetary Influences
Ruling planets: Saturn and Jupiter.
First decan: Personal planet is Saturn.
First cusp: Capricorn with Sagittarian tendencies.

♄ ♃

Sacred and Cultural Significance
Saint's day: Francis Xavier Cabrini (d. 1917), patron saint of emigrants.

A woman of integrity, First Lady Claudia Alta Johnson (nicknamed Lady Bird) has demonstrated her birthdate's qualities of perseverance and dedication in both public and private life. A loyal family member who supported Lyndon B. Johnson's program for the Great Society during his presidency, she has continued her commitment to public service in environmental and other causes since she was widowed in 1973.

Planetary Influences
Ruling planets: Saturn and Jupiter.
First decan: Personal planet is Saturn.
First cusp: Capricorn with Sagittarian tendencies.

♄ ♃

Sacred and Cultural Significance
The Laurentina ceremony held in Rome by Pagans; Balomain honored by Kalash people.
Saints' day: Frithebert (8th century AD); Thorlac of Skalholt (1133–93); John of Kanti (1390–1473), patron saint of university lecturers.

This day's promise of innovation in the public interest was fulfilled in 1977 by completion of Minoru Yamasaki's World Trade Center—then the world's tallest building—in New York City. The twin towers of this landmark skyscraper reflect the soaring aspirations characteristic of December 23 ventures.

DECEMBER 23

The fulfillment of many December 23 individuals is bound up with the welfare of the social group with which they identify most strongly—whether family and friends, members of their local community, compatriots or the larger fellowship of humankind. Some feel a real emotional connection; others may be prompted by the recognition that group endeavors can often effect more than individual ventures. However, all are fueled by their drive to lead others along what they believe to be the optimum path to communal success. Their clarity of perception enables them to identify areas in need of improvement, and they can formulate original, yet practical, solutions. Gifted organizers, December 23 people are in many respects suited to positions of leadership in the realms of politics, law enforcement, or commerce, although the more individualistic may be attracted by the opportunities to exert their influence in scientific, artistic or spiritual pursuits.

Others respect their strength of conviction and determination, but do not always view them with affection, sensing the tendency to disregard their emotions and aspirations, and focus on their usefulness. Such negative perceptions are usually inaccurate, resulting from the urgency with which those born on this day (especially men) bring to their tasks. In fact, they can be extremely impatient with those who do conform to their beliefs, especially family members and friends, but they form deep and loyal relationships.

VIRTUES: Not only do those born on this day feel a strong sense of connection with, and responsibility for, those around them, but their predisposition toward directing others along lines intended to advance the greater good makes them natural leaders. Decisive, organized and extremely active, they display resourcefulness and fixity of purpose in working toward their goals, and a dependable, steady demeanor.
VICES: December 23 people might well be deeply hurt if they thought that those whose well-being they have at heart doubted their motives. But it is nevertheless the case that the subjects of their concern may consider them authoritarian types whose propensity to control others manifests the need for power.
VERDICT: It is important that these individuals try to develop a greater insight into the possibly negative effects that the unequivocal demands—however well-intentioned—that they make of those around them may produce. Listening to, and, where possible, adopting the viewpoints of others, as well as respecting their right to think and act autonomously, will help not only December 23 people to retain their goodwill and cooperation, but will also give them a wider perspective on life.

On This Day

Famous Births: Axel Frederic Cronstedt (1722); Richard Arkwright (1732); Czar Alexander I of Russia (1777); Jean-François Champollion (1790); Joseph Smith (1805); Karl Richard Lepsius (1810); Samuel Smiles (1812); "Lord" George Sanger (1827); Connie Mack (1862); Sarah Breedlove (1867); Joseph Arthur Rank (1888); Yousuf Karsh (1908); Maurice Denham (1909); Jose Greco and Helmut Schmidt (1918); Harry Guardino (1925); Paul Hornung (1935); Harry Shearer (1943); Susan Lucci (1949); Corey Haim (1971).

Significant Events and Anniversaries: This is a day that promises innovations designed to contribute to the communal welfare, as was demonstrated on this day when British architect Joseph Hansom patented his "safety," or hansom, cab—a forerunner of the taxi (1834). On a day that often highlights somewhat ruthless actions on the perceived behalf of the common interest: seven prominent Japanese leaders, including the former premier Hideki Tojo, were hanged by the Allies, having been sentenced to death for war crimes committed during World War II (1948); Lavrenti Beria, the political ally of the recently deceased Joseph Stalin and former head of the N.K.V.D. secret police, was executed, along with six others, on the orders of the U.S.S.R.'s "collective leadership" (1953); and Reza Shah Pahlavi, the shah of Iran, raised the price of the crude oil exported by his country by 100 per cent (1973).

DECEMBER 24

The single-minded focus with which those born on this day pursue the visions that inspire them is awesome in its intensity. Their fulfillment is bound up with the achievement of their goals. Some are determined to better themselves personally; others may be more concerned with benefiting society at large—but all show remarkable vigor and determination in working toward the realization of their aims. Many have identified their goals and principles early in life (perhaps as early as childhood). However, they are not coldly rational individuals—on the contrary, their aspirations usually reflect intuitive responses to the plight of those who are suffering from emotional or physical deprivation.

The careers to which December 24 individuals are drawn offer opportunities for initiating progress. Many will choose to work as commercial, technical, political or educational innovators, or as pioneers in the artistic realm. Coworkers may feel unable to match their dedication, and they often appear isolated within the professional sphere. However, they are positive, reliable people who make devoted friends, partners and especially parents, whose affection is reciprocated by their loved ones.

VIRTUES: Those born on this day draw upon their astute and rational intellectual talents in devising plans intended to effect positive action as directly and effectively as possible. When pursuing their progressive visions they display enormous energy and resourcefulness, along with immense fixity of purpose—all qualities that augur well for their success.
VICES: December 24 people are so convinced of the veracity of their beliefs and so determined to effect their aims that they have a tendency to focus on the causes and ambitions that fire their imaginations to the exclusion of all else, including their own needs for physical relaxation and intellectual diversification. Inherent in their certainty as to correctness of their views and methodologies is the risk that they may become intolerant of different viewpoints.
VERDICT: These individuals should try to recognize that in devoting their energies to their intellectual interests they may inadvertently be limiting the amount of time and attention that they would otherwise have available to pay to those whose well-being is so important to them: their loved ones. Indulging in jointly enjoyed simple pleasures will not only prove mutually beneficial in reinforcing strong emotional bonds, but will also give them a more balanced and relaxed perspective on life's priorities.

On This Day
Famous Births: King John of England (1167); Ignatius Loyola (1491); George Crabbe (1754); Augustin Eugène Scribe (1791); Kit Carson (1809); Henry Norris Russell (1812); James Prescott Joule (1818); Matthew Arnold (1822); Emanuel Lasker (1868); Michael Curtiz (1888); Harry Warren (1893); Georges Guynemer (1894); Howard Hughes (1905); Ava Gardner (1922); Jill Bennett (1931); Colin Cowdrey (1932).

Significant Events and Anniversaries: On a day that promises innovative technical achievements: Canadian-born U.S. physicist Reginald Fessenden made the world's first broadcast by radio telephone, from Brant Rock, Massachusetts, to ships sailing off the eastern coast of the U.S.A. (1906); a German monoplane became the first aircraft to bomb Britain, when it dropped its payload on Dover, England (1914); and, during World War II, German engineers working at Peenemünde launched the *Vergeltungswaffe* ("revenge weapon") the V1, an unmanned flying bomb nicknamed the "doodle-bug" or "buzz bomb," the first ever surface-to-surface guided missile (1942). The strength of conviction that is featured by this day is paralleled in warfare, and December 24 marks the anniversary of: the appointment of U.S. general, Dwight D. Eisenhower, as commander-in-chief of the Allied Expeditionary Force during World War II (1943); and the compounding of the Soviet invasion of Afghanistan when the country's premier, Hafizulah Amin, was executed and replaced by the pro-U.S.S.R. Babrak Karmal (1979).

Planetary Influences
Ruling planets: Saturn and Jupiter.
First decan: Personal planet is Saturn.
First cusp: Capricorn with Sagittarian tendencies.

♄ ♃

Sacred and Cultural Significance
In Christianity, Christmas Eve.
Saints' day: Mochua of Timahoe (d. c.657);

According to folklore, December 24 is an auspicious day on which to form an engagement: the marriage that ensues will be a long and happy one. The romantic Victorians symbolized such a union with signs of good fortune like lovebirds, flowers and horseshoes.

Thinking of You

With tender love

Planetary Influences
Ruling planets: Saturn and Jupiter.
First decan: Personal planet is Saturn.
First cusp: Capricorn with Sagittarian tendencies.

♄ ♃

Sacred and Cultural Significance
In Christianity, Christmas Day; in ancient Rome, the Birthday of the Invincible Sun celebrated.
Saints' day: Anastasia (d. c.304); Alburga (d. c.810).

More than one billion Christians around the world celebrate the traditional date of Christ's birth with a variety of rites and customs. Europeans enshrined the evergreen Christmas tree as a symbol of eternal life, along with the holly, ivy, Yule log and candles that became emblems of the season of light in winter's darkness.

DECEMBER 25

Those born into Christian families on this day will inevitably have felt themselves marked out as special from an early age, yet they will also have learned to compromise: today's celebrations are not focused exclusively on them. In fact, they receive less attention on their birthdays than their siblings and friends, and may feel that they are missing out. These dual feelings often persist throughout the lives of December 25 people, who are notable for their determination to achieve ambitious aspirations. Although they are pragmatic and objective, the concepts that fire them reflect an imaginative and progressive outlook. Whether they are drawn to the potential inherent in science, business, politics or the arts, they show a real ability to combine practical skills with intellectual insight.

Individualistic as they are, December 25 people also have a sense of social responsibility (especially when they were born in the Chinese year of the snake). This leads them to enlist the support of others for causes they believe will illuminate or otherwise benefit the lives of those around them, or humanity as a whole. Originality, resourcefulness and charisma contribute to their leadership qualities and their easy popularity. However, their ambition, strength of conviction and high standards may place a heavy burden of expectation upon those whose interest they have most deeply at heart.

VIRTUES: December 25 people are stimulated by their idealistic goals and convinced that their implementation will contribute to the greater good. They bring high energy, strength of purpose and a gift for organization to all their endeavors.
VICES: Those born on this day are perfectionists who will not rest until they have realized their goals. However, they can become impatient with those who are unwilling or unable to meet their demands or to do things their way, thus alienating potential allies.
VERDICT: In order to help them to both achieve their goals and retain the goodwill of those around them, it is vital that these people recognize the wisdom of the adage "Live and let live." Conciliation and compromise can help them to develop a more *laissez-faire* approach—even if they disagree with the premises of others.

On This Day
Famous Births: Jesus Christ (c.4 BC); Isaac Newton (1642); William Collins (1721); Dorothy Wordsworth (1771); Mohammed Ali Jinnah (1876); Charles Pathé and Maurice Utrillo (1883); Conrad Hilton (1887); Robert Ripley (1893); Humphrey Bogart (1899); Ernst Ruska (1906); Cab Calloway and Lew Grade (1907); Tony Martin (1912); Mohammed Anwar El-Sadat (1918); Rod Serling (1924); Kenny Everett (1944); Jimmy Buffett (1946); Barbara Mandrell (1948); Sissy Spacek (1949); Annie Lennox (1954); Jilly Mack (1957).

Significant Events and Anniversaries: On a day that highlights outstanding leadership potential, December 25 marks: the coronation in Rome by Pope Leo III of Charlemagne, king of the Franks, as the first Holy Roman Emperor (800); the crowning at Westminster Abbey in London of William the Conqueror, duke of Normandy, as King William I of England (1066); and the accession of Hirohito to the Japanese throne (1926). Conversely, this day also warns that leaders who fail to enlist the support of their followers may be repudiated, as when: repressive and corrupt former Communist dictator of Romania Nicolae Ceausescu was executed, along with his wife Elena in a revolutionary coup (1989); and Soviet president Mikhail Gorbachev resigned in the face of political fragmentation within the U.S.S.R. (1990). The importance of conciliation is indicated on December 25, and this quality was displayed when, during World War I, opposing British and German troops fraternized in no-man's land during a temporary, informal truce (1914). Innovative advances of all kinds are promised on this day, when: the first Welsh *eisteddfod* ("sitting"), a festival bringing together musicians and bards, was held at Cardigan Castle (1176); the temperature scale invented by Swedish astronomer Anders Celsius was first integrated into a thermometer (1741); U.S. yacht *Henrietta* became the first such vessel to win a transatlantic race (1866); and Sony unveiled its TV 8-301, a pioneering transistor television set (1959).

DECEMBER 26

Such is the vigorous nature of the people born on this day that they are not content simply to dream of their visionary aspirations but seek to transform them into reality. December 26 people are blessed with incisive perspicacity, supplemented by profound empathy with those whom they perceive as victims of society's failings or abuses. When they identify such faults, they invariably take remedial action. This combination of characteristics attracts them to fields that are concerned with effecting human progress, perhaps by instituting more enlightened political systems, technical innovations, social service work or creative use of the media. They relish the opportunity to rise to a demanding challenge, but their ultimate goal is to further the common good through their work. While they project themselves as intense, serious people, those born on December 26 are dependable, loyal friends who are admired and loved for their supportive, committed presence. They may, however, be very slow to form their deep relationships, because their ideals sometimes generate unrealistic expectations of others.

Their sense of social concern does not preclude their insistence on freedom of thought and action, which may lead them to adopt a combative stance when they believe their right to personal autonomy is threatened, or when others behave in a manner contrary to their convictions. And although their determination and ability to lead by example marks them out as dynamic team leaders, their unwillingness to brook ideological dissent in coworkers, or even family members and friends, may disrupt the harmony they seek in promoting the common purpose.

VIRTUES: December 26 people are incisive and objective thinkers, whose interest is engaged by subjects with the potential for wide-ranging or concrete improvements. Remarkably single-minded in their determination to effect their plans, they draw upon their intellectual and physical energy, practicality and resourcefulness in promoting their goals.
VICES: Those born on this day are so intent on realizing their ideals, which often generate opposition, that they may disregard potentially helpful alternatives proposed by others and push forward with their original plans.
VERDICT: It is important that these individuals recognize that their decisive approach may alienate those who might be persuaded to adopt their convictions and close their minds to alternative viewpoints that may be valid and useful. Greater tolerance and a more approachable manner—particularly in their personal relationships—will give them intellectual and emotional perspective.

On This Day

Famous Births: Thomas Gray (1716); Charles Babbage (1792); Dion Boucicault (1822); Henry Valentine Miller (1891); Mao Tse-tung (1893); Richard Widmark (1914); Steve Allen (1921); Alan King (1927); Rohan Babulal Kanhai (1935); Fred Schepisi (1939); Phil Spector (1940); Carlton Fisk (1947); Jared Leto (1971).

Significant Events and Anniversaries: This day promises innovations beneficial to the public, as seen in the realm of entertainment when: Britain's first pantomime (now a Boxing Day tradition), *Harlequin Executed*, was performed at London's Lincoln's Inn Fields Theatre (1717); and what is believed to be the world's earliest feature film, *The Story of the Kelly Gang*, had its premier in Melbourne, Australia. This pioneering potential was reflected in the field of scientific research when Polish-born scientific researcher Marie Curie discovered radioactivity while experimenting with pitchblende ore in Paris (1898). Inherent in this day is the willingness to adopt combative strategies in the defense or pursuit of ideals, as when: Count Lévin A. Bennigsen's Russian troops beat off Napoleon's army at the Battle of Pultusk in eastern Europe during the Napoleonic Wars (1806); U.S. pugilist "Galveston Jack" Johnson became the first boxer of African origin to win the world heavyweight title, beating Tommy Burns in a championship bout in Sydney, Australia (1908); and British naval forces sank German battleship the *Scharnhorst* off Norway during World War II (1943).

Planetary Influences
Ruling planet: Saturn.
First decan: Personal planet is Saturn.

♄

Sacred and Cultural Significance
In British tradition, Boxing Day.
Saints' day: Stephen (d. c.35), patron saint of brick-layers, deacons and headache sufferers; Tathai (5th–6th century AD).

The dynamic Chinese leader Mao Tse-tung, born in 1893, used the qualities inherent in his birthdate to make radical changes in the world's most populous country. His revolutionary power politics, advanced "through the barrel of a gun," made China a People's Republic under Communist auspices at a high cost in human lives and centuries of indigenous culture.

✳✳✳✳✳✳✳✳✳✳✳✳✳✳✳✳✳✳✳✳✳✳✳✳✳✳✳✳✳✳✳✳✳✳✳✳✳✳✳

Planetary Influences
Ruling planet: Saturn.
First decan: Personal planet is Saturn.

Sacred and Cultural Significance
The birthday of Freya, the Norse goddess of fertility, celebrated.
Saint's day: John the Evangelist (d. 1st century AD), patron saint of publishers, theologians and writers.

German-born actress Marlene Dietrich, the epitome of Hollywood's glamour years, had all the talent and ambition associated with this day. Born in 1901, she became a star in Berlin with such films as The Blue Angel *(1930), entertained American soldiers during World War II and refused to return to Germany after the Nazi regime. Her reserved, contemplative side, characteristic of those born in the Chinese year of the ox, became more pronounced as she grew older.*

The majority of December 27 people have two distinct sides to their personalities: not only do they have a strong feeling of social responsibility and present a positive and dependable persona to the wider world, they are also deep thinkers who need time and space to pursue their own interests. Inherent in this duality is the danger that those born on this day may feel torn between what they perceive as their duty to others and their own personal prerequisites for fulfillment, and imbalance may lead them to become frazzled and frustrated. Because their goodwill makes it difficult for them to refuse requests for help, they may become overburdened with problems not of their own making—especially the women born on this day. When they can reconcile their desire to help others with their own interests, their potential is truly remarkable. Provided they center themselves emotionally and spiritually, they will attract friends readily for their steady, reliable, supportive qualities, but they can appear unapproachable when immersed in their careers or favorite forms of recreation.

Intellectual and intuitive perception, logical minds and tenacity draw those born on this day to professions wherein they can make contributions to as science, engineering, commerce, sporting or artistic ventures. Despite their concern with the well-being of others, their intellectual focus may isolate them professionally. Typically, they seek an outlet for their emotional needs in their personal relationships and value the comfort and support offered by their nearest and dearest, reciprocating with affection and loyalty.

VIRTUES: Those born on this day are blessed with keenly perceptive intellects, which enable them to pinpoint areas in need of improvement and apply their talents to formulating effective, often pioneering, strategies. They are also kind and thoughtful as friends, lovers and parents.
VICES: As well as being talented problem-solvers, December 27 people are socially concerned individuals who will rarely stand idly by when others are in need of assistance. Their benevolent willingness to address the dilemmas and difficulties of others may, however, divert their energies and attention from the promotion of their own interests, with the result that they may eventually become disgruntled and resentful.
VERDICT: To safeguard their equilibrium, it is crucial that these individuals strike a balance between their need to fulfill their personal aspirations and their more altruistic urges. Before acceding to the demands that others may make of them, they should weigh up the pros and cons and, if necessary, gently encourage those who approach them for assistance to seek their own solutions.

On This Day
Famous Births: Johannes Kepler (1571); George Cayley (1773); Louis Pasteur (1822); Sydney Greenstreet (1879); Marlene Dietrich (1901); Oscar Levant (1906); John Charles (1931); John Amos (1942); Gerard Depardieu (1948); Tovah Feldshuh (1952); Arthur Kent (1953); Gerina Dunwich (1959).

Significant Events and Anniversaries: This is a day that highlights the pursuit of innovative visions aimed at contributing to the greater good, as was reflected: in the scientific realm when English naturalist Charles Darwin embarked from Plymouth, England, for South America in the H.M.S. *Beagle*, on the first leg of the voyage that would result in his pioneering work on evolution, *On the Origin of the Species* (1831); and in the artistic world, when Scottish playwright J. M. Barrie's seminal piece *Peter Pan* was premiered in London, England (1904); the world's first state-supported theater, Ireland's The Abbey in Dublin, was officially opened to the public (1904); and U.S. composer Jerome Kern's operetta *Show Boat* was first staged on Broadway (1927). The instigation of practical solutions to complicated problems is furthermore emphasized by December 27, on which the International Monetary Fund (I.M.F.), an agency of the United Nations charged with stabilizing international trade, was instituted in Washington, D.C. (1945).

DECEMBER 28

The image that December 28 people present to the world at large is one of confidence, dependability and capability: thus they are often regarded as pillars of support and sources of advice and help. They are, in fact, socially responsible—a benevolent, but also somewhat dutiful, quality that makes it hard for them to turn away requests for assistance. Yet their competent exterior overlies a constant and profound search for inner understanding and knowledge in realms that do not necessarily coincide with the more immediate demands that others may make of them. Thus their personal magnetism may be both a gift and a drawback, in that although December 28 individuals may derive transitory satisfaction from lending their energies and talents to the resolution of the problems of others, they may thereby neglect the exploration of interests that are essential to their personal fulfillment. Yet when a serendipitous conjunction of their external and internal orientations occurs—perhaps within their careers—the dynamic synergy produced can have excellent results.

Their natural inclinations, combined with their practical and technical expertise, admirably equip those born on this day for professions in which by furthering their own interests and insights, they may simultaneously help, guide, inform, enlighten or delight a wider audience. Such pursuits include politics, spiritual studies, communications and art. Typically admired for their abilities and self-reliance, there is a risk that these individuals may be regarded primarily as competent providers of support—an image that they themselves may unwittingly foster—and their own emotional needs will be disregarded. It is vital that they and those around them (especially their nearest and dearest) realize that they, too, are emotionally vulnerable and require the mutual support and affection that is inherent in strong emotional bonds.

VIRTUES: Those born on this day are assured individuals who are blessed with the ability to inspire the confidence of those around them by means of their practical abilities, astute yet sympathetically expressed judgements, and their real concern with effecting others' progress. Also profound thinkers who wish to advance their personal knowledge and comprehension, these are integrated and progressive types, who have pronounced innovative potential.

VICES: December 28 people are liable to intellectual and physical burnout, for by seeking to satisfactorily address their multitude of externally and internally directed concerns—to all of which they have a propensity to devote their total attention—they have a tendency to spread their energies too thinly and may thereby prohibit their ability to attain their ultimate individual fulfillment.

VERDICT: Although they should never ignore either their personal predilections or their innate sense of responsibility with regard to promoting the welfare of others, these people should recognize that they are not superhuman and therefore cannot achieve everything as perfectly as they would like—that is, unless they adhere to the pursuit of the priorities that are most important to them, a policy that means that they may inevitably have to decline requests for assistance from others.

On This Day

Famous Births: Woodrow Wilson (1856); Wilson Steer (1860); Arthur Stanley Eddington (1882); Cliff Arquette and Earl "Fatha" Hines (1905); Lew Ayres (1908); Sam Levenson (1911); Johnny Otis (1924); Simon Raven (1927); Maggie Smith (1934); Edgar Winter (1946); Denzel Washington (1954); Nigel Kennedy (1956); Chad McQueen (1960).

Significant Events and Anniversaries: On a day that emphasizes a strong propensity to act on behalf of the perceived common good, the state of Iowa elected to join the U.S. Union (1846). December 28 is governed by the element of earth, as was reflected when: tragically, a devastating earthquake killed over 75,000 individuals in the Sicilian town of Medina (1909); and, more happily, the Peak District area in Britain was proclaimed the country's first national park (1950).

Planetary Influences
Ruling planet: Saturn.
First decan: Personal planet is Saturn.

♄

Sacred and Cultural Significance
An annual festival of peace celebrated in China.
Saints' day: the Holy Innocents (d. 1st century BC).

Actor Denzel Washington, born on this day in 1954, has worked steadily toward the goals suggested by his December 28 birthday since he studied at Fordham University and won a scholarship to the American Conservatory Theater. His memorable films include The Mighty Quinn (1989), Mo' Better Blues (1990) and He Got Game (1998), and his career is balanced by a stable family life and involvement in many humanitarian causes.

Planetary Influences
Ruling planet: Saturn.
First decan: Personal planet is Saturn.

♄

Sacred and Cultural Significance
The Day of Nymphs celebrated in ancient Greece.
Saints' day: Evroult (626–706); Thomas of Canterbury (1118–70).

The elusive inner quality of people born on this day is reminiscent of the beautiful nature-centered Nymphs of Greek mythology who were the focus of a celebration on December 29 in ancient times. People born on this day have gifts that mark them out for public attention and leadership roles, but their private lives are sacred to them. They cannot compromise their autonomy, even for the highest motives, without suffering a loss of self.

DECEMBER 29

✦ ★ ✦

The positive and capable approach of December 29 people inspires admiration and respect: thus they are often seen in leadership positions. Although their strong sense of responsibility leads them to discharge their duties with diligence, those born on this day would often prefer to pursue their own interests unburdened by the demands of others. Harmonizing their external and internal orientations is essential to realizing their own potential for fulfillment, and many—consciously or unconsciously—pursue careers that absorb their personal interests while providing real benefits for the greater good. Along with a penchant for logical and straightforward thought, December 29 people are blessed with keenly perceptive and progressive minds, a combination of qualities that makes them alert to flawed social systems. Because they are vigorous and resourceful, they seek new ways of moving forward, drawing upon their highly developed organizational skills.

Those born on this day will thrive in any career that offers challenging opportunities to assist or enlighten. They are especially suited to those realms where they can provide ideological guidance to others (as parents, politicians or writers, for example), or make innovations that advance knowledge and prosperity (perhaps as scientists or engineers). Others respond to the benevolent aura that December 29 people emanate, but in many respects this personal magnetism can cause unwanted complications in their lives. In essence, they are private individuals who are happiest when working toward their personal goals, bolstered by the love and support of those closest to them, who contribute profoundly to their emotional well-being.

VIRTUES: Those born on this day are multitalented individuals: energetic and tenacious, intellectually imaginative and astute, and blessed with practical abilities. Their natural gifts and concern with promoting the welfare of others bestow clear leadership potential upon them and promise pioneering achievements.
VICES: Their tendency to take responsibility for the problems of those in need of assistance makes it hard for December 29 people to resist requests for help. In working on behalf of others, they run the dual risk of sublimating their own cherished desires and aspirations and of trying to do too much at once.
VERDICT: To avoid the danger of becoming overworked and stressed by their attempts to satisfy their own needs and those of others, it is vital that these people focus on the pursuit of what is most meaningful to them.

On This Day
Famous Births: Jeanne Antoinette (1721); Charles Macintosh (1766); Charles Goodyear (1800); Andrew Johnson (1808); William Gladstone (1809); Alexander Parkes (1813); Pablo Casals and Lionel Tertis (1876); Jess Willard (1881); Vera Brittain (1893); Emile Julius Klaus Fuchs (1911); Albert Tucker (1914); Robert Ruark (1915); Viveca Lindfors (1920); Bernard Cribbens (1928); Mary Tyler Moore (1937); Harvey Smith and Jon Voight (1938); Marianne Faithfull (1946); Ted Danson (1947); Gelsey Kirkland (1952); Ed Autry (1954); Jude Law (1972).

Significant Events and Anniversaries: December 29 is a day that promises outstanding leadership potential, as seen when: Sun Yat-sen, founder of the Guomindang, became his nation's first post-revolutionary president (1911); and Czech playwright and activist Vaclev Havel became president of Czechoslovakia after the overthrow of Communism (1989). A day that also highlights the active promotion of communal goals (for good or ill), December 29 marks the anniversary of: the Republic of Texas' admission to the U.S. Union (1845); the massacre of more than 150 members of the Oglala Sioux tribe, led by Chief Big Foot, by members of the 7th Cavalry at Wounded Knee, South Dakota (1890); the onset of the Jameson Raid, when the anti-Boer raiders attempted to overthrow the Boer government (1895); and the implementation of the Republic of Ireland's constitution and the nation's adoption of the name Eire (1937). This day's potential for conflicts of interest was seen when Thomas à Becket, archbishop of Canterbury, was murdered at the altar of Canterbury Cathedral (1170).

DECEMBER 30

The thoughts and actions of those born on this day are profoundly influenced by their need to bring order to confused situations and concepts—to effect dynamic progress in place of stasis. These individuals are not only skilled at identifying areas in need of improvement, but also have the vision and imagination to make effective changes. Strong organizational talents and resourcefulness help them to promote the common welfare, whether of family and friends, co-workers, fellow citizens or even the world community. Their ability to channel the energy and talents of those around them makes them natural leaders, successful not only in material terms, but in making significant contributions to the wider world. Their occasionally taciturn demeanor can sometimes mislead others; though prone to pessimism, these are people who prefer a straightforward approach and appreciate humor and the lighter side of life.

The professions to which December 30 people are drawn offer opportunities for innovation and advancement within set—although flexible—parameters (for they prefer to build upon existing foundations rather than branch off in radically new directions). Their talents and inclinations suit them well to business and commercial ventures (especially if they were born in the Chinese year of the snake). Politics, diplomacy and positions that require forceful negotiating skills are other possibilities. Their decisive tendency to take charge of people whom they wish to help can have impressive results, but their associates may resent perceived attempts to limit their personal freedom.

VIRTUES: December 30 people are stimulated by the challenge to create orderly systems of operation, and set out to bring harmony and cohesion with single-minded tenacity. Always focused on their long-term aims, they also display strong attention to detail and their abilities as organizers. Despite appearing somewhat abrupt, they are down-to-earth people who make valuable and trusted friends and allies.
VICES: Inherent in their aptitude for problem-solving is their confidence in the veracity of their viewpoints and solutions. This apparently superior attitude may irritate, or even alienate, those who disagree with them.
VERDICT: If they are to attain their aims without losing the goodwill of others, those born on this day should learn to appreciate that not everyone will agree with their proposals. Rather than rejecting instances of dissent and engendering confrontation, they should employ conciliatory tactics, particularly within their personal relationships.

On This Day

Famous Births: André Messager (1853); Rudyard Kipling (1865); Stephen Leacock (1869); Albert Einstein (1879); L.P. Hartley (1895); Dmitri Kabalevsky (1904); Carol Reed (1906); Bert Parks (1914); Stan Tracey (1927); Bo Didley (1928); Jack Lord (1930); John Hillerman (1932); Barry Briggs and Russ Tamblyn (1934); Sandy Koufax (1935); Gordon Banks and Noel Paul Stookey (1937); Michael Nesmith (1942); Davy Jones (1945); Tracy Ullman (1959); Tiger Woods (1975).

Significant Events and Anniversaries: A day that highlights the desire to direct the actions of others, December 30 is the anniversary of: the Battle of Wakefield during the English Wars of the Roses, when Lancastrian forces led by the dukes of Somerset and Northumberland defeated their Yorkist opponents under Richard, Duke of York (1460); and the murder of Russian "holy man" Grigori Yefimovich Rasputin by a group of aristocrats led by Prince Yusupov, outraged by his debauchery and influence over the czarina, Alexandra (1916). December 30 also indicates the institution of organizational systems, as seen in the realm of national politics when: the Transvaal region of southern Africa was proclaimed a republic, with Paul Kruger as its premier (1880); and the Soviet Union was formed by the nations of Russia, Belorussia, Transcaucasia and the Ukraine (1922). Artistic innovations promised by the imaginiative aspects of this day were shown when: British collaborators W.S. Gilbert and Arthur Sullivan first staged their comic opera *The Pirates of Penzance* (1879); and American composer Cole Porter's musical *Kiss Me Kate* had its premiere performance (1948).

Planetary Influences
Ruling planet: Saturn.
First decan: Personal planet is Saturn.

Sacred and Cultural Significance
Saint's day: Egwin (d. 717).

The British writer Rudyard Kipling synthesized his bicultural background in literary works that won him the Nobel Prize in 1907. Born in India in 1865 to British parents, and educated in England, he returned to the East as a journalist. There his qualities of imagination and energy—two of the positive traits often seen in December 30 people—resulted in Anglo-Indian classics including two Jungle Books *(1894–95),* Soldiers Three *(1889) and* The Seven Seas *(1896).*

Planetary Influences
Ruling planet: Saturn.
First decan: Personal planet is Saturn.

♄

Sacred and Cultural Significance
New Year's Eve; Hogmanay in Scotland.
Saint's day: Sylvester (d. 335).

The independent and self-starting qualities of those born on December 31 were exemplified by the French artist Henri Matisse, who repudiated a career in law during his twenties to study painting. Influenced by Cubism and Impressionism, he became the leader of the movement disparaged by critics as "les Fauves" ("wild beasts") and pursued his mastery of line and color, profoundly influencing modern art.

DECEMBER 31

Those born on December 31 are both idealists and pragmatists. With their progressive objectives, they aim toward perfection, but they possess the insight to recognize personal and practical limitations. As a rule, they are reformers rather than revolutionaries, with good leadership abilities and independent minds. Their talent for devising original strategies to solve problems is joined with tenacity of purpose. Leaders by example, they set high standards for others to follow, but never demand more than they themselves are prepared to give. Reasonable and fair, they are respected and admired by friends and colleagues.

December 31 individuals are well suited to careers in which they can not only satisfy their need to create harmony and excel, but direct coworkers in efforts that will benefit all concerned. Politics, the military or commercial ventures may attract them, and they make skilled and effective team-builders, bringing out the best in others when they temper their own somewhat controlling behavior and encourage others' efforts. Others admire their dedication but do not always concur with their convictions and methods. Although their personal relationships are characterized by love and concern for their nearest and dearest, they must beware of imposing their elevated standards and expectations on them.

VIRTUES: December 31 people are blessed with astute and rational intellects, as well as the ability to focus on the projects that inspire them while paying attention to detail. Fueled by their compulsion to bring order and progress to all their endeavors, they promote their aims with remarkable vigor and resourcefulness.
VICES: Their urge to construct cohesive and organized teams or methods for advancement includes confidence in the veracity of their views and approaches. They can manifest impatience with those whose objections hinder them, which may cause them to lose the support of coworkers, friends and potential allies.
VERDICT: If they are not to become somewhat narrow-minded and intolerant of the individuality of others, those born on this day should temper their occasionally self-righteous tendency to stick rigidly to principles, encouraging those around them to express their opinions, however much they may differ.

On This Day
Famous Births: Jacques Cartier (1491); Charles Edward Stuart, "Bonnie Prince Charlie"/"The Young Pretender" (1720); Charles Cornwallis (1738); George Gordon Meade (1815); John Taliaferro Thompson (1860); Henri Matisse (1869); George Catlett Marshall (1880); Jule Styne (1905); Peter May (1929); Odetta (1930); Anthony Hopkins (1937); Sarah Miles (1941); John Denver and Ben Kingsley (1943); Barbara Carrera (1945); Patti Smith (1946); Tim Matheson and Donna Summer (1948); Jean-Pierre Rives (1952); Val Kilmer (1959).

Significant Events and Anniversaries: December 31 highlights organized action intended to improve upon existing systems, as was demonstrated on this day when: having suffered religious persecution in France, a group of Protestant Huguenots intent on securing their right to freedom of worship embarked on a sea journey bound for the Cape of Good Hope (1687); the U.S. government opened a reception center for steerage-class immigrants to the U.S.A. on New York's Ellis Island (1890); and the British government ordered the rationing of sugar during World War I, in order to distribute the country's dwindling stocks equitably (1917). A similarly practical propensity was reflected in the various technical innovations and advances that were introduced on this day including: the B.B.C.'s first-ever broadcast of the chimes of Big Ben—the bell that hangs in the clock tower of Britain's houses of parliament— to usher in the new year (1923); the first use of a breathalyzer, the invention of Dr. R. N. Harger, to measure the amount of alcohol consumed by motorists, in this instance by the Indianapolis Police Department (1938); and the maiden flight of the Soviet-built supersonic aircraft the TU-44, a pioneering feat that preceded the subsequent achievement of the Anglo-French Concorde (1968).

JANUARY 1

* *

Those born on January 1 are blessed with the characteristics that caused Janus, the Roman god of doorways, to be named patron of the first month of the year: intellectual balance, a willingness to look forward and embrace change, as well as the ability to recall the lessons learned from past experiences. Yet the duality inherent in the double-faced Roman deity is also an integral part of these people's natures. While they are prized for their affable characters and ability to think rationally and clearly, for example—and nowhere more so than in the workplace, where such qualities usually make them respected and appreciated coworkers—under certain circumstances they may lose their equilibrium and stubbornly go off on a startling tangent. Indeed, these people are renowned for their determination, capacity for hard work, organizational abilities and strong willpower, and will see a cherished project through any obstacle, sometimes at the expense of their personal lives. They are suited for any career in which their formidable intellectual powers can be stretched, but are especially effective as teachers, lawyers and financial analysts—professions in which their enviable mastery of their chosen field of expertise can prove invaluable.

Their ability to think coolly and incisively makes January 1 people sought after for advice, all the more because their natural kindness and empathy with others make them loyal friends. Trusted and valued by their peers, they do, however, have a tendency to think the best of people, a quality which makes them popular, but which can lead them to be deceived by those who harbor an ulterior agenda. While their trusting natures may thus set them up to be profoundly let down, January 1 people are wise enough to learn from such devastating experiences and to be more cautious in the future. They also have a pronounced intuitive streak and, if this inner voice is heeded, will achieve a balance of "head" and "heart" which will stand them in good stead in their personal and professional relationships.

VIRTUES: January 1 people are charming and affectionate, and thus earn the devotion and lasting friendship of others. Intellectually, they are fair and thoughtful, considering all sides of a problem impartially and arriving at a sound conclusion.
VICES: If riled or opposed over something about which they feel particularly strongly, these people have a tendency to lose their famed equanimity, and can astound others with their displays of temperamental behavior. Their natural propensity to take people at face value may cause them to be taken advantage of by more unscrupulous characters.
VERDICT: January 1 people are blessed with many positive qualities of character—such as fairness, affability and single-mindedness—which both stand them in good stead in all their activities and make them popular with their peers. They should, however, take care to control their tempers and should also beware of being too trusting.

On This Day

Famous Births: Lorenzo de' Medici (1449); Paul Revere (1735); Betsy Ross (1752); James Frazer (1854); Pierre de Coubertin (1862); Alfred Stieglitz (1864); E.M. Forster and William Fox (1879); Martin Niemoller (1892); J. Edgar Hoover (1895); Dana Andrews (1909); Kim Philby (1912); J.D. Salinger (1919); Idi Amin Dada (1925); Joe Orton (1933); Frank Langella (1940).

Significant Events and Anniversaries: Reflecting this day's connotation of change, German and Swiss states were among the first to introduce the new Gregorian Calendar (1583), Samuel Pepys began his famous *Diary* (1660) and, indicating a desire to record and judge the passing of time, the first issue of the British *Daily Universal Register [The Times]* appeared (1788). The day's progressive influence can be seen in the opening of the Iron Bridge (the world's first such bridge) in Shropshire, England (1781), the Trans-Siberian Railway in Russia (1905) and Britain's Manchester Ship Canal (1894). Momentous political events also occurred on this day: the importing of slaves into the U.S.A. was banned (1808); Queen Victoria became empress of India (1887); the European Economic Community (E.E.C.) was inaugurated (1958); and Fidel Castro's coup caused the downfall of the Batista regime in Cuba (1959).

Planetary Influences
Ruling Planet: Saturn.
Second decan: Personal planet is Venus.

Sacred and Cultural Significance
New Year's Day in the Gregorian Calendar.
Saints' day: The Blessed Virgin Mary (1st century AD), the patron saint of mothers, nuns and virgins, in veneration of her role in the incarnation and redemption; Concordius (2nd century AD); Odilo (c. 962–1049).

The Emancipation Proclamation is read to a family of slaves by a Union soldier. The document was issued by President Abraham Lincoln on January 1, 1863, a day noted for progressive and humanitarian influences.

Planetary Influences
Ruling planet: Saturn.
Second decan: Personal planet is Venus.

Sacred and Cultural Significance
Inanna's birthday celebrated in Sumeria;
Advent of Isis from Phoenicia.
Saints' day: Gregory of Nazianzus (329–89);
Basil the Great (c.330–79); Munchin
(7th century AD); Seraphim of Sarov
(1759–1833); Gaspare del Bufalo (1786–1837).

January 2 people are particularly closely attuned to their senses, drinking in the finer details of their surroundings that are invisible to less sensually observant people. This sensitivity to their environment makes them outstanding artists, for their perceptiveness will frequently be manifested through the medium of their chosen craft. This quality of perception also applies to their interpersonal relationships, with the result that January 2 people are blessed with an almost uncanny ability to tune in to the nature or moods of other people. Strongly committed to their personal ambitions and goals, these clear-sighted and objective people also harbor a marked critical streak which, when imposed on their work, often produces wonderful results. Less positively, there is a danger that they will demand the impossible of themselves, or that they will set such stringent parameters on their personal relationships that they will be left emotionally isolated.

These people are extremely motivated and diligent, requiring the most of themselves and also of others, qualities which make them valuable employees and exacting bosses. Having intuitively absorbed the information inherent in a given situation, they will then determine their goal and work single-mindedly toward its achievement. Curiously, although they are driven by their desire for perfection, January 2 people often manifest a marked reluctance to have their high ideals disappointed; they are therefore sometimes averse to making irrevocable decisions, preferring to hedge their bets rather than make a commitment about whose outcome they are uncertain. This indecision can be particularly pronounced in January 2 men with regard to their personal relationships. If they throw their natural caution to the wind, however, and apply their undoubted qualities of intuition and self-discipline to the relationship or task as it develops, they will often be successful.

VIRTUES: The acute sensitivity, creativity and objectivity of January 2 people are complemented by their capacity for unusual industriousness and commitment, a potent combination which often produces magical results.
VICES: Feeling that others—or, indeed, even they themselves—cannot live up to their lofty standards and expectations, January 2 people have a tendency to retreat into their own world, or to avoid taking gambles if they do not feel that the risk will result in perfection.
VERDICT: These people have exceptional potential to succeed in their chosen professions and relationships, but must ensure that they do not compromise their chances for personal happiness and fulfillment by imposing unrealistic standards upon themselves or others.

Several events in the history of human observation of the Moon (shown here in a sketch by Galileo) occurred on January 2, a day with strong lunar connections.

On This Day
Famous Births: James Wolfe (1727); Mily Alexeyevich Baldkirev (1837); Gilbert Murray (1866); Michael Tippett (1905); Isaac Asimov (1920); Roger Miller (1936); David Bailey (1938); Jim Bakker (1939); Cuba Gooding, Jr. (1968); Christy Turlington (1969).

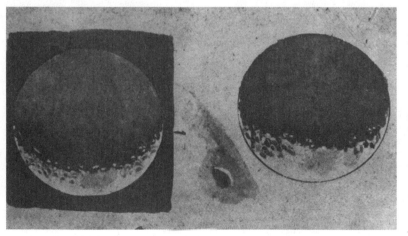

Significant Events and Anniversaries: The creative influence that pervades this day can be seen in the origins of two great artistic establishments on January 2: the *Academie Française* in France, which was founded by Cardinal Richelieu (1635), and Britain's Royal Academy of Arts, established with Sir Joshua Reynolds as its president (1769). Intuition—a quality associated with the Moon—is also a characteristic of this day, on which the pioneering French photographer Louis Daguerre took the first photograph of the Moon (1839) and the unmanned Soviet spacecraft *Luna I* was launched on its journey to pass the Moon (1959). Imperial idealism motivated the British general Clive of India to capture Calcutta (1757), while the Russians saw similar ambitions collapse when they surrendered Port Arthur, in Manchuria, to the Japanese (1905).

JANUARY 3

* *

The magnetic aura of easy personal charm exuded by January 3 people masks the fact that at their core lies a single-minded commitment to the pursuit of their ideals. Once a venture captures their imagination, they will go to almost any lengths to see it through, refusing to compromise or be deflected from their chosen path. Affable, humorous and quirky, their highly individualistic characters draw others to them, and January 3 people can be quick to take advantage of the effect that they have on other people in order to gain their participation in a pet project; this tendency is reinforced if they were born in the Chinese year of the dragon. Such a combination of idealism and manipulative skills makes them imaginative and gifted team leaders, and they will not hesitate to use a whole armory of tactics to ensure that their coworkers achieve a common goal. The quality of wholehearted commitment may be a double-edged sword, however, for it can simultaneously inspire and exasperate others. January 3 people can become obsessive, so convinced of the rightness of their chosen course that they will ignore alternative viewpoints.

Loyalty is a key component in the make-up of January 3 people, and this applies just as much to their domestic as to their professional lives—provided, that is, that their friends and loved ones fall into line with them. Other related features displayed by these people are trustworthiness and reliability, qualities which mean that they will not only deliver anything that is required of them, but will furthermore provide a stable environment for their families. Although others can depend upon their support, January 3 people will suffer disappointment and disillusionment if this loyalty is not reciprocated.

VIRTUES: In every sphere of life January 3 people have clear ambitions, as well as the necessary iron will to carry them out. Such is the power of attraction exerted by their personalities that they have no trouble in winning the friendship and devotion of others.
VICES: Their strong wills, highly developed reliance on self, and determination to succeed can be so overwhelming that these people run the dual risk of alienating others or of becoming blind to the feasibility of their chosen projects. Such stubbornness has its advantages, but must not be misplaced.
VERDICT: January 3 people should ensure that they do not dismiss out of hand those opinions with which they do not initially agree, and that they strive to remain constantly open-minded; in this way their considerable talents will not be misdirected and they will avoid being disappointed by the failure of unrealistic ideals.

Planetary Influences
Ruling planet: Saturn.
Second decan: Personal planet is Venus.

Sacred and Cultural Significance
Annual performance of the Deer Dances, a Pueblo fertility ceremony; Lenaia, ancient Greek religious ceremony honoring Dionysus.
Saint's day: Geneviève (d. c.500).

Martin Luther nailing his theses protesting corruption in the Catholic Church to the door of a church in Wittenberg, Germany. He was excommunicated for his zealous campaign for reform on January 3, 1521, an illustration of the conflicts of ideals and beliefs that have historically come to a head on this day.

On This Day
Famous Births: Marcus Tullius Cicero (106 BC); Robert Whitehead (1823); Father Damien (1840); Clement Attlee (1883); Herbert Morrison (1888); Osip Mandelsthan (1891); J.R.R. Tolkien (1892); Ray Milland (1905); Victor Borge (1909); George Martin (1926); Dabney Coleman (1932); John Thaw (1942); Victoria Principal (1946); Stephen Stills (1945); Mel Gibson (1956).

Significant Events and Anniversaries: Certain events of this day illustrate the conflicts that may inevitably result from the single-minded pursuit of ideals and ambitions: the Catholic Church, infuriated by the beliefs and activities of Martin Luther, excommunicated him (1521); during the American War of Independence, George Washington's army defeated the British forces at the Battle of Princeton (1777); and the U.S.A. severed all diplomatic relations with Cuba (1961). Other events illustrate the rewards that can be won through sheer perseverance in the furtherance of cherished aims, such as the discovery of the tomb of Tutankhamen in the Valley of the Kings, Egypt, by British explorer Howard Carter (1924), and the attainment of his goal of reaching the South Pole by New Zealand explorer Edmund Hillary (1958).

JANUARY 4

Planetary Influences
Ruling planet: Saturn.
Second decan: Personal planet is Venus.

♄ ♀

Sacred and Cultural Significance
In Korea, Chilseong-je (Sacrifice to the Seven Stars).
Saints' day: Roger of Ellant (d.1160); Elizabeth Seton (1774–1821).

Benjamin Rush, born on January 4, 1785, combined his practical skills as a physician with his firm abolitionist beliefs to work effectively for social and economic change. Born in the Chinese year of the dragon, he was characteristically decisive, hard-working and tenacious.

People born on this day manage to combine an impressive capacity for organization in their working and domestic habits with a notable independence of thought, with the result that they often come up with ideas of startling originality, and then implement them with meticulous thoroughness. Their perceptive and incisive minds cut straight to the heart of a problem and, once they have identified their preferred solution, they will be unswerving in its pursuit. They will sometimes manifest a deep and genuine concern for the well-being of humanity and may act on their convictions by becoming involved in political activism. On an individual level, this means that they are sensitive, empathetic and supportive friends and partners, while on a more global scale their desire to improve the lot of those who are less fortunate, as well as their capacity for inventiveness, frequently makes them gifted teachers, charity workers or social pioneers. These people may also prove successful in business ventures, because of their ability to back up their innovative ideas effectively with solid and efficient organizational practices.

Although they enjoy the good things of life and tend to indulge in hedonistic pleasures, especially when young, January 4 people will not be diverted by the trivial for very long, preferring to exert their considerable energies on tasks and projects that will give them a deeper sense of fulfillment. If taken too far, however, such behavior could cut them off from many new experiences and potential friendships. They should also recognize that,while others may not share their goals or methodology, this does not invalidate the worth of alternative opinions, and that there is much to be gained from embracing diversity, whatever form this takes.

VIRTUES: Widely admired as "can-do" people, those born on January 4 possess the ability to reconcile easily their tendency for social idealism with uncompromisingly practical methods, and therefore have the potential to see their visions realized.
VICES: Because these people are quick to identify both the nub of a problem and its possible solution, they may become impatient with, and dismissive of, colleagues and acquaintances who do not share their clear-cut convictions.
VERDICT: January 4 people have considerable potential to succeed in every area of life, but must remember that other people's opinions—even if they conflict with their own—may have equal validity. They should therefore guard against a tendency toward intolerance.

On This Day
Famous Births: Jakob Grimm and Benjamin Rush (1785); Louis Braille (1809); Sir Isaac Pitman (1813); George Washington Carver (1861); Josef Suk (1874); Augustus John (1878); C.L. James (1901); Sterling Holloway (1905); Jane Wyman (1914); Floyd Patterson (1935); Dyan Cannon and Grace Bumbry (1937); John McLaughlin (1942).

Significant Events and Anniversaries: Reflecting this day's propensity for problem-solving, the first chess column to be printed in a newspaper appeared in *Bell's Life in London* (1835); the Fabian Society—a socially concerned organization intended to improve the lot of humankind—was founded in Britain (1884); while in Iowa, Dr. Williams West Grant performed the first successful appendix operation—a significant step forward in medical history—on twenty-two-year-old Mary Gartside (1885). The conflict that is often the consequence when strong views collide with each other can be seen in three events that occurred on this day: the British pronouncement of Gandhi's National Congress of India as illegal (1932); the start of the British Fifth Army's onslaught on Monte Cassino, Italy, during World War II (1944); and the Communist capture of Seoul, South Korea, during the Korean War (1951). Among the many political achievements that have occurred on January 4 are: Utah's confirmation as the 45th state of the U.S.A. (1896); Burma's attainment of independence from the British Commonwealth (1948); and the appointment of the first woman judge, Rose Heilbron, to London's High Court (1972).

JANUARY 5

Individuals born on this day are natural adventurers, their questing minds leading them readily to explore the fascination of the unknown. Yet they are not flighty types: mixed in with this independent streak is a strong tendency toward employing practical methods and finding pragmatic solutions to any obstacles that they may encounter on their journeys of discovery. Thus, while they believe in following their highly developed instincts, they will pursue their ideological aims with logical thoroughness and rigorous self-discipline. Their tendency toward optimism furthermore gives them an impressive capacity to withstand or dismiss any setbacks. Such personal characteristics signal the potential for great success in whichever career they choose, but since they often manifest outstanding artistic talents, January 5 people will especially excel in the creative or performing arts, as well as in the political or scientific spheres.

In common with many who rely strongly upon their intuition when it comes to decision-making and questions of judgement, January 5 people are unusually sensitive in tuning in to those around them. Empathetic and understanding, they are valued as friends, but are nevertheless not prepared to give of themselves limitlessly, and may grow impatient if those who seek their support and advice are reluctant to accept the benefit of their wisdom. Having arrived at a carefully considered set of convictions, and having developed a corresponding *modus operandi*, there is an inevitable tendency for those born on this day to stick rigidly to these preferences and close their minds to alternative approaches. Their self-belief is more often than not justified, but they should remember that there is much to be gained from personal interaction and constant re-evaluation.

VIRTUES: Those born on this day are imaginative and independent, and their sensible, grounded approach tempers any tendency to pursue unrealistic goals. Self-confident and yet sensitive to others, they are respected by those around them and make outstanding leaders.
VICES: There is a danger that January 5 people may become too self-reliant, rejecting the contributions of those people not of the same mind.
VERDICT: January 5 people contain all the ingredients for personal success within them, but must take care that they neither exclude those who profess different opinions from their lives, nor become too rigidly set in their own ways. Keeping an open and accepting mind is of paramount importance.

Planetary Influences
Ruling planet: Saturn.
Second decan: Personal planet is Venus.

Sacred and Cultural Significance
Saints' day: Simeon Stylites (390–459); John Neumann (1811–60).

Multicultural Jerusalem was the site of the historic meeting of Roman Catholic and Orthodox leaders, which occurred on January 5, 1964, a day on which open-mindedness and respect for others are important values.

On This Day
Famous Births: Stephen Decatur (1779); John Burke (1787); Konrad Adenauer (1876); Stella Gibbons (1902); Jeane Dixon (1918); Arturo Benedetti Michelangeli (1920); Walter Mondale (1928); Zulfikar Ali Bhutto (1928); Alvin Ailey, Alfred Brendel and Robert Duvall (1931); King Juan Carlos I of Spain (1938); Maurizio Pollini (1942); Eusébio (1943); Diane Keaton (1946).

Significant Events and Anniversaries: Two advances in technical development were first demonstrated this day, illustrating the successful consummation of this day's potential for problem-solving: X-rays were unveiled by German scientist Wilhelm von Röntgen (1896) and FM radio was invented by U.S. army officer Edward H. Armstrong (1940). The political field is starred by this day, and in Europe the German Workers Party (later the Nazi Party) was founded by Anton Drexler (1919), while Alexander Dubcek became the leader of the Polish Communist Party (1968), and in the U.S.A., the determined Nellie Taylor Ross of Wyoming became the nation's first female governor (1925). Demonstrating the importance of the spirit of reconciliation and mutual tolerance highlighted by January 5, Pope Paul VI met the ecumenical patriarch of Constantinople in Jerusalem, the first meeting of the Roman Catholic and Orthodox churches for five centuries (1964).

JANUARY 6

Planetary Influences
Ruling planet: Saturn.
Second decan: Personal planet is Venus.

Sacred and Cultural Significance
In Christianity, Twelfth Night.
Saints' day: Peter of Canterbury (d. 607); the feast of the Magi: Caspar, Melchior and Balthasar (d. 1st century AD), patron saints of travelers.

The dedicated, inspirational St. Joan of Arc, born on January 6, 1412.

Underpinning many of the beliefs and actions of people born on January 6 is a profoundly mystical sense of union with the unseen forces that govern the earth. This empathy may take the form of ecological crusades, or else may find its spiritual expression in religion. Either way, these people form firm moral judgements and are determined enough to overcome their natural tendency to gentleness both to defend their convictions and spread their message to others. Such propagation is greatly aided by their ability to connect with others, and thus effectively to impart their vision to the world. This potent combination of intellectual conviction and communication skills makes people born on this day talented teachers, politicians and artists, but they will flourish in any area in which they can provide focused leadership. Depending as they do so deeply on their instincts, there is a danger that these people will rely on these exclusively, politely rejecting alternative viewpoints. Parents of January 6 children should therefore encourage them to appreciate the value of both personal experience and the wisdom of others.

Because they are inherently self-disciplined, service oriented, and driven by their ideals, these people manifest an unusual degree of both tenacity and determination to see a task through, in order that humanity can enjoy the fruits of their visions. Such drive is commendable, but these people should remember that not only is perfection rarely achievable, but that it also exacts a considerable personal toll. They should therefore take care not to neglect their private lives, and should accept the fact that their friends and families appreciate them for what they already are.

VIRTUES: People born on this day have a highly developed sense of fair play and morality, as well as the determination and capability to impart their ideals in inspirational fashion.
VICES: So convinced are they of the urgency of spreading their message to society that these people have a tendency to become obsessed with achieving their ideological objectives, to the detriment of their own needs and personal relationships.
VERDICT: January 6 people should remember to retain an element of objectivity and tolerance in all their ventures, and to devote as much time to their personal life as to their professional and ideological concerns in order to find complete fulfillment.

On This Day
Famous Births: King Richard II of England (1367); St. Joan of Arc (1412); Heinrich Schliemann (1822); Gustave Doré (1832); Max Bruch (1838); Carl Sandburg (1878); Loretta Young (1912); Danny Thomas (1914); Sun Myung Moon (1920); John DeLorean (1925); P.J. Kavanagh (1931); E.L. Doctorow (1931); Bonnie Franklin and Henry Kravis (1944); Rowan Atkinson (1955); Kapil Dev (1959); Joey Lauren Adams (1971).

Significant Events and Anniversaries: January 6 is a day that augurs well for the realm of communication, as was seen when Samuel Morse demonstrated his innovative electromagnetic telegraph that would revolutionize long-distance contact (1838). One event of this day especially underlines the conflict that can be the tragic result of unyielding idealism: in a bloody battle, King Alfred of Wessex defeated the Danes at the Battle of Ashdown (871). Unshakably convinced of his right to the monarchy, Harold II was crowned king of England (1066), an event that would lead to the Norman Conquest; while as a result of his obsession to breed sons and thus secure the succession, King Henry VIII of England rashly contracted an ill-fated marriage with Anne of Cleves (1540).

JANUARY 7

January 7 people have little difficulty in attracting others to them: cheerful, affectionate, loyal and generous in their personal lives, these qualities, which are reinforced if they were born in the Chinese year of the dog, are cherished by friends, family members and coworkers alike. These people have the instinctive gift of being able to sense the moods of other people, a talent which, when combined with their genuine empathy and desire to smooth the way for their fellows, makes their company much sought after. Such qualities make them ideally suited to social work and medicine, or similar activities where their considerable interpersonal and communicative skills can best be employed. It would amaze many to realize, however, that despite their reputation as being pillars of strength, these sensitive people frequently harbor a deep lack of self-confidence and therefore seek to gain a sense of validation and worth from the affection and respect of others.

Personal connection is therefore of great importance to people born on this day, but they also possess a real sense of integration with the natural world, as well as a pronounced otherworldly, mystical side, which fuels an extraordinarily imaginative capacity. It is thus not hard for these people not only to accept, but also to manifest, a marked fascination with unexplained phenomena. Although they would be well advised to pursue their instincts, many do not, apprehensive of being branded cranks. When backed up with the methodical and disciplined approach characteristic of January 7 people, however, this tendency toward original thought can find satisfying fruition.

VIRTUES: These open-minded, sensitive people are genuinely concerned with the welfare of others and will exert their considerable energies on other people's behalf. Imaginative and tenacious, they are unfettered by conventional beliefs.
VICES: January 7 people are in danger of placing too high a value on receiving the approval of others, often to the extent of suppressing their true opinions for fear that they will cause alienation and ridicule.
VERDICT: People born on this day should work on bolstering their sense of self-belief and should accept that the convictions of others, although valuable, are not paramount. In this way, they will be able to find a greater capacity for the freedom of expression that is so important to their emotional well-being.

On This Day

Famous Births: Jacques Etienne Montgolfier (1745); Joseph Bonaparte (1768); Millard Fillmore (1800); St. Bernadette of Lourdes (1844); Carl Laemmle (1867); Charles Péguy and Adolf Zukor (1873); François Poulenc (1899); Zora Neale Hurston (1901); Charles Addams (1912); Vincent Gardenia and Jean-Pierre Rampal (1922); Gerald Durrell (1925); Kenny Loggins (1948); Erin Gray (1952); Donna Rice (1958); Katie Couric (1957); Nicolas Cage (1964).

Significant Events and Anniversaries: Others branded them eccentrics, but three individuals pursued their particular interests with notable success, thus demonstrating the potential for scientific breakthrough favored by this day. While studying the planet Jupiter, the astrologer Galileo discovered its four satellites naming them: Europa, Io, Callisto and Ganymede (1610). The first aerial crossing of the English Channel was made by Dr. John Jeffries and Jean-Pierre Blanchard in a hot-air balloon (1785). A desire for social welfare is heralded by this day, as is reflected in the holding of its first nationwide elections by the fledgling democracy of the U.S.A. (1789). An important quality of this day is communication, and it marks the anniversary of the inauguration of the first telephone service between New York and London (1927).

Planetary Influences
Ruling planet: Saturn.
Second decan: Personal planet is Venus.

Sacred and Cultural Significance
Saints' day: Brannoc (dates unknown); Lucian of Antioch (d.312); Kentigerna (d. c.733); Canute Lavard (c.1096–1131); Raymund of Pennafort (c.1180–1275), patron saint of canonists.

Galileo, who discovered the satellites of Jupiter on this day in 1610, demonstrates his telescope to senators of Venice. Scientific breakthroughs are favored on January 7.

JANUARY 8

****

Planetary Influences
Ruling planet: Saturn.
Second decan: Personal planet is Venus.

Sacred and Cultural Significance
Saints' day: Gudule (c.648–712), patron saint of Brussels, Belgium; Nathalan (d. c.678); Pega (d. c.719); Wulsin (d. 1002); Thorfinn (d. 1285).

Stephen Hawking, one of the most brilliant, original and acclaimed scientists of the twentieth century, was born on this day in 1942. With his Moon in Virgo, Hawking is especially analytical and logical, and his Chinese star sign, the snake, reinforces his cerebral focus.

Exceptionally single-minded and highly motivated, those born on this day possess the potential to achieve outstanding success in whatever field they choose, be it in the creative arts, where their artistic imaginations can be given full rein; in scientific pursuits, where they can best employ their considerable aptitude for analysis; or in philanthropic work, where their empathetic instincts can be satisfied. January 8 people often harbor burning personal ambition but, being pragmatic and somewhat saturnine personalities, realize that the recognition they desire will have to be assiduously worked for. Yet although they possess the necessary radical vision, determination and drive to realize their dreams, they may find that their achievements are somewhat empty if they have sacrificed their personal relationships in pursuit of their cherished goals.

The irony is that while these people may appear almost intimidatingly poised and self-possessed, underneath lies a very real sense of anxiety and insecurity which is masked by an outward façade of cool reserve. Perhaps January 8 people believe that it is only by spectacular success that they will gain the affection of others, but this is far from the case, and they run the risk of loneliness and disillusionment if they persist in this conviction. They should therefore ensure that they actively seek out and nurture honest and relaxed relationships with others, for it is ultimately from such loving and supportive bonds that they will find the key to personal happiness and fulfillment.

VIRTUES: January 8 people display an unusual level of imagination, originality, self-discipline and motivation, and are therefore capable of rising to the highest levels in their chosen professions.
VICES: The personal ambition inherent in these people may develop into an overwhelming compulsion, with the danger that in extreme cases they may withdraw from society and become obsessive, self-involved and isolated from others.
VERDICT: People born on this day should remember that professional triumph alone is not enough to bring about their ultimate personal contentment. They should therefore cherish their personal contacts and beware of taking themselves too seriously.

On This Day
Famous Births: Wilkie Collins (1824); John Curtin (1885); Dennis Wheatley (1897); Solomon Bandaranaike (1899); Georgi Malenkov (1901); José Ferrer (1912); Ron Moody (1924); Charles Osgood (1933); Elvis Presley (1935); Shirley Bassey (1937); Yvette Mimieux (1939); Stephen Hawking (1942); David Bowie (1947); Calvin Smith (1961); Ami Dolenz (1969).

Significant Events and Anniversaries: Reflecting this day's empathetic indication, the world's first soup kitchen dedicated to feeding the poor was opened in London (1800). The importance of maintaining and promoting equality and harmony in relationships applies just as much to nations as to individuals, a lesson learned by the British when they were defeated by U.S. forces under Andrew Jackson at the Battle of New Orleans (1815) and a principle underlined by the passage in Congress of a bill granting suffrage to African Americans in Washington, D.C. (1867). Tenacity and self-belief can bring victory laurels, as demonstrated when the Severn Railway Tunnel (which remained Britain's longest until the construction of the "Chunnel" in the 1990s) was successfully completed and opened (1886), and by Dr. Herman Hollerith when he patented the first computer, which was later marketed by I.B.M. (1889), or when General Charles de Gaulle was elevated to the presidency of the French Fifth Republic (1959).

JANUARY 9

✦✦

Blessed with sharp, analytical intellects, keen powers of perception, and great reserves of energy, January 9 people demand high standards from themselves as well as others, and will not easily accept defeat. They are sometimes intensely ambitious, but their desire is fueled more by perfectionism—by the need to see a task done as well as possible—than by a craving for plaudits or adulation. People born on this day are therefore valued employees, for when given charge of any project they will quickly identify the best course of action, and then set about accomplishing it with characteristic focus and drive. Yet January 9 people are not really corporate animals, cherishing freedom of thought, expression and movement over the restrictions that are usually imposed by large organizations, and they generally thrive better when they are self-employed.

Family is extremely important to people born on this day. Deeply committed to providing the best possible opportunities for their children, they will often work long hours to gain the necessary financial means to achieve them, but in doing so they inevitably sacrifice time spent together. They may also make enormous demands of their children in terms of academic attainments, albeit with the highest motives. It is therefore important that these people do not push their children too hard, but accept their true selves and limitations, love them for who they are, and support them uncritically. They will also gain personally from a more relaxed approach to family life, which will provide a valuable safety valve to release the pressures built up by their professional commitments.

VIRTUES: Formidable drive, determination and tenacity are combined in these efficient people, who have both the intellectual and temperamental ability to shrug off obstacles in the pursuit of their career and personal goals.
VICES: Their characteristically single-minded approach can lead January 9 people to deprive themselves of the simple pleasures of life, notably relaxation and the satisfaction that can be gained from the company of friends and family members.
VERDICT: People born on this day should strive to maintain a balance, to compromise and to recognize that giving priority to intellectual or professional pursuits can have a pernicious effect and will deprive them of the liberating benefits of a full personal life.

On This Day

Famous Births: John Jervis, Earl of St. Vincent (1735); Jenny Jerome, Lady Randolph Churchill (1854); Karel Capek (1890); Gracie Fields (1898); Chic Young (1901); Rudolf Bing (1902); George Balanchine (1904); Simone de Beauvoir (1908); Richard Nixon (1913); Gypsy Rose Lee (1914); Joan Baez and Susannah York (1941); Jimmy Page (1944); Crystal Gayle (1951).

Significant Events and Anniversaries: Resourcefulness and uncompromising demands are indicated by this day, and, indeed, January 9 was the day that income tax was introduced in Britain (1799). Reflecting the day's tendency to sacrifice personal pleasures in pursuit of the common good, New York State banned flirting in public (1902), while the Bolsheviks finally defeated the White Russians, heralding the introduction of the Communist ideology of the Soviet Union (1920). Confirming the tenacity and potential that this day promises, Alexander Fleming used penicillin successfully for the first time (1929), and the first trial of the supersonic Anglo-French Concorde took place in Bristol, England (1969).

Planetary Influences
Ruling planet: Saturn.
Second decan: Personal planet is Venus.

Sacred and Cultural Significance
Saints' day: Berthwald (693–731); Adrian of Canterbury (d. 709–10); Fillan (8th century AD).

The Bolsheviks gained ascendancy over White Russia on this day in 1920. This achievement occurred on a day governed by the tendency to sacrifice personal fulfillment in favor of an abstract goal.

Planetary Influences
Ruling planet: Saturn.
Second decan: Personal planet is Venus.

Sacred and Cultural Significance
The Feast of Dreams, Iroquois New Year's celebration.
Saints' day: Paul the First Hermit (d. c.345); Dermot (6th century AD); Saethrith (7th century AD).

January 10 marks the anniversary of a number of significant British "firsts," including the introduction of Indian tea in 1839.

JANUARY 10

★★★

Energetic, realistic and forthright to the point of bluntness, the qualities manifested by people born on January 10 inspire respect and not a little awe in others. The force that drives them is usually their unceasing quest for knowledge, their deep-rooted need to understand, judge the situation and then bring about improvement, never fearing to manipulate others to further their cause. Indeed, such is the boldness of their approach that they will often confidently propose an outrageously radical solution to a problem, and then watch it either fail or succeed spectacularly. Such self-confidence, originality and uncompromising certainty makes these people ideally suited to the speculative end of the financial sector, where their appetite for risk-taking can be amply satisfied, and they can gain the recognition that they feel their talents merit. They will rarely find fulfillment as a small cog in a large wheel, and will only thrive in those situations where their individuality and need to take control can be given full expression.

Blessed with considerable personal charm and an infectious aura of optimism, January 10 people often find themselves the center of attention, but run the risk of hurting others' feelings by their honest observations. They should therefore be aware of the fact that judicious use of tact will often help them achieve their objectives more effectively, and will help to win them the lasting loyalty of their friends. Despite the robust face that they present to the world, these people are also highly sensitive, and perform best when they are bolstered by the affection and esteem of those around them. By actively working on maintaining their friendships, they stand to gain as much as they invest.

VIRTUES: Vibrant, positive and incisive, January 10 people have the confidence and optimism of approach to realize their inherent potential and make a valuable contribution to anything that they undertake.
VICES: These people feel an irresistible urge to speak their minds, a feature that has undoubted merits in certain situations, but is best tempered in their interpersonal relationships. They should restrain their tendency to dominate and manipulate others.
VERDICT: January 10 people are livewires, possessed of boundless enthusiasm and an infectiously positive attitude. If they just remember to treat others as they themselves would wish to be treated, they will go far.

On This Day
Famous Births: Michel Ney (1769); Jesse James (1847); Robinson Jeffers (1887); Barbara Hepworth (1903); Ray Bolger (1904); Paul Henreid (1908); Galina Ulanova (1910); Gustav Husak (1913); Max Roach (1924); Giselle MacKenzie and Johnny Ray (1927); Sherrill Milnes (1935); Burnum Burnum (1936); Sal Mineo (1939); Rod Stewart (1945); George Foreman (1949); Pat Benatar (1953).

Significant Events and Anniversaries: Reflecting this day's potential for progress, it is the anniversary of many administrative and technical advances, including the introduction of the "Penny Post" by Sir Rowland Hill in Britain (1840), and the opening of the London Underground railway by the British prime minister, William Gladstone (1863). In the political arena, too, positive advances are starred: the U.S. House of Representatives took a large constitutional step forward when it voted in favor of women's suffrage (1918), and the U.N. Assembly held its first meeting (1946). Although the Treaty of Versailles, which ended World War I, was ratified on this day, the League of Nations was inaugurated (1920), and British inventor Sir Clive Sinclair demonstrated his C5 electric car (1985), neither the treaty, organization nor automobile were ultimately successful, demonstrating that success will not always result from the boldness indicated by this day. The execution of scapegoat Marinus van Lubbe for allegedly starting the Reichstag fire in Berlin (1934) tragically illustrates the powers of manipulation that are indicated on this day.

JANUARY 11

Those born on January 11 are blessed with unusually sharp powers of perception, which, when combined with their keen intellects, result in a formidable talent for objective, thorough evaluation and effective decision-making. Little escapes these people, and when there is a problem to be solved they typically display an impressive ability to marshal the facts available to them, impartially weigh up the merits or disadvantages inherent in alternative approaches, and then come to an intelligent, closely argued strategy. This talent for objectivity, logical thought and intellectual clarity makes January 11 people especially well suited to careers in academic research, or else in business, areas in which these qualities—as well as their characteristic refusal to allow their judgement to become clouded by emotional concerns—are greatly prized. Because these people possess such highly developed critical faculties, and are furthermore articulate and quick-witted, they should beware of pronouncing their opinions too forcefully and thereby offending those who may not share their point of view or sense of certainty.

January 11 people are intensely loyal to those people and things that they consider merit their devotion. Though they may seem unapproachable at first, they have the potential to make excellent friends and parents. They should, however, beware of a tendency toward stubbornness and becoming impatient with those who do not quickly fall into line with their own way of thinking, especially as parents. By ensuring that they keep a check on their propensity to judge others against their own exacting standards, and relaxing their inclination to maintain a certain structured formality in their relationships, they will benefit from a richer personal life.

VIRTUES: Coolly logical, exceptionally clear-sighted, responsible and reliable, January 11 people can be trusted to make impeccably evaluated decisions, and then carry them out with unfailing efficiency.
VICES: Confident in their own capabilities, these people have a tendency toward extreme obstinacy, rarely making concessions if they feel convinced of the correctness of their approach. They are liable to appear arrogant and unwilling to listen to advice or criticism. A further cause for concern is their tendency to envisage a range of possible future scenarios, which leads them to harbor and dwell on unnecessary anxieties, especially if they were born in the Chinese year of the rat.
VERDICT: Inherent in these people are admirable intellectual powers, but they should beware of becoming too inflexible, and should make a concerted effort to accept and accommodate differences of opinion and approach and to temper their judgemental responses.

On This Day

Famous Births: Daniel Dancer (1716); Alexander Hamilton (1757); Ezra Cornell (1807); Alexander MacDonald (1815); William James (1842); Christian Sinding (1856); Fred Archer and Henry Gordon Selfridge (1857); George Nathaniel Curzon (1859); William Stephenson (1896); Alan Paton (1903); Ellery Queen and Tex Ritter (1907); Neville Duke (1922); Grant Tinker (1926); Rod Taylor (1929); Naomi Judd (1946); Ben Crenshaw (1952).

Significant Events and Anniversaries: The first state lottery was held in England (1569), reflecting an unusual blend of the powers of inventiveness and financial acumen that are inherent in this day. Canadian patient Leonard Thompson was the first person to be successfully treated with insulin at Toronto General Hospital, Canada (1922), again illustrating the benefits that can result from the day's tenacity and intellectual rigor, as is also seen in the exemplary medical care that allowed the world's first surviving sextuplets to be delivered to Mrs. Rosenkowitz in Cape Town, South Africa (1974). Joachim Murat, king of Naples, deserted Napoleon to join forces with the Allies (1813), and King Zog of Albania was deposed on this day (1946), testimony, perhaps, to the obstinacy involved in maintaining conflicting, inflexible ideological viewpoints, and Australia's assistant police commissioner Colin Winshester was fatally shot (1989).

Planetary Influences
Ruling planet: Saturn.
Third decan: Personal planet is Mercury.

Sacred and Cultural Significance
Carmentalia celebrated in ancient Rome; Juturna honored in Italy.
Saints' day: Theodosius (d. AD 529).

Alexander Hamilton, first secretary of the treasury (1789–95), helped influence the adoption of the U.S. constitution. He was endowed with all the potential virtues of January 11 people.

Planetary Influences
Ruling planet: Saturn.
Third decan: Personal planet is Mercury.

Sacred and Cultural Significance
Hindu ceremony of Makara-Sankranti.
Saints' day: Benedict Biscop (628–89);
Salvius (7th century AD); Ailred of
Rievaulx (1110–67); Antony Mary Pucci
(1819–92).

*In 1970 the first transatlantic flight by a Boeing
747 was accomplished on January 12—a day of
adventure and pioneering influences.*

JANUARY 12

Challenging, entertaining, sharp and self-assured, these people tread a fine line between introversion and extroversion. While their incisive intelligence and tendency toward nit-picking criticism may signal an unusual level of self-reliance, they also enjoy the attention that their outspokenness and unabashed individuality brings them, and frequently relish playing to the crowd. January 12 people do not do things by half-measures, and once their mercurial minds have alighted on a topic that intrigues them, they pursue their interests with near-obsessive intensity. They are unafraid of promoting their opinions, and, indeed, welcome a challenging argument in which they will attempt to their utmost to convince others of the veracity of their point of view. Somewhat maverick in their approach, these people flourish best either in those organizations that allow them complete freedom of thought and action, or when working on their own account. They will find the greatest satisfaction engaged in any business activity—such as sales and marketing—within which they can perhaps bend the rules to promote their own beliefs and aims.

In their personal lives, January 12 people often manifest the need to be at the center of attention, and absolutely hate being ignored. They will frequently manufacture confrontational scenarios for the sheer enjoyment of provoking a reaction, and enjoy nothing more than playing devil's advocate. This occasionally pugnacious approach carries its risks, however, and these people should ensure that they do not get carried away with themselves and thus hurt the feelings of those who are less emotionally robust—particularly their family members, whom they may inadvertently discourage by their cynicism.

VIRTUES: Independently minded, quick-witted and confident, January 12 people are adventurous and welcome intellectual stimulation. Their sometimes unusual convictions are supported by a strong level of commitment, a combination that promises great success.
VICES: If taken to its extreme, the pronounced self-certainty manifested by these people can lead to arrogance which, when expressed in the dismissive, sarcastic terms to which they are prone, can alienate others and thereby cause their own marginalization.
VERDICT: January 12 people should remember to temper their natural impatience with sensitivity and respect for the feelings and opinions of others. They undoubtedly have much to offer, but may need to adjust their approach to ensure that their better qualities are appreciated and that they do not drive others away.

On This Day
Famous Births: Charles Perrault (1628); Edmund Burke (1729); Johann Heinrich Pestalozzi (1746); Jean Joseph Etienne Lenoir (1822); Joseph Joffre (1852); John Singer Sargent (1856); Jack London (1876); Hermann Goering (1893); Paul Hermann Muller (1899); Luise Rainer (1910); P.W. Botha and Ray Price (1926); Des O'Connor (1932); Long John Baldry (1941); Joe Frazier (1944); Anthony Andrews (1948); Howard Stern (1954); Kirstie Alley (1955).

Significant Events and Anniversaries: Among the auguries of this day are unusual and farsighted ideas, as seen in the establishment of the Aeronautical Society of Great Britain before humanity had fully realized the possibilities of flight (1866), while this was also the day that the first Boeing 747 jet made its maiden transatlantic flight from New York to London (1970). Potential collision is indicated on this day, and tragically the British submarine *Truculent* crashed into a Swedish ship, causing the loss of sixty-five lives (1950). Boxing is perhaps the ultimate manifestation of human confrontation, and on this day Henry Cooper became the British and European heavyweight boxing champion when he defeated Brian London (1959).

JANUARY 13

January 13 people are highly motivated—even driven—by the desire to effect improvement, be it in the personal, material sense by "bettering" themselves, or by instituting a global, philanthropic scheme to help the lot of humanity. Nor are such grandiose ambitions doomed to remain mere pipe dreams, for these people have sufficient intellectual capability, directness of approach, and boundless energy to see them realized. When faced with an unsatisfactory position, be it in these people's careers or in society as a whole, they will quickly and surely identify a solution and then doggedly work toward its implementation, cutting aggressively through obstructions and pushing ever onward toward their ultimate objective. Whatever it is that inspires them, they will give it their all, but in doing so will inevitably encounter confrontation and resistance, which they will typically handle with perfunctory disdain. Social reform is therefore a natural area of interest for January 13 people, but their imagination and single-mindedness give them the potential to succeed in many arenas.

Although such all-consuming clarity of focus and clear-cut goals are admirable qualities, they may leave little room for human relationships, and those born on this day would do well to remember that, while saving the world is laudable, they may simultaneously neglect those who are close to them, with often far-reaching, destructive consequences. This *caveat* applies particularly to men, whose partners or children may suffer from a devastating loss of self-esteem if they perceive that their personal needs and concerns are being dismissed or are considered of secondary importance. They should take heed of their own need for relaxation and the simpler pleasures of life, and ensure that they do not sacrifice their physical or emotional health to their aspirations.

VIRTUES: People born on this day are imaginative, determined to the point of obsession, and motivated by the highest of ideals for improvement. They will let nothing stand in the way of their objectives and are capable of implementing far-reaching changes.
VICES: In their determination to achieve their goals, these people may ride roughshod over others; they should be aware of the attendant risk of creating alienation and even enmity in others and should weigh up the pros and cons of their actions.
VERDICT: In all their activities, January 13 people should strive to retain a sense of balance, ensuring that they do not disregard either their own personal needs, or those of their family and friends, in the struggle to move the world forward on their own terms.

On This Day

Famous Births: Horatio Alger (1832); Peter Dawson (1882); Sophie Tucker (1884); Ted Willis (1918); Robert Stack (1919); Harry Worth (1920); Johannes Bjelke-Petersen (1921); Gwen Verdon (1925); Michael Bond (1926); Charles Nelson Reilly (1931); Richard Moll (1943); Julia-Louis Dreyfus (1961).

Significant Events and Anniversaries: Mirroring the capacity for ideological and social change indicated by this day, Keir Hardie established the socialist Independent British Labour Party (1893); writer Emile Zola published his letter "*J'accuse!*" in the French newspaper *L'Aurore*, condemning the prevailing antisemitic sentiments exposed by the Dreyfus Affair (1898); and Dr. Robert Weaver became the first African American to serve in a presidential cabinet when President Lyndon B. Johnson appointed him head of the newly created Department of Housing and Urban Development (1966). Confirming the day's ceaseless quest for improvement, opera was first broadcast from the stage of the Metropolitan Opera House in New York, thus bringing the voice of Enrico Caruso to a wider audience (1910); N.A.S.A. selected its first women astronauts (1978), thereby advancing the cause of female equality; and the world's largest airport was opened at Dallas, Texas (1974).

Planetary Influences
Ruling planet: Saturn.
Third decan: Personal planet is Mercury.

Sacred and Cultural Significance
Feast of Brewing celebrated by Druids.
Saints' day: Hilary of Poitiers (c.315–c.368); Kentigern (d. 612).

Years of dedicated research bore fruit when the first live radio transmission brought music from the Metropolitan Opera House to the public in 1910. Both progress and determination are abundant in January 13's stars.

****

Planetary Influences
Ruling planet: Saturn.
Third decan: Personal planet is Mercury.

Sacred and Cultural Significance
Pongal festival held in India.
Saints' day: Felix of Nola (d. 260);
Macrina the Elder (d. 340); Sava
of Serbia (1173–1236).

*Glamorous and self-possessed, Faye Dunaway
knows what she wants and achieves it, living
up to her January 14 potential. With Venus in
Sagittarius, she is naturally inclined to acting,
and her Chinese influences as a metal snake
underline her quiet determination and her
love of elegance and the arts.*

Those born on this day incorporate an intriguing mixture of iron wills and self-indulgence—frequently manifested by their tendency to abandon themselves totally to the pleasures of the senses, to the exquisite. Indeed, their instinctive appreciation of art and music, which is reinforced if they were born in the Chinese year of the snake, as well as their charming and magnetic personalities, mask their very real concern with social injustice and their pronounced determination to change the world for the better. Another apparently paradoxical quirk of their personalities is the juxtaposition of their strongly held ethical beliefs and concomitant desire to impose collective improvements on human society, while at the same time operating on a fiercely individualistic basis. Yet these people, who are governed by a very real sense of right and wrong and are skilled at evaluating the cause of any perceived injustice, will take a fierce personal stance on those issues they hold dear, from which they will refuse to be deflected.

Curiously, for people who are driven by their humanitarian convictions, January 14 people often harbor a deep aversion to making commitments in their personal lives. This may stem from a reluctance to divert their energies from their intellectual ambitions, but may also result from their fear of making the wrong decision. In order to avoid future isolation and loneliness, they should therefore ensure that they do not apply their own ideal moral standards to potential friends and partners, and should learn to appreciate and respect people as they are, compromising accordingly.

VIRTUES: Hawks in doves' clothing, January 14 people are strong-willed and usually possess the enviable facility to identify and then implement their often radical objectives in the most charming and convincing manner.
VICES: These people must beware of misplaced obstinacy, an inevitable danger of their highly developed sense of certainty, which may lead them in a direction from which there is no return and lose them many allies along the way.
VERDICT: People born on this day should take care to remember to respect and make allowances for others who do not share their views and opinions. Fulfillment lies in relaxed and harmonious personal and professional relationships, and not in making brave, lone stands.

On This Day
Famous Births: Benedict Arnold (1741); Ludwig von Köchel (1800); Henri Fantin-Latour (1836); Jean de Reszke (1850); Albert Schweitzer (1875); Hugh Lofting (1886); Hal Roach (1892); Cecil Beaton (1904); William Bendix (1906); Joseph Losey (1909); J. Skelly Wright (1911); Andy Rooney (1919); Yukio Mishima (1925); Tom Tryon and Warren Mitchell (1926); Richard Briers (1934); Jack Jones (1938); Trevor Nunn (1940); Faye Dunaway (1941); Jason Bateman (1969).

Significant Events and Anniversaries: Appreciation for the arts is highlighted on this day, on which Puccini's opera *Tosca* was first performed in Rome (1900), Walt Disney's innovative full-length, Technicolor cartoon *Snow White and the Seven Dwarfs* had its first screening in the U.S.A. (1938), and Britain's Covent Garden Opera Company presented its first performance, *Carmen,* in London (1947). Persistence and determination bore fruit when the king of Sweden acquired present-day Norway, which was ceded by the king of Denmark (1814). Yet this day also carries the danger of moral or religious intransigence, as is reflected in the ritual burning of Salman Rushdie's controversial work, *The Satanic Verses,* by outraged Muslims in Bradford, England, who regarded it as blasphemous (1989). January 14 has seen an unusually high incidence of natural disasters in the Northern Hemisphere, including the earthquake in Kingston, Jamaica, that claimed over one thousand lives (1907).

JANUARY 15

****

January 15 people aspire to perfection, but this desire is generally not fueled by the need to be top dog and reach the pinnacle of their profession (although this may indeed be the culmination of their efforts). Rather than being driven primarily by personal ambition or materialism, they are motivated by idealistic and ethical concerns, and demonstrate a strong urge to lead a moral and useful life, thereby often secretly or openly hoping to inspire others by their example. From a very early age these people may manifest a sure, almost intuitive, sense of right and wrong. This tendency may, however, result in a propensity to see things in black and white, and to dismiss the various shades of gray in between without according them the necessary sympathetic and thorough consideration.

These people are especially sensitive to the suffering of others, and because they are blessed with strong analytical and rational intellectual powers, they are also able to channel their emotional responses into the formulation of a carefully considered plan of action in an attempt to alleviate injustice or distress. They perform best within a team framework that offers the mutual support and encouragement of others, and where their strong convictions will provide inspiration and leadership. For this reason January 15 people are particularly suited to careers in the caring professions, or in the emergency services, but some are also talented artists. They are devoted to their family and friends, desiring to bring about their happiness rather than see them succeed at all costs. They should take care to draw a clear demarcation line between their professional and personal concerns so that they do not impose the crushing burden of living up to their own lofty idealistic expectations on those closest to them.

VIRTUES: Caring, empathetic and highly motivated, these people are driven by an altruistic desire to make the world a better place. As well as being emotionally responsive, they are organized in their activities, determined, and possess the quality of visionary foresight, a combination that gives them the potential to achieve whatever they set out to do.
VICES: January 15 people have a tendency to form unshakable convictions, albeit with the highest possible motives, and will stick stubbornly by them through thick and thin, even when events throw doubt upon their veracity. They must remember to retain a sense of perspective, and demonstrate flexibility in certain circumstances.
VERDICT: People born on this day should try to temper their natural inclination toward idealism by cultivating a grounding sense of realism and greater open-mindedness. This will help them to form a less instinctual and more pragmatic outlook, and will help to protect both them and those closest to them from the bitter disappointment of failing to achieve unattainable expectations.

On This Day

Famous Births: Jean Baptiste Poquelin (Molière) (1622); William Prout (1785); Pierre Joseph Proudhon (1809); Mary MacKillop (1842); Louis Terman (1877); Ivor Novello (1893); Edward Teller (1908); Gene Krupa (1909); Lloyd Bridges (1913); Gamal Nasser (1918); Martin Luther King, Jr. (1929); Margaret O'Brien (1937); Charo (1951); Chad Lowe (1968).

Significant Events and Anniversaries: Appreciation for the arts is indicated by this day, on which: one of the largest such institutions in the world, the British Museum was opened at Montague House, London, with the intention of education and enlightenment (1759); and Tchaikovsky's ballet *Sleeping Beauty* was first performed (1890). Demonstrating the strongly held convictions that frequently collide in warfare, Italian aircraft dropped the world's first propaganda leaflets during the Italo-Turkish War of 1911–12 (1912), while President Nixon called a halt to the U.S.A.'s Vietnam offensive in recognition of the suffering that the martial stalemate was causing (1973). The Irish Free State came into being, reflecting the idealism indicated by this day, which in this case found its expression in a new nation and constitution (1922). The Aswan High Dam was opened in Egypt, the culmination of a project whose benefits, it was hoped, would be manifold (1971).

Planetary Influences
Ruling planet: Saturn.
Third decan: Personal planet is Mercury.

Sacred and Cultural Significance
In ancient Rome, the Feast of the Ass.
Saints' day: Macarius the Great (c.300–90); Ita (d. c.570); Ceolwulf (d. 764–60).

Dr. Martin Luther King, Jr., an idealist, humanitarian and prophet whose leadership and oratory inspired the world, embodied the best of January 15 characteristics. The influence of his Chinese sign, the dragon, served to reinforce his steadfast determination and endow him with extraordinary personal charisma.

Planetary Influences
Ruling planets: Saturn and Uranus.
Third decan: Personal planet is Mercury.
Second cusp: Capricorn with Aquarian tendencies.

Sacred and Cultural Significance
Betoro Bromo honored in Indonesia.
Saints' day: Marcellus (d. 309); Sigebert (d. 635); Fursey (d. 650); Henry of Coquet Island (d. 1127).

As a result of escalating pressure from activists like these, the 18th Amendment was ratified on this day in 1919, bringing Prohibition to the U.S.A. January 16 favors ambitious achievements, though these can sometimes be controversial.

JANUARY 16

Those born on January 16 somehow combine an unusual level of sensitivity with razor-sharp, analytical minds. These are often the people who instinctively absorb the indefinable, sublimely elevating qualities of an artistic masterpiece at the same time as consciously deconstructing and evaluating the technicalities of its composition. These multifaceted qualities (an affinity with the finer things in life as well as rigorous intellectual analysis) make them perfectly suited for careers in arts administration or teaching, and doubly so when their gift for communication is taken into consideration. With such a talent for perceiving and integrating both the mystical and rational, little passes them by, and their abilities are such that they are often much sought after for their opinions and advice. In the business sphere, they make successful management consultants or troubleshooters, where their diplomatic skills are also greatly appreciated.

Valued as these people are by others, their sensitive dispositions, when coupled with their tendency toward intellectual criticism, can result in a feeling of internal crisis or *angst*. Together, their farsightedness and emotional receptiveness may cause January 16 people to become unnecessarily anxious about their future direction, or to believe that they can never live up to their own expectations. The respect and support of their family and friends is therefore of the greatest importance in providing a loving and stable framework in which those born on this day will thrive, particularly when they are young. In turn, January 16 people should remember that little is more important than nurturing personal bonds.

VIRTUES: Sensitive and intuitive, but also possessed of great cerebral clarity and vision, these people possess the rare twin gifts of being in tune with both their emotions and their intellects. They are considerate, tactful and talented communicators.
VICES: These people have a natural tendency toward introspection which, if allowed to develop to its most negative extreme, can result in crushing feelings of inferiority and despair, a state of depression which, once reached, can be hard to overcome.
VERDICT: January 16 people should not allow themselves to become too self-reliant or isolated, but should ensure that they actively foster and maintain strong interpersonal relationships in order to benefit from the encouragement and appreciation of others.

On This Day
Famous Births: Charles H. Davis (1807); Johnston Forbes-Robertson and André Michelin (1853); Robert Service (1874); Laura Riding (1901); Diana Wynyard (1906); Alexander Knox (1907); Ethel Merman (1908); Lord Thomson of Monifieth (1921); Susan Sontag (1933); Ronnie Milsap (1943); John Carpenter (1948); Debbie Allen (1953); Sade (1960); Kate Moss (1974).

Significant Events and Anniversaries: On January 16 visionary aspirations are highlighted, and on this day the British explorer Ernest Shackleton achieved his ambition to reach the area of the South Magnetic Pole (1909). Prohibition was introduced to the U.S.A., a policy which had been carefully evaluated before its implementation, but which eventually proved unsuccessful (1919). Reflecting this day's cultural overtones, Duke Ellington and his orchestra first recorded "It Don't Mean a Thing" (1932), and the famous Cavern Club opened in Liverpool, England (1957). Diplomatic talents are starred on this day, on which General Dwight Eisenhower was appointed Supreme Commander of Allied Forces in Europe (1944). His future success owed as much to his personal tact as to his strategic abilities.

JANUARY 17

****

January 17 people rarely fail to impress others with their forceful sense of purpose and drive. Possessing the enviable ability to evaluate all aspects of a situation and swiftly discard the chaff from the wheat, these people quickly reach a firm opinion which they then promote with an unwavering certainty of purpose. Tenacious and strong-willed, people born on this day have the confidence to brush aside their detractors and proceed on their chosen course undeterred. This direct approach is the mark of the leader, a role which January 17 people are happy to assume—not out of a sense of ambition, but because, having applied their considerable judgemental skills to the formation of their convictions, they are genuinely convinced of the correctness of their actions. They also work well as part of a team, being naturally gregarious and appreciative of other people's input, provided, of course, that they share the same motivations. They will find the greatest fulfillment in any career, such as within the military or police force, in which they can combine their strategic talents with their flair for organizational implementation.

The danger of having such a strong sense of self-belief is that if ever these people are thwarted they can lose their tempers in spectacular fashion. They must therefore try to apply their undoubted capacity for intellectual discipline to their emotions, ensuring that they maintain a sense of equilibrium in their dealings with others, and trying not to become temperamentally unsettled when they encounter inevitable obstacles. Furthermore, they should allow their family members freedom of expression and should not try to be all-controlling or to impose unnecessary demands upon them.

VIRTUES: Independently minded, confident and clear-sighted, these people find it easy to reach a decision and pursue it with single-minded tenacity. Their originality and directness are admired by others, who often regard their qualities as being inspirational.
VICES: People born on this day have a tendency to be domineering, to attempt to control both impersonal situations and the people around them absolutely. If opposed, they may lose their self-control, undoing much of the respect that they otherwise command by petulant displays of temper.
VERDICT: Although they should never allow their major strengths, those of self-belief and integrity, to be compromised, January 17 people should always be mindful of the value of mutual respect and cooperation, and must try not to dominate others. This is particularly important in their personal relationships.

On This Day
Famous Births: Benjamin Franklin (1706); Anne Brontë (1820); David Lloyd George (1863); Mack Sennett (1884); Compton Mackenzie (1883); Al Capone and Nevil Shute (1899); Betty White (1922); Eartha Kitt (1927); Vidal Sassoon (1928); Ita Buttrose and Muhammad Ali (1942); Larry Fortensky (1952); Paul Young (1956); Jim Carrey (1962).

Significant Events and Anniversaries: The qualities inherent in this day are especially propitious for military leadership, and on January 17 Bonnie Prince Charlie and his Highland supporters won the Battle of Falkirk against the English forces arraigned against them (1746); the Duke of Wellington, among the most gifted of generals, was appointed commander-in-chief of the British Army (1827); and following the invasion of Kuwait by Saddam Hussein's forces, the Gulf War began in earnest, with the allied U.S., British and Saudi forces instigating their air raids of Iraq (1991). Reflecting the day's tenacity, Captain Robert Falcon Scott and the surviving members of his doomed expedition finally reached the South Pole after untold hardship (1912).

Planetary Influences
Ruling planets: Saturn and Uranus.
Third decan: Personal planet is Mercury.
Second cusp: Capricorn with Aquarian tendencies.

Sacred and Cultural Significance
Wassailing the Apple Trees, a Celtic ritual.
Saints' day: Antony of Egypt (251–356), patron saint of pigs and basket-makers; Mildgyth (7th century AD); Sulpicius (d. 647).

Benjamin Franklin, born on January 17, 1706, was an original thinker who displayed the tenacity and decisiveness of his birth destiny.

JANUARY 18

Planetary Influences
Ruling planets: Saturn and Uranus.
Third decan: Personal planet is Mercury.
Second cusp: Capricorn with Aquarian
tendencies.

Sacred and Cultural Significance
In China, Zao Jun honored.
Saints' day: Prisca (dates unknown);
Ulfrid (d. 1028).

Their innate sense of fun and unlimited imaginative powers make these people fascinating to others and their company a pleasure. Possessing questing minds, perceptive powers and a desire to explore all that the world has to offer, these people embrace the unusual with infectious enthusiasm, and since they generally find it easy to communicate their ideas to others, will often have a rapt audience. Once they have found a subject that absorbs them, they will pursue it with determination, in doing so demonstrating an impressive level of tenacity and unflagging interest. Although highly self-disciplined, January 18 people chafe under the rules and regulations of others, particularly if they do not appreciate their underlying purpose, and unless they are truly convinced of the merits of a task will not thrive as part of a strictly regulated organization or team. Indeed, given the value that they place on independent thought and their highly developed sense of fantasy, people born on this day have a natural inclination toward such creative activities as writing, acting or painting.

It may take these people some time to find the métier that ideally suits their talents and inclinations, however, and the impatience that may be engendered by adverse circumstances may cause them either to give in to childish displays of willfulness, or to take refuge in their own private world. In children, these strong-willed tendencies may give their parents cause for concern, but such is the resourcefulness of these people that they will eventually find a fulfilling outlet for their intellectual and emotional requirements. They will be happiest if those around them respect their need for freedom, while at the same time providing them with stability and support.

VIRTUES: Stimulating, independently minded, boundlessly inquisitive, and possessing strong determination, these people are potentially both great intellectuals and born entertainers, delighting others with their enthusiastic flights of fantasy and irreverent opinions.
VICES: If their need for an enduring interest, or the conditions in which to explore it, are not satisfied, these people may become bored and disillusioned, and may divert their considerable energies either to slightly subversive maneuvers, or retreat into a world of fantasy. They are also prone to feelings of frustration, which, if not resolved, may explode in fits of temper.
VERDICT: January 18 people must learn to be realistic, to work effectively within existing situations, and to find alternative expressions for their inclinations and interests if the ideal is not within reach.

On This Day

Leaders at the Versailles Conference, which opened on January 18, 1919. This day predicts a determined pursuit of ideals.

Famous Births: Peter Mark Roget (1779); Daniel Webster (1782); Joseph Farwell Glidden (1813); Emmanuel Chabrier (1841); Ruben Dario (1867); A.A. Milne (1882); Arthur Ransome (1884); Thomas Sopwith (1888); Oliver Hardy (1892); Cary Grant (1904); Danny Kaye (1913); David Bellamy (1933); Raymond Briggs (1934); Bobby Goldsboro (1941); Paul Keating (1944); John Hughes (1950); Kevin Costner (1955).

Significant Events and Anniversaries: Reflecting January 18's prevailing conjunction of determination and vision, this was the day on which Captain Cook discovered Hawaii, which he named the Sandwich Islands (1778). Wilhelm of Prussia, a man whose tendency toward fantasy tended toward the grandiose and self-delusionary, had himself proclaimed emperor of the German *Reich* in the fairy-tale setting of the Hall of Mirrors at Versailles (1871). A fantasy of a far less dangerous variety was realized with the publication of the first edition of the British *Boy's Own Paper* (1879). With its participants determined to build a better future for the world, the Versailles Peace Conference opened in the aftermath of World War I (1919). After a sixteen-month siege by the German invaders, Leningrad was relieved by the Soviet Army in a superhuman effort fueled by national idealism and dogged tenacity (1943).

JANUARY 19

Latent in January 19 people is a tendency toward intensity that can all too easily develop into extremism. Although possessed of mercurial, curious minds, they will pursue whatever it is that especially excites their interest—often profoundly mystical and somewhat nebulous concepts—with a single-minded determination that can become obsessive in its attention to detail. Yet if the vision proves short-lived or easily exhausted, such is their desire for intellectual stimulation and knowledge that another subject will soon be found and investigated with equal dedication. This is the day of true originality, of those whose idiosyncrasies may be misunderstood and dismissed by the more conventional, but whose obstinacy will not brook dissuasion from their chosen course. Consequently, people born on this day usually perform their best work in solitary conditions. They frequently receive acclaim in the scientific or artistic fields, and it may well take some time before others appreciate and acknowledge their undoubted talents.

In their personal lives, the restless dynamism of these people will attract baffled admiration, but their natural unconventionality may frighten and alienate those who are not brave or farsighted enough to stand prolonged exposure to them. Indeed, without the grounding support of sympathetic, easy-going friends and relatives, January 19 people may find themselves isolated and, without meaningful personal contact, tend to become prone to depression. They must therefore strive to balance their lives, to ensure that they not only spread their energies equally between work and relaxation, but that they pay genuine attention to the opinions and emotional requirements of those around them; mutually supportive relationships are crucial.

VIRTUES: January 19 people are blessed with an extraordinary gift of focus which, when combined with their drive and inherent tendency toward investigation, will not only inspire others, but offers the potential for true greatness. They have the potential to lead others and may make an unforgettable mark on the world.
VICES: When inspired by a visionary concept, these people are in danger of losing their sense of perspective, and may give themselves up so completely to the pursuit of their ideal that they neglect every other aspect of their lives. They run the risk of intimidating others and becoming isolated and depressed.
VERDICT: These people must make a concerted effort to calm their wilder, more obsessive tendencies and to ground themselves in caring and respectful relationships; intellectual talents are already in place, but will find positive expression only when contained within a stable emotional framework. Failure to heed this advice can be dangerous for January 19 people, who lack the perspective to moderate their own behavior.

On This Day

Famous Births: King François I of France (1544); James Watt (1736); Robert E. Lee (1807); Edgar Allan Poe (1809); Paul Cézanne (1839); Alexander Woollcott (1887); John Raitt (1917); Javier Pérez de Cuéllar (1920); Patricia Highsmith (1921); Jean Stapleton (1923); Phil Everly (1939); Michael Crawford (1942); Janis Joplin (1943); Dolly Parton (1946); Simon Rattle (1955).

Significant Events and Anniversaries: Illustrating this day's tendency toward extremism motivated by idealism or political ambition, Czech patriot Jan Pallach set fire to himself in Wenceslas Square in Prague in protest at the Soviet domination of his country (1969), while imperialist ambitions led Japan to invade Burma (1942) and Germany to instigate the first Zeppelin raids on England at Great Yarmouth and King's Lynn (1915). This day favors the artist, and marks both the anniversary of the first performance of Giuseppe Verdi's opera *Il Travatore* (1853), as well as the premiere of Massenet's *Manon* (1884). The day's potential for greatness was indicated when Indira Gandhi became prime minister of India, the culmination of the political aspirations for which she had worked with unwavering determination (1966).

Planetary Influences
Ruling planet: Saturn and Uranus.
Third decan: Personal planet is Mercury.
Second cusp: Capricorn with Aquarian tendencies.

Sacred and Cultural Significance
Thorrablottar celebrated in Iceland.
Saints' day: Branwalader (6th century AD); Wulfstan (c.1008–95); Canute (d. 1086); Henry of Finland (d. 1156); Marguerite Bourgeoys (1620–1700).

Robert E. Lee, the greatest general of the American Civil War, was born on January 19, 1807.

AQUARIUS

January 20 to February 18
Ruling planet: Uranus (traditionally Saturn)   **Element:** Fixed air
Symbol: The water carrier   **Polarity:** Positive (masculine)
Physical correspondence: The blood vessels, calves, ankles and heels
Stones: Sapphire, onyx, amethyst, black pearl, hematite
Flowers: Myrtle, rosemary, dandelion, orchid, goldenrod
Colors: Violet and blue

The constellation of Aquarius is known as the water carrier, personified as a human figure bearing, or pouring, a pot of water. This portrayal corresponds to the ancient Egyptian tales of the god Hapi (equated with the River Nile), who filled the sacred river with life-giving water, as well as to the Greek myth of Ganymede, the beautiful youth whom the enamored Zeus (Jupiter), in the form of an eagle, transported into the heavens to act as his cup bearer. Other astrological traditions, however, depersonalized Aquarius and identified it as a vessel containing water: in Hindu astrology, for example, it is called Khumba; and in Mesopotamian belief it was Dul, both names that signify a water-pot. Yet the Babylonians equated this sign with the goddess Gula, the deity who regulated childbirth and possessed the gift of healing. Until the planet Uranus was discovered in 1781, Aquarius was believed to be governed by Saturn (the Greek Kronos, an agricultural deity), but since the Greek god after which Uranus is named, Ouranos, was a sky god, whose domain was the element of air that influences this sign—and who was additionally the consort of the mother goddess Gaia (associated with the fecund powers of water)—in many respects the more recent pairing is appropriate.

The defining characteristic of Aquarians is independence, particularly manifested in their intellectual originality and progressiveness (with which Uranus is also credited), and the water that Aquarius represents is symbolically equated with the water of knowledge. Yet since this is a sign that is governed by the element of air—which not only signifies a desire for freedom of thought and action, but may also imply a lack of staying power—those born under this sign may tend toward aloofness and impulsiveness, while their personal relationships are often relegated to second place when competing with the Aquarian fascination for exploring abstract ideas.

JANUARY 20

These exuberant individuals relish the attention that their manifold interests, outgoing personalities and love of life attract. Their kindness and sense of fun make them popular companions, but unless these people keep their feet on the ground and develop a more pragmatic attitude their heads may be turned by the admiration that they inspire. In their efforts to entertain others (and humor is strongly indicated by this day) they have a tendency to become somewhat out of control. This is not to say that people born on this day lack discipline (far from it), but if bored or frustrated they may either withdraw completely, succumb to temper tantrums or play the fool in an attempt to enliven things. Indeed, this need for stimulation is paramount for January 20 people, and when they find a subject that truly interests them they display unusually intense powers of concentration and tenacity, rarely giving up on a task until it is completed.

Running parallel with these people's capacity for solid, intellectual pursuits is a marked sensitivity for the feelings of others, as well as a desire to please their audience. These qualities mark them out as natural performers and also indicate a latent talent for diplomacy and politics—particularly if they were born in the Chinese year of snake—areas in which their resilience, self-belief and aptitude for problem-solving may find their full expression. In their personal relationships, people born on this day should cultivate patience, and try to develop a more relaxed and accepting attitude toward both themselves and others.

VIRTUES: Energetic and inquisitive, yet also boasting analytical minds and an impressive capacity for hard work, these people have the potential to make a real mark on the world. Their considerable personal charm and ability to tune in to the moods of others indicate a potential for well-rounded personalities.

VICES: Because they are self-confident and relish being the center of attention, January 20 people are prone to arrogance and vanity, and may seek to dominate those around them. This behavior is not prompted by megalomaniac tendencies, however, but rather the unshakable belief that they know best.

VERDICT: People born on this day must ensure that they take things calmly and do not allow themselves to become distracted and disruptive when bored. They should also remember that other people's opinions have equal validity to their own, and that they do not always hold all the answers.

On This Day

Famous Births: Theobald Wolfe Tone (1763); Johannes Jensen (1873); Mischa Elman (1891); George Burns (1896); Aristotle Onassis (1906); Roy Welensky (1907); Joy Adamson (1910); Frederico Fellini (1920); Slim Whitman (1924); Patricia Neal (1926); Edwin "Buzz" Aldrin (1930); Nalin Chandra Wickransinghe (1939); David Lynch (1946); Malcolm McLaren (1947); Lorenzo Lamas (1958).

Significant Events and Anniversaries: This day favors imaginative and problem-solving qualities, as well as a structured approach, characteristics which can be clearly linked to governance; not only did the first English parliament meet on this day (1265), but it is also the day of inauguration for U.S. presidents since the second inauguration of Franklin Delano Roosevelt (1937). Diplomatic pursuits are indicated by this day, on which Britain was ceded Hong Kong by the Chinese at the Chuenpi Convention (1841) and fifty-two American hostages were released from the U.S. Embassy in Tehran, Iran (1981). Prompted by a rock-solid certainty and belief in their cause, the Cromwell-led English parliament tried King Charles I (1649), and also on this day the R.A.F. dropped 2,300 tons of bombs on Berlin (1944). Appropriately, on the day of the patron saint of athletes, this day also marks the anniversary of the first game of basketball, which was played at the YMCA in Springfield, Massachusetts (1892).

Planetary Influences
Ruling planets: Uranus and Saturn.
First decan: Personal planet is Uranus.
First cusp: Aquarius with Capricorn tendencies.

Sacred and Cultural Significance
In Christianity, St. Agnes' Eve.
Saints' day: Fabian (d. 250); Sebastian (3rd. century AD), patron saint of archers and athletes; Fechin (d. 665); Eustochium Calafato (1434–68).

Berlin's most famous landmark, the Kaiser Wilhelm Memorial Church, before it was partially destroyed by bombing on January 20, 1944. Political, diplomatic and strategic military events have all occurred frequently on this day.

JANUARY 21

* *

Planetary Influences
Ruling planets: Uranus and Saturn.
First decan: Personal planet is Uranus.
First cusp: Aquarius with Capricorn tendencies.

Sacred and Cultural Significance
Saints' day: Agnes (d. c.305), patron saint of girls; Meinrad (d. 861).

January 21 is St. Agnes' day, and those born on her day often display kindness and compassion.

AGNES: VIRG: ET MART

Crucial to January 21 people is their profound thirst both for unfettered freedom of expression and for an emotional haven to which they can retreat for the privacy that is so essential to them. These people will never find fulfillment if they are forced to submit unquestioningly to the rules of others, for their urge to explore and follow their natural inclinations is as vital to them as the air that is their element. Indeed, in order to understand what exactly it is that makes these libertarian people tick, one must appreciate their need to be allowed to act upon their instincts. The important thing is that even if they end up following the wrong course, the decision to do so was their own and, indeed, they will be quick to learn from their experiences. These twin qualities of sensitivity and waywardness, as well as a marked sensuality, bestow upon people born on this day the especial potential to succeed in the world of the arts.

Inevitably somewhat unpredictable, their idiosyncratic behavior may ultimately exasperate those around them who prefer a more organized and logical approach. Any attempt to place impositions upon January 21 people is, however, doomed to disaster; they must be accepted as they are. Related to their individuality is their occasional craving for solitude, the time for reflection and to be themselves, and this too should be respected. Yet while people born on this day are stubbornly resistant to coercion, their inherent respect for personal liberty means that they will never consciously attempt to dominate others, despite their talent for persuasion. Since they are consumed by a strong desire for the happiness of other people, their ideals will often lead them into humanitarian activities and pursuits.

VIRTUES: Since January 21 people are free spirits, who are deeply sensitive to their emotions and instincts, their boldly original personalities draw others to them. Idealistic and caring, they will strive to improve the lives of other people without material reward.
VICES: Because they respond so strongly to their instincts, these people may find it difficult to concentrate on a single cause, and may moreover succumb to indecision. Their escapist tendencies may, if unchecked, result in isolation from other people.
VERDICT: There are occasions when there is no alternative but to conform or accept the situation's limitations, and people born on this day therefore benefit by cultivating staying power in every aspect of their lives.

On This Day
Famous Births: John Charles Fremont (1813); Thomas "Stonewall" Jackson (1824); King Oscar II of Sweden and Norway (1829); John Moses Browning (1855); Duncan Grant and Leadbelly (1885); Christian Dior (1905); Paul Scofield (1922); Telly Savalas (1924); Benny Hill (1925); Wolfman Jack (1938); Jack Nicklaus (1940); Placido Domingo (1941); Martin Shaw (1945); Jill Eikenberry (1947); Robby Benson (1956); Geena Davis (1957); Michael Hutchence (1960); Emma Lee Bunton (1976).

Significant Events and Anniversaries: Mirroring the potential for innovation heralded by this day, this is the anniversary of the first edition of England's *Daily News*, edited by Charles Dickens (1846) and the start of the first Monte Carlo Rally (1911). As befits an Aquarian day, the U.S.A. launched the world's first nuclear submarine, *Nautilus* (1954). Appropriately for a day ruled by the element of air, this is the anniversary of the inaugural flights of the supersonic Anglo-French airliner Concorde, from London to Bahrain and Paris to Rio de Janeiro (1976).

JANUARY 22

✦✦

People born on this day have a craving for stimulation, a need that endows them with the potential to be polymaths, provided that they are disciplined enough to develop their interests beyond the superficial level. Because they are quick-witted and instinctual, they are gifted at speedily summing up a situation, but may then persist with their initial response and fail to explore it deeper. Tedium is their greatest enemy, and if forced to carry on with a task that bores them, their impatience may lead them into performing hastily or carelessly, or, indeed, to abandon the project altogether in favor of the lure of pastures new. Whichever profession they choose, whether it be in the arts or not, they blossom when allowed to express their creativity unhindered, and when not stultified by petty procedures.

In common with most Aquarians, January 22 people are not generally motivated by personal ambition or monetary aims, but rather by the desire for personal and collective human improvement. They also feel strong empathy and appreciation for the natural world, and their ideals and inclinations may lead them to become environmentalists. In order to enjoy fulfilling personal lives, people born on this day must control their inherent tendency to behave impetuously and inconsiderately, and should seek to ground themselves in stable, mutually respectful relationships.

VIRTUES: January 22 people are versatile, multifaceted personalities with wide-ranging interests. Their restless vigor and natural enthusiasm give them the potential to be extraordinarily successful at whatever they choose.
VICES: Easily bored, these people must try to control their tendency to flit from subject to subject without exploring any fully, and benefit by developing patience and tenacity. If frustrated, they have a tendency to lose their tempers quite spectacularly.
VERDICT: If these people succeed in overcoming their natural impulsiveness and learn the importance of both paying attention to detail and developing their powers of concentration, they will find stability and satisfaction in all areas of their lives.

Planetary Influences
Ruling Planets: Uranus and Saturn.
First decan: Personal planet is Uranus.
First cusp: Aquarius with Capricorn tendencies.

Sacred and Cultural Significance
Pagan Festival of the Muses.
Saints' day: Vincent of Saragossa (d. 304); Anastasius (d. 628), patron saint of goldsmiths; Berhtwald (995–1045); Vincent Pallotti (1795–1850).

Rorke's Drift, one of the many crucial military engagements that have been fought on January 22, illustrates the day's propensity for impulsive action.

On This Day
Famous Births: Ivan the Great (1440); Francis Bacon (1561); André Ampère (1775); Lord Byron (1788); August Strindberg (1849); Beatrice Potter Webb (1858); Rasputin (1871); D.W. Griffith (1875); Charles Morgan (1894); Dixie Dean (1907); Ann Southern (1909); Alf Ramsey (1922); Sam Cooke (1931); Piper Laurie (1932); Bill Bixby (1934); John Hurt (1940); Linda Blair (1959).

Significant Events and Anniversaries: At its extreme, the tendency toward impatience that is inherent in this day can explode, which, in national contexts, may lead to armed conflict, as when four thousand Zulu warriors attacked ninety-two British soldiers at the Battle of Rorke's Drift in southern Africa (1879); when Russian soldiers fired on a crowd of demonstrators in St. Petersburg on "Red Sunday" (1905); and when the Allied forces landed their troops in Anzio during World War II, initiating their invasion of Italy (1944). Illustrating the success that can be achieved if a vision is fully explored, Marconi made his first successful radio transmission from Cornwall to the Isle of Wight in Britain (1902).

✴ ✴

Planetary Influences
Ruling planets: Uranus and Saturn.
First decan: Personal planet is Uranus.
First cusp: Aquarius with Capricorn tendencies.

Sacred and Cultural Significance
Day of Hathor in Egypt.
Saints' day: Emerentiana (d. c.304);
Ildephonsus of Toledo (c.607–77); John
the Almsgiver (c.620).

*During the January 23 Egyptian festival
honoring Hathor, the goddess of heaven,
beauty and love, prayers to the goddess are
spoken as a libation of cow's milk is poured
into the River Nile.*

To their enthusiasts, their deep convictions, original thinking, manifest integrity and natural sense of style make those born on this day inspirational figures. Yet January 23 people are unintentional and reluctant role models, and often feel uneasy at being regarded as such. While they might well occasionally seek to influence others, they are motivated by the wish to achieve impersonal ideals, and not by the desire to become the subjects of admiration. Yet it is precisely this refreshing disregard for human vanity that, along with their individualistic approach, other people find so magnetic. The intellectual qualities of people born on this day (curiosity, objectivity, inventiveness and a dash of adventurousness) signal a distinct aptitude for science, as well as for those artistic spheres in which they can combine their natural sensitivity with their independent approach. Naturally open to outside influences, and enthusiastic travelers, these people will drink in new experiences and then reinterpret them in their inimitably unique fashion.

Because January 23 people are easily absorbed by intellectual pursuits and are highly self-reliant (especially if they were also born in the Chinese year of the tiger), their friends and relatives may feel somewhat excluded. Although they are usually considerate and generous partners who tend to think the best of others (and thus also make extremely good parents), there are times when their fascination with ideas will cause them to withdraw into their own world and to neglect those close to them. They benefit by remembering that, in their desire to advance the greater good of humanity, they must not sacrifice the individual.

VIRTUES: January 23 people combine a splendid disregard for convention with a highly original approach, and yet somehow manage to remain grounded in reality.
VICES: Their cool single-mindedness and tendency to withdraw into themselves can inadvertently cause hurt to others.
VERDICT: If people born on this day ensure that their exploration of the abstract does not take precedence over their personal relationships, they will benefit from the essential emotional support that results from a wholehearted commitment to human bonds.

On This Day
Famous Births: John Hancock (1737); Muzio Clementi (1752); Marie Henri Beyle (Stendhal) (1783); Edouard Manet (1832); Katherine Tynan Hinkson (1861); Rutland Boughton (1878); Sergei Mikhailovich Eisenstein (1898); Humphrey Bogart (1899); Django Reinhardt (1910); Bob Paisley (1919); Jeanne Moreau (1928); Chita Rivera (1933); Bill Gibb (1943); Rutger Hauer (1944); Richard Dean Anderson (1953); Princess Caroline of Monaco (1957); Tyrone Power, Jr. (1959); Tiffani-Amber Thiessen (1974).

Significant Events and Anniversaries: Natural sciences are emphasized by this day, and in a tragic manifestation of seismicity in action, an earthquake in Shensi Province, China, resulted in the deaths of about 830,000 people (1556). During World War II, motivated by their desire to defeat the Nazi regime, the British forces captured Tripoli and thrust into Tunisia (1943); twenty-five years later, soldiers on North Korean patrol boats boarded the U.S. intelligence-gathering ship *Pueblo,* killing several crew members (1968). Reflecting the originality of this day, which may border on the eccentric, Professor Piccard descended 35,800 feet into the Pacific Ocean in his "bathyscaphe" contraption, *Trieste* (1960). A day of conspiracies, sixteen U.S. oil companies were convicted of price-fixing (1938) and Kim Philby, the British spy who regarded his political ideals as more important than national loyalty, defected to the U.S.S.R. (1963).

JANUARY 24

⁎ ⁎

Those born on this day are imaginative to the point of feyness, and are fascinated by topics that less free-thinking people might dismiss as being oddball. Indeed, so accustomed are they to being branded eccentric when they moot their wildly original ideas and theories, that to avoid experiencing the hurt of a negative reaction, they frequently keep quiet about what it is that really excites them. This defensive mechanism may be effective in the short term, but such suppression of the true self will ultimately cause emotional damage. The paradox is that although January 24 people are generally greatly admired for their original qualities, they are reluctant to believe that others appreciate them just as they are and may reject such esteem, either suspecting underlying motives or feeling that their essence has been misunderstood.

Their sensitivity, love of nature, and genuine desire to work for good propels many January 24 people into working with animals, with whom they feel a deep empathy and trust that they sometimes feel are lacking in their relationships with their human peers. They thrive best in those small-scale, more personal, working environments in which they do not feel inhibited or under pressure to perform artificially. Similarly, they need to be constantly reassured by the love and support of their friends and family if they are to achieve their true potential.

VIRTUES: Possessing exceptionally high levels of empathy, sensitivity and originality, people born on this day seem effortlessly to draw others to them. Their attraction to all that is different, along with their outstanding intellectual abilities, bestow upon them the potential to make real breakthroughs in their careers.
VICES: These people benefit by not allowing themselves to become oversensitive in their relationships with other people, and by maintaining their integrity in the face of others' expectations. They may nurture a belief that no one else understands their true nature, and therefore may cultivate a deceptive air of aloofness.
VERDICT: January 24 people are blessed with rare talents and qualities and must remain true to themselves if they are to find fulfillment. While they should guard against a tendency to becoming overly self-absorbed, at the same time they should work on becoming more confident in their dealings with others.

On This Day

Famous Births: Hadrian (76); William Congreve (1670); Frederick the Great, King of Prussia (1712); Pierre de Beaumarchais (1732); Charles James Fox (1749); Ernst Hoffmann (1776); Edith Wharton (1862); Vicki Baum and Ernst Heinkel (1888); Ann Todd (1909); Ernest Borgnine (1917); Oral Roberts (1918); Desmond Morris (1928); Trent Nathan (1940); Neil Diamond (1941);Michael Ontkean (1946); John Belushi (1949); Yakov Smirnoff (1951); Natassja Kinski (1960); Mary Lou Retton (1968).

Significant Events and Anniversaries: Highlighted by this day is an affinity with the natural world, as is reflected by the discovery of gold at Sutter's Sawmill, California, by James Marshall, thus sparking a gold rush (1848), and by the sadness engendered by the death of the lioness Elsa, who won the hearts of millions through the movie *Born Free* (1961). Impelled by the desire to act for the common good against the imperialist threat of Germany, the British Navy was victorious at the Battle of Dogger Bank, during which the cruiser *Blücher* was sunk (1915). This day is under the influence of the element of air, and sadly this is the anniversary of two air accidents: that of a U.S. B–52 bomber breaking up in mid-flight, thereby killing three crew members (1961), and the collision of a Soviet satellite with the earth in the Northwest Territory in Canada (1978).

Planetary Influences
Ruling planet: Uranus.
First decan: Personal planet is Uranus.

Sacred and Cultural Significance
Traditional purification ceremony, Blessing of the Candle of the Happy Women, in Hungary.
Saints' day: Babylas (d. c.250); Cadoc (dates unknown); Francis of Sales (1567–1622), patron saint of authors, writers and journalists.

Panning for gold in California during the 1848 gold rush, which began on this day of natural connotations.

JANUARY 25

★★★

Planetary Influences
Ruling planet: Uranus.
First decan: Personal planet is Uranus.

Sacred and Cultural Significance
Burns Night in Scotland; Lunar New Year
Festival in Vietnam.
Saints' day: The conversion of Paul (d. c.62),
patron saint of missionary bishops; Dwyn
(c.5th to 6th century AD); Praejectus (d. 676).

*Michelangelo's depiction of the conversion of
St. Paul, which is believed to have occurred
on this day.*

To the less sensitive, those born on January 25 present something of an enigma. Such is the complexity of their characters that they may at one moment entertain others with their humor, wit and charisma, and at the next retreat into a shell of introversion and solitude. Indeed, these people are drawn to extremes, a reflection of their inherent curiosity, craving for stimulation and thirst to explore and satisfy the many facets of their personalities. Their behavior, pursuits and moods may sometimes appear erratic, but underlying them is an overwhelming interest in all aspects of life, which may often be manifested in an enthusiasm for travel and a willingness to experience new things.

Those born on January 25 are extremely sensitive and are highly receptive to the feelings of others. This gift, combined with their powers of perception and genuine interest in the welfare of others, suits them especially to the caring professions, in which they often make outstanding contributions. There will be times, however, when they will feel almost overwhelmed by the strength of their empathy, which may be intensified by the strong sense of fatalism to which they are prone. On such occasions they must actively strive to be positive and not to succumb to feelings of helplessness and despair. The unqualified love and support of those close to them is crucial to these people's emotional well-being, and will in turn be amply and loyally rewarded.

VIRTUES: Blessed with questing minds and a love of variety, these people are unusually dynamic and therefore fascinate others. Yet beneath the mercurial, multitalented surface lies a tendency toward profound thought, and the gift of humanitarian vision, as well as a deep feeling of empathy with other people.
VICES: Such is their power to absorb the moods of others, that people born on this day may be prey to emotions of overpowering identification, which may cause them to lose their rational perspective. In extreme cases, their farsightedness may lead to undue anxiety.
VERDICT: January 25 people benefit by maintaining equilibrium in every aspect of their lives, and especially between their emotional and intellectual needs.

On This Day
Famous Births: Edmund Campion (1540); Robert Boyle (1627); Joseph Louis Lagrange (1736); Robert Burns (1759); Lord Lonsdale (1857); William Somerset Maugham (1874); Virginia Woolf (1882); Wilhelm Furtwängler (1886); Paul Henri Spaak (1899); Witold Lutoslawski (1913); Ernie Harwell (1918); Edwin Newman (1919); Edvard Shevardnadze (1928); Corazon Aquino (1933); Dean Jones (1935); Leigh Taylor-Young (1944); Kay Cottee (1954).

Significant Events and Anniversaries: As befits a day indicating such wide-ranging interests, this is the anniversary of a rich variety of innovations, including the firing of the first torpedo in anger, when the Russian Navy targeted and sank a Turkish steamer (1878); the holding of the first international hockey match, between Wales and Ireland (1895); the production of the world's first radio commercial sets by the British Wireless Telegraph & Signal Company (1899); and the ordination of the first Anglican female priest, Macao's Reverend Florence Tim-Oi Lee (1944). The day furthermore indicates foresight, which in the national sphere is reflected by the purchase by the U.S.A. of the Virgin Islands for $25 million (1917). The British Social Democratic Party held a press conference to announce its establishment (1981), stressing the day's social concerns.

JANUARY 26

Their energy, drive and boldly expressed convictions make many January 26 people larger-than-life figures who follow their hunches and deeply held convictions in characteristically individual style. There is a dual side to these personalities: on the one hand they are physically vibrant, combative and confident in their sensitivity and intellects, while on the other they are prone to follow their instincts and beliefs with steely determination, thereby also demonstrating their capacity for organization and tenacity. The combination of their highly developed talents of intuition, ambitious vision and intellectual perceptiveness, as well as their willingness to take risks if they feel these justify the potential rewards, mark these people out as potentially successful players of the financial markets, where they often have a gift for investment. Yet despite this commercial bent, people born on this day also have a propensity to spend their money as though it were water.

In their personal lives, these people must beware of using the same tactic of determined confrontation that frequently serves them so well in their careers. Although they may have a deep and genuine affection for their loved ones, they may inadvertently cause upset if they give their well-meant words of advice too bluntly, or try to make others follow a course of action to which they are not suited. These people therefore benefit by becoming less controlling and more accepting of the limitations and viewpoints of others; when they apply this strategy to their own lives, they will also discover that there is much to be gained from a more relaxed attitude and willingness to compromise.

VIRTUES: Impossible to ignore, these dynamic, quick-witted, confident people can have a resounding impact on others. The conjunction of outstanding intellectual gifts and instinct that is inherent in these people gives them outstanding potential to achieve their aims and realize their visions.
VICES: Because they have strong convictions and are not afraid of expressing them, January 26 people must beware of their tendency to intimidate or browbeat others, a policy which may have short-lived success but which will rarely benefit them in the long run.
VERDICT: These people should attune their undoubted sensitivity to others' feelings and try to become more receptive to what their family and coworkers have to say. They must not allow one side of their personality to dominate the other, maintaining balance in all things.

On This Day
Famous Births: Douglas MacArthur (1880); Henry Cotton (1907); Stéphane Grapelli (1908); Jimmy Van Heusen (1913); Michael Bentine (1922); Paul Newman (1925); Eartha Kitt and Roger Vadim (1928); Angela Davis (1944); Jacqueline du Pré (1945); Christopher Hampton (1946); Kim Hughes (1954); Eddie Van Halen (1955); Anita Baker and Ellen DeGeneres (1958); Wayne Gretzky (1961).

Significant Events and Anniversaries: This days favors visions that are realized through tenacity, and as a result of these qualities explorer Vicente Yáñez Pinzón discovered Brazil, which he claimed for Portugal (1500); Michigan became the twenty-sixth U.S. state (1837); Hong Kong was first proclaimed British sovereign territory (1841); the first regiment composed entirely of African American soldiers (the 54th Massachusetts Volunteers) was established (1863); and German inventor Karl Benz patented his three-wheeled motor car and internal combustion motor (1886). Mahatma Gandhi was released by the British from one of his prison terms in 1931 on the day that would become India's Republic Day. Conflict is indicated by this day, on which British General Gordon was murdered by the followers of the Mahdi in Khartoum (1885), and Franco's Nationalist forces captured Barcelona during the Spanish Civil War (1939).

Planetary Influences
Ruling planet: Uranus.
First decan: Personal planet is Uranus.

Sacred and Cultural Significance
Australia Day; Republic Day in India.
Saints' day: Timothy (d. 97); Titus (1st century AD); Paula (d. 404), patron saint of widows; Conan (d. 648); Bathild (d. 680); Tortgirth (d. 681); Alberic (d. 1109); Augustine of Trondheim (d. 1188); Margaret of Hungary (1242–70).

Mahatma Gandhi, symbol of India's independence.

Planetary Influences
Ruling planet: Uranus.
First decan: Personal planet is Uranus.

Sacred and Cultural Significance
Day of Ishtar in ancient Babylonia.
Saints' day: Julian of Le Mans (4th century AD); Angela Merici (1474–1540).

JANUARY 27

★★

Perhaps the strongest characteristic of January 27 people is their inherent need to be challenged and stimulated, and this is often manifested by a ceaseless questing to experience and master all that life has to offer. Running parallel to their strong sense of purpose and deep desire to succeed is a pronounced streak of courage, which enables them doggedly, and sometimes apparently recklessly, to tread new paths without being deflected from their purpose. Yet although they are daring, those born on this day will generally not take chances without first having weighed up the risks and having carefully examined potential pitfalls. Although they are personally ambitious, these people are rarely motivated by a desire for financial reward, instead being driven by a desire to test and prove themselves. Their intellectual talents, including those of perceptiveness and objectivity, suit them for most professions, that is, as long as their attention is held and they are allowed to be creative.

Away from work, these people greatly enjoy the good things of life and as appreciative gourmets are ever willing to sample new sensual experiences. Unusually, for such active people, their propensity for self-indulgence and love of luxury can seduce them into idleness, especially if they were born in the Chinese year of the snake. Generous to a fault, they are deeply attached to their family and friends, desiring their happiness above all. In turn—perhaps as a result of their intellectual restlessness—they need a stable and secure personal life, and to receive the constant reassurance and encouragement of those closest to them, as well as the occasional firm hand.

VIRTUES: Pioneering spirits, these people respond instinctively to challenge, and possess the necessary determination to rise to the occasion. Benevolent and relaxed in their dealings with others, they accept and appreciate variety, accepting others as they are.
VICES: If their need for intellectual stimulation is denied them, these people will become so frustrated that they have a tendency to withdraw into their own self-satisfying world. They must also guard against their propensity toward sensation-seeking and physical indulgence.
VERDICT: Balance is the key for these people. While they should never suppress their natural inclinations, they benefit by knowing when to give themselves over to the lure of sensory excitement and when it is necessary to buckle down and impose some self-discipline.

January 27 indicates challenge and new horizons, and was the legendary day on which Sir H.M. Stanley met missionary-explorer Dr. Livingstone (1868).

On This Day
Famous Births: Henry Greathead and Wolfgang Amadeus Mozart (1756); Lewis Carroll or (Charles Lutwidge Dodgson) (1832); Kaiser Wilhelm II of Germany (1859); William Randolph Hearst (1863); Jerome Kern (1885); Art Rooney, Sr. (1901); Skitch Henderson (1918); Donna Reed (1921); Sir Brian Rix (1924); Troy Donahue (1936); John Ogdon (1937); Mairead Corrigan-Maguire (1944); Mimi Rogers (1956); Bridget Fonda (1964).

Significant Events and Anniversaries: On this day of the pioneer spirit, the meeting in Africa of celebrated explorers Sir Henry Morton Stanley and Dr. Livingstone took place (1868). A day that bestows the potential to successfully meet a challenge: on January 27 Greece finally won her independence from Turkey (1822); John Logie Baird demonstrated the television that he had developed to members of the Royal Institution, London (1926); yachtsman Francis Chichester was knighted by Queen Elizabeth II for his achievement in sailing round the world (1967); and a ceasefire was signed in the Vietnam War (1973). Sadly, the brave will not always be successful in their quest, as was illustrated when U.S. astronauts Virgil "Gus" Grissom, Ed White and Roger Chafee were killed when the *Apollo I* ignited during a ground test (1967). On this Aquarian day, disastrous flooding in California resulted in many deaths (1969).

JANUARY 28

Although these people have extremely strong views regarding what is right and what is wrong, and relish the stimulating cut and thrust of intellectual debate, these qualities are motivated more by a sense of justice than by a need to impose their convictions by dominating others. Indeed, while they may not always agree with them, January 28 people are remarkably tolerant in their appreciation of inevitable differences of opinion, respecting what other people have to say but not allowing their integrity to be swayed in the process. These qualities are often best employed in the judicial, diplomatic or political sphere, in which they can objectively seek to advance the humanitarian causes that are dear to them without dismissively rejecting alternative convictions. Their natural charm, capacity for penetrative thought and compelling articulateness will also stand them in good stead in such pursuits. January 28 people are also intuitive, and if they nurture their creative impulses, they can achieve memorable artistic success.

Just as they are frequently motivated by humanitarian aims in their professional lives, in their personal relationships people born on this day place the happiness and well-being of their families above all else. They greatly value the sense of security that they gain from strong, supportive relationships. Highly sensitive, they have an instinctive distate for emotional conflict and will do their utmost to avoid unpleasant confrontation with members of their family, whom they may often infuriate by appearing to duck issues and retreating into their own world.

VIRTUES: The compassion and idealism of these people, as well as their objective intellects, are qualities that are greatly admired by others. Their realism, tolerance toward others and powers of persuasion make them talented and respected negotiators and parents.
VICES: There is a danger that these intuitive people may allow their empathy with those who are less fortunate than themselves to overwhelm them. They must furthermore ensure that their preference for maintaining an even keel does not prevent them from personal advancement or emotional involvement.
VERDICT: January 28 people desire above all an easy and civilized life—for themselves and for others. They must, however, recognize that the confrontation to which they are naturally averse is occasionally necessary in order to move forward.

On This Day

Famous Births: King Henry VII of England (1457); Charles Gordon (1833); Henry Morton Stanley (1841); José Marti (1853); William Burroughs (1855); Colette (1873); Vsevold Meyerhold (1874); Auguste Piccard (1884); Artur Rubinstein (1887); Ernst Lubitsch (1892); Jackson Pollock (1912); Ronnie Scott (1927); James Callaghan (1928); Acker Bilk and Claes Oldenburg (1929); Alan Alda (1936); Mikhail Baryshnikov (1948); Barbi Benton (1950); Nick Carter (1980); Elijah Wood (1981); Athina Onassis (1985).

Significant Events and Anniversaries: This is a day that indicates both tolerance and desire for human progress, and in Spain the rule of the dictator Miguel Primo de Rivera was today ended, raising the people's hopes for democracy (1930); while Iceland, in a controversial decision, became the first country to legalize abortion (1935). Aspirations to advance human knowledge of space were tragically dashed when the U.S. shuttle *Challenger* exploded after lift-off, with the loss of the lives of seven people (1986).

Planetary Influences
Ruling planet: Uranus.
First decan: Personal planet is Uranus.

Sacred and Cultural Significance
Up-Helly-Aa fire festival in the Shetland Islands.
Saints' day: John the Sage (dates unknown); Peter Nolasco (c.1182–1256); Thomas Aquinas (c.1225–74), patron saint of students and theologians.

Mikhail Baryshnikov, one of a number of outstanding performing artists with January 28 birthdays, dances with Natalia Makarova in Swan Lake. Baryshnikov's perfectionism and discipline are indicated by the presence of the Moon in Virgo at the time of his birth.

Planetary Influences
Ruling planet: Uranus.
First decan: Personal planet is Uranus.

Sacred and Cultural Significance
Parade of the Unicorns in Vietnam.
Saints' day: Julian the Hospitaller (dates unknown), patron saint of hoteliers; Gildas (c.500–c.570).

Reflecting the sensitivity to others associated with January 29, Queen Victoria of England established the Victoria Cross, awarded for military bravery, on this day in 1856.

JANUARY 29

★★

The forceful personalities and profound convictions of January 29 people frequently evoke extremes of emotion in others, to whom they may be either the subject of deep esteem or dismissive derision. Either way, they refuse to be ignored, a quality for which they are sneakingly admired even by their detractors. Inherently empathetic to the plight of others, and blessed with quick-witted minds, those born on this day are, invariably drawn to social causes, impelled by their natural sense of justice to fight for those whom they feel have been wronged. When inspired they make formidably determined campaigners, despite—or perhaps because of—the fact that they usually prefer to achieve their ends through reasoned argument rather than direct confrontation. Such qualities indicate that these people are predisposed to be politicians or social campaigners.

The downside of their innate sensitivity is that when they provoke negative responses January 29 people may feel deeply hurt by this rejection. This makes it all the more important that they are supported by stable personal relationships so that they are buoyed up by the love and understanding of those who appreciate their qualities. A happy personal life will also put a brake on these people's martyr and obsessive tendencies, and will help to provide them with a sense of perspective.

VIRTUES: These people are extremely bright, strong-willed and possessed of a burning desire to right perceived wrongs. Their ardent espousal of their ideals has the potential to inspire others, enlisting support for their cause.
VICES: January 29 people are often so determined to see their idealistic convictions implemented that, when met with opposition, they may become infuriated and petulant. They also have a tendency to take too much upon themselves, which may result in physical and emotional exhaustion.
VERDICT: In order to fully realize their ambitions, people born on this day must sometimes temper their passions and adopt a more pragmatic approach in their dealings with others. By compromising and being more conciliatory, they will not only find that their aims are more easily achieved, but that they also benefit personally. Physical and mental relaxation is crucial to these people's well-being.

On This Day
Famous Births: Emmanuel Swedenborg (1688); Daniel Bernoulli (1700); Thomas Paine (1737); William McKinley (1843); Frederick Delius (1862); Vicente Blasco Ibáñez (1867); W.C. Fields (1880); Huddie "Leadbelly" Ledbetter (1885); Victor Mature (1916); John Forsythe (1918); Paddy Chayefsky (1923); Leslie Bricuse (1931); Sacha Distel (1933); Germaine Greer (1939); Tom Selleck (1945); Katharine Ross (1943); Jody Schecter (1950); Ann Jillian (1951), Oprah Winfrey (1954); Greg Louganis (1960).

Significant Events and Anniversaries: In reflection of the sensitive nature of the day, this is the anniversary of the first performance of John Gay's *The Beggar's Opera* (1728). In recognition of the selfless bravery exhibited by certain individuals during times of military conflict, Queen Victoria instituted Britain's highest decoration, the Victoria Cross (1856). Throwing in its lot with the U.S.A.'s national ambitions, Kansas became the thirty-fourth state to join the Union (1861). Conflict may be an inevitable consequence of the day's influence, as was manifested when German Zeppelins dropped their first bombs on Paris during World War I (1916).

JANUARY 30

These dynamic people are possessed of a burning desire to impose their individual stamp on all that they undertake, confident as they are in the absolute veracity of their convictions. Although they will have arrived at their judgements by means of reasoned and practical thought, January 30 people rely heavily on their instincts to guide them, and indeed often retrospectively justify their initially emotional responses with impeccably constructed, rational arguments. This remarkable ability to channel their sensitivity through their intellects and then transmit their opinions lucidly and convincingly is a rare one, and will gain them acclaim, especially when employed in artistic pursuits, but also in politics or the military forces. Whichever professional path they follow, however, it is important that these people be allowed to follow their natural urge to lead others and to act independently. They do not function well in subordinate roles, either in the professional or personal realm, and can be somewhat passive-aggressive toward anyone who tries to dominate them.

There is a distinct danger that such a high level of self-belief, particularly when it is apparently confirmed by others, can result in excessive egotism or complacency. These people furthermore crave the approval of their peers and may play to their audience, instinctively picking up on the prevailing mood and mirroring it. On such occasions they should step back and calm their propensity to respond impulsively and instead remain true to themselves and their own convictions. They may demand (and receive) the unquestioning support of their family and friends, but should remember that any dissension is not a personal betrayal, but rather a healthy manifestation of the rich benefits that are gained from diverse opinions and approaches.

VIRTUES: The strength of these people's characters, their ability to transform their feelings of empathy into direct action, as well as their talent for persuasion, equip these people as natural, effective leaders.
VICES: The inevitable result of January 30 people's self-belief is their tendency toward vanity, and they must therefore ensure that they do not become convinced by their own propaganda. They should also moderate their propensity to become impatient and dismissive if they do not get their own way.
VERDICT: While ensuring that they never neglect the direction in which their prodigious talents lead them, people born on this day must learn genuinely to appreciate and welcome the views and criticisms of others. Mutually honest and trusting relationships will bring them personal fulfillment.

On This Day
Famous Births: William Jenner (1815); Osceola (1838); Anton Chekhov (1860); Franklin Delano Roosevelt (1882); Roy Eldridge (1911); Percy Thrower (1913); John Profumo (1915); Dorothy Malone (1925); Olaf Palme (1927); Harold Prince (1928); Gene Hackman (1930); Tammy Grimes (1936); Vanessa Redgrave and Boris Spassky (1937); Z. Budapest (1940); Dick Cheney (1941); Marty Balin (1942); Phil Collins (1951); Brett Butler (1958).

Significant Events and Anniversaries: Reflecting the artistic potential of this day; in Manchester, Britain, Charles Hallé founded his Hallé Orchestra (1858); Dior designer Yves St. Laurent held his first fashion show in Paris (1958); and archaeologists discovered five magnificent pharaonic statues near Luxor, Egypt (1989). The day of leadership, Adolf Hitler came to power when he was appointed chancellor of Germany (1933), while their ideological convictions caused three leaders to meet their ends: King Charles I of England by execution (1649); Austrian Crown Prince Rudolf (1889); and Mahatma Gandhi by assassination (1948). The British people mourned the loss of their great wartime leader, Sir Winston Churchill, whose state funeral was held on this day (1965). The day's potential for extreme intolerance can be seen in the tragic events of "Bloody Sunday," when thirteen people were killed by British paratroopers in Londonderry, Northern Ireland (1972).

Planetary Influences
Ruling planet: Uranus.
First decan: Personal planet is Uranus.

Sacred and Cultural Significance
Feast of Spring in ancient Rome.
Saints' day: Martina of Rome (d. 230).

Franklin Delano Roosevelt, born on January 30, 1882, manifested the powerful qualities of courage, fortitude and leadership associated with this day.

JANUARY 31

Planetary Influences
Ruling planet: Uranus.
First decan: Personal planet is Uranus.

Sacred and Cultural Significance
Sacred festival of Sarasvati in the Katmandu Valley of Nepal.
Saints' day: Maedoc of Ferns (d. 626); John Bosco (1815–88), patron saint of editors, schoolboys and youth.

Both artistry and originality are notable characteristics of January 31 people; Franz Schubert displayed both in abundance.

January 31 people have an all-consuming need to be taken seriously, to gain the regard of their peers for those qualities that they value most in themselves: their originality, compassion, sensitivity and vision. And indeed these people are admired by others yet, despite their best efforts, it may be for entirely different, and perhaps more superficial, reasons—such as for their personal charm, physical appearance or the entertainment that they give others. Perhaps these people have a tendency to send mixed messages in their attempts to gain the undivided attention of others, but it is frequently the case that they undervalue the particular talents that attract others to them, placing greater worth on their more profound characteristics. Their extreme sensitivity, fascination with mystical concepts and innate appreciation of beauty will often find fulfilling expression in the artistic world, but their considerable penetrative intellectual powers will also bring them success.

To console and reinforce them in the throes of their personal struggles to be accepted on their own terms, it is vital that January 31 people receive frequent demonstrations of the unconditional support of those closest to them, whose encouragement they will reward many times over. Yet, as in all other areas of their lives, people born on this day must beware of making unreasonable demands on the good will of others. Developing a more relaxed, pragmatic and less intense approach will benefit them in all areas of their lives.

VIRTUES: Empathetic, idealistic and effortlessly attractive to others, these are truly magnetic personalities, whose unusual gifts not only have the potential to bring great joy to the wider world, but also to influence and inspire.
VICES: These people tend to be oversensitive, to read meanings into the actions of others that may not be entirely accurate. When their expectations are disappointed, they have a propensity to react abruptly in their frustration, either cutting themselves off completely and becoming depressed, or startling others by the vehemence or waywardness of their responses.
VERDICT: January 31 people must learn to accept the recognition of others gracefully, even if they perceive it to be misplaced. They should remember to moderate their high demands both of themselves and other people and attempt to be more realistic and less intense in their personal relationships.

On This Day
Famous Births: Franz Schubert (1797); Zane Grey (1875); Irving Langmuir (1881); Anna Pavlova (1882); Eddie Cantor (1892); Freya Stark (1893); Tallulah Bankhead and Lord Soper (1903); Jackie Robinson (1919); Mario Lanza (1921); Carol Channing and Norman Mailer (1923); Jean Simmons (1929); Christopher Chataway (1931); James Franciscus (1934); Philip Glass and Suzanne Pleshette (1937); Queen Beatrix of the Netherlands (1938); Richard Gephardt (1941); Nolan Ryan (1947); Johnny Rotten (1956).

Significant Events and Anniversaries: On this day of outstanding and complex artistry, Chekhov's play *The Seagull* had its first performance (1901) and RCA introduced the world's first musical synthesizer (1955). Inventiveness and progress is further indicated by this day, on which Isambard Kingdom Brunel and John Scott Russell's innovative, five-funneled steamship, *The Great Eastern*, was finally launched at Millwall, England, after a three-month delay (1858); the U.S. House of Representatives passed the 13th Amendment to the Constitution, abolishing slavery (1865); the massive project to build the Trans-Iranian oil pipeline was completed (1957); and *Explorer I,* the U.S.A.'s first earth satellite, was launched (1958). Potential disillusionment is a characteristic of the day, on which, having bitterly disappointed the Soviet leader's demanding expectations for conformity, Leon Trotsky was exiled from the U.S.S.R. by Josef Stalin (1929). Reflecting the day's lesson that pragmatism is often the best course, German Field Marshal von Paulus surrendered his Sixth Army to the Soviets at Stalingrad, in direct defiance of Hitler's orders (1943). Finally, on this day that is governed by the sign of the water-carrier, the Thames Estuary broke its banks, thereby killing 307 people (1953).

FEBRUARY 1

February 1 people are blessed with so many talents that they often have difficulty in deciding which to concentrate on, a tendency that is complicated by the conflict between their heads and hearts. Indeed, these people have powerful perceptive qualities, as well as the enviable ability to evaluate a situation quickly and formulate an appropriate course of action—often a humanitarian course motivated by their natural sense of justice and desire to effect improvement. Their gifts and disposition suit them for careers in politics or education, as well as the medical and other caring professions, but since they are sensitive and communicative, they may also find success in the arts. Whichever area they decide to favor, however, these strong-willed people must be allowed to follow their own course, for if frustrated or forced to espouse a cause in which they do not believe, they will become obdurate and uncooperative.

Their grounded and sensible intellectual approach does not mean that these people are dull and plodding. On the contrary, their empathetic and intuitive qualities can result in startlingly impulsive behavior. February 1 people are often extremely sensual and sociable, giving themselves over to the enjoyment of the good things of life with enthusiasm. These characteristics make them popular and attractive to others, who are drawn to their company for the fun and excitement that they generate. Children and less disciplined individuals may become carried away by their wayward impulses and propensity for self-indulgence, a predilection toward the extreme that should be curbed.

VIRTUES: February 1 people are multitalented, combining a bright but tenacious intellect with a marked level of sensitivity and compassion toward others. They also possess outstanding powers of communication and personal magnetism, which draw others to them.
VICES: People born on this day have a tendency toward stubbornness when confronted with others' objections; they benefit by learning to compromise a little more rather than rejecting other opinions out of hand. Their propensity to speak their minds may cause offense.
VERDICT: Their personal abilities and willingness to strike out boldly on new paths give these people the potential to be real trail-blazers. However, they will gain by cultivating a more patient approach to others, which will enable them to achieve their objectives more easily.

On This Day
Famous Births: Clara Butt (1872); John Ford (1895); Stephen Potter (1900); Clark Gable (1901); Langston Hughes (1902); S.J. Perelman (1904); George Pal (1908); Stanley Matthews (1915); Muriel Spark (1918); Renata Tebaldi (1922); Boris Yeltsin (1931); Don Everly (1937); Sherman Hemsley (1938); Princess Stephanie of Monaco (1965); Lisa Marie Presley (1968).

Significant Events and Anniversaries: Reflecting the potential for medical advances indicated by this day, the first world's dental college was instituted in Baltimore, Maryland (1840). The artistic qualities of the day found their expression in: the establishment of the first film studio, by Thomas Alva Edison in New Jersey (1893); the first performance of Puccini's opera *La Bohème* (1896); and the opening in Paris of the Pompidou Centre for the Arts (1977). The natural justice starred by this day can be seen in the first session of the U.S. Supreme Court (1790) and the arrest of British "Great Train Robber" Ronald Biggs in Brazil (1974), while the day's tendency to extremism can be seen in Austrian chancellor Dollfus's action in banning all political parties except his own (1934) and the return of the Ayatollah Khomeini to Iran from exile, bent on instituting a strictly religious Islamic regime (1979).

Planetary Influences
Ruling planet: Uranus.
Second decan: Personal planet is Mercury.

Sacred and Cultural Significance
Lesser Eleusinian Mysteries celebrated in ancient Greece; first day of Black History Month in the United States.
Saints' day: Brigid of Ireland (d. c.525), patron saint of scholars and dairymaids; Seiriol (6th century AD).

On this day of awareness of justice and humanitarian interests, on which Black History month now commences in the U.S.A., the first lunch-counter sit-in protesting racial segregation was staged by Civil Rights Movement demonstrators in Greensboro, North Carolina, in 1960.

FEBRUARY 2

* *

Planetary Influences
Ruling planet: Uranus.
Second decan: Personal planet is Mercury.

Sacred and Cultural Significance
Saints' day: Candlemas Day, celebrating
the purification of the Blessed Virgin Mary
(d. 1st century AD), patron saint of mothers,
nuns and virgins; Jeanne de Lestonnac
(1556–1640); Theophane Vénard (1829–61).

Bustos's Immaculate Conception, 1880, *illustrates
the purification of the Blessed Virgin Mary on
Candlemas Day.*

Control is vitally important to February 2 people, who need to feel in command of a given situation, of their emotions, as well as of their image and how others perceive them. There are many possible reasons for this fundamental necessity, including a wish to hide perceived weakness, a yearning to attain perfection, or, perhaps, a genuine desire for domination. These people will frequently cultivate a suave exterior or a coldly logical approach—whatever the personal implications of such a stance—and may terrify others by the apparently unattainable level of their demands. Yet it must be remembered that, despite their tough image, these people aspire to the approval and admiration of their peers for their outstanding qualities, which are, indeed, considerable.

People born on this day possess the talent to analyze a problem with crystal clarity, weigh alternative courses of action dispassionately, and strive to achieve their objectives with single-minded determination. They revel in competition: when not climbing their way to the top of the corporate tree—and they usually excel in the business sphere, especially in sales—they will often be winners in the sporting field, or in politics. Unfortunately, particularly if they are male, their preferred tactics may be less welcome in more intimate relationships, where, in spite of their willingness to offer instant and practical advice, their reluctance to appear vulnerable may be seen as a hurtful lack of interest.

VIRTUES: Driven and dynamic, February 2 people possess the intellectual capacity to cut straight to the heart of an issue and to formulate a logical and measured response. Masters of detail, they have the enviable faculty of seeing the larger picture.
VICES: Because these people have a tendency to suppress their instinctive impulses and project a chosen, idealized image to the outside world, others sometimes perceive them as cold fish, lacking in warmth and empathy. In fact, in extreme cases, February 2 people regard emotional responses as inferior to the more impersonal qualities of discipline and intellectual clarity.
VERDICT: People born on this day should not work so hard at proving their worth, but should concentrate instead on developing the empathetic skills that they undoubtedly possess and focusing more on emotional needs—both their own, and those of the people closest to them. By being candid about their failings and mindful of the need to be connected to their inner feelings, they will not only be better understood and appreciated by others, but will also find greater personal satisfaction.

On This Day
Famous Births: Nell Gwyn (1650); Charles Maurice de Talleyrand-Périgord (1754); Jesse Boot (1850); Havelock Ellis (1859); Fritz Kreisler (1875); James Joyce (1882); Jascha Heifetz (1901); Jussi Björling (1911); Hughie Green (1920); Valéry Giscard d'Estaing (1926); Stan Getz and Elaine Strich (1927); Les Dawson (1933); Tommy Smothers (1937); David Jason (1940);Farrah Fawcett (1947); Christie Brinkley (1953); Kim Zimmer (1955).

Significant Events and Anniversaries: Image is a strong feature of this day, on which Alexander Selkirk, who would later serve as the model for Daniel Defoe's *Robinson Crusoe*, was rescued after spending five solitary years on the "desert" island Mas à Tierra (1709); the funeral of Queen Victoria, a British national icon, was held (1901); and Lichtenstein at last granted the vote to women (1986). The controlling tendencies of February 2 were reflected in Greece's declaration of war on Turkey (1878), and in Major-General Idi Amin's proclamation of himself as the absolute ruler of Uganda (1971). After a remarkable display of determined resistance, a marked characteristic of the day, by the Soviets, the German army surrendered at Stalingrad (1943).

FEBRUARY 3

asy-going, affable and kind to those whom they perceive as vulnerable, February 3 people are popular individuals, whose apparently relaxed approach to relationships draws others to them. While they generally enjoy their powers of attraction, their personal magnetism can also create the unwelcome feeling of being trapped by the attention of others. Their greatest fear is of having their wings clipped and their freedom curtailed by the stifling demands of partners or friends for wholehearted commitment. This is not to say that these people do not experience deep and genuine emotions, but that they need to feel they have not sacrificed the personal liberty that is so dear to them. This tendency is particularly pronounced in February 3 men, and in those also born in the Chinese year of the horse: partners who desire an enduring relationship with them should accept the fact that they cannot tolerate being "suffocated."

However, these people are not usually intellectual butterflies who flit from subject to subject without stopping long enough to delve deeper. When a concept truly stimulates them, they will probe every minute aspect of it, driven by their insatiable curiosity and determination to master attendant challenges. Their inherent sensitivity, originality and technical aptitude is an ideal combination for success in the arts—a career in music may be particularly auspicious—or in the scientific field, where their willingness to strike out boldly may lead them along previously untrodden paths.

VIRTUES: Charming, adventurous and intelligent, those born on this day are especially admired by others for their quick minds and fascinating individualism. When they alight upon a subject or task that interests them, they will pursue it with dedication, often resulting in exciting consequences.
VICES: Because they have a horror of being hemmed in by personal commitment, these people may often be regarded as unreliable, or lacking in perseverance or emotional depth. If they feel that they are being pressured to concede to a demand that makes them uncomfortable, they may abandon a relationship or project, or even resort to fits of temper.
VERDICT: February 3 people should cultivate a greater sense of realism and objectivity in their personal relationships, which will enable them to realize that others do not harbor agendas for entrapment in seeking their affection. Moderation, pragmatism and resisting the tendency to react defensively will benefit them in every area of life.

On This Day
Famous Births: Felix Mendelssohn (1809); Elizabeth Blackwell (1821); Walter Bagehot (1826); Robert Cecil, Marquess of Salisbury (1830); Hugo Junkers (1859); Gertrude Stein (1874); Clarence E. Mulford (1883); Carl Theodore Dreyer (1889); Norman Rockwell (1894); Alvar Aalto (1898); James Michener (1907); Simone Weil (1909); Joey Bishop (1918); Glen Tetley (1926); Frankie Vaughan (1928); Val Doonican (1929); Jeremy Kemp (1935); Blythe Danner (1943); Melanie (1948); Morgan Fairchild (1950).

Significant Events and Anniversaries: The adventurous nature of this day was reflected in Portuguese navigator Bartholomew Diaz's triumph in landing at Mossel Bay, on the east side of the Cape of Good Hope, making him the first European to land on southern African soil (1488), and in the first controlled moon landing, by the Soviet unmanned spacecraft *Luna IX* (1966). On this day of commitment to freedom, the 15th Amendment to the U.S. Constitution was ratified, bringing the vote to African American men (1870); the first meeting of the League of Nations was held in Paris (1919); and the execution of Ronald Ryan was Australia's last under the death penalty (1967). The temperamental aspect of the day was confirmed by three disasters: Ottawa's parliament building burned to the ground (1916); an earthquake hit New Zealand, killing 216 people in Napier and Hastings (1931); and 280 people died in eastern England after flooding and storms (1957). Governed by the element of air, this day is the anniversary of British politician Harold Macmillan's "Wind of Change" speech to the South African parliament (1960).

Planetary Influences
Ruling planet: Uranus.
Second decan: Personal planet is Mercury.

Sacred and Cultural Significance
In Christianity, the Blessing of the Throats.
Saints' day: Blaise (dates unknown), patron saint of throat sufferers; Ia (dates unknown); Laurence of Canterbury (d. 619); Werburga (d. c.700); Anskar (801–65); Margaret of England (d. 1192).

In this image from a medieval Book of Hours, a mother-to-be is offered a protective hand. February 3 is St. Margaret's day, honoring the patron saint of pregnant women.

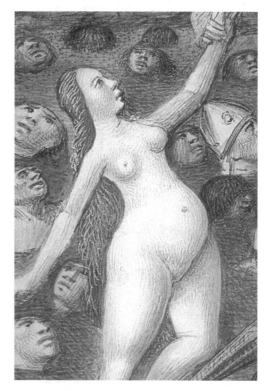

Planetary Influences
Ruling planet: Uranus.
Second decan: Personal planet is Mercury.

Sacred and Cultural Significance
In Japan, Setsu-bun, an annual purification and protective festival.
Saints' day: Phileas (d. 306); Gilbert of Sempringham (c.1083–1189), patron saint of paralyzed people; John de Britto (1647–93).

FEBRUARY 4

* *

Such is their originality, their speed of thought and their prodigious energy that people born on this day sometimes exhaust their less mercurial companions. The whirlwind of activity that they create around them is driven by their darting curiosity and compulsion to act—characteristics that, if focused, may lead them into uncharted realms. Lacking such focus, their relish for discovery and variety may cause them to bounce from one enthusiasm to the next, often spending vast quantities of money in the process. Indeed, if bored, they tend to lack staying power, dismissing an unstimulating project or relationship as unworthy of their attention. They should make an effort to curb this impatience, especially in their personal lives in which, because of their flighty behavior, they may be seen as superficial and unable to reciprocate profound emotions.

Yet despite their sometimes inconsistent image, February 3 people do harbor great emotional depths: the level of their empathy with others, or the strength of their humanitarian vision, will often manifest itself in a stubbornly brave refusal to be deflected from their position. When they are truly fired up by a cause they will pursue it with fierce intensity and such a tenacious sense of purpose that others may label them eccentric. They will fare especially well in the artistic field, where their idiosyncratic blend of sensitivity and originality will be accepted and appreciated, but their potential may generate success in any professional area they choose, as long as they remember the importance of self-discipline.

VIRTUES: These positive, inquisitive and quick-thinking personalities stamp their remarkable originality upon everything that they undertake. Others may be stimulated by their typically unconstrained and exuberant imaginative powers, which also give them the capacity to bring about real innovations.
VICES: Their speed of thought and enormous vigor can lead these people to act impulsively without having thought through the full implications of their actions. They may be easily and frequently distracted and thus may become somewhat scatty, unable to keep on top of their various interests.
VERDICT: February 4 people should take care to look before they leap, with characteristic enthusiasm, into a situation. Developing a more focused approach will help them to realize their full potential in both their professional and personal lives.

On This Day
Famous Births: Tadeusz Andrzej Bonawentura Kosciusko (1746); Fernand Léger (1881); Raymond Arthur Dart (1893); Ludwig Erhard (1897); Charles Lindbergh (1902); Dietrich Bonhoeffer (1906); Byron Nelson (1912); Ida Lupino (1918); Norman Wisdom (1920); Betty Friedan (1921); David Brenner (1945); Dan Quayle (1947); Alice Cooper (1948); Lisa Eichhorn (1952); Lawrence Taylor (1959).

Significant Events and Anniversaries: February 4 is a day that indicates latent originality bordering on the eccentric, and is the day when Pierre van Ryneveld and C.J. Quinton embarked on the first flight from Britain to Cape Town, southern Africa (1920); Malcolm Campbell achieved a speed of over 174 m.p.h. in *Bluebird* in Wales, thus setting a new land speed record (1927); and also marks the launching of the world's biggest hovercraft at Cowes, on the Isle of Wight in Britain (1968). Obstinacy in support of a cherished cause is a further feature of this day, on which the American Confederacy of southern states was established (1861), and the Yalta Conference between the Allied powers began to discuss the imminent defeat of Nazi Germany (1945). Reflecting the extravagance indicated by the day, Rolls-Royce was declared bankrupt (1971). The mercurial aspect of this day was tragically highlighted by an earthquake in Guatemala, resulting in the death of around 23,000 people (1976).

From the chaos of world war, the Yalta conference, which began on this day in 1945, laid the groundwork for the international humanitarian goals of the defeat of Nazism and the founding of the United Nations.

FEBRUARY 5

February 5 people are often much admired by others for their fluently competent manner and apparent capacity to undertake any task with effortless ease. Yet life is no easier for people born on this day than for others—it is just that they have cultivated a calm and efficient external manner to mask their internal difficulties. The smooth façade that they present to the world may conceal a deep-rooted sense of insecurity, however, which—particularly if they are women—they strive to resolve by seeking the admiration of other people. Perfection, however, is not a natural human condition, and not only will they find this ideal impossible to achieve, but they run the risk of driving others away by their unrealistic demands or intimidatingly lofty manner.

Their hypersensitivity is perhaps the key to February 5 people, who respond instinctively to the moods of others. Their twin qualities of intuition and mental farsightedness may, however, cause them great emotional anxiety, which they will suppress with a polished veneer that falsely indicates control. Indeed, the combination of their desire to be seen in the best possible light and their perceptive intellectual powers may sometimes lead them to offer practical help over the emotional support that is perhaps more valuable to others and which, moreover, they also crave for themselves. Their unusually diverse personal talents make them naturally well-rounded, with the potential to excel in either the arts or in academic or scientific pursuits. They generally work better as part of a team or cause, where they can simultaneously satisfy their need for human contact and utilize their flair for administration and management.

VIRTUES: Highly controlled and extremely self-disciplined, those born on February 5 impress others with both their clarity of vision and their competence. The unusual juxtaposition of great sensitivity and organizational powers that is inherent in them gives them extraordinary potential for achievement.
VICES: These people are perhaps too oriented toward presenting an idealized image to the world in order to gain the admiration and respect that is so important to them. In doing so, however, they may not only mislead others as to their real natures, but may alienate others by their apparently superior air.
VERDICT: February 5 people should remember that maintaining outward appearances that conflict with their true selves can be emotionally damaging. They must therefore open up, for they will find ultimate fulfillment by allowing others to know them properly.

On This Day

Famous Births: Robert Peel (1788); John Boyd Dunlop and Hiram Stevens Maxim (1840); Joris Karl Huysmans (1848); Adlai Ewing Stevenson (1900); John Carradine (1906); William Seward Burroughs (1914); Red Buttons and Andreas Papandreou (1919); Frank Muir (1920); John Pritchard (1921); Hank Aaron (1934); Susan Hill (1942); Bob Marley (1945); Charlotte Rampling (1946); Barbara Hershey (1948); Jennifer Jason Leigh (1962).

Significant Events and Anniversaries: This day has enormous artistic potential, and marks the first performance of Rossini's opera *The Barber of Seville* (1816); the discovery of a hitherto unknown Mozart symphony in Odense, Denmark (1983); and the general release of Walt Disney's *Peter Pan* (1953). Reflecting the day's outstanding, often martial, organizational abilities, three military and diplomatic forces scored notable successes: when the Third Treaty of Nijmegen ended the Seven Years' War in Europe (1679); the British captured Minorca from the Spanish (1782); and when the U.S. Army entered Manila during World War II (1945). February 5 is ruled by the element of air, and is the anniversary of the foundation of Britain's Royal Air Force College at Cranwell (1920), but also of the bankruptcy of Laker Airlines, Sir Freddy Laker's independent aviation company (1982).

Planetary Influences
Ruling planet: Uranus.
Second decan: Personal planet is Mercury.

Sacred and Cultural Significance
Feast of Ia, a Pagan celebration.
Saints' day: Agatha (dates unknown), patron saint of bell-founders, fire-fighters, nurses, Malta and diseases of the breast.

Florence Nightingale, perhaps the most famous nurse in history. February 5 is St. Agatha's day, celebrating the patron saint of nurses.

FEBRUARY 6

Planetary Influences
Ruling planet: Uranus.
Second decan: Personal planet is Mercury.

Sacred and Cultural Significance
New Zealand Day (Waitangi Day);
Aphrodite honored in ancient Greece.
Saints' day: Dorothy (d. c.313), patron saint
of florists; Mel (d. 488); Vedast (d. 539);
Amand (c.584–c.675), patron saint of
hoteliers and the wine industry; Paul Miki
and Companions (d. 1597).

*As an actor and statesman, Ronald Reagan,
who was born on this day in 1911, constantly
sought (and won) popularity, a desire reinforced
by the influence of the Chinese year of the pig.
Characteristically for February 6 people,
liberty was his most cherished value throughout
his career.*

In common with most Aquarians, February 6 people have a profound need for liberty, not necessarily in the physical sense—although these people may be restless and have a love of travel and sporting pursuits—but more crucially in their intellectual pursuits and dealings with others. They hate feeling constrained by the demands of others and will rarely thrive in tightly run organizations or in relationships in which they feel that too great a level of commitment is being required of them. That having been said, they will often display remarkable focus when they find a topic or person that intrigues them, and will be driven by the almost irresistible urge to investigate further. For this reason they show a special aptitude for scientific research, into which their willingness to anticipate the unexpected and explore new avenues will be profitably channeled. More artistically inclined February 6 people may find similar satisfaction in the realms of music and literature.

Ironically, given their fiercely independent outlook, people born on this day prize the approval of others. This desire for popularity is generally not motivated by the desire to have their talents recognized, but rather by a more emotional craving to be cocooned by the love and admiration of those around them. Since they are intuitive beings, they will absorb the prevailing mood of the company within which they find themselves, and are prone to reflect it—a policy which may endear them to others in the short term, but which may ultimately gain them a reputation for inconstancy. Even so, others frequently feel affinity and enthusiasm for these people, and may elevate them to positions of leadership.

VIRTUES: People born on this day respond exceptionally well to sensory and intellectual stimuli, reacting intelligently and originally to any challenge that inspires them, however daunting. Their twin powers of intuition and curiosity will often lead them into new and fascinating fields of inquiry.
VICES: These people need to control their tendency to become bored and skittish when they find themselves in situations that do not stimulate them. When their attention is not held, they have a propensity to flee from commitment and seek new pastures. They should moderate their yearning to be all things to all people.
VERDICT: February 6 people should remember that their desire to be loved may cause them to act in a manner that is incompatible with their true emotional needs. They should endeavor to recognize their insecurities and work on resolving these; increased self-awareness and patience will bring them a greater degree of emotional stability.

On This Day
Famous Births: Christopher Marlowe (1564); Queen Anne of Britain and Ireland (1665); Sir Henry Irving (1838); Babe Ruth (1895); Claudio Arrau (1903); Wladyslaw Gomulka (1905); Ronald Reagan (1911); Eva Braun (1912); Zsa Zsa Gabor (1915); Patrick McNee (1922); Keith Waterhouse (1929); Fred Trueman (1931); François Truffaut (1932) Leslie Crowther (1933); Tom Brokaw and Jimmy Tarbuck (1940); Natalie Cole (1950); Axl Rose (1962); Rick Astley (1966).

Significant Events and Anniversaries: February 6 is governed by the element of air, and the day marks the anniversary of two notable events in aviation: the formation of the German airliner company Lufthansa (1919), and, tragically, the plane crash that caused the death of twenty-three people, including seven "Busby's Babes," members of Britain's Manchester United soccer team, at Munich (1958). The gift of personal popularity bestowed by this day may ultimately result in leadership, and it is the day on which: Maximilian I was pronounced Holy Roman Emperor (1508); Robert E. Lee was appointed commander-in-chief of the Confederate Armies (1865); Ramsay MacDonald was voted chairman of the British Labour Party (1911); and, upon the death of her father, George VI, Princess Elizabeth became Queen of England (1952).

FEBRUARY 7

Those born on February 7 view the world around them in a somewhat naive way, in that they have an inherent sense of justice and respond on a deeply emotional level to any perceived social abuse. They are quick to identify solutions to problems, which they will then pursue with idealistic enthusiasm, but in their zeal they are unlikely to have thought their plans through sufficiently. These people, who are quick-witted and original thinkers, are furthermore possessed with great communicative and persuasive skills, which they will characteristically employ to enlist the support of others. Such interpersonal talents indicate potentially successful salespeople, but they will often also thrive in social work, and make gifted journalists and technicians, too.

A vital characteristic of these people is their instinctive aversion to authority. It is not that they lack discipline—far from it—just that they chafe under regulations with which they do not agree and, if constricted, they will typically resort to subversion as a manifestation of their independence. Self-starters, they will always perform best when given autonomy and freedom of action; this applies as much to their personal as to their professional lives. If this crucial criterion is satisfied, they make empathetic and even indulgent partners, and—since they always maintain a youthful outlook and tend to persuade rather than dictate—are often particularly good parents.

VIRTUES: Their humanitarian concern, endearing sense of optimism, and boundless energy give these people the potential to be real forces for good. Their capacity for incisively original thought bestows on them great problem-solving abilities.
VICES: Because they are so sensitive, February 7 people may suffer great disappointment when insurmountable obstacles hinder their progressive aspirations, and may then hide their disillusionment with a dismissive mask of cynicism.
VERDICT: February 7 people must recognize that life is too complicated to be seen in terms of black-and-white or quick-fix solutions. They should learn to respect diversity of opinion, develop a greater sense of realism with regard to people, and accept that they will not always be able convert others to their viewpoints.

Planetary Influences
Ruling planet: Uranus.
Second decan: Personal planet is Mercury.

Sacred and Cultural Significance
Li Chum, annual Spring fertility festival, celebrated in China.
Saints' day: Richard (d. 720); Romuald of Ravenna (c.950–1027); Ronan (dates unknown).

On This Day
Famous Births: Thomas More (1478); Philippe Buache (1700); Charles Dickens (1812); Frederick Douglass (1817); Laura Ingalls Wilder (1867); Alfred Adler (1870); James "Eubie" Blake (1883); Sinclair Lewis (1885); Larry "Buster" Crabbe (1908); Russel Drysdale (1912); Eddie Bracken (1920); Dora Bryan (1924); Peter Jay (1937); Rolf Benirschke (1955); Garth Brooks (1962).

Significant Events and Anniversaries: This day highlights freedom of thought and action and is the anniversary both of Grenada's attainment of independence (1974) and of the U.S.S.R.'s ruling Communist Party's agreement to amend the Soviet constitution to make the government less authoritarian, thereby taking the first step toward democracy (1990). On this day of natural justice, "Baby Doc" Duvalier, the dictator of Haiti, was deposed and forced to seek refuge in France (1986) and Switzerland gave women the right to vote (1971). This day of the water-carrier tragically commemorates the loss of 185 people's lives when the British vessel H.M.S. *Orpheus* foundered on the New Zealand coast (1863). Joan Bazely was rewarded for her persistence against officialdom, when she was appointed the first woman referee of an English football match at Croydon (1976), and the originality indicated by February 7 found its most bizarre expression in Ipswich, Australia, when it rained sardines (1989).

This is a day on which anything can happen, as illustrated when a violent storm caused sardines to "rain" from the sky over Ipswich, Australia, on February 7, 1989.

FEBRUARY 8

Planetary Influences
Ruling planet: Uranus.
Second decan: Personal planet is Mercury.

Sacred and Cultural Significance
Saints' day: Kew (5th century AD); Elfleda (653–714); Cuthman (d. 8th century AD); Stephen of Muret (c.1047–1124); Jerome Emiliani (1481–1537).

James Dean, a gifted actor who achieved cult status, was born on this day in 1931. With his Moon in Scorpio, his innate sensitivity and vulnerability were tempered with a grounded, hard-working approach to his craft.

Inherent in February 8 people is a curious mixture of extreme intuition and technical flair which, if balanced, can make them extraordinarily successful in the world of the arts—especially if they were also born in the Chinese year of the tiger. Of further benefit to them in their musical, artistic, dramatic or literary pursuits are their strong imaginative powers, which, in combination with their instinctive ability to assess a situation and their gift of interpretation, will delight their audiences with their originality. Although intellectual freedom is as vital to these people as the air that is their element, they do not limit this requirement to themselves alone and are always ready to respect and consider other people's opinions. Furthermore, they shrink from confrontation, and therefore generally seek to smooth over conflict by finding a compromise.

It is their profound—occasionally almost psychic—sensitivity that drives these people to try to create peace and harmony around them. They delight others with their unique sense of humor and refreshing company, although they remain reserved and avoid personal topics of conversation. Their ability to effortlessly attune themselves to the moods of other people, as well as their limitless imaginations, leads them not only to identify themselves with others' situations, but also to envisage possibly negative future scenarios. Thus the easy-going façade that they generally adopt may mask a deep sense of distress and emotional turmoil. Their friends and partners should therefore give them unquestioning support and understanding in order to create the stable, loving background which is so important to them.

VIRTUES: Creative, intuitive and accomplished, people born on this day possess both the necessary talent and vision to make an outstanding success of their chosen career. They are great respecters of personal liberty, and aim to achieve concord by consensus in their interpersonal relationships.
VICES: Such is the sensitivity of February 8 people that they may be beset with feelings of anxiety and depression over which they feel they have no control and from which they see no escape. They have a tendency to try to conceal their true feelings and vulnerability from others in order to avoid being hurt.
VERDICT: While always guarding against the cynicism that can result from disappointment, these people should actively strive to develop a more pragmatic approach to all areas of their lives, and must moderate their propensity to become overwhelmed and confused by their emotional responses. They should, moreover, ensure that they reveal their true selves to their loved ones.

On This Day
Famous Births: John Ruskin (1819); William Tecumseh Sherman (1820); Jules Verne (1828); Dimitri Ivanovich Mendeleyev (1834); Dame Edith Evans (1888); King Wallis Vidor (1894); Lyle Talbot (1902); Chester Floyd Carlson (1906); Lana Turner (1920); Jack Lemmon (1925); James Dean (1931); John Williams (1932); Ted Koppel and Nick Nolte (1940); Robert Klein (1942); Gary Coleman (1968).

Significant Events and Anniversaries: The element of February 8 is air, and this day marks the anniversary of the Boeing 747's maiden flight (1969) and the day on which U.S. astronauts Gerald Carr, Edward Gibson and William Pogue safely returned to Earth after spending eighty-five days in the Skylab space station (1974). On this day of particular artistry, the seminal British band the Beatles arrived in New York on their first tour of the U.S.A. (1964) and eighteen-year-old Debi Thomas won the women's Senior Singles U.S. Figure Skating Championship, making her the first African American to win this title (1986). Reflecting Elizabeth I of England's abhorrence of direct confrontation, a characteristic of February 8, she had Mary, Queen of Scots, beheaded at Fotheringhay Castle for allegedly conspiring to overthrow her, without ever having met her cousin face to face (1587). Russia celebrated the accession of a new empress, Catherine, who exhibited so many of the gifts starred by this day that she became termed "the Great" (1725).

FEBRUARY 9

For many who are close to them, February 9 people appear to possess two diametrically opposed characteristics: whereas they are unfailingly optimistic while addressing other people's problems, when it comes to their own situation, they often appear unduly negative. This apparent inability to apply their considerable gift for encouraging others to themselves has many possible causes—perhaps it results from a feeling of fatalism founded on the accumulation of previously unhappy experiences, or it may be the manifestation of an unjustified sense of unworthiness. Such is their natural vigor and appetite for tasting all that life has to offer, that these people will indeed be exposed to a wide variety of situations—with both positive and negative ramifications—in their lives, and will draw upon their wealth of experience to assist those who seek their advice.

The complex personal qualities displayed by those born on this day are the products of their great sensitivity and highly developed powers of perception and imagination. Practical as well as empathetic, they make gifted counselors, as well as excellent parents (especially in the case of February 9 women). Yet when they apply their talent for penetrating insight to their own personalities, they have a tendency to measure themselves against an impossible ideal and will inevitably consider themselves lacking. By reciprocating the love and support of these people, their friends and family members will give them the stability and sense of self-affirmation that they need if they are to thrive.

VIRTUES: These kind and empathetic people are strongly motivated by humanitarian concerns, and are unflagging in devoting their prodigious energies to furthering a worthy cause. Their sympathetic natures and wisdom gained by experience makes them greatly sought after for advice and support.

VICES: Those born on this day have an endearing tendency to think the best of others, and should therefore beware of allowing their natural goodwill to be exploited, either in their personal lives or in professional ventures. They should also strive to regard themselves more positively and make fewer demands of themselves.

VERDICT: February 9 people should try to value themselves as much as they do others and remember that they cannot be effective pillars of support if those pillars are crumbling on the inside. Retaining their sense of humor and perspective will help them to overcome feelings of depression and to bolster their self-esteem.

On This Day

Famous Births: William Harrison (1773); Anthony Hope (1863); Mrs. Patrick Campbell (1865); Alban Berg (1885); Ronald Colman (1891); Jim Laker (1922); Brendan Behan (1923); Garret Fitzgerald (1926); Roger Mudd (1928); Janet Suzman (1939); Carole King (1942); Joe Pesci (1943); Alice Walker (1944); Mia Farrow (1945); Bernard Gallacher and Judith Light (1949); Sandy Lyle (1958); Amber Valetta (1974).

Significant Events and Anniversaries: On this day, whose element is air, the Soviet airline Aeroflot was founded (1923) and Halley's Comet returned to the skies above the Earth (1986). February 9 indicates progressiveness, and was the day on which Giuseppe Mazzini proclaimed a Roman Republic (1849, February to May)—believing republicanism to be the best possible system for enlightened government—as well as the day on which Nelson Mandela, an outstanding exponent of beneficence and tolerance, was inaugurated as South Africa's first African president (1994). This Aquarian day marks the anniversary of Charles Sturt's identification of the terminating point of Australia's longest river, the Murray (1830).

Planetary Influences
Ruling planet: Uranus.
Second decan: Personal planet is Mercury.

Sacred and Cultural Significance
Narvik Sun Pageant in Norway.
Saints' day: Apollonia (d. c.249), patron saint of dentists and those who suffer from toothache; Teilo (6th century AD).

Nationalist revolutionary Giuseppe Mazzini, who fought for political liberty against the Risorgimento, *established the short-lived Roman Republic on this day in 1849, attempting to reinstate ancient Rome's republican system and the concept of leadership by "first citizens." Astrology played a major role in decision-making for the leaders of ancient Rome.*

Planetary Influences
Ruling planet: Uranus.
Third decan: Personal planet is Venus.

Sacred and Cultural Significance
New Year's Day celebrated by the Kebbawa tribe of Nigeria.
Saints' day: Scholastica (d. c.543), patron saint of convulsive children and nuns; Trumwin (d. c.704); William of Malavalla (d. 1157).

The auspicious marriage of Victoria and Albert on this day of alliances in 1840 marked a union that would bestow outstanding political success for Great Britain and emotional stability for the royal family.

FEBRUARY 10

Those people born on February 10 are centered on achievement. It is vitally important to them to win the respect and recognition of others—possibly as a result of a sneaking sense of insecurity—and it is generally to this end that they concentrate their considerable talents. Blessed with great determination, imagination and a confident belief in their own potential, they will strive to make their mark on the world, secretly hoping to have their sense of self validated by the approval of others. Yet however great their ambition, these are not people who trample roughshod over others on their upward path; intuitive and kind, their aspiration is to achieve their goals and not to harm others in the process. Indeed, when channeled toward problem-solving, their gift of empathy and genuine desire for progress makes them notable peacemakers. Inevitably, however, these people will experience competition, particularly since many are drawn to active sports.

Because they are so oriented toward realizing their goals, these people may not pay adequate heed to their undoubted gift of empathy, and may inadvertently neglect those close to them, becoming emotionally isolated. They have a tendency to externalize their sensitivity, picking up the mood of others and in turn projecting it back again to gain approval—a propensity that suits many February 10 people to careers in the performing arts. Ironically, given that much of their energies are ultimately directed toward gaining the esteem and affirmation of others—whether or not they are consciously aware of it—they may find themselves admired from afar but lacking intimate friends to rejoice and share in their success.

VIRTUES: These original and multitalented people are exceptionally clear-sighted with regard to their aspirations. Driven and dynamic, they have the enviable ability single-mindedly to focus their energies on achieving their potential.
VICES: People born on this day should guard that the pursuit of their guiding vision does not become obsessive. They should seek to discover the real motivation behind their ambition and ensure that they do not lose sight of it.
VERDICT: February 10 people benefit from paying as much attention to their personal relationships as they do to their careers. They have the capability to achieve their ambitions, but the triumph will be a hollow one if there is no one to genuinely and unselfishly celebrate with them.

On Ths Day
Famous Births: William Congreve (1670); Charles Lamb (1775); Samuel Plimsoll (1824); William Pember Reeves (1857); Boris Pasternak (1890); Jimmy "Schnozzle" Durante and William Taten Tilden (1893); Harold Macmillan (1894); Bertold Brecht (1898); Joyce Grenfell (1910); Larry Adler (1914); Alex Comfort (1920); Leontyne Price (1927); Robert Wagner (1930); Roberta Flack (1940); Peter Allen (1944); Mark Spitz (1950); Greg Norman (1955); Laura Dern (1967).

Significant Events and Anniversaries: The potential success indicated by the single-minded ambition starred by February 10 was reflected in the resolution of the Seven Years' (French and Indian) War on the signing of the Treaty of Paris, by which Britain received Canada from France (1763), while on the same day Upper and Lower Canada were unified (1840). This day indicates singular originality and tenacity, and is the Aquarian day on which British inventor Andrew Becker tested his "practical diving suit" in the River Thames (1774). On this day, Queen Victoria of Britain married Albert of Saxe-Coburg-Gotha (1840), a union which gave the reigning monarch vital emotional support in her devoted pursuance of her royal duties. The wartime U.S. bandleader Glenn Miller received the music business's first gold disk for his recording of "Chattanooga Choo Choo" (1942), a tangible symbol of both his, and the song's, enormous popularity.

FEBRUARY 11

T he urge to implement progress is a vital component of February 11 people's personal makeup. With their complementary need for mental stimulation and natural capacity for problem-solving, they are constantly casting around for a challenge against which they can apply their talents and, because they are usually rather domesticated beings, will often find it close to home. Indeed, these cheerfully original and multitalented people have something of a knack for invention and, when also technically minded, enjoy nothing more than designing and constructing their own, improved version of a household appliance, or devising a scheme to make everyday life easier. Yet their wish to bring about improvement is not merely limited to their immediate sphere of influence, and people born on this day may, for example, become charity workers or dedicated volunteers, actively pioneering practical ways in which to help others.

Their originality and optimism frequently exert a magnetic influence on other people, who are drawn irresistably to their affability and sense of fun. In turn, February 11 people, who are in any case naturally gregarious, relish the cut-and-thrust excitement of intellectual sparring. Extremely hospitable, they are welcoming and solicitous in their care of their guests. The combination of their great sociability and intellectual enthusiasms, however, can mean that they may not devote enough attention to the emotional needs of their family and friends, and they should therefore ensure that they do not neglect the less tangible needs of their nearest and dearest, especially as parents.

VIRTUES: Creative, enthusiastic and original to the point of eccentricity, these people have the potential not only to make their mark on the world in their own, inimitable fashion, but in so doing, helping—as well as charming—others.
VICES: Their often exclusive absorption in a current enthusiasm may cause these people unwittingly to forget the importance of nurturing their personal relationships. They should also be aware that, while they enjoy filling their houses with people and parties, those who share their homes may come to resent this open-door policy as an invasion of their privacy and personal space.
VERDICT: February 11 people must not allow their propensity for fantasy and their desire to see their dreams realized interfere with the reality of their existence. While never suppressing their creativity and essential drives, they should remember the importance of retaining a sense of equilibrium in all things.

On This Day
Famous Births: William Henry Fox Talbot (1800); Auguste Edouard Mariette (1821); Josiah Willard Gibbs (1839); Thomas Alva Edison (1847); Vivien Ernest Fuchs (1908); Joseph L. Mankiewicz (1909); Sidney Sheldon (1917); King Farouk I of Egypt (1920); Eva Gabor (1921); Kim Stanley (1925); Leslie Nielsen (1926); Tina Louise, Mary Quant and John Surtees (1934); Burt Reynolds (1936); Bill Lawry (1937); Manuel Noriega (1940); Sergio Mendes (1941) Sheryl Crow (1963); Jennifer Aniston (1969).

Significant Events and Anniversaries: This is a day of practical innovation, and marks the anniversary of the publication of the world's first weekly weather bulletin, by Britain's Meteorological Office (1878), while on this day Margaret Thatcher took a pioneering step forward in the annals of women's history when the Conservatives voted her the first female leader of a British political party (1975) and Joan Child followed her lead when she became Australia's first woman speaker of the House of Representatives (1986). February 11 also heralds independent action, and was the day on which Honduras became an independent republic (1922), and the Lateran Treaty proclaimed the Vatican in Rome to be a sovereign state under the rulership of the pope (1929). Reflecting this day's compassionate qualities, Nelson Mandela, a man who came to embody humanitarian concern, was released from captivity in South Africa (1990).

Planetary Influences
Ruling planet: Uranus.
Third decan: Personal planet is Venus.

Sacred and Cultural Significance
National Founding Day, Japan; pilgrimage to shrine of Our Lady of Lourdes in France.
Saints' day: Gobnet (5th century AD); Caedmon (d. 680); Gregory II (d. 731); Benedict of Aniane (750–821).

Thomas Alva Edison, born on this day in 1847, was one of the most prolific and ingenious inventors in history. Largely self-taught (he had only three months of formal education), he achieved phenomenal success in his career by maximizing the drive, creativity and originality that are characteristic of February 11 people.

Planetary Influences
Ruling planet: Uranus.
Third decan: Personal planet is Venus.

Sacred and Cultural Significance
Saints' day: Ethilwald (d. 740).

Charles Darwin, who was born on the same day as Abraham Lincoln in 1809, shared with him some noteworthy February 12 characteristics, including clear, original thinking, courage in the face of opposition and boundless energy.

FEBRUARY 12

****

Admired by others for their inspirational qualities and concern for social justice, these people often find themselves in leadership positions. And while they are indeed sympathetic to the plight of others, February 12 people are motivated less by feelings of empathy than by a burning desire to right perceived wrongs and to set the world moving along a more enlightened course. When faced with a situation that requires resolution, they have an enviable facility to marshal the facts available to them, evaluate them impartially, and then determine an effective plan of action. Such is their faith in the veracity of their moral judgements that they will rarely be deflected from their chosen path, and will work toward their goal with confidence and single-minded tenacity. Such qualities may make them ideally equipped for senior positions in military or political careers, especially if they were also born in the Chinese year of the dragon.

Yet although they are driven, these people are not all earnestness and ambitious zeal—far from it. They are also highly sensual beings, who have a real and instinctive appreciation for the good things in life, including the arts, fine cuisine and stimulating company. Indeed, most recognize that indulging their hedonistic side is a necessary release from the pressures of their intellectual or professional pursuits. They also typically make loving and concerned partners and parents, although they should beware of being overly paternalistic and should allow their children in particular to follow their own course.

VIRTUES: February 12 people have strong convictions developed through using their great powers of objectivity, perception and original thought. They are fueled by their wish to implement progressive action, which, for some, may become almost a mission.
VICES: Because they find it easy to think in terms of black and white, and form their opinions by a careful process of intellectual consideration, these people may find it difficult to compromise their most deeply held convictions.
VERDICT: People born on this day are blessed with many positive characteristics, including courage, energy and a desire to create harmony. Yet because they possess such a profound sense of certainty of purpose, they must beware of a tendency toward closing their minds to alternative viewpoints.

On This Day
Famous Births: Thomas Campion (1567); John Winthrop (1588); Jan Swammerdam (1637); Cotton Mather (1663); Charles Darwin and Abraham Lincoln (1809); George Meredith (1828); Marie Lloyd (1870); Omar Bradley (1893); Roy Harris (1898); Ted Mack (1904); Lorne Green (1915); Dom DiMaggio (1917); Franco Zeffirelli (1923); Joe Garagiola (1926); Bill Russell (1934); Judy Blume (1938); Simon MacCorkindale (1953); Joanna Kerns (1955); Arsenio Hall (1958); Sigrid Thorton (1959); Christina Ricci (1980).

Significant Events and Anniversaries: Social justice is strongly indicated by this day on which: Chile gained its independence (1818); the NAACP (National Association for the Advancement of Colored People) was founded in the U.S.A. (1909); China became a republic after the imperialist Manchu dynasty was deposed (1912); Ernie Bridge became the first Aboriginal cabinet minister in Australian government history (1986); and Dr. Carmen Lawrence became the first woman premier of an Australian state (1990). The firm—often intolerant—upholding of convictions is also a feature of February 12, which saw Lady Jane Grey, queen of England for only thirteen days, executed for what Mary Tudor regarded as her treasonous presumption (1554). Reflecting its propensity for progress, this day marks the demonstration of Alexander Graham Bell's "articulating" telephone, in a call made between Boston and Salem (1887). On a more prosaic note—but one extremely appropriate for an Aquarian day—the world's first rubber galoshes were sold commercially by the Boston, England, firm of J.W. Goodrich (1831).

FEBRUARY 13

February 13 people are natural extroverts. Brimming with energy, sensation-seeking, and open and unaffected in all they undertake, they are difficult to ignore and relish being the center of attention. Their strong imaginative powers and irresistible urge to seek out new paths, combined with their boldness and a tendency toward exhibitionism, mean that these people are often regarded as trend-setters, especially within the realm of the arts. Indeed, these people are oriented toward interpersonal contact, and shine brightest when playing to an audience. Whichever career they choose, they will not flourish when constricted by petty rules and regulations, and rarely find satisfaction in solitary pursuits that deprive them of acclaim.

Despite their need for intellectual stimulation and love of novelty, these good-hearted people are genuinely and deeply attached to their family and friends, desiring nothing more than their happiness and comfort. In turn, they require profound love and a large amount of emotional support, and may thereby unwittingly demand that those dear to them sacrifice a certain amount of independence of action and thought. While they appreciate the material things that money can buy, and aspire to surround themselves with luxurious objects, this yearning is motivated less by a wish to flaunt wealth than by the sheer sensory pleasure derived from beauty and opulence.

VIRTUES: February 13 people are exuberant, out-going, original and daring, and have a propensity to make waves wherever they go. Their quick-witted intelligence and apparently inexhaustible vigor is, however, balanced by a natural willingness to give themselves up to sensory indulgence.

VICES: These vibrant people have a tendency to become carried away with the excitement of their own performance on the stage of life and may behave erratically when following their hearts rather than their heads. Their boisterous self-confidence and predilection toward speaking their minds may lead them inadvertently to hurt or exclude less robust types.

VERDICT: In every area of their lives, people born on this day benefit from taking things a little more steadily, considering calmly the implications of their actions before setting off on their characteristically impulsive course. They should also remember to allow others the time and space within which to express themselves, and to respect their opinions.

Planetary Influences
Ruling planet: Uranus.
Third decan: Personal planet is Venus.

♅ ♀

Sacred and Cultural Significance
Parentalia in ancient Rome.
Saints' day: Modomnoc (6th century AD), patron saint of bee-keepers; Huna (7th century AD); Ermengild (d. c.700); Catherine dei Ricci (1522–90).

February 13 is a day of forceful action, as seen in the aftermath of the Allied bombing of Dresden on this day in 1945.

On This Day

Famous Births: Randolph Churchill (1849); Feodor Ivanovich Shalypin (1873); Bess Truman (1885); Georges Simenon (1903); Rosa Parks (1913); Tennessee Ernie Ford (1919); Kim Novak (1933); George Segal (1934); Oliver Reed (1938); Carol Lynley (1942); Stockard Channing (1944); Peter Gabriel (1950).

Significant Events and Anniversaries: On this day of boldness and exhibitionism, the notorious James-Younger gang robbed its first bank in Liberty, Missouri (1866) and Mata Hari, the Dutch-born exotic dancer, was arrested by the French for spying (1917). This is a day indicating self-belief and action, qualities that had two tragic manifestations: when John Campbell's English troops massacred members of the MacDonald clan at Glencoe, Scotland (1692); and when nearly two thousand British and American planes bombed the German town of Dresden, laying it to waste (1945). As a direct consequence of his independence of thought, dissident writer Alexander Solzhenitsyn was expelled from the Soviet Union (1974).

FEBRUARY 14

✴✴

Planetary Influences
Ruling planet: Uranus.
Third decan: Personal planet is Venus.

Sacred and Cultural Significance
Juno-Lupa honored in ancient Rome.
Saints' day: Valentine (3rd century AD), patron saint of lovers; Zeno of Rome (dates unknown); Conran (7th century AD); Cyril (826–69) and Methodius (c.815–85), patron saints of ecumenists; Sava of Serbia (1173–1236).

Hearts and flowers, symbolizing romantic love, are traditionally exchanged on St. Valentine's Day.

February 14 people think quickly and analytically, express themselves succinctly and often wittily, and are progressive—both in their ceaseless personal need to move onward and upward, and in their desire to set the world to rights. While the purposeful and clear-thinking manner in which they direct their considerable energies frequently garners them admiration, their impatience with those who think and act less quickly may well intimidate others, driving them away. Furthermore, their biting sense of humor, when combined with their great articulateness can, if not checked, be a deeply wounding weapon. They must remember to respect the sensibilities of other people—especially those closest to them—and anticipate the consequence of impulsive words, however satisfying their impact may be in the short term.

Yet these people are not solely governed by their intellectual qualities. They are extremely receptive to their instincts, and respond on a profound level to such sensual stimuli as a wonderful painting, a haunting piece of music, a gourmet dish or a fine vintage wine. Such is the varied nature of their talents that they have the potential to be equally successful in the artistic or scientific fields, but their compulsion for action gives them an especial aptitude for such business spheres as manufacturing. They enjoy making money, but mainly so that they have the financial means to be able to surround themselves with beautiful objects.

VIRTUES: February 14 people are blessed with incisive and questing intellectual powers coupled with highly developed communication skills, qualities which potentially enable them to achieve their goals with enviable ease. In addition to their practical skills, they also have a deeply sensual side and appreciate luxury.
VICES: These quick-thinking people must guard against a tendency to express their impatience with those who are either unable or unwilling to fall into line with their demands. They have a tendency to manifest their frustration by going on the attack, either verbally or by losing their tempers spectacularly.
VERDICT: People born on this day must ensure that they use their many talents to the good, and that they remain positive and relaxed in the face of adversity. If they allow themselves to succumb to the destructive impulses to which they are prone, they will find themselves emotionally isolated from the support of others.

On This Day
Famous Births: Francesco Cavalli (1602); Thomas Robert Malthus (1766); Christopher Latham Scholes (1819); Jack Benny (1894); John Longden (1907); Juan Pujol Garcia (1912); Hugh Downs (1921); Vic Morrow (1932); Florence Henderson (1934); Carl Bernstein and Alan Parker (1944); Gregory Hines (1946); Kevin Keegan (1951); Meg Tilly (1960).

Significant Events and Anniversaries: A facility with words is indicated by this day on which: the play *The Importance of Being Earnest*, by the noted wit Oscar Wilde, was first performed (1895); Nikita Khrushchev unambiguously denounced Stalin's dictatorship at the Twentieth Soviet Communist Party Conference (1956); and the Ayatollah Khomeini of Iran proclaimed a *fatwa* on Salman Rushdie for having offended Islamic sensibilities with his work *The Satanic Verses* (1989). The innovative and progressive potential of this day was reflected by the opening of London's Great Ormond Street Hospital for Sick Children (1852); the booting-up of I.B.M.'s computer at the University of Pennsylvania (1946); and the inauguration of the first satellite telephone service, Skyphone, on British Airways' transatlantic flights (1989). And, ironically on a day that is dedicated to love, seven gangsters were gunned down by members of a rival gang in Chicago, an event that became known as the St. Valentine's Day Massacre (1929).

FEBRUARY 15

Perhaps the overriding characteristics inherent in February 15 people are their need for stimulation and their related enthusiasm for exploring new areas of interest, both in their intellectual pursuits, and—since these energetic people often feel a strong connection with the natural world—also in the more physical sense. They furthermore rely to a large extent upon their highly developed instincts in their dealings with other people, attuning themselves to others' moods and responding with kindness and courtesy. Motivated by their desire to bring happiness to those closest to them, as well as to the wider world, they will employ their skills of communication and diplomacy to smooth over potentially explosive situations. They are thus greatly valued by their friends and family, who may, however, become irritated by what is sometimes perceived as a certain waywardness and aversion to being hemmed in by parameters that have been dictated by others.

Because they are multitalented, people born on this day will find professional success in a variety of fields—science, the creative arts, outdoor and sporting pursuits, as well as business—just as long as they are allowed to follow their own, idiosyncratic course. If they feel themselves to be stifled by external constrictions, they have a marked propensity to escape into the more congenial world of the senses, compensating for their frustration by indulging their love for entertainment, company and the good life, especially if they were also born in the Chinese year of the rabbit.

VIRTUES: These charming, enthusiastic and empathetic people genuinely desire to bring happiness and joy to other people, and have both the originality and intellectual potential to bring about humanitarian improvement.
VICES: Because these people are so strongly oriented to mental and physical excitement, they have a propensity to lack discipline and to yield to their instincts in order to avoid those tedious situations which they find so frustrating.
VERDICT: Those born on February 15 must acknowledge and honor those responsibilities that are unavoidable in human existence, and should therefore apply their often dormant capacity for focus to those areas of their lives that they instinctively find disagreeable or mundane.

On This Day

Famous Births: Pedro Menendez de Aviles (1519); Galileo Galilei (1564); King Louis XV of France (1710); Jeremy Bentham (1748); Cyrus Hall McCormick (1809); Charles Lewis Tiffany (1812); Susan Brownell Anthony (1820); Elihu Root (1845); Sir Ernest Henry Shackleton (1874); John Barrymore (1882); Cesar Romero (1907); Harvey Korman (1927); Norman Graham Hill (1929); Claire Bloom (1931); Melissa Manchester and Jane Seymour (1951); Matthew Groening (1954); Chris Farley (1964).

Significant Events and Anniversaries: This day indicates a strong humanitarian streak—a desire for human happiness and progress that can take many forms—and, appropriately, the first refrigerated cargo of meat was sent from New Zealand to Britain on the S.S. *Dunedin* (1882); while the U.S.A. launched its battleship *Maine* on a conciliatory mission to Cuba (1898) (unfortunately it sank in Havana's harbor after colliding with a mine); and the first session of the Permanent Court of International Justice was held in the Hague, Holland (1922). Motivated by their desire to destroy the iniquitous regime of Nazi Germany, the Allies began to bombard Monte Cassino in Italy (1944) and, on their push into the heart of Germany, British troops reached the River Rhine (1945). The potential for change on this day was reflected by the official retirement of the Union Jack as Canada's national flag, and replacement by the Maple Leaf (1956) and the introduction of decimal coinage into Britain, displacing the imperial system (1971).

Planetary Influences
Ruling planets: Uranus and Neptune.
Third decan: Personal planet is Venus.
Second cusp: Aquarius with Piscean tendencies.

Sacred and Cultural Significance
Lupercalia celebrated in ancient Rome.
Saints' day: Sigfrid (d. c.1045).

The eccentric Susan B. Anthony, who was born on this day of originality in 1820, renounced the traditional responsibilities of marriage and family to dedicate herself to the cause of women's suffrage.

FEBRUARY 16

* *

Planetary Influences
Ruling planets: Uranus and Neptune.
Third decan: Personal planet is Venus.
Second cusp: Aquarius with Piscean
tendencies.

Sacred and Cultural Significance
Saints' day: Juliana (4th century AD).

*John McEnroe, born on February 16, 1959,
has an anxious, sensitive and volatile
personality characteristic of his birth date.
Those qualities are, however, tempered by the
strong determination and focus bestowed by
the presence of his Moon in Gemini, and he
has achieved high honors in his demanding
tennis career.*

February 16 people respect life in all its forms, and are deeply troubled by manifestations of social injustice, since they feel an instinctive empathy and a burning desire to effect improvement. Yet although these people may be guided by their intuition and compassion, they rarely act impulsively, preferring instead to apply their highly developed powers of intellectual analysis and foresight to a problem before deciding upon their preferred course of action. Furthermore—perhaps because they are so perceptive—they have an impressive capacity to be realistic, both in their assessment of others and in their personal goals. Such qualities, along with their originality and energy, give them the potential to perform particularly well in business, especially if they are able to take charge. Since these people are profoundly receptive to the intuitive, life-enhancing quality inherent in the arts, they may also find success as entertainers and performers.

Many February 16 people consciously control their propensity toward extreme sensitivity, applying a rational system of checks and balances to their emotional responses in what may be an unconscious self-defensive mechanism. Indeed, such is their concern for the welfare of others that they may believe that they will be overwhelmed with sadness and anxiety unless they maintain a level of emotional detachment. They have a tendency, however, to internalize their deepest feelings, and may therefore become beset with feelings of inadequacy, while their quality of vivid foresight may cause them to resist, or even avoid, emotional commitment. Their partners should therefore be patient, considerate and encouraging in their treatment of these sensitive people.

VIRTUES: Although February 16 people are intellectually discerning and dispassionate, their empathy toward others, as well as their desire to improve the human condition, evokes in them a desire to harness their many talents in a selfless quest.
VICES: Their sensitivity and capacity for critical thought can sometimes make these people pessimistic and prone to feelings of depression and self-doubt. Their ability to envisage many possible scenarios can result in anxiety and indecision.
VERDICT: Those born on this day should take care not to allow their emotional and intellectual equilibrium to become unbalanced, neither becoming overly rational and thus ignoring their instincts, nor allowing their inherent desire to bring about good to be obstructed by their emotional responses.

On This Day
Famous Births: Philip Melanchthon (1497); Gaspard de Coligny (1519); Henry Brookes Adams (1838); Charles T. Russell (1852); George Macaulay Trevelyan (1876); Robert Flaherty (1884); Hugh Beaumont (1909); Patty Andrews (1920); Geraint Llewellyn Evans (1922); John Schlesinger (1926); Barry Humphries (1934); Sonny Bono (1935); Anthony Dowell (1943); William Katt (1955); Le Var Burton (1957); Ice-T (1958); John McEnroe (1959).

Significant Events and Anniversaries: This is a day that celebrates life, freedom and social justice, and marks the anniversary of the granting of an amnesty to, and the release of, 25,000 Indian prisoners to honor the birthday of Queen Victoria of England (1887), as well as the rescue by a boarding party from the H.M.S. *Cossack* of 299 British prisoners of war held on the German vessel *Altmark* in a Norwegian fjord (1940); the U.S. capture of Japanese-occupied Bataan, in the Philippines (1945); and the opening of the trial of John Demanjuk, who was accused of perpetrating atrocities at the Treblinka concentration camp in Israel (1987). On this day of the water-carrier, the U.S. nuclear submarine U.S. *Triton* embarked on its voyage to be the first such vessel to circumnavigate the world while submerged under water (1960). On a day that is characterized by the desire to improve the human condition, the magazine *Ladies Home Journal* premiered (1883) and the first cheque was used in England (1659).

FEBRUARY 17

These people are extraordinarily sensitive individuals, who never miss a detail, nuance or undertone of a situation. Their inherent powers of perception, combined with their soft hearts and their profoundly empathetic identification with the weak and defenseless, are rare qualities, but may often cause emotional complications for February 17 people. Indeed, as children they will often be deeply hurt by the careless words or actions of others, and their parents should recognize this propensity and support them with consistently kind and considerate behavior and reinforcement. As they mature, they will be forced to develop self-protective strategies and will mask their vulnerability with a veneer of toughness, but although they may often thus present a hardened image, their sensitivity will always remain an integral part of their natures.

Building a better world is of vital importance to those born on this day, and this desire to effect improvement may take a variety of forms, depending on the particular talents of the individual. Although they are not especially organized types, they will typically devote their passions toward implementing national, social, physical or technical ideals in a characteristically determined manner. Because they are such firm believers in individual freedom, and, being free spirits, chafe at being subjected to the unimaginative regimes of others' making, they will be unhappy (and possibly insecure) unless they are allowed to operate either independently or within an unstructured and enlightened framework.

VIRTUES: These people are defined by their sensitivity; deeply empathetic to the downtrodden, they will direct their considerable vitality toward fighting on behalf of the less fortunate, and will pursue their crusade with single-minded determination.
VICES: Their personal characteristics may drive February 17 people to extremes: they will either obey their emotions exclusively, thereby condemning themselves to a life of inner turmoil, or they will adopt an impenetrable façade in order to avoid being wounded. Ironically, in their mission to overcome intolerance, they may become equally inflexible.
VERDICT: While it is vital to the emotional well-being of these people that they control their overwhelming tendency to respond exclusively to their instincts, in doing so they should ensure that they do not cut their true selves off from others by manufacturing insurmountable barriers.

On This Day

Famous Births: Horace Bénédict de Saussure (1740); René Laënnec (1781); Frederick Eugene Ives (1856); Andrew Barton "Banjo" Paterson (1864); André Maginot (1877); Marion Anderson (1902); John Allegro (1923); Hal Holbrook (1925); Yasser Arafat (1929); Ruth Rendell (1930); Alan Bates (1934); Jim Brown (1936); Mary Ann Mobley (1939); Rene Russo (1954); Lou Diamond Phillips (1962); Michael Jordan (1963); Jerry O'Connell (1974).

Significant Events and Anniversaries: The zeal to create a better social system that is starred by this day may often result in conflict, as when the Confederate submarine *H.L. Hunley* fired the first torpedo in anger at the Federal corvette *Housatonic* in Charleston Harbor, thereby sinking both vessels (1864), and when radical Russian anti-imperialists intent on ending the autocratic rule of Czar Alexander II bombed the Winter Palace in St. Petersburg (1880). The pursuit of human excellence was reflected in the triumph of skier Jean-Claude Killy in winning three gold medals at the Winter Olympics in Grenoble, France (1968). Technical innovation is also a feature of this day, on which Baron Karl von Drais de Sauerbrun patented his "Draisine"—an early form of bicycle (1818); Londoner Mr. A. Ashwell registered his "vacant" and "engaged" signs for public lavatories (1833); and the Volkswagen Beetle broke the Model "T" Ford's record when the 15,007,034th vehicle was sold (1972).

Planetary Influences
Ruling planets: Uranus and Neptune.
Third decan: Personal planet is Venus.
Second cusp: Aquarius with Piscean tendencies.

Sacred and Cultural Significance
In Hinduism, the birthday of Kali.
Saints' day: Loman (d. c.450); Fintan of Clonenagh (d. 603); Finan of Lindisfarne (7th century AD); the Seven Servite Founders (13th century AD).

Kali, the most powerful goddess in the Hindu pantheon, whose birthday is celebrated on February 17, is often portrayed as here, dancing on the supine body of the god Shiva.

FEBRUARY 18

* *

Planetary Influences
Ruling planets: Uranus and Neptune.
Third decan: Personal planet is Venus.
Second cusp: Aquarius with Piscean
tendencies.

Sacred and Cultural Significance
Persian festival Spenta Armaiti.
Saints' day: Colman of Lindisfarne (d. 676);
Fra Angelico (1387–1455).

Reflecting the misguided convictions of this day, Jefferson Davis was inaugurated as president of the short-lived Confederacy, a political entity formed in 1861 because of a refusal by the Southern states to entertain the prospect of social change.

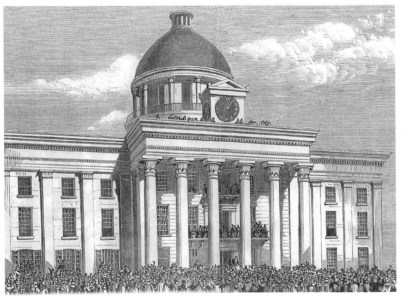

Their strong convictions—which will often have been shaped by their hearts rather than their heads—may give February 18 people a very idiosyncratic and optimistic view of the world which, although altruistic, may not be entirely realistic. These sensitive, and occasionally spiritual, people are quick to perceive those areas in which humanity's lot could be improved and, being idealistic and determined types, will energetically marshal their talents to the cause. Since they are inspired by the desire to realize their sometimes grandiose utopian visions, and impatiently refuse to allow themselves to be distracted by petty details in the urgent promotion of their aims, those born on this day have the potential to achieve remarkable success. Although they care deeply for those closest to them, and, indeed, have a profound need to receive their support and encouragement, they may inadvertently neglect their loved ones in favor of their cherished cause, particularly if they are men.

Despite their propensity to pursue their ambitions with apparently boundless vigor and tenacity, these people are not solely given over to their instinctual responses. They have a tendency to rationalize their predilections, and will evolve a sense of certainty from knowing that they have verified their instincts by means of their talents for analysis and perception. Moreover, they will listen to other people's points of view and, if convinced of their veracity, will adopt certain tenets. Because they are charismatic and inspiring figures, others are drawn to them for leadership, and these multitalented individuals will therefore flourish in any professional discipline, provided they can follow their own path.

VIRTUES: Visionary, tenacious and progressive, these idiosyncratic people tend to be guided by their hearts, yet they also have the ability to support their instincts with a single-minded and clear-cut intellectual approach.
VICES: February 18 people have a propensity to focus to the exclusion of all else on their particular passion, a characteristic which may alienate them from those people upon whom they rely for their own emotional support.
VERDICT: These people should make an effort to remain rooted in the real world, ensuring that they devote as much attention to the needs of their friends and relatives as they do to the purpose that drives them. They will find that fulfillment lies in maintaining a balance between their personal and professional lives.

On This Day
Famous Births: Queen Mary I of England (1516); Count Alessandro Volta (1745); Nicolo Paganini (1782); Ernst Mach (1838); Wendell Lewis Willkie (1892); Andres Segovia (1894); André Breton (1896); Enzo Ferrari (1898); Phyllis Calvert (1915); Jack Palance (1920); George Kennedy (1925); Len Deighton (1929); Toni Morrison and Ned Sherrin (1931); Milos Forman (1932); Yoko Ono and Bobby Robson (1933); Beatrice Faust (1939); Cybill Shepherd (1950); John Travolta (1954); Vanna White (1957); Matt Dillon (1964); Molly Ringwald (1968).

Significant Events and Anniversaries: This day, which indicates a level of human idealism that may tend toward the spiritual, marked the occasion of the first publication of John Bunyan's Christian allegory *The Pilgrim's Progress* (1678). An altogether more practical form of human progress was reflected in the establishment of the first direct telegraph line between Britain and New Zealand (1876), and the inauguration by Henri Pecquet of the world's first official airmail service, from Allahabad in India to Naini Junction (1911). It is apt that, on this day that is governed by the element of air, Clyde Tombaugh, at the U.S.A.'s Lowell Observatory, identified the planet Pluto in the night sky (1930).

PISCES

♓

February 19 to March 20
Ruling planet: Neptune (traditionally Jupiter)   **Element:** Mutable water
Symbol: Two fishes   **Polarity:** Negative (feminine)
Physical correspondence: The feet
Stones: Coral, jasper, bloodstone, white opal, pearl, amethyst, moonstone
Flowers: Poppy, waterlily, pink, thyme
Colors: White, mauve, red

Many astrological traditions have identified this constellation with a marine creature: both the ancient Greeks and Persians envisaged Pisces as a single fish, named Ikhthues and Mahik respectively; Hindu astrologers, too, term it Mina, "the fish," and link it to Vishnu's *avatar* as a fish, Matsya. It was the Babylonians who first conceived of the constellation as a pair of fishes, the Kun, or "two tails," one of which was the goddess of Simmah ("the swallow"), and the other Anunitum ("the Goddess"). An ancient Greco-Roman myth tells of how the ogre Typhon pursued the goddess Aphrodite/Venus and her son Eros/Cupid until they finally escaped him by transforming themselves into fishes and swimming away. Because Aphrodite/Venus was born from the sea (and most goddesses are associated with water) and since this sign is ruled by the sea god Neptune (who supplanted Jupiter following the planet's discovery in 1846), it is appropriate that the element of water governs this sign. Another astral body that is symbolically sacred to feminine deities is the Moon, whose ability to regulate the oceanic tides links it unequivocally with water. The twin curves of Pisces' sigil mimic the crescents that represent the waxing and waning of the Moon. This duality is mirrored within the annual natural cycle, for since Pisces' realm of influence is the last month of winter it simultaneously looks back over the past agricultural year and forward to the next, the rains associated with this time of year preparing the world for the growth heralded by spring.

Pisces represents duality, and in psychological terms this is taken to denote the often conflicting concerns of the spiritual and worldly realms. The Piscean personality may be symbolically linked to a fish swimming through the water seeking enlightenment (and the influence of Neptune indicates that Pisceans may tend toward spiritual and mystical concerns), but the potential for undirected restlessness and emotional instability is also indicated. Many iconic representations of Pisces show the two fishes bound together by the Nodus, or silver cord, which represents the link to the spirit world, suggesting Pisceans' dreamy natures.

PISCES

FEBRUARY 19

****

Planetary Influences
Ruling planets: Neptune and Uranus.
First decan: Personal planets are Neptune and Jupiter.
First cusp: Pisces with Aquarian tendencies.

♆ ♅ ♃

Sacred and Cultural Significance
In Greco-Roman mythology, the birthday of Athena (Minerva).
Saints' day: Conrad of Piacenza (1290–1351), Franciscan.

Thomas Edison patented his innovative phonograph on February 19, 1897, bringing light relief, through the pleasure of music, to the "long, dark evenings" of winter. The day is characterized by a concern for improving quality of life.

February 19 people value independence of thought and action and many exhibit a near-compulsive need to impose the stamp of their individuality on everything that they undertake. Although they are undoubtedly sensitive to the needs of other people, they usually direct their concern more toward humanity as a collective entity rather than toward individuals. Like the rather global quality of their empathy, their powers of perception are conditioned by their predilection to rational thought, and they therefore cultivate a rather lofty air of impartiality. Yet despite the impersonal projection of their empathetic insights, February 19 people nurture deep aspirations to effect progress and contribute to the greater good. For this reason they often make outstanding social and care workers who do not allow themselves to become ineffective through overidentification with their clients, as well as gifted environmental campaigners. The more artistically inclined among them—and many have a mystical side—possess the enviable potential to delight and inspire others with the power and focus of their performances.

Because they are able to balance empathy and rational idealism, these people typically exude a sense of stability. They make responsible and supportive parents—particularly if they are women—whose natural sense of authority, combined with their respect for individual opinions, draws others to them. On the other hand, their quest for knowledge and need to be challenged can lead them to take increasingly hair-raising risks, bolstered as they are by their self-confidence and faith in their own abilities.

VIRTUES: People born on this day are extremely perceptive and enormously capable in terms of formulating practical solutions to human problems. Stimulated by challenge, these energetic and original thinkers like nothing more than to test their limits.
VICES: These people should ensure that their relish for experiencing novel situations and for expressing their individuality does not become addictive. They also have a predilection or tendency to suppress their natural instincts.
VERDICT: February 19 people are right to balance their rational and emotional tendencies, but should beware of a propensity to lose sight of their quieter, more contemplative, inner selves in their active quest to devote their boundless energies to the pursuit of intellectual progress.

On This Day
Famous Births: Nicolaus Copernicus (1473); David Garrick (1717); Luigi Rodolfo Boccherini (1743); Adelina Patti (1843); Cedric Webster Hardwicke (1893); Merle Oberon (1911); Stan Newcomb Kenton (1912); Carson McCullers (1917); Lee Marvin (1924); Smokey Robinson (1940); Cass Elliot (1943); Peter Hudson (1946); Steven Nichols (1951); Jeff Daniels and Margaux Hemingway (1955); Prince Andrew of Britain and Holly Johnson (1960); Justine Bateman (1966).

Significant Events and Anniversaries: It is perhaps appropriate that, on a day governed by the sign of the fish, the "cod war" over fishing rights should cause Iceland to sever diplomatic relations with Britain (1976). Autonomy, authority and self-belief are indicated by this day, on which Napoleon Bonaparte proclaimed himself first consul—*de facto* dictator—of France (1800) and Cyprus's independence was guaranteed by the signing of an agreement by Britain, Turkey and Greece (1959). The day's concern with improving the collective lot of humanity was mirrored by the founding of the Women's Institute in Ontario, Canada, by Mrs. Hoodless (1897) and the opening of the Pan-African Congress at the Grand Hotel in Paris, which was attended by fifty-seven delegates who represented sixteen countries or colonies (1919), while Thomas Alva Edison contributed to the mass enjoyment of music by patenting his phonograph (1897). Reflecting the daring highlighted by this day, as well as the ideological conviction, Japanese aircraft bombed Darwin, Australia (1942).

FEBRUARY 20

It is ironic that although those born on this day are thoughtful and highly oriented toward pleasing other people, they may sometimes cause hurt to those who are drawn to them. For while they usually feel a global concern for the welfare of others, it is the acclaim and validation of their contemporaries that brings them security, and in seeking this recognition they may disregard the sensibilities of individuals. These people are intuitively perceptive, and find it easy to attune themselves to the moods of those around them, adjusting their responses accordingly. They are possessed with considerable personal charm, which they may sometimes consciously exploit in order to manipulate others in the furtherance of their ambitions. Given such driving personal qualities, these people have the potential to achieve great success in the caring professions, but especially in the artistic sphere, where they can employ their sensitivity and energy and in turn receive the attention and applause that they so deeply desire.

Coupled with this yearning to be appreciated for their achievements is a need to be stimulated, to experience novel sensations and excitement. February 20 people have an urge to travel, and will often choose to work in tourism, where they can satisfy their sense of adventure while also retaining the interpersonal contact that is so important to them. This restlessness may cause them difficulties in their personal lives, however, especially since they have a fear of emotional commitment in the first place.

VIRTUES: Dynamic, charismatic and highly aware of the emotional welfare of others, February 20 people are extremely ambitious and seek to make a difference, and, indeed, have sufficient originality and energy to do so.
VICES: These people must beware of misusing their capacity to instinctively relate and appeal to other people in the single-minded pursuit of their aims; they need their friends more than they realize, but may end up taking advantage of them.
VERDICT: Those born on this day must strive to develop a more rational, considered approach to all that they do, and curb their tendency to be ruled by their emotions and instincts alone. They should also moderate their desire for external stimulation, and ground themselves in stable personal relationships.

Planetary Influences
Ruling planets: Neptune and Uranus.
First decan: Personal planets are Neptune and Jupiter.
First cusp: Pisces with Aquarian tendencies.

Sacred and Cultural Significance
Saints' day: Wulfric of Haselbury (c.1080–1154).

On This Day
Famous Births: Karl Czerny (1791); William Prescott (1796); Honoré Daumier (1808); Marie Rambert (1888); Alexei Niklayevich Kosygin (1904); Sidney Poitier and Gloria Vanderbilt (1924); Robert Altman (1925); Jimmy Greaves (1940); Buffy Sainte-Marie (1941); Peter Strauss (1947); Jennifer O'Neill (1948); Ivana Trump (1949); Patty Hearst (1954); Kelsey Grammer (1955); Cindy Crawford (1966); Kurt Cobain and Andrew Shue (1967).

Significant Events and Anniversaries: The unsettled nature of this day was reflected in the violent storms that blew away the steeple of Chichester Cathedral in England (1861), and—on a day governed by the element of water—in the abnormally heavy rains that resulted in the deaths of around five hundred people in Rio de Janeiro, Brazil (1988). Indicating this day's inherent desire for prestige and acclaim, two individuals rose to positions of prominence: Lord Louis Mountbatten, on his appointment as the last British viceroy of India (1947), and Idi Amin, who made himself both a general and the president of Uganda (1971). February 20's potential for success can also be seen in astronaut John Glenn's achievement in becoming the first person to orbit the Earth three times in his Mercury space capsule *Friendship 7* (1962).

Severe rain storms deluged Rio de Janeiro on this mercurial day in 1988, causing 500 deaths and widespread devastation.

FEBRUARY 21

Planetary Influences
Ruling planets: Neptune and Uranus.
First decan: Personal planets are Neptune and Jupiter.
First cusp: Pisces with Aquarian tendencies.

Sacred and Cultural Significance
Feralia Festival celebrated in ancient Rome.
Saints' day: Fructuosus, Augurius and Eulogius (d. 259); Peter Damian (1007–72).

The most influential English-language poet of his generation, Wystan Hugh Auden embodied the sensitivity and intuition of his birthdate, February 21 1907, as well as the imagination and creativity of his Chinese influences as a fire goat. His works communicate a passionate commitment to his antiwar and anti-Fascist beliefs as well as encompassing emotional and spiritual themes, and he experimented with numerous styles, indicating his willingness to embrace adventure and change—another characteristic of those born on this day.

Their profound sensitivity is the defining characteristic of February 21 people, although this may not be immediately apparent to those who do not know them well, for they may have developed a tough outer shell in order to protect themselves from experiencing pain. These inherently guileless and trusting people instinctively think the best of others, an endearing characteristic which, unfortunately, means that unscrupulous individuals are liable to abuse their confidence and take advantage of them. Having suffered as a result of such disappointments, those born on this day will therefore consciously harden themselves, building a protective wall around their soft centers. They must, however, ensure that they do not take this strategy too far and become overly cynical—especially if they are men—for their emotions are at the core of their being.

When they have achieved the perfect balance between their intuitive and emotional urges and their rational consciousness, these highly original people have the potential to make outstanding artists and craftsmen in particular, although their intellectual inquisitiveness, predilection toward careful consideration and natural spirit of adventurousness also indicate possible success in the fields of science, business and research. They should, however, ensure that their inherent restlessness, as well as their fear of being hurt if they commit themselves to one individual totally, does not prevent them from finding the fulfillment in their closest personal relationships that is so vital to them.

VIRTUES: Those born on February 21 are extraordinarily intuitive, caring and self-perceptive people, who recognize that they need to develop their impersonal intellectual capabilities in order to perform at their best.
VICES: In their need to shield themselves from being wounded, these people may adopt a steely exterior, to the extent that they may either delude others as to their real natures or—more damagingly—even suppress their true selves completely.
VERDICT: It is important that, by their self-protective behavior, these people do not completely conceal their innermost emotions—either from themselves or from others—and it is especially crucial that they do not exclude their loved ones in this way. While they are right to protect their vulnerable nature, they should recognize that they will damage their psyches if they suppress their real feelings and needs.

On This Day
Famous Births: Czar Peter III of Russia (1728); Antonio López de Santa Anna (1794); Cardinal John Newman (1801); Léo Delibes (1836); August von Wasserman (1866); Gertie Millar (1879); Sacha Guitry (1885); Anais Nin and Madeleine Renaud (1903); W.H. Auden (1907); Robert Gabriel Mugabe (1924); Nina Simone (1933); Rue McClanahan (1936); Jilly Cooper (1937); Tyne Daly (1947); Alan Trammell (1958); Christopher Atkins (1961); Jennifer Love Hewitt (1979).

Significant Events and Anniversaries: Highlighted by February 21 is the need for self-protection, and on this day: Edwin T. Holmes of Boston, Massachusetts, installed the first electric burglar alarm (1858); the Battle of Verdun began when German troops attacked the French fortifications (1916); Israeli forces shot down a Libyan airliner for flying over an Israeli military airfield, causing the death of seventy-four people (1973); while in Soweto, South Africa, two men whom Winnie Mandela had employed as her bodyguards were charged with the murder of Stompie Mocketsi (1989). Humanitarian concerns and scientific ability are indicated by this day on which: British engineer Richard Trevithick demonstrated the first steam engine to run on rails (1804); a device to monitor the workings of the human heart was patented by King Hassan of Morocco (1969); and the Polaroid Land camera was demonstrated (1947). The originality of the day was indicated when Richard Nixon became the first U.S. president to visit China (1972) and the first woman graduated from dental school (1866).

FEBRUARY 22

Strong-willed and determined, February 22 people are inspired by high humanitarian ideals, toward the achievement of which they direct their considerable powers of mental clarity and great energy. These are sensitive individuals, whose empathy with the less fortunate and concurrent desire to improve their lot drives them to formulate a well-thought-out plan of action and then implement it with characteristic tenacity. Although they respond to their instincts, they rarely allow themselves to be deflected from pursuing the realization of their aims by strictly rational means. This combination of qualities is a particularly powerful one, and suits them to a variety of careers, including those within the realm of scientific research—especially if they were also born in the Chinese year of the rooster—the military and politics, but also within the performing arts.

These are steady and responsible people, who are relied upon by their families and friends for the advice and support that they rarely fail to provide. Because they are also generally self-reliant types and desire to protect their loved ones from anxiety, they may, however, fail to share their personal worries with those closest to them, thereby denying themselves emotional comfort and release. A further danger that results from their lofty ideals and high personal standards is that they will inevitably experience disappointment when others fail to live up to them, a feeling that they find hard to conceal.

VIRTUES: Possessed of a pronounced intellectual focus and abundant compassion, as well as of a strong measure of moral integrity and a burning desire to help other people by their service, February 22 people are furthermore blessed with the necessary energy, focus and drive to accomplish their aims.

VICES: As a result of their humanitarian vision and sense of duty toward their fellow human beings, these people have a tendency to carry all the burdens of the world upon their shoulders, assuming a role of responsibility that can sometimes be overwhelming and ultimately damaging to their emotional well-being.

VERDICT: It is of vital importance that these people try to be more forgiving and understanding of those who do not—indeed cannot—meet their high expectations, and they should include themselves in this *caveat*. They should cultivate a more relaxed and dispassionate approach to their careers in order to cope with disillusionment, which will help alleviate their natural propensity toward depression and pessimism.

On This Day

Famous Births: George Washington (1732); Arthur Schopenhauer (1788); Robert Baden-Powell and Heinrich Hertz (1857); Eric Gill (1872); Luis Buñuel (1900); Robert Young (1907); John Mills and H.E. Todd (1908); Sybil Leek (1917); Kenneth Williams (1926); Edward Kennedy (1932); Sheila Hancock and Katharine Worsley, Duchess of Kent (1933); Niki Lauda (1949); Julius Erving and Julie Walters (1950); Michael Chang (1972); Drew Barrymore (1975).

Significant Events and Anniversaries: The concern for humanity as a collective entity that is indicated by February 22 can take the form of patriotic fervor, and on this day Britain experienced its last invasion when a force of 1,400 Frenchmen burning with nationalist zeal landed at Fishguard in Wales (1797); the U.S.A. gained Florida from Spain (1819); and American troops defeated their Mexican counterparts at the Battle of Buena Vista (1847). Many of the characteristics of this day are associated with leadership, as was reflected when five-year-old Tenzin Gyatso was enthroned as the fourteenth Dalai Lama in Lhasa, Tibet (1940), and Harold Washington was elected the first African American mayor of Chicago (1983). As a result of his desire to aid humanity by means of medical progress, Dr. Selman Abraham Waksman revealed his discovery of streptomycin (1946). A rather less altruistic innovation, but one that was nonetheless ultimately enormously popular, was the opening of Frank Winfield Woolworth's first "five and ten cent" store in Utica, New York (1879), while *The Times* of London published the world's first classified personal column (1886).

Planetary Influences
Ruling planets: Neptune and Uranus.
First decan: Personal planets are Neptune and Jupiter.
First cusp: Pisces with Aquarian tendencies.

Sacred and Cultural Significance
Saints' day: Margaret of Cortona (c.1247–97), patron saint of repentant prostitutes.

A dedicated and accomplished military leader before he became the first president of the U.S.A., George Washington embodied the best of February 22's characteristics: vision, duty, integrity and drive.

PISCES

Planetary Influences
Ruling planet: Neptune.
First decan: Personal planets are Neptune and Jupiter.

Sacred and Cultural Significance
Terminalia, ancient Roman festival.
Saints' day: Polycarp (c.69–c.155); Jurmin (7th century AD); Milburga (d. 715); Willigis (d. 1011).

A commemorative Iwo Jima stamp.

UNITED STATES POSTAGE

3¢

IWO JIMA

FEBRUARY 23

Although other people are drawn to them for their cheerful, "can-do" approach to life, underneath their confident exterior February 23 people are in reality less optimistic and certain than their projected image suggests. Those born on this day are blessed with both great analytical skills and tenacity, and gain much satisfaction from worrying away at an issue, examining every angle and thinking through all the possible permutations and consequences of a proposed solution. Their self-confidence is born of a recognition of their talents, and also of an awareness of the respect and affection that they engender in others. These characteristics make them particularly well equipped to attain success in business, where their positive approach and natural gregariousness will further endear them to their coworkers. Since their intellectual talents are complemented by profound sensitivity, they also have the potential to make their marks as artists, writers or actors.

Geared as they are toward smoothing the path for other people, unless they feel as though they are supported by the uncritical love and encouragement of their loved ones, however, the sensitivity of those born on this day may be manifested in negative feelings. If they feel that their efforts are not being appreciated by others, they will feel exploited and may therefore become resentful. Another disadvantage of being simultaneously mentally perceptive, imaginative and responsive to their intuitive side is that not only do they have the propensity to envisage a variety of scenarios, but they also have a natural predilection to focusing on the less positive ones.

VIRTUES: Intellectually perceptive, rational and determined, these people are also inherently empathetic toward others, whom they feel compelled to assist in soundly considered, practical ways.
VICES: These people need to feel that their endeavors on behalf of others are appreciated. If they believe that they are being taken advantage of they will either sulk or disguise their hurt with a somewhat martyred type of behavior that masks the seething bitterness underneath.
VERDICT: When faced with an impersonal situation that requires action, these people typically adopt a pragmatic approach. They should strive to apply this realism to their personal lives, and recognize that it is important to accept people as they are—with all their limitations—and that they should not always expect to receive plaudits for their actions.

On This Day
Famous Births: Samuel Pepys (1633); George Frederic Handel (1685); Meyer Amschel Rothschild (1743); Sir George Frederick Watts (1817); William Edward Burghardt DuBois (1868); Victor Fleming (1883); Erich Kästner (1899); Leslie Halliwell (1929); Sylvia Chase (1938); Peter Fonda (1939); Johnny Winter (1944); Howard Jones (1955).

Significant Events and Anniversaries: Handel's *Oratorio* was premiered in Britain on the composer's forty-seventh birthday (1732). This day indicates that well-meaning actions will not always receive the recognition that they deserve, and on this day author Emile Zola was imprisoned as a result of the publication of his *"J'accuse!"* letter, which accused the French establishment of anti-Semitism (1898). Reflecting the apparently bold self-confidence of this day, American forces fighting Japanese imperialism raised the U.S. flag on Iwo Jima (1945); the February Revolution began in Russia (1917), and Benito Mussolini founded the Italian Fascist Party (1919)—both the latter actions intending to impose what the protagonists believed to be a better political system on their countries—while, on a more practical note, the Rotary Club was founded in Chicago (1905).

FEBRUARY 24

Others turn to February 24 people when they are in need of a helping hand—be it practical aid or emotional support—knowing that not only will they not be turned away, but that they will receive committed and sympathetic assistance. Those born on this day generally have a real desire to engage their energies on behalf of their fellow human beings. Their motivations may vary. It may be that they have experienced unhappiness at the hands of others—especially during their childhoods—and are determined to save others from a similar plight; many believe in the power of karma and the notion that they will benefit spiritually from their unselfishness; some have a real humanitarian vision; while others experience the superiority of martyrdom from self-sacrifice.

Whatever it is that fuels them, these people will find satisfaction in such public services as the military or police force, or else in the caring and medical professions, where they can feel that they are actively doing good. The empathy that informs many of their actions is a manifestation of the extreme sensitivity of these people, but these are not vague and dreamy types—on the contrary, they are resolutely practical and will harness their intuitive tendencies to their impressive capacity for self-discipline and intellectual clarity. There are twin dangers inherent in this devotion to others, however: that the no less pressing needs of those closest to February 24 people are neglected in favor of the greater good, or that they suppress their own, less "worthy"—but no less important—urges.

VIRTUES: February 24 people feel impelled to dedicate their considerable talents and vigor to the service of other people. They manage to transform their enormous powers of empathy into practical action, and, moreover, have the tenacity to achieve their aims.
VICES: While their humanitarian aspirations are eminently laudable, these people have a tendency to throw themselves wholeheartedly into their mission, thereby forgetting that they, as well as their families and friends, also need to be cherished. They should also beware of a propensity to think in black-and-white terms.
VERDICT: These people must not allow themselves to become blinkered and unbalanced by their single-minded focus on achieving their visionary objectives. They should remember to indulge their own need for relaxation and pleasure, and also ensure that they do not take their loved ones for granted, or sacrifice their personal lives in pursuit of the cause.

On This Day

Famous Births: Don John of Austria (1545); Samuel Wesley (1766); Wilhelm Grimm (1786); George Moore (1852); Arnold Dolmetsch (1858); Chester Nimitz (1885); Brian Close (1931); Michel Legrand (1932); Renata Scotto (1935); James Farentino (1938); Dennis Law (1940); Paul Jones (1942); Barry Bostwick (1945); Edward James Olmos (1947); Alain Prost (1955).

Significant Events and Anniversaries: Sacrifice is a major characteristic of this day, on which the Roman Empire officially began to persecute Christians, thereby creating the first Christian martyrs (303). Aspirations for human progress are highlighted by February 24, which marks the anniversary of Nancy Astor's—Britain's first female member of parliament—maiden speech to the House of Commons (1920); Malcolm Campbell's beating of his own land-speed record, when he reached 253.96 m.p.h. in *Bluebird* at Daytona Beach (1932); the marketing of the world's first nylon product—a toothbrush—in New Jersey (1938); and, in a major advance in the treatment of infertility, the birth of the world's first baby developed through in vitro fertilization (following the freezing and subsequent implantation of a fertilized donated egg) in London, England (1988).

Planetary Influences
Ruling planet: Neptune.
First decan: Personal planets are Neptune and Jupiter.

Sacred and Cultural Significance
Shivaratri honored in Hinduism.
Saints' day: Matthias (1st century AD).

Among the noteworthy achievements that have occurred on February 24 was the new land-speed record set by Malcolm Campbell in 1932.

PISCES

Planetary Influences
Ruling planet: Neptune.
First decan: Personal planets are Neptune and Jupiter.

Sacred and Cultural Significance
Carnival in Christianity.
Saints' day: Ethelbert of Kent (560–616); Walburga (d. 779).

Pierre Auguste Renoir's The Luncheon of the Boating Party. *Renoir's sensitivity, idiosyncrasy and intuitiveness are typical of February 25 people, whose originality of vision makes them well suited for artistic pursuits.*

FEBRUARY 25

✶✶✶✶✶✶✶✶✶✶✶✶✶✶✶✶✶✶✶✶✶✶✶✶✶✶✶✶✶✶✶✶✶✶✶✶✶✶✶

February 25 people nurture passionately held convictions and ideals, world views that are dictated by their emotional response to perceived social injustices and abuses of power. They are profoundly empathetic to the vulnerable—and their pity is often directed toward animals—who arouse in them a fiercely protective instinct and a single-minded desire to reverse their situation. Although they are tenacious, perceptive and visionary, they are guided more by their emotions than by dispassionate, intellectual considerations, and will therefore often act impulsively and thereby sabotage their efforts through their overhasty and rash enthusiasm. Moreover, since they are convinced that theirs is the right course of action, they may contemptuously dismiss those who express their reservations, not believing it worth the effort to recruit a potential convert by patient and reasoned argument; this dismissive attitude is particularly pronounced during adolescence.

Other people admire them for their energy and ardent commitment, but may regard them as being radical to the point of eccentricity and erratic when disappointment causes them to move on to a new crusade. Friends and family members should be tolerant of, and patient with, these people, always keeping in mind the truly noble motivations that fuel them. When these people accept that there are limitations to everything, and become more realistic and self-disciplined, they will often fulfill their enormous potential in such intellectual fields as scientific research, but also within the artistic world.

VIRTUES: These are energetic and compassionate people, who burn to right social wrongs, and are selfless in the pursuit of their ideals. Although they have undoubted intellectual powers, they have a propensity to obey their hearts rather than their heads.
VICES: Because February 25 people have such a profound sense of natural justice and respond so strongly to their emotions, they have a tendency to stride out in a noble cause without having calmly considered the full implications of their actions.
VERDICT: Those born on this day must try to take a step back when they are overwhelmed with a compulsion to throw themselves into a deserving cause, and to consider the situation rationally. They must also remember to heed and respect the opinions of others, especially when they are instinctively opposed to them.

On This Day
Famous Births: Carlo Goldoni (1707); José de San Martin (1778); Pierre Auguste Renoir (1841); Enrico Caruso (1873); John Foster Dulles (1888); Myra Hess (1890); Zeppo Marx (1901); Daisie Adelle Davis (1904); Jim Backus and Gert Frobe (1913); Leslie Thomas and John Arlott (1914); Anthony Burgess (1917); Tommy Newsom (1929); Tom Courtenay (1937); Herb Elliot (1938); David Puttnam (1941); George Harrison and Sally Jesse Raphael (1943).

Significant Events and Anniversaries: Reflecting the day's capacity for intolerance that can result from the devoted adherence to a concept or cause, Pope Pius V excommunicated Queen Elizabeth I of England for her refusal to abandon Protestantism (1570). Impulsive behavior is indicated by this day, on which the married U.S. evangelist Jimmy Swaggart's career was ruined when he was suspended by the elders of his church for succumbing to the charms of a prostitute (1988). The success that can result from pursuing a cherished vision was illustrated by the screening of a three-dimensional movie to the Académie des Sciences in France by the film pioneer Louis Lumière (1935). Mirroring the confrontation inherent in this day, boxer Cassius Clay (Muhammad Ali) became the world heavyweight boxing champion when he knocked out Sonny Liston (1964).

FEBRUARY 26

The authoritative, somewhat detached, persona that these people often adopt masks a profoundly sensitive and caring nature. Thus while others stand in awe of the rather impersonal and abrupt image that those born on this day project, underneath the façade lies an intuitive and compassionate being. Indeed, their natural powers of perception and moral certainty arouse in February 26 people a determined desire to improve the world around them. Rather than impulsively launching themselves into their mission, they prefer to stand back, rationally consider the merits of a strategy, and then work quietly but tenaciously toward its implementation. Personal independence is vital to those born on this day, and they demand that they be allowed to follow their consciences.

The natural empathy that informs these people's conscious actions remains a guiding principle, and the combination of humanitarianism, shrewd pragmatism and originality that is inherent in these people suits them for careers in the judiciary, as well as in the arts, where they will typically put forward their critical message in a misleadingly palatable—but in fact subversive—form. In their personal lives, they are steady and caring, but they do have a tendency to be authoritarian or caustic when those close to them appear to deviate from the straight and narrow path of which they approve.

VIRTUES: February 26 people have the outstanding ability to fuse their feelings of compassion with their intellectual propensity for reasoned evaluation and independence of thought into a particularly effective package.
VICES: Because they are so convinced of the veracity of their opinions, these people have a tendency to condemn behavior that does not conform to their high ideals. They should therefore guard against becoming too morally rigid and thereby unnecessarily emotionally isolated from other people.
VERDICT: Those born on this day are blessed with a diversity of talents that are generally well balanced. They should, however, remember to relax their often lofty standards on occasions, and not to take themselves so seriously.

On This Day
Famous Births: Victor Hugo (1802); Honoré Daumier (1808); "Buffalo Bill" Cody (1846); Emile Coué (1857); Frank Bridge (1879); Lotte Lehmann (1888); Richard Gatling and Orde Wingate (1903); Tony Randall (1920); Betty Hutton (1921); "Fats" Domino (1928); Johnny Cash (1932); Sandie Shaw (1947); Michael Bolton (1953).

Significant Events and Anniversaries: February 26 indicates resourcefulness and independence, and on this day three events that variously illustrate these qualities occurred: Napoleon Bonaparte escaped from the island of Elba, to which he had been exiled following his defeat at the Battle of Waterloo (1815); the Second French Republic came into being (1848); and Robert Watson-Watt unveiled his radar system in Daventry, England (1935). Justice is also a characteristic of this day, on which Chi-hsui and Cheng-yu, the leaders of the Boxer Rebellion, were executed in China (1901), and the corrupt President Marcos in the Philippines was deposed (1986). This day is governed by the element of water, and marks two tragic incidents at sea: the sinking of the British troopship *Birkenhead* off Simon's Bay in southern Africa, with the loss of 485 lives (1852); and the sinking of the French vessel *Provence II* following an attack by the German Navy, with 930 casualties (1916).

Planetary Influences
Ruling planet: Neptune.
First decan: Personal planets are Neptune and Jupiter.

Sacred and Cultural Significance
Saints' day: Porphyry, bishop of Gaza (353–420).

"Buffalo Bill" Cody, born on February 26, 1846, carved out for himself a truly unique career, using his originality of thought and a practical streak (both characteristic of this day) to the full.

PI/CES

FEBRUARY 27

✴✴✴

Planetary Influences
Ruling planet: Neptune.
First decan: Personal planets are Neptune and Jupiter.

Sacred and Cultural Significance
Saints' day: Leander (c.550–600); Alnoth (d. c.700); Herefrith of Louth (d. c.873); Gabriel Possenti (1838–62).

A symbol of the passionate ideals and optimism of the day, the United Nations building in New York City housed its first meeting on February 27, 1952.

As these pragmatic and charismatic people stride confidently through their professional lives, others admire them for their apparent sense of certainty and purpose, but may secretly wonder why it is that they often have such tumultuous personal lives. The answer to this apparent contradiction is that those born on this day are highly responsive to their often explosive emotions, and while they may successful conquer their impulse to listen exclusively to their hearts in impersonal situations, they find this strategy virtually impossible in their dealings with those closest to them—in those relationships that are, after all, founded on passionate emotions. Another exacerbating factor is that while these people demand the right of freedom of action and thought for themselves, they expect total commitment and support from others. Those who wish to build a stable relationship with February 27 people should therefore recognize this inconsistency and avoid head-on confrontations in favor of more subtle approaches.

While they may be prone to extremely impulsive behavior when "off duty," these people tend to show greater focus when it comes to their careers. Hand-in-hand with their sensitivity go highly developed powers of perception, and those born on this day find it easy to absorb all the various elements of a situation and then decide on the appropriate course of action. They perform particularly well in business ventures, where their empathy for others will also stand them in good stead when working as part of a team, but they will probably find greatest fulfillment in the artistic sphere, where they can project their intuition outward to inform or entertain other people.

VIRTUES: These people are independent, energetic and perceptive, but are above all governed by their emotions; when self-disciplined, their rich inner lives will delight and inspire those around them.
VICES: February 27 people have a propensity to be distracted by the calling of their hearts, as well as by their need for constant stimulation. These qualities may lead them to flit from impulse to impulse, never halting long enough to explore a situation or person more deeply.
VERDICT: Those born on this day should make a concerted effort to discipline themselves and to develop their undoubted potential for intellectual tenacity. They should beware of making unreasonable demands of others, and should try to maintain balance and perspective in all areas of their lives.

On This Day
Famous Births: Constantine the Great (274); Henry Wadsworth Longfellow (1807); Ellen Terry (1847); Hubert Parry (1848); Rudolf Steiner (1861); Charles Herbert Best (1899); John Steinbeck (1902); Elizabeth Welch (1908); Joan Bennett (1910); Lawrence Durrell (1912); Joanne Woodward (1930); Elizabeth Taylor (1932); Ralph Nader (1934); Antoinette Sibley (1939); Paddy Ashdown and Howard Hesseman (1940); Mary Frann (1943); Robert de Castella (1957); Chelsea Clinton (1980).

Significant Events and Anniversaries: One aspect of this day is the potential for confrontation when conflicting emotional ideals collide, and February 27 marks the anniversary of two battles between the British and Boers in southern Africa: that of the Battle of Majuba, won by the Boers (1881), and that of the Battle of Paardenberg, in which the British were the victors (1900); the Reichstag in Berlin was burned down, causing a considerable boost to the Nazis' popularity as "defenders of the state" (1933); in Czechoslovakia President Benes was deposed by the Communists (1948); and the Gulf War ended with the retreat of Iraqi forces from Kuwait (1991). Guided by more positive visionary aspirations, the British Labour Party was founded (1900) and the United Nations met for the first time in its new building in New York City (1952).

FEBRUARY 28

February 28 people are adventurers on the sea of life, enthusiastically following wherever their impulses lead them in their search for the gratification of sensual excitement. These highly intuitive people have an almost irresistible compulsion to obey their instincts, and, since they are usually hyperactive as well as hypersensitive, will bounce from one enthusiasm to the next with breakneck speed, particularly if they were also born in the Chinese year of the horse. This sensation-seeking behavior is compounded by their inherent horror of standing still and subjecting themselves to boredom. Although more steady people are drawn to those born on this day for the hedonistic excitement that they generate, they will rarely be able to stand the erratic pace. February 28 people are regarded with deep affection by others, especially since they regard others positively, wish to please and entertain those around them and, moreover, harbor no ulterior motives. They may often find it difficult to stay committed in their personal relationships, however.

It is vitally important that these endearing people learn to develop greater self-control, otherwise they will find themselves spiraling on a path to self-destruction at breakneck speed, and parents of February 28 people should do their utmost to instill a sense of realism—as well as an understanding of cause and effect—in their children when young. Those born on this day will thrive in professions in which they can channel their vigor and natural inquisitiveness along a more focused course; tourism is a particularly propitious field for them, while the arts and sport will allow them to fulfill their twin needs for sensuality and action. Financial careers should be avoided, since these people have a tendency to be as extravagant with their money as they are with their emotions.

VIRTUES: Charming, original and extraordinarily energetic, those born on this day are compelled to seek out stimulating and different encounters, an impulse which, if anchored in a steady intellectual approach, may have pioneering consequences.
VICES: February 28 people are driven by their compulsion to indulge their impulses and experience every sensation that life has to offer. Self-discipline has no attraction for them, and hence their behavior is often out of control. Because they think and believe the best of people, they are in danger of being exploited.
VERDICT: These people must strive to conquer and overcome their overwhelming propensity to act impulsively. While they should never suppress their natural curiosity and prodigous energy, they should try to moderate these characteristics, look before they leap, and consider the consequences of their actions.

Planetary Influences
Ruling planet: Neptune.
First decan: Personal planets are Neptune and Jupiter.

Sacred and Cultural Significance
Pagan celebration honoring Earth Goddesses.
Saints' day: Oswald of Worcester (d. 992).

On this day of adventure and pioneering, the world's first parachute jump was made by Albert Berry in 1912.

On This Day
Famous Births: Michel Eyquem de Montaigne (1533); Réné Reaumur (1683); John Tenniel (1820); Charles Blondin (1824); Ben Hecht (1894); Philip Showalter Hench (1896); Linus Pauling (1901); Stephen Spender (1909); Vincente Minnelli (1910); Zero Mostel (1915); Peter Alliss (1931); Tommy Tune (1939); Mario Andretti (1940); Brian Jones (1942); Stephanie Beacham (1947); Bernadette Peters (1948); Barry McGuigan (1951).

Significant Events and Anniversaries: This is the day of the adventurer, and marks the world's first parachute jump, made by Albert Berry over Missouri (1912). Monetary acumen is not starred by this day, as is reflected by the bankruptcy declaration of Liverpool's famous Cavern Club in Britain (1966). Illustrating the uncontrolled tendency of this day, in Britain a London Underground train crashed at Moorgate station, resulting in the death of forty-one people (1975). Emotional responses and perceptions may be diverted into the political arena, and on this day Oswald Mosley founded the New Party—a Fascist political party—in Britain (1931).

PISCES

Planetary Influences
Ruling planet: Neptune.
First decan: Personal planets are Neptune and Jupiter.

Sacred and Cultural Significance
Leap Year Day, which occurs every four years to make the calendar year catch up with the solar year (which takes 365.242199 days); in Western tradition, the day on which women propose marriage to men.
Saints' day: Cassian (c.360–433).

A day that harbors inexplicable associations, arrest warrents were issued on this day in 1692 for three women who were believed to be practicing witchcraft, thereby beginning the infamous Salem Witch Trials.

FEBRUARY 29

From their earliest years, these people will have felt different from others, and, indeed, so they are, since they can only celebrate their true birthdate every four years. As a further result of this quirk of the calendar, they will have had to learn the value of pragmatism and of entering into the spirit of compromise by choosing an alternative date upon which to mark the passing of the years. A positive side effect of their unusual birthday, however, is that in chronological terms these people are technically still children when they reach middle age, and adolescents in old age. Their characteristic youthful vibrancy, sense of optimism and risk-taking, and determination to experience all that life has to offer moreover seems to confirm their youthfulness in years.

Their natural tendency to indulge their senses in hedonistic pursuits is therefore tempered by a more grounded intellectual attitude to life, although February 29 people still retain their restlessness and inquisitive qualities, which are augmented by a streak of daring. They have a strong sense that they are special individuals, a belief that manifests in their self-confidence, as well as in a compulsion to make others appreciate their unique qualities. They will therefore flourish in any competitive profession—especially if they are men—where they can harness their instincts, realism and need to prove their worth. In their personal lives, they should, however, try to temper any aggressive tendencies and recognize that others already accept them as they are.

VIRTUES: February 29 people are individualistic and original, as well as possessing a pragmatic and rational turn of mind. Although they are highly attuned to their instincts, they have the potential to moderate these when necessary.
VICES: Those born on this unusual day may sometimes feel as though they are out of synch with their contemporaries, and may feel driven to validate aggressively their self-perceived uniqueness by forcing others to take notice of them—a policy which they may have a tendency to take to excessive proportions.
VERDICT: These people possess a rare combination of intellectual and emotional qualities, which, when supported by their profound sense of self-reliance, bestows upon them enormous potential to effect innovation. They should, however, ensure that they do not alienate others by overpromoting either themselves or their convictions.

On This Day
Famous Births: Marquis de Montcalm Gezan de Saint Véran (1712); Ann Lee (1736); Gioacchino Rossini (1792); John Phillip Holland (1840); Herman Hollerith (1860); Ranchhodji Morarji Desai and William Wellman (1896); Jimmy Dorsey (1904); Joss Ackland (1928).

Significant Events and Anniversaries: Self-belief is a quality highlighted by this day, on which the Jewish Stern Gang, confident in the veracity of their crusade, blew up a Cairo-to-Haifa train, resulting in the death of twenty-seven British military personnel (1948), and Pakistan officially became an independent Islamic republic (1956). Innovative potential is indicated by February 29, on which: the St. Gotthard tunnel, which linked Switzerland and Italy, was completed (1880); solid helium was produced by Dutch scientists (1908); and the first pulsar was revealed to the world by Dr. Jocelyn Burnell of Cambridge University in Britain (1968). Neatly combining the hedonism of this day with its pioneering qualities, the first Playboy Club was opened by Hugh Heffner in Chicago (1960). Traditionally associated with the mysterious, little-understood powers of women to influence events through their own will, Leap Day marked the issuing of arrest warrants for three women accused of witchcraft in Salem, Massachusetts (1692).

MARCH 1

Beneath the charming and easy-going manner of March 1 people lies a real and heartfelt concern for other people's well-being, and hence with a variety of social issues and humanitarian causes. These people are sensitive in the extreme, but instinctively recognize that acting impulsively, or revealing their often tumultuous emotions, may result in disastrous consequences. By controlling the more erratic urges that may lead them into irreversible situations, and by cultivating a calm and nonconfrontational approach, they therefore not only provide themselves with a safety net, but inspire confidence in others, although they may not feel this confidence themselves. Indeed, when their problems appear insurmountable, the rising panic felt by those born on this day may cause them to abandon the situation altogether and resort to a comforting strategy of cutting themselves off from the cause of their emotional distress by ignoring it or moving on.

Despite the propensity toward self-doubt and depression that is engendered by their sensitivity, these people are blessed with remarkably positive qualities. As well as possessing great personal magnetism, they have a highly original intellectual approach and an optimism that is inspired by their fascination with new and stimulating ideas. In their professional lives they will generally find personal satisfaction as artists, or when they run their own enterprises, in which they can operate independently of alienating regulations and exploit their imaginative concepts profitably. And when they achieve the financial rewards that they unashamedly relish, they will generously share the fruits of their success with those whose unstinting emotional support and affection has played such a crucial part in its achievement.

VIRTUES: March 1 people are imaginative, independent and instinctive—all qualities that derive from their great sensitivity. They possess the intellectual sensibility to moderate extreme feelings and harness them by following a rational course of action.
VICES: When overwhelmed by their intuitive responses, those born on this day are prone to suffering from feelings of anxiety, and may believe that they are spiraling out of control. In such instances, they may feel compelled to abandon the problems of the real world and retreat to a less tormenting scenario.
VERDICT: These people have the capability to balance the emotional extremes to which they are prone with a more reasoned strategy. Crucial to their well-being is a stable personal background, which will allow them to moderate erratic impulses and give them the stability within which they can thrive.

On This Day
Famous Births: Frédéric Chopin (1810); Lytton Strachey (1880); Oskar Kokoschka (1886); Glenn Miller (1904); David Niven (1910); Robert Lowell and Dinah Shore (1917); Yitzhak Rabin (1922); Harry Belafonte (1927); Robert Conrad (1935); David Broome (1940); David Scott Cowper (1942); Roger Daltrey (1944); Alan Thicke (1947); Leigh Matthews (1952); Catherine Bach and Ron Howard (1954); Nik Kershaw (1958).

Significant Events and Anniversaries: Reflecting the social concerns of this day, Pennsylvania abolished slavery, the first U.S. state to do so (1780), while the collective U.S. states ratified the Articles of Confederation, stating their national purpose (1881). Charles Lindbergh's baby son was kidnapped for ransom by Bruno Hauptmann, illustrating the day's propensity toward extremes of behavior, and also its concern for personal enrichment (1932). This day indicates a dislike of direct confrontation, and marks the retirement of the "Brown Bomber," the U.S. world heavyweight champion Joe Louis, from the boxing arena (1949); the formation of the Peace Corps of Young Americans by President Kennedy (1961); and the landing of the Soviet unmanned spacecraft, *Venus 3*, on Venus—the planet named for the Roman goddess of love (1966). On a day noted for artistic pursuits, Vivien Leigh won an Oscar for her role as Scarlett O'Hara in *Gone with the Wind* (1940).

Planetary Influences
Ruling planet: Neptune.
Second decan: Personal planet is the Moon.

Ψ ☽

Sacred and Cultural Significance
Sacred fire in Temple of Vesta rekindled to celebrate the Old Roman New Year's Day; in Bulgaria, Granny March's Day celebrated; first day of Women's History Month in the United States.
Saints' day: David, patron saint of Wales (d. 601 or 589); Swithbert (d. 713); Rudesind (907–77).

Conservation was a relatively new concept—especially for the vast American West—when, on this day in 1872, the U.S. Congress established Yellowstone as the first national park—a visionary action on this day of social concerns.

Planetary Influences
Ruling planet: Neptune.
Second decan: Personal planet is the Moon.

Sacred and Cultural Significance
Saints' day: Joavan (d. c.562); Chad (d. 672), patron saint of medical springs.

The American statesman Sam Houston was born on this day in 1793. His political career was noteworthy for his loyalty, dedication and commitment to progress for the common good—qualities indicated by his birthdate. As a teenager, Houston lived with the Cherokee and learned their language and lifeways, an experience that endowed him with a sensitivity toward Native American issues that was extraordinary for his time.

MARCH 2

Still rivers run deep, as the saying goes, and this maxim certainly applies to those born on March 2. These people are deeply intuitive beings, who generally would rather explore their own inner world of thoughts and dreams than launch themselves at the challenges of the real world. Indeed, although they are often passionate about social issues, these gentle people detest the emotional upset that direct confrontation causes them, and will do their utmost to promote a peaceful resolution to problems—if they have not previously managed to avoid them altogether. It therefore goes without saying that March 2 people will be unhappy in competitive business situations, and are better suited to the artistic world. However, they are also suited to those careers, such as politics or the caring professions, in which they feel that their services can make a real contribution to the welfare of others.

Despite—or perhaps because of—their rather introverted personalities, these people crave the security that results from happy and stable personal relationships. They have a deep need to receive the unconditional love of those closest to them, which they will reciprocate loyally. The unstinting devotion—and even uncritical adoration—that they have a propensity to direct toward their partners, children or individuals that inspire them, creates the risk of stifling the objects of their affection, however. These people should therefore try to develop a more detached approach within their personal liaisons. Indeed, a less dependent attitude to others will benefit them in all areas of their lives.

VIRTUES: Blessed with enormous sensitivity and compassion, these people yearn to bring harmony both to the wider world and to their own personal circumstances. Their profoundly intuitive qualities, and unwavering loyalty toward those things that they believe in, give them the potential to be real forces for good.
VICES: Such is their steadfast and unflagging commitment to an individual or cause that these people hold dear, that there is a danger that they may lose their capacity for critical objectivity. Furthermore, they may drive other people away with their intensity and unspoken demands for a similar level of emotional support.
VERDICT: While never suppressing their gentle qualities, these people should try to toughen themselves up, to be more pragmatic and not to shy away from conflict when necessary. By developing a more relaxed and robust approach, they will not only protect themselves from being hurt, but will benefit from the richness of life's experiences.

On This Day
Famous Births: Samuel Houston (1793); Bedrich Smetana (1824); Kurt Weill (1900); Theodore Geisel (Dr. Seuss) (1904); Desi Arnaz (1917); Jennifer Jones (1919); Cardinal Basil Hume (1923); Mikhail Gorbachev and Tom Wolfe (1931); George Benson (1943); Lou Reed (1944); Naomi James (1949); Karen Carpenter (1950); Laraine Newman (1952); Ian Woosnam (1958); Jon Bon Jovi (1962); Suzette Charles (1963).

Significant Events and Anniversaries: This day possesses the potential for outstanding artistic achievements, and marks the performance of the first recorded ballet in England: John Weaver's *The Loves of Mars and Venus* (1717). Reflecting this day's abhorrence of face-to-face confrontation, Rutherford Birchard Hayes became the only U.S. president to be appointed by electoral commission, to settle disputed election results (1877), while in Britain, the Social Democratic and Liberal parties merged to form the Social and Liberal Democratic Party rather than continue battling against each other (1988). The potential achievement of the visionary dreams indicated by this day was illustrated by the completion of the first nonstop round-the-world flight by Captain James Gallagher and his U.S. Airforce crew (1949); the unveiling of the revolutionary optical telegraph (semaphor machine) in Paris (1791); and the completion of Sir Vivian Fuchs' and his British Commonwealth Trans-Antarctic team's crossing of the surface of the South Pole (1958). This day is ruled by the element of water, and tragically marks the dramatic flooding of areas of north and western Australia, resulting in the death of two hundred people (1955).

MARCH 3

It may surprise those who do not know them intimately, that beneath the confident and direct manner of people born on March 3 lie deeply sensitive and reflective beings. Indeed, some of these people may consciously have cultivated a brisk, no-nonsense approach to shield their emotional vulnerability and their unfounded sense of insecurity. In general, however, they are naturally inclined toward combining their considerable powers of intellectual clarity with their instincts. Their inherent ability to unite such qualities of compassion and rational perspicuity is a rare gift, and augurs well for success in such careers as charity or social work, in which they can promote their desire for human progress by means of a carefully considered and logical plan of action. This conjunction of sensitivity and discipline also bestows great artistic potential upon those born on this day.

These empathetic and caring people make loyal and affectionate partners and parents, supplying the right balance of emotional support and domestic organization. It is essential, however, that they do not allow their propensity for intellectual criticism to become overdeveloped. Because—whether they realize it or not—these people are motivated by their emotional responses, they have a tendency to promote the beliefs that are supported by their intuition with convincing justifications, and then to discredit counterarguments by picking holes in them.

VIRTUES: Sensitive, perceptive and humanitarian, these people's gentler characteristics are complemented by such practical qualities as intellectual incisiveness, self-discipline, professional competence and tenacity. Their compassion therefore takes an unusually pragmatic form, redoubling their potential.

VICES: Because these people's opinions are formed primarily by their emotions, they have a predilection to instinctively dismiss opinions with which they do not feel comfortable, without first having given them sufficient objective consideration. Their convictions are usually founded on the best of motivations, but may cause these people to become resistant to accepting new approaches.

VERDICT: Although March 3 people intuitively understand the importance of maintaining balance in every aspect of their characters and lives, they often find this balance elusive, and must ensure that they refrain from smothering their emotional side by relying too much on their rational qualities.

On This Day

Famous Births: William Godwin (1756); Georg Cantor and George Mortimer Pullman (1831); Alexander Graham Bell (1847); Henry Wood (1869); Edward Thomas (1878); Jean Harlow (1911); Ronald Searle (1920); John Irving (1942); Fatima Whitbread (1961); Jackie Joyner-Kersee and Herschel Walker (1962).

Significant Events and Anniversaries: March 3 indicates great artistic ability, and this day, which also comes under the influence of the Moon, marks the anniversary of the publication of Ludwig van Beethoven's *Moonlight Sonata* (1802), as well as the premieres of Georges Bizet's opera *Carmen* (1875) and the classic movie *King Kong* (1933). *Apollo 9* was launched into Earth orbit to test the Lunar Module, an important step toward the first Lunar landing (1969). This day is furthermore one of humanitarian vision, which may be expressed in the form of nationalism, and on this day: Kemal Atatürk abolished the Turkish Caliphate, and Islam as the official state religion, in his quest to modernize and liberalize Turkey (1924); "The Star-Spangled Banner," with its message of freedom and justice, became the U.S.A.'s national anthem (1931); Allied air attacks on the Japanese Navy concluded the Battle of the Bismarck Sea during World War II (1943); Florida became the 27th state of the Union (1845); and Latvia and Estonia voted to secede from the Soviet Union (1991). Illustrating the day's capacity for human progress, the U.S. Congress created the Freedmen's Bureau to aid and support impoverished blacks and whites in the South (1865).

Planetary Influences
Ruling planet: Neptune.
Second decan: Personal planet is the Moon.

Sacred and Cultural Significance
National Day of Morocco.
Saints' day: Marinus of Caesarea (d. c.260); Non (5th century AD); Winwaloe (6th century AD); Cunegund (c.978–1033).

Alexander Graham Bell, born on March 3, 1847, is best remembered for his intellectual achievements as the inventor of the telephone, which he patented in 1876. His sensitivity and humanitarian concerns, however, were just as strong as his intellect, as evidenced by his dedication to teaching the deaf and developing an early form of sign language.

PISCES

Planetary Influences
Ruling planet: Neptune.
Second decan: Personal planet is the Moon.

Sacred and Cultural Significance
Saints' day: Owin (d. c.670); Adrian of May (d. 875); Casimir (1458–84).

MARCH 4

March 4 people are typically self-contained individuals, whose rich imagination and profound sensitivity do not require the trigger of external stimuli. Those born on this day are fascinated by abstract concepts, and their compulsion to explore these further will be expressed with remarkable tenacity—indeed, sometimes to the exclusion of all else. Yet despite their twin intellectual talents of great concentration and inquisitiveness, these intuitive and humanitarian people are governed by their hearts rather than their heads and not only respond to their emotional impulses, but experience deeply empathetic feelings with regard to the problems of others. Therefore, although they may isolate themselves from the world when exploring an idea that absorbs their full attention, they are never completely unaware of the parallel world of reality.

These are gentle people, who abhor confrontation and will withdraw smartly within themselves at the first sign of discord. This tendency, combined with their other personal characteristics, means that they will be unhappy in competitive professional situations, but will flourish when they can move within parameters set by themselves. Careers as artists, musicians and writers are especially well starred, but they may also make gifted teachers, whose infectious enthusiasm for their subject will inspire their pupils. Receiving the emotional support of friends and family members is vital to these people's holistic well-being, but they may involuntarily neglect the needs of those closest to them when their minds are in thrall to an impersonal interest.

VIRTUES: These sensitive people are true introverts, whose interests are directed internally rather than externally, and yet they are highly empathetic toward others. Receptive to innovative concepts, and themselves possessed of an original—often visionary—turn of mind, they have the potential to inspire others when they choose to share their talents.
VICES: Because March 4 people are both so intellectually and emotionally self-reliant, they have a predilection toward retreating from the company of other people, especially when faced with a potentially difficult situation.
VERDICT: Those born on this day must ensure that they do not overindulge their natural propensity for self-absorption. They must try to participate more in the interaction of everyday life, and to pay greater attention to the individual needs of others in order to avoid becoming cut off from reality.

The Forth Bridge, Britain's longest and a major technological achievement for its time, was opened on this day that is so strongly associated with water in 1890.

On This Day
Famous Births: Prince Henry the Navigator (1394); Antonio Vivaldi (1678); Henry Raeburn (1756); Knute Rockne (1888); Patrick Moore and Alan Sillitoe (1928); Bernard Haitink (1929); Miriam Makeba (1931); Jim Clark (1936); Barbara McNair (1937); Paula Prentiss (1939); Chris Squire (1948); Kenny Dalglish (1951); Kay Lenz (1953); Chastity Bono (1969).

Significant Events and Anniversaries: This day highlights tenacity in the pursuit of a vision, a quality which augurs well for success, and on March 4 the Communist International (Comintern) was inaugurated by Lenin, after years of political struggle (1919). The artistry that is such a crucial component of this day was illustrated by the first performance of the ballet *Swan Lake* (1877), by the publication of the song "Happy Birthday to You" by Clayton F. Summy (1924), and by the knighting of comic actor Charlie Chaplin by Queen Elizabeth II of Britain in recognition of his outstanding contribution to the world of entertainment (1975). That the ruling element of this day is water is reflected in it being the anniversary of three aquatic events: the opening of Britain's longest bridge, the Forth Bridge (1890); the achievement of the U.S. nuclear submarine *Nautilus* in becoming the first such vessel to pass under the North Pole's icecap (1958); and the piping ashore of the first North Sea gas to Durham in Britain (1967).

MARCH 5

Like the water that is the ruling element of March 5, people born on this day can at one moment appear calm and tranquil, and at the next be making spectacular waves. The emotional undercurrent that flows beneath these people's attractive exterior is a strong one and, since they are sensitive types who respond to their instincts, they may feel powerless to resist the shifting directions to which they are being drawn. When they feel happy and secure, those born on this day are capable of being charming and sympathetic companions who will do their utmost to put others at their ease; when their equilibrium is unbalanced, however, the passionate expression of their frustration can be manifested in a veritable squall of temper. Given the emotional extremes to which they are prone, these people need to receive the unconditional understanding and support of those closest to them, who in many ways may be equated to ports in a storm.

The empathy which gives them such a strong rapport with others frequently manifests itself in a fervent desire to work toward the good of humanity, and these people will find satisfaction in careers which allow them to pursue this aim—in such areas as social or volunteer work, for example. But underneath the often assured and gregarious façade presented by these people lies a more pensive soul, which needs occasionally to retreat from the demands of the world to indulge in quiet and solitary reflection—a mark of the artist. Their intellectual powers of perception and analysis are great and, when harnessed to their empathy, can achieve remarkable results.

VIRTUES: March 5 people are blessed with the quality of profound empathy, which enables them to attune themselves to the feelings of others and to identify themselves with the less fortunate. They also possess a more rational talent for evaluation and incisive thought, qualities that can bring them success when they are emotionally secure.

VICES: Such is the sensitivity of these people that they often feel compelled to obey their instincts and may thus not only behave irrationally and impulsively, but may lose their fragile emotional control completely.

VERDICT: Maintaining a balance in every area of their lives is vital if those born on this day are to find fulfillment. They should cultivate a strategy of consciously regulating their innermost thoughts and feelings, which will help them to sail on a smooth and direct course through the waters of life.

On This Day

Famous Births: King Henry II of England (1133); Gerhardus Mercator (1512); William Oughtred (1575); Giovanni Battista Tiepolo (1696); James Madison (1751); Augusta Gregory (1852); Rosa Luxemburg (1871); William Beveridge (1879); Heitor Villa-Lobos (1887); Rex Harrison (1908); James Noble (1922); James B. Sikking (1934); Dean Stockwell (1936); Samantha Eggar (1939); Michael Warren (1946); Elaine Page (1952); Andy Gibb (1958); Niki Taylor (1975).

Significant Events and Anniversaries: This day is characterized by impulsive and often extreme behavior, as was reflected in the panic-stricken action of British troops in Boston, Massachusetts, when they fired on a hostile mob and killed five people—a tragedy which became known as the "Boston Massacre" (1770), and the fact that almost half the seats in the German elections were won by the extremist Nazi party (1933). The potential for loss of emotional control was seen in the abrupt ending of Elvis Presley's U.S. Army career when he was officially discharged (1960), and the more drastic collapse of John Belushi, who died of a drug overdose (1982). Reflecting the perspicacity indicated by this day, Sir Winston Churchill, the former British premier and wartime leader, made his famous "iron curtain" speech at Fulton, Missouri, warning of the dangers of the Soviet policy of increasing isolationism (1946).

Planetary Influences
Ruling planet: Neptune.
Second decan: Personal planet is the Moon.

Sacred and Cultural Significance
In North Africa and Rome, Egyptian goddess Isis honored.
Saints' day: Piran (d. c.480); Ciaran of Saighir (c.5th to 6th century AD).

The infamous 1770 Boston Massacre, which began when British soldiers fired shots on a crowd of Americans, was one of a number of extreme, ill-judged events that have occurred on this day of volatile behavior.

PISCES

Planetary Influences
Ruling planet: Neptune.
Second decan: Personal planet is the Moon.

Sacred and Cultural Significance
National Day of Ghana.
Saints' day: Conon (3rd century AD); Fridolin (c. 6th century AD); Tibba (7th century AD); Cyniburg (d. c.680); Baldred (8th century AD) and Billfrith (8th century AD; Chrodegang of Metz (d. 766); Colette (1381–1447).

Michelangelo exemplified the outstanding aesthetic sensibilities of people born on March 6. His Delphic Sybil, *below, is part of the Sistine Chapel ceiling that is one of the world's best-known masterpieces of fine art.*

MARCH 6

Those born on this day are idealists, but their quest for perfection is not motivated by austerely intellectual objectives, but rather by a desire to experience the pleasure and satisfaction that are engendered by true excellence. The orientation of this overriding ambition may vary according to the personal interests of March 6 individuals, but since all are profoundly sensitive and thus inherently appreciative of the arts, this sphere of life is particularly important to them. Whether or not they actively direct their highly imaginative talents toward the creation of sublime pieces of music, paintings, sculptures or poems, those born on this day are stimulated and uplifted by aesthetic beauty. Some of these people passionately wish to create an ideal political or social regime. Whatever their career choice, be it in business, the arts or in the caring professions, these people will typically invest their considerable gifts of energy and perception in the attainment of their high ideals.

The disadvantage of this high regard for excellence, however—and this is especially true for March 6 men—is that others will inevitably fail to match their lofty standards. In their personal lives especially, the disappointment that these people feel when the object of their affection turns out to have feet of clay can be shattering, and they may therefore have difficulty in making and maintaining emotional commitments. They must therefore try to develop a more realistic and less demanding attitude to those closest to them.

VIRTUES: March 6 people are primarily motivated by the desire to experience perfection, which results in an unceasing pursuit to translate an often intangible ideal into reality. Extraordinarily sensitive, these people are blessed with heightened emotional and sensory perceptions, and also have the tenacity and intellectual ability to channel these effectively.
VICES: Unfortunately, perfection is not a natural—or a globally attainable—human state, so these people's compulsion toward perfection may doom them to disillusionment and may alienate them from other people.
VERDICT: These people must learn not to dismiss or denigrate the ordinary and mundane in life. Although it is laudable to aspire to perfection, this tendency should not be allowed to prevent a more healthy acceptance and appreciation of the true natures of people and things.

On This Day
Famous Births: Michelangelo Buonarroti (1475); Savinien Cyrano de Bergerac (1619); Elizabeth Barrett Browning (1806); Philip Henry Sheridan (1831); George du Maurier (1834); Oscar Strauss (1870); Lou Costello (1908); Frankie Howerd (1922); Ed McMahon (1923); Andrzej Wajda (1926); Marion Barry (1936); Valentina Nikolayeva-Tereshkova (1937); Kiri Te Kanawa and Mary Wilson (1944); Rob Reiner (1945); Tom Arnold (1959); Shaquille O'Neal (1972).

Significant Events and Anniversaries: The artistic excellence that is promised by this day was reflected in the first performance of Verdi's opera *La Traviata* (1853), but the success that can result from March 6's constant quest to realize an ideal can also be manifested in many different forms, illustrated by the patenting of the aspirin—a "wonder drug"—by Felix Hoffman (1899), and the marketing of Birds Eye's first frozen foods in Springfield, Massachusetts (1930). Less happily, Davy Crockett and Colonel James Bowie, among two hundred Texans, spectacularly failed to achieve their aims and were killed by three thousand Mexicans at the conclusion of the Battle of the Alamo (1836). On this day, which is governed by the element of water, Australian Christopher Massey set a water skiing record of 143.08 mph (228.9 kph) (1983), while, on a more tragic note, the *Herald of Free Enterprise* capsized outside Belgium's Zeebrugge harbor, causing the deaths of over two hundred people (1987). The organizational qualities of this day were seen when the U.S. Congress created the Census Bureau (1902), and York, in Upper Canada, was incorporated as Toronto (1834).

MARCH 7

Although they can be immensely practical and, as a result of their sensitivity, empathetic toward other people, those born on March 7 have a propensity to direct their interest and attention to what really fascinates them—the ideas and ideals that are products of their vivid imaginations. These people possess the gift of extraordinary vision; they will typically perceptively survey their surroundings, analyze the situation's faults and merits and formulate an ideal scenario, which they will then tenaciously strive to achieve. Although they may be gripped by one specific aim, since they are inherently receptive to all kinds of emotional and intellectual stimuli, this perspicuity and urge to act may be manifested in diverse enthusiasms. Within whichever area they ultimately choose to make their profession—be it in the arts, for which they have such a natural affinity, politics or sport—they will generally mount a determined and organized campaign to attain their ambitions.

There is a danger, however, given their focus on impersonal concepts, that those born on this day may allow their focus to be diverted from the very real needs of their family and friends, who will not necessarily understand these people's frequent desire for periods of solitary reflection or their enthusiastic devotion to a cause that may seem remote. Cultivating a spirit of compromise and give and take is therefore vital in giving March 7 poeple the balance that will result in self-fulfillment.

VIRTUES: March 7 people are naturally compelled to explore, implement and ultimately realize their visionary and usually nonmaterialistic goals. In doing so, they are aided by their intuitive, perceptive and intellectual capabilities.
VICES: These people are attracted by a range of interests, and may experience difficulty in concentrating on one priority. When a goal is identified, however, they will devote their exclusive attention to it, and thereby run the risk of ignoring less demanding—though no less important—areas of their lives.
VERDICT: Despite the fact that these multitalented people instinctively employ both their emotional and rational talents in the pursuance of their ideals, they should also attend to their undoubted ability to empathize with others, in order to ensure that they do not neglect the needs of those closest to them.

On This Day

Famous Births: Joseph Nicéphore Niepce (1765); Alessandro Manzoni (1785); John Herschel (1792); Edwin Landseer (1802); Luther Burbank (1849); Thomas Garrigue Masaryk (1850); Piet Mondrian (1872); Maurice Ravel (1875); Ernest Bevin (1881); Jacques Chaban-Dalmas (1905); Willard Scott (1934); Daniel J. Travanti (1940); Tammy Faye Bakker (1942); John Heard (1947); Viv Richards (1952); Rik Mayall (1958); Ivan Lendl (1960).

Significant Events and Anniversaries: March 7 highlights artistic potential, and on this day the legendary "Swedish Nightingale," the vocalist Jenny Lind, made her debut at the Stockholm Opera in Weber's *Der Freischutz* (1838), while Nick La Rocca and his Original Dixieland Jazz Band made the world's first jazz record, courtesy of the U.S. Victor Company, which featured "The Dixie Jazz Band One-step" and "Livery Stable Blues" (1917). This day indicates the pragmatic execution of an ideal and, reflecting their desire to reinvent their radical past, marks the changing of the Bolsheviks' name to the Russian Communist Party (1918). The success that can be achieved by the single-minded pursuit of a cherished ambition was illustrated by the patenting of the world's first workable telephone by Alexander Graham Bell (1876) and the triumph of French aviator Henri Seimet in flying nonstop from Paris to London—the first person to do so (1912). Reflecting the pursuit of visionary goals that characterizes March 7, in Switzerland men voted to give women the right to vote and hold federal office (1971), while England's King Hennry VIII's declaration that he was the head of the Church of England illustrates the emotional fervor of the day (1530).

Planetary Influences
Ruling planet: Neptune.
Second decan: Personal planet is the Moon.

Sacred and Cultural Significance
Saints' day: Perpetua and Felicitas (d. 203); Eosterwine (650–86).

Known as the "Swedish Nightingale" for her exceptionally clear, sweet singing voice, Jenny Lind made her famous debut at the Stockholm Opera on this day of artistic associations in 1838.

Planetary Influences
Ruling planet: Neptune.
Second decan: Personal planet is the Moon.

Sacred and Cultural Significance
In China, Mother Earth Day festival.
Saints' day: Senan (d. c.544); Felix of
Dunwich (d. 647); Duthac (d. 1065); John
of God (1495–1550), patron saint of book-
sellers, heart patients, hospitals, nurses,
printers and the sick.

Most famous for her role in Singin' in the
Rain, *actress and dancer Cyd Charisse was an
individualist from the beginning—a March 8
trait. Her Chinese sign, the pig, bestows
creativity and charm, qualities that are evident
in her screen performances.*

MARCH 8

March 8 people harbor a fiercely independent spirit beneath their outward veneer of
endearing affability, so while they may give the impression of conforming to the norm,
to some extent they are often actually working to undermine accepted conventions. This
somewhat subversive approach is not prompted by a need to be perverse for defiance's sake—
although the free-spirited individuals born on this day are naturally resistant to submitting
to hidebound rules and regulations—but rather because they find it easy to identify the flaws
and contradictions of a previously unchallenged approach and to formulate a better solution.
Indeed, these people are blessed with highly developed intellectual qualities of inquiry and
lateral thinking, as well as being inherently sensitive and empathetic toward others. Such
characteristics mark them out as potentially great reformers or inspirational trailblazers,
especially in the academic, scientific, artistic and social spheres.

As children, March 8 people will have to accept the hard lesson that society demands
adherence to its mores, but if their parents respect their individuality and give them understanding and a sufficient degree of sympathetic guidance, they will benefit from the opportunity to learn to channel their talents positively. Otherwise there is a danger that the
compulsion experienced by these people will find negative outlets, or that they will cut themselves off from others altogether.

VIRTUES: Those born on this day possess intuitive and intellectually questing minds, which
compel them to follow their own, sometimes highly original, course of inquiry. Perceptive
and individualistic, they are true to themselves and usually refuse to submit to the constraints
of systems with which they do not agree.
VICES: Such is their inherent need for autonomy of thought and action that these people
may find themselves plowing a lonely furrow, having alienated themselves from more conventional souls by persisting in what their friends and family members may perceive to be
obstinate and radical behavior.
VERDICT: While they should never suppress their independent approach, March 8 people should not lose sight of the fact that, in the interests of the greater good, compromise is
the glue that holds the fabric of human society together. By tempering their unconventional
nature and grounding themselves in supportive relationships with their family and friends,
they will achieve greater equilibrium in all areas of their lives.

On This Day
Famous Births: Carl Philipp Emanuel Bach (1714); Karl Ferdinand von Graefe (1787);
Ruggiero Leoncavallo (1858); Kenneth Grahame (1859); Otto Hahn (1879); Eric Linklater
(1899); Cyd Charisse (1923); Douglas Hurd (1930); Lynn Seymour (1939): Susan Clark
(1940); Lynn Redgrave (1943); David Wilkie (1955); Gary Numan (1958); Aidan Quinn
(1959); Kathy Ireland (1963).

Significant Events and Anniversaries: Illustrating the allied tendencies of innovation and
independence that are important characteristics of this day, the daring experimental use of
an artificial heart was first achieved (1952) and two aviators gained the world's first pilot's
licenses: J.T.C. Moore-Brabazon of Britain and Mlle Elise de Laroche of France (1910).
Reflecting the day's propensity to ignore accepted social norms in pursuit of a personal agenda,
gangster Ronnie Kray murdered George Cornell in an East End pub in London (1966); former Beatle Paul McCartney was charged with growing the illegal drug marijuana on his land
in Scotland (1973); and John McPherson entered the record books for kissing more than
4,000 women in eight hours (1985). The capacity for changing previously set rules on a collective level is also characteristic of this day, as seen when: soap opera writers in the United
States went on strike for improved terms to their contracts (1988); and in India, 3,000 resi-
dents were restricted to their homes in order to enforce a government ban on the nude wor-
shipping of a Hindu god (1988).

MARCH 9

Those born on this day are uncompromisingly individualistic in every aspect of their lives. Their energy is fueled by a burning compulsion to gather knowledge and seek out the truth of a situation for themselves rather than accepting the interpretation of others. And, because they are extraordinarily imaginative, their curiosity will lead them to explore a variety of avenues, then to evaluate their findings objectively before expressing them in their unique fashion. March 9 people have high nonmaterialistic ideals—a result both of their visionary qualities and of their sensitivity. Because they desire harmony in life, and because their empathy with others bestows on them a profound sense of natural justice, these people will often make gifted social campaigners and reformers. Indeed, into whatever career their interests lead them—be it in the artistic realm, politics or sport—these people will never allow the excitement of discovery to obliterate their humanitarian concerns.

Because they retain their inherent feeling of connection with other people, especially if they were also born in the Chinese year of the horse, March 9 people will rarely forsake the real world for the isolation of an ivory tower. Yet this does not mean that these profound thinkers will not withdraw temporarily from the society of others in order to ponder an irresistibly absorbing concept. Those closest to them should therefore respect that occasional periods of solitude are crucial to these normally gregarious people.

VIRTUES: These people often arouse great admiration in others for their intellectual originality and daring, yet also for the empathy and support that they typically have to offer. The combination of such characteristics is an unusual gift, and these people have the perception and enthusiasm to utilize it fully.

VICES: Those born on this day are highly responsive to both intellectual and emotional stimuli, a propensity which, if uncontrolled, can result in a confusing diversity of interests and impulses, which will inevitably cause emotional unsettlement.

VERDICT: Although March 9 people generally manage to maintain an even balance between their introverted and extroverted sides, they should ensure that neither gains the upper hand, causing them either to become overwhelmed by conflicting emotions, or to suppress their more human qualities in the single-minded furtherance of an idea.

On This Day

Famous Births: Amerigo Vespucci (1454); William Cobbett (1763); Vyacheslav Mikhailovich Molotov (1890); Vita Sackville-West (1892); Samuel Barber (1910); André Courrèges (1913); Micky Spillane (1918); Irene Pappas (1926); Keely Smith (1932); Yuri Alekseyevich Gagarin (1934); Micky Gilley (1936); Raul Julia (1940); Bobby Fischer and Trish Van Devere (1943); Micky Dolenz (1945); Bill Beaumont (1952); Linda Fiorentino (1960); Emmanuel Lewis (1971).

Significant Events and Anniversaries: March 9 is a day that indicates the successful reconciliation of emotional and rational characteristics, as well as of social concern. Such qualities are often manifested by national, military or political leaders, and on this day: Pu-Yi, the last Chinese emperor, was installed as head of the Japanese puppet state of Manchukuo (1932); General Ulysses Grant was named the commander-in-chief of the Union side during the American Civil War (1864); and Eamon de Valera became president of Ireland (1932). This day highlights the potential for innovation, and marks the anniversary of the formation of the French Foreign Legion (1831). Independence of thought and action are further features of this day, on which Svetlana Alliluyeva, the daughter of the former dictator of the Soviet Union, defected to the West (1967). The unrealistic consequences that may result when intellectual considerations are promoted at the expense of emotional expression can be seen in one instance in Naples, Italy, when kissing in public was banned on pain of death (1562).

Planetary Influences
Ruling planet: Neptune.
Second decan: Personal planet is the Moon.

Sacred and Cultural Significance
Tibetan Buddhist Butter Lamp festival.
Saints' day: Forty Martyrs of Sebaste (d. 320); Gregory of Nyssa (c.330–c.395); Constantine (dates unknown); Boso (7th and 8th centuries AD); Frances of Rome (1384–1440), patron saint of motorists; Dominic Savio (1842–57).

During the Butter Lamp Festival, which is celebrated on March 9 by Tibetan Buddhists, yak-butter sculptures of Buddhist heroes are paraded through the streets and then cast into a river. It is believed that this annual ritual will ensure the gods' benevolence. The fluttering flags adorning the chörten *below are thought to carry believers' prayers.*

PISCES

Planetary Influences
Ruling planet: Neptune.
Second decan: Personal planet is the Moon.

Sacred and Cultural Significance
Saints' day: Kessog (6th century AD); John Ogilvie (1580–1615).

This spiritual day marks the anniversary of the completion of the rebuilding of the Temple of Jerusalem after the return of the Jews from their Babylonian exile. Doré's depiction of the desolated temple, below, shows the illumination of the temple by the Divine light, symbolizing hope.

Although they are blessed with the intellectual gifts of objectivity and discernment, as well as with practical, organizational skills, it is their inner world of visions and ideals that primarily defines and occupies March 10 people. These are profoundly sensitive and thoughtful people, whose deeply felt compassion with those who are less fortunate arouses in them the ardent ambition to bring about improvement. And because they are inclined to think both innovatively and seriously, they will often come up with a visionary, but also pragmatic, plan of action. Most will find greatest fulfillment when serving the common good, and they are therefore especially well suited to such caring professions as social work or medicine, or in fields in which they can devote their considerable talents to bringing happiness to others in less tangible ways, such as in the arts.

Despite their humanitarian concerns, and the value that they place on the intimacy of family life, these people are relatively solitary beings who need to retreat within themselves every so often for periods of reflection. Their sensitivity furthermore instills in them an inherent dislike of conflict, and when they feel upset or under pressure they will go within rather than confront an unpleasant situation; this tendency is particularly pronounced in March 10 males. They therefore need to receive frequent manifestations of the unconditional love and support of their friends and family if they are to thrive.

VIRTUES: March 10 individuals are extremely empathetic to the problems of other people, and will typically direct their considerable capacity for perceptive, reasoned and original thought toward the reversal of social ills.
VICES: Because these people are idealistic and motivated by altruistic concerns, they have a propensity both to think the best of people and to expect a similar level of commitment from others as they themselves display. When inevitably disappointed or hurt, they are prone to withdraw from the real world to seek solace in their personal universe of beauty and fantasy.
VERDICT: These caring, contemplative and visionary people must ensure that they do not become victims of their own sensitivity and other outstanding qualities. They should therefore make a concerted effort to develop a more robust acceptance of their own and other people's imperfections, rather than fleeing to the safety of their shell when emotionally wounded.

On This Day
Famous Births: Marcello Malpighi (1628); Lorenzo da Ponte (1749); Edward Hodges Baily (1788); Wyatt Earp (1848); Henry Watson Fowler (1858); Tamara Platonova Karsavina (1885); Arthur Honegger and Eva Turner (1892); Bix Beiderbecke (1903); Gerard Croiset (1909); Charles Groves (1915); Pamela Mason (1922); Chuck Norris (1942); Katharine Houghton (1945); Shannon Tweed (1957); Sharon Stone (1958); Prince Edward of Britain (1964).

Significant Events and Anniversaries: Communal and spiritual aspiration are features of this day, on which, following their return from exile in Babylon, the Jewish people completed the rebuilding of the Temple of Jerusalem (512 BC), which had been destroyed by Nebuchadnezzar. Driven by her egalitarian mission to help bring about equality for women, British suffragette Mary Richardson took drastic action by slashing Velásquez's painting *The Rokeby Venus* at the National Gallery in London (1914). A measure of peace was found by millions of mourners of Dr. Martin Luther King, Jr., when James Earl Ray pleaded guilty to his murder (1969). March 10 is ruled by the element of water, and on this day a car ferry capsized during a severe storm in Wellington harbor, New Zealand, tragically causing the death of two hundred people (1968), while Britain's Prince Charles narrowly avoided death in the avalanche that took the life of a companion during a skiing trip in the Swiss Alps (1988).

MARCH 11

Those individuals born on this day share the intuition that characterizes their Piscean fellows, but in their case it is less static and contemplative in quality, since they tend to use it more as a tool for gathering information and, if necessary, manipulating others. Indeed, March 11 people are shrewd judges of character, a talent partly informed by their instincts, and partly by their gift for detached perception. Similarly, although they nurture high ambitions, these are generally personal rather than global, and are furthermore realistically pitched. These people are geared toward making progress, especially in their professional lives, within which they will work tirelessly, not only to reach the top of the corporate ladder, but also to make their organization the best of its type. Because they are also imaginative and positive people who are willing to put aside personal differences in favor of building a dynamic team, they usually fare extremely well when directing commercial enterprises and managing complex projects, particularly when they were also born in the Chinese years of the monkey or snake.

Domestic harmony is also important to March 11 people, who regard their personal sphere as a retreat from the hurly-burly of work in which they can relax and be themselves. They make indulgent parents, partners and friends, although—especially if they are men—they may occasionally adopt their professional persona in their relationships with those closest to them and behave in a somewhat high-handed manner. They furthermore expect the unquestioning loyalty and support of their loved ones, and have a tendency to lose their tempers spectacularly if they detect dissension.

VIRTUES: These enthusiastic and energetic people display clear-sightedness in the pursuit of their goals and, by virtue of their capacity to effectively marshal their talents of perception, interpersonal skills, drive and imaginative vision, have the potential to realize their ambitions.
VICES: Although they will generally do so in a charming manner, these people have a propensity to deliberately manipulate others to enlist their support. When presented with obdurate resistance, however, they will explode with frustration. Cultivating a greater respect for the opinions of others is therefore vital.
VERDICT: As they progress onward and upward, those born on this day must not forfeit their empathetic talents. They should remember the worth of simple human values, and take time out every so often to give themselves the time and space in which to engage in honest personal reflection.

On This Day
Famous Births: Torquato Tasso (1544); Urbain Jean Joseph Leverrier (1811); Marius Petipa and Henry Tate (1819); Malcolm Campbell (1885); Raoul Walsh (1892); Dorothy Gish (1898); Lawrence Welk (1903); Jessie Matthews (1907); Harold Wilson (1916); Ralph Abernathy (1926); Althea Louise Brough (1928); Rupert Murdoch (1931); Nigel Lawson (1932); Sam Donaldson (1934); Douglas Adams (1952).

Significant Events and Anniversaries: This day favors business ventures, and marks the anniversary of: the opening of London's Theatre Royal in Drury Lane (1794); the formulation of self-raising flour by Henry Jones (1845); the passing of the Lend-Lease Bill by the U.S. Congress, which agreed to lend armaments to Britain during World War II in return for the lease of military bases (1941); and the purchase of London's famous Harrods store by the Al-Fayed brothers (1985). In a more destructive manifestation of this commercial characteristic, during World War II Allied bombers destroyed the Krupps manufacturing plant in Germany (1945). Leadership potential is highlighted by this day, on which Mikhail Gorbachev became the youngest general secretary of the Communist Party of the Soviet Union (1985). March 11 is influenced by the element of water, and on this day a reservoir flooded disastrously near Sheffield, England, claiming around 250 lives (1864).

Planetary Influences
Ruling planet: Neptune.
Third decan: Personal planets are Mars and Pluto.

Sacred and Cultural Significance
Saints' day: Oengus the Culdee (d. c.824); Eulogius of Cordoba (d. 859).

The potential to succeed in realizing ambitious visions was a central characteristic of civil rights activist Ralph Abernathy (shown at left in the 1956 photograph below), who was born on this day in 1926. Born in the Chinese year of the tiger, his leadership skills were reinforced, and he typified the forceful, magnetic, passionate qualities of the fire tiger.

Planetary Influences
Ruling planet: Neptune.
Third decan: Personal planets are Mars and Pluto.

Sacred and Cultural Significance
Babylonian Feast of Marduk.
Saints' day: Pionius (d. c.250); Maximilian (d. 295); Paul Aurelian (6th century AD); Mura (7th century AD); Alphege (10th century AD).

Marduk, the Babylonian king and founding father, was fêted on March 12 in ancient times. In this carving, he is depicted standing guard over the waters with a dragon.

MARCH 12

A crucial component of the characters of those born on this day is the need to explore as many aspects of life as they can, in order to gain knowledge, to expose themselves to new experiences, and often also to test themselves against demanding challenges. In view of their adventurous spirits, it is hardly surprising that March 12 people are also energetic and daring individuals, who carry the less imaginative along on the tide of their enthusiasm, although few would dare to travel as impulsively or, indeed, as far. Some regard these individuals as reckless—and they unquestionably sometimes are—but since they have the gift of clarity of vision they will generally have considered any risks and will have evaluated the odds. These people have the potential to succeed as stockbrokers, or in any field in which they can take gambles. Yet it is not only external stimuli that invigorate those born on this day: they possess an originality and vision—as well as a fascination with the metaphysical—that borders on the radical, and augurs well for personal success in such diverse realms as politics or the arts.

Although they relish competition—against themselves rather more than against others—March 12 individuals are not motivated by the need to score victories over other people. They are empathetic and compassionate beings who have no real desire to succeed at another's expense, and who moreover also need to be rooted in the secure bonds of an emotionally stable and happy personal life. They sometimes find it hard to reciprocate the quiet and unconditional support that they crave from their friends and family, however, a difficulty that is caused by their inherent mental restlessness.

VIRTUES: March 12 individuals are defined by their intellectual curiosity and their propensity to pursue radical quests—to discover where they will be led, as well as to gauge themselves against the challenges thereby presented. Yet they also have a profoundly intuitive and reflective side, although they will rarely allow themselves the opportunity to explore it deeply.
VICES: Such is the enthusiasm and gusto with which these people respond to both intellectual and physical challenges that they may tend toward extreme, sensation-seeking behavior that can, for some, become addictive.
VERDICT: Those born on this day are not only open to, but positively invite, innovation and excitement. This characteristic, when combined with their infectious enthusiasm, gives them the potential to lead others in radically new directions. They should, however, remember to look before they leap, as the saying goes, to ensure that they do not end up propelling themselves into a cul-de-sac.

On This Day
Famous Births: Thomas Augustine Arne (1710); John Daniell (1790); Gustav Robert Kirchoff (1824); William Henry Perkin (1838); Gabriele d'Annunzio (1863); Stuart Edward White (1873); Kemal Atatürk (1881); Vaslav Nijinsky (1890); Joseph Meyer (1894); Max Wall (1908); Googie Withers (1917); Jack Kerouac (1922); Edward Albee (1928); Andrew Young (1932); Al Jarreau (1940); Barbara Feldon (1941); Paul Katner (1942); Liza Minnelli (1946); James Taylor (1948); Daryl Strawberry (1962).

Significant Events and Anniversaries: This is a day that indicates the testing of character, and marks the anniversary of Juliette Gordon Low's founding of the Girl Guides in the U.S.A., an organization designed to do precisely that (1912); while Mahatma Gandhi demonstrated this propensity when he set out on his 320 km "Salt March," intending to manufacture salt from the Indian Dandi Sea as a protest against the British taxes on salt (1930). Illustrating the radical behavior that is a tendency of this day, Russian troops mutinied in support of the February Revolution (1917) and Britain banned all travel to and from Ireland and Ulster (1944). The intellectual clarity that is highlighted by March 12 was paralleled in the natural world by De Beers's much-fêted exhibition of a spectacular diamond, at 599 carats the second largest ever discovered (1988).

MARCH 13

With their marked interest in metaphysical and even paranormal concepts, March 13 people are instinctively fascinated by ideas and ideals that less imaginative types would brand as being fanciful or naive at best, and outrageously implausible at worst. Such is their acceptance of otherworldly possibilities, as well as their consequent tendency to challenge conventional "truths," that as children these people will have taxed their parents to the limit with their endless questioning as to the hows and whys of life. If properly channeled, their curiosity and free-ranging intellects, coupled with their refusal to be dissuaded from pursuing the interests that excite them, can have remarkable consequences. Those born on this day will not find fulfillment by following a structured career path, and will be stifled within large organizations. If their many talents are to flourish, they must be allowed to follow their own route, and they are therefore best suited to working in the academic, artistic or sporting sphere, in which they will be relatively unconstrained.

There is a danger that other people's denigration of their world views and opinions may wound these deeply sensitive individuals, causing them to conceal their true natures in an attempt to conform to a less original norm. Alternatively, they may feel tempted to opt out of conventional society altogether. It is therefore important that those closest to them not only bolster their self-belief, but that they gently steer them on to a straighter course when their equilibrium threatens to become unbalanced.

VIRTUES: March 13 people are highly original in their way of thinking, intuitively recognizing that there is more to the universe than has yet been discovered, and fired by their enthusiasm to learn hidden truths. They have the potential and courage to lead others along previously untrodden paths.
VICES: Those born on this day are extraordinarily sensitive, a quality that informs many of their beliefs and actions, but also makes them vulnerable to the dissent or mockery of others. They must accept the occasional need to compromise, but must not abandon their fundamental selves because of their inherent lack of confidence.
VERDICT: While never stifling their compulsion for exploring the abstract or otherworldly, those born on this day must ensure that they remain securely rooted in the physical world. Adopting a more pragmatic approach will help them to reconcile their visionary tendencies with the reality of the everyday world.

On This Day
Famous Births: Joseph Priestley (1733); Daniel Lambert (1770); Percival Lowell (1855); Hugo Wolf (1860); Hugh Walpole (1884); Henry Hathaway (1898); Oscar Nemon (1906); L. Ron Hubbard (1911); William Casey (1913); Tessie O'Shea (1918); Neil Sedaka (1939); Joe Bugner (1950); Deborah Raffin (1953); Adrian Zmed (1954); Dana Dlany (1956).

Significant Events and Anniversaries: This day indicates imaginative vision which, if pursued, can result in pioneering discoveries, and to illustrate, March 13 marks the discovery of the planet Uranus by William Herschel (1781), as well as the launching of the Soviet *Soyuz T-15* spacecraft which would later dock at the Mir space station, the first human outpost in space (1986). The struggle to implement radical concepts can, however, be at the expense of individual lives, as was illustrated when the American Revolutionary War claimed its first victim, William French, on this day (1775), when Czar Alexander II of Russia died from wounds inflicted by antimonarchist bombers (1881), and when Nazi Germany invaded Austria, claiming to have been invited—an action which it termed the *Anschluss* ("annexation" or "joining together") (1938). This day is ruled by the element of water, and in a tragic demonstration of aquatic force, around 450 people died when a dam burst near Los Angeles (1928). Reflecting the day's quest for enlightenment and truth, Harvard University was named (1639), while the pioneering nature of March 13 was seen in the first permanent settlement at Shikai-o, known today as Chicago (1773).

Planetary Influences
Ruling planet: Neptune.
Third decan: Personal planets are Mars and Pluto.

Sacred and Cultural Significance
Burgonndeg, a Pagan fire festival.
Saints' day: Mochoemoc (7th century AD); Gerald of Mayo (d. 732).

William French, whose gravestone in Westminster, Vermont, is shown below, was the first to die in America's Revolutionary War. The 22-year-old lost his life to a grand cause that was an example of March 13's radical, yet risky, associations.

Planetary Influences
Ruling planet: Neptune.
Third decan: Personal planets are Mars and Pluto.

Sacred and Cultural Significance
Ghanaian New Year celebration; in Egypt, Ua Zit honored.
Saints' day: Matilda of Quedlinburg (897–966), mother of Holy Roman Emperor Otto I.

Nobel Prize-winner Albert Einstein, born on this day in 1879, is regarded as one of the greatest geniuses in the history of science. As the visionary formulator of the General Theory of Relativity, he demonstrated the extraordinary originality that March 14 bestows. He was also an outspoken critic of intolerance and injustice.

Those born on March 14 frequently exasperate others by their apparent inability to make a decision and stick by it. Yet this indecisive tendency is not the result of a lack of perception or conviction—on the contrary, these sensitive individuals are extremely astute, and furthermore possess strong principles. It is just that because they have the ability to evaluate a situation and then visualize many possible future scenarios, they find it hard to decide on a single course of action when the alternatives seem equally viable or fraught with problems. Since they are furthermore intellectually open to a variety of viewpoints, as well as being profoundly intuitive when it comes to the emotions of those around them, they shrink from bigotry and intolerance and from accepting other people's certainties. It is precisely their combination of open-mindedness, empathy and abhorrence of injustice that informs their deeply humanitarian concern.

Human company is important to these sociable people, and others are drawn to them on account of their cheerful kindness, sympathy and infectious originality. Wonderful friends, they also have potential to make exceptionally good, nonjudgemental parents, but—as in all things—may initially find it hard to commit themselves to a single partner. Professionally, they will thrive when working within small teams, although they instinctively rebel against the rigidity of large corporations. The artistic sphere is especially auspicious for March 14 people, in which their powers of imagination and sensuality can be given the opportunity to flower.

VIRTUES: Like the water that is their astrological element, these people refuse to be constrained by artificial boundaries, and travel through life searching out and soaking up new experiences. Their capacity for tolerance and perceptive skills give them the capability to be real forces for good.
VICES: Such is their ability to absorb the information that emanates from every source—be it intellectual, emotional or sensory—that these people have a tendency to become somewhat confused by the sheer diversity of the plethora of choices available to them, and thus feel unable to reach concrete decisions.
VERDICT: In order to move forward, those born on this day must try to conquer their propensity toward intellectual stasis, a state that can be caused by their inherent aversion to condemning any principle or plan out of hand. It is sometimes necessary to champion and act upon a specific stance—even when it means opposing or dismissing another or perhaps to fly in the face of conventional wisdom.

On This Day
Famous Births: Georg Philipp Telemann (1681); Johann Strauss the Elder (1804); King Victor Emmanuel II of Italy (1820); Giovanni Viginio Schiaparelli (1835); Mrs. Isabella Beeton (1836); Paul Ehrlich (1854); Maxim Gorky (1868); Albert Einstein (1879); Hank Ketcham (1920); Frank Borman (1928); Michael Caine and Quincy Jones (1933); Eleanor Bron (1940); Rita Tushingham (1943); Jasper Carrott and Steve Kanaly (1946); Billy Crystal (1947); Tessa Sanderson (1957); Taylor Hanson (1983).

Significant Events and Anniversaries: The artistic qualities highlighted by this day were reflected by the first performance of Gilbert and Sullivan's comic opera *The Mikado* at the Savoy Theatre in London (1885). On this water-governed day, telephone cable was first laid along the bed of the English Channel (1891), English explorer Samuel White Baker became the first European to sight Lake Albert Nyanza, through which the River Nile flows (1864), and the German cruiser *Dresden* sank (1915). Marking a move toward greater open-mindedness, the New English Bible was first published on this day (1961). Intellectual, although not necessary physical, promiscuity is a feature of this day, on which five lionesses at the Singapore Zoo were prescribed contraceptive pills to prevent the leonine colony from becoming overpopulated (1985).

MARCH 15

The adventurousness of March 15 people may take many forms: they may be intrepid travelers, fearless athletes, dynamic business people, visionary scientists or inspirational artists. In whatever area these people choose to make their careers, their progress will be rapid, driven by their compulsion for exploration and their inherent courage when it comes to taking risks. Yet despite their ceaseless quest to be stimulated by new experiences, those born on this day will not generally set off blindly on a voyage of discovery, for they are furthermore blessed with keen and perceptive intellectual powers, as well as the capacity for great concentration in the pursuit of their aims. These individuals will inform themselves of the facts of a particular situation and impartially evaluate alternative approaches before throwing themselves at a challenge with their typical enthusiasm and energy.

Their need for independence of thought and action defines those born on this day, and their strength of purpose—as well as their natural magnetism—make them charismatic figures who have great leadership potential. Despite their undoubted empathy, they have a tendency to become impatient with those who do not share their visions and willingness to take chances, dismissing such individuals as being dull or obstinate. It is therefore important that they do not isolate themselves from other people—particularly their family and friends—by failing to acknowledge the merits of less intrepid viewpoints and approaches.

VIRTUES: March 15 people are perceptive, independent in all things, and bold enough to explore avenues that may appear dangerous to others. Potential leaders of others, they possess the originality and courage to blaze a decisive trail in life.

VICES: These people have the propensity to overwhelm other people with their restless energy and incisively searching approach to life. They may denigrate or ignore those who are unwilling to cooperate with them, and tend to dominate those who do.

VERDICT: It is important that these people moderate their desire for action and adventure and ground themselves within a supportive domestic or professional framework; by doing so, they will achieve the necessary emotional and intellectual equilibrium, and thereby find greater personal satisfaction.

Planetary Influences
Ruling planet: Neptune.
Third decan: Personal planets are Mars and Pluto.

$$\Psi \quad \male \quad P$$

Sacred and Cultural Significance
The Ides of March; in ancient Rome, the Festival of Attis and Cybele.
Saints' day: Longinus (d. 1st century AD); Zacharias (d. 752); Louise de Marillac (1591–1660); Clement-Mary Hofbauer (1751–1820).

On This Day
Famous Births: Andrew Jackson (1767); William Lamb, Viscount Melbourne (1779); John Snow (1813); Eduard Strauss (1835); Emil von Behring (1854); Leslie Stuart (1866); Macdonald Carey (1913); Harry James (1916); Judd Hirsch (1935); Phil Lesh (1940); Mike Love (1941); Sylvester Stone (1944); David Wall (1946); Fabio and Terence Trent d'Arby (1961).

Significant Events and Anniversaries: March 15 indicates leadership potential which, if unchecked, may tend toward tyranny, and on this day: fervent republicans assassinated the Roman emperor, Julius Caesar (44 BC); Czar Nicholas II was forced to abdicate by Russian revolutionaries (1917); and the German chancellor, Adolf Hitler, proclaimed the Third Reich (1933). The energy inherent in this day augurs well for sport, and on this day the Cincinnati Red Stockings became the first baseball team to have all professional members (1869), and the first test match was played between the English and Australian cricket teams (1877). The day also highlights innovation of all types, and marks the anniversary of the election of the first female members of parliament in Finland (1907), the opening of England's first department store in London by G.S. Selfridge (1909), as well as the establishment of the first U.S. central blood bank (1937).

On the Ides of March in 44 BC, Julius Caesar was assassinated—an event that had been predicted by his astrological diviners.

Planetary Influences
Ruling planet: Neptune.
Third decan: Personal planets are Mars and Pluto.

Sacred and Cultural Significance
In India, Hindu festival of Holi.
Saints' day: Finan Lobur (6th century AD); Abraham Kidunaia (6th century AD).

Thelma Catherine Ryan was born on this day in 1912 and was nicknamed "Pat" because of her birth on the eve of St. Patrick's day. After marriage, she became known simply as Pat Nixon, the confident, ambitious, charismatic and organized woman whose performance as First Lady would make these March 16 characteristics evident. With her combination of the water sign of Pisces, the Chinese element of water and the Chinese sign of the rat, she possessed great loyalty and empathy for others whose causes she championed.

MARCH 16

Those born on March 16 generally appear to others to be exceptionally well-balanced characters, who somehow manage to reconcile their imaginative and fun-loving qualities with a steady and practical approach. These people are blessed with incisive powers of perception, logic and penetrating vision, all of which they utilize in formulating effective plans with which to attain their goals. They may often be personally ambitious, and enjoy the trappings that material success can bring as an affirmation of their status, but because of their sensitive nature, they are more anxious to gain respect and friendship. They will flourish in those professional situations in which they can lead and inspire a team, and are therefore especially suited to careers in teaching or business.

Such is their originality of thought that these people will remain unsatisfied if they cannot impress their personal stamp on everything that they do, especially if they were also born in the Chinese year of the dragon. In their personal lives, they are active types who will competently organize a vibrant social event or recreational expedition, but have a tendency to sulk if others fail to fall into line with their current enthusiasm. Similarly, although they make generous and gregarious friends and family members, they may have a propensity to become overly authoritarian, particularly with regard to their children.

VIRTUES: These multitalented people have a remarkable ability to channel their qualities of imagination and perception into schemes that are simultaneously visionary and realistic, thereby giving them great potential. Yet despite their intellectual focus, they never lose their capacity for hedonistic behavior.
VICES: The self-belief and confidence manifested by those born on this day is tremendous, but if unchecked it can result in their abrupt dismissal or marginalization of those whose beliefs do not conform with their own.
VERDICT: As a result of their ability to maintain a stable emotional and intellectual equilibrium, March 16 people have the capacity to succeed in whichever area of life they choose. However, they should moderate their propensity to dominate others, or to become cynical, and should remember to acknowledge the validity of different viewpoints.

On This Day
Famous Births: James Madison (1751); Matthew Flinders (1774); Georg Simon Ohm (1787); William Henry Monk (1823); René Prudhomme (1839); Emile Cammaerts (1878); Thelma Catherine "Pat" Nixon (1912); Leo McKern (1920); Jerry Lewis (1926); Daniel Patrick Moynihan (1927); Bernardo Bertolucci (1940); J.Z. Knight (1946); Erik Estrada (1949); Kate Nelligan (1951); Isabelle Huppert (1955).

Significant Events and Anniversaries: Leadership potential is a quality highlighted by this day, on which West Point, the U.S. military academy for officers, was established (1802), and William of Orange became king of the Netherlands (1815). Profound self-belief is a further characteristic indicated by March 16 which can, however, have negative consequences, as was reflected in Adolf Hitler's renunciation of the Versailles Treaty that prohibited German rearmament, and his introduction of conscription (1935); as well as in the massacre of around 175 inhabitants of the village of My Lai in Vietnam by U.S. troops (1968). A combination of visionary and organizational powers is also starred by this day, a conjunction that can be seen in the playing of the first English Football Association cup final in London (1872), in the publication of the first issue of Freedom's Journal, the first African American newspaper (1827), in archaeologist Sir Arthur Evans's announcement that he had excavated the city of Knossos in Crete (1900), in Dr. Robert Goddard's launching of the world's first rocket fueled by gasoline and liquid oxygen in Massachusetts (1926), and in the official opening of the newly rebuilt London Bridge by Queen Elizabeth II (1973). Reflecting the materialistic associations of this day, Émile Roger of Paris made the first recorded purchase of a manufactured automobile, a Benz (1888).

MARCH 17

The natures of March 17 people can be compared to that of their watery element, for they have a propensity to drift fluidly from interest to interest, and, rather than be impeded by a difficult obstacle, simply to sidetrack and flow around it. This characteristic behavioral pattern has many possible causes, including these people's inquisitiveness and desire for progress, their dislike of confrontation, or, indeed, often a fundamental sense of insecurity and lack of self-esteem which discourages them from standing their ground. Whatever the reason for their restless and elusive nature, those born on this day are unsuited to strictly structured careers in which they are subject to external controls and the rule of others, and must be indulged in their need for independence of action and thought. Their talents will often find their best expression in crafts, design and the arts, in which they can delight others with their sensitive interpretations of the beauty that inspires them.

Although they are fired by humanitarian concern and hate witnessing others' unhappiness, these people may inadvertently hurt those closest to them by their inherent aversion to commitment in close relationships (especially if they are men) and to the mundane constraints imposed by domestic life. They may therefore initially find it difficult to settle down, and, when they do, have a propensity to shirk responsibility. Their partners will thus need to be tolerant types, who can respect March 17 people's need for freedom and imaginatively work around their fear of entrapment.

VIRTUES: Those born on this day are imaginative, intuitive and optimistic individuals, who are driven by their curiosity and quest for discovery. When properly channeled, these qualities can bring exciting rewards and the admiration of others.
VICES: March 17 people have a tendency to evade potentially thorny problems, preferring to abandon a project or relationship rather than deal with any inherent difficulties, with the result that they may gain a reputation of being unreliable.
VERDICT: These people must strive to develop a more focused and tenacious approach, and not simply move on or attempt to run away and dissociate themselves when they encounter unpleasant or tedious issues. They will derive a far greater sense of satisfaction from achievements made in the face of adversity than from drifting though life pleasantly but aimlessly.

On This Day

Famous Births: Edmund Kean (1787); Gottlieb Wilhelm Daimler (1834); Kate Greenaway (1846); Margaret Grace Bondfield (1873); Eileen J. Garrett (1895); Shemp Howard (1895); Anna Jensen Shufelt (1901); Bobby Tyre Jones (1902); Patrick Hamilton (1904); Mercedes McCambridge (1918); Nat "King" Cole (1919); Robin Knox-Johnston and Rudolf Hametovich Nureyev (1939); John Sebastian (1944); Patrick Duffy (1949); Kurt Russell (1951); Lesley-Ann Downe (1954); Gary Sinise (1955); Rob Lowe (1964).

Significant Events and Anniversaries: Inherent in this day is the quality of flexibility, a characteristic accurately—if prosaically—reflected in the patenting of the elastic band by Londoner Stephen Perry (1845). The day's artistic potential was underlined by the publication of the famous Neopolitan song *"O Sole Mio!"* with lyrics by G. Capurro and music by E. di Campna (1899), and the opening of the Bastille Opera House in Paris (1990). In an attempt to address the inevitable consequence of the propensities for sensory indulgence and impulsiveness that are indicated by this day, Marie Stopes opened The Mothers' Clinic, a pioneering birth-control clinic in London (1921). March 17 highlights an abhorrence of conflict, and marks the anniversary of a huge anti-Vietnam War demonstration in front of the U.S. Embassy in London which, ironically, culminated in violence (1968). On a day governed by the element of water, Noah is said to have entered the ark with his family and menagerie of animals as the Flood began, and the *Amoco Cadiz* oil tanker ran aground off Brittany in France, causing an environmental disaster by spilling its cargo of 220,000 tons of crude oil (1978). The day's progressive nature was illustrated when Golda Meir became prime minister of Israel (1969).

Planetary Influences
Ruling planets: Neptune and Mars.
Third decan: Personal planets are Mars and Pluto.
Second cusp: Pisces with Arian tendencies.

Sacred and Cultural Significance
Traditionally said to be the day on which the Flood began and Noah entered the ark.
Saints' day: Patrick (c.390–461?), patron saint of Ireland; Gertrude of Nivelles (626–59), patron saint of the recently dead; Withburga (d. c.743).

March 17 is St. Patrick's Day, honoring the patron saint of Ireland.

PISCES

Planetary Influences
Ruling planets: Neptune and Mars.
Third decan: Personal planets are Mars and Pluto.
Second cusp: Pisces with Arian tendencies.

Sacred and Cultural Significance
Pagan fertility goddess Sheela-na-gig honored in Ireland.
Saints' day: Cyril of Jerusalem (c.315–86); Finan of Aberdeen (6th century AD); Edward the Martyr (c.962–79); Christian (d. 1186).

The opening of the landmark Sydney Harbour Bridge on March 18, 1932, was one of the many technical and civil engineering achievements that have occurred on this day of progress and advancement.

MARCH 18

Individuals born on March 18 are fueled by a constant quest to make progress, to move a step further on in life, and while this compulsion may be manifested in personal ambition, these compassionate people are typically motivated by a more global concern to improve the lot of humanity. Indeed, these visionary people have the gift of seeing the wider picture—of how things are and how they ought to be—a talent that results primarily from their perceptiveness and also from their profound sense of natural justice. While this ability, combined with their trademark enthusiasm, gives them the potential to achieve real success, it also can influence them to ignore the seemingly minor, yet often crucial, details of a situation. This is particularly true if the details involve unpleasant or controversial issues, which those born on this day would prefer not to confront.

Their aversion to conflict can result in these people employing their considerable skills of diplomacy in the pursuit of a solution, but may equally cause them to make inadvisable concessions or to prevaricate. They are particularly suited to careers as sympathetic caregivers, or in the arts, in which they will not be forced to compromise their principles, and in which they can use their talents to inspire a larger audience. Similarly, in their personal liaisons, they will thrive best if they are not pushed into following a lifestyle or complying with emotional demands that are alien to their natures.

VIRTUES: Sensitive, empathetic and geared toward humanitarian improvement, these people are characterized by their visionary desire to effect positive human progress.
VICES: Such is their instinctive dislike of confrontation in any form that these people will go to considerable lengths to avoid it, a generally laudable principle which, however, may cause them either to ignore a difficult situation when it should more properly be addressed, or to sacrifice their own convictions in favor of compromise.
VERDICT: March 18 people should try to overcome their tendency to resort to evasionary tactics when faced with potential unpleasantness, and should realize that the most successful route is not necessarily always the smoothest.

On This Day
Famous Births: King Frederick III of Denmark and Norway (1609); Stephen Grover Cleveland (1837); Stéphane Mallarmé (1842); Nikolai Rimsky-Korsakov (1844); Rudolf Diesel (1858); Neville Chamberlain (1869); Edgar Cayce (1877); Lavrenti Pavlovich Beria (1889); Wilfred Owen (1893); Peter Graves (1926); John Updike (1932); Frederik Willem de Klerk (1936); Charlie Pride (1938); Wilson Pickett (1941); Alex "Hurricane" Higgins (1949); Pat Eddery (1952); Irene Cara (1959); Vanessa Williams (1963); Queen Latifah (1970).

Significant Events and Anniversaries: March 18 highlights a desire for human advancement, and on this day technical progress was made when: the first public bus service was inaugurated in Paris, France (1662); the first gasoline-driven bus was unveiled in the German Rhineland (1895); the world's first electric shavers were produced by Schick, Inc., in Connecticut (1931); the Sydney Harbour Bridge was opened in Australia (1932); and Soviet cosmonaut Aleksey Arkhipovich Leanor stepped out of his craft *Voskod II* and floated in space (1965). The humanitarian concern that is a feature of this day was reflected in the Communards' uprising in Paris, France (1871). Compromise is indicated by this day, on which the western military powers collaborated in setting up the North Atlantic Treaty Organization (N.A.T.O.) (1949). The element of March 18 is water, and on this day the oil tanker *Torrey Canyon* foundered off Land's End in England, with tragic consequences for the environment (1967).

MARCH 19

Inherent in the characters of March 19 people is a curious mixture of imaginative qualities that tend toward the fanciful and a blunt directness and tenacity that will seldom be swayed. If properly channeled, this combination of visionary idealism and single-minded determination can give these people the potential to be startlingly successful in the pursuit of their aims, that is, as long as they have focused on a realistically achievable target. While these people are fueled by a righteous desire to effect social improvements, because they are highly original thinkers, their seemingly radical solutions may cause others to balk. However, once those born on this day have identified a worthy task to which to devote their prodigious energies, they will work unswervingly toward its completion, employing their considerable powers of organization and persistence in the process.

As a result of these qualities, March 19 people are happiest working in fields in which they feel that they are actively doing good, a requirement that encompasses a diversity of professional interests, including politics, science, the military, the caring professions and, of course, the arts. Because they frequently encounter opposition to their ideas, it is important to these people's emotional well-being that they receive the consistent and unjudgemental support of their nearest and dearest, so that their homes become havens of security in which they can retire from the battle and simply be themselves.

VIRTUES: March 19 people are driven by a burning desire to move the world forward, to identify and then rectify human ills. Although their ambitions are inspired by their sensitivity, empathy and innate sense of natural justice, they will typically utilize more intellectually rigorous methods in their attempts to fulfill their ideals.
VICES: The profound idealism inherent in these people gives them a tendency to lose sight of either the viability of their aims or the possibility that others may not concur with them. When held in the grip of an enthusiasm, they also have a propensity to become obsessive and blind to alternative viewpoints.
VERDICT: It is vital that these people strive to be more pragmatic in all their dealings, and that they not only recognize that other people are entitled to different convictions, but that they should respect and encourage these rather than riding roughshod over them. By listening to others, they may achieve far more than by closing their ears and clinging to their own, private world views.

On This Day

Famous Births: George de la Tour (1593); Tobias George Smollett (1721); David Livingstone (1813); Richard Burton (1821); Wyatt Earp (1848); Alfred von Tirpitz (1849); Sergei Pavlovich Diaghilev (1872); Max Reger (1873); Jean Joliot-Curie (1900); Adolf Eichmann (1906); Adolf Galland (1912); Smoky Dawson (1913); Patrick McGoohan (1928); Ornette Coleman (1930); Philip Roth (1933); Phyllis Newman (1935); Ursula Andress (1936); Glenn Close (1947); Bruce Willis (1955); Courtney Pine (1964).

Significant Events and Anniversaries: March 19 is a day of exceptionally far-sighted vision, as was illustrated by two astronomical events: the first recording of an eclipse by Babylonian star-gazers (721 BC); and the inauguration of Britain's first planetarium at Madame Tussaud's waxworks museum in London (1958). It is also a day on which façades are penetrated, and was the date on which American television evangelist Jim Bakker was forced to resign in the wake of his sex and corruption scandal (1987). This day indicates the desire to alleviate human ills, inequalities and discomfort, and marks the anniversary of the granting of equal rights to French- and English-speaking settlers in Canada (1791) and the marketing of Alka-Seltzer (1931). The determination that characterizes this day is often manifested in the political and military spheres, as was reflected in the U.S. Senate's decision against joining the League of Nations, preferring to maintain its isolationist stance (1920), and the invasion of the Caribbean island of Anguilla by British forces to quell a disorderly uprising against St. Christopher Nevis (1969).

Planetary Influences
Ruling planets: Neptune and Mars.
Third decan: Personal planets are Mars and Pluto.
Second cusp: Pisces with Arian tendencies.

Sacred and Cultural Significance
Akitu, Babylonian New Year Festival; in India, Stala honored as part of Hindu New Year.
Saints' day: Joseph (d. 1st century AD), patron saint of bursars, carpenters, the dying, fathers, holy death, procurators and workers; Alcmund (d. c.800).

On this day of clear vision, the first sighting of an eclipse was recorded by Babylonian astronomers in 721 BC.

Planetary Influences
Ruling planets: Neptune and Mars.
Third decan: Personal planets are Mars and Pluto.
Second cusp: Pisces with Arian tendencies.

Sacred and Cultural Significance
Traditionally said to be the last day of winter and end of the astrological year; Rosicrucian New Year celebrated; in ancient Egypt, the Spring Harvest Festival.
Saints' day: Cuthbert (c.634–87), patron saint of shepherds; Herbert of Derwentwater (d. 687); Wulfram (7th century AD).

In ancient Egypt, the goddess Isis was honored on this day of the Spring Harvest Festival. In the region now known as the Middle East, the hot, arid summer months were the agricultural fallow period, and seeds were sown in early winter for a spring harvest.

MARCH 20

Those born on this day possess such a wealth of attributes that it is difficult to identify a specific quality as a defining characteristic. But underlying their perceptiveness, tenacity, imagination and idealism is their great sensitivity, a gift that can have both negative and positive consequences for March 20 people. Although their inherent ability to relate to others with kindness and empathy makes them valued colleagues and friends, these people may sometimes feel overwhelmed by the intensity of their feelings of compassion, and therefore have a propensity to become depressed in the face of human suffering, particularly if they are women. Yet these individuals are natural optimists and, when buoyed up by their enthusiastic determination to make the world a better place, will intuitively follow a clear-sighted and logically considered plan of action.

A further characteristic that results from March 20 people's humanitarianism is their endearing propensity to think the best of others; sadly, this may make them vulnerable to being taken advantage of by less scrupulous types, and such abuses of trust will wound them deeply. A stable and supportive domestic background is vital in maintaining these people's emotional equilibrium, since they need to be assured of the love of those closest to them and will reciprocate it unflaggingly. Professionally, the best—and potentially least damaging—outlet for the sensitivity of those born on this day lies in the realm of the arts, especially if they were also born in the Chinese year of the rat, or in the service industries.

VIRTUES: Those born on this day are multitalented individuals, who possess acutely sensitive powers of intuition, compassion and vision. Because they are practical as well as idealistic, these people have real potential to achieve their dreams.
VICES: These individuals are prone to becoming victims of their empathetic qualities, and run the risk of becoming confused to the point of stasis when they attune themselves to the emotional turmoil of others.
VERDICT: In every area of their lives, March 20 people must strive to become more emotionally robust, while never suppressing the sensitivity that is one of their greatest assets. By cultivating a more pragmatic and objective attitude to the demands of others, they will not only safeguard their own emotional well-being, but will make themselves more effective instruments for good.

On This Day
Famous Births: Ovid (43 BC); Henrik Ibsen (1828); Beniamino Gigli and Lauritz Melchior (1890); B.F. Skinner (1904); Ozzie Nelson (1907); Michael Redgrave (1908); Sviatoslav Richter (1915); Vera Lynn (1917); Carl Reiner (1922); Fred Rogers (1928); Hal Linden (1931); David Malouf (1934); Brian Mulroney (1939); Pat Riley (1945); William Hurt (1950); Spike Lee (1957); Holly Hunter (1958).

Significant Events and Anniversaries: This day augurs well for the realization of visions, and marks the anniversary of the manufacturing of the world's first duplicator by James Watt (1780); the patenting of a revolutionary automatic Shoe Lasting Machine by African American inventor Jan Ernst Matzeliger (1883); as well as the unveiling of a German radar system at Kiel Harbor (1934). Reflecting the outstanding humanitarian and artistic potential of this day, Harriet Beecher Stowe's seminal book *Uncle Tom's Cabin* was published (1852). On a day on which an attempt to abduct Princess Anne of Britain was foiled by police and bystanders (1974), newspaper heiress Patty Hearst was found guilty of abetting an armed robbery carried out by her kidnappers, the Symbionese Liberation Army, demonstrating the day's sometimes misguided susceptibilty to emotionally identifying with others (1976).

THE INTERACTION OF OTHER BIRTH INFLUENCES

Numerous systems of mystical belief have been shaped by astrological principles, and particularly by the influence credited to the seven traditional "planets": the Sun and Moon (both of which are more properly termed "luminaries"), Mercury, Venus, Mars, Jupiter and Saturn. Their significance is due in part to the profound importance once attributed to the roles of the planets and constellations in regulating the universe and all its components. Another vital feature of astrological links with "occult" practices is the archetypal symbolism inherent in both the planets and zodiacal signs, an aspect that retains a strong resonance today, when practitioners are perhaps geared more toward expanding inner consciousness than toward seeking to effect a material influence on the world around them. Many esoteric systems could be discussed in relation to their connection with birth influences, but we focus here upon four of the most important and enduring: numerology, Tarot, the Kabbalah and alchemy—interrelated traditions, which, when studied singly and together, can help us to discover more about the cosmic "vibrations" and significances inherent in our names and dates of birth.

NUMEROLOGY

Although most early cultures ascribed divine significance to numbers, especially in relation to their deities, it was Pythagoras (580–500 BC) who originated the Western mystical belief that numbers are imbued with cosmic power. He proposed that mathematical laws govern such diverse systems as music, geometry and astrology. He also noted the special importance of single numerals: that is, those between one and nine, to each of which he assigned a symbolic, cosmic meaning. Kabbalists, too, use numbers as a tool to further mystical understanding, especially through such numerical systems as gematria, which equates every letter of the Hebrew alphabet with a numerical equivalent. The basic theory of numerology in relation to the interpretation of birth influences is that individuals' names and birthdates encapsulate cosmic "vibrations," and that the key to their personalities, and perhaps even their futures, may therefore be discovered by numerological diagnosis.

Onomancy concerns the translation of the individual letters comprising words and names into their numerical correspondents. This standard means of working out an individual's "number of development," or "fadic number," uses the following grid:

1	2	3	4	5	6	7	8	9
A	B	C	D	E	F	G	H	I
J	K	L	M	N	O	P	Q	R
S	T	U	V	W	X	Y	Z	

Once the number that corresponds to each letter has been identified, each is added together, the sum produced being added again until a single number is left. It is this number that is subject to interpretation. Thus if the name being examined is Sara Hunt, S = 1; A = 1; R = 9; A = 1; H = 8; U = 3; N = 5; and T = 2. The total is 30, and because 3 + 0 = 3, which cannot be reduced further, 3 is the number of development.

The birth number is usually regarded as the most significant in defining individual personality, and a similar process is used to identify it. The months of the year are assigned the following numbers: January = 1; February = 2; March = 3; April = 4; May = 5; June = 6; July = 7; August = 8; September = 9; October = 1 (1 + 0 = 1); November = 2 (1 + 1 = 2); December = 3 (1 + 2 = 3). For example, if an individual's birth date is August 1, 1964, the birth number would be identified as: 8 + 1 + 1 + 9 + 6 + 4 = 29; 2 + 9 = 11; 1 + 1 = 2. Therefore, two is the crucial number.

In numerology, each primary number is either masculine and active (odd numbers), or feminine and passive (even numbers). Every number has a meaning, but the inclusive numerals of one to nine are the most important. Thus numerologists reduce dual-digit numbers to single numerals by adding the two together. Profound symbolism imbues the numbers one to nine:

1: Unity and the potential for creation and renewal. Active and determined individuals.

2: Duality, with inherent equilibrium. Potentially indecisive but well-balanced people.

3: Harmonious triplicity; dynamic and generative power. Energetic and assured people.

4: Stability, orderliness and wholeness. Steady and practical personalities.

5: The "golden number," that of humanity. Questing and restless individuals.

6: Beauty and harmony. Integrated and positive people.

7: The number of mystical knowledge and creation. Idealistic and profound thinkers.

8: Material and spiritual equilibrium. Perfectionistic and progressive people.

9: The harmonious reconciliation of component parts. Intellectually decisive personalities.

Although they are not usually used by numerologists in their calculations, 0 is regarded as signifying embryonic potential, while 10 is the Pythagorean *tetraktys*, the number of perfection, which signifies both the successful completion of a cycle and a new beginning.

These simple principles have been widely applied, with variations, in related spheres including the Tarot, Kabbalah symbolism and alchemy.

TAROT

The derivation of the word "Tarot" can be traced to the Italian *tarocchi* ("triumphs" or "trumps"). Although the true origins of this system of divination are obscure—the eighteenth-century French practitioner Antoine Court de Gébelin, for example, claimed that it dated from ancient Egyptian times—the first Tarot cards as we know them today were created in Italy during the fifteenth century.

The Tarot deck consists of seventy-eight cards in total, comprising: (1) the twenty-two, originally unnumbered, major-arcana ("secrets") cards (which the nineteenth-century French occultist Eliphas Levi saw as having symbolic links to the twenty-two letters of the Hebrew alphabet); (2) the fifty-six minor-arcana cards, which are themselves divided into four suits: wands (scepters or batons), representing the element of fire, vitality and action; swords (or epées), symbolizing the element of air, destruction and intelligence; cups (or coupes), signifying the element of water, fertility and intuition; and pentacles (deniers or coins), symbolizing the element of earth and material matters. The minor arcana also have Kabbalistic links, in that their groupings may be said to correspond to the four worlds defined within Kabbalism. Many versions of the Tarot deck are in use today, but most are based on the Rider-Waite deck designed by Arthur Edward Waite and Pamela Colman Smith in 1910.

Some astrologers believe that the major-arcana cards are related to astrological personality tendencies, equating the major-arcana numbers with the degree of the sign under which the person was born. Thus, for example, someone born in the first degree of Aquarius (usually January 20) would tend to display the characteristics of the Juggler or Magician, ie, willfulness or selfishness; the twenty-second degree is equated with zero, or the Fool; and the twenty-third to thirtieth degrees are reduced to their numerological root, eg, 2+3=5, indicating the characteristics of the Pope or Hierophant.

There are various shapes in which the cards may be laid ready for interpretation, including the cross, circle, square, seven-pointed star and horseshoe. Whichever pattern is preferred, it is important that the cards are well shuffled before being laid. Although each minor-arcana card also has a divinatory meaning, the major-arcana cards are of greater significance, for they represent both archetypal symbols and the progressive steps inherent in the attainment of enlightenment. Their meanings are briefly summarized as follows:

0. **(or unnumbered) The Fool:** the unconscious.
1. **The Juggler, or Magician:** the will.
2. **The High Priestess:** feminine wisdom and intuition.
3. **The Empress:** feminine fertility, abundance and nurture.
4. **The Emperor:** masculine power and determination.
5. **The Pope or Hierophant:** spiritual wisdom and authority combined.
6. **The Lover(s):** the necessity of choice.
7. **The Chariot:** consciously controlled progress.
8. **Justice:** impartial judgement.
9. **The Hermit:** introspection.
10. **The Wheel of Fortune:** change and opportunity.
11. **Strength:** controlled intellectual power.
12. **The Hanged Man:** the sacrifice of the ego.
13. **Death:** transition and new beginnings.
14. **Temperance:** equilibrium and harmony.
15. **The Devil:** the need to overcome temptation.
16. **The Lightning-struck Tower:** release through unexpected challenge.
17. **The Star:** renewal and future promise.
18. **The Moon:** need to conquer emotional confusion.
19. **The Sun:** achievement and contentment.
20. **(The Last) Judgement:** evaluation and renewal.
21. **The World or The Universe:** completion and unity.

It should also be mentioned that each Tarot card has an opposite, negative significance, indicated when the card is reversed. The exception is the Sun, which indicates happiness under either aspect.

Tarot cards present a powerful means of promoting spiritual illumination, particularly when their implications are considered in conjunction with those indicated by other birth influences.

THE KABBALAH

The Jewish mystical system known as the Kabbalah (the Hebrew for "received tradition") was originally passed down orally and secretly (initially, it is said, from God to the angel Raziel, to Adam, and thence to the Jewish elders). Eventually, it became known to a wider audience, primarily through the work of the Judeo-Spanish philosopher Solomon Ibn Gabirol (1021–58), as a result of the thirteenth-century flowering of Jewish scholastic communities in Provence, France, and Spain. Many of Kabbalism's guiding precepts were set down in three seminal works of varying dates: the *Sefer Ha-Bahir* ("the book of brilliance"), reportedly written in the first century; the *Sefer Yetzirah* ("the book of creation"), thought to date from the third century; and the *Sefer Ha-Zohar* ("the book of splendor"), composed by Moses de Leon in the thirteenth century. After the Jews were expelled from Spain in 1492, Kabbalism spread all over Europe.

The tenets encompassed by Kabbalism, which seeks union with God, may be summarized as follows: God the creator is at the apex of a system of cosmic governance and delegates degrees of authority and powerful properties to the angels, the constellations and the material world. Thus the Godhead (*en sof*, "without end") is present in everything, and humans must try to reconcile the various components representing aspects of divine power to achieve enlightenment. Symbols vital to Kabbalism include the twenty-two letters of the Hebrew alphabet (underlying the esoteric practices of gematria, notariqon, temura and tsiruphim, which are used to search out hidden meanings in the sacred Torah); and the numbers one to ten (collectively termed the *sephiroth*, individually, *sephira*). In their totality, these numbers form the symbolic structure of reality, while the letters represent the foundation of all things. Indeed, the *Sefer Yetzirah* states that God created the universe by emanating these thirty-two paths of wisdom.

The importance of the inclusive numbers one to ten appears in such Kabbalistic symbols as the tree of life, ten concentric spheres and the ten-branched candelabrum (similar to the *menorah*). Each consists of the ten *sephiroth*, their interlinked arrangement symbolizing their inextricable connection. In the tree of life, for example, the ten *sephiroth* are represented as a trunk (the "pillar of equilibrium") with two branches: that on the left is the "pillar of severity or judgement"; the right is the "pillar of mercy." Viewing the tree from left to right, the pillar of severity (representing masculine principles) contains: 3, Binah (intelligence); 5, Gevurah (severity); and 8, Hod (splendor). The pillar of equilibrium comprises: 1, Kether (crown); 6, Tifereth or Rahamin (beauty); 9, Yesod (foundation); and 10, Malkuth (kingdom). The pillar of mercy (representing the feminine qualities) includes: 2, Hokhmah (wisdom); 4, Hesed (love); and 7, Netsah (victory).

Four worlds are also symbolized by the tree of life, for the grouping of the *sephiroth,* 1, 2 and 3 also represents an upward-pointed triangle, which equates to spirituality and the archetypes (*olam atziluth*); 4, 5 and 6, a downward-pointed triangle representing creation (*olam briah*); and 7, 8 and 9, another inverted triangle symbolizing the world of forms (*olam yetzirah*). These significances are also contained within each *sephira*, the fourth quadrant representing *olam assiah*, the material world. And just as Kabbalists believed that the tree of life contained the mystical name of God, or Tetragrammaton, YHWH, so each of the four worlds corresponds to one of its four component letters, as well as to three signs of the zodiac: Y = Aries, Taurus and Gemini; H = Cancer, Leo and Virgo; W = Libra, Scorpio and Sagittarius; and H = Capricorn, Aquarius and Pisces.

According to occultist Athanasius Kircher's work *Oedipus aegyptiacus* (1642), seven of the *sephiroth* relate to the planets and luminaries, and also to the angels of God. This reconciles the Kabbalistic *sephiroth* with astrological principles (similarly, the seven-branched menorah has planetary symbolism). Another important Kabbalistic symbol, derived from the teachings of Isaac Luria (1543–72), is that of Adam Kadmon, the cosmic man.

ALCHEMY

There are two major alchemical traditions: the Eastern (Chinese), which dates from the third century BC, and the Western, said to have originated in ancient Egypt. The evolution and principles of both were strongly influenced by astrological precepts, along with other systems of mystical belief. Chinese alchemists, for example, drew heavily upon the dualistic Taoist tenets of *yin-yang* and the *I Ching*, as well as the *Wu-hsing* (the five elements); while Western alchemy incorporated ancient Egyptian, Hermetic, Neoplatonist, Gnostic and also Christian elements, along with early forms of chemistry and metallurgy.

The ultimate purpose of both alchemical traditions centers on achieving spiritual enlightenment and eventual perfection, although the primary goal of the Chinese alchemists was specified as the attainment of immortality. Thus while popular belief envisages alchemists as seeking to enrich themselves materially by transmuting base metals into gold—or, in China, cinnabar (mercuric sulfide)—their quest may actually be regarded as a symbolic metaphor for the spiritual and intellectual refinement of the individual. This is particularly clear within Chinese alchemy, in which two complementary principles are inherent: *wai tan*, which concentrates on working toward physical immortality by experimentation with chemical substances; and *nei tan*, spiritual alchemy, which is concerned with directing and purifying the three aspects of the life force, *chi'i*, by means of yoga and meditation. Similarly, Western alchemy seeks to transmute the impure and disparate into perfection, each "base" mineral, chemical or metallurgical component used in the *magnum opus* ("the great work") representing a human quality. The alchemist's objective of creating the elusive "philosopher's stone" (*lapis philosophorum*), or "elixir of life," is both internally and externally directed: the elixir represents what was once perceived to be the incorruptible metal, gold, that itself symbolizes the spiritual ideal which confers immortality.

The psychologist Carl Jung, in his seminal study of alchemical symbolism, compared alchemy to the search for psychological individuation, in which such symbols as the *rebis* (the hermaphrodite) correspond to the archetypes present in the human psyche, this symbol, for example, representing the successful reconciliation of the animus and the anima.

According to Western alchemical thought, everything in the universe consists of the *materia prima* ("first matter"), comprising various combinations of the four elements of air (*aeris*, symbolized by sylphs), fire (*ignis*, salamanders), water (*aquae*, undines) and earth (*terrae*, gnomes). From these four, it is said, a fifth, ideal element, the quintessence, ether, can be distilled. There are also three other "philosophical elements": sulfur (representing the will, solar and masculine powers), mercury (the spirit, lunar and feminine forces), and salt (the material or intellect). By breaking down and reassembling (*solve et coagula*) these components in a more perfect form, it is hoped that the desired elixir will be created.

Astrology also plays an important part in alchemy. Each of the planets is equated with a deity, metal and color, as follows: the Sun = Apollo or Sol, gold, red; the Moon = Diana or Luna, silver, blue; Mercury = Mercury, mercury/quicksilver, white; Venus = Venus, copper, green; Mars = Mars, iron, orange; Jupiter = Jupiter, tin, purple; Saturn = Saturn, lead, black. Furthermore, the *magnum opus* can begin properly only when the Sun is in Aries, Taurus or Gemini (preferably Aries), and it is believed that the conjunction of soul and spirit will occur when Leo is ascendant, while the elixir will be produced during the period of Sagittarius's dominance. Twelve steps make up the *opus*: (1) *calcinatio* (calcination); (2) *solutio* (dissolution); (3) *elementorum separatio* (separation); (4) *coniunctio* (conjunction); (5) *putrefactio* (putrefaction); (6) *coagulatio* (coagulation); (7) *cibatio* (cibation); (8) *sublimatio* (sublimation); (9) *fermentatio* (fermentation); (10) *exaltatio* (exultation); (11) *augmentatio* (augmentation); and (12) *proiectio* (projection). Each is associated with a zodiacal sign. An alternative method, consisting of seven steps, links the stages of the *opus* to the influence of the seven planets.

ASTROLOGICAL COMPATIBILITIES

		Aries			Taurus			Gemini			Cancer			Leo			Virgo		
		March 21–March 31	April 1–April 10	April 11–April 20	April 21–April 30	May 1–May 11	May 12–May 20	May 21–May 31	June 1–June 10	June 11–June 21	June 22–June 30	July 1–July 11	July 12–July 22	July 23–July 31	Aug 1–Aug 10	Aug 11–Aug 22	Aug 23–Aug 31	Sept 1–Sept 11	Sept 12–Sept 22
Aries	Mar 21–Mar 31	10	11	12	4	5	6	10	11	12	19	20	21	4	5	6	10	11	12
	April 1–April 10	11	10	12	5	4	6	11	10	12	20	19	21	5	4	6	11	10	12
	April 11–April 20	12	11	10	6	5	4	12	11	10	21	20	19	6	5	4	12	11	10
Taurus	April 21–April 30	7	8	9	7	8	9	16	17	18	10	11	12	1	2	3	7	8	9
	May 1–May 11	8	7	9	8	7	9	17	16	18	11	10	12	2	1	3	8	7	9
	May 12–May 20	9	8	7	9	8	7	18	17	16	12	11	10	3	2	1	9	8	7
Gemini	May 21–May 31	10	11	12	13	14	15	13	14	13	19	20	21	7	8	9	16	17	18
	June 1–June 10	11	10	12	14	13	15	14	13	15	20	19	21	8	7	9	17	16	18
	June 11–June 21	12	11	10	15	14	13	15	14	13	21	20	19	9	8	7	18	17	16
Cancer	June 22–June 30	16	17	18	7	8	9	19	20	21	4	5	6	16	17	18	10	11	12
	July 1–July 11	17	16	18	8	7	9	20	19	21	5	4	6	17	16	18	11	10	12
	July 12–July 22	18	17	16	9	8	7	21	20	19	6	5	4	18	17	16	12	11	10
Leo	July 23–July 31	10	11	12	4	5	6	1	2	3	4	5	6	16	17	18	16	17	18
	Aug 1–Aug 10	11	10	12	5	4	6	2	1	3	5	4	6	17	16	18	17	16	18
	Aug 11–Aug 22	12	11	10	6	5	4	3	2	1	6	5	4	18	17	16	18	17	16
Virgo	Aug 23–Aug 31	19	20	21	7	8	9	4	5	6	13	14	15	18	14	15	16	17	18
	Sept 1–Sept 11	20	19	21	8	7	9	5	4	6	14	13	15	14	13	15	17	16	18
	Sept 12–Sept 22	21	20	19	9	8	7	6	5	4	15	14	13	15	14	13	18	17	16
Libra	Sept 23–Sept 30	13	14	15	4	5	6	4	5	6	13	14	15	7	8	9	16	17	18
	Oct 1–Oct 11	14	13	15	5	4	6	5	4	6	14	13	15	8	7	9	17	16	18
	Oct 12–Oct 22	15	14	13	6	5	4	6	5	4	15	14	13	9	8	7	18	17	16
Scorpio	Oct 23–Oct 31	7	8	9	10	11	12	16	17	18	4	5	6	7	8	9	7	8	9
	Nov 1–Nov 11	8	7	9	11	10	12	17	16	18	5	4	6	8	7	9	8	7	9
	Nov 12–Nov 21	9	8	7	12	11	10	18	17	16	6	5	4	9	8	7	9	8	7
Sagittarius	Nov 22–Nov 30	1	2	3	13	14	15	10	11	12	16	17	18	7	8	9	7	8	9
	Dec 1–Dec 11	2	1	3	14	13	15	11	10	12	17	16	18	8	7	9	8	7	9
	Dec 12–Dec 21	3	2	1	15	14	13	12	11	10	18	17	16	9	8	7	9	8	7
Capricorn	Dec 22–Dec 31	10	11	12	10	11	12	16	17	18	4	5	6	16	17	18	13	14	15
	Jan 1–Jan 10	11	10	12	11	10	12	17	16	18	5	4	6	17	16	18	14	13	15
	Jan 11–Jan 19	12	11	10	12	11	10	18	17	16	6	5	4	18	17	16	15	14	13
Aquarius	Jan 20–Jan 31	7	8	9	13	14	15	13	14	15	16	17	18	7	8	9	16	17	18
	Feb 1–Feb 9	8	7	9	14	13	15	14	13	15	17	16	18	8	7	9	17	16	18
	Feb 10–Feb 18	9	8	7	15	14	13	15	14	13	18	17	16	9	8	7	18	17	16
Pisces	Feb 19–Feb 29	13	14	15	4	5	6	10	11	12	7	8	9	7	8	9	10	11	12
	Mar 1–Mar 10	14	13	15	5	4	6	11	10	12	8	7	9	8	7	9	11	10	12
	Mar 11–Mar 20	15	14	13	6	5	4	12	11	10	9	8	7	9	8	7	12	11	10

ASTROLOGICAL COMPATIBILITIES

Sept 23–Sept 30	Oct 1–Oct 11	Oct 12–Oct 22	Oct 23–Oct 31	Nov 1–Nov 11	Nov 12–Nov 21	Nov 22–Nov 30	Dec 1–Dec 11	Dec 12–Dec 21	Dec 22–Dec 31	Jan 1–Jan 10	Jan 11–Jan 19	Jan 20–Jan 31	Feb 1–Feb 9	Feb 10–Feb 18	Feb 19–Feb 29	March 1–March 10	March 11–March 20
Libra			Scorpio			Sagittarius			Capricorn			Aquarius			Pisces		
4	5	6	1	2	3	7	8	9	7	8	9	10	11	12	19	20	21
5	4	6	2	1	3	8	7	9	8	7	9	11	10	12	20	19	21
6	5	4	3	2	1	9	8	7	9	8	7	12	11	10	21	20	19
4	5	6	7	8	9	19	20	21	4	5	6	4	5	6	7	8	9
5	4	6	8	7	9	20	19	21	5	4	6	5	4	6	8	7	9
6	5	4	9	8	7	21	20	19	6	5	4	6	5	4	9	8	7
1	2	3	10	11	12	10	11	12	16	17	18	13	14	15	19	20	21
2	1	3	11	10	12	11	10	12	17	16	18	14	13	15	20	19	21
3	2	1	12	11	10	12	11	10	18	17	16	15	14	13	21	20	19
16	17	18	19	20	21	13	14	15	7	8	9	16	17	18	19	20	21
17	16	18	20	19	21	14	13	15	8	7	9	17	16	18	20	19	21
18	17	16	21	20	19	15	14	13	9	8	7	18	17	16	21	20	19
7	8	9	10	11	12	7	8	9	16	17	18	13	14	15	16	17	18
8	7	9	11	10	12	8	7	9	17	16	18	14	13	15	17	16	18
9	8	7	12	11	10	9	8	7	18	17	16	15	14	13	18	17	16
13	14	15	4	5	6	10	11	12	7	8	9	16	17	18	1	2	3
14	13	15	5	4	6	11	10	12	8	7	9	17	16	18	2	1	3
15	14	13	6	5	4	12	11	10	9	8	7	18	17	16	3	2	1
16	17	18	10	11	12	10	11	12	19	20	21	1	2	3	7	8	9
17	16	18	11	10	12	11	10	12	20	19	21	2	1	3	8	7	9
18	17	16	12	11	10	12	11	10	21	20	19	3	2	1	9	8	7
7	8	9	16	17	18	13	14	15	7	8	9	13	14	15	1	2	3
8	7	9	17	16	18	14	13	15	8	7	9	14	13	15	2	1	3
9	8	7	18	17	16	15	14	13	9	8	7	15	14	13	3	2	1
7	8	9	19	20	21	7	8	9	19	20	21	16	17	18	16	17	18
8	7	9	20	19	21	8	7	9	20	19	21	17	16	18	17	16	18
9	8	7	21	20	19	9	8	7	21	20	19	18	17	16	18	17	16
16	17	18	4	5	6	19	20	21	4	5	6	1	2	3	4	5	6
17	16	18	5	4	6	20	19	21	5	4	6	1	1	3	5	4	6
18	17	16	6	5	4	21	20	19	6	5	4	3	2	1	6	5	4
1	2	3	13	14	15	10	11	12	13	14	15	4	5	6	16	17	18
2	1	3	14	13	15	11	10	12	14	13	15	5	4	6	17	16	18
3	2	1	15	14	13	12	11	10	15	14	13	6	5	4	18	17	16
4	5	6	7	8	9	16	17	18	4	5	6	16	17	18	1	2	3
5	4	6	8	7	9	17	16	18	5	4	6	17	16	18	2	1	3
6	5	4	9	8	7	18	17	16	6	5	4	18	17	16	3	2	1

This chart and those on the following pages represent levels of compatibility in personal relationships as indicated by dates of birth. The chart at left is based upon Western astrology, while the one on pages 426–29 reflects the Chinese system. The table of Chinese lunar years on pages 424–25 will help the reader to determine his or her birthday animal and that of the partner concerned. The dominant element for both parties can be worked out using the method described on page 32.

In the Western astrological table, the vertical column represents the masculine influence in a relationship while the horizontal column, the feminine. Using the Chinese astrological chart, the vertical column represents the person who is consulting the table, and the horizontal, the person of interest. "Scores" have been allocated as follows: 1 to 21 for the Western chart, with 1 representing a relationship that is extremely well starred, and 21 a relationship that will be challenging; and 2 to 12 for the Chinese table, 2 being the most auspicious, and 12 indicating the need for considerable input from partners. Westerners may be surprised that 2, rather than 1, is the highest score, but this reflects the Chinese yin-yang theory, whereby true harmony is achieved only when the universal components yin and yang work together in perfect synergy.

THE CHINESE LUNAR YEARS

LUNAR YEAR			SIGN	POLARITY	ELEMENT
January 31, 1900	to	February 18, 1901	Rat	Positive/Yang	Metal
February 19, 1901	to	February 7, 1902	Ox	Negative/Yin	Metal
February 8, 1902	to	January 28, 1903	Tiger	Positive/Yang	Water
January 29, 1903	to	February 15, 1904	Rabbit	Negative/Yin	Water
February 16, 1904	to	February 3, 1905	Dragon	Positive/Yang	Wood
February 4, 1905	to	January 24, 1906	Snake	Negative/Yin	Wood
January 25, 1906	to	February 12, 1907	Horse	Positive/Yang	Fire
February 13, 1907	to	February 1, 1908	Goat	Negative/Yin	Fire
February 2, 1908	to	January 21, 1909	Monkey	Positive/Yang	Earth
January 22, 1909	to	February 9, 1910	Rooster	Negative/Yin	Earth
February 10, 1910	to	January 29, 1911	Dog	Positive/Yang	Metal
January 30, 1911	to	February 17, 1912	Pig	Negative/Yin	Metal
February 18, 1912	to	February 5, 1913	Rat	Positive/Yang	Water
February 6, 1913	to	January 25, 1914	Ox	Negative/Yin	Water
January 26, 1914	to	February 13, 1915	Tiger	Positive/Yang	Wood
February 14, 1915	to	February 2, 1916	Rabbit	Negative/Yin	Wood
February 3, 1916	to	January 22, 1917	Dragon	Positive/Yang	Fire
January 23, 1917	to	February 10, 1918	Snake	Negative/Yin	Fire
February 11, 1918	to	January 31, 1919	Horse	Positive/Yang	Earth
February 1, 1919	to	February 19, 1920	Goat	Negative/Yin	Earth
February 20, 1920	to	February 7, 1921	Monkey	Positive/Yang	Metal
February 8, 1921	to	January 27, 1922	Rooster	Negative/Yin	Metal
January 28, 1922	to	February 15, 1923	Dog	Positive/Yang	Water
February 16, 1923	to	February 4, 1924	Pig	Negative/Yin	Water
February 5, 1924	to	January 24, 1925	Rat	Positive/Yang	Wood
January 25, 1925	to	February 12, 1926	Ox	Negative/Yin	Wood
February 13, 1926	to	February 1, 1927	Tiger	Positive/Yang	Fire
February 2, 1927	to	January 22, 1928	Rabbit	Negative/Yin	Fire
January 23, 1928	to	February 9, 1929	Dragon	Positive/Yang	Earth
February 10, 1929	to	January 29, 1930	Snake	Negative/Yin	Earth
January 30, 1930	to	February 16, 1931	Horse	Positive/Yang	Metal
February 17, 1931	to	February 5, 1932	Goat	Negative/Yin	Metal
February 6, 1932	to	January 25, 1933	Monkey	Positive/Yang	Water
January 26, 1933	to	February 13, 1934	Rooster	Negative/Yin	Water
February 14, 1934	to	February 3, 1935	Dog	Positive/Yang	Wood
February 4, 1935	to	January 23, 1936	Pig	Negative/Yin	Wood
January 24, 1936	to	February 10, 1937	Rat	Positive/Yang	Fire
February 11, 1937	to	January 30, 1938	Ox	Negative/Yin	Fire
January 31, 1938	to	February 18, 1939	Tiger	Positive/Yang	Earth
February 19, 1939	to	February 7, 1940	Rabbit	Negative/Yin	Earth
February 8, 1940	to	January 26, 1941	Dragon	Positive/Yang	Metal
January 27, 1941	to	February 14, 1942	Snake	Negative/Yin	Metal
February 15, 1942	to	February 4, 1943	Horse	Positive/Yang	Water
February 5, 1943	to	January 24, 1944	Goat	Negative/Yin	Water
January 25, 1944	to	February 13, 1945	Monkey	Positive/Yang	Wood
February 14, 1945	to	February 1, 1946	Rooster	Negative/Yin	Wood
February 2, 1946	to	January 21, 1947	Dog	Positive/Yang	Fire
January 22, 1947	to	February 9, 1948	Pig	Negative/Yin	Fire
February 10, 1948	to	January 28, 1949	Rat	Positive/Yang	Earth
January 29, 1949	to	February 16, 1950	Ox	Negative/Yin	Earth
February 17, 1950	to	February 5, 1951	Tiger	Positive/Yang	Metal
February 6, 1951	to	January 26, 1952	Rabbit	Negative/Yin	Metal
January 27, 1952	to	February 13, 1953	Dragon	Positive/Yang	Water
February 14, 1953	to	February 2, 1954	Snake	Negative/Yin	Water

THE CHINESE LUNAR YEARS

LUNAR YEAR			SIGN	POLARITY	ELEMENT
February 3, 1954	to	January 23, 1955	Horse	Positive/Yang	Wood
January 24, 1955	to	February 11, 1956	Goat	Negative/Yin	Wood
February 12, 1956	to	January 30, 1957	Monkey	Positive/Yang	Fire
January 31, 1957	to	February 17, 1958	Rooster	Negative/Yin	Fire
February 18, 1958	to	February 7, 1959	Dog	Positive/Yang	Earth
February 8, 1959	to	January 27, 1960	Pig	Negative/Yin	Earth
January 28, 1960	to	February 14, 1961	Rat	Positive/Yang	Metal
February 15, 1961	to	February 4, 1962	Ox	Negative/Yin	Metal
February 5, 1962	to	January 24, 1963	Tiger	Positive/Yang	Water
January 25, 1963	to	February 12, 1964	Rabbit	Negative/Yin	Water
February 13, 1964	to	February 1, 1965	Dragon	Positive/Yang	Wood
February 2, 1965	to	January 20, 1966	Snake	Negative/Yin	Wood
January 21, 1966	to	February 8, 1967	Horse	Positive/Yang	Fire
February 9, 1967	to	January 29, 1968	Goat	Negative/Yin	Fire
January 30, 1968	to	February 16, 1969	Monkey	Positive/Yang	Earth
February 17, 1969	to	February 5, 1970	Rooster	Negative/Yin	Earth
February 6, 1970	to	January 26, 1971	Dog	Positive/Yang	Metal
January 27, 1971	to	January 15, 1972	Pig	Negative/Yin	Metal
January 16, 1972	to	February 2, 1973	Rat	Positive/Yang	Water
February 3, 1973	to	January 22, 1974	Ox	Negative/Yin	Water
January 23, 1974	to	February 10, 1975	Tiger	Positive/Yang	Wood
February 11, 1975	to	January 30, 1976	Rabbit	Negative/Yin	Wood
January 31, 1976	to	February 17, 1977	Dragon	Positive/Yang	Fire
February 18, 1977	to	February 6, 1978	Snake	Negative/Yin	Fire
February 7, 1978	to	January 27, 1979	Horse	Positive/Yang	Earth
January 28, 1979	to	February 15, 1980	Goat	Negative/Yin	Earth
February 16, 1980	to	February 4, 1981	Monkey	Positive/Yang	Metal
February 5, 1981	to	January 24, 1982	Rooster	Negative/Yin	Metal
January 25, 1982	to	February 12, 1983	Dog	Positive/Yang	Water
February 13, 1983	to	February 1, 1984	Pig	Negative/Yin	Water
February 2, 1984	to	February 19, 1985	Rat	Positive/Yang	Wood
February 20, 1985	to	February 8, 1986	Ox	Negative/Yin	Wood
February 9, 1986	to	January 28, 1987	Tiger	Positive/Yang	Fire
January 29, 1987	to	February 16, 1988	Rabbit	Negative/Yin	Fire
February 17, 1988	to	February 5, 1989	Dragon	Positive/Yang	Earth
February 6, 1989	to	January 26, 1990	Snake	Negative/Yin	Earth
January 27, 1990	to	February 14, 1991	Horse	Positive/Yang	Metal
February 15, 1991	to	February 3, 1992	Goat	Negative/Yin	Metal
February 4, 1992	to	January 22, 1993	Monkey	Positive/Yang	Water
January 23, 1993	to	February 9, 1994	Rooster	Negative/Yin	Water
February 10, 1994	to	January 30, 1995	Dog	Positive/Yang	Wood
January 31, 1995	to	February 18, 1996	Pig	Negative/Yin	Wood
February 19, 1996	to	February 7, 1997	Rat	Positive/Yang	Fire
February 8, 1997	to	January 27, 1998	Ox	Negative/Yin	Fire
January 28, 1998	to	February 5, 1999	Tiger	Positive/Yang	Earth
February 6, 1999	to	January 27, 2000	Rabbit	Negative/Yin	Earth
January 28, 2000	to	January 23, 2001	Dragon	Positive/Yang	Metal
January 24, 2001	to	February 11, 2002	Snake	Negative/Yin	Metal
February 12, 2002	to	January 31, 2003	Horse	Positive/Yang	Water
February 1, 2003	to	January 21, 2004	Goat	Negative/Yin	Water
January 22, 2004	to	February 8, 2005	Monkey	Positive/Yang	Wood
February 9, 2005	to	January 28, 2006	Rooster	Negative/Yin	Wood
January 29, 2006	to	February 17, 2007	Dog	Positive/Yang	Fire
February 18, 2007	to	February 6, 2008	Pig	Negative/Yin	Fire

CHINESE COMPATIBILITY CHART

		Rat					Ox					Tiger					Rabbit					Dragon					Snake			
	METAL RAT	WATER RAT	WOOD RAT	FIRE RAT	EARTH RAT	METAL OX	WATER OX	WOOD OX	FIRE OX	EARTH OX	METAL TIGER	WATER TIGER	WOOD TIGER	FIRE TIGER	EARTH TIGER	METAL RABBIT	WATER RABBIT	WOOD RABBIT	FIRE RABBIT	EARTH RABBIT	METAL DRAGON	WATER DRAGON	WOOD DRAGON	FIRE DRAGON	EARTH DRAGON	METAL SNAKE	WATER SNAKE	WOOD SNAKE	FIRE SNAKE	EARTH SNAKE
METAL RAT	4	3	3	6	5	4	3	3	6	5	7	6	6	9	8	5	4	4	7	6	3	2	2	5	4	5	4	4	7	6
WATER RAT	5	4	3	3	6	5	4	3	3	6	8	7	6	6	9	6	5	4	4	7	4	3	2	2	5	6	5	4	4	7
WOOD RAT	6	3	4	5	3	6	3	4	5	3	9	6	7	8	6	7	4	5	6	4	5	2	3	4	2	7	4	5	6	4
FIRE RAT	3	6	3	4	5	3	6	3	4	5	6	9	6	7	8	4	7	4	5	6	2	5	2	3	4	4	7	4	5	6
EARTH RAT	3	3	6	5	4	3	3	6	5	4	6	6	9	8	7	4	4	7	6	5	2	2	5	3	4	4	4	7	6	5
METAL OX	4	3	3	6	5	5	4	4	7	6	8	7	7	10	9	5	4	4	7	6	5	4	4	7	6	3	2	2	5	4
WATER OX	5	4	3	3	6	6	5	4	4	7	9	8	7	7	10	6	5	4	4	7	6	5	4	4	7	4	3	2	2	5
WOOD OX	6	3	4	5	3	7	4	5	6	4	10	7	8	9	7	7	4	5	6	4	7	4	5	6	4	5	2	3	4	2
FIRE OX	3	6	3	4	5	4	7	4	5	6	7	10	7	8	9	4	7	4	5	6	4	7	4	5	6	2	5	2	3	4
EARTH OX	3	3	6	5	4	4	4	7	6	5	7	7	10	9	8	4	4	7	6	5	4	4	7	6	5	2	2	5	4	3
METAL TIGER	7	6	6	9	8	8	7	7	10	9	5	4	4	7	6	7	6	6	9	8	5	4	4	7	6	8	7	7	10	9
WATER TIGER	8	7	6	6	9	9	8	7	7	10	6	5	4	4	7	8	7	6	6	9	6	5	4	4	7	9	8	7	7	10
WOOD TIGER	9	6	7	8	6	10	7	8	9	7	7	4	5	6	4	9	6	7	8	6	7	4	5	6	4	10	7	8	9	7
FIRE TIGER	6	9	6	7	8	7	10	7	8	9	4	7	4	5	6	6	9	6	7	8	4	7	4	5	6	7	10	7	8	9
EARTH TIGER	6	6	9	8	7	7	7	10	9	8	4	4	7	6	5	6	6	9	8	7	4	4	7	6	5	7	7	10	9	8
METAL RABBIT	5	4	4	7	6	5	4	4	7	6	7	6	6	9	8	4	3	3	6	5	5	4	4	7	6	5	4	4	7	6
WATER RABBIT	6	5	4	4	7	6	5	4	4	7	8	7	6	6	9	5	4	3	3	6	6	5	4	4	7	6	5	4	4	7
WOOD RABBIT	7	4	5	6	4	7	4	5	6	4	9	6	7	8	6	6	3	4	5	3	7	4	5	6	4	7	4	5	6	4
FIRE RABBIT	4	7	4	5	6	4	7	4	5	6	6	9	6	7	8	3	6	3	4	5	4	7	4	5	6	4	7	4	5	6
EARTH RABBIT	4	4	7	6	5	4	4	7	6	5	6	6	9	8	7	3	3	6	5	4	4	4	7	6	5	4	4	7	6	5
METAL DRAGON	3	2	2	5	4	3	4	4	7	6	5	4	4	7	6	5	4	4	7	6	4	3	3	6	5	4	3	3	6	5
WATER DRAGON	4	3	2	2	5	6	5	4	4	7	6	5	4	4	7	6	5	4	4	7	5	4	3	3	6	5	4	3	3	6
WOOD DRAGON	5	2	3	4	2	7	4	5	6	4	7	4	5	6	4	7	4	5	6	4	6	3	4	5	3	6	3	4	5	3
FIRE DRAGON	2	5	2	3	4	4	7	4	5	6	4	7	4	5	6	4	7	4	5	6	3	6	3	4	5	3	6	3	4	5
EARTH DRAGON	2	2	5	3	4	4	4	7	6	5	4	4	7	6	5	4	4	7	6	5	3	3	6	5	4	3	3	6	5	4
METAL SNAKE	5	4	4	7	6	3	2	2	5	4	8	7	7	10	9	5	4	4	7	6	4	3	3	6	5	4	3	3	6	5
WATER SNAKE	6	5	4	4	7	4	3	2	2	5	9	8	7	7	10	6	5	4	4	7	5	4	3	3	6	5	4	3	6	6
WOOD SNAKE	7	4	5	6	4	5	2	3	4	2	10	7	8	9	7	7	4	5	6	4	6	3	4	5	3	6	3	4	3	3
FIRE SNAKE	4	7	4	5	6	2	5	2	3	4	7	10	7	8	9	4	7	4	5	6	3	6	3	4	5	3	6	3	4	5
EARTH SNAKE	4	4	7	6	5	2	2	5	4	3	7	7	10	9	8	4	4	7	6	5	3	3	6	5	4	3	3	6	5	4

CHINESE COMPATIBILITY CHART

	Metal Horse	Water Horse	Wood Horse	Fire Horse	Earth Horse	Metal Goat	Water Goat	Wood Goat	Fire Goat	Earth Goat	Metal Monkey	Water Monkey	Wood Monkey	Fire Monkey	Earth Monkey	Metal Rooster	Water Rooster	Wood Rooster	Fire Rooster	Earth Rooster	Metal Dog	Water Dog	Wood Dog	Fire Dog	Earth Dog	Metal Pig	Water Pig	Wood Pig	Fire Pig	Earth Pig
METAL RAT	10	9	9	12	11	7	6	6	9	8	3	2	2	5	4	6	5	5	8	7	5	4	4	7	6	5	4	4	7	6
WATER RAT	11	10	9	9	12	8	7	6	6	9	4	3	2	2	5	7	6	5	5	8	6	5	4	4	7	6	5	4	4	7
WOOD RAT	12	9	10	11	9	9	6	7	8	6	5	2	3	4	2	8	5	6	7	5	7	4	5	6	4	7	4	5	6	4
FIRE RAT	9	12	9	10	11	6	9	6	7	8	2	5	2	3	4	5	8	5	6	7	4	7	4	5	6	4	7	4	5	6
EARTH RAT	9	9	12	11	10	6	6	9	8	7	2	2	5	4	3	5	5	8	7	6	4	4	7	6	5	4	4	7	6	5
METAL OX	6	5	5	8	7	10	9	9	12	11	7	6	6	9	8	3	2	2	5	4	8	7	7	10	9	6	5	5	8	7
WATER OX	7	6	5	5	8	11	10	9	9	12	8	7	6	6	9	4	3	2	2	5	9	8	7	7	10	7	6	5	5	8
WOOD OX	8	5	6	7	5	12	9	10	11	9	9	6	7	8	6	5	2	3	4	2	10	7	8	9	7	8	5	6	7	5
FIRE OX	5	8	5	6	7	9	12	9	10	11	6	9	6	7	8	2	5	2	3	4	7	10	7	8	9	5	8	5	6	7
EARTH OX	5	5	8	7	6	9	9	12	11	10	6	6	9	8	7	2	2	5	4	3	7	7	10	9	8	5	5	8	7	6
METAL TIGER	3	2	2	5	4	7	6	6	9	8	10	9	9	12	11	6	5	5	8	7	3	2	2	5	4	4	3	3	6	5
WATER TIGER	4	3	2	2	5	8	7	6	6	9	11	10	9	9	12	7	6	5	5	8	4	3	2	2	5	5	4	3	3	6
WOOD TIGER	5	2	3	4	2	9	6	7	8	6	12	9	10	11	9	8	5	6	7	5	5	2	3	4	2	6	3	4	5	3
FIRE TIGER	2	5	2	3	4	6	9	6	7	8	9	12	9	10	11	5	8	5	6	7	2	5	2	3	4	3	6	3	4	5
EARTH TIGER	2	2	5	4	3	6	6	9	8	7	9	9	12	11	10	5	5	8	7	6	2	2	5	4	3	3	3	6	5	4
METAL RABBIT	8	7	7	10	9	3	2	2	5	4	6	5	5	8	7	10	9	9	12	11	4	3	3	6	5	3	2	2	5	4
WATER RABBIT	9	8	7	7	10	4	3	2	2	5	7	6	5	5	8	11	10	9	9	12	5	4	3	3	6	4	3	2	2	5
WOOD RABBIT	10	7	8	9	7	5	2	3	4	2	8	5	6	7	5	12	9	10	11	9	6	3	4	5	3	5	2	3	4	2
FIRE RABBIT	7	10	7	8	9	2	5	2	3	4	5	8	5	6	7	9	12	9	10	11	3	6	3	4	5	2	5	2	3	4
EARTH RABBIT	7	7	10	9	8	2	2	5	4	3	5	5	8	7	6	9	9	12	11	10	3	3	6	5	4	2	2	5	4	3
METAL DRAGON	5	4	4	7	6	5	4	4	7	6	3	2	2	5	4	4	3	3	6	5	10	9	9	12	11	5	4	4	7	6
WATER DRAGON	6	5	4	4	7	6	5	4	4	7	4	3	2	2	5	5	4	3	3	6	11	10	9	9	12	6	5	4	4	7
WOOD DRAGON	7	4	5	6	4	7	4	5	6	4	5	2	3	4	2	6	3	4	5	3	12	9	10	11	9	7	4	5	6	4
FIRE DRAGON	4	7	4	5	6	4	7	4	5	6	2	5	2	3	4	3	6	3	4	5	9	12	9	10	11	4	7	4	5	6
EARTH DRAGON	4	4	7	6	5	4	4	7	6	5	2	2	5	4	3	3	3	6	5	4	9	9	12	11	10	4	4	7	6	5
METAL SNAKE	8	7	7	10	9	7	6	6	9	8	8	7	7	10	9	3	2	2	5	4	5	4	4	7	6	10	9	9	12	11
WATER SNAKE	9	8	7	7	10	8	7	6	6	9	9	8	7	7	10	4	3	2	2	5	6	5	4	4	7	11	10	9	9	12
WOOD SNAKE	10	7	8	9	7	9	6	7	8	6	10	7	8	9	7	5	2	3	4	2	7	4	5	6	4	12	9	10	11	9
FIRE SNAKE	7	10	7	8	9	6	9	6	7	8	7	10	7	8	9	2	5	2	3	4	4	7	4	5	6	9	12	9	10	11
EARTH SNAKE	7	7	10	9	8	6	6	9	8	7	7	7	10	9	8	2	2	5	4	3	4	4	7	6	5	9	9	12	11	10

CHINESE COMPATIBILITY CHART

		Metal Rat	Water Rat	Wood Rat	Fire Rat	Earth Rat	Metal Ox	Water Ox	Wood Ox	Fire Ox	Earth Ox	Metal Tiger	Water Tiger	Wood Tiger	Fire Tiger	Earth Tiger	Metal Rabbit	Water Rabbit	Wood Rabbit	Fire Rabbit	Earth Rabbit	Metal Dragon	Water Dragon	Wood Dragon	Fire Dragon	Earth Dragon	Metal Snake	Water Snake	Wood Snake	Fire Snake	Earth Snake
Horse	METAL HORSE	10	9	9	12	11	6	5	5	8	7	3	2	2	5	4	8	7	7	10	9	5	4	4	7	6	8	7	7	10	9
Horse	WATER HORSE	11	10	9	9	12	7	6	5	5	8	4	3	2	2	5	9	8	7	7	10	6	5	4	4	7	9	8	7	7	10
Horse	WOOD HORSE	12	9	10	11	9	8	5	6	7	5	5	2	3	4	2	10	7	8	9	7	7	4	5	6	4	10	7	8	9	7
Horse	FIRE HORSE	9	12	9	10	11	5	8	5	6	7	2	5	2	3	4	7	10	7	8	9	4	7	4	5	6	7	10	7	8	9
Horse	EARTH HORSE	9	9	12	11	10	5	5	8	7	6	2	2	5	4	3	7	7	10	9	8	4	4	7	6	5	7	7	10	9	8
Goat	METAL GOAT	7	6	6	9	8	10	9	9	12	11	7	6	6	9	8	3	2	2	5	4	5	4	4	7	6	7	6	6	9	8
Goat	WATER GOAT	8	7	6	6	9	11	10	9	9	12	8	7	6	6	9	4	3	2	2	5	6	5	4	4	7	8	7	6	6	9
Goat	WOOD GOAT	9	6	7	8	6	12	9	10	11	9	9	6	7	8	6	5	2	3	4	2	7	4	5	6	4	9	6	7	8	6
Goat	FIRE GOAT	6	9	6	7	8	9	12	9	10	11	6	9	6	7	8	2	5	2	3	4	4	7	4	5	6	6	9	6	7	8
Goat	EARTH GOAT	6	6	9	8	7	9	9	12	11	10	6	6	9	8	7	2	2	5	4	3	4	4	7	6	5	6	6	9	8	7
Monkey	METAL MONKEY	3	2	2	5	4	7	6	6	9	8	10	9	9	12	11	6	5	5	8	7	3	2	2	5	4	8	7	7	10	9
Monkey	WATER MONKEY	4	3	2	2	5	8	7	6	6	9	11	10	9	9	12	7	6	5	5	8	4	3	2	2	5	9	8	7	7	10
Monkey	WOOD MONKEY	5	2	3	4	2	9	6	7	8	6	12	9	10	11	9	8	5	6	7	5	5	2	3	4	2	10	7	8	9	7
Monkey	FIRE MONKEY	2	5	2	3	4	6	9	6	7	8	9	12	9	10	11	5	8	5	6	7	2	5	2	3	4	7	10	7	8	9
Monkey	EARTH MONKEY	2	2	5	4	3	6	6	9	8	7	9	9	12	11	10	5	5	8	7	6	2	2	5	4	3	7	7	10	9	8
Rooster	METAL ROOSTER	6	5	5	8	7	3	2	2	5	4	6	5	5	8	7	10	9	9	12	11	4	3	3	6	5	3	2	2	5	4
Rooster	WATER ROOSTER	7	6	5	5	8	4	3	2	2	5	7	6	5	5	8	11	10	9	9	12	5	4	3	3	6	4	3	2	2	5
Rooster	WOOD ROOSTER	8	5	6	7	5	5	2	3	4	2	8	5	6	7	5	12	9	10	11	9	6	3	4	5	3	5	2	3	4	2
Rooster	FIRE ROOSTER	5	8	5	6	7	2	5	2	3	4	5	8	5	6	7	9	12	9	10	11	3	6	3	4	5	2	5	2	3	4
Rooster	EARTH ROOSTER	5	5	8	7	6	2	2	5	4	3	5	5	8	7	6	9	9	12	11	10	3	3	6	5	4	2	2	5	4	3
Dog	METAL DOG	5	4	4	7	6	8	7	7	10	9	3	2	2	5	4	4	3	3	6	5	10	9	9	12	11	5	4	4	7	6
Dog	WATER DOG	6	5	4	4	7	9	8	7	7	10	4	3	2	2	5	5	4	3	3	6	11	10	9	9	12	6	5	4	4	7
Dog	WOOD DOG	7	4	5	6	4	10	7	8	9	7	5	2	3	4	2	6	3	4	5	3	12	9	10	11	9	7	4	5	6	4
Dog	FIRE DOG	4	7	4	5	6	7	10	7	8	9	2	5	2	3	4	3	6	3	4	5	9	12	9	10	11	4	7	4	5	6
Dog	EARTH DOG	4	4	7	6	5	7	7	10	9	8	2	2	5	4	3	3	3	6	5	4	9	9	12	11	10	4	4	7	6	3
Pig	METAL PIG	5	4	4	7	6	6	5	5	8	7	4	3	3	6	5	3	2	2	5	4	5	4	4	7	8	10	9	9	12	11
Pig	WATER PIG	6	5	4	4	7	7	6	5	5	8	5	4	3	3	6	4	3	2	2	5	6	5	4	4	7	11	10	9	9	12
Pig	WOOD PIG	7	4	5	6	4	8	5	6	7	5	6	3	4	5	3	5	2	3	4	2	7	4	3	6	4	12	9	10	11	9
Pig	FIRE PIG	4	7	4	5	6	5	8	5	6	7	3	6	3	4	5	2	5	2	3	4	4	7	4	5	6	9	12	9	10	12
Pig	EARTH PIG	4	4	7	6	5	5	5	8	7	6	3	3	6	5	4	2	2	5	4	3	4	4	7	6	5	9	9	12	11	10

CHINESE COMPATIBILITY CHART

	Horse					Goat					Monkey					Rooster					Dog					Pig				
	METAL HORSE	WATER HORSE	WOOD HORSE	FIRE HORSE	EARTH HORSE	METAL GOAT	WATER GOAT	WOOD GOAT	FIRE GOAT	EARTH GOAT	METAL MONKEY	WATER MONKEY	WOOD MONKEY	FIRE MONKEY	EARTH MONKEY	METAL ROOSTER	WATER ROOSTER	WOOD ROOSTER	FIRE ROOSTER	EARTH ROOSTER	METAL DOG	WATER DOG	WOOD DOG	FIRE DOG	EARTH DOG	METAL PIG	WATER PIG	WOOD PIG	FIRE PIG	EARTH PIG
METAL HORSE	4	3	3	6	5	4	3	3	6	5	7	6	6	9	8	6	5	5	8	7	3	2	2	5	4	5	4	4	7	6
WATER HORSE	5	4	3	3	6	5	4	3	3	6	8	7	6	6	9	7	6	5	5	8	4	3	2	2	5	6	5	4	4	7
WOOD HORSE	6	3	4	5	3	6	3	4	5	3	9	6	7	8	6	8	5	6	7	5	5	2	3	4	2	7	4	5	6	4
FIRE HORSE	3	6	3	4	5	3	6	3	4	5	6	9	6	7	8	5	8	5	6	7	2	5	2	3	4	4	7	4	5	6
EARTH HORSE	3	3	6	5	4	3	3	6	5	4	6	6	9	8	7	5	5	8	7	6	2	2	5	4	3	4	4	7	6	5
METAL GOAT	4	3	3	6	5	4	3	3	6	5	7	6	6	9	8	7	6	6	9	8	8	7	7	10	9	3	2	2	5	4
WATER GOAT	5	4	3	3	6	5	4	3	3	6	8	7	6	6	9	8	7	6	6	9	9	8	7	7	10	4	3	2	2	5
WOOD GOAT	6	3	4	5	3	6	3	4	5	3	9	6	7	8	6	9	6	7	8	6	10	7	8	9	7	5	2	3	4	2
FIRE GOAT	3	6	3	4	5	3	6	3	4	5	6	9	6	7	8	6	9	6	7	8	7	10	7	8	9	2	5	2	3	4
EARTH GOAT	3	3	6	5	4	3	3	6	5	4	6	6	9	8	7	6	6	9	8	7	7	7	10	9	8	2	2	5	4	3
METAL MONKEY	7	6	6	9	8	7	6	6	9	8	4	3	3	6	5	7	6	6	9	8	5	4	4	7	6	5	4	4	7	6
WATER MONKEY	8	7	6	6	9	8	7	6	6	9	5	4	3	3	6	8	7	6	6	9	6	5	4	4	7	6	5	4	4	7
WOOD MONKEY	9	6	7	8	6	9	6	7	8	6	6	3	4	5	3	9	6	7	8	6	7	4	5	6	4	7	4	5	6	4
FIRE MONKEY	6	9	6	7	8	6	9	6	7	8	3	6	3	4	5	6	9	6	7	8	4	7	4	5	6	4	7	4	5	6
EARTH MONKEY	6	6	9	8	7	6	6	9	8	7	3	3	6	5	4	6	6	9	8	7	4	4	7	6	5	4	4	7	6	5
METAL ROOSTER	6	5	5	8	7	7	6	6	9	8	7	6	6	9	8	8	7	7	10	9	7	6	6	9	8	7	6	6	9	8
WATER ROOSTER	7	6	5	5	8	8	7	6	6	9	8	7	6	6	9	9	8	7	7	10	8	7	6	6	9	8	7	6	6	9
WOOD ROOSTER	8	5	6	7	5	9	6	7	8	6	9	6	7	8	6	10	7	8	9	7	9	6	7	8	6	9	6	7	8	6
FIRE ROOSTER	5	8	5	6	7	6	9	6	7	8	6	9	6	7	8	7	10	7	8	9	6	9	6	7	8	6	9	6	7	8
EARTH ROOSTER	5	5	8	7	6	6	6	9	8	7	6	6	9	8	7	7	7	10	9	8	6	6	9	8	7	6	6	9	8	7
METAL DOG	3	2	2	5	4	8	7	7	10	9	5	4	4	7	6	7	6	6	9	8	5	4	4	7	6	5	4	4	7	6
WATER DOG	4	3	2	2	5	9	8	7	7	10	6	5	4	4	7	8	7	6	6	9	6	5	4	4	7	6	5	4	4	7
WOOD DOG	5	2	3	4	2	10	7	8	9	7	7	4	5	6	4	9	6	7	8	6	7	4	5	6	4	7	4	5	6	4
FIRE DOG	2	5	2	3	4	7	10	7	8	9	4	7	4	5	6	6	9	6	7	8	4	7	4	5	6	4	7	4	5	6
EARTH DOG	2	2	5	4	3	7	7	10	9	8	4	4	7	6	5	6	6	9	8	7	4	4	7	6	5	4	4	7	6	5
METAL PIG	5	4	4	7	6	8	2	2	5	4	5	4	4	7	6	7	6	6	9	8	5	4	4	7	6	5	4	4	7	6
WATER PIG	6	5	4	4	7	4	3	2	2	5	6	5	4	4	7	8	7	6	6	9	6	5	4	4	7	6	5	4	4	7
WOOD PIG	7	4	5	6	4	5	2	3	4	2	7	4	5	6	4	9	6	7	8	6	7	4	5	6	4	7	4	5	6	4
FIRE PIG	4	7	4	5	6	2	5	2	3	4	4	7	4	5	6	6	9	6	7	8	4	7	4	5	6	4	7	4	5	6
EARTH PIG	4	4	7	6	5	2	2	5	4	3	4	4	7	6	5	6	6	9	8	7	4	4	7	6	5	4	4	7	6	5

Row groups (right margin labels): Horse, Goat, Monkey, Rooster, Dog, Pig